Composers of Yesterday

Books by David Ewen

Hebrew Music
The Unfinished Symphony
From Bach to Stravinsky
Wine, Women and Waltz
The Man With the Baton
Composers of Today

COMPOSERS OF YESTERDAY

A Biographical and Critical Guide to the Most Important Composers of the Past

Compiled and Edited by
DAVID EWEN

NEW YORK
THE H. W. WILSON COMPANY
NINETEEN HUNDRED THIRTY-SEVEN

1937

To
LAZARE SAMINSKY
in friendship and admiration

INTRODUCTION

In presenting *Composers of Yesterday*—a companion volume to *Composers of Today*, published two years ago—the editor and publisher feel that a definite gap in musical literature has been filled.

Both the publisher and the editor have felt that the musical layman (whose number is increasing prodigiously with each year) was in need of a reference book on composers especially designed to satisfy his own particular needs. *Composers of Yesterday* has attempted to provide, in each of its sketches, such information as the average music-lover invariably desires about composers. The average music-lover is interested in copious biographical material, generously sprinkled with the spice of anecdotes; he is avid for a glimpse at the personality of the composer—the man as distinguished from the artist. Finally, music-lovers are eager to know what leading critics of all time have said about the composer's major works, about the nature of his style, about his contribution to musical development and about his position in musical history. To satisfy such curiosity, the editor has combed the writings of leadings critics and biographers, has tapped all sources contemporary with each composer, has referred to all available material in books, magazines and newspapers and collated the most important information into these sketches. Thus each sketch is, for the most part, a synthesis of the leading critical thought available about each composer.

It was the original intention of the editor to make this volume the last word in comprehensiveness by including some three hundred and fifty composers, including many whose significance was only transitory. As the work on this book progressed, it became appallingly evident that— if the book were not to expand to prohibitive size—either the space devoted to each composer must be curtailed or else a number of the composers must be deleted from the table of contents. To abbreviate the sketches would have defeated the very purpose of this book. It would have been impossible to include all that information which musical laymen seek about an important composer, information which he is unable to find in other reference books. The editor, therefore, decided to eliminate the less significant composers from the book. None of these omissions, the editor is confident, will be seriously felt by the reader.

In selecting composers for inclusion in this volume, the editor has chosen either those whose work still affords aesthetic pleasure, or else those who have played so important a part in the development of the musical art that their names live on, even though their music does not. Each sketch was prepared with the intent of giving the reader a historical perspective; in this connection, the editor urges the reader to consult frequently the synthetic historical outline in the appendix.

Each sketch includes a list of the principal works of each composer, a listing of the more important phonograph recordings of his music, and a bibliography. Where more than one recording of a work existed, the editor listed the one which, in his opinion, was the best, both from the point of view of performance and of quality of reproduction.

DAVID EWEN

November 11, 1936

CONTENTS

Key to Pronunciations

The correct pronunciation of foreign, unusual, or difficult names is indicated in footnotes to the biographies. The following simplified group of symbols is used:

ä, as in father; ă, as in at; ā, as in mate; à, as in miracle.

ĕ, as in pet; ē, as in tree; ē̄, as in her; è, as in prevail.

ĭ, as in tin; ī, as in wine.

ŏ, as in not; ō, as in note; ô, as in obey; oo, as in foot; o͞o, as in boot.

ŭ, as in cut; ū, as in amuse.

ou, as in out.

th, as in thee; TH, as in thin.

N indicates that the n itself is silent, but that the preceding vowel has a nasal quality.

H represents the German guttural ch, as in *ich*; and the Spanish guttural g or j, as in *gente*.

The main accent is indicated by a single stress

COMPOSERS OF YESTERDAY

Adolphe Adam *1803-1856*

AN important member of that school of French light opera (*opéra-comique*) of which Auber was dean and which included Hérold and Boieldieu, was Adolphe Charles Adam, who was born in Paris on July 24, 1803.

His father, Louis Adam, was well known as a pianist, teacher, and author of several books on piano method. Adolphe Adam was, therefore, brought into contact with music at an early age. It cannot be said that he was an alert pupil. "They tried to teach me music," he confessed in later years, "but in spite of my pronounced taste for it, I couldn't bring myself to do very much studying. I tore the method of my father to shreds; I simply refused to devote myself to scales. But I improvized incessantly."

His first important instructor was Benoist, the organist, at the Paris Conservatory, which he had entered in 1817. Even at the Conservatory, he was an apathetic student, until he came into contact with Boieldieu who, as his teacher and friend, turned Adam in a new direction in his music study. Thru Boieldieu's advice and influence, Adam turned from the composition of serious music in pretentious forms to that sphere which was so much more congenial to his gifts—that of the *opéra-comique*. In the words of Jacques Halévy, Boieldieu was Adam's "master, his guide and his friend. . . . He disengaged him from the labyrinth in which he had until now been enmeshed, and brought him to Melody which until now he had ignored. . . . Certainly, Adam had an instinct for the theatre, and would ultimately have discovered the road of which, at first, he lost sight; but Boieldieu avoided for him a long and circuitous route."

Adam's first creative effort in the lighter vein was an overture to Boieldieu's operetta, *Dame blanche*. This, in turn, was succeeded by a one-act

ADOLPHE ADAM

comic-opera, *Pierre et Catherine*, produced at the Opéra Comique in 1829. The following year, Adam produced his first success, the three-act *Danilowa* which encouraged him to continue along the path Boieldieu had pointed out to him.

In 1847, Adam started at his own expense a new operatic theatre which he called the Théâtre National, whose mission was to bring to the fore the work of young neglected composers who failed to procure a hearing elsewhere. Unfortunately, the revolution of 1848 crushed this venture in its infancy; the theatre was forced to close, involving its owner in great debt. Upon its closing, Adam assumed the responsibility of paying off each one of the many debts which he had incurred during the short life of his theatre. He succeeded in doing this during the next five years by producing a series of comic-operas, each of which proved to be more successful than the preceding one.

Adam enjoyed a triumphant career such as has been the fate of only a few composers. He was, perhaps, the most popular composer of his time. His melodies were heard everywhere; and his comic operas were the talk of the town. He was continually met with honor and adulation. He became a member of the Legion of Honor in 1836. Eight years later he was elected a member of the Institut; and in 1849 he became professor of composition at the Conservatory.

His death came suddenly on May 3, 1856, in Paris. The evening before his death he wrote several letters and reminded his wife to awaken him promptly at eight the following morning so that he might be punctual for a nine o'clock appointment with the composer, Auber. At the appointed hour, his wife came to his bedroom to arouse him. "His face was calm," described a friend of the family, "his eyes, half-open. He had merely pushed back the quilt ever so lightly. But the movement had been so slight that the little dog lying at his feet had not budged. Nor was the dog awakened, until a horrible cry arose from Mme. Adam's lips, when she could no longer doubt that tragedy had stricken her."

A grandiose funeral was the last honor that Paris extended to its beloved composer. The ceremony, which took place at the church Notre Dame de Lorette, was attended by the foremost musicians, writers and actors of the day.

During the height of his career, Adam led a life intense with activity and hard creative labor. "It is the fever of creation and hard work that prolongs my youth and succors me," he once wrote. He devoted the hours of night to composition. He slept infrequently, and never more than a few hours at a stretch.

His days were devoted to the many duties of the theatre, and to audiences given to the many people who besieged his door either to do him honor or to ask a favor. He was known to have been excessively generous; it was said that he never refused or neglected to do a favor, even to mere passing acquaintances.

He was a Parisian to the tips of his fingers. He possessed a contagious vivacity and an intriguing lightness of spirit which made him always a desirable companion. He loved good food, which he frequently ate gluttonously; he was a connoisseur of wines, with a most discriminating palate. The luxuries of soft living were essential to his happiness.

As a composer, he knew his own shortcomings only too well. "The misfortune about me," he said to a friend, "is that I write with too much facility— far too much facility."

While Adam occasionally turned his creative pen to serious efforts—producing several rather unfortunate grand operas —his entire significance as a composer rests with his lighter achievements, particularly with his light operas of which *Le Postillon de Longjumeau* is a characteristic example.

"If he failed completely in grand lyric drama, in spite of his desires and ambitions. . . he knew, despite the number of his rivals, how to bring into the field of light-opera a truly personal style, touched at the same time with grace and coquetry, with sentiment of emotion, with gaiety and comic verve," wrote Arthur Pougin in his valuable biography on the composer. "Much more versatile . . . than his rival [Auber] Adam possessed qualities for which one would search in vain in the former's music. If he was, to the general viewpoint—and this was quite evident!—less salty, less sustained, less pure in style; if he never had—and it was a fault!—that serenity, that equality of musical humor, which was in one way or another the distinctive characteristic or trade-mark of Auber's genius, he had to a greater degree than Auber, a tenderness of emotion . . . a sort of juvenile and naive grace . . . finally, a great poetic feeling."

When inspired by the sweet simplicity of French popular song," commented Sterling MacKinlay, "he produced effects of the tenderest pathos. Sometimes, however, his melodies are trivial in the extreme; his structure of concerted pieces is of the flimsiest kind, his dance rhythms used without moderation. . . He shares . . . the flowing melodiousness, rhythmical piquancy of style, precision of declamatory phrasing, and charming effects of graceful, though sketchy, instrumentation."

Adolphe Adam's ballet, *Giselle*, was a *pièce de resistance* in the repertoire of the famous Russian Ballet, and as danced by Nijinsky and Anna Pavlova, enjoyed preeminent success.

Principal works by Adolphe Adam:

OPERA: *Richard en Palestine*; *Le Châlet*; *Le Postillon de Longjumeau*; *Le Brasseur de Preston*; *Le Roi d'Yvetot*; *Cagliostro*; *Si j'étais roi*; *Le fidèle berger*.

BALLET: *Giselle*; *Le Corsaire*.

About Adolphe Adam:

Halévy, Jacques. *Souvenirs et Portraits*; MacKinlay, Sterling. *Origin and Development of Light Opera*; Pougin, Arthur. *Adolphe Adam*.

Important recordings of music by Adolphe Adam:

SELECTIONS FROM OPERAS: *Le Châlet*, "Arrêtons-nous ici," and "Chant de la montagne" (ODEON); "Entendez-vous ces airs touchants" (ODEON); "Dieu soutient mon courage" and "Il faut me céder" (ODEON). *Le Postillon de Longjumeau*, "Mes amis, écoutez l'histoire" and "Villabella" (PATHE). *Si j'étais roi*, "Overture" (PARLAPHONE-Bodanzky); "Regard de ses yeux" and "J'ignorais son nom" (ODEON).

Isaac Albéniz *1860-1909*

"In him—sensual and melancholy, joyous and passionate, wild and chivalrous—the soul of Spain has found, and embodied, itself."—MARLIAVE

ISAAC ALBÉNIZ, one of the most distinguished of Spanish composers, was born at Camprodón, in the province of Gerona, on May 29, 1860. It is curiously appropriate that his life, which was thruout rich with adventure and travel, should have begun on a dramatic note: Immediately after Isaac Albéniz's birth, his father was compel'ed to take the child to a different town—on a night electric with storm, and thru almost impassable roads—in order to procure a nurse capable of satisfying the infant's voracious appetite.

Albéniz's musical education began early. At the age of four, he made an appearance as a pianist in Barcelona and played with such self-assurance that the audience was convinced that a mature pianist was performing behind the curtains. Two years later, he entered a competition for piano-playing held at the Conservatory of Paris. His performance was brilliant and, with the prize virtually in the palm of his hand, he expressed his contempt for competitions in general and for the Conservatory in particular by taking a ball out of his pocket, and by throwing it with all his strength, smashing the mirrors in the contest hall.

He was back in Madrid in 1868, and was entered in the Madrid Conservatory for routined musical instruction. Routine could not discipline a boy of Albéniz's restless temperament. At that time he was an insatiable reader of adventure stories, particu'arly those of Jules Verne. Inspired by his reading, he suddenly decided to satisfy a hunger for travel by running away from home. He escaped on the first train, but hardly had he settled comfortably in his seat when he was accosted by the alcalde of the Escurial who, impressed by the boy's story, took him to his home where, at the Casino, the boy gave a sensational piano recital. The concert over, the boy was put upon a train by the alcalde who, with threats and commands, ordered the boy to return directly home. Isaac listened meekly to the commands, promising faithfully to obey them. Then, at Villalba, he slipped from the train, boarded another one which was going in the opposite direction and began what was soon to become a solitary pilgrimage

thru the principal cities of northern Spain. He visited Avila, Zamora, and Salamanca, giving concerts and earning a sizable income. His pockets bulging with his earnings, young Albéniz decided that he would, at last, return home. En route, he was robbed, and rather than face the humiliation of returning with empty pockets, he decided to undertake another concert tour to regain his lost money. This time he traveled for two years, earning, as a prodigy, a reputation which spanned the borders of Spain.

In his eleventh year, he was back in his father's home. The inactivity of home life soon proved too stifling to a born rover. Once again young Albéniz escaped. He had reached Cadiz when he was apprehended by the governor of the city who was determined to send him back home. Late one night, Albéniz escaped from his temporary prison and boarded a boat for Porto Rico. From Porto Rico he smuggled himself to Cuba, from Cuba to Buenos Aires, and from Buenos Aires to the United States. He played the piano in concert halls and in café-houses, and when he had amassed two thousand dollars he decided to sail for Europe for serious music study.

For a short while, he settled in Leipzig, studying under Jadassohn and Reinecke. But his blood was warm for adventure, and his spirit eager for more travel. A few months of study, and he took the road to Spain. Here, thru the intervention of Count Morphy, he was introduced to the King, Alphonso XII, who was so stirred by the boy's musical gifts that he endowed him with a pension to enable him to continue his study. Albéniz went to Brussels to become a pupil of François Gevaert. It was here that he first met his life-long friend, Enrique Fernández Arbós (today, a celebrated orchestral conductor) who, at that time, was also a student.

It cannot be said that Albéniz was even now a very diligent pupil. He became acquainted with a group of dissolute young men, neglected his studies, and dissipated his time and energies in drink and gambling. At this time, he entered into a compact with a friend in which they promised each other to enjoy life to the full and then to commit suicide. One evening, Albéniz learned that his young

friend had hung himself. The news sobered Albéniz, and for the first time he promised himself to brush aside all manner of dissipation, to surrender all thought of travel and adventure, and to turn seriously to music study.

For a long while he kept his promise. In Brussels, he gave a concert the proceeds of which enabled him to make a trip to Weimar to meet Franz Liszt. Liszt was greatly impressed with the boy's pianistic talents, and from that time on there developed between the great composer and Albéniz a close friendship which persisted until the former's death.

In 1880, Albéniz went on an extensive concert-tour which brought him to Cuba, Mexico, Argentina and the principal cities of Spain. The following year, he devoted himself strictly to routine work —to the teaching of the piano, to concertizing and, at night, to the composition of pot-boilers. Two years later he settled in Barcelona where he married, deciding, at last, to lead a domestic and sedentary existence. Unfortunately, he invested his money in unwise stock speculations and became so involved in debt that he was forced to flee. He came to Madrid where he remained for several years. It was here that he became a pupil of Felippe Pedrell—often considered the father of modern Spanish music [1]—who was to have an inestimable influence upon Albéniz's career. It was Pedrell who turned Albéniz from a pianistic career and hack composition to important artistic creation; and it was Pedrell who first instilled into Albéniz the mission of producing an autochthonic Spanish music.

Albéniz's last public appearance occurred in Berlin in 1893. He settled in Paris shortly thereafter, and from that time on devoted himself entirely to serious composition. At first he composed scores for musical comedies. Then, feeling increasing strength in his fingers, he turned his pen to giving expression to the Spanish idiom in significant musical forms. In 1899, his *Catalonia*—a piano work which he himself orchestrated—was performed at the Colonne concerts in Paris.

In 1900, a serious illness brought him to Spain, and for the remainder of his

[1] See sketch on Felippe Pedrell.

life he was to make his home in his native country. Here he knew misery and despair, heightened by his own illness, by the prolonged maladies of his wife, and by the death of a daughter. It was while his spirit was thus darkened that, in 1904, he composed what is generally recognized as his masterpiece, his suite for the piano, *Iberia*. It is interesting to point out that Albéniz almost burned the manuscript of *Iberia* because he thought that it was technically so complex that no pianist could possibly perform it!

Isaac Albéniz died in Cambó on June 16, 1909. His daughter, Laura, has touchingly described the last evening. "The Spring has been damp and chill, and the flowers refused to bloom. My father's room opened on a terrace filled with woodbine and rosetrees, and every day he asked me would the roses never bloom. Two days before my father's death the sun shone in fullest radiance, and on the morning, as though by magic, we found that all the roses had opened. They were the purest pink in color. And that evening, my sister and I went out on the terrace and cut all the roses to cover our father with them. . . ."

Albéniz died lamenting the fact that he had spent so much of his time and energy in the composition of operas, and so little in a field in which he was a master—the composition of Spanish music for piano or orchestra. After his death, his body was transferred from Cambó to Barcelona; and to the accompaniment of the *Requiem* of Gabriel Fauré, and the funeral marches of Beethoven, Chopin and Wagner, Albéniz was interred in the South-West Churchyard.

Albéniz was as gentle and lovable as he was impractical and, upon occasion, irrational. He was extravagant financially because he could never learn to value money, and he detested contemplating the problems of everyday existence. He possessed a pungent sense of humor, and one of his essential traits was a roguishness which, thruout his life, made his personal friends helpless victims of his pranks. Like so many other great composers, he adored Nature, and the outdoors; and his life attests to the fact that he was passionately fond of travel. He

had three children, and his favorite was his youngest daughter, Laura.

Isaac Albéniz's importance in musical history rests in the fact that, together with Granados, he gave a further impetus to that movement begun by Felippe Pedrell—namely, the creation of a Spanish musical art based on a native idiom. This movement has reached culmination in the works of such modern Spanish composers as Manuel de Falla and Joaquin Turina.

In his most important works, Albéniz is essentially a Spanish composer, and his music, as J. B. Trend carefully points out, "is very much in 'the Spanish idiom'; but it is the Spanish idiom employed by a master, and in the best of them . . . one can forget the 'idiom' in the beauty of the musical thought. . . . The more one gets to know. . . Albéniz, the more it becomes apparent that the 'Spanish idiom' is something to which one has to become so accustomed that one no longer notices it—in other words, it is impossible to see what a composer means until his idiom is so familiar that one is no longer distracted by it."

Georges Jean-Aubry has astutely analyzed Albéniz's crowning creative achievement, the *Iberia*, for piano. "*Iberia* marks the summit of the art of Albéniz. . . . One finds here all that emotion and culture can desire. The composer here reached a sureness of touch and grasped an originality of technique which demanded much attention and which have no ulterior object. . . . There are no doubt fastidious critics who will find blemishes, but such blemishes as exist are not detrimental to expression, and this alone is important. In music there are many excellent scholars but few poets. Albéniz has all the power of the poet—ease and richness of style, beauty and originality of imagery, and a rare sense of suggestion.

"A list of the themes alone of *Iberia* would suffice to show their richness in melody and the variety of their rhythm. But more wonderful than the beauty of the themes is their suppleness and fluidity; their languorous intonation, or their heat and energy. That in which Albéniz is inimitable is the atmosphere he creates around a theme, the scenery with which he surrounds the 'melodic personage'—a word, a song, or a murmured confession. The method of Albéniz, if one can use such a word with regard to him, is almost inscrutable. It obeys only subtle and personal laws. An expressive counterpoint, always ductile and full of movement, supports his themes, plays with them or crosses them. The parts seem at times inextricably intermingled, and suddenly all is again resolved in lucidity."

Iberia has been orchestrated by Enrique Fernández Arbós, and in this form has been prominently featured by symphony orchestras.

Principal works by Isaac Albéniz:

OPERA: *The magic opal*; *Enrico Clifford*; *Poor Jonathan*; *San Antonio de la Florida*; *Pepita Jiménez*, etc.

ORCHESTRA: *Iberia* (orchestrated by Arbós); *Catalonia*.

PIANO: *Suite Española*; *Pavana*; *Iberia*; *Cantos de España*; *La Vega*; *Navarra*; *Azulejos*; *Malagueñas*; *Tango*, etc.

CHORAL: *Cristo*.

About Isaac Albéniz:

Collet, Henri. *Albéniz et Granados*; Van Vechten, Carl. *In the Garret*.

British Musician 5:91 April 1929; *Chesterian* N.S. 6:43 November 1924; *Musical Quarterly* 15:117 January 1929.

Important recordings of music by Isaac Albéniz:

ORCHESTRA: *Iberia*, orchestrated by Arbós (COLUMBIA-Arbós); *Jota Aragonesa* (ODEON).

SELECTIONS FROM OPERA: *Pepita Jiménez*, "Intermezzo" (COLUMBIA-Arbós).

PIANO: *Córdoba* and *Evocación* (VICTOR-Rubinstein); *Málaga* (POLYDOR-Borowsky); *Granada* (COLUMBIA-Viñes); *Triana* (PATHE); *Malagueñas* and *Seguidillas* (VICTOR-Cortot); *Sevillanas* (VICTOR-Iturbi); *Tango* (VICTOR-Bachaus).

Eugène d'Albert *1864-1932*

EUGÈNE FRANCIS CHARLES D'ALBERT was born in Glasgow on April 10, 1864. His father, of German nationality, and a dancing master, was a composer of much dance music. Eugène's childhood was an unhappy one. He had no friends or playmates, and at home was misunderstood by parents who failed to realize that their son had great musical talent. Loneliness and abuse were his fate for several years.

EUGÈNE D'ALBERT

Until his twelfth year, he was virtually self-taught in music. When he finally undertook systematic instruction at the National School of Music, he learned his lessons with such rapidity that he was soon elected Queen Victoria Scholar. He was known to have been an unusually industrious pupil, and it is related that when Sir Arthur Sullivan started a composition class at the school, D'Albert brought in so much work that Sullivan was forced to comment: "Good gracious, my dear boy, do you expect me ever to go thru with all this?"

Eugène d'Albert made his first important public appearance as a pianist in 1880 when he performed at a Monday Popular Concert in London, his facile technique attracting attention. The following year, he performed the *Piano concerto* of Robert Schumann both at the Crystal Palace Saturday concerts and at the Royal Philharmonic Orchestra concerts. Once again his performance aroused enthusiasm.

Towards the close of 1881, Hans Richter, the eminent conductor, met Eugène d'Albert, and was so impressed by the young man's musical intelligence and talents that he invited him to introduce his own *First piano concerto* at the Hans Richter concerts in London. The concert was successful, and the *Concerto*—D'Albert's first major work—received high praise. As a result of this success,

Hans Richter brought D'Albert to Vienna for a repetition of the same concert with the Vienna Philharmonic. The concert was widely publicized in view of the fact that Eugène d'Albert was the youngest pianist ever to appear with the Vienna Philharmonic. The spontaneous charm and melodic originality of the *Concerto* found many enthusiastic admirers even among discriminating Viennese audiences.

It was at this time that D'Albert decided to make Germany his permanent home, principally because he wished to be near that master of all pianists, Franz Liszt. There developed a friendship between Liszt and D'Albert which was all-significant in the development of the latter both as pianist and as composer. Liszt admired the young artist—whom he playfully called "Albertus Magnus"— and frequently said that, were he only a young man again, he would have liked having D'Albert as his rival at the piano.

In 1882, D'Albert was appointed *Hofpianist des Grossherzogs* of Weimar. The following year, he gave his first piano recital in Berlin, introducing at the same time his own *Piano suite*. There followed, for the next few years, concert-tours thruout the world which definitely established him as one of the greatest pianists of his generation, and one of the foremost interpreters of Bach and Beethoven.

It was, however, not all triumph. In 1905, he made an extensive tour of America, and was so exhausted by the strain of travel that his performances suffered severely. In Cincinnati, he played so far below his customary standards that a local critic viciously attacked him. D'Albert took the criticism as a personal affront, and instituted a legal suit against the reviewer. This action aroused the antagonism of the American music public, and during the remaining concerts his audiences were so embittered against him that, for a while, D'Albert seriously feared an attempt would be made on his life. The legal suit was hurriedly dropped, and D'Albert cancelled the remainder of his American concert-tour.

Upon returning to Germany, D'Albert succeeded Joseph Joachim as director of the Hochschule in Berlin, holding this position with great distinction for many years.

D'Albert's first opera, *Der Rubin*, was given a performance in Karlsruhe in 1893 only because D'Albert was willing to pay 5,000 marks into the treasury of the opera house. It was not favorably received. There followed other operas, none of which impressed the German music public deeply. It was not until 1910 that Eugène d'Albert was accepted as a composer of importance. In that year, Gustave Brecker performed in Dresden *Tiefland,* an opera which had been introduced in Prague seven years previously. Performed in a slightly abridged version, *Tiefland* now created such a vivid impression that, soon afterwards, it was introduced into the repertory of important opera houses thruout the world. It was exhibited to the American music public in 1914 by the Century Opera Company.

Discussing *Tiefland,* Felix Borowski has written: "In his score, D'Albert followed the Italians only partly down the road which they had made. He, as they, caused the music to deepen and enhance the message of the play, but D'Albert did not open the sluices of vocal melody that caused Italian opera to be a synonym for song. With him, as with most German composers for the theatre, the orchestra carries the burden of the music, and the vocal element is declamation, only occasionally transmuted into tune. For the rest, the score is often charming and not infrequently stirring to the ear. Originality may not stream richly thru its pages, but that perhaps may explain some of the opera's success."

During the last years of his life, Eugène d'Albert lived in seclusion and retirement, devoting all his time and energy to composition. He died in Riga, Latvia, on March 3, 1932, after placing the final strokes on his last opera, *Mister Wu. Mister Wu* was given its first performance in Dresden on September 29, 1932, five months after D'Albert's death, and it was generally considered an unimpressive achievement. "In D'Albert's watered version," wrote Geraldine de Courcy in review, "the lacklustre meanderings of uninspired music shear the dramatic impulse of its thrust, and we have neither good music nor good melodrama."

Eugène d'Albert was married six times. His third wife was Teresa Carreño, the distinguished pianist, who also, curiously enough, had been married twice before. His last divorce was procured two months before his death.

He was a robust man with an inexhaustible capacity for hard work, and an incredible fund of energy. He was a fond devotee of sports, cycling and tennis being his major diversions. The study of medica¹ science was his favorite intellectual pastime.

He received n, less than ten official decorations for h,s musical achievements.

Principal works by Eugène d'Albert:

OPERA: *Der Rubin*; *Die Abreise*; *Kain*; *Tiefland*; *Flauto solo*; *Die toten augen*; *Mister Wu*.

ORCHESTRA: Two concertos for piano and orchestra; *Concerto for violoncello and orchestra*; *Symphony*; Overtures: *Esther*, *Hyperion*.

CHAMBER MUSIC: Two string quartets.

About Eugène d'Albert:

Raupp, Wilhelm. *Eugène D'Albert*.

Musical Courier 104:5 March 12, 1932; *Musical Times* 45:697 November 1, 1904.

Important recordings of music by Eugène d'Albert:

SELECTIONS FROM OPERAS: *Tiefland*, "Fantasia" (PARLAPHONE); "Entr'acte, Act I." (PARLAPHONE-D'Albert); "Wolfserzählung" (ODEON-Tauber); "Traumerzählung" (ODEON-Tauber). *Die toten augen*, "Fantasia" (GRAMOPHONE); "Arie der Psyche" (PARLAPHONE-Lehmann).

Gregorio Allegri *1582-1652*

GREGORIO ALLEGRI, who continued the traditions of the sixteenth century Roman polyphonic school, was born in Rome in 1582 to a family which included among its members the celebrated painter Correggio.

For five years (from 1591 until 1596) Allegri was a choir-boy, participating as a tenor in the festivals at San Luigi. He turned after that to composition, and produced several motets and concertini of such merit that they attracted

the attention of Pope Urban VIII who, on December 6, 1629, appointed Allegri singer in his Chapel. Allegri held this position until his death, which took place in Rome on February 17, 1652. He was buried in the chapel of Santo Filippo Neri of the Chiesa Nuova in Rome.

Gregorio Allegri, who composed an entire library of polyphonic music, is famous in musical history by virtue of one major work, the *Miserere*, which for many years was sung each Holy Week at the Sistine Chapel. The score of the *Miserere* was kept secret for a long time, to prevent any performance of this work elsewhere, and it was decreed by the Pope that any attempt to copy it was punishable with excommunication. It is one of the most famous anecdotes in musical history that Wolfgang Mozart in 1770—then a boy of thirteen—heard the *Miserere*, during a visit to Rome, and after one hearing was able to put the entire score upon paper from memory. The pope was so impressed by this incredible feat that, instead of excommunicating this amazing genius, he honored him with a decoration.

George Hogarth, in commenting upon the *Miserere*, informs us that the work does not appear very impressive upon paper. "It is a piece of very plain and simple harmony." Its effectiveness was due exclusively to the skill and invention with which the chapel singers performed the work.

It is related, as a matter of fact, that Emperor Leopold I of Austria, a patron of music, ordered his ambassador at Rome to apply to the Pope for permission to copy the score of the *Miserere*. The Pope decided to cede to the Emperor's request, and ordered the composer to copy the music and send it to Austria. When the Emperor received the music he was so amazed at its mediocrity that he believed that he had been duped by the Pope, ever intent upon keeping the precious *Miserere* a secret. He sent to Rome a bitter note which resulted in Allegri's dismissal from the papal service. For a long time, the Pope refused to see the composer or to hear his defense. Finally, at the inter-

GREGORIO ALLEGRI

Principal works by Gregorio Allegri:

CHORAL: *Miserere*; motets; magnificats; concertini, etc.

About Gregorio Allegri:

Burney, Charles. *A General History of Music*; Halévy, Jacques. *Souvenirs et Portraits*; Hogarth, George. *Musical History, Biography and Criticism*; Mendelssohn, Felix. *Letters from Italy and Switzerland.*

Anton Arensky *1861-1906*

ANTON STEPANOVITCH ARENSKY was born at Nijny-Novgorod on August 11, 1861. His environment was a musical one, his father—a doctor—being an accomplished violoncellist, and his mother capable of playing the piano with professional competence. Arensky was, therefore, brought early into contact with music for which he showed marked aptitude. At the age of nine, still ignorant of the rules of composition, he produced his first string quartet.

His unusual flair for music encouraged his parents to send him to St. Petersburg in 1879 where he became a student at the Conservatory, and ultimately a pupil of Rimsky-Korsakoff. He was an adept pupil, winning a gold medal and arousing considerable comment with a symphony and a piano concerto which he composed at this time and which were performed in St. Petersburg and Moscow. No less a musician than Tschaikovsky became vitally interested in him and began to intercede for him to Rimsky-Korsakoff, urging the latter to substitute an Arensky work for the previously scheduled *Romeo and Juliet* of Tschaikovsky at one of the forthcoming orchestral concerts.

Upon completing his studies at the Conservatory, Arensky came to Moscow where he now made his home for thirteen years. Shortly after his arrival, he was appointed professor of counterpoint at the Moscow Conservatory, and it was during this period of pedagogy that he produced the most important part of his musical output. Of this, his opera, *A dream on the Volga*, produced in Moscow in 1892, enhanced his reputation considerably.

He was uniquely honored in 1895 by an appointment as director of the

vention of a Cardinal, the Pope gave Allegri an audience enabling him to explain the entire situation. The Pope asked that a paper be drawn and sent to Vienna. The situation was finally alleviated when Leopold urgently requested the Pope to send him a few papal choristers to teach his own singers how the work should be performed most effectively. Unfortunately, before their arrival, a Turkish-Austrian war drew the Emperor from Vienna.

Felix Mendelssohn, the celebrated composer, has commented upon the *Miserere* which he had occasion to hear during his voyage to Italy. "The *Miserere*," he wrote, "is a simple sequence of chords, grounded either on tradition, or what appears to be much more probable, merely embellishments, introduced by some clever maestro for the fine voices at his disposal, and especially for a very high soprano. These embellishments always recur on the same chords, and as they are cleverly constructed and beautifully adapted for the voice, it is invariably pleasing to hear them repeated. I could not discover anything unearthly or mysterious in the music; indeed, I am perfectly contented that its beauty should be earthly and comprehensible."

Imperial Choir, one of the most significant musical posts in Russia at the time.
He held this position with esteem for
six years, relinquishing it only because
he wished to devote himself completely
to composition. Upon his resignation,
he found himself in enviable circumstances, indeed. He was drawing a yearly pension of 6000 rubles, and was left
unhampered to devote his entire effort
to creative work.

It is to be greatly regretted that his
health had by this time become considerably undermined by hard work and
more especially by dissipation (thruout
his life, Arensky had been a heavy
drinker and an inveterate gambler). He
developed consumption, and in attempt
to recover his lost strength he went to
Nice. His last days were spent in a
sanitarium in Finland. He died in
Terioki on February 25, 1906.

The outstanding features of Arensky's
composition, as pointed out by Cobbett
in a succinct resumé, are "the brevity
of his finales and the extreme brilliancy
of his scherzos. That contained in the
piano quintet is one of the brightest
movements in chamber-music repertory.
It sparkles like diamonds in the sun."

Arensky was never numbered among
the more important members of Russian
music—even though some of his
chamber-works are still performed by
prominent string quartets—primarily because he lacked an authentically original
vocabulary. Too frequently his music
revealed imitative speeches. In his writing for orchestra, and in many of his
chamber-works, he disclosed the indelible
influence that both Tschaikovsky and
Rimsky-Korsakoff had exerted upon
him. It is precisely this derivative
quality of Arensky's music that has
tempted Rimsky-Korsakoff to say of its
composer that "he will soon be forgotten."

Principal works by Anton Arensky:

OPERA: *Raphael*; *Nal and Damayanti*; *A
dream on the Volga.*
CHORAL: *The Fountain of Bakhchisarai*;
The Diver.
ORCHESTRA: Two symphonies; *Concerto
for piano and orchestra*; *Fantasia on Russian
folk-songs* (for piano and orchestra); *Con-
certo for violin and orchestra.*
CHAMBER MUSIC: Two string quartets;
Intermezzo (for string quartet); *Piano trio*;
Piano quintet; pieces for piano, for two
pianos, etc.

About Anton Arensky:

Cobbett, Walter Willson. *Cyclopedic Survey
of Chamber Music*; Pougin, Arthur. *A Short
History of English Music*; Rimsky-Korsakoff,
Nicholas. *My Musical Life.*

Important recordings of music by
Anton Arensky:

SELECTIONS FROM OPERA: *Raphael*, "Sere-
nade" (VICTOR).
CHAMBER MUSIC: *Trio*, "Scherzo"
(COLUMBIA); *Suite, no. 2*, "Waltz" (VICTOR-
Bauer, Gabrilowitsch).

Thomas Arne *1710-1778*

THOMAS AUGUSTINE ARNE,
one of the significant figures in
eighteenth-century English music, was
born in London on March 12, 1710. His
father was a London tradesman, who
enjoyed some reflected glory by virtue of
the fact that he was used as the model
for Addison's *Political Upholsterer.*

It was that eminent musicologist,
Charles Burney, who gave Thomas Arne
his first systematic instruction in music.
Arne's father, however, was vigorously
opposed to music as a career. And so,
in his adolescence, Thomas Arne was
sent to Eton for the purpose of studying
law. But, as Burney wrote, "his love
for music operated upon him too powerfully for his own peace, or that of his

ANTON ARENSKY

companions; for with a miserable cracked flute, he used to torment them night and day when not obliged to attend school."

As the years passed, music drew Arne more and more ineluctably to its bosom. When he left school, he borrowed a servant's uniform so that he might gain admission to the upper gallery of the opera which was reserved for domestics. As an articled clerk in an attorney's office, he saved his earnings in order to buy a spinet which he smuggled into his bedroom; muffling its strings with handkerchiefs, he would practice upon it during the night when his family was in bed. With equal secrecy he took lessons upon the violin, and so amazed his father, one day, by playing upon it, that he finally succeeded in gaining permission to follow the study of music seriously.

In 1732, Arne produced his first creative effort of importance—*Rosamond,* an opera, based upon a libretto of Addison. This was performed at the Lincoln's Inn Fields Theatre the following year and was well received. Encouraged, Thomas Arne produced that same year a masque, *Dido and Aeneas,* which in turn was succeeded by several operas.

His reputation, however, was not firmly established until 1738. In that year he was commissioned to compose music for Dr. Dalton's adaptation of Milton's *Comus,* and it was in this work that Arne for the first time revealed his great ability as a composer. In *Comus,* as we are informed by William H. Cummings, "Arne made it quite evident that he possessed a style of melody peculiarly English and wholly his own. Graceful, flowing, and elegant, full of expression and just accent; jolly when the poetry required animation, and simple when the situation demanded it."

From that time on, Arne's position in the English music of his day was firmly established. That position he further solidified in 1740. Commissioned to compose music for a masque to be performed at a fête held by Frederick, Prince of Wales, at his residence, *Cliefden,* near Maidenhead, to commemorate the Hanoverian Accession to the throne of England and the birthday

of the Princess Augusta, Arne composed the music for *Alfred,* a masque which contained among its numbers the immortal anthem, *Rule Britannia.* It might not be out of place to point out that *Rule Britannia* was considered by Beethoven sufficiently important as a musical work for him to utilize it in his *Battle symphony* and, in still another work, in a series of five variations on the theme. Richard Wagner arranged it for grand orchestra in 1836.

After a short sojourn in Dublin—where he earned particular success with an operatic oratorio, *Abel*—Arne returned to London to become in 1745, composer to Vauxhall Gardens, for which he wrote some of his most famous songs. During this period, too, he wrote incidental music extensively for Shakespeare's plays—and some of his Shakespearean airs (*Where the bee sucks,* for example) have earned him immortality. In 1759, Arne was honored with a doctorate degree in music by the University of Oxford.

His later years were darkened by grief. Domestic troubles, pecuniary difficulties and illness combined to embitter his life, and his one-time glory and prestige became a thing of the distant past. He died on the fifth of March, in 1778, of a spasm of the lungs, "retaining his faculties to the last moment of his existence," as we learn from the writings of a contemporary. "He had originally been instructed in the principles of the Roman Church. These, however, he had for many years wholly neglected, as inconsistent with a life of ease and gallantry, in which he indulged to the full extent of his purse and constitution. In his last stage, the dormant seeds of early maxims revived in his bosom, too strong to be checked. A priest was sent for, and he was soon awed into a state of submissive repentance. For about an hour before his death he sang an harmonious Hallelujah, calculated to usher him into another world."

Thomas Arne was a scholar, well-versed in Italian and Latin, and intimately familiar with great literature. During his entire life he had an unusual attachment for women. He was an epicure and would frequently neglect important

THOMAS ARNE

engagements to partake of a good dinner. His correspondence further reveals him to be a "jealous and self-seeking tradesman," an opportunist of the first water. When he was eager to compose music for Dryden's *King Arthur*, for which Purcell, too, composed a score, he could write in a letter to Garrick that Purcell's songs were "infamously bad—so bad that they are privately the objects of sneer and ridicule to musicians," a fact which he knew to be false.

As a composer, Arne "carries light armor," as W. H. Hadow has written "He wins by readiness of attack and dexterity of movement, he is less at his ease in the larger and more stately exercises of art than in those of the . . . playing ground; but his sentiment, if a little shallow, is always sincere and his melody is delightfully fresh and spontaneous. In an age when English music had become dull and academic, he lightened it with a native wood-note of genuine sweetness and charm; and though he seldom rises to the first order, and that only for moments, he takes an honorable rank in the second."

"But, unequal composer though he was," to conclude with a critical comment of Ernest Walker, "Arne at his best possessed an individual vein of melody which, if not for a moment comparable with Purcell is, nevertheless, genuine and pure; it is true that his range is not wide, and his emotion not deep, but still his music lives and breathes, even after one hundred and fifty years have elapsed."

Principal works by Thomas Arne:

OPERA: *Rosamond*; *Opera of operas*; *Dido and Aeneas*; *Comus*; *Alfred*; *The prophetess*; *The sultan*; *The ladies' frolic*; *The portrait*; *The fairy prince*; *May day*; *Phoebe at court*; *Phillis*, etc.

ORCHESTRA: Incidental music to innumerable plays, including Shakespeare's *Tempest*, *Merchant of Venice*, etc.; overtures.

Songs, glees, catches, canons, sonatas for harpsichord, masses, organ concertos, etc.

About Thomas Arne:

Burney, Charles. *A General History of Music*; Cummings, William H. *Arne*; Horner, Burnham W. *Life and Works of Dr. Arne*; Sharp, R. Farquharson. *Makers of Music*.

Monthly Musical Record 62:179 October 1932; *Musical Times* 42:713 November 1, 1901; *Proceedings of the Musical Association* (1909-1910), 36 Session, p. 75.

Important recordings of music by Thomas Arne:

SONGS: *Blow, blow thou winter wind* and *Under the greenwood tree*, arranged by Fellowes (GRAMOPHONE); *Celia's charms* (DECCA); *Rule Britannia* (COLUMBIA); *Where the bee sucks* (COLUMBIA).

Thomas Attwood   *1765-1838*

THOMAS ATTWOOD, distinguished composer of English church music, was born in London on November 23, 1765, the son of a coal-merchant who was a very devoted musical amateur.

At the age of nine, Thomas Attwood became a chorister in the Chapel Royal, studying music at that time under Dr. Ayrton. Seven years later, he performed in a concert at Buckingham Palace, where his talents were immediately recognized by the Prince of Wales (later George IV), who sent the boy to Italy for further musical study. For two years, Attwood remained in Naples as a pupil of Filippo Cinque and Gaetano Latilla.

From Naples, Attwood went to Vienna where, for a brief period, he was a pupil of Wolfgang Mozart. Mozart was deeply impressed with Attwood's abilities, and at one time said of his pupil: "Attwood is a young man for whom I

THOMAS ATTWOOD

have a sincere affection and esteem. . . . He partakes more of my style than any scholar I ever had, and I predict that he will prove a sound musician."

When Attwood returned to England, in 1787, he was appointed organist of the St. George-the-Martyr Church. In 1791, he was named private musical instructor to the Duchess of York, and five years later assumed still greater importance when he became organist of St. Paul Cathedral, and composer for the Chapel Royal.

From that time on, he enjoyed a fruitful musical career. In 1813, he became one of the founders of the Royal Philharmonic Orchestra, which he conducted for a few performances. Eight years later, he was appointed organist of the George IV private chapel in Brighton, and in 1823 he became one of the professors of the newly-founded Royal Academy of Music. Between 1791 and 1816, he composed many operas which were performed in England, but none of these enjoyed great success.

Thomas Attwood died at his home in Chelsea on March 24, 1838, and was buried in St. Paul's Cathedral, under the organ which he had played for so many years.

While he composed prolifically for the stage, Attwood is best known for the music which he composed for church services; until the end of the nineteenth century no church music enjoyed greater popularity in England than his. W. H. Hadow has characterized Attwood's compositions as "distinguished by purity and taste, as well as force and expression."

Principal works by Thomas Attwood:
CHORAL: Five services; Seventeen anthems; Nine chants, etc.
OPERA: *The Adopted child; The Castle of Sorrento; The Magic oak; Harlequin's tour; The Escape; Adrian and Orilla; The Curfew,* etc.
Songs, pieces for piano, etc.

About Thomas Attwood:
Barrett, William Alexander. *English Church Composers;* Kelly, Michael. *Reminiscences.*

Daniel François Auber   *1782-1871*

DANIEL FRANÇOIS ESPRIT AUBER, "prince of the *opéra-comique,*" was born in Caen, Normandy, on January 29, 1782. His father was something of an aristocrat, by virtue of his position as officer of the Royal Hunt. The Revolution deprived him of his sinecure, and he became a publisher and storekeeper—prospering sufficiently to earn a respectable livelihood, and to give his son a competent education.

By the time Auber reached his sixteenth birthday, he was deemed an accomplished boy. He could play the violin and piano well, and he possessed a pleasing singing voice. He knew Italian fluently, and could write a graceful prose. And he was already composing small musical pieces of noticeable merit.

In late adolescence, he was sent by his father to London to become fluent in a language valuable in the publishing business, as well as to acquire closer contact with English business methods. The rupture of the Treaty of Amiens forced young Auber to return to Paris in his twentieth year. However, he vigorously refused to affiliate himself with his father's establishment, and devoted his hours instead to composition. That these hours were well spent was proved soon thereafter; in 1806, his *Violin concerto* was performed by Mazas at the Conservatory concerts and disclosed ripe creative talent.

His father decided to consult some musical authority on the extent of his son's musical capabilities. He turned to

Cherubini, one of the most important musical figures in Paris at the time. Cherubini carefully evaluated the manuscripts brought to him, and gave the following equivocal verdict: "Your son does not lack imagination; but it is necessary for him to begin by forgetting everything he knows so that he can start learning something." Mild praise, indeed; but that Cherubini did not think too lightly of Auber's gifts was emphatically proved when Cherubini offered to teach the young musician. For three years, Auber studied with Cherubini, and after this period of study he emerged fully equipped, technically, to enter upon composition in all seriousness.

He soon turned to composing music for the stage. His early efforts—*Julie* (1811), *Jean de Couvin* (1812) and *Le Séjour militaire* (1813)—were, to be sure, immature, and received so unfavorable a reception that for six years Auber was discouraged from composing anything further for the theatre. In 1819, Auber re-emerged as a composer of operas when the Opéra Comique presented his *La Bergère châtelaine*. Once again the reception was frigid—but by this time Auber had become so convinced that in this medium lay his greatest potentialities as a composer that he would permit no discouragement to smother his enthusiasm.

It was not until Auber acquired the librettos of Augustin-Eugène Scribe, that he was to reach full maturity as a composer for the stage. Until his death, Scribe furnished Auber with a series of librettos for light and serious operas whose dramatic variety and sparkle of treatment kindled the embers of Auber's talent, causing it to burst into flame. *La Muette de Portici* came in 1828; *Fra Diavolo* in 1830; *Gustave III*, in 1833; *Le Domino noir*, in 1837, each enjoying success and bringing their composer prestige which made him the most popular composer of his time.

It is interesting to note, in connection with *La Muette de Portici*, that it had political as well as musical significance. Its revolutionary theme was largely responsible for the outbreak of riots in Brussels immediately after its per-

DANIEL FRANÇOIS AUBER

formance on August 25, 1830, which resulted in the ejection of the Dutch from that country.

The remaining years of Auber's life were crowned with triumph. In 1829, he was appointed member of the Académie, succeeding Gossec. In 1842, Louis Philippe made him director of the Conservatory, a position he held with considerable honor until the end of his life. And in 1857, Napoleon III further honored him by appointing him Imperial *Maître-de-la-chapelle*.

Daniel François Auber died in Paris on May 12, 1871, after having witnessed the first riots of the Paris Commune. His death was mourned by all Paris, who regarded him as one of its beloved sons and its most popular composer.

Francis Grierson has described Auber as a man of unimpressive appearance. "He might have passed for an old-clothes man," was his acid comment. However, Auber's personality more than compensated for his lack of physical dignity. He was known to possess great charm and a suave manner. His bon mots and quips were said to have been almost as famous as the airs of his comic-operas, and his conversation was fluent and rich with anecdote.

He was remarkably humble. "I have no self-conceit," he once said. "If I had any, I should have more talent." And at another occasion, in commenting upon

Gluck, he added: "A man like Gluck lived three flights up, and I have a gilded drawing room and English horses!"

He was, however, fond of living ostentatiously and sumptuously, and he was fastidious about his comforts. He ate only one meal a day.

In estimating Auber's musical position, it must be recalled that he was at his strongest in lighter moments, that in *opéra-comique*—rather than in serious opera—did his greatest talent lie. Henri Lavoix, in *Histoire de la Musique Française,* has emphasized this point: "One must expect from Auber neither a profound dramatic sentiment, nor poetical outbursts, nor powerful effects, nor sensibility, nor tenderness, nor—especially—passion. Wit in melody, wit in the general style, wit in the harmonies—which are ingenious and distinguished—wit in the orchestra, notwithstanding more *brio* than brilliancy, more sound than sonority—wit in the rhythms (altho these are sometimes vulgar)—wit especially in the disposition of the scenes—wit ever and always, even when the heart should be moved: this is the predominating character of his talent."

Though Auber's genius expressed itself most felicitously in flippant accents, it would be a mistake to underestimate his importance. Someone once remarked to Rossini that Auber's music was, after all, quite petty, to which Rossini answered: "If that is petty music, you must admit that it was, at least, grandly put together!" Another musical master—Richard Wagner—was equally enthusiastic about Auber's ingenuity. "His music, at once elegant and popular, fluent and precise, graceful and bold, bending with marvelous facility to every turn of his caprice, had all the qualities to win and dominate public taste. He mastered vocal music with a keen vivacity, multiplied its rhythms to infinity, and gave the ensemble pieces an *entrain,* a characteristic briskness scarcely known before his time."

It is generally accepted that Auber's masterpiece is *La Muette de Portici,* certainly one of the glories in *opéra-comique* repertory. "Here, indeed, was a fresh departure both in text and music," writes Arthur Hervey enthusiastically. "Rising to the occasion and putting forward all his skill, he surpassed his previous efforts and produced a work of wondrous brilliancy, replete with melody, admirably characteristic, and effectively scored. The diminished seventh with which the overture commences sounds as a defiance hurled against conventionality. In form, Auber had adhered to consecrated models and he had adopted some of the vocal acrobatics of Rossini. But he had also displayed a pronounced individuality of his own, an extraordinary gift of tune, and distinct qualities of musical characterization."

Principal works by Daniel François Auber:

OPERA: *Emma; Fiorella; La Muette de Portici; La Fiancée; Fra Diavolo; Le Philtre; Le Cheval de bronze; Gustave III; Le Domino noir; Zanetta; La Barcarolle; Zerline; Le Premier jour de bonheur,* etc.

About Daniel François Auber:

Lavoix, Henri. *Histoire de la Musique Française;* Malherbe, Charles. *Auber;* Wagner, Richard. *Collected Writings.*

English Review 18:173 August 1914.

Important recordings of music by Daniel François Auber:

SELECTIONS FROM OPERA: *Le Cheval de bronze,* "Ouverture" (GRAMOPHONE-Goossens). *Le Domino noir,* "Ouverture" (GRAMOPHONE-Blech). *Fra Diavolo,* "Ouverture" (COLUMBIA-Klemperer); "Ne craignez rien" and "Quel bonheur" (PARLAPHONE); "Voyez sur cette roche" (VICTOR); "C'est grande fête" and "Oh, Sainte Vierge" (GRAMOPHONE). *La Muette de Portici,* "Ouverture" (VICTOR-Boult); "L'Amour sacre de la patrie" (POLYDOR); "Du Pauvre seul ami fidèle" (GRAMOPHONE). *Zanetta,* "Ouverture" (GRAMOPHONE-Sargent).

Johann Christian Bach 1735-1782

"He is the Benjamin of the Bach family."—PHILIPP SPITTA

JOHANN CHRISTIAN BACH—frequently referred to by the musical historian as the "English Bach"—was the youngest son of Johann Sebastian Bach and Anna Magdalena. He was born in Leipzig on September 5, 1735.

In his fifteenth year, his father, Johann Sebastian, died, and Johann Christian was taken to Berlin by his half-brother, Friedemann Bach. There he was placed under the charge of Philipp Emanuel Bach, who for four years gave him rigorous musical schooling. While in Berlin, Johann Christian became intimately acquainted with Italian opera which aroused his enthusiasm and admiration.

In 1754, Bach came to Italy (for a long time it was falsely believed that he left for Italy in the company of an Italian prima donna), and shortly afterwards was appointed chapel master to Comte Agostino Litta, who provided him with sufficient means to enable him to continue his music-study under Padre Martini. During this period, Johann Christian became converted to the Catholic faith, and immersed himself deeply in the composition of church music. His first significant work—a Mass—was given a successful performance in 1757. Three years later, Bach was appointed organist of the Milan Cathedral.

By this time, Bach's musical enthusiasm had been partially diverted from the church to his first love—the theatre; and, together with masses, requiems and motets, he began the composition of operas. In 1761, *Artaserse* was presented in Turin, followed by a production in Naples of *Catone in Utica*. One year later, Naples saw the first performance of *Allesandro nell'Indie*. These three operas were successful, and Bach's reputation now grew so great that it penetrated beyond the boundaries of Italy.

In 1762, the directors of Italian opera in London began negotiations with Johann Christian Bach, and on February 19, 1763 his first Italian opera for England, *Orione*, was produced at the King's Theatre. The King and the Queen attended the opening night performance and were so delighted with the music that they returned the following evening for a second hearing. *Orione* ran for three months, and obtained for Bach the position of music-master to Queen Charlotte, a post which he kept until his death.

Early in 1764, Johann Christian Bach became intimately acquainted with Karl Friedrich Abel, a pupil of the great Sebastian, and a talented performer on the viol da gamba. Abel had been appointed chamber-musician to the Queen, and thus came frequently into contact

JOHANN CHRISTIAN BACH

with Johann Christian. Between the two a close friendship arose, and they not only decided to live together but also planned to give joint concerts in London. For more than seventeen years, Bach and Abel concertized together in London. Their performances acquired considerable fame and artistic significance.

The year of Bach's meeting with Abel was likewise made momentous by his acquaintance with the child-genius, Wolfgang Amadeus Mozart. Mozart had come to London, and when he was introduced to the Queen's chapel-master, a great affection arose between the two. Bach frequently tested Mozart's genius by giving him increasingly difficult musical tests to perform, and was bewildered at the ease with which the child coped with every problem. Bach and Mozart gave several sonata performances.

During his years as music-master to Queen Charlotte, Johann Christian Bach composed orchestral, chamber and piano music prolifically. His was an industrious pen which knew no recess. As Philipp Emanuel Bach once commented: "My brother lives merely to compose; while I compose merely to live!"

Johann Christian Bach died in London on January 1, 1782, and—having lived in elegant style during the last fifteen years of his life— left behind him debts amounting to five thousand pounds. It has been recorded that only the effort of friends prevented pressing creditors from seizing the corpse.

Johann Christian Bach was buried in an obscure corner of St. Pancras Church in London; it is not known precisely where his remains lie. In life, he had been the most famous musician in England, but in death his name was twice misspelled in the burial register of the St. Pancras Church, where he was referred to as "John Cristian Back." *Sic transit.* . . .

"Literally it was true, as an English poet sang of him, 'Bach stands on the summit of Olympus,' " wrote Rochlitz, the eminent critic of Beethoven's day. "His operas, written for England, Italy and Germany, betray all the magnificence of the composer's art. This Bach would have accomplished anything. . . . This man could write every kind of music, in the style of his father or brother, music for the church, theatre and chambre. An ever-ready invention, lovely melodies, rich instrumentation, surprising modulations, magnificent duets, masterly chorus and recitatives characterize his operas. . . . His *Te Deum Laudamus* for double choir is one of the finest things in existence. . . . His symphonies are great and magnificent."

As the present-day German critic, Dr. Alfred Einstein, has pointed out, the music of Johann Christian Bach has almost no relation to the art of his father. "His work is in sweetness, grace and fineness of style the elegant forerunner, the most influential force in Mozart."

It was the astute Charles Burney who perceived that, in his method of composition, Johann Christian Bach was the important precursor of Haydn and Mozart. "Bach seems to have been the first composer who observed the law of contrast as a principle. Before his time, contrast frequently was to be found in the work of others, but it seems to have been accidental. Bach in his symphonies and other instrumental pieces. . . . seldom failed after a rapid and noisy passage to introduce one that was slow and soothing."

Johann Christian Bach cut a magnificent figure in the London society of his time. He was handsome, with soft feminine lines of the face, refinement of feature, and expressive eyes. This, combined with his personal charm and the attractiveness of his dress, made him— as one of his contemporaries termed him—"the darling of the English ladies." He lived elegantly and extravagantly, was fond of mingling with high society, and borrowed money continually, even from his coachman. He was famous for his wit and poise. His most familiar portrait is the one painted by Gainsborough.

Principal works by Johann Christian Bach:

OPERA: *Catone in Utica*; *Orione*; *Zanaida*; *Adriano in Siria*; *Caratacco*, etc.

CHORAL: *Gioas*; masses; requiems; motets; cantatas, etc.

ORCHESTRA: Symphonies for small orchestra; Concertos for piano and smal' orchestra, etc.

Sonatas for harpsichord; arias; canzonets, etc.

About Johann Christian Bach:

Bitter, C.H. *C.P.E. Bach, W.F. Bach und deren Brüder*; Terry, Charles Sanford. *Johann Christian Bach.*

Musical Opinion 52:921 July 1929; *Sammelbände der Internationalen Musik Gesellschaft* 2:401 (1901-1902); *Strad* 24:360 February 1914.

Important recordings of music by Johann Christian Bach:

ORCHESTRA: *Sinfonia in B-flat major* (VICTOR-Mengelberg); *Concerto for piano and strings in G-major* (GRAMOPHONE).

PIANO: *Sonata in E-major*, "Rondo" (COLUMBIA-Samuel).

Johann Sebastian Bach *1685-1750*

"Music owes as much to Bach as religion to its founder."—ROBERT SCHUMANN

FOR two full centuries the Bachs passed on from father to son the tradition of music-making. Johann Sebastian Bach, therefore, was descended from a long line of musicians—a line so famous that, at one time in its history, every musician in Erfurt was termed a "Bach."

Johann Sebastian Bach, the youngest son of a violinist from Erfurt, was born in Eisenach on March 21, 1685, and received his first musical instruction from his father. Johann Sebastian's parents died when he was ten years old, and he was placed under the care of his oldest brother, Johann Christoph Bach, an organist at Ohrdruf. For five years,

JOHANN SEBASTIAN BACH

Johann Sebastian lived at the home of his brother, and was his pupil at the clavier.

His talent for music was so extraordinary that, it has often been said, he aroused the envy and malice of his brother-teacher. His love for music was equally formidable. Johann Christoph was in the possession of a manuscript edition of famous clavier pieces which he kept jealously hidden under lock and key. Young Sebastian succeeded in gaining a duplicate key and for the next few months, while the family was asleep, he copied the music by the light of the moon. One night, he was discovered by his brother, and the fruits of his labor—which practically ruined his eyesight for life—were confiscated.

In 1700, Johann Sebastian Bach became a chorister at the Convent of St. Michel at Lüneburg. Freed from his brother's malice, he knew several happy years. He had access to an excellent library of music which he virtually studied by rote. He was permitted to indulge freely not only in composition but also in the study of the organ, clavier and the violin, in all of which he made vast progress. His love for music kept pace with his knowledge. He frequently made the thirty-mile journey by foot from Lüneburg to Hamburg in order to hear the celebrated organist, Reinken, perform. He even marched the still

¹ See sketch of Buxtehude.

greater distance to Celle where the duke sponsored a French orchestra, and where Bach was able to become acquainted with the works of French composers, particularly those of Couperin.

He was eighteen years old when he was engaged as a violinist for the church band of Duke Johann Ernst. He held this post for a short period, and resigned when the more attractive position of organist at Arnstadt was offered to him. Arnstadt was not far distant from Lübeck, where the great organist, Buxtehude, gave performances and conducted his celebrated *Abendmusiken*.¹ For a long period, Bach directed envious glances towards Lübeck, the scene of so much great music. Finally, he applied for a month's leave-of-absence to enable him to partake of some study under Buxtehude. His delight in associating himself with a master like Buxtehude proved to be so intense that Bach forgot Arnstadt and his duties and, without permission, extended his absence from one to three months. These were all-important months in Bach's artistic development. Buxtehude directed Bach more forcefully towards organ music and introduced him to those supple forms— toccatas, passacaglias, fantasias, etc.— into which Bach was, in the near future, to pour his copious ideas.

It was said that Bach could have secured the organ-post in Lübeck as Buxtehude's successor if he were willing to marry Buxtehude's spinster-daughter. Her age made an otherwise attractive position undesirable and, regretfully, Bach returned to Arnstadt. Here he was severely reprimanded by the Consistory not only for his prolonged absence, but also for introducing "strange harmonies" and "perplexing variations" into his musical performances during the services. The position at Arnstadt, therefore, soon became intolerable, and in 1707 he eagerly accepted another post at Mühlhausen. His salary, together with free cartage, consisted of eighty-five gulden, three measures of corn, two trusses of wood and six trusses of faggots a year. It was not an abundant income, to be sure, but it was sufficient to enable Bach to marry his first cousin, Maria Barbara, and to enter upon a domestic existence.

Bach's first important position came in 1708 when he was appointed organist of the Ducal Chapel in Weimar. Here he remained for nine years, and these nine years constituted the first of the three great creative periods in Bach's artistic career—the period of the organ-works. By this time, Bach had become one of the greatest organists of his generation and, having profited from his instruction under Buxtehude, he now began the composition of an entire library of magnificent organ music which remains the richest collection in the history of the organ. During this period, Bach composed his sublime *Passacaglia and fugue in C-minor*, his great fantasias, toccatas and fugues (many of which have been transcribed for orchestra by musicians of our time), as well as his transcriptions of concertos by Vivaldi.

Directing a critical glance towards this incomparable wealth of organ music, C. Hubert Parry wrote: "His work in this line seems to comprise all the possibilities of pure organ music. Everything that has been written since is but a pale shadow of his splendid conceptions. . . . He had complete mastery of all genuine organ devices which tell in the hearing— the effects of long sustained notes accompanied by wonderful ramifications of rapid passages; the effects of sequences of linked suspensions of great powerful chords; the contrast of whirling rapid notes with slow and stately march of pedals and harmonies. He knew how the pearly clearness of certain stops lent itself to passages of intricate rhythmic counterpoint, and what charm lay in the perfect management of several simultaneous melodies—especially when the accents came at different moments in different parts; and he designed his movements so well that he made all such and many other genuine organ effects exert their fullest impressions on the hearers. He rarely allows himself to break into a dramatic vein, though he sometimes appeals to the mind in phrases which are closely akin to the dramatic— as in the great *Fantasia in G-minor*, the *Toccata in D-minor*, and the *Prelude in B-minor*. He occasionally touches on tender and pathetic strains, but for the most part adopts an attitude of great

dignity which is at once generous in its warmth and vigor, and reserved in the matter of sentiment."

Life in Weimar was not particularly eventful, but its routine monotony was interrupted from time to time by visits to neighboring cities in Germany where Bach gave unforgettable performances on the organ. "He played with so easy and small a motion of the fingers," we learn from Forkel, "that it was hardly perceptible. Only the first joints of his fingers were in motion; his hand retained, even in the most difficult passages, its rounded form; his fingers rose very little from the keys, hardly more than in a shake, and when one was employed the others remained still in their position. Still less did the other parts of his body share in his playing." "Friends and foes alike," to continue with a sentence from Philip Spitta, "bowed to the irresistible force of an unheard-of power of execution, and could hardly comprehend how he could twist his fingers and his feet so wonderfully and so nimbly without hitting a single false note or displacing his body with violent swaying."

In Cassel, in 1714, Bach gave a performance on the organ which so swept Frederick I of Sweden with its dazzling virtuosity that the monarch, in gratitude, gave Bach the diamond ring from his finger. In the Autumn of 1717 occurred the famous organ competition between Bach and Louis Marchand, organist of Louis XV. Bach had come to Dresden expressly to hear Marchand play, and at this time it was arranged that a contest take place between the two great organists. Bach consented, and an arrangement was made whereby each organist was to perform at sight whatever music his opponent chose to designate. At the hour of the contest, however, a messenger arrived announcing that Marchand had tacitly admitted defeat by hurriedly escaping from Dresden.

The second of Bach's great creative periods—the "instrumental period"— began in 1717 when he left Weimar, for a reason which has never been adequately explained, and accepted the appointment of chapel-master to Prince Leopold of Anhalt-Cöthen. His principal duty, in his new post, was to arrange concerts of instrumental music, and for these he composed—during six years of activity—a rich library of music for chamber-orchestra and solo instruments which is not less remarkable than his output for organ had been during the Weimar years.

It was during this period that Bach composed his six Brandenburg concertos for chamber-orchestra, altho it was not for the Cöthen concerts that these works were created. In 1719, Christian Ludwig, Margraf of Brandenburg, commissioned Bach to produce music especially for his chamber-orchestra. In the Spring of 1721, Bach sent his six concertos to his patron, with a dedication in which, prostrating himself humbly at the feet of the prince, he begged him not to judge the imperfections of the concertos too harshly, but rather to discover in them "the profound respect and the very humble allegiance which they seek to convey." Taking up the idea of the old concerto grosso, Bach undertook to prove that he could write effective orchestral works for solo instruments other than strings. Each concerto was, therefore, written for a different group of instruments—and all with equal pliancy and effectiveness, inexhaustible imaginativeness, and often awe-inspiring sublimity. Albert Schweitzer has referred to these Concertos as "the purest product of Bach's polyphonic style," and purity of writing is certainly their most distinguishing characteristic.

It was at this time, too, that Bach created not only his great solo sonatas for violin and his concertos for piano and orchestra, and violin and orchestra, but also his epoch-making *Well-tempered clavichord,* which came from his pen in 1722.

W. R. Anderson clearly explains why the *Well-tempered clavichord* is of momentous historical importance. "The old method of tempering (tuning) the keyboard was based on a system which (to put it briefly and as untechnically as possible) left some keys well in tune and some out of tune. Bach advocated little adjustments so that music in *every* key be equally pleasant, even if the tune were not mathematically exact. Such tuning is, of course, a commonplace today, but it was by no means so in Bach's time, or even for a good while afterwards."

But Bach's *Well-tempered clavichord* is not only important as a technical development in the history of piano music, but—genius that Bach was—he filled the work with a grandeur, variety and often depth of expression such as piano music before his time had never known. It was Goethe who said that in the *Well-tempered clavichord* he seemed "to hear the eternal harmony conversing with itself, as it might have done in God's bosom shortly before cosmocreation."

In 1720, Bach's first wife died, and Bach—being essentially a domestic soul—married a second time, one year later. His second wife was the charming Anna Magdalena, twenty-year-old daughter of a town musician. It was in order to facilitate her study of the harpsichord that Bach composed his delightful *Anna Magdalena clavierbuch,* utilized so extensively today by beginners of piano-playing.

Early in May of 1723, Bach entered upon the third, and final period of his creative career when he accepted an appointment as cantor of the St. Thomas Schule in Leipzig, as successor to Kuhnau. In the same manner that the Weimar period was characterized by the production of organ music, and the Cöthen period by instrumental works, so the years spent in Leipzig marked Bach's creation of great religious music—his grandiose masses, oratorios, passions, motets and chorales. There can be little question—without attempting to disparage Bach's contribution to the organ, orchestra or solo instruments—that this was the greatest and crowning phase of his career.

To this period belong those gargantuan musical structures, the *Passion according to St. Matthew,* the *Passion according to St. John,* the *Christmas oratorio,* and the greatest of them all, the *Mass in B-minor.*

The *Mass* was composed in 1733 when Bach, seeking a post in the royal chapel, sent a portion of it to Augustus III, as an "insignificant example of my skill." That eminent conductor, Leopold Stokowski, has made some discerning remarks about the *Mass* which are well worth repeating, for they sum up the qualities which make the *Mass* one of the sublime productions in musical history. "The *Mass in B-minor*," wrote Mr. Stokowski, "is planned on a vast scale, and the texture of the music is complex and highly concentrated, revealing a slow and rich outwelling of his inspiration. . . . While it is cast in a form similar to the great Masses preceding Bach, this form is greatly enlarged and extended. . . . It has cosmic vastness of expression and consciousness. . . . The parts which are in reality prayers, such as the beginning of the first *Kyrie,* have the intensity and simple directness that probably is always one of the chief elements in prayer. . . . In many places, such as the great choruses of the *Gloria in excelsis Deo*, the *Credo*, the *Sanctus*, the *Osanna*, there is a blazing jubilation like radiant sunlight. It is as if all Nature, man, the planets, the whole universe were singing together. . . . At certain moments in the *Mass,* such as the *Qui tollis* and *Et incarnatus* and *Crucifixus,* there is in the music profound mystical intensity that could only have come from the spirit of a man who was moved to the uttermost of his being."

It is the opinion of many Bach authorities that it is in his cantatas, even more than in his larger choral works, that Bach expressed his personality most felicitously. His cantatas were pieces of concerted music for voice and orchestra, requiring twenty to thirty minutes for performance. Usually consisting of six or seven movements, they frequently terminated in a four-part chorale. In Leipzig, Bach's cantatas were performed on alternate Sundays. "Their range is so wide," wrote Charles Sanford Terry, "their diversities are so numerous, they touch so many moods, that in themselves they form a gallery which exhaustively represents his art and exhibits his personality. They dissipate the illusion, not yet wholly removed, that he was of cold, mathematical precision. They reveal him as one of the tenderest and most emotional of men, with a poet's soul and a painter's eye. As a musician, they declare him a Master whose workmanship was perfect, his technical skill marvelous. Above all, they proved him

a large-hearted, simple-minded Christian."

There is not much need to dwell in detail upon the remainder of Bach's life, which—despite occasional friction with the church authorities of the St. Thomas Schule who could not realize that they were dealing with an incomparable genius—was placid and industrious. He created children (no less than twenty of them) and masterpieces with equal productivity. His life was a whirlwind of musical activity—performances on the organ, teaching, the training of choirs, the preparation of musical performances, and composition. And while he was never accorded that recognition as a composer that he so well deserved, honors beat a path to his door by virtue of his undisputed gifts at the organ. Frequently, great musicians thruout Europe made pilgrimages to Leipzig to hear him play and to perform for him. One of the greatest honors came to him towards the close of his life when he was invited to the court of Frederick the Great in Potsdam and was received with great reverence.

Towards the close of his life, Bach's eyesight failed him. An English occulist was called upon to operate and, the operation being unsuccessful, Bach became totally blind. On July 18, 1750, vision momentarily returned; but the end was not far off. A few hours later, Bach was stricken with paralysis. After ten days of suffering, he passed away, on July 28, 1750. He was buried in the churchyard of St. John's Church, and for almost a century and a half the exact spot of his burial was unknown.

Johann Sebastian Bach was a man of incomparable simplicity and piety. Believing with all the power of his being in God, he saw everything—including his own genius—as manifestations of God's greatness. Biographers inform us that he was of happy disposition, with a warm and human sense of humor, and was frequently very jolly company. His intellectual range was extremely limited, his entire world consisting of music, his family and God. Worldly matters interested him but slightly. He worked prodigiously, and approached his art with an unassuming modesty that is startling. Asked once by a friend how he explained the unique mastery of his technique, his simple answer was: "I worked hard."

It is one of the striking phenomena in musical history that for almost a century after his death, the music of this incomparable genius was completely forgotten, except by a scattered few disciples. When he died, Johann Sebastian Bach was esteemed as a great organist, and not as a great composer. It was believed that his music had already become sadly dated, and that—the art of music having passed from polyphony to homophony—his day and art were definitely over. After Bach's death, his widow, who suffered great poverty, sold a whole bundle of cantatas for $40. His son, Friedemann, disposed of sixty others at ten cents each. The copper-plates of Bach's final masterpiece, *The Art of the fugue*, was sold as scrap-metal. And a century after his death, the solo violin sonatas were found among a pile of old papers, on their way to a butcher shop to be used for wrapping meat. Only a handful of Bach's works had reached publication, and the rest were scattered to the four winds, collecting dust in obscure and forgotten corners. For many years, when the name of Bach was mentioned, it was Philipp Emanuel or Johann Christian who was being spoken of, and never Johann Sebastian.

Then, in 1802, Nikolaus Forkel—a close friend of Bach's sons, and an unswerving disciple of the great master—published a monograph in which he lamented the neglect of a great genius. "This sublime genius, this prince of musicians, German or foreign, dwarfs all others from the height of superiority," he wrote. "Let Germany be proud of him, but worthy of him, too."

Twenty years later, a copy of the *Passion according to St. Matthew* came to the attention of Felix Mendelssohn, who was bewildered to find in it such majesty and greatness. He was determined to bring it to public notice and, in 1829, Mendelssohn organized a special chorus for this purpose. On March 11, after one hundred years of silence, Bach's grandiose work was heard again. Four years later, there took place a performance of the *Passion according to St. John*. And, in 1850, a complete edition of Bach's works was undertaken by the Bach Gesellschaft Society. Over a period of fifty years, more than ten editors labored on the monumental task of publishing everything Bach had composed, finally producing an edition which extended to sixty volumes. It was then that the world realized what an inexhaustible wealth of immortality had been produced by the simple and devout-hearted musician of Leipzig.

It is the opinion of Charles Sanford Terry that of all the forms in which Bach expressed himself, the fugue "was the mode of utterance most attuned to his nature. His fugues are unique because, among his predecessors and contemporaries, he alone fully realized the romantic and artistic possibilities of the fugal form. His personality is behind every bar of them. They are the poetry of a master who found it natural and congenial to express himself in that form. His relation to the fugue, in fact, is that of Beethoven to the sonata, or of Haydn to the quartet. . . . His technical skill in them remains unique and unsurpassed. No one has approached him in the miraculous complexity of his part-writing, or in his ingenuity in weaving melodic strands into a single fabric. No one equally displays his gift of melody, his sense of form, the virile quality of his themes, the boldness of his technique, even the daring of his harmonic coloring. Thus, even within the forms he used, Bach is dateless, his art perennial, immortalized by the intense individualism that informed it. Directed by a faith childlike in its simplicity, he used it to interpret the infinite saw the heavens opened, and was prophetically oracular."

Principal works by Johann Sebastian Bach:

CHORAL: More than 250 church cantatas; *Mass in B-minor;* four small masses; five passions (including the *Passion according to St. Matthew,* and the *Passion according to St. John*); two magnificats; *Trauerode;* motets; *Christmas oratorio;* Secular cantatas (including the comic *Bauern* and *Caffee* cantatas), etc.

ORCHESTRA: Six Brandenburg concertos; four orchestral suites; *Musikalisches opfer* (for harpsichord and accompanying strings); Concertos for violin and orchestra; Concertos for one to four pianos, with accompanying strings, etc.

PIANO: *The Well-tempered clavichord*; *Inventions* (in two and three parts); six French suites; six English suites; six partitas; *The Goldberg variations*; *The Art of the fugue*; *Chromatic fantasy and fugue; Concerto in the Italian style,* etc.

VIOLIN: Six sonatas for violin and piano; Six solo sonatas for unaccompanied violin; Partitas for violin (the *D-minor Partita* including the *Chaconne*), etc.

An entire library of music for the organ; Sonatas for violoncello; Sonatas for flute and piano, etc.

About Johann Sebastian Bach:

Boughton, Rutland. *Bach*; Forkel, Johann Nikolaus. *Johann Sebastian Bach: His Life, Art and Work*; Fuller-Maitland, J.A. *The Age of Bach and Handel*; Grace, Harvey. *The Organ Works of Bach*; Parry, C. Hubert. *Johann Sebastian Bach: The Story of the Development of a Great Personality*; Schweitzer, Albert. *Johann Sebastian Bach*; Spitta, Philipp. *Johann Sebastian Bach*; Terry, Charles Sanford. *Bach: A Biography*; Terry, Charles Sanford. *Bach: The Historical Approach*.

Important recordings of music by Johann Sebastian Bach:

CHORAL: *Passion according to St. Matthew,* abridged (VICTOR); *Mass in B-minor,* complete (VICTOR-Coates); *Passion according to St. John,* principal excerpts (COLUMBIA; PARLAPHONE); *Magnificat in D-minor* (GRAMOPHONE); *Christmas oratorio,* "Betreite dich Zion" (LUMEN), "Sinfonia" (VICTOR-Stokowski); innumerable recordings of the principal cantatas.

ORCHESTRA: Six Brandenburg concertos (COLUMBIA-Busch); *Suite in B-minor* (COLUMBIA-Mengelberg); Suite in D-major (COLUMBIA-Defauw); *Suite in G-major* (VICTOR-Goosens); *Musikalisches opfer,* "Ricercare," arranged by Fischer (VICTOR-Fischer); *Concerto in D-minor for piano and orchestra* (VICTOR-Fischer); *Concerto in F-minor for piano and orchestra* (NATIONAL GRAMOPHONIC SOCIETY-Bartlett); *Concerto in G-minor for piano and orchestra* (PARLAPHONE); *Concerto for two pianos and orchestra* (GRAMOPHONE); *Concerto for three pianos and orchestra* (GRAMOPHONE); *Concerto for four pianos and orchestra* (TELEFUNKEN); *Concerto in A-minor for violin and orchestra* (COLUMBIA-Huberman); *Concerto in E-major for violin and orchestra* (VICTOR-Menuhin); *Concerto in D-minor for two violins and orchestra* (VICTOR-Menuhin, Enesco); Arrangements of famous Bach works for orchestra by Leopold Stokowski, including the *Passacaglia in C-minor,* the *Chaconne,* etc. (VICTOR), etc.

PIANO: *The Well-tempered clavichord,* complete (HIS MASTER'S VOICE-Fischer); French suites in G-major and E-major (COLUMBIA-Cumpson); *English suite in A-minor* (VICTOR-Samuel); *Goldberg variations* (SOCIETY ALBUM-Landowska); *The Art of the fugue,* arranged for string-quartet by Harris and Norton (COLUMBIA-Roth); *Chromatic,*

fantasy and fugue (VICTOR-Fischer); *Concerto in the Italian style* (COLUMBIA-Cumpson); fantasias, partitas, etc.

SONATAS: *Unaccompanied sonata in G-minor* (VICTOR-Menuhin); *Unaccompanied sonata in A-minor* (COLUMBIA-Szigeti); *Unaccompanied sonata in D-minor* (VICTOR-Menuhin); Sonatas for violin and piano, nos. 4, 5, 6 (COLUMBIA-Dubois, Maas); Sonatas for flute and piano, nos.1, 6 (COLUMBIA-Laurent, Cumpson, etc.

ORGAN: *Bach's organ music,* a collection of the greatest of Bach's organ works (COLUMBIA-Schweitzer).

Philipp Emanuel Bach *1714-1788*

"For what I know, I have to thank Philipp Emanuel Bach."—JOSEF HAYDN

CARL PHILIPP EMANUEL BACH, the son of Johann Sebastian and Maria Barbara Bach, was born in Weimar on March 8, 1714. His godfather was Georg Philipp Telemann, a distinguished composer of the time and chapel-master at Hamburg.

Philipp Emanuel Bach was trained musically at an early age by his father (who remained his only teacher) and disclosed unusual precociousness. He learned to play the clavier skillfully, and his musical intelligence was so great that, one day in his eleventh year, he glanced over his father's shoulder at a manuscript, and then sat down and played the entire piece from memory.

Needless to say, he was continua'ly in contact with music. He frequently attended rehearsals and performances at the St. Thomas Schule, and continually rubbed elbows with great musicians. For, as he himself has written, "altho I was kept at home many years, and therefore saw little of the world, yet no master of music passed thru this place without coming to make himself known to my father and play before him."

It is strange, indeed—particularly in view of his unusual musical talents—that Philipp Emanuel was, at first, directed by his father towards law, rather than music. In 1724, he was registered at the St. Thomas Schule, and nine years later his father sent him to Frankfort-on-the-Oder to complete his legal studies at the University. Music, however, remained an important part of his life, and in Frankfort Bach founded a choral society which performed some of his music.

PHILIPP EMANUEL BACH

By 1738, Philipp Emanuel was convinced that his direction was music and not law. He went to Berlin to make his own way as a musician, and his extraordinary ability at the clavier attracted the notice of Crown Prince Frederick. When Frederick ascended the throne in 1740, he had not forgotten Philipp Emanuel Bach, and immediately engaged him as a court-musician. Bach has written in his brief autobiography that the first flute solo that Frederick played—as king—was accompanied by him.

It was Bach's task, each day, to accompany the flute-playing of Frederick-the-Great—not a particularly pleasant task, in view of the fact that the king was not meticulous about correct tempo. His salary was 300 thalers a year. In 1744 Philipp Emanuel married Johanna Maria Daneemann, the daughter of a Berlin wine-merchant, which automatically made him subject to the king's favor.

Altho Philipp Emanue' Bach remained in his post at Frederick's court for many years, he chafed considerably, and frequently sought an avenue for escape. This did not come to him until 1767 when the death of his godfather, Telemann—chapel-master in Hamburg—brought him an offer to assume the vacant post. Frederick was reluctant to have his favorite musician go, and it was only after Bach repeatedly entreated and urged the king for an acceptance of his resignation that he was finally permitted to leave.

In Hamburg—where Bach now remained until the end of his life—he reached the height of his fame as a musician. He was generally recognized as one of the great c'avier performers of his day, and his compositions enjoyed great prestige. Mozart, himself, was tempted to say of Bach: "He is the father, and we his children. Those of us who know what is right, have learned it from him; and those who have not confessed it, are scoundrels."

Carl Philipp Emanuel Bach died in Hamburg on December 14, 1788 of pulmonary consumption.

That distinguished musicologist, Charles Burney, met Bach personally, and has recorded his impressions: "The instant I entered, he conducted me upstairs into a large and elegant music-room, furnished with pictures, drawings and prints of more than one hundred and fifty Englishmen, and original portraits in oil of his father and grandfather. After I had looked at these, Bach was so ob'iging as to sit down to his Silbermann clavichord, a favorite instrument, upon which he played three or four of his choicest and most difficult compositions, with the delicacy, precision and spirit for which he is so justly celebrated among his countrymen. . . . After dinner, which was elegantly served, and cheerfully eaten, I prevailed upon him to sit down again to a clavichord, and he played, with little intermission, until 11 o'clock at night. During this time, he grew so animated and possessed that he not only played but looked like one inspired. His eyes were fixed, his under lip fell, and drops of effervescence distilled from his countenance. He said, if he were to be set to work frequently in this manner, he would grow young again. He is now fifty-nine, rather short in stature, with black hair and eyes, and brown complexion, has a very animated countenance, and is of cheerful and lively disposition."

While Bach composed prolifically in many branches of the musical art, his outstanding contribution has been in his symphonies and works for the clavichord. Here, he was the bridge from his father to Haydn, from the age of polyphony to the period of homophonic music. Curiously enough, his music shows very little of Johann Sebastian's influence. As Charles Burney wrote: "How he formed his style would be difficult to trace; he certainly neither inherited it nor adopted it from his father who was his only master." He was essentially of the new period of homophonic music.

He inherited the germs of the sonata-form from Stamitz, and brought it to such full development that there are many musical historians who believe that the symphony and the piano-sonata were really born with him. It is well known that, as a student, Haydn memorized Philipp Emanuel Bach's sonatas, and acquired from them many valuable lessons about piano-style and form.

"The position of Philipp Emanuel Bach," wrote C. Hubert Parry in the *Evolution of the Art of Music*, "was important, though not quite in conformity with the tendencies of his age. In his best symphonies, he adopted a line of his own. . . . [His works] have an underlying basis of harmonic form. . . . His management of the various instruments shows considerable skill and clear perception of the effective uses to which they can be put; and he treats them with thoro independence and variety."

"Though Bach's compositions still interest us greatly," remarks Karl Nef, "they seldom satisfy us with their bold runs, their harmonic and rhythmic surprises, and their sudden pianissimos and fortissimos. Philipp Emanuel Bach, like most of his contemporaries, appears more genuine and profound when he surrenders himself to sentimentality. An illustration of this will be found in the *cantabile e mesto* from a clavier sonata in D minor (1781) in which bold harmony and expression mingle strangely with rococo figuration."

Not the least of Emanuel Bach's accomplishments was his pedagogic *Versuch über die wahre Art das Klavier zu spielen* whose importance rests not only upon the fact that it was the first important method of piano-playing, but also that it today gives us a striking insight into the manner in which the clavier was played in the day of Bach.

Principal works by Carl Philipp Emanuel Bach:

CHORAL: *The Israelites in the wilderness*; *The Resurrection*; *Magnificat*; works for Easter, Michaelmas, Christmas, etc.; Nine sacred choruses, with instrumental accompaniment; Five motets; Ninety-five songs and choruses, etc.

ORCHESTRA: Fifty-two concertos for clavichord and orchestra; Eighteen symphonies, etc.

More than 200 pieces for clavichord; 47 trios, etc.

About Carl Philipp Emanuel Bach:

Bitter, C. H. *C. P. E. Bach, W. F. Bach und deren Brüder*; Nef, Karl. *An Outline of the History of Music*; Parry, C. Hubert. *Evolution of the Art of Music*; Schmid, Ernest Fritz. *C. P. E. Bach und seine Kammermusik*; Vrieslander, Otto. *C. P. E. Bach.*

Important recordings of music by Carl Philipp Emanuel Bach:

ORCHESTRA: *Concerto in A-major for violoncello and orchestra* (COLUMBIA); *Suite in D-major*, arranged by Casadesus (VICTOR).

PIANO: *Sonata in F-minor*, first movement (COLUMBIA-Samuel); *Sonata in G-major*, second movement (COLUMBIA-Samuel).

Wilhelm Friedemann Bach *1710-1784*

"He could replace our father better than all the rest of us put together."—PHILIPP EMANUEL BACH

WILHELM FRIEDEMANN BACH was the second child, but oldest son, of Johann Sebastian and Maria Barbara Bach. He was born in Weimar on November 22, 1710, and when he passed out of childhood, he was given a thoro and intensive musical training by his father in theory, composition, and the playing of the organ, clavichord, harpsichord and violin. It was for his benefit that Johann Sebastian Bach wrote famous instruction pieces for the clavichord, including the first part of the *Well-tempered clavichord*, and the *Inventions*.

In 1723, the Bach family came to Leipzig, and Wilhelm Friedemann was enrolled at the Thomas Schule. Shortly afterwards, he was entered in the University of Leipzig, from which he was graduated in 1729. In the meanwhile, the study of music was followed industriously, and a talented concerto for the clavier, composed at this time, proved that he was in the possession of formidable creative gifts.

WILHELM FRIEDEMANN BACH

In 1733 the position of organist at the St. Sophia Church in Dresden was left vacant, and Wilhelm Friedemann applied as a candidate in the competition conducted to select the successor. His performance on the organ was so unquestionably superior to that of his competitors that he was immediately engaged. Here, he remained for thirteen years, and the position gave him sufficient leisure to enable him to compose industriously. Wilhelm Friedemann Bach was greatly esteemed in Dresden for his musical gifts, and enjoyed a high position in its social life.

From Dresden, Wilhelm Friedemann came to Halle, as organist of the Liebfrauen Kirchen. For eighteen years—until 1764—he held this post with high honor, performing on the organ at services and, during holidays, directing the orchestra.

On May 12, 1764 Wilhelm Friedemann suddenly resigned from his Halle post, feeling somewhat peevishly that his eminence as a musician was not sufficiently recognized. During the years that followed, he earned a precarious living, giving recitals on the organ, devoting himself to the teaching of music, dedicating his compositions to wealthy patrons—and with all that, earning an income so slender that it was hardly sufficient to supply the necessities of life for himself and his family. The closing years of Bach's life were, therefore, touched with bitterness and disappointment. He died in Berlin on July 1, 1784, leaving his wife and daughter in great want.

Wilhelm Friedemann Bach, as a personality, has been the subject of many paragraphs and chapters; a romantic novel, by Brachvogel, utilized him as a central figure. He was known to have been excessively lazy, a man of ungracious disposition even to relatives and friends, boorish in manner, intensely selfish—and eccentric, to boot. He drank to excess, and was a victim of dissolute habits. It is amazing, indeed, that with a temperament such as his, he was able to produce an abundant output of music, and much of extraordinary quality.

Nikolaus Forkel informs us that "Wilhelm Friedemann approaches the nearest to his father in the originality of all his thoughts. All his melodies have a different turn from those of other composers, and yet they are not only extremely natural, but, at the same time, uncommonly ingenious and elegant."

C. H. Bitter, speaking of Wilhelm Friedemann as a composer of high significance, points out that he has left "distinguished work to posterity, and opened up new paths and ways which lead to higher completion and greater perfection. His position in the history of music lies in his unity of purpose as the son of a great father."

Principal works by Wilhelm Friedemann Bach:

OPERA: *Lausus und Lydie.*

ORCHESTRA: Nine symphonies; Concertos for piano and orchestra; Concertos for two pianos and orchestra, etc.

CHORAL: About 25 cantatas; *German mass,* etc.

CHAMBER MUSIC: Trio sonatas for flute; Two sonatas for strings; Duets for viola and continuo, etc.

About Wilhelm Friedemann Bach:

Bitter, C.H. *C.P.E. Bach, W.F. Bach und deren Brüder*; Falck, Martin. *Wilhelm Friedemann Bach*; Zehler, C. *Wilhelm Friedemann Bach und seine Hallische Wirksamkeit.*

Mily Balakirev *1837-1910*

THE founder of that world-famous school of Russian music, known as the "Russian five," was Mily Alexeivich Balakirev.

He was born in Nijny-Novgorod on January 2, 1837. Balakirev received a solid academic education before he turned to music, graduating from the University of Kazan. The diplomat Alexander Oulibishev, an excellent musician, first interested Balakirev in music, and undertook to teach him the rudiments. From Oulibishev, Balakirev acquired a competent background and a comprehensive technique.

Shortly after his eighteenth birthday, Balakirev set out for St. Petersburg in order to adopt a musical career officially. In St. Petersburg, he met that great national composer, Glinka, who influenced his direction vitally and pointed out to him the significance of Russian national music. Balakirev soon became a devoted disciple of Glinka who looked upon the younger composer as the one most worthy to carry on his banner.

At this time, Balakirev became a friend of César Cui, another young Russian composer deeply interested in nationalistic music, and from their daily conversations the new school of Russian music was evolved.

César Cui has himself written about the origin of this new school: "In 1856, two young musicians, passionately devoted to their art, met at St. Petersburg. The Russian capital being the chief musical and intellectual center of the country, they took up their permanent residence there. One of the was Balakirev, and the other was the author of these pages. Some little time afterwards they were joined by Rimsky-Korsakoff, Borodin and Moussorgsky; and thus a little circle was formed of friends who were drawn together by a common enthusiasm for music.

"These informal meetings of theirs gave rise from that time onwards to most interesting and instructive debates, which ranged conscientiously over the whole of the then existing literature of music. . . . In this way, the little brotherhood ended by acquiring fixed convictions and by forming criteria, which they applied to a number of questions in the realm of art that frequently lay far outside the current ideas of the public and press. While each member of the group retained his own characteristics and capacity, an ideal common to all soon began to be sharply defined, and an effort was made to imprint it on their compositions."

What was the common ideal uniting this "brotherhood" of musicians? It was, as M. D. Calvocoressi points out, twofold. "In the matter of musical drama, it was alleged that operatic routine ought to be strongly counteracted; and that the choice of subject, the management of the plot, and the musical style, should become more simple, more in conformity with reality; while in music, generally speaking, the aim was to profit by the example that popular art afforded; viz., to write works of art in the style of national songs. . . as well as with various highly valuable modes until then not put to use in modern music."

In 1862, Balakirev took over the direction of the St. Petersburg symphony concerts which were vitally instrumental in bringing to the attention of their audiences the work of this new school of composers. At the same time, he devoted his conscientious efforts to the study of folk-music, and in 1866 he published a valuable collection of forty folk-songs. His work as a prophet of this new music received wide attention, and it was in recognition of his achievements in this direction that he was offered the direction of the Russian Musical Society.

Unfortunately, at this time, Balakirev succumbed to a madness of superstition. He paid secret visits to fortune-tellers who, by gazing into a mirror, told him the future, in which he believed with childlike implicitness. This growing madness brought with it temporary seclusion from musical activity, and in 1873 he obtained a position as stores-superintendent of the Warsaw Railway.

Referring to this mental malady of Balakirev, Rimsky-Korsakoff wrote: "I found him very much changed. In every room in his home were holy images with a little lamp burning in front of each. He was ever attending services. He had given up wearing furs, smoking, and eating meat. He liked to eat fish, provided it had not been knocked on the head. His love for all living creatures had become so great, that if a noxious insect found its way into his room, he would catch it with care and throw it out of the window, wishing it 'God speed.' At the end of his talks on religion with people he was fond of, he used to press them to cross themselves. And if they demurred, he would insist: 'Please do! For my sake, just this once! Why not try?' He believed in the supernatural efficiency of this symbolic gesture—believed that it might help to turn the minds of irreligious people who made it."

In 1883, Balakirev returned to musical activities, and from 1883 until 1895 he was a conductor at the Court Chapel, at the same time returning with renewed vigor to musical composition.

The last years of Balakirev's life were lonely ones. His closest friends were dead, and he lived in almost complete isolation. At the same time, his former superstition had now mounted to religious mania. He became a recluse, and gave himself up to religious meditation and prayer. He would cross himself when passing a church or upon hearing a loud noise; he filled his room with images and burning lamps.

MILY BALAKIREV

Yet, notwithstanding this obsession— and, with it, ill-health brought on by a disease of the heart—Balakirev's last years were uniquely productive. He composed his C-major symphony in 1898, and followed it with a piano sonata, a second symphony, a cantata in the memory of Glinka, and a piano concerto which, left uncompleted by his death, was finished by Liapounoff.

Mily Balakirev died a lonely death in St. Petersburg on May 29, 1910.

He was, as Rimsky-Korsakoff has written, a striking character. "The spell of his personality was tremendous. Young, with marvelously alert fiery eyes, with a handsome beard—unhesitating, authoritative and straight-forward in speech. . . . His influence over those around him was boundless; and resembled some magnetic or mesmeric force. . . . He despotically demanded that the tastes of his pupils should exactly coincide with his own. The slightest deviation from his taste was severely censured by him."

Balakirev was not a prolific composer, but his small output has sufficient strength and the power of originality to place its composer in the front rank of Russian composers.

"He is, first and foremost, a symphonic writer," declared his friend, César Cui. "As far as vocal music is concerned, he has written . . . songs which have broad, simple melodies with graceful accompaniments, and are often characterized by vehemence and passion. Lyrical feeling predominates in them, for they are the spontaneous expression, in terms of lovely music, of the impulse of the heart. In form, Balakirev's songs are the link between those of Glinka and Dargomijsky, on the one hand, and those of later composers on the other."

Perhaps the most striking characteristic of Balakirev's music is its resemblance in form to that of his master, Glinka. Turning once again to the writings of M.D. Calvocoressi, we learn: "Balakirev resembled Glinka in the straightforward, simple warmth of his utterance, in his love for intensity of color, his dislike for glare, his lack of conscious artifice, and his disdain for the more obvious ways of formulism. . . . He owes to Glinka . . . the rare limpidity, the perfectly mellow quality of his scoring; and to Glinka, alone—apart, of course, from Russian and Eastern folk-music—the range of colors for which he evinces the most marked predilection."

Principal works by Mily Balakirev:

ORCHESTRA: *Russia*; *Overture on three Russian themes*; *Tamara*; *Symphony*; Overture to *King Lear*.

PIANO: *Islamey*; nocturnes; waltzes; mazurkas, etc.

Songs.

About Mily Balakirev:

Abraham, Gerald. *Studies in Russian Music*; Pougin, Arthur. *A Short History of Russian Music*; Rimsky-Korsakoff, Nicholas. *My Musical Life.*
Monthly Musical Record 51:101 May 1921; *Musical America* 53:5 March 10, 1933.

Important recordings of music by Mily Balakirev:

ORCHESTRA: *Russia* (COLUMBIA-Harty); *Tamara* (VICTOR-Coppola); *Islamey*, arranged by Casella (VICTOR-Goossens).

PIANO: *Islamey* (GRAMOPHONE).

Michael Balfe *1808-1870*

"Others may come with skill more great,
But hardly one to emulate,
A soul like his, to blazen forth
At once, mind, genius, taste and worth."
—EDWARD FITZBALL

MICHAEL WILLIAM BALFE was born in Dublin on May 15, 1808. He showed his first inclination for music at the age of four when he attended band concerts at Wexford and revea'ed a keen delight in them. His father, a good musician, decided to train his son musically, and taught him the violin. Michael made such extraordinary progress that a more efficient instructor was soon sought, and found in William O'Rourke. By his ninth birthday, Balfe was ready for his first public appearance. "By most particular desire," read an advertisement in *Saunders News Letter,* of 1817, "and positively for this night only, that wonderful child, Master Balfi (*sic*!), pupil of Mr. William O'Rourke, will perform a concerto for violin, introducing the popular air *The Minstrel Boy,* and a rondo composed expressly for the occasion by Mr. O'Rourke.

Shortly after his sixteenth year, Michael Balfe was left destitute by the death of his father. He decided to go to London to earn his livelihood with fiddle and bow. For a period, he was successful as a performer of violin solos at oratorio performances, and as a substitute director of the orchestra at Drury Lane. It was then that he met Count Mazzara, who interested himself in the boy, and decided to take him to Italy. In 1825, Balfe reached Rome, living at the home of his patron, and studying counterpoint under Frederici. From Rome, he went to Milan, becoming a pupil at the Conservatory. His studies were soon to bring first fruit, for it was at this time that his first large opus reached performance, a ballet, *La Pérouse,* which aroused great praise upon its presentation in Milan.

It was yet many years before Balfe emerged as a full-fledged composer. Meanwhile, he launched upon a career as professional singer. Returning to Paris, he became a friend of Rossini, the great composer, who was greatly impressed with his baritone voice and offered him the post of principal baritone at the Italian Opera. For the next few years, Balfe sang opera in Paris, Italy and London, and achieved a great reputation.

A singing career, however, could not appeal permanently to Balfe. In 1835 he definitely turned from the interpretative to the creative field of music. In that year, his *Siege of Rochelle* was produced at Drury Lane, and was so markedly successful that it convinced its composer that his future rested with creation rather than with singing. The following Spring, he produced *Maid of Artois,* the success of which was further heightened by the presence of the sensational Mme. Malibran in the cast. There followed in its footsteps a string of other operas which unmistakably placed Balfe at the head of English composers for the theatre of his day.

Balfe's reputation as a composer was soon to penetrate beyond the shores of England. In 1840, he settled in Paris where, in collaboration with such distinguished librettists as Scribe and St. George, he won Parisian hearts with his seductive music for *Le Puits d'amour* and *Les quatre fils d'Aymon,* presented at the Opéra Comique. In 1849, he was a guest in Berlin, in honor of special

MICHAEL BALFE

performances of his operas which took place at that time, and was offered by the King the decoration of the Prussian Eagle—a distinction he was compelled to decline as a British subject. Three years later, Balfe was to conquer Russia as well—coming, as he did, with letters of introduction from the Prince of Prussia—being welcomed with profuse honor, receptions and gifts.

What is generally accepted as Balfe's crowning operatic achievement, *The Bohemian girl*, was presented in London on November 27, 1843. The appeal of *The Bohemian girl* was so universal that, after a sensational run in London, it was translated into virtually every European language, and performed with unquestioned success. In December of 1869, the French version of this opera was introduced at the Théâtre Lyrique, where it was so enthusiastically acclaimed by audiences and critics that, immediately thereafter, Balfe was honored by Emperor Louis Napoleon with the Legion of Honor.

The last few years of Balfe's life were spent in seclusion on a small property, named Rowney Abbey, which he had purchased in Hertfordshire. Here he died on October 20, 1870, after a cold he had caught the previous September developed into bronchitis. After his death, a statue of him by Malampré was erected in the vestibule of the Drury Lane Theatre in London.

In estimating Balfe's importance as a composer, present-day criticism concedes almost unanimously that the enthusiasm of Balfe's contemporaries for his operas was undeserving. Balfe's operas died almost simultaneously with their composer. Ernest Walker, in gaging the artistic merits of *The Bohemian girl*, from a twentieth century perspective, writes: "Artistically, it is not worth a moment's consideration—the tunes are empty beyond expression, and there is not a particle of workmanship to carry them off; yet, there is nothing worse than emptiness, and the rubbish is quite unpretentious and decent. . . . We go to sleep over his middle-class melodies, but we are not actively irritated by them. No doubt, in his day Balfe was thought a great man; he strove to rival the favorite Italian operas, and wrote in the fashionable bravura style for the prima-donnas. . . . But it is all artistically dead, beyond the very faintest hope of resurrection; and we need not feel any cause for lament."

Principal works by Michael William Balfe:

OPERA: *The Siege of Rochelle*; *Maid of Artois*; *Joan of Arc*; *Falstaff*; *The Bohemian girl*; *The Enchantress*; *The Maid of honour*; *The Sicilian bride*; *The Rose of Castile*; *Bianca*; *The Puritan's daughter*; *Blanche de Nevers*; *Il Talismano*, etc.

About Michael William Balfe:

Baptie, David. *Sketches of English Glee Composers*; Barrett, William Alexander. *Balfe: His Life and Works*; Kenney, Charles Lamb. *A Memoir of Michael William Balfe*.

Important recordings of music by Michael William Balfe:

SELECTIONS FROM OPERA: *The Bohemian girl*, "Overture" (GRAMOPHONE-Barbirolli); "I dreamt I dwelt in marble halls" (COLUMBIA); "Then you'll remember me" (BRUNSWICK). *The Siege of Rochelle*, "Travelers of every station" (GRAMOPHONE).

SONGS: *Killarney* (GRAMOPHONE-Crooks); *The Arrow and the song* (GRAMOPHONE); *Come into the garden Maud* (COLUMBIA); *Excelsior* (GRAMOPHONE).

Ludwig van Beethoven *1770-1827*

"He was a Titan wrestling with the Gods."
          –RICHARD WAGNER

IN 1767, Johann van Beethoven, a tenor-singer of Flemish origin—formerly a member of the private chapel of the Elector of Cologne—married Maria Magdalena Laym, a cook. Their first child died in infancy. Their second child was Ludwig van Beethoven, who was born in the small city of Bonn, on the Rhine, on December 16, 1770.

His early childhood was sordid. His father was a drunkard who consistently dissipated his small earnings in drink, and the earliest years of Ludwig van Beethoven's life were made sombre by poverty and drunken scenes. The only warm touches in an otherwise bleak childhood were the tenderness of his mother, and the warm generosity and affection of his grandfather, formerly a chapel-master, and a musician of high attainments.

Increasing poverty soon inspired Johann van Beethoven with a dream. He had noticed that his boy, Ludwig, had evinced an unusual curiosity for music, and—having heard startling stories of the fame and fortune which Mozart had received as a child-prodigy—he decided to develop his own son as a similar attraction. He engaged his companion, Pfeiffer, to teach Ludwig the clavier. For endless hours Ludwig was kept at the instrument, threatened by the shadow of a rod that wou'd follow each mistake or pause with blows. It is related that frequently, when Pfeiffer and Johann van Beethoven returned home late from one of their drunken spells, they would arouse Ludwig from his bed and compel him to begin practicing his lessons.

As a boy, Beethoven was both ugly and clumsy. There was not much about him to arouse affection or interest. Ries Beethoven's life-long friend, has informed us that "in behaviour, Beethoven was awkward and helpless; his uncouth movements were often destitute of grace. He seldom took anything into his hands without dropping and breaking it. No piece of furniture was safe with him. He frequently knocked his ink-pot into the pianoforte." As a result, Beethoven had few friends in early life, and his youth was spent in comparative loneliness. Such attention as he did receive usually consisted of ridicule.

In 1782, Beethoven became a pupil of Christian Gottlob Neefe, the court organist of Bonn, and one-time cantor of the St. Thomas Schule of Leipzig. Under Neefe, Beethoven made rapid strides in his music-study, and aroused the high admiration of his teacher. "Beethoven, son of the court tenor singer of that name, a boy of eleven years old, possesses talent of great promise," wrote Neefe in *Cramer's Magazine*. "He plays the piano with wonderful execution, and reads very well at sight. . . . He will certainly be a second Wolfgang Amadeus Mozart, if he continues as he has begun."

Beethoven remained Neefe's pupil until 1787, and during this period of study he officiated for a time as assistant organist in the Electoral chapel. In 1787, Beethoven came to Vienna where he knocked at Mozart's door and asked for a hearing. Mozart was not particularly impressed with Beethoven's style of performance on the pianoforte, but when Beethoven began to improvise upon a theme given him by Mozart, the master knew that he was in the presence of genius. "He will make a noise in the world some day," was his prophetic comment.

LUDWIG VAN BEETHOVEN

It is not known definitely whether Beethoven was a pupil of Mozart or not. In any case, Beethoven's stay in Vienna was fated to be brief. Two months after his arrival, he heard the tidings of his mother's serious illness, and he rushed back to Bonn to be at her death-bed. Her death, on July 17, was a severe blow to Beethoven, who felt that he had lost the only person who understood him. "She was indeed a kind mother to me," he wrote shortly after her death. "Ah, who was happier than I when I could still utter the sweet name of mother, and it was heard? To whom can I now say it? Only to the silent form which my imagination pictures to me!"

With the death of his mother, Beethoven personally assumed the management of his household. It was not an easy task, for his father was growing more and more dissolute. By 1789 he had become so hopeless a drunkard that he was summarily dismissed from his post. The entire burden of support fell on Beethoven's shoulders, and he assumed it heroically, without question or complaint.

His existence, during these years, might have been drenched with misery, were it not for the fact that at this time Beethoven became acquainted with the Breuning family and with Count Waldstein who apreciated his genius and extended to him the warmth of affection and friendship. It is the belief of Prof. Ludwig Schiedermair that Elenore von Breuning was Beethoven's first love. In any case, Beethoven became closely attached to his new friends, and received from them the encouragement and sympathy he needed so sorely at this time.

In 1792, Beethoven made his second visit to Vienna, this time to become a pupil of Josef Haydn, whom he had already casually met once before when the master passed thru Bonn. It cannot be said that this association of the two great musical figures of the late eighteenth century proved felicitous. To a man of Haydn's aristocratic background, Beethoven was, as a personality, unforgivably boorish and uncouth. Moreover, in his composition, Beethoven was too free in spirit to accept meekly Haydn's academic formalism. The lessons, therefore, soon came to an end, and Beethoven turned to Albrechtsberger for further instruction. It was hardly a distinguished change. Albrechtsberger was even more a pedant than Haydn, and was at a complete loss to understand or appreciate his pupil. He regarded Beethoven contemptuously, and at one time told an enquirer not to have anything to do with the young musician because "he had never learned anything, and would never do anything in a decent style."

During these early years in Vienna, Beethoven earned a living by playing the viola in a theatre orchestra. At the same time, letters of introduction from Count Waldstein enabled him to meet several influential aristocrats — particularly Prince Karl Lichnowsky, who immediately recognized Beethoven's genius and offered the composer a home in his palace. Beethoven accepted the invitation with the express conditions that he be left to himself much of the time and that he be under no obligation to conform to court etiquette. That Prince Karl Lichnowsky was able to remain Beethoven's host for several years, speaks favorably not only for his tact and generosity but for his ability to make allowances in human behaviour where genius was concerned. Truth to tell, Beethoven was not a gracious companion, and he could frequently try one's patience. He was extremely sensitive, and more than once flew into a violent temper at the slightest provocation. He was, moreover, arrogant, volatile, and even bumptious. More often rude than affable, and surly than charming, he rewarded his host's generosity time and again with a passion of anger or impatience.

Yet, so great was Prince Lichnowsky's faith in Beethoven's genius that he not only tolerated him but accorded him great honor and reverence. Beethoven was, therefore, in a setting conducive to creative work, and at this time he produced those early works in which genius first glimmered with unmistakable brightness—the first trios, the first *Concerto for piano and orchestra*, and the early piano sonatas including the *Sonata pathétique*.

Beethoven's first published work, a set of three piano trios—which made their appearance in 1795—was Beethoven's official bow as a composer. "And a portentous bow it was!" remarks Robert Haven Schauffler. "These compositions instantly overshadowed all that Haydn and Mozart had composed in that form. The older trios had been written with an eye to the fashionable taste of the Austrian aristocracy. Opus I, on the other hand, while keeping many a rococo characteristic, was writen with an eye single to the expression of strangely personal feeling. It has pages where one can almost overhear the proud commoner exucting in his own mental and spiritual resources."

In March of 1795, Beethoven made his first public appearance as pianist, in two charity concerts. He took Vienna by storm. It was not only his phenomenal technique and powerful interpretative insight which aroused the wonder and admiration of musicians, but his genius at improvisation which was said to have been without comparison. "Apart from the beauty and originality of the ideas," Czerny has recorded concerning Beethoven's improvisations, "there was something extraordinary in the expression."

From this time on, Beethoven's regal position as a pianist was not questioned; and it was as a pianist, and not as a composer, that the Viennese music public did him honor towards the close of the century.

By 1800, Beethoven had composed those works which comprise the first period of his creative career, including the first ten of the pianoforte sonatas, the first five of the sonatas for violin and piano, the first eight trios, the first two piano concertos, the *Septet*, the *Serenade*, and the *First symphony*. In these works, to be sure, the influence of Haydn and Mozart is noticeable; but Beethoven's fingerprints are easily discernible.

In the music of the first period, summarizes Daniel Gregory Mason, "Beethoven had in the first place thoroly assimilated the sonata form developed by his forerunners as the most convenient and natural medium for the expression of the free, direct, and widely eclectic

secular spirit in music. He had, in the second place, raised this form to higher potencies of beauty and expressiveness, by rigorous exclusion of what was superfluous and inorganic in it, by purification of its texture and strengthening of its essential structural features, and by introduction into it, thru the power of his genius for composition, of more subtle and more thorogoing contrasts of rhythm, harmony, and general expressive character. Still he was not content. His soaring idealism demanded a still greater flexibility of form, as we'l as a more intense and intimate utterance of feeling. 'I am not satisfied,' he wrote in 1802, 'with my works up to the present time. From today I mean to take a new road.'"

In 1801, Beethoven—who thruout his life was susceptible to the lure of women —fell deeply in love. She was Countess Giuletta Guicciardi, a charming girl who had become fascinated with the magnetic personality of the great composer. There was talk of marriage which, unfortunately, Beethoven took too seriously. Count Guicciardi intervened, and the affair collapsed. That Beethoven was powerfully attached to Giuletta cannot be denied. The *Moonlight sonata* is dedicated to her. Moreover, after Beethoven's death there was discovered a secret drawer in his desk which contained a medallion portrait of Giuletta together with the most passionate letter written by him a—letter dedicated to his "Immortal Beloved." There are some biographers who believe strongly that the "Immortal Beloved" is none other than Giuletta Guicciardi.

Simultaneous with his disappointment in love came a far greater tragedy. In 1801, Beethoven wrote to a friend: "Know then that my noblest faculty, my hearing, has been sadly deteriorated. When you were still with me I had intimations of this, but said nothing about them; now it has been growing steadily worse, and whether it can be cured remains to be seen, the trouble probably coming from the condition of my abdomen. . . What a sorrowful life I must now live, avoiding all that is dear and precious to me; and, too, among such miserable and egotistical people. . . . Sorrowful resignation—in this must I find refuge."

His deafness gradually became worse and, as one doctor after another failed to find a remedy, Beethoven's depression of spirit increased. In 1802, he spent the summer in the quaint village of Heiligenstadt, near Vienna, where he wrote a gloomy suicidal Testament—a document of utter despair and futility, caused by the oncoming Silence. By the close of 1802, his illness had become so acute that he was compelled to give up all of his piano-performances in public and much of his conducting, and devote himself almost exclusively to composition. At the same time, he segregated himself from all society, and preferred to live in solitude.

Deafness marked the prelude of the second creative period in Beethoven's life —a period that produced some of his most famous masterpieces. "I am now making a fresh start," he wrote at this time. A fresh start, indeed! For between 1803 and 1804, he produced the *Piano concerto in C-minor*, the *Kreutzer sonata*, for violin and piano, the *Waldstein* and *Appassionata* piano sonatas, and the *Eroica symphony*.

The circumstances surrounding the composition of the *Eroica* are too well known to require detailed repetition. It is common knowledge that Beethoven had originally intended calling it the "Buonaparte symphony," in honor of a great republican. When Ries brought Beethoven the tidings that Napoleon had declared himself Emperor of France, Beethoven broke out angrily: "Then he is nothing but an ordinary man. Now he'll trample on all the rights of men to serve his own ambition; he will put himself higher than all others, and turn tyrant!" Following this cry, he tore the dedicatory page of the symphony to shreds, and entitled the work merely the *Eroica*.

The flood of masterpieces had begun, and until 1812 it was to continue virtually without intermission. Beethoven's only opera, *Fidelio*, came in 1805. Between 1806 and 1808, he composed his *Fourth*, *Fifth* and *Pastoral* symphonies. At the same time, came his *Fourth* and *Emperor* piano concertos, the *Concerto for violin and orchestra*, the Rasoumovsky quartets, the magnificent overtures to *Egmont*

and *Coriolanus*, and the most famous of his piano and violin-piano sonatas. In 1812, this sublime output was climaxed by the creation of the *Seventh* and *Eighth* symphonies.

The distinguishing quality of Beethoven's masterpieces of this period—a quality which sharply differentiates this music from all other—is what Paul Bekker apt'y called the "poetic idea." In these works, it is not merely the sound patterns, the melodic line or the subtlety of rhythmic or harmonic construction which intrigues us, but the expression of profound thoughts and of the most poignant emotions. "Music is no longer sonority pure and simple," wrote Paul Bekker, explaining his thesis. "It contains abstract ideas. Beethoven did not write music to preconceived ideas, but the ideas and the music went inseparably together. With him the dynamic urge which is an organic part of all harmonic music, goes far beyond the ordinary scope of dynamic impulses and becomes the means of interpreting the idea. . . . It is . . . impossible to dismiss the idea from Beethoven's music without misrepresenting the man. It is the idea which constitutes the constructive power, the dynamic principle of form in his compositions. It is the idea which determines the character of his work and which makes possible the further development of harmonic music. Beethoven's true relationship with Schiller and Kant lies in their being men who stood for ideas, though they worked along different creative lines. But in his particular type of ideas, Beethoven is the great child of a great imaginative era—an era in which the gods and heroes of idealism throve, an era which believed in man as a spiritual being, in freedom and brotherhood, in the joy of divine inspiration, in the everlasting peace and happiness of mankind."

In 1810, Beethoven was once again in love, this time with Fraülein Theresa Malfatti, a girl of fifteen; and once again he seriously contemp'ated marriage. Pathetically enough, he now grew fastidious about his dress, bought handsome cravats and shirts, and went to excessive pains to make himself more presentable to his beloved. This affair culminated in acute disappointment for

Beethoven, when the girl's uncle firmly refused to sanction such a marriage. Beethoven had hardly recovered from his affair when he fell in love again, with his life-long friend, Bettina Brentano, friend of Goethe. Bettina was singularly attracted to the great composer. "When I saw him," she wrote to Goethe, "I forgot the whole world, as the world still vanishes when the memory grips me. . . . It is Beethoven of whom I now wish to tell you, and in whose presence I forgot the world and you. . . . He strides far ahead of the culture of all humanity. And shall we overtake him?" Beethoven responded sensitively to such adoration. "God, how I love you," he wrote to her.

In the Summer of 1811, Beethoven was attracted to still another woman, the beautiful and flirtatious Amalie Sebald, whom he met at the baths of Teplitz. There are some musicologists who consider Amalie Sebald, and not Giuletta, Beethoven's "Immortal Beloved."

Between the years of 1812 and 1817, Beethoven confronted comparative sterility in composition, which can be explained to a great extent by the disagreeable litigation which he suffered at this time in connection with his nephew, Karl. When his brother, Caspar, died, Beethoven—in horror that Caspar's son should now be put under the influence of a dissolute mother, whom he called "The Queen of the Night"—decided to adopt the boy. The mother decided to fight the adoption, and for several years the affair was fought in Viennese courthouses. The ugly litigation—which cost Beethoven much mental pain—finally ended favorably for Beethoven.

But the victory proved hardly worth while. As Beethoven grew more and more attached to his nephew, he was faced with the harrowing discovery that the boy had inherited the less desirable traits of his mother and father. Karl was shiftless, irresponsible and corrupt. He contracted large debts and stole to defray them. He was perpetually in trouble and, though Beethoven always treated his faults with kindness and mercy, blamed his uncle for his own failings. He was expelled from one school after another, then attempted suicide in the picturesque ruins of the Castle of Rauhenstein. He was, finally, incarcerated in an asylum.

In 1817, Beethoven's productive flame burned once again. He began work simultaneously on three gargantuan ventures, including the *Missa solemnis,* the *Ninth symphony* and the piano sonata Opus 106. With these works Beethoven entered upon the final phase of his artistic development, the phase often spoken of as the "metaphysical period," in which he became more experimental than ever before, and compressed his music with greater profundity of ideas and thought. During this final period, Beethoven composed his last piano sonatas and the last quartets, which for many years were the subject of great controversy.

What J. W. N. Sullivan wrote about the *C-sharp minor quartet* might very aptly describe all of Beethoven's music of the last period. "It is the completely unfaltering rendering into music of what we can only call the mystic vision. It has the serenity which, as Wagner said, speaking of these quartets, passes beyond beauty. Nowhere else in music are we made so aware, as here, of a state of consciousness surpassing our own, where our problems do not exist, and to which even our highest aspirations, those that we can formulate, provide no key. Those faint and troubling intimations we sometimes have of a vision different from and yet including our own, of a way of apprehending life, passionless, perfect and complete, that resolves all our discords, are here presented with the reality they had glimpsed. This impression of a superhuman knowledge, of a superhuman life being slowly frozen into shape, as it were, before our eyes, can be ambiguous. That passionless, remote calm can seem, as it did to Wagner, like a melancholy too profound for any tears. To Berlioz it was terrifying. To Beethoven himself it was the justification of, and the key to, life. In the light of this vision he surveys the world. That this vision was permanent with Beethoven is inconceivable. No man ever lived who could maintain such a state of illumination. This, we may be sure, is the last and greatest of Beethoven's spiritual discoveries, only to be grasped in the moments of his profoundest abstraction from the world."

In 1826, Beethoven visited his brother in Gneixendorf to settle a dispute which arose concerning their nephew, Karl. On his return to Vienna, he caught cold. Pneumonia set in and, subjected to great care, was partially cured. However, an unexpected relapse followed, bringing with it jaundice and dropsy. Beethoven was an acutely sick man and an entire world held its breath.

During the final days of his life, Beethoven was in good temper. He read Scott and Ovid whom he enjoyed immensely, and was greatly pleased at the gifts which came to his sick-bed— including a magnificent edition of Handel, a sum of five hundred dollars from the London Philharmonic Orchestra, and a case of Rhine wine from his publishers, Schott. But Beethoven knew that his end was near. On March 23, he signed his will, and the following day submitted quietly to the Last Sacraments. On the 25th of March he slipped into unconsciousness. "The strong man lay," wrote Gerhard von Breuning, "completely unconscious. . . . breathing so stertorously that the rattle could be heard at a distance. His powerful frame, his unweakened lungs, fought like giants with approaching death."

The following day there was thunder and lightning in Vienna. Suddenly, at a peal of thunder, Beethoven raised himself in his bed, directed a defiant fist at the growling heavens, and then fell back. He was dead.

The funeral took place on the 29th, and in Beethoven's honor the schools of Vienna were closed. A military force was called out to keep the 25,000 admirers—who had come to pay their last respects to the great composer— under control. Among the torch and pall bearers were Schubert, Hummel, Czerny and Kreutzer.

Forty-five years later, Beethoven's body was exhumed and reburied in the Central Friedhof of Vienna where it lies today, near the remains of Mozart, Schubert and Brahms.

Beethoven was five feet five inches in height, solidly built and broad-shouldered. His face—strikingly un-

attractive—had a magnificent strength which Reichardt described as "cyclopean." He was almost austerely simple in his everyday habits, placed little importance on food—altho he enjoyed a dish of fish and a grass of good wine— and seemed oblivious to material comforts. He was incredibly absent-minded; he was always forgetting something— sometimes his washing, sometimes that he had engaged rooms in which he was not living, sometimes to eat his meals. He often paid waiters for meals he had not as yet been served. Upon many occasions, his friends would creep into his bedroom and substitute an entirely new outfit for the decrepit one they found in the closet; in the morning, Beethoven dressed, and never noticed that his wardrobe had been changed.

Hot-headed, volatile, erratic, he was far from being a pleasant friend; and he could often be unreasonably demanding. At one time—in 1804—he came to live in the home of his boyhood friend, Stephen von Breuning. He fell seriously ill, and was tenderly nursed back to health by his friend. Upon recovery, Beethoven discovered that he had forgotten to give notice to his former landlady and that he was now compelled to pay an imposing bill for back rent. In his anger, Beethoven completely forgot all of his friend's kindness, and bitterly attacked him for not having been thoughtful enough to arrange the cancellation of that apartment. They quarrelled, and Beethoven left in hot anger as though he had been viciously imposed upon.

He alternated between insane wrath and exaggerated repentance. Frequently he broke out into wild transports of rage, sometimes on the most negligible provocation, and his invectives could drip poison. On the other hand, he had moments of touching softness and whenever he recognized that he had been in the wrong, he would write letters of the most affectionate and self-denunciatory character.

He was idealistically democratic, his sympathies always with the masses. Never would he bend his knee to aristocracy. When he was performing for nobility and one of them would disturb his performance with conversation, he would shout out vehemently at them: "I will not play for such hogs." When asked to be ceremonious before his social superiors, his answer was: "I, too, am king!" He was once walking with Goethe, when he saw the Empress coming towards them. At the sight of Goethe assuming an obsequious pose, Beethoven lost his temper: "It is they who must make way to us, not we to them!" he growled.

"He was fond of the company of women," his friend Reis has informed us, "especially if they had young and pretty faces, and generally when we passed a somewhat charming girl he would turn back and gaze keenly at her thru his glasses, and if he noticed that I observed him, he would laugh or grin. He was frequently in love." In love, as in everything else, Beethoven was the high-idealist. "Sensual gratification, without union of souls," he wrote, "is and remains bestial."

Strangely enough, Beethoven was always a cool and calculating business man who was capable of driving a hard bargain; nor was he always scrupulously honest in his business dealings. Where money matters were concerned, Beethoven was not only careful but almost avaricious. Otherwise, he was hopelessly impractical. He was unable to shave himself without cutting himself deeply, and he was as incapable as a child of taking care of himself.

When he was hard at work, he concentrated so deeply that he frequently forgot himself completely. Sometimes he would run out of doors, without hat or coat, and wander in the fields for hours as his mind busily developed themes into elaborate tonal structures. He would return home late at night, cold, wet, and famished, but altogether oblivious of his condition, and spend further hours at the piano translating his mental dreams into music.

His method of working was to jot down his ideas on paper or in sketchbooks as they came to him, and these ideas he would continually polish and revise until they reached their most crystallized form. "I carry my thoughts about with me long, often very long, before I write them down," he himself has explained. "In doing this my memory stands me in such good stead that even years afterwards I am sure not to forget a theme that I have once grasped. I alter some things, eliminate and try again until I am satisfied. Then begins the mental working out of this stuff in its breadth, its narrowness, its height and depth. And, as I know what I want, the fundamental idea never deserts me. It mounts, it grows in stature; I hear, see the picture in its whole extent, standing all of a piece before my spirit, and there remains for me only the labor of writing it down, which goes quickly whenever I have time for it. For many times I have several pieces in hand at once, but am perfectly sure not to confuse them. You will ask me where I get my ideas. I am not able to answer that question positively. They come directly, indirectly; I can grasp them with my hands. Out amid the freedom of nature, in the woods, on walks, in the silence of the night, early in the morning, called forth by such moods as in the minds of poets translate themselves into words, but in mine into tones which ring, roar, storm until at last they stand as notes before me."

Robert Haven Schauffler has written a notable book on Beethoven, in which he refers to this great composer as "the man who freed music." This is a singularly appropriate designation, for few composers in musical history have been the iconoclast so fearlessly as Beethoven. Schauffler, in several discerning paragraphs, has pointed out the monumental change to which music was subjected under Beethoven, "By his choice of texts, he presented vocal music with the freedom of the world of great literature—a pioneer accomplishment. Thru the accidental circumstance that the *B-minor Mass* was not published until years after Beethoven's *Missa solemnis*, our hero became the Luther among composers, extricating the Mass from the bonds of convention and dogma. He released the dramatic overture from subservience to that hybrid thing, opera; and the concerto orchestra from its abject servility as a mere accompanist to the solo part. More than any previous composer, he rid music of the exhibitionistic taint of virtuosity for virtuosity's sake, and the reproach of composing to the order of outer compulsion rather than from inner necessity.

"His ingenuity helped to throw open to the piano and the orchestra a new world of richness and sonority. The accident of deafness freed the art in another way, by decreeing a divorce between composer and virtuoso and smashing the harmful old convention that the creative musician must necessarily fritter away his energies in interpretative work.

"Perhaps his supreme achievement as emancipator was the exertion of a more potent influence than that of his greatest predecessors towards freeing music from the shackles of literature, whose servant it was in the beginning. By pouring into music a wealth of suggestive factors which made it so much more opulent and self-contained than ever before, he made it easier for the imagination of the ordinary listener at length to escape from the weakening incubus of cliché programs and, under the stimulus of this powerfully independent art, to fashion its own poetic interpretations.

"Beethoven found the art of music narrowed to the pastime of a special class. He made it broadly human. He left it superhuman. Of course, he was far from being the only man who ever freed music. In many ages and lands the art has been enslaved and has found its liberators. But the most potent of all these was Beethoven."

Principal works by Ludwig van Beethoven:

CHORAL: Two masses (including the *Missa solemnis*); *Christ on Mount of Olives*; Ten cantatas.

OPERA: *Fidelio.*

ORCHESTRA: Nine symphonies (the last with chorus); *Egmont, Coriolanus, Leonore* (1, 2, 3, 4) overtures; Five piano concertos; *Fantasie* (for piano, orchestra and chorus); *Concerto for violin and orchestra*; Two romances (for violin and orchestra); *Triple concerto* (for piano, violin, violoncello and orchestra), etc.

BALLET: *Prometheus.*

CHAMBER MUSIC: Sixteen string quartets; *Grosse fugue* (originally composed as last movement of Quartet Opus 130); *Septet*; *Sextet* (for strings and wind); Eight piano trios; Five trios for other instruments; Two string quintets; Ten sonatas for violin and piano; Five sonatas for violoncello and piano.

PIANO: Thirty-two sonatas; over 100 smaller pieces including variations, rondos, preludes, etc.
Over 250 songs.

About Ludwig van Beethoven:

D'Indy, Vincent. *Beethoven*; Ewen, David (editor) *From Bach to Stravinsky*; Mason, Daniel Gregory. *Beethoven and His Forerunners*; Newman, Ernest. *The Unconscious Beethoven*; Rolland, Romain. *Beethoven and Goethe*; Rolland, Romain. *Beethoven the Creator*; Schauffler, Robert Haven. *Beethoven: The Man Who Freed Music*; Shedlock, J. S. *The Letters of Beethoven*; Sullivan, J. W. N. *Beethoven: His Spiritual Development*; Thayer, A. W. *The Life of Ludwig van Beethoven*; Turner, W. J. *Beethoven: The Search for Reality.*

Important recordings of music by Ludwig van Beethoven:

CHORAL: *Missa solemnis,* complete (VICTOR).

OPERA: *Fidelio,* complete (VICTOR).

ORCHESTRA: *Symphony no. 1* (VICTOR-Mengelberg); *Second symphony* (COLUMBIA-Beecham); *Eroica symphony* (VICTOR-Koussevitzky); *Fourth symphony* (COLUMBIA-Weingartner); *Fifth symphony* (VICTOR-Koussevitzky); *Pastoral symphony* (COLUMBIA-Paray); *Seventh symphony* (VICTOR-Toscanini); *Eighth symphony* (VICTOR-Koussevitzky); *Ninth symphony,* with chorus (VICTOR-Stokowski); *Egmont overture* (VICTOR-Boult); *Coriolanus overture* (VICTOR-Boult); *Leonore overture no. 3* (COLUMBIA-Mengelberg); Five concertos for piano and orchestra (VICTOR-Schnabel); *Concerto for violin and orchestra* (VICTOR-Kreisler); *Romance in G-major* (GRAMOPHONE-Elman); *Romance in F-major* (GRAMOPHONE-Elman).

PIANO: Thirty-two sonatas for piano (HIS MASTER'S VOICE-Schnabel).

CHAMBER MUSIC: *String quartet Opus 18, no. 1* (VICTOR-Busch); *String quartet Opus 18, no. 2* (VICTOR-Flonzaley); *String quartet Opus 18, no. 3* (VICTOR-Budapest); *String quartet Opus 18, no. 4* (GRAMOPHONE-Rosé); *String quartet, Opus 18, no. 5* (COLUMBIA-Capet); *String quartet Opus 18, no. 6* (COLUMBIA-Lener); *String quartet Opus 59, no. 1* (GRAMOPHONE-Budapest); *String quartet Opus 59, no. 2 and no. 3* (COLUMBIA-Lener); *"Harp" quartet* (COLUMBIA-Lener); *"Serious" quartet* (COLUMBIA-Roth); *String quartet Opus 127* (VICTOR-Flonzaley); *String quartet Opus 130* (VICTOR-Budapest); *String quartet Opus 131* (COLUMBIA-Capet); *String quartet Opus 132* (COLUMBIA-London); *String quartet Opus 135* (VICTOR-Busch); *Grosse fugue* (VICTOR-Budapest); *Septet* (COLUMBIA-Lener); *Archduke trio* (VICTOR); *Clarinet trio* (POLYDOR); *Sonata for violoncello and piano in A-major* (VICTOR-Casals); *Sonata in G-major for violoncello and piano* (VICTOR-Piatigorsky); Ten sonatas for violin and piano (HIS MASTER'S VOICE-Kreisler), etc.

Miscellaneous songs, pieces for violin, for piano, etc.

Vincenzo Bellini *1802-1835*

"Whoever ignores Bellini, ignores true melody."—ROGER ALLARD

VINCENZO BELLINI was born at Catania, Sicily, on November 1, 1802. His father, a descendant of a long line of musicians, was an organist and conductor, and it was from him that Vincenzo acquired the first rudiments of music. He took to musical instruction easily, learning his lessons rapidly and well. One day, a Sicilian nobleman, speaking to Vincenzo, was struck by the boy's talent and asked the father for permission to finance the young musician's career.

Thus Bellini came to Naples in late adolescence to attend the Conservatory, and he remained here for several years acquiring technical maturity. He was by no means an extraordinary student, but his original composition showed sufficient talent to attract notice. In 1825, his first work to receive performance was introduced at the Conservatory— a cantata, *Ismene*; and it was sufficiently impressive to arouse the enthusiasm and personal congratulations of the King.

Bellini was as precocious a lover as he was a musician. Possessing a striking appearance, and a suave and agreeable manner, he—like Mozart before him—attracted female hearts from boyhood days. At the age of sixteen, he was already writing to the daughter of a notary in his native city: "It seems to me that you are at my side, that you caress my face with your fairy-like fingers. . . . Your love inflames me, exalts me. . . ." With these words still fresh upon paper, he could direct affectionate glances in other corners as well. There was a seamstress in Catania who embroidered a handkerchief for him when he left for Naples, as a love-token. And, in Naples, there were several minor amorous incidents to color an otherwise routine existence.

While he was still at the Conservatory, Bellini composed his first opera, *Adelson e Salvina*, which was played in the presence of Barbaja, the eminent impresario of the La Scala in Milan and the San Carlo in Naples. Barbaja had keen perception, and he recognized talent even in this early work. He therefore com-

VINCENZO BELLINI

missioned its young composer to prepare an opera expressly for him. In 1826, *Bianca e Fernando* was performed at the San Carlo. While it was not a particularly striking success, it elicited some praise and admiration from the audience.

Barbaja, however, still had faith in his young composer and engaged him to prepare an opera for Rubini, the famous tenor of the time. It was partially Rubini's great fame and talent, but more specifically Bellini's sun-bathed melodies that brought phenomenal esteem to *Il Pirata,* introduced at the La Scala in Milan. *Il Pirata* was soon afterwards performed in Paris, and before long it made its appearance in the repertory of leading opera houses in Europe, establishing its creator as one of the most promising operatic composers of his time.

It was not until four years later that Bellini fully fulfilled the promise of *Il Pirata.* In his succeeding two operas he was still the faltering artist. But in 1831 he pushed his apprentice years far behind him, and produced a work which, by critics everywhere, was esteemed his masterpiece, *La Sonnambula.* Introduced at La Scala in Milan, it created a sensation. There followed performances thruout all of Europe. Finally, Mme. Malibran, the distinguished prima-donna, appeared in an English version which made the opera equally popular with English-speaking audiences.

Bellini, now having found his stride, produced two more operas of unquestionable importance. One year after *La Sonnambula* came *Norma*, the opera which contains what is probably Bellini's greatest melody, *Casta Diva*. In 1834, on the advice of Rossini, Bellini came to Paris for the purpose of composing an opera expressly for the Théâtre Italien. This, the third of Bellini's masterpieces, was *I Puritani*.

Vincenzo Bellini died of intestinal fever in Paris on September 24, 1835. On the eve of his funeral, the Théâtre Italien in Paris opened its new season with *I Puritani*.. After this performance, the singers and musicians combined in a monumental requiem service for the dead composer, directed by such eminent musicians as Cherubini and Rossini. The mass took place in the Church of the Invalides, and Bellini's body was brought to Père Lachaise, where it rests at the present time.

Heinrich Heine, in his *Florentinische Nächte*, has given us a striking verbal portrait of Bellini. "Bellini was a tall, up-shooting, slender figure, which always moved gracefully; coquettish, looking as if just emerged from a band-box; a regular, but large, delicately rose-tinted face; light, almost golden hair, worn in wavy curls; a high, very high marble forehead, straight nose, light blue eyes, well-sized mouth, and round chin. His features had something vague in them, a want of character, something milk-like; and in this milk-like face flitted sometimes a painful-pleasing expression of sorrow. It was this shallow sorrow that the young maestro seemed most willing to represent in his whole appearance. His hair was dressed so fancifully sad; his clothes fitted so languishingly round his delicate body; he carried his cane so idyllike, that he reminded me of the young shepherds we find in our pastorals, with their crooks decorated with ribbons. His whole walk was so innocent, so airy, so sentimental. The man looked like a sigh in pumps and silk-stockings."

Bellini's important position in the history of Italian opera cannot easily be doubted. He carried on the traditions of Italian opera and brought to it new spheres of expressiveness. Bellini did not pave new roads in the operatic art. He was satisfied with the forms which Rossini and Cherubini had employed successfully; but into these he poured an altogether new flood of beauty.

Certainly, Bellini's greatest strength as a composer lies in his ability to produce melodies of stabbing beauty. As Ildebrando Pizzetti, the distinguished modern Italian composer, has written: "The lyricism of Bellini expresses itself in a song that gushes forth with the essence of an emotion that springs from the drama, that gushes forth especially at moments that bring the drama to a resolution, similar to a fire which is ignited after it emits hot sparks. And this song, gushing forth, becomes a stream, a river, finally an ocean that rolls away to the distance towards the immense horizon. . . . Bellini has created a song that is ample, marvelous and unique. Unique is the song of the final scene of *Norma*, unique is the one which accompanies the closing of the first act of the *Sonnambula*, and unique is the song which can be found in the most important scenes of *Puritani*."

While Bellini's unusual gifts at melodic invention have always been accepted, he has frequently been accused of poverty in harmonic construction. Cecil Gray has eloquently answered such critics: "His vocal writing could only be impaired by such treatment," wrote Gray in discussing the possibility of a more elaborate harmonic treatment for Bellini's exquisite arias. "Like folk-song, it instinctively rejects harmonic elaborateness as foreign to its nature. . . . In the same. way that a jewel is displayed to better advantage in a simple setting than in none at all, but overshadowed by the brilliance of an elaborate one, so a melody of Bellini requires a certain degree of accompaniment which must never be allowed to become so obtrusive as to distract our attention from the melody, or to impress itself too strongly on our consciousess." Incidentally, both Georges Bizet and Cherubini considered Bellini's accompaniments the last word in harmonic good-taste.

But, as Richard Wagner was not slow to realize, Bellini was not merely an inspired singer of song; he was also a vital factor in the development of music-drama. By composing recitatives that are crisp and dramatic, by permitting his music to express the emotional sentiments of each dramatic situation, Bellini was unconsciously working in the direction of a stronger union between music and text, thereby paving the way for such future composers as Wagner himself. "Never," wrote Wagner in his *Memoirs,* "will I forget the impression which Bellini's operas made upon me at a time when I was perfectly weary of the eternally abstract complexity of our orchestrations, and when a simple and noble song manifested itself as something new to me. . . ." And, elsewhere, Wagner wrote: "People believe that I hate all the Italian school of music and specifically Bellini. No, no, a thousand times no! Bellini is one of my predilections, because his music is strongly felt and intimately bound up with the words."

It is the interesting opinion of Igor Stravinsky, distinguished modernist composer, that Bellini was not merely far ahead of his own time, but also so far in advance of our own, that it will yet be many years before the music-world will fully appreciate his genius.

Bellini has recorded for us his method of working: "I study attentively the dispositions of the characters, the passions which sway them, and the sentiments which they express. Possessed by the feelings of each of them, I imagine myself for the moment to have become the one who is speaking, and I make an effort to feel like him, and to express myself in his manner. Knowing that music results from the employment of a variety of sounds, and that the passions of mankind manifest themselves by means of utterance of diverse tones, I have reproduced the language of passion in my art thru incessant observation.

"Then, in the seclusion of my study, I begin to declaim the parts of the different characters in the drama with the utmost warmth, observing in the meanwhile the inflexions of my voice, the degree of haste or languor in their delivery—the accent, in short—and the tone of expression which nature gives to the man who is in the throes of emotion: and I find in this way the musical mo-tives and tempi best adapted to their communication to others thru the medium of sounds.

"I transfer the results to paper, try it over on the piano and if I feel in it the corresponding emotion, I consider myself to have succeeded. If I do not, then I begin again."

Principal works by Vincenzo Bellini:

OPERA: *Il Pirata; La Sonnambula; I Puritani; Norma.*

About Vincenzo Bellini:

Bellaigue, Camille. *Musical Studies and Silhouettes;* Lloyd, William A. *Bellini. Monthly Musical Record* 21:270 December 1, 1891; *Music and Letters* 7:49 January 1926; *La Revue Musicale* No. 156 (Special issue) May 1935.

Important recordings of music by Vincenzo Bellini:

SELECTIONS FROM OPERA: *Columbia Bellini Centenary Albums,* 2 vols., including principal selections from *Norma, I Puritani, La Sonnambula* (COLUMBIA).

Sterndale Bennett *1816-1875*

WILLIAM STERNDALE BENNET was born in Sheffield, England, on April 13, 1816. In his fourth year, he lost his father—who had been an organist of the parish church—and, soon afterwards, his mother as well. He was, therefore, adopted by his grandfather, who was the first to recognize the child's musical talent. At five, William received his first piano instruction; and two years later he was admitted as a chorister in the choir of King's College.

After studying music with local teachers, William Sterndale Bennett was enrolled, in his tenth year, at the Royal Academy of Music in London. Here he was considered an apathetic and disinterested student, even though his playing of the piano was unusually competent. His sincere love for music, however, could not be questioned. He would take scores of Mozart's music to bed with him, and would memorize the orchestration. His spare hours belonged to composition. During his student days at the Academy he composed his first symphony, which was of sufficient merit to warrant publication, and—in 1833—to attract the favorable attention of Felix Mendelssohn.

STERNDALE BENNETT

A small sum of money, inherited from his mother, came due at this time and enabled him to realize a long-cherished ambition: to go to Leipzig and meet Mendelssohn personally. He came to this musical Mecca in 1836. Mendelssohn was so impressed with the compositions that Bennett had brought with him that he took the young student under his wing. He introduced him to the foremost musicians in Leipzig, including Robert Schumann, and gave him personal advice in his composition.

Bennett literally absorbed the musical life in Leipzig. He studied with an unparalleled assiduity, attended all the concerts, and composed with a fertile pen. He would take daily walks with Robert Schumann and Felix Mendelssohn and discuss music with them tirelessly. It is interesting to point out that Schumann soon became so attached to Bennett that he dedicated his famous *Études symphoniques* to him.

In Leipzig it was that Bennett first achieved fame. Thru Mendelssohn's influence his *Concerto for piano and orchestra* and the *Naiades overture* were performed by the Leipzig Gewandhaus Orchestra, and were acclaimed. Robert Schumann wrote about the young composer in glowing terms in his *Zeitschrift für Musik*. By his twenty-first birthday, Bennett found himself a famous

composer, one of the most significant to have come from England.

Upon returning to his native country, Bennett earned his livelihood by playing and teaching the piano. His pen, however, had lost none of its productiveness. During the next few years, performances of his symphonic works were frequent in London and Leipzig. In 1844, he married Mary Wood, the daughter of a Navy Commander.

Beginning with 1849, Sterndale diverted his musical talents into channels other than composition. In that year he founded the Bach Society, whose first president he became; this was largely instrumental in acquainting England with the—then—unknown music of Johann Sebastian Bach. In 1856, Bennett became the principal conductor of the Royal Philharmonic Society, holding the position with great honor for ten years. In 1866, he was appointed director of the Royal Academy of Music, the duties of which he fulfilled with industry and foresight until his death. By 1871, he was accepted as the undisputed dean of English music, in recognition of which fact he was knighted by the King.

William Sterndale Bennett died in London on February 1, 1875, and was buried in Westminster Abbey, not far from the tomb of Henry Purcell.

William Sterndale Bennett's son has given us the following description of his father: "His head, as Millais noticed, was certainly on a large scale in relation to his whole figure. . . . His hair was black, his eyes of a deep blue color, but no floridness. He looked his best in the height of summer. . . . His large eyes often attracted attention by reason of the intense and prolonged earnestness of their gaze." "I was particularly struck by the character and refined beauty of his hands," is an added note of Sir Charles Villiers Stanford.

He was, in the words of Ferdinand Hiller, "extremely simple, unaffected, open, honorable, good-tempered, cheerful and sociable." He dressed in the old style, with a dark coat, high collar and flowing tie. He rarely spoke about music; a friend once said that it was possible to spend several days with him without knowing that he was a musician by profession. In politics he was a

Liberal. He had a comprehensive knowledge of English poetry. He loved, above all other things, long walks, good humor and circus-shows.

W. H. Hadow has pointed out the amazing fact that Sterndale Bennett's best composition was done before his twenty-fifth birthday. His innumerable activities in later life exacted a precious toll from his creative efforts. In his later works "there is something left of the old skill, and all of the old sincerity, but the freshness of inspiration is gone: it is tired work, 'numbers ratified' and the 'golden cadence of poetry' is wanting."

However, Bennett assumed an important position in English music. He left an indelible impression upon the history of music in his country. "When Bennett appeared on the scene"—to quote Sir Charles Villiers Stanford—"chamber music of native origin had been dormant for nearly a century. There had been no outstanding composer of absolute music since Purcell. It is to Bennett's initiative that England owes the awakening which since his day has spread over the artistic life of the country."

Sterndale Bennett is, perhaps, most impressive in his piano music. "He was, so to speak, a pianist by nature," wrote H. Heathcote Statham. "His numerous compositions for his favorite instrument have not that orchestral largness and breadth of manner which belongs to the pianoforte compositions of Beethoven, and to a lesser degree to those of Mendelssohn. But they are remarkable and most interesting, in addition to their intrinsic beauty, as specimens of composition in which the capabilities of the instrument are strictly consulted—which represent precisely what the pianoforte can best do, and that only, and what no other instrument can imitate. There is not anywhere in art an instance of finer perception of means to an end than is furnished by the pianoforte works of Bennett."

Principal works by William Sterndale Bennett:

ORCHESTRA: Four concertos for piano and orchestra; *The Naiades*; *The Wood nymphs*; *Paradise and the Peri*; *Symphony in G-minor*.

CHORAL: *The Woman of Samaria*; Four sacred duets, etc.
Songs; works for the piano, etc.

About William Sterndale Bennett:

Bennett, James Robert Sterndale. *The Life of William Sterndale Bennett*; Stanford, Charles Villiers. *Interludes*; Statham, H. Heathcote. *My Thoughts On Music and Musicians*; Walker, Bettina. *My Musical Experiences*.
Musical Quarterly 2:628 October 1916; *Musical Times* 57:233 May 1, 1916.

Alban Berg *1885-1935*
(See *Composers of Today*)

Charles de Bériot *1802-1870*

CHARLES AUGUSTE DE BÉRIOT was born in Louvain, Belgium, on February 20, 1802. His parents who were of noble extraction died when Charles was aged nine, leaving him completely destitute. He was adopted by Monsieur Tiby, a professor of music, who was attracted to the boy because of his unaffected devotion for music. It was Monsieur Tiby who gave Charles de Bériot his first lessons on the violin.

When de Bériot reached his nineteenth birthday, he came to Paris with a letter of introduction to Viotti, the great violinist, who at that time was director of music at the Opéra. Viotti heard de Bériot play and praised his performance

CHARLES DE BÉRIOT

effusively. Thru Viotti's influence, de Bériot was enrolled as a student at the Paris Conservatory, where he became a pupil of Baillot. But de Bériot had little patience with schools and school-book exercises, and before long he withdrew from the Conservatory to study by himself.

He began his career as a concert violinist. In 1826, he performed with the Royal Philharmonic of London, and made such a vivid impression that he was urged to make an extensive tour. He travelled widely, and scored a great success wherever he went. Finally, returning to his native country, he was appointed solo violinist to the King of the Netherlands. In 1830, the revolution deprived him of this position.

He returned to Paris where he became acquainted with Mme. Malibran, the world-famous prima donna. Their friendship developed, and Mme. Malibran urged the violinist to accompany her on a concert-tour thru Italy. In 1835, Mme. Malibran divorced her American husband, a merchant. Soon afterwards she was married to Charles de Bériot. Their marriage was idyllic but brief. A few months after the wedding ceremony, Mme. Malibran was thrown off her horse. Internal injuries caused her death. In 1841, de Bériot married a second time—Mlle. Huber, daughter of a Viennese magistrate.

At the invitation of music-lovers of Belgium, de Bériot went to Brussels to become the director of the violin classes at the Conservatory. He held this post until 1852. Finally, failing eyesight compelled him to withdraw from all musical activity. He died in the city of his birth, on April 8, 1870.

Charles de Bériot composed extensively for the violin. His works "have a certain easy, natural flow, and bring out the characteristic effects of the instrument in the most brilliant manner," notes Henry C. Lahee. While de Bériot's works for the violin are pleasing melodically and technically adroit, they never succeed in rising above sheer ingenuity and good-taste to genuine artistic importance.

Principal works by Charles de Bériot:
VIOLIN: Ten concertos for violin and orchestra; Eleven *airs variés*; Forty-nine duos; caprices, etc.

About Charles de Bériot:
Bachmann, Alberto. *Les Grands Violinistes du Passé*; Ferris, George T. *Great Violinists and Pianists*; Lahee, Henry C. *Famous Violinists of Today and Yesterday*; Phipson, Thomas Lambe. *Biographical Sketches and Anecdotes of Celebrated Violinists.*

Hector Berlioz *1803-1869*

"Berlioz is a genius without talent."
—GRILLPARZER

"He is unique, without a predecessor, without a successor, a moment of our race, of our history, of our poetry."
—EDOUARD HERRIOT

HECTOR LOUIS BERLIOZ was born at La Côte-Sainte-André, France, on December 11, 1803. Music played a very negligible rôle in the Berlioz household: the father, a country doctor, looked upon the musical art with disdain. As a result, Hector Berlioz, though revealing imposing gifts in music, received little training.

His musical inquisitiveness attracted the notice of the leader of the village orchestra who was inveigled, by the boy, into giving him haphazard instruction upon the guitar and the piano. Late each night, young Berlioz would sit up in bed and memorize the harmony text-books of Rameau, d'Alembert and Catel. This was his only contact with music. Until his arrival in Paris, he had heard no music greater than the quartets of Pleyel and orchestral and vocal excerpts of Boieldieu and Martini.

As a boy, Berlioz disclosed unusual sensitivity for beauty. He would sit at the side of his father, and together they would read Horace and Virgil, whose noble metres held young Berlioz spellbound. He was helplessly attracted to the pageantry of religion, and it is said that the beauty of the Catholic service threw him into something resembling mystic raptures during his first communion. He was similarly sensitive to feminine beauty. At the age of twelve he was already in love with a girl six years his senior, Estelle Gautier. "I had no idea what was the matter with me," Berlioz wrote in his *Memoirs* in

HECTOR BERLIOZ

later-life, "but I suffered acutely, and spent my nights in sleepless anguish. In the daytime, I crept away like a wounded bird and hid myself in the maize fields and orchards. I suffered agonies when any man approached my idol, and it makes me shudder even now when I recall the ring of my uncle's spurs as he danced with her."

Father Berlioz was determined to have his son follow in his footsteps, and carefully planned a medical career for him. Hector, therefore, was sent to Paris to be enrolled in medical school. His first contact with dissection disgusted him so violently that he fled from school, swearing that he would never undertake medicine as a career. His next decision came soon afterwards—to pursue the study of music seriously. Entering the Conservatory, he became a pupil of Lesueur, under whose technical guidance Berlioz composed his first works. In 1825, a *Mass*—his first work to reach the public —was performed at the Saint Roch Church. Lesueur was among the solitary few to recognize its independence and talent. "You will not be a doctor or a druggist," he told the young composer, "but a great composer. You have genius. I say it, because it is true."

Such happiness as Berlioz knew at this first performance was soon enough dispelled. Entering a cantata for the Prix de Rome, he met his first acute

disappointment on learning that, far from winning the award, it failed to receive even honorary mention. Shortly thereafter, he was ordered home by his father; father Berlioz would not tolerate his son becoming a musician. Disappointed in himself, and exhausted by physical hardships, Berlioz decided to yield to fate and to return to his father's household.

His stay there was brief. Separation from music proved so painful to Berlioz that, for a while, he was obsessed with stifling despondency and despair. In the face of such suffering, his father could not persist in his stubbornness. He decided that he would support his son for a specified period in Paris. During that time, Berlioz would have to prove definitely that he was uniquely gifted as a musician, or return to medical study.

In 1826, Berlioz was back in Paris, once again a student at the Conservatory, and pursuing music more devotedly than before. He spent his leisure hours committing to memory voluminous orchestral and operatic scores—particularly those of Gluck. But once again he was to know unhappiness. Having incurred numerous debts, he exhausted the patience of his father who peremptorily discontinued the allowance. With starvation continually at his elbow, Berlioz continued his hard work with music. In 1828, he again entered a composition for the Prix de Rome, and was greeted a second time with failure. Two years later, he once again competed for the much-desired prize. But this time perseverance won. A cantata, *La mort de Sardanapale*, attracted the attention of the judges for its originality and strength, and earned the award for its composer.

It was during these early years in Paris that Berlioz first met Henrietta Smithson. The English Shakespearean actress and her company were performing *Hamlet* in Paris, and Berlioz, who was in the audience, fell in love with the enchanting Ophelia. He felt that he would know neither peace nor rest until he had met this actress personally and had expressed his admiration to her. He attempted to meet her, and to impress her with his musical talent, but with small success. He took lodgings opposite her home, only to discover that she was soon leaving Paris. Finally, he confessed his plight to his friend Hiller, who in turn confided the story to his sweetheart, Camille Moke. Camille Moke took it upon herself to console the distressed Berlioz for his unrequited love, and in consoling him, she learned that she herself was in love with the composer, and that the composer generously returned this affection. In the heat of this affair, Henrietta Smithson was sufficiently forgotten for Berlioz to announce his formal engagement to Camille Moke.

With the Prix de Rome in his possession, Berlioz left for Rome to take up his three year residence at the Villa Medici. Rome proved far less attractive in contact than it had appeared from the glamorous distance of several hundred miles, and Berlioz was not happy in the Italian capital. He detested Italian music and Italian performances, and chafed under the rigorous routine of Conservatory life there. It was while he was in such despondent mood that, one day, he heard the news that his fiancée, Camille Moke, had suddenly married another man. He swore vengeance for such treachery. He planned to disguise himself as a lady's maid, to return to Paris and murder his unfaithful beloved. To bring this plan into realization, he bought a set of pistols as well as a complete diguise, began the journey to Paris, lost his disguise, bought a second one, and then—by the time he reached Genoa—was so thrilled by the beauty of the Italian scene and the gentleness of Italian climate, and suddenly became so terrified at the possibility of smothering a musical career that had begun so auspiciously, that he decided to forget his picaresque plan and returned humbly to Rome. During the months that followed, he enjoyed the happiest days of his life, tramping the slopes of Roman hills, bathing in the ocean and absorbing the beauty of Nature.

In 1832 he returned to Paris, somewhat impatient for the active musical life which Paris had to offer him. He discovered that his name was not unknown in music circles; that, as a matter of fact, his independent compositions (particularly his *Symphonie fantastique*) which were so charged with originality and daring, had created a considerable amount of comment in music circles.

He was to make an even more important discovery in Paris: Henrietta Smithson was there with a special English company. Relentlessly, Berlioz set out to meet her, and then, when the meeting was finally consummated, attempted to convince the actress that he loved her. The courtship between them was a stormy one. Henrietta was temperamental and volatile, now carrying Berlioz to extreme happiness by her profuse love, and now bringing him to despair by indifference and apathy. But Berlioz was indomitably insistent, and finally succeeded in getting Henrietta Smithson's consent for marriage.

But the tempest was yet to come, as Berlioz soon realized. His father, and Henrietta's family, objected violently to a marriage such as this, and when Berlioz made preparations for a civil wedding, he was to see the marriage contract torn up by his father before his very eyes, at the notary's office. To intensify this situation, Henrietta suddenly lost financial independence, because the English company slipped into bankruptcy, and because she broke her leg on stepping out of her carriage, which accident resulted in her permanent withdrawal from the stage. Berlioz, however, permitted nothing to alter his plans. In October, 1833, they were married at the British Embassy. They were miserably poor, but—as Berlioz wrote so triumphantly—"she was mine, and I defied the world!"

It is not surprising that their marriage was not a happy one. For a great part of their lives Berlioz and his wife lived apart. However, he remained devoted to Henrietta until the very end—even though with time, she developed into a shrewish invalid—often working slavishly so that her every desire and whim might be satisfied. Henrietta Berlioz died on March 3, 1854.

The years that followed Berlioz's marriage to Henrietta Smithson were difficult ones. In addition to domestic problems, his enemies—who were numerous and powerful—prevented him from procuring remunerative teaching posts at the Gymnase Musicale and at the Conservatory. For a long period, Berlioz knew financial difficulties. However, he would not permit discouragement and unhappiness to smother his inspiration. His pen was even more active than it had been before, and during these years of despondency he produced several of his most famous works. These included *Harold en Italie*—which had been commissioned by Paganini who was seeking a large symphonic work featuring a viola solo—the *Roméo et Juliette*, the *Requiem*, and his opera, *Benvenuto Cellini*, the prelude to the second act of which was in later years to become independently famous as the *Roman Carnival overture*.

This imposing production brought Berlioz his first recess from financial distress. In 1838, the *Symphonie fantastique* brought Berlioz a cash gift of 20,000 francs. For a long time, it was believed that Paganini was the donor of this munificent sum; recent research, however, has disclosed the fact that the benefactor was Armand Bertini, editor of the *Journal des Débats* and a great admirer of Berlioz, who felt that the gift would be more impressive if it was extended by one great artist to another and, therefore, urged Paganini to present it. Two years after this, Berlioz received another 10,000 francs for his *Symphonie funèbre et triomphale*. To this sum, the French government added 4,000 francs for the *Requiem*.

These handsome gifts enabled Berlioz to give up all hack work and criticism and, in 1843, to embark upon a tour of Germany as a conductor of his own works. This tour was one of the crowning triumphs of Berlioz's career. His performances were so enthusiastically acclaimed that Berlioz was tempted to make several more tours during the next few years which brought him to England, Austria and Russia.

The last twenty years of Berlioz's life were depressing. His best work had been done, and Berlioz knew that his creative powers had lost their one-time vigor and freshness. Moreover, Berlioz knew additional marital problems. He had married a second time—a singer, Mlle. Recio, by name; and his second marriage was hardly more fortunate than the first. Deprived by death of his best

friends, and his son Louis, Berlioz was a sick and lonely man.

It was probably the chilly solitude of his last years that tempted him, one day, to make a strange, romantic pilgrimage to Geneva to see once again his first love —Estelle Gautier—whom he had adored when he was twelve years old, and whom he had not seen since. He found before him a gentle, lovable, gray-haired lady—and together they spent many pleasant hours in reminiscence.

By 1868, Berlioz's health was completely broken; one year later—on March 9, 1869—he passed away at his home in Paris.

His pall-bearers were the famous composers, Gounod and Ambroise Thomas. His bier was decorated with wreaths sent from Italy, Hungary and Russia. At the head of the funeral procession marched the band of the National Guard which performed the funeral march from Berlioz's *Symphonie funèbre et triomphale*. Berlioz was buried in the cemetery of Montmartre.

Romain Rolland has graphically described Berlioz in his *Musicians of Today*. "He was really very fair and had blue eyes, and Joseph d'Ortigue tells us they were deep-set and piercing, though sometimes clouded by melancholy and languor. He had a broad forehead, furrowed with wrinkles by the time he was thirty, and a thick mane of hair, or, as E. Legouvé puts it, 'a large umbrella of hair, projecting like a movable awning over the beak of a bird of prey.' His mouth was well cut, with lips compressed and puckered at the corners in a severe fold, and his chin was prominent. He had a deep voice, but his speech was halting, and often tremulous with emotion; he would speak passionately of what interested him, and at times be effusive in manner, but more often he was ungracious and reserved. He was of medium height, rather thin and angular in figure, and when seated seemed much taller than he really was. He was very restless, and inherited from his native land, Dauphine, the mountaineer's passion for walking and climbing, and love of a vagabond life, which remained with him nearly to his death. He had an iron constitution, but he wrecked it by privation and excess, by his walks in the rain, and by sleeping out-of-doors in all weather, even when snow was on the ground."

He was, by temperament, a true Romantic. He was impulsive, emotional, hypersensitive, excitable and hot-headed. "When I hear certain pieces of music," he confessed in his Memoirs, "my vital forces at first seem doubled. I feel a delicious pleasure, in which reason has no part. The emotion, increasing in proportion to the energy or the grandeur of the ideas of the composer, soon produces a strange agitation in the circulation of the blood; tears, which generally indicate the end of the paroxysm, often indicate only a progressive state of it, leading to something still more intense. In this case, I have a spasmodic contraction of the muscles, a trembling in all my limbs, a complete torpor of the feet and the hands, a partial paralysis of the nerves of sight and heart; I no longer see, I scarcely hear. . . ."

Berlioz had very little respect for convention, nor was he patient with social formalities. He frequently shocked his friends not only by his unorthodox behavior but by his irreverent speech. As a Prix de Rome scholar, he frequently astonished his acquaintances in Rome by wandering thru the streets with a guitar under his arm, singing popular songs at the top of his voice. Neither physical nor spiritual restraint were known to him. He was a man of great courage, enormous self-confidence, and stinging intolerance.

As the man, so his music. In his works, Berlioz adopts the same unconventional pose that he assumed in everyday life; in his composition, as in his living, he was the enemy of formality and tradition. He was a prophet who peered into the future, and fearlessly walked towards it. Beginning with his early *Symphonie fantastique*, he was always the experimentalist, always the innovator. Not merely did this Symphony foreshadow for the first time the effective use of the *leit-motif* (later to be employed so effectively by Richard Wagner), but almost single-handed it launched music towards a new direction —that of 'program music', of which Franz Liszt and Richard Strauss were to be the principal exponents. "He was a

good iconoclast," wrote Daniel Gregory Mason. "He helped to break the bonds of a narrow conservatism which was in danger of confining all music to the forms of the symphony and the sonata, and to the type of expression perfected by the classicists. By his daring imagination he abashed pedantry and opened up vistas of new possibilities. And he was at least in one department, that of orchestration, a triumphant innovator."

It is quite ture, as Arthur Hervey points out, that Berlioz "was never gifted with a very rich vein of melody. His themes are often poor and trivial." But Berlioz more than compensated for this deficiency with an enormous gift at instrumentation and a genius for rhythmic effects. Certainly, as an orchestrator he has few equals. He had the ability to think orchestrally, to know intuitively how to combine the various instruments most effectively. Often his indefatigable search for new colors and timbres led him to introduce the most unorthodox instruments into the orchestra, but frequently he emerged with new qualities never before heard in symphonic music. "He possessed," to quote W. H. Hadow, "in a high degree every quality which successful scoring implies, a complete knowledge of the strength and weakness of each instrument, great skill in treatment and combination, ready invention, and boundless audacity. Further, he displays in this department of his art that sense of economy and reticence which has been noticed as absent elsewhere. He can be as light-handed as Mozart, (witness the *Invitation à la valse*, the opening of the Rakócky march, the first number of the Tempest fantasy), and yet when the moment comes to be vigorous and impressive there is no one more strong to wield the thunderbolt or direct the whirlwind. Even the crude violence of his Brigand's Orgy or his Witches' Sabbath becomes almost humanized when we observe the marvelous, matchless skill with which its horrors are presented."

Although Berlioz is best known by those works by which he is represented on symphony-programs—the *Symphonie fantastique* and the *Roman Carnival overture*—critics are generally agreed that his greatness is most clearly manifest in such works as the *Requiem*, the *Roméo et Juliette* and *Benvenuto Cellini*. "Berlioz has now an eye for something more in life than his own unshorn locks and his sultry amours," wrote Ernest Newman, in contemplating these three works. "He no longer thinks himself the centre of the universe; he no longer believes in the Berliozcentric theory, and does not write with one eye on the mirror half the time. In place of all this we have a Berlioz who has sunk his aggressive subjectivity and learned to regard life objectively. His spirit touched to finer issues, he sings, not Berlioz, but humanity as a whole. He is now what every great artist is instinctively—a philosopher as well as a singer; by the *Requiem* he earns his right to stand among the serious, brooding spirits of the earth. So again in the final scene of *Roméo et Juliette*, where he rises to loftier heights than he could ever have attained while in the throes of egoistic Romanticism."

Principal works by Hector Berlioz:

ORCHESTRA: *Symphonie fantastique*; *Roman Carnival overture*; *Symphonie funèbre et triomphale*; *Harold en Italie*; *Roméo et Juliette* (with chorus); *Corsair overture*.

OPERA: *Benvenuto Cellini*; *Béatrice et Bénédict*; *Les Troyens*; *La Damnation de Faust*.

CORAL: *Requiem*; *Tristia*; *Te Deum*; *L'Enfance du Christ*; *L'Impériale*; *L'Apothéose*. Songs, arrangements, etc.

About Hector Berlioz:

Berlioz, Hector. *Memoirs*; Hadow, W. H. *Studies in Modern Music*; Newman, Ernest. *Musical Studies*; Rolland, Romain. *Musicians of Today*; Tiersot, Julien. *Berlioz*.

Important recordings of music by Hector Berlioz:

ORCHESTRA: *Symphonie fantastique* (VICTOR-Monteux); *Roman Carnival overture* (COLUMBIA-Harty); *Roméo et Juliette*, selections from Part II and Part IV (COLUMBIA-Harty); *Corsair overture* (COLUMBIA-Harty); *Benvenuto Cellini overture* (VICTOR-Monteux).

OPERA: *La Damnation de Faust*, slightly abridged (GRAMOPHONE-Coppola).

Heinrich von Biber *1644-1704*

HEINRICH IGNAZ FRANZ VON BIBER, one of the earliest of German instrumental composers, was born in Wartenburg, Bohemia, on August 12,

HEINRICH VON BIBER

1644. His father was a forester. He began the study of music at an early age, specializing in the playing of the violin.

In 1670, he was appointed violinist in the Arch-Episcopal chapel of Kremsier. Soon afterwards he was called to Salzburg by the Archbishop, and here he remained the major portion of his life. In 1679 he became vice-chapel-master, and six years later he rose to the rank of chapel-master.

Heinrich von Biber occupied a pre-eminent position among the violin virtuosi of his day, and in his travels thru Italy, France and particularly Germany, he created a profound impression. Emperor Leopold frequently awarded him generous gifts for his performances, and in 1681 elevated him to nobility.

Heinrich von Biber died in Salzburg on May 3, 1704.

His principal importance in the history of music rests with his sonatas for violin and figured bass, in which he proved to be one of the important pioneers to lay the foundations for true sonata form. Here, his influence upon Mozart was known to have been far-reaching.

"His work brought native art to respect," wrote Guido Adler, "and encouraged the deserved estimation, even the wonder, of his contemporaries. He was the first German violin composer who could enter into direct competition with those rulers and followers of the

Italian and French tonal art. . . . His mastery over his art bespeaks the existence and influence of his German heritage."

Heinrich von Biber, we learn from Constantin Schneider, has likewise been an important influence in the development of German opera, by virtue of his "dramma-musicale," *Chi la dura la vince*. "Only the pitiable circumstance that all other opera works of the period have disappeared, has made it impossible to recognize his importance in this field until now. But this isolated and preserved witness of a vanished world proves that Biber's creation was equally important in all musical fields. As a matter of fact, this work is even more illuminating than his instrumental music in showing us the . . . unknown paths that this sometimes perplexed but always sincere artist traveled upon."

Principal works by Heinrich von Biber:

INSTRUMENTAL: Six sonatas for violin and figure bass; Twelve sonatas in four and five parts; Seven partitas for three instruments, etc.

CHORAL: *Vesperae longiores ac breviores*.

OPERA: *Chi la dura la vince*; *Alessandro in Pietra*; *L'ossequio di Salisburgo*.

About Heinrich von Biber:

Denkmäler der Tonkunst in Österreich, vol. 11; Schneider, Constantin. *Geschichte der Musik in Salzburg von der ältesten Zeit bis zur Gegenwart*.
Archiv der Musikwissenschaft 3:20 April 1927.

William Billings *1746-1800*

WILLIAM BILLINGS shares with Francis Hopkinson the distinction of being chronologically the first American composer.

He was born in Boston on October 7, 1746. Nature had handicapped him severely. He was born blind in one eye, one of his arms was withered, his legs were of uneven length and his voice was rasping. But he came to the world with an instinctive love for music, to which he turned during his earliest years. As a boy, he taught himself the rudiments of the art by memorizing Tansur's *Musical Grammar*. This was virtually his entire musical education.

As a profession, he chose tannery, but he would devote his entire time to marking the walls, and even the hides, of his tannery with pieces of musical composition. In 1778, he turned to music more actively by teaching the choir boys in Brattle Street Church in Boston. "He had a rasping voice which refused to blend with any other in the choir," we learn from George Upton. "It was also so stentorian that the singers could barely hear their own voices. But this did not prevent them from singing with enthusiastic effort."

This was the beginning of his association with church choirs. For the remainder of his life he was intimately connected with church music, both as a choirmaster and as a composer, and he earned the title of "Father of the American Church Choir."

In 1764, Billings married Mary Leonard, and ten years later he was married a second time, to Lucy Swan. He had six children, five of whom were boys. He died in indigent circumstances in Boston on September 26, 1800.

A contemporary of Billings, William Bentley, wrote in his diary about the personality of the composer: "He was a singular man of moderate size, short of one leg, with one eye, without any address, and with an enormous negligence of person. Still, he spake and sang and thought as a man above the common abilities."

William Billings was a very intimate friend of Samuel Adams, the statesman, with whom he frequently sang duets for diversion.

Billings' compositions are principally for voice, and enjoyed in their day great popularity. We are informed by the *Musical Reporter* that, for many years, "no other music . . . was heard thruout New England. Many of the New England soldiers who, during the Revolutionary war, were encamped in the southern states, had his popular tunes by heart, and frequently amused themselves by singing them in camp to the delight of all who heard them."

In his church compositions, Billings "seems to have been fond of rhythmic melody and a melodic bass," comments Isaac Goldberg. "Often he had his bass run parallel to the melody in thirds and sixths, in a manner that is still current among such of the clergy as feel impelled to sing impromptu harmonies to a hymn. . . . He made his music live in a day when, utterly out of touch with the wonders that were happening in Europe, it threatened to become a series of undifferentiated dirges. He woke up his native Boston; he flooded the church with a little fresh air and a tonic sunlight. He enriched the music of his country with something of the energy that thrilled in his own misshapen body and cantankerous soul. The fellow was, in his generation, alive."

Principal works by William Billings:

VOCAL: *The New England psalm singer*; *The Singing master's assistant*; *Music in miniature*; *Psalm singer's amusement*; *Suffolk harmony*; *Continental harmony*.

About Wi liam Billings:

Howard, John Tasker. *Our American Music*; Metcalf, Frank J. *American Writers and Compilers of Sacred Music*; Upton, George. *Musical Pastels*.
American Mercury 14:68 May 1928.

Georges Bizet *1838-1875*

GEORGES BIZET was born in Paris on October 25, 1838, as Alexandre César Léopold Bizet. His father was a teacher of singing; his mother, an even more sensitive musician, was the sister of a world-famous singer. Thus, as a child, Georges Bizet moved in a musical environment, and acquired a great love for the art at an early age. By the time he reached his tenth birthday, it had been definitely decided by his parents to train him as a professional musician. He became a student at the Paris Conservatory where he remained for nine years, and in 1857 he won the much-coveted Prix de Rome award.

The three years spent at the Villa Medici were, in many respects, the happiest in Bizet's life. He was enraptured by the splendors of Rome, and he was surrounded by a musical environment which enabled him to work with fecundity and enthusiasm. His musical development was so marked during this Italian sojourn that when he returned to Paris he was already the self-assured musician. In his valise he carried the manuscripts of a descriptive symphony

with chorus, *Vasco di Gama,* and an opéra-comique, *La Guzla de l'Emir.* Neither of these works were of outstanding artistic importance, but they disclosed the fact that their composer was rapidly acquiring maturity.

Bizet was twenty-five when his first significant work reached public attention. On September 29, 1863, the Théâtre Lyrique introduced *Les Pêcheurs de perles,* a work whose distinction, in its best pages, is generally recognized today. "The Oriental coloring so vividly imparted to the music," writes Arthur Hervey, "constitutes an undeniable charm. The languidly enervating melodies, full of luscious sweetness, are redolent of Eastern climes. The score is imbued with poetical sentiment, besides which it reveals a strong dramatic temperament."

Les Pêcheurs de perles was not successful, and there followed many years of struggle and disappointment for Bizet. On December 26, 1867, he brought his *La Jolie fille de Perth* to the public, and five years after that *Djamileh,* but neither work succeeded in lifting the composer from the abyss of obscurity and neglect.

On June 9, 1869, Georges Bizet was married to Genevieve Halévy, the daughter of his teacher at the Conservatory, and their marriage was one of the few sources of happiness to the composer during his life.

GEORGES BIZET

In June of 1872, Georges Bizet wrote to a friend that "I am asked to write three acts for the Opéra Comique. Meilhac and Halévy will do the piece. It will be bright, but of a brightness that allows style." A story by Prosper Mérimée was selected as the subject, and its lambent Spanish theme inspired Bizet to compose his masterpiece. On March 3, 1875, *Carmen* was given its first performance at the Opéra Comique.

Sentimentalists would have us believe that the first performance of *Carmen* was a complete failure. This is not warranted by historical fact. The audience was appreciative at the first performance, and the critics, if not as enthusiastic as the work deserved, were by no means apathetic. "Monsieur Bizet is a past master in orchestration, and no one knows better the secret of fine harmony and suitable scoring," wrote Ernest Reyer in *Le Journal des Debats*. "The work is one of those which rebound to the credit of a musician," was the verdict of *Le Courier de Paris*. The opera enjoyed thirty-seven performances—a respectable figure. However, it would be exaggerated enthusiasm to call *Carmen's* entrance into the operatic world a triumphant one.

It was not until its second début in Paris, on April 21, 1883, that the full greatness of *Carmen* became apparent. Introduced once more to a masterpiece, Paris now took it to its bosom, acclaiming it with cheers. From that time on, *Carmen* conquered the music-world. In 1878, it was performed in Marseilles, Lyon, Bordeaux, Leningrad, Naples, Florence, Ghent, Hanover and Mayence. Nietzsche heard *Carmen* twenty times and considered it an incomparable masterpiece. Tschaikovsky, who became acquainted with the work in 1880, prophesied that in ten years *Carmen* would be the most popular opera in the world. By the end of the century, there was hardly an opera house that did not feature this popular work.

Contemporary criticism is of the opinion that in its atmospheric color, in its orchestration, in its full-blooded melody and in its harmonic ingenuity and dramatic intensity *Carmen* is among the great operas of the world. "*Carmen* is unique in two senses," wrote D.C. Parker,

in his biography of Bizet. "It is unique in the realm of opera; there is no work quite like it. It is unique also in that it stands head and shoulders above anything else Bizet has produced . . . I place *Carmen* high by reason of the quality of its inspiration, the attraction of its themes, the handling of its ideas, and the musicianship displayed thruout. There is characterization, too, skilfully devised."

Upon one point there has risen controversy in connection with *Carmen*—namely, its Spanish idiom. Spanish musicians—Joaquin Turina, for example—cannot accept it because they regard the score as pseudo-Spanish music. However, Bizet had no intention of composing essentially Spanish music for *Carmen*. True, he utilized Spanish folk-material and Spanish rhythms, but only discreetly and to give a more authentic flavor and color to the opera. It is merely in mood and atmosphere that Bizet attempted to imitate the Spanish; in style of composition he remained himself thruout—French to the core.

Altho the initial performance of *Carmen* was by no means a complete failure, its reception was a source of disappointment and grief to the composer. A short period after the final performance, he decided, to escape from the scene of his disappointment, and to retire to his country home at Bougival. During his first day in the country, he passed the time in quiet enjoyment. That night, however, he suddenly suffered suffocation. The doctor who was summoned prescribed long rest. The following morning an even more severe attack kept Bizet in bed. On the night of June 3, 1875, Georges Bizet passed away. He died without seeing his beloved opera accepted the world over as a masterpiece.

The funeral took place on the 5th of June at the church of the Trinity in Paris. Bizet was buried in Père Lachaise.

Georges Bizet's appearance was impressive. He had a shock of curly black hair, a majestic beard, a square jaw and alert and sparkling eyes. His personality was, as Frederick Niecks pointed out, "simple and straight forward. You could not meet a stauncher friend or a more honest enemy. Naturally and fundamentally gay and good-natured, he was easily roused. But along with these traits there seems to have been also, at least early in life, some phlegm and a good deal of love of ease about him. In short, his was a good-hearted and hotheaded character."

His greatest enjoyment was in taking long walks in the country. He rarely went to the opera, and when he did it was only because the music of Mozart and Rossini—his two idols—was being performed. He was supremely sensitive to criticism. In regard to women, he was surprisingly indifferent. "I would readily risk my life for a friend," he once wrote to his mother, several years before his marriage, "but should consider myself an idiot if I lost a hair of my head on account of a woman."

He worked best at night, and once having begun work he would continue uninterruptedly until dawn. He conceived all of his works clearly in his mind before attempting to transfer them on paper.

It is not generally known that Bizet composed a talented *Symphony*. This work, in the key of C major, was recently resurrected in London by Sir Hamilton Harty at a concert of the London Symphony Orchestra. A critic in the *Morning Daily Telegraph* of London wrote as follows about this work: "The first movement has no suggestion of the epic style. It might have been written by one who had never heard of Beethoven. The second movement opens in the style of a serenade. Then the music grows in intensity, glowing with the warmth that makes the Flower Song in *Carmen* one of the greatest of all love songs. The scherzo, of a Schubertian cut, and the finale, with a 'perpetuum mobile' figure for the first violin, command respect."

Principal works by Georges Bizet:

OPERA: *Les Pêcheurs de perles*; *La Jolie fille de Perth*; *Djamileh*; *Carmen*.

ORCHESTRA: *Symphony in C-major*; *Overture to Sardou's Patrie*; Incidental music to Daudet's *L'Arlésienne*; *Petite suite.*

Songs, pieces for the piano, etc.

About Georges Bizet:

Delmas, Marc. *Georges Bizet*; Gallet, Louis. *Notes d'un Librettiste*; Parker, D. C. *Georges*

JOHN BLOW

Bizet: His Life and Works; Weissman. Adolph. *Bizet.*

Important recordings of music by Georges Bizet:

OPERA: *Carmen*, complete (COLUMBIA-Opera Comique).

SELECTIONS FROM OPERA: *Les Pêcheurs de perles*, "Au fond du temple saint" (VICTOR); "Je crois entendre encore (VICTOR-Gigli); "De mon amie, fleur endormie" (COLUMBIA).

ORCHESTRA: *Overture to Sardou's Patrie* (GRAMOPHONE-Sargent); Incidental music to Daudet's *L'Arlésienne*, Suite 1 (VICTOR-Stokowski), Suite 2 (POLYDOR-Schreker); *Petite suite* (VICTOR).

John Blow *1648-1708*

"One of the greatest masters in the world."—HENRY PURCELL

JOHN BLOW, one of England's great composers for the church, is believed to have been born in North Collingham, either in 1648 or 1649. Possessing a very striking voice as a child, he was made a member of the first Chapel organized by Captain Cooke in 1660. An amusing comment in the diary of Samuel Pepys is believed to refer to Master Blow, chorister. Under the date of August 21, 1667, Pepys wrote: "This morning came two of Capt. Cooke's boys, whose voices are broke, and are gone from the chapel, but have extraordinary skill; and they and my boy, with broken voice, did sing three parts; their names were Blaew (*sic*!) and Loggins; but notwithstanding their skill, yet to hear them sing with their broken voices, which they could not command to keep in tune, would make a man mad—so bad it was."

In 1669, Blow was appointed organist of Westminster Abbey, and, in 1674, he was sworn in as Gentleman of the Chapel Royal. His popularity as a composer and organist grew rapidly from this time on, and he was granted leases on property as a mark of royal favor.

Much of Blow's life is veiled in obscurity. It is believed that, in 1676, he succeeded Christopher Gibbons as one of the organists of the Chapel Royal, but definite proof does not exist. It is also believed that he was compelled to resign his position as organist of Westminster Abbey, in 1679, to make room for his pupil, Purcell; at any rate, on Purcell's death, Blow was reappointed organist and maintained this position until the end of his life.

It is known that Blow was held in high esteem by the royalty of England. When James II ascended the throne, he appointed Blow a member of the royal band, and court composer. In 1692, he rose to the rank of master of royal vocal music at a salary of a 100 pounds a year. During this period he composed with fertility, and produced an imposing number of anthems and services.

John Blow died at his home in Westminster on October 1, 1708, and was buried near his pupil, Purcell, in Westminster Abbey. The inscription on his monument reads in part: "His own musical compositions, especially his church musick, are a far nobler monument to his memory than any other that can be raised for him."

"Eliminating his pupil, Henry Purcell," comments Jeffrey Pulver, "John Blow is certainly the most considerable musician of the period, and he has left a large quantity of music marked by real nobility, depth of feeling and sincerity."

His music was generally marked by its harmonic daring—which startled even so discerning a musicologist as Charles Burney—its complete independence of form, and its melodic vitality.

"Granting his limitations," wrote Heathcote D. Statham, "he is far from being a small figure. There is breadth, dignity and sincerity about the best of his Church music which will ensure its being sung as long as Church music is sung at all. And it is beautifully singable; in the flowing grace of his interweaving melodies, he can meet and sometimes beat Elizabethans on their own ground. Above all, he was an experimenter. . . . He combines the characteristics of a Church musician . . . with a gay bravado which compels him to 'throw his notes about at random.' "

Principal works by John Blow:

VOCAL: Anthems, Services, Hymns, etc. Suites for harpsichord.

About John Blow:

Barrett, William Alexander. *English Church Composers*; Bridge, Frederick. *Twelve Good Musicians*; Fuller-Maitland, J. A. *The Contemporaries of Purcell*, vol. 1; Pulver, Jeffrey. *A Biographical Dictionary of Old English Music*.
Musical Times 43:81 February 1902, 67:987 November 1926.

Luigi Boccherini *1743-1805*

LUIGI BOCCHERINI was born in Lucca, Italy, on February 19, 1743. He was taught music at an early age by his father, a professional bass-player, and the Abbé Vannucci, chapel-master to the Archbishop. Luigi Boccherini proved to be an adept pupil, and in 1757 he was sent to Rome to perfect his technique under expert instruction.

He returned to his native city a professional musician, and he joined the town theatre orchestra as violoncellist. At the same time, he introduced himself to his fellow citizens as a composer by giving a special concert—with the cooperation of Filippo Manfredi, violinist —devoted entirely to his sonatas. The success of this concert was so great that the two artists decided to tour the principal cities of France. Their reception everywhere surpassed their wildest expectation, including Paris, which they reached in 1768.

The fame of the two artists had become so considerable that the Ambassador of Spain in Paris invited them to come to Madrid. They were disappointed by their Spanish tour because their reception was not half so cordial as they had anticipated, and royal patronage—which had been promised them—was not forthcoming. For Boccherini, however, there were consolations. The Prussian Emperor was impressed with his abilities both as virtuoso and as composer, and engaged him as a chamber-composer at a generous annual salary. For several years, Boccherini held this position, enjoying during this period comfort and high esteem. With the death of his royal benefactor, however, Boccherini was compelled to seek employment elsewhere, and he decided to return to Spain.

For a long period he lived in Madrid, in obscurity and want. He occupied, together with his family, a dreary backroom where his only escape from squalor and darkness was in the production of music. He had few friends, and—ill-health having necessitated his complete retirement from violoncello playing—he was removed from public notice. For a brief span he knew some recess from poverty when Lucien Buonaparte, ambassador of the French republic at Madrid, an admirer of Boccherini's music, commissioned him to compose some chamber-music. However, this was only a fleeting respite from want. The last years of Boccherini's life were spent in appalling poverty, which he tried to alleviate by doing hack-work—principally arrangements of his own works for the guitar at the request of some rich patrons. His misery was further heightened by the death of two sons.

Luigi Boccherini died in Madrid on May 28, 1805, and his death passed virtually unnoticed.

While few of Boccherini's compositions are performed in our day (one excepts, of course, the world-famous *Minuet*), his name is prominent in musical development. He definitely established the string-quartet form, in which he composed more than a hundred works. If he did not possess the strength and character of Haydn (Giuseppe Puppo, the violinist, pointedly referred to Boccherini as "Haydn's wife"), he possessed melodic invention and a charm-

LUIGI BOCCHERINI

ing poise to almost as great a degree as his celebrated contemporary.

François Joseph Fétis, the distinguished musicologist of Boccherini's time, was one of the few of his age to recognize Boccherini's distinction. "Rarely has a composer had the merit of originality, to a greater degree than Boccherini. His ideas are always original, and his works are so remarkable . . . that one would be tempted to believe that he has never known any other music but his own. . . . His harmony is rich in effects. . . . His adagios and his minuets are always delicious. . . . With a merit so remarkable, it is strange that Boccherini should not be better known today in France."

Passing to the judgment of a present-day critic, we learn from R. Sodenheimer that Boccherini is "the first great perfecter in modern music. Everything for which his predecessors worked, singly and laboriously, was garnered and absorbed by him. Sammartini's beginning, Stamitz's radicalism, Pugnani's tentative efforts and Beck's inspiration—all these had their experimental value for Boccherini, and the achievements of all these hot-bloods of the new art are at last justified and brought to fulfillment. In his hands, the new style yields up its most secret properties and possibilities. . . . In Boccherini . . . a sensitive and exuberant spirit is seen inhabiting, as it were, a tropical world. Of this spirit, subtle melodies are first conceived. Boccherini then concentrates on the independent leading of the parts (based on a plurality of motifs) achieving at times truly plastic effects, which belong rather to the romantic epoch than to the severe linear art of the classics. . . . What constitutes an epoch-making characteristic of Boccherini's work is the skilful manner in which he continues to vary his forms of expression within the sma'lest framework. . . . In this respect none of Boccherini's contemporaries can compare with him."

The world-famous Boccherini *Minuet* appears in the *String quintet in E major*, Opus 13 no. 5.

Principal works by Luigi Boccherini:

ORCHESTRA: Suite; Twenty symphonies; Eight concertante; Four concertos for violoncello and orchestra.

CHORAL: *Stabat Mater*; *Mass*; *Christmas cantata*, etc.

CHAMBER MUSIC: 102 string quartets; Eighteen quintets for flute, oboe, two violins, viola and violoncello; Twelve piano quintets; Sixteen sextets; Two octets; Forty-eight trios, etc.

About Luigi Boccherini:

Cobbett, W. W. *Cyclopedic Survey of Chamber Music*; Meugy, A. *La Poésie de la Musique*.

Important recordings of music by Luigi Boccherini:

CHAMBER MUSIC: *Minuet*, arranged for chamber orchestra (VICTOR-Stokowski); *Sonata in A-Major*, for violoncello and piano, "Adagio" and "Allegro" (VICTOR-Casals).

François Boieldieu *1775-1834*

FRANÇOIS ADRIEN BOIELDIEU, a member of that celebrated triumvirate of composers of *opéra-comique* which included Adam and Auber, was born in Rouen on December 16, 1775. His father, secretary to the Archbishop, placed François in the choir school which was a part of the Rouen Cathedral. Here, as a boy, Boieldieu heard a performance of Grétry's *Barbe-bleu*, which made so vivid an impression upon him that, from that moment, he knew he would become a composer.

Domestic troubles drove François Boieldieu from his father's home; and

FRANÇOIS BOIELDIEU

the household of Monsieur Broche, organist of the Cathedral, accepted him. The home of Monsieur Broche was hardly a happy asylum for young Boieldieu; Monsieur Broche was an inveterate drunkard and, at regular intervals, he abused the boy. From such unpleasant surroundings, Boieldieu found escape in his music. He composed several songs which found such favor in the eyes of his fellow townspeople that, in 1793, he was commissioned by them to compose a special *Hymn to Reason*, in honor of the revolutionary fêtes in Paris. Simultaneously came his first assay in operatic form *La Fille coupable*.

In his twentieth year, Boieldieu escaped from Rouen; Paris, the musical Mecca of France, was his destination. He traveled a portion of the way by cart, some of the way by foot, spending nights either in shepherds' huts or in the field. He reached Paris, finally, with eighteen francs in his pocket, unknown and homeless, but with high hopes for the future.

He discovered with discouraging promptness that Paris could be mercilessly callous to strangers. For a long period, starvation and cold crushed him physically and spiritually. He did not eat for several consecutive days at a time, and, at one period he thought seriously of drowning himself as the only possible escape from the gruesome hunger he was experiencing. At the dramatic eleventh hour, a messenger from home brought him some money.

For a while, he earned a pitiable income by tuning pianos and singing his own songs at receptions. It was not until he met such musicians as Cherubini, Méhul and Grétry that his fate took a turn for the better. Cherubini was almost immediately impressed with Boieldieu's talent, accepted him as a pupil and, when he felt that Boieldieu had mastered his lessons, offered him a professorship at the Conservatory.

From that moment on, success smiled broadly at him. In 1800, his opera, *Zoraïme et Zulnare* was presented in Paris with such acclaim that Boieldieu engaged himself upon the composition of more operas with renewed enthusiasm. The end of the year saw the performance of the *Caliph of Bagdad,* a sensational success which realized seven hundred performances. There followed *Ma tante Aurore* which, though much slighter in texture and content than its important predecessor, was no less successful. Boieldieu was now a famous composer, one of the most famous in Paris.

In 1802, Boieldieu entered upon an ill-fated marriage with Mlle. Clotilde, of questionable background and reputation. Their union was sordid from the first and, to escape from it, Boieldieu accepted an invitation to visit Russia in 1803. Here he was received with high honors. The Tsar appointed him chapel master, and the leading opera houses offered him a contract to compose three new operas each year. When Boieldieu finally left Russia, he was laden with numerous gifts sent to him by the nobility.

In 1817, Boieldieu succeeded Méhul as a member of the Institut. But his measure of success had not, as yet, reached its summit. Eight years later, he produced *La Dame blanche*—generally recognized as his masterpiece. *La Dame blanche* achieved the magnificent total of 1500 performances, and earned for its composer a handsome government pension.

With *La Dame blanche* Boieldieu seemed to have exhausted himself artistically. There followed one failure after another, and it was not long before the grandiose success of former years was followed by misery. In 1830, the fall of the French king deprived Boieldieu of his pension, and soon afterwards ill health compelled the composer to give up his teaching position at the Conservatory. For a short period, Boieldieu again knew want and suffering; finally, the government—remembering his one-time achievements—came to his rescue with an annual grant of 3000 francs.

The end of Boieldieu's life found him in complete retirement from musical activity. He had completely lost his voice, as a result of laryngeal consumption, and secluded himself in a small house near the ruined abbey of Jarcey, where he found some diversion in gardening and painting. He died on the eighth of October of 1834; Cherubini's *Requiem* accompanied his body to Père Lachaise.

Boieldieu was a man of considerable personal charm as well as attractive appearance. His facile tongue and pointed wit were as famous in Paris as his melodies. He was a man of extreme generosity, and his purse was continually at the service of friends and acquaintances.

He was a very industrious worker, but composition came easily to him and he worked with amazing rapidity. It was Cherubini who complained that Boieldieu too often touched the superficial in his composition only because he worked with such facility.

Superficial Boieldieu most certainly was; however, his importance in his own realm—that of the *opéra-comique*—should not be minimized. No less a musician than Robert Schumann considered one of Boieldieu's operas, *Jean de Paris,* "one of the first three opera-comiques of the world, placed together with Mozart's *Figaro* and Rossini's *Barber.*" Gifted with a fresh melodic vein, a supple and fluid style, and a charming grace, his music was uniquely suited for the requirements of *opéra-comique.*

"His speech is supple, elegant, well-ordered," is the critical comment of Arthur Pougin, "and the grace of his language, its clarity, and the amiable spirit with which it is endowed are constantly of a nature to satisfy the listener and to procure for him delicate and ever renewed pleasure. No great force, no audacious strains . . . no sublime flashes of light arouse our enthusiasm; but an abundant and varied inspiration, an imagination that is always fertile, a truly poetic sentiment, a unity and perfection of style. . . . The qualities of Boieldieu were . . . melodic richness, the excellence and solidity of his plan, a warm instrumentation that was brilliant and colorful, possessing charm and taste and distinction. . . . From the dramatic point of view, we have tenderness and grace, on the one hand, and, on the other, a rare comic sentiment and profound intelligence of the resources and needs of the theatre."

Principal works by François Boieldieu:

OPERA: *The Caliph of Bagdad*; *Zoraïme et Zulnare*; *Ma tante Aurore*; *La Dame invisible*; *Rien de trop*; *Jean de Paris*; *La Dame blanche*; *Les Deux nuits*; *Marguerite*, etc.

Sonatas for piano; Sonatas for violin and piano; Duos; Trio; Romances; Concerto for piano; Concerto for harp, etc.

About François Boieldieu:

Hargrave, Mary. *Earlier French Musicians*; Lassus, Lucien Augé de. *Boieldieu*; Pougin, Arthur. *Boieldieu*.

Important recordings of music by François Boieldieu:

SELECTIONS FROM OPERA: *The Caliph of Bagdad*, "Overture" (COLUMBIA). *La Dame blanche*, "Ouverture" (GRAMOPHONE-Blech); "Ah! quel plaisir" (COLUMBIA); Déjà, la nuit plus sombre" (ODEON); "Rêverie de Georges Brown" (PARLAPHONE); "Viens, gentille dame" (PATHE).

Arrigo Boito *1842-1918*

ARRIGO BOITO has earned the double distinction in musical history of being the composer of *Mefistofele,* and the librettist of Verdi's *Falstaff* and *Othello.*

He was born in Padua on February 24, 1842 as Enrico Boito. His father, a talented painter, was an irresponsible rover who, a few years after Arrigo's birth, deserted the family. Penniless, the mother bravely assumed the burden of supporting her two sons, providing both for their physical well-being and for their intellectual upbringing. She was determined to make musicians of them both. Arrigo, however, revealed much more adaptability for music than his brother Camillo, and it was upon

Arrigo, therefore, that the mother lavished her hopes and dreams.

After completely severing relationship with her vagrant husband, Arrigo's mother brought him to Milan for the purpose of entering him in the Conservatory; and, at the price of enormous personal sacrifice, made it possible for him to begin a serious study of music. Arrigo, at first, was not a distinguished scholar, and it is more than likely that he would have been dismissed from the Conservatory were it not for the fact that the officials were familiar with his mother's trying circumstances. However, as Arrigo's love for music developed, he began to apply himself to his studies with greater assiduity; before his school career came to a close he was recognized as one of the best pupils in the Conservatory.

In 1860, his cantata, *Il 5 giugno*, was presented at the Conservatory with success, and the following year, in collaboration with Franco Faccio, he produced *Le sorelle d'Italia,* a work of such merit that the Italian government gave both composers a traveling scholarship. Their travels brought them to Paris where they were influenced by the ideology of Victor Hugo, Berlioz and Rossini. From there, they went to Poland, where Boito was first inspired with the idea of composing an opera on the life of Nero. Following a circuitous route which brought him into Germany, Belgium and England, Boito returned to Milan, greatly matured by his travels.

Upon his return, Boito engaged himself passionately in the battle of reforming Italian music. His ideal was to interest his apathetic compatriots in the great symphonic music of Europe, and also to bring about a radical reform in the stilted operatic form of his own country. To bring this ideal to realization, Boito turned from composition to literature, and for the next few years enlisted his vigorous prose style on behalf of musical reform. His fearless condemnation of many Italian composers of the time brought him many enemies —so much so that, at one time, he was forced to fight a duel in which his right arm was wounded.

The friendship between Verdi and Boito began in 1862 when Boito wrote the words for Verdi's *Hymn of the nations*. Their relationship did not begin happily. Verdi took many of Boito's robust remarks about contemporary Italian opera as a personal affront, and was therefore violently prejudiced against this young upstart. It was only after their acquaintance ripened that Verdi recognized the flaming artistic sincerity of the young man and appreciated his high ideals.

Composition soon drew Boito back to its bosom. In 1866, Boito began work upon his opera, *Mefistofele*. Unfortunately, the outbreak of war between Austria and Italy in 1866 compelled him to abandon his creative work temporarily, and Boito enlisted with the Garibaldian volunteers. Upon his return to Milan, he resumed his work on the opera, completing it in two years.

La Scala of Milan accepted it for performance, principally because by this time Boito's energetic criticisms had earned for him a nation-wide reputation. On March 5, 1868, therefore, the first performance of *Mefistofele* was given under the baton of the composer, and developed into one of the most devastating fiascos in musical history. The opera house swarmed with Boito's enemies, many of whom had been bitterly stung by his vitriolic thrusts and who, therefore, had come to avenge themselves. During the performance, the opposition to the opera mounted and grew into a riot. There ensued catcalls, hisses, shouts. Fist-fights developed. Similar demonstrations greeted *Mefistofele* during its next two performances, and by the order of the chief of police the opera was removed from the La Scala repertoire.

In 1912, Boito entered politics, and was elected Senator. When the World War broke out, he paid a visit to the Front, and the strenuous trip undermined his health considerably. In November of 1917, he attended a religious ceremony at the church of Sant' Ambrogio, where he caught a chill from which he never fully recovered. For a while he rallied, but a few months later he took to his bed permanently. He died in Milan on June 10, 1918.

His second opera, *Nerone*, was completed on October 12, 1916, after having

ARRIGO BOITO

absorbed Boito's interest and attention for almost half a lifetime. It was produced at La Scala on May 1, 1924, six years ·after Boito's death, under the direction of Arturo Toscanini. The audience was comprised of visitors from all parts of the world, who had come to Milan to make this gala occasion a glorious tribute to Boito.

It is, however, because of *Mefistofele* that Boito's name is prominent. "In *Mefistofele*," to quote H. C. Colles, "Boito made a serious attempt to convey in his music something of the philosophy underlying the Faust drama of Goethe. He succeeded sufficiently, at any rate in his prologue, to be ranged with the German masters, Schumann, Wagner and Liszt, who had essayed a similar task. As originally produced at the La Scala, Milan, five acts followed the prologue, but Boito subsequently reduced them to four. It was a bewildering scheme of prodigious length, in which daring experiment and conventional operatic procedure jostled one another, and its immediate failure was inevitable, quite apart from the conflict of prejudice in which it was received by the audience. Boito lacked the first-rate creative musical power to enable him to weld together the divergent elements of music-drama and to surmount all the difficulties which Wagner was presently to do in *Götterdammerung*."

Despite many beautiful pages in the opera, *Mefistofele* is a work of obvious weaknesses. James Gibbons Huneker pointed this out when he wrote: "*Mefistofele* was once music of the future. Now it reminds one of some strange, amorphous survival from a remote period. It is such a tremendous attempt to embrace all of Goethe's profound world philosophy, poetry, dramatic symbolism, that it is a failure—a remarkable failure. There is little melodic invention; the prison-scene being the top-notch of its dramatic passion. . . . It is mostly music of the head, not of the heart."

However, it would be a mistake to underestimate the significance of *Mefistofele*. "Despite the composite style of Boito's music, there can be no doubt of its value to Italy," wrote Arthur Elson. "He was the pioneer in many things that were new and good, and not alone Verdi, but even Mascagni was forced to follow his lead in adopting the modern vein of polyphonic composition."

Not the least of Boito's accomplishments were the superb librettos which he fashioned from Shakespeare for Verdi's two last operas. Essentially a fine and sensitive poet, he carved out of the Shakespeare plays, librettos of remarkable operatic qualities, and was responsible to a great extent for directing Verdi's genius into altogether new channels. "Theirs was a union of brain and creative impulses, intellect and genius," commented H. C. Colles.

Principal works by Arrigo Boito:
OPERA: *Mefistofele*; *Nerone*.

About Arrigo Boito:
Blackburn, Vernon. *The Fringe of An Art*; Colles, H. C. *Oxford History of Music*, vol. 7; Elson, Arthur *The History of Opera*; Streatfeild, R. A. *The Opera*.

Important recordings of music by Arrigo Boito:
OPERA: *Mefistofele*, complete (COLUMBIA-La Scala).

Alexander Borodin *1833-1887*

A LEXANDER PORPHYRIEVICH BORODIN, one of the prominent figures in the celebrated group of Russian composers known as the "five," [1] was born at St. Petersburg on November 12, 1833—not in 1834 as has been believed until recently. He was the illegitimate son of Prince Lucas Semenovitch Gedezanof—a descendant of the royal family of Imeretia, in the Caucasus —and Evdokia Kleineke, and as was required by Russian law, he was registered as the son of a serf.

As a child, Alexander Borodin disclosed an amazing mentality. He could speak several languages, among them English, French and German. He evinced an unusual curiosity for, and alertness in, the sciences. He constructed a puppet theatre for which he himself wrote little dramatic pieces. And he expressed himself musically as naturally as though tones were a native language to him: he learned to play the flute and the violoncello, and he acquired the rudiments of musical theory by reading text books. At the age of ten, he turned to composition—inspired by his first love affair—and produced a polka, entitled *Hélène*, dedicated to his beloved.

His "mother," realizing that of his many gifts young Borodin was most talented in music, decided to give him an intensive education in that art. A member of the Semeonsky Regiment band was called upon to teach the boy the flute; and a friend Michale Shtchiglef (later famous as a music teacher) filled in the gaps in the boy's theoretical learning. Alexander Borodin proved to be an extraordinary pupil. He fed upon music study with an insatiable appetite, and in his thirteenth year produced a concerto for flute and piano, and a trio for two violins and violoncello.

Meanwhile, his academic studies were not neglected. Having displayed a strong penchant for science, Borodin was permitted to follow the study of medicine. For this reason he was entered in the Academy of Medical and Physical Sciences, from which he graduated in 1850. After two years of service in a military hospital, he was sent at government expense to study abroad (1859-1862). Upon his return to St. Petersburg, he received an appointment as assistant professor of chemistry at the Academy.

Early in 1862, Borodin met Balakirev, whose conversations on music revived in

[1] See sketch of Balakirev for a more detailed account of the "Russian Five."

him his early passion for the art. Intrigued by Balakirev's theories, Borodin decided to affiliate himself with the principles to which his friend subscribed so strongly, and soon became one of the major spirits of that group of five composers who dedicated their lives to the revivification of Russian musical art.

From that time on, Borodin's life was divided between two major pursuits: science and music. In both of these fields, he was a tireless and valuable worker. As a scientist, he did intensive research in the branches of botany and chemistry, and actively interested himself in medicine. He established medical courses for women, and he was the principal lecturer until his death. He was deluged with meetings and important academic conferences. "In winter," Borodin once wrote to a friend, "I can only compose when I am too unwell to give my lectures. So my friends, reversing the usual custom, never say to me, 'I hope you are well,' but 'I do hope you are ill.' "

And he was almost as industrious a musician, devoting long nights to the composition of chamber and symphonic works. Shortly after his first meeting with Balakirev, he began the composition of his *First symphony*. His celebrated *Symphony in B-minor* followed nine years later. The first string-quartet was produced in 1878 and, two years later, came that symphonic masterpiece, *In the steppes of Central Asia*.

He also produced a fragment for the opera house, written under ususual circumstances. The director of the Opera, Etienne Gedeonov, had written a libretto for a fantastic ballet-opera, entitled *Mlada,* and asked Borodin to compose the music for it. Borodin was moved by the idea of making this ballet-opera an expression of the aims and ideals of the "Russian Five." He decided, therefore, instead of composing the work himself, to ask Cui, Moussorgsky and Rimsky-Korsakoff to join him and compose one act each. While they were thus engaged upon this project, Gedeonov's enterprise collapsed. It was therefore decided to abandon the entire venture. Borodin had however sketched the fourth act; after his death it was orchestrated and brought to completion by

ALEXANDER BORODIN

Rimsky-Korsakoff, who was also to compose an entirely new opera upon this very same libretto.

In 1863, Borodin was married to Catharine Protopopova, a gifted pianist. She was of delicate health, and not long after her marriage was confined almost permanently to a sick-bed. Thruout her life, Borodin remained tender and solicitous, and took devoted care of her.

In 1877, Borodin made a pilgrimage to Germany, which brought him as far as Weimar, where he came into personal contact with Franz Liszt. "Do not let criticism beguile you into altering the form of your works," Liszt advised him. "You have gone very far, but have not erred: your path is the right path, and your artistic instinct is a sure guide to you."

Eight years later, Borodin visited Belgium to be present at several successful performances of his two symphonies and his tone-poem, *In the steppes of Central Asia.*

At this time, Borodin felt himself drawn ineluctably to the theatre, for which he yearned to compose one major work. Towards the close of his life the ambition to create a folk-opera intensely Russian in theme and treatment became something of an obsession. Finally, turning to a legendary epoch in Russian history for his subject (the epoch of Prince Igor's army), Borodin composed the score for *Prince Igor*, a work that is generally regarded as his masterpiece. "*Prince Igor*," explained Borodin himself, "is essentially a national opera which can only be of interest to us Russians who like to refresh our patriotism at the fountain-head of our history, and to see the origins of our nationality revived upon the stage." It was performed in St. Petersburg on November of 1890 (three years after the composer's death), and was immediately accepted as one of the outstanding Russian operas of the time.

Alexander Borodin's death came with catastrophic suddenness. It was the last day of the carnival of 1887—February 28—and Borodin had invited a group of intimate friends for an evening celebration at his home. He was in unusually high spirits, boisterous and exuberant. He sang fragments from an unfinished symphony to his friends, and participated vigorously in the dancing. Suddenly, he stopped short in his loud merry-making, turned deathly pale, and losing his balance, fell backwards. When his friends rushed towards him, they found that he had died instantly.

Alexander Borodin was "a man of strong physique and health; a man of no whims and easy to get along with," as his eminent friend, Rimsky-Korsakoff, described him. "He slept little, but could sleep on anything and anywhere. He could dine twice a day, or go dinnerless altogether, both of which happened frequently."

"Borodin lived in the building of the former Imperial Medical Academy," we learn from an illuminating article by M. M. Kurbanoff. "The lecture-room in which he gave his lectures on chemistry was situated in the same building, the flat being occupied by himself, his wife and his ward. . . . The flat was pleasant, with big windows facing the river Neva. From a dark hall, the way led to a small drawing-room containing a piano, and then to a dining room. To the left of the drawing-room was Borodin's study which, as a rule, was in a state of great disorder. In this study, Borodin wrote many of his compositions. . . .

"They were at home chiefly in the evenings, altho even then Borodin would often disappear on some pretext or other. . . . I usually found them in the dining room drinking tea; at one end of the big table sat Mrs. Borodin, at the other end he himself, drinking his tea out of a tiny, almost miniature coffee-cup. Of such cups he drank an infinite number, passing his cup every time to his wife, who poured the tea, causing great discomfiture to those who sat between them. When I asked him why he did not drink out of a larger cup, he would reply: 'You see when I have drunk ten such thimbles as this with all the paraphernalia of passing them to and fro and pouring, I have the illusion of having drunk an immense quantity, yet, in reality, I have drunk very little, for tea has a bad effect on me.' In spite of great fatigue from his lectures and the work on innumerable committees, Borodin took a lively interest in the conversation. His sense of humor and happy disposition kept the whole company in a perpetual state of merriment."

Borodin's favorite diversions consisted in painting, modelling and drawing. At one time in his life he was an expert in the art of manufacturing fireworks. He frequently entertained his guests by conjuring strange tricks thru the medium of chemistry.

Borodin possessed a strong social and political consciousness, and he was a vigorous supporter of all societies devoted to youth and feminine movements.

What are Borodin's qualities as a musician? Writes Arthur Pougin: "He had a complex, subtle mind; in his harmonies, he was delicate, refined and bold, and was not afraid to assault the ears of the audience of his day; he was a skilful contrapuntist; and he handled his orchestra with distinction. His weakness, such as it was, lay in a certain absence of unity in conception and in a lack, which is occasionally noticeable, of calmness and simplicity in all the nervous vigor he has at command."

That celebrated Russian critic, Stassov, pointed out that Borodin, like Glinka, "is an epic poet. He is not less national than Glinka, but the oriental element plays with him as it plays for Glinka, Dargomijsky, Moussorgsky, Rimsky-Korsakoff. He belongs to the composers of program music. He can say with

Glinka: 'For my limitless imagination I must have a precise and given text.' Of Borodin's two symphonies, the second is the greater, and it owes its force to the maturity of the composer's talent, but especially to the national character with which it is impregnated by the program. The old heroic Russian form dominates it as it does *Prince Igor*. . . . Borodin was haunted when he wrote this symphony by the picture of feudal Russia, and tried to paint it in his music."

Principal works by Alexander Borodin:

OPERA: *Mlada* (fragment); *Prince Igor*.

ORCHESTRA: Two symphonies; *Scherzo*; *In the steppes of Central Asia*; Two movements of a third symphony.

CHAMBER MUSIC: *Quartet in A-major*; *Quartet in D-major.*

Songs, pieces for the piano, etc.

About Alexander Borodin:

Abraham, Gerald. *Studies in Russian Music*; Pougin, Arthur. *A Short History of Russian Music*; Rimsky-Korsakoff, Nicholas. *My Musical Life.*

Important recordings of music by Alexander Borodin:

SELECTIONS FROM OPERA: *Prince Igor,* "Overture" (VICTOR-Coates); "Prologue" (ODEON); "I hate a dreary life" (VICTOR-Chaliapin); "Girls' dance" (GRAMOPHONE-Blech); "Daylight is fading away" (PARLAPHONE-Rosing); "How goes it prince?" (VICTOR-Chaliapin); "Polovtsian dances" (COLUMBIA-Beecham).

ORCHESTRA: *In the steppes of Central Asia* (COLUMBIA-Gaubert); *Symphony in B-minor* (VICTOR-Coates).

CHAMBER MUSIC: *Quartet in D-major* (VICTOR-Pro Arte).

Marco Enrico Bossi *1861-1925*

MARCO ENRICO BOSSI, distinguished composer of organ-music, was born in Salò, near Brescia, on April 25, 1861. His father was an organist in Morbegno who acquired some fame in the world of music as a result of several popular compositions for his instrument.

Marco Enrico Bossi showed unusual interest in the organ as a child, and was, consequently, given an intensive training on the instrument by his father. Proving himself considerably gifted, Marco Bossi was placed, at the age of ten, in the Liceo Musicale in Bologna. Here he remained for three years, passing on to the Milan

MARCO ENRICO BOSSI

Conservatory where he became a pupil of Ponchielli in composition and Fumagalli in organ-playing.

Six years of study at the Milan Conservatory prepared him for a professional musical career. Upon graduating from the school, he was appointed organist and chapel-master at the Cathedral of Como. For ten years, he remained at this post, where his talents were so great that, during this time, his reputation spread thruout Italy.

In 1891, he was appointed professor of organ and theory at the Naples Conservatory. Five years later, a still more significant post became his when he became director of the Liceo Musicale Benedetto Marcello in Venice, and was placed in charge of the Benedetto Marcello orchestral concerts. In 1902, Bossi was called to Bologna to assume the direction of its Liceo Musicale, and after ten years of outstanding achievement as its musical director, he decided to resign in order to enjoy greater tranquility for composition. In 1916, however, he returned once again to pedagogy, when he became director of the Academy of St. Cecilia in Rome.

Marco Enrico Bossi died aboard the steamship De Grasse on February 24, 1925, on his way back to Italy after a successful concert tour in America. He was unquestionably one of the great organists of his time.

While Bossi composed abundantly in every musical form—including that of the opera and the symphony—his great contribution as an artist was in the field of organ music, of which he produced a significant library.

"It is his organ works . . . that will make his fame enduring," remarks Harvey B. Gaul. "Bossi's organ style . . . lies chiefly in his harmonic structure. It is characterized by aggressive masculine chords. . . . His themes are rarely ingratiating. . . . He is what is called 'tuneless'. . . . He weaves a fine contrapuntal fabric, working towards full organ climaxes. Fugal development interests him more than mere lateral melody. His sense of nuance and the facilities of the concert organ are ever in the fore part of his mind. He has the austerity of the early German school and none of the melodic fecundity of his compatriots—and this is his greatest fault."

Principal works by Marco Enrico Bossi:

ORCHESTRA: *Concerto for organ and orchestra*; *Concertstück* (for organ and orchestra); *Inno trionfale*; *Marcia eroica*; *Étude symphonique*; *Processional march*; *Suite*; *Symphony*; *Concerto for violin and orchestra*.

OPERA: *Paquita*; *Il Viandante*; *L'Usignuola e la rosa*, etc.

CHORAL: *Messa a S. Marco*; Two requiems; *Tota pulchra*; *Marinesca*; *Il Cieco*; *Giovanna d'Arco*; *Il Paradiso perduto*, etc.

CHAMBER MUSIC: *String trio*; *Piano trio*; etc.

About Marco Enrico Bossi:

Dagino, Eduardo. *Marco Enrico Bossi*; *Monographien Moderner Musiker*, vol. 2; Paribeni, Giulio Cesare. *Marco Enrico Bossi*. *Musical America* 41:47 February 28, 1925; *Musical Quarterly* 4:353 July 1918.

Important recordings of music by Marco Enrico Bossi:

ORCHESTRA: *Concerto for organ and orchestra in A-minor*, "Adagio" (POLYDOR); *Suite for string orchestra*, "Prelude and Minuet" (VICTOR-Sevitzky); *Burlesca* (VICTOR).

William Boyce *1710-1779*

WILLIAM BOYCE, eminent English Church composer, was born in London on February 7, 1710. His father, a cabinet-maker, placed him under the musical instruction of Charles King at the St. Paul's Cathedral, where William Boyce became a chorister. When his voice broke, he was dismissed from the choir, and became a pupil at the organ of Maurice Greene. When his apprenticeship ended, Boyce became organist of Oxford Chapel, in 1734, at the same time giving private lessons on the harpsichord.

While still a young man, Boyce knew the tragedy of partial deafness, but, fortunately, it did not interrupt his musical career. In 1736, he became the organist of St. Michael's Parish Church in Cornhill, and a few months later he was appointed composer to His Majesty, his duty consisting of the composition of anthems for the Royal Chapel. His musical activities soon branched out in other directions: in 1737 he became the conductor of the Three Choirs in Gloucester, a post he held with distinction for several years. Six years after this, he made a new mark for himself as a composer, when a gifted serenata, entitled *Solomon*, reached publication.

During the last twenty years of his life, Boyce occupied a position of first importance in the musical life of England. Upon the death of Maurice Greene in 1755, he became—at the nomination of the Duke of Grafton—master of the royal band of musicians, and conductor of the annual festival held at St. Paul's Cathedral by the Sons of the Clergy. In 1758, the most important organ post in England became his—that of the Chapel Royal. In the meanwhile, his pen had not ceased its activity. He continued the composition of many anthems and services, and added to these several works for the theatre, as well as much incidental music to Shakespeare's plays (at the request of his friend, David Garrick).

In 1760, William Boyce published the first volume of his monumental *Cathedral Music*, a work for which he is, probably, best known. This work was originally planned by Maurice Greene who collected considerable material on early English Church music which he bequeathed to Boyce upon his death. William Boyce's *Cathedral Music* (which, finally, appeared in three volumes) succeeded in snatching from

WILLIAM BOYCE

Sir John Hawkins, contemporary of Boyce, has characterized his music as follows: "In musical erudition, he emulated Tallis and Byrd; in harmony and various modulations, Orlando Gibbons; and in the sweetness of me'ody, Purcell. . . . In a word, it may be said that in skill, in powers of invention, he was not surpassed by any of the most celebrated of his predecessors or contemporaries."

Recently, the young modern English composer, Constant Lambert, edited and rescored one of the symphonies of William Boyce, which, in this new form, was presented by Sir Thomas Beecham in London and New York.

Principal works by William Boyce:

THEATRE: *The Chaplet*; *The Shepherd's lottery*; *Lethe*; *Peleus and Thetis*; etc.

ORCHESTRA: Symphonies; Incidental music to many of Shakespeare's plays including *Cymbeline, Romeo and Juliette* and *The Winter's tale*; *Concerto for violin and orchestra*.

CHORAL: Anthems; odes; services; *Te Deum*; *Jubilate*; *David's lamentation*; *Noah*.

CHAMBER MUSIC: Twelve sonatas for two violins and bass. Songs, duets, pieces for the harpsichord, etc.

About William Boyce:

Barrett, William Alexandre. *English Church Composers*; Boyce, William. *Cathedral Music*, vol. 1 (introduction by Sir John Hawkins).

Monthly Musical Record 43:284 November 1, 1913.

oblivion a great library of old English Church music, and in establishing a repertoire for English cathedrals utilized extensively for more than a century after its publication.

His increasing difficulties in hearing compelled Boyce to give up all pedagogical activity and, in 1770, to retire to Kensington and devote himself entirely to the preparation of the second and third volumes of *Cathedral Music*. The third vo!ume of this anthology was published in 1778.

During the final years of his life, Boyce suffered acutely from gout. He died in London on February 16, 1779, and was buried in St. Paul's Cathedral.

Altho Boyce was a contemporary of the great Handel, and was closely acquainted with this master's music, it has been noted that "with all due reverence for the abilities of Handel, Boyce neither pillaged nor serviley imitated him." In his music, Boyce succeeded in retaining his own individuality, and in endowing his music with a strength of character uniquely its own.

"Boyce's style," writes William Alexander Barrett, "as expressed in his church music, is massive, dignified and impressive. In what is now called picturesque writing, he was probably without a rival. His anthems . . . are as good as anything in the whole repertory of cathedral music."

Johannes Brahms   *1833-1897*

"He is the most notable musician I ever met."—JOSEPH JOACHIM

"He has burst upon us fully equipped, as Minerva sprang from the head of Jupiter."—ROBERT SCHUMANN

JOHANNES BRAHMS was the second child, but the oldest son, of Jakob Brahms, a contrabass player in a Hamburg orchestra, and Johanna Henrinka Christiane Brahms, a needlewoman of delicate health. He was born in Hamburg on May 7, 1833.

Altho poverty was prevalent in the Brahms household, Johannes Brahms' childhood was not an unpleasant one. His parents were sympathetic and tender with him and made every effort to bring him the essential comforts and necessities of life. They soon noticed that he showed unusual curiosity in music—

JOHANNES BRAHMS

such curiosity that, as a matter of fact, he invented a notation of his own, when he was six years old, enabling him to put upon paper the little melodies that came into his head!—and they began to teach him the elements of music. One year later, they called upon Otto Cossel, a pianist, to give him intensive piano lessons. Johannes was an apt pupil, and he was soon able to earn a few *pfennigs* a day by playing the piano in a sextet in a summer garden.

By the time he reached his tenth birthday, a new and more competent teacher was acquired—Edouard Marxsen, later the director of music at Altona—under whose rigorous schooling, Brahms acquired an education in harmony and form as well as the playing of the piano. He attained sufficient technical competence in his piano performances to be able to make his official debut in his fourteenth year, playing a program which included a fugue of Bach and a set of original variations on a folk-theme.

Notwithstanding the fact that Brahms made an auspicious entrance into the world of music at an early age, the five years following his debut were difficult ones. He earned his living by playing cheap pot-boilers in dancing saloons, earning so miserable an income—from labor that was arduous and exacting— that he was compelled to supplement this

work with the teaching of the piano (at twenty-five cents a lesson). To these duties was added that of hack-work, in the form of popular transcriptions, which were published under the nom-de-plume of "G.W. Marks." However, it was not all work during these trying years. Brahms devoted rest periods to prolific reading, particularly poetry. And there was some composition—a few songs and a piano trio. The latter work was given a private performance in 1851 and, modestly enough, Brahms concealed his identity under another psuedonym, that of "Karl Würth."

It was at this time that the great Hungarian violinist, Eduard Reményi, came to Hamburg—after a triumphant American tour. Introduced to Brahms, he was so pleased with the young musician's personality that he engaged him as accompanist. Reményi introduced Brahms to Hungarian folk-music which made a vital impression on the young musician; the famous Hungarian Dances, composed in a later year, were the direct result of Reményi's influence.

In 1853, Brahms and Reményi left for a concert-tour. This tour was of outstanding importance in Brahms' life because it brought him for the first time into contact with his life-long friend, Joseph Joachim. Reményi and his accompanist had come to Celle, where the *Kreutzer Sonata* of Beethoven was the feature of the program. At this concert, Brahms noted that the piano was tuned one semi-tone too low, and unhesitatingly set about the task of transcribing his accompaniment at sight. Joseph Joachim was in the audience. He was so impressed with this feat that he sought Brahms out to congratulate him. That was the beginning of a long and devoted friendship between the two musicians. Brahms visited Joachim at his home, performing for him some of his own songs. "It was a revelation to me," Joachim said in later years, "when the song *O versenk* struck my ears. Besides, his piano playing was so tender, so full of fancy, so free, so fiery that it held me enthralled."

From Celle, Brahms and Reményi came to Weimar where, at their first concert, Brahms introduced his *Scherzo in E-flat minor*. The day following this concert, Brahms visited Liszt—equipped with a letter of introduction from Joachim. A relationship that began with a regrettable incident (Liszt performed for Brahms his prolonged *Sonata in B-minor,* only to discover that his young disciple had fallen asleep!) culminated more happily when Liszt had an opportunity to appraise Brahms' talents. Brahms remained in Weimar six weeks, too enchanted with Liszt's company to leave. When, finally, he was compelled to continue his journey it was with a deep sense of regret.

The journey now brought Brahms to Göttingen, and from there to Düsseldorf, the home of Robert Schumann. A few years before this, Brahms had sent Schumann a bundle of songs for criticism, but, at that time, Schumann was too preoccupied with other duties to study them. This time, however, Brahms found the door of Schumann's house open to him, principally because of Joachim's introduction. Brahms performed his own music, to Schumann's great delight. "Clara must hear this," Schumann cried out enthusiastically, in the middle of one piece. "Hear! my dear Clara," Schumann added, when Clara came into the room, "you will hear such music as you never heard before." From that moment on, Brahms became a household friend of the great composer and his wife.

It was Schumann's efforts on behalf of Brahms that definitely launched the latter's career as a composer. Schumann interested his own publishers, Breitkopf and Härtel, in Brahms' works. They accepted some of them for immediate publication. And on October 28, 1853, Schumann published his epoch-making essay in the *Neue Zeitschrift für Musik,* an essay which focused the limelight of attention and fame upon the young, and until now obscure, composer.

Schumann's effusive encomium brought Brahms an invitation to perform at a concert at the Gewandhaus in Leipzig on December of the same year. Brahms included in his recital his own *First piano sonata* and *Scherzo.* Following this performance, a storm of controversy burst, with Brahms as its victim—a storm which persisted until after Brahms' death. There were those who felt that this new composer was too academic, too pedantic and too sterile; on the other hand, there were some musicians who felt that this music possessed the high inspiration and power of Beethoven.

During the next few years, Brahms —now an intimate friend of the Schumanns—profited by the composer's encouragement and advice; much of his artistic development at this time was the direct result of Schumann's guidance. With Robert Schumann's illness, which developed startlingly during the early part of 1854, Brahms became even more attached to the household of his friend. He frequently quieted the sick man with music; he likewise did everything in his power to prevent the Schumann household from becoming enmeshed in financial entanglements. After Robert Schumann's death, Brahms remained Clara's closest companion, her indefatigable guardian and adviser.

In 1854, Brahms accepted a position as music-master to the Prince of Lippe-Detmold. The duties were not exacting; there were many leisure hours which Brahms could devote to his personal musical interests. Brahms devoted this period to an intensive study of the piano, acquiring a masterly technique. Composition likewise absorbed his energies. At this time, he produced several serenades for orchestra, a *Piano trio,* and what is undoubtedly his greatest work up to this period, the *First piano concerto.* The piano concerto was introduced by Brahms himself at the concerts of the Leipzig Gewandhaus Orchestra, in January of 1859. A work, which today is recognized as one of Brahms' mature achievements, was referred to by the Leipzig *Signale,* after the first performance, as music which is "ungrateful as possible," consisting of orchestration which was nothing more than a "series of lacerating chords."

At this time, Brahms met a charming lady from Göttingen—Agathe von Seibold—with whom he fell seriously in love. He contemplated marriage, but with almost schoolboyish diffidence hesitated to confide in her his ambitions for their future life. He failed to find the courage to broach the subject of marriage, and their friendship petered out.

In 1862, Brahms came to Vienna, making this musical metropolis his permanent home for the remainder of his life. Soon after his arrival, his *Sextet* was performed by the Hellmesberger chamber organization, receiving glowing praise. Brahms' importance was now generally recognized in Vienna, and he received an appointment as conductor of the Vienna Singakademie.

The death of Brahms' mother inspired him to compose his greatest choral work, *The German requiem.* Its first complete performance took place in Bremen on Good Friday of April, 1868, in the cathedral; Frau Schumann had come halfway across Germany to attend the performance. The impression which Brahms' music made upon the audience was a stirring one. There were some academic theologians who condemned the work because Brahms had not utilized a Latin text. The audience, in general —little interested in such technicalities —was deeply moved.

The German requiem was followed by three other impressive vocal works, the *Song of fate,* after a poem by Friedrich Hölderlin, the *Rhapsody,* for alto solo, male chorus and orchestra, and the *Liebeslieder-walzer* for vocal quartet and four hands. Successful performances of these works brought increased prestige to Brahms, in the form of an appointment as director of the *Gesellschaft der Musikfreunde* in Vienna, and a decoration of the Maximilian Order of Arts and Sciences from the King of Bavaria.

It has frequently been pointed out that Brahms was reluctant to begin the composition of a major symphonic work until he was fully confident of his creative powers. Thus—though he was frequently goaded on by Schumann and Joachim, and though time and again he put to paper random sketches or a symphony—it was not until comparatively late in life that Brahms produced his first symphony. His admiration for Beethoven was so great, that he found it difficult to compose in a form which his great predecessor had brought to such heights of sublimity. "I shall never compose a symphony!" he once told a friend—a few months after he had made some sketches for a first symphony.

"You have no conception of how the likes of us feel when we hear the tramp of a giant like him (Beethoven) behind us!"

In 1873, Brahms produced a major orchestral work in his *Variations on a theme of Haydn.* His satisfaction in this achievement, no doubt, convinced him that the symphonic form was not beyond his grasp. In September of 1876, therefore, after working more than ten years upon sketches for a symphony, he brought to completion the *First symphony*—probably the greatest "first symphony" ever created. "From the first notes," as Lawrence Gilman wrote, "we are aware of a great voice, uttering superb poetic speech."

Recognition did not come overnight to the great first *C-minor symphony.* Eduard Hanslick spoke of it as "music more or less clear, more or less sympathetic, but difficult of comprehension." And when Hermann Levi gave it a scond performance in Munich it was vigorously hissed. It was not until recently that audiences began to realize that Brahms' *C-minor symphony* was not difficult of comprehension, and that it was not merely a cold slab of musical architecture, but, rather, recognized the warmth, compassion, tenderness and sublimity of its poetic flights.

His *First symphony* composed finally, others were not slow in coming. The *Second symphony* came in 1877, and was successfully introduced by the Vienna Philharmonic under Hans Richter. The *Third symphony*—called by Hans Richter, Brahms' *Eroica symphony*—was completed in 1883, and the *Fourth symphony* followed it approximately one year later.

Throwing a *coup d'oeil* over the four symphonies of Brahms, Walter Niemann has written as follows in his illuminating biography: "The *First symphony* is Brahms' 'Pathetic symphony.' Movement by movement, third by third, it struggled upwards, in a titanic striving against the most grievous tribulation, to a triumphant paean of confident vitality. . . The *Second symphony* . . . may be called Brahms' 'Pastoral symphony.' Just as the *First symphony,* with its sombre pathos, struggled upwards in thirds from movement to movement out of darkness into the sun, to a godlike serenity and freedom, so the *Second,* with its loftily anacreontic tragedy, descends in a peaceful cycle of descending thirds. . . . Its quiet, unconscious tragedy, hidden beneath the blossoms of a soft idyll of man and nature, with a subdued evening tinge and prevailing pastoral spirit, carried direct conviction to a discriminating and unprejudiced listener. . . . The *Third symphony* . . . is Brahms' '*Eroica*'; heroic, that is to say in the Brahmsian spirit. In spite of its truly heroic and virile strenuousness and conflicts, its last supreme word of wisdom is a serene resignation. This is, moreover, expressed with such wonderful truth and moving effect in the music form in which it is clothed that we may venture to say that in its purely human qualities the *Third symphony* is Brahms' most typical, personal and important symphonic work. In no other symphony has Brahms unveiled his own individual nature so wonderfully, in no other has his whole personality found such marvelously pure and undisguised expression, in no other symphony has he displayed such spiritual independence as in this. . . . The *Fourth symphony* . . . may be called Brahms' 'Elegiac' symphony. The virile, energetic hero of the *Third,* with its conflicts and strivings, has become transformed in the *Fourth,* into a resigned philosopher, withdrawing by degrees into inward solitude with advancing years. In this lies the deeply moving and genuine quality of the *Fourth symphony.* . . . The tone of defiant, concentrated and superior strength, such as is found in the first movement of the *Third symphony,* is intensified in the *Fourth,* with his growing maturity, into the most concise and monumental symphonic style."

In the opinion of H.C. Colles: "Of Brahms' four symphonies, each one a masterpiece of its kind, the *Fourth* is most fit to stand beside the *Jupiter* and *Eroica*."

In 1878, the degree of doctor of philosophy was conferred upon Brahms by the University of Breslau. In recognition of this honor Brahms composed his *Academic Festival Overture,* which utilized student melodies.

The last years of Brahms' life were happy ones. He traveled frequently, principally to Italy, a country he adored; his summer months were spent peacefully in his mountain home near Vienna. His significant position as a composer was not questioned; security and recognition were his. From all parts of the world, honors beat a path to his door.

The death of his dearest friend— Clara Schumann—was, perhaps, the severest blow in his declining years. She died on May 20, 1895. With her death, Brahms felt, an integral part of him had passed away. He attended her funeral, and generously offered his services to the stricken daughters.

At this funeral, Brahms caught a severe cold which affected his health seriously. In September of 1896 he was forced to go to Carlsbad for a cure. During the entire winter that followed, he suffered illness, requiring the persistent attention of a physician.

When the end finally approached, he did not know that he was dying. He was in unusually good spirits. It was only when he saw his housekeeper silently weeping in a corner of the room that he guessed the truth. He died on the morning of April 3, 1897 at his home at 4 Carlgasse, where he had been living for twenty-five years. He was buried in the Vienna Friedhof.

Sir George Henschel, the English composer who knew Brahms well, described the master as follows: "He was broadchested, of rather short stature, with a tendency to stoutness. The healthy and rather ruddy color of his skin indicated a love of nature and a habit of being in the open air in all kinds of weather; his thick hair fell nearly down to his shoulders. His clothes and boots were not exactly of the latest pattern, nor did they fit particularly well, but his linen was spotless. What, however, struck me most was the kindliness of his eyes. They were of a light blue, wonderfully keen and bright, with now and then a roguish twinkle in them, and yet of almost childlike tenderness."

"He was not fussy in his dress," Philip Hale remarked in his valuable program notes. "At home he went about in a flannel shirt, trousers, a detachable white collar, no cravat, slippers. In the country he was happy in a flannel shirt and alpaca jacket, carrying a soft felt hat in his hand, and in bad weather wearing on his shoulders an old-fashioned bluish-green shawl, fastened in the front by a huge pin. . . . He preferred a modest restaurant to a hotel table d'hôte. In his music room were pictures of a few composers, engravings (the Sistine Madonna among them), the portrait of Cherubini by Ingres, with a veiled Muse crowning the composer ('I cannot stand that female,' Brahms said to his landlady), a bronze relief of Bismarck, always crowned with a laurel. There was a square piano on which a volume of Bach was usually standing open. On the cover lay notebooks, writing tablets, calendars, cigar cases, spectacles, purses, watches, keys, portfolios, recently published books and music, also souvenirs of his travels. He was passionately patriotic, interested in politics, a firm believer in German unity. He deeply regretted that he had not done military duty as a young man."

He was known to have been a practical joker, and more than once his pranks—as well as his acid humor—afforded him much more pleasure than it did those near him. He could, at alternate times, be a most charming friend and a disagreeable companion. Consideration for the feelings of others was not his strong point; frequently he left fellow-musicians stung with pain as a result of his verbal darts. And yet, he could be intensely human, lovable, capable of excessive devotion, self-sacrifice and tenderness where his personal friends were concerned.

He died a bachelor, but he was an enemy of neither women nor marriage, esteeming both highly. He was attached to more than one lovely girl in his life. He frequently regretted his bachelorhood.

His daily existence was of the barest simplicity: he worked, read, prepared his own coffee, took long walks, visited friends and spent many hours at his favorite cafés reading the current periodicals and indulging in conversation. He detested interviewers, avoided all newspaper publicity fastidiously, would not tolerate sitting for either photographers or painters.

Brahms, as a composer, distinguished himself equally in the symphony and the song, and in chamber and piano music.

In his piano music, wrote James Gibbons Huneker, "Brahms has an individual voice. . . . His Spartan simplicity sometimes unmasks the illusory and elusive qualities of the instrument. . . . His techniques are peculiar, but they make the keyboard sound beautifully. . . . His piano music is gay, is marmoreal in its repose, is humorous, jolly, sad, depressing, morbid, recondite, poetic, severe and fantastic. He pours into the elastic form of the sonata romantic passion, and in the loosest texture of his little pieces he can be as immovable as bronze, as plastic as clay. But even in the more invertebrate pieces—if Brahms could ever construct without vertebra—there is a sense of form, a pattern weaving. . . . He is sometimes frozen by grief and submerged by the profundity of his thought, but he is ever interesting. . . . Above all, he is deeply human."

In the song, Brahms may not—as Cecil Gray noted—"attain quite to the heights which Schubert does in a small handful of unexcelled masterpieces, but with this one glorious exception it is difficult to see whom one could place above him. . . . A song of Brahms is not . . . a mere turgid flow of notes without any intrinsic value apart from the poem, but a delicately organized and articulated structure with a logic of its own. . . . Brahms . . . was never content until he had created a vocal line of intrinsic melodic beauty and an accompaniment as full of musical subtlety as he could make it."

It is the opinion of Herbert Antcliffe, that, in the chamber works, Brahms achieved his most personal expression. "Brahms . . . was happier by far in this than in any other mode of composition. Great as is his symphonic music, truthful and dramatic though his choral works, sensuous and brilliant his piano pieces, none appeals to our finer feelings so forcibly and effectively as the concerted chamber works. In these he meets and discourses with his friends. Perfect in their workmanship, they never smell of the lamp or wear the scholar's gown. They are the intimate thought of a man spoken only to his friends. . . . They will always be musicians' music."

What is Brahms' importance in musical history? Writes W.H. Hadow: "So far as concerns the technical problem of composition . . . the work of Brahms is the actual crown and climax of our present musical art. . . . In him converge all previous streams of tendency, not as into a pool, stagnant, passive, motionless, but as into a noble river that receives its tributary waters and bears them onward in larger and statelier volume.

"Are we to say, then, that Brahms is more consummate a master of his medium than Bach and Beethoven? By no means; but, in consequence of their work, his medium is more plastic than theirs. . . . To Brahms we may apply Dryden's famous epigram, in which the force of nature 'to make a third has joined the other two.' By his education, he learned to assimilate their separate methods; by his position, in the later days of romance, he found anew emotional language in established use; by his own genius he has made the forms wider and more flexible, and has shown once more that they are not artificial devices, but the organic embodiment of artistic life."

Principal works by Johannes Brahms:

ORCHESTRA: Four symphonies; *Academic Festival overture*; *Tragic overture*; *Variations on a theme of Haydn*; Two serenades; Two concertos for piano and orchestra; *Concerto for violin and orchestra*; *Concerto for violin, violoncello and orchestra*.

CHORAL: *Liebeslieder-walzer* (for quartet and four hands); *The German requiem* (for chorus and orchestra); *Song of Fate*; *Triumphlied*; *Rinaldo*; *Rhapsody* (for alto, male chorus and orchestra); *Ave Maria*; *Psalm 13*; *Geistliches lied*; A cappella motets, etc.

CHAMBER MUSIC: Two sextets for strings; Two quintets for strings; *Clarinet quintet*; Two string quartets; Three piano quartets; Three piano trios; Trio for piano, violin and horn; Trio for piano, clarinet and violoncello; Three sonatas for violin and piano; Two sonatas for violoncello and piano; Two sonatas for clarinet and piano.

PIANO: Two piano sonatas; *Scherzo in E-flat minor*; *Variations on a theme of Schumann*; *Variations on a theme of Haydn* (two pianos); *Variations and fugue on a theme of Handel*; *Variations on a theme of Paganini*; Ballades; Rhapsodies; Intermezzos; Waltzes; Hungarian dances, etc.

About 230 songs.

About Johannes Brahms:

Kalbeck, Max. *Johannes Brahms*; Maitland, J. A. Fuller. *Brahms*; May, Florence. *The Life of Johannes Brahms*; Murdoch, William. *Brahms*; Niemann, Walter. *Brahms*; Schauffler, Robert Haven. *The Unknown Brahms*; Schumann, Clara. *Letters of Clara Schumann and Johannes Brahms*; Specht, Richard. *Johannes Brahms*.

Important recordings of music by Johannes Brahms:

ORCHESTRA: *Symphony in C-minor* (VICTOR-Stokowski); *Symphony in D-major* (VICTOR-Stokowski); *Symphony in F-major* (VICTOR-Stokowski); *Symphony in E-minor* (VICTOR-Walter); *Academic Festival overture* (COLUMBIA-Mengelberg); *Tragic overture* (VICTOR-Boult); *Variations on a theme of Haydn* (VICTOR-Casals); *Concerto for Piano and orchestra in D-minor* (VICTOR-Bachaus); *Concerto in B-flat major* (VICTOR-Schnabel); *Concerto for violin and orchestra* (COLUMBIA-Szigeti); *Concerto for violin, violoncello and orchestra* (VICTOR-Casals, Thibaud).

CHORAL: *Rhapsody* (VICTOR); *A German requiem*, "Blest are they that mourn" (GRAMOPHONE); "Behold all flesh" (GRAMOPHONE); "How lovely is thy dwelling place" (GRAMOPHONE); "Ye that are sorrowful" (PARLAPHONE).

CHAMBER MUSIC: *Sextet in B-flat major* (VICTOR-Pro Arte, Hobday, Pini); *Quintet in G-major* (VICTOR-Budapest, Mahlke); *Clarinet quintet* (COLUMBIA-Lener, Draper); *Piano quintet* (VICTOR-Flonzaley, Bauer); *String quartet in C-minor* (VICTOR-Busch); *String quartet in A-minor* (VICTOR-Budapest); *Piano quartet in G-minor* (VICTOR-Pro-Arte, Rubinstein); *Piano quartet in A-major* (GRAMOPHONE-Busch, Serkin); *Trio in B-major* (BRUNSWICK); *Trio in C-major* (COLUMBIA); *Trio for violin, horn and piano* (VICTOR); *Sonata for violoncello and piano in E-minor* (COLUMBIA-Feuermann); *Sonata for viola and piano* (COLUMBIA-Tertis); *Sonatas for violin and piano in G-major and A-major* (VICTOR-Busch, Serkin); *Sonata for violin and piano in D-minor* (COLUMBIA-Zimbalist).

PIANO: *Sonata in F-minor* (COLUMBIA-Grainger); *Variations and fugue on a theme of Handel* (VICTOR-Moisevitch); *Variations on a theme of Paganini* (VICTOR-Bachaus); *Representative piano works of Brahms*, selected Ballades, Capriccios, Hungarian dances, Rhapsodies, Waltzes, etc. (VICTOR-Bachaus).

SONGS: *Brahms lieder album* (VICTOR-Bampton); *Brahms lieder group* (VICTOR-Gerhardt).

Tomás Bretón *1850-1923*

TOMÁS BRETÓN Y HERNÁN-DEZ was born in Salamanca on December 29, 1850. He received musical training at an early age. In his

TOMÁS BRETÓN

tenth year, he was already engaged professionally in musical activity as a member of an orchestra in his native city.

In his fifteenth year, Bretón went to Madrid where for several years he earned his livelihood by playing in theatres and cafés. Following this, he traveled thru Spain with a touring operatic company, as a member of its orchestra.

Meanwhile, Bretón had become more and more actively interested in native Spanish music. He was, finally, driven by the desire to express this native music in artistic forms larger than mere folk-songs. In order to solidify his technique—to bring this ideal to fruition —he entered the Madrid Conservatory in 1875. One year later, his influence asserted itself when he founded the Unión Artistico Musical, its purpose being to introduce important new Spanish works to the music public.

From this time on, Bretón's career was rich with activity and achievement. For a long period, he was conductor at the Madrid Opera House, and of symphony concerts, once again serving as an all-important medium in bringing important new Spanish works to the attention of the music world. Pedagogy also absorbed his attention. In 1901, Bretón was engaged as teacher at the

Conservatory of Music in Madrid; two years later he became its director.

However, it is with his compositions that Bretón's greatest importance in Spanish music rests. In 1889, *Los Amantes de Teruel,* the first of Bretón's outstanding *zarzuelas* (operettas), reached performance, and was received so enthusiastically that Bretón was encouraged to produce a long string of similar works which endeared him to Spaniards. These *zarzuelas,* remarks Adolfo Salazar, "are quite after the heart of the public and are full of real character."

Analyzing Bretón's style of composition painstaking'y in his authoritative study on modern Spanish music, Salazar pointed out that Bretón's technique is more cerebral than inspired, and that his art is almost rudimentary "in the manner in which it utilizes the popular chant whose gracefulness and freshness he spoiled on account of the treatment to which he submitted it."

Bretón may not have been a great composer (it is doubtful if he can even be numbered among the outstanding composers of Spain), notwithstanding the fact that he produced some chamber-music of brilliant construction and freshness of ideas. But Bretón was an important factor in the movement to nationalize Spanish music. His historical importance, therefore, should not be underestimated.

Tomás Bretón died in Madrid on December 2, 1923.

Principal works by Tomás Bretón:

OPERA: *Los Amantes de Teruel*; *La Verbena de la Paloma*; *Juan Garín*; *Dolores*; *El Domingo de Ramos*; *Raquel*; *Farinelli*; *Taboré,* etc.

CHORAL: *Apocalipsia.*

ORCHESTRA: *Las Escenas andaluzas*; *Salamanca*; *En la Alhambra*; *Concerto for violin and orchestra,* etc.

CHAMBER MUSIC: Three string quartets; *Piano quintet*; *Wind sextet.*

About Tomás Bretón:

Salazar, Adolfo. *La Música Contemporánea en España*; Salcedo, Angel S. *Tomás Bretón. Chesterian* N.S. 11:263 February 1919.

Important recordings of music by Tomás Bretón:

OPERA: *La Verbena de la Paloma,* abridged version (ODEON).

SELECTIONS FROM OPERA: *Dolores*, "Duo" and "Jota" (GRAMOPHONE).

ORCHESTRA: *Las Escenas andaluzas* (COLUMBIA-Arbós); *En la Alhambra* (COLUMBIA-Arbós).

Max Bruch *1838-1920*

MAX BRUCH was born in Cologne on January 6, 1838. He was the son of a government employee, and the grandson of a famous clergyman.

As a boy, Bruch disclosed talent in two different directions—for music and for painting. For a long while it seemed uncertain which art would claim him. His mother, a gifted singer, discerned that her son showed greater adaptability for music; she therefore urged him to follow its study most conscientiously. Music soon acquired such prominence in Bruch's life that, by his fourteenth birthday, he had composed no less than seventy works. One of these, a symphony, was performed in Cologne in 1852 so successfully that it definitely convinced Bruch he was meant for music.

A scholarship of four hundred gulden enabled him to become a pupil of Ferdinand Hiller in Cologne. Hiller soon became deeply impressed with the capabilities of his student, exerting his influence in procuring a publisher for Bruch's early works.

During the winters of 1857 and 1858, Bruch was in Leipzig, where he came in contact with Moscheles and David. The musical environment of Leipzig was a healthy spiritual influence for him; his composition now acquired greater poise and maturity.

Returning to his native town, Bruch turned to pedagogy for self-support. At the same time he composed an operetta, *Scherz, List und Rache* (to words by Goethe) which received performance in 1858.

In 1861, Bruch went to Munich where he received an introduction to the well-known poet, Geibel. At the express wish of Mendelssohn, Geibel had written a libretto for an opera, entitled *Die Loreley*, for which Mendelssohn did not compose the score only because of his untimely death. Geibel was sufficiently convinced of Bruch's genius to turn the libretto over to him. In 1863, Bruch's

MAX BRUCH

opera, *Die Loreley*—his first major work—was performed in Mannheim. It was a great success, and was soon afterwards repeated in Leipzig.

One year later, Bruch produced another major work, a cantata, *Frithjof*. Upon its première in Aix-la-Chapelle in 1864, it was so well received that it was soon thereafter performed in principal cities thruout Germany. With the *Loreley* and *Frithjof*, Bruch's reputation as a composer was firmly established.

In 1865, Bruch was appointed conductor of orchestral concerts in Coblenz. One year later a still more important appointment became his, that of chapelmaster at Sonderhausen. These years with the baton turned Bruch's interest towards orchestral music; during this period he composed several significant works, including two symphonies and a *Concerto for violin and orchestra*, dedicated to Joseph Joachim. Of these works, the Concerto (it was the one in G-minor) was the most important of his achievements. "Grave and earnest from beginning to end, yet rising into passionate outbursts of almost tragic intensity," wrote J. A. Fuller-Maitland, "this work acquired at once a place of its own among violin concertos. Its melodies have a character deeper, nobler and more genuinely expressive than any former work of its composer."

In 1871, Bruch temporarily surrendered his conductorial duties to devote himself more completely to composition. The first fruit of his newly acquired leisure was an opera, *Hermione* (after Shakespeare's *A Winter's Tale*) first produced in Berlin in 1872 with only moderate success. The outbreak of the Franco-Prussian War brought Bruch to Berlin where he settled permanently. Shortly afterwards, he composed two outstanding choral works, *Odysseus* and *Achilleus.* Arno Kleffel wrote as follows about these two works: "In *Odysseus* and *Achilleus,* Bruch had found a field of material which made a strong appeal to his instincts and aesthetic feelings, a field in which he found opportunity to develop to the highest degree both in the masterful treatment of choral masses and in his ever growing art of instrumentation. . . . Bruch's music not only brought the Homeric world nearer to us again, but more, the musical setting has revealed to us for the first time various poetic phrases in their entire depth and purity."

Bruch's rising prestige as a composer brought him an invitation to visit England, in 1877, in conection with the first performance of his G-minor Violin concerto by Pablo Sarasate in London. Bruch's visit to England resulted in performances of his principal choral and orchestral works thruout the country. In 1880, he was appointed conductor of the Liverpool Philharmonic Society.

In 1883, Bruch crossed the Atlantic as a guest of several important singing societies in America which had scheduled performances of his more important choral works. He was given a royal welcome, and treated with great honor and reverence by music audiences thruout the East. Upon returning to Europe, he became conductor of the Breslau Symphony Orchestra.

Bruch's last important musical post came to him in 1892 when he was appointed head of the master school of composition at the Royal High School in Berlin. He fulfilled this important position with honor and dignity. In 1912, he resigned from his professional duties. For the remainder of his life he sought seclusion in a suburb of Berlin.

Max Bruch died in Friedenau, Berlin, on October 2, 1920.

While Bruch is best known as a composer of the deservedly celebrated *Violin concerto in G-minor*, the *Kol Nidrei* variations (for violoncello and orchestra) and the *Romance*, it is Hugo Riemann's opinion, in his monumental study of music after the time of Beethoven, that Bruch's chief artistic importance rests with his choral works. Riemann finds that in this field Bruch possessed a modern style of harmony, counterpoint and instrumentation, and a masterly sense of form. Riemann goes so far as to maintain that Bruch's musical writing in his choral pieces contains even greater lucidity than that of Brahms.

Principal works by Max Bruch:

ORCHESTRA: Three symphonies; Three concertos for violin and orchestra; *Concerto for two pianos ' and orchestra; Fantasia* (for violin and orchestra); *Conzertstück* (for violin and orchestra); *Romance* (for violin and orchestra); *Kol Nidrei* (for violoncello and orchestra), etc.

OPERA: *Die Loreley; Hermione.*

CHAMBER MUSIC: Two string quartets; *Piano trio.*

CHORAL: *Arminius; Achilleus; Moses;* Cantatas (including *Frithjof, Odysseus, Leonidas, Die Macht des Gesanges, Heldenfeier,* etc.). About 40 songs, pieces for the piano, etc.

About Max Bruch:

Fuller-Maitland J. A. *Masters of German Music;* Riemann, Hugo. *Geschichte der Musik seit Beethoven.*

Important recordings of music by Max Bruch:

ORCHESTRA: *Concerto in G-minor for violin and orchestra* (VICTOR-Menuhin); *Kol Nidrei* (PARLAPHONE-Piatigorsky).

CHORAL: *Heldenfeier* (PARLAPHONE).

Anton Bruckner *1824-1896*

"I know of only one who may be compared to Beethoven, and he is Bruckner."
—RICHARD WAGNER

ANTON BRUCKNER, who was born in Ansfelden, Austria, on September 4, 1824, was the oldest of eleven children. He was descended from a long line of schoolmasters.

Music rather than academic studies first appealed to Bruckner. At the age of four he could play the violin agreeably; he could also compose tunes of an attractive quality. At school, any studies removed from music found him an apathetic pupil. He was, therefore, permitted to study music. A cousin of the family was enlisted to teach him theory and the organ, and to give him direction in his abortive composition.

Anton Bruckner's father died when the boy was thirteen years old, making it imperative for the mother to send him as a choir-boy to the St. Florian secular music school. He remained there for four years, getting private instruction with the intention of entering the teachers' preparatory school in Linz.

When Bruckner reached his seventeenth birthday, he received his first pedagogical assignment at Windhaag. Negligence in his duties brought about his transference to an even smaller town, Kronsdorf. What was intended as a punishment soon turned out to be a blessing in disguise for young Bruckner. Kronsdorf was midway between Enns and Steyr. At Enns, Bruckner came into contact with the organist, Zanetti, who taught him theory; at Steyr, could be found one of the best pipe-organs in Europe, upon which Bruckner was permitted to practice.

In 1845, Bruckner—having passed his schoolmaster's license examination—was appointed to the St. Florian school where he had spent his boyhood years as chorister. Pedagogy, however, could not draw him away from music. Composition and the playing of the organ remained his favorite pastimes. In 1849, he produced the first work to disclose his originality and talent as a composer, the *Requiem in D-minor.*

By 1853, he came to the decision of abandoning pedagogy for music. Bruckner set out for Vienna in an attempt to establish himself in this musical metropolis. He subjected himself to a rigorous course of study under Simon Sechter, the distinguished theorist. He was so diligent a pupil that, when asked for written exercises, he brought his professor seventeen books of studies. "I never had a more serious pupil than you," Sechter told Bruckner.

It was about this time, too, that Bruckner revealed his musical capabili-

ANTON BRUCKNER

ties in a convincing manner. He decided to enter the examination which was regularly given in Vienna by a high tribunal of musical authorities, whose purpose it was to test the background of young musicians. One of the judges would write down a theme and would then ask the aspiring musician to improvise upon it. When Bruckner entered the contest, a second judge maliciously doubled the length of the theme, and passed the paper on to Bruckner at the organ. Bruckner, with slight hesitation, composed extemporaneously a prelude and fugue upon the given theme with such technical adroitness that the judges were astounded. "He should examine us," one of them said. "If I knew one tenth of what he knows, I would be a happy man!"

In 1860, Bruckner was appointed choral director of the *Frohsinn society.* It was thru this organization that Bruckner was able for the first time to introduce a work of his to the Viennese music public, an *Ave Maria* for seven voices.

Three years later came one of the great musical experiences in Bruckner's life. He heard Wagner's *Tannhäuser,* which opened a new world to him. To Bruckner, *Tannhäuser* seemed to blaze a new direction, a new goal for musical art. From that moment on, Bruckner decided to abandon classical rigidity in his composition and permit himself free and unrestricted expression in more plastic and more ambitious forms.

With this ideal in mind, Bruckner composed his first symphony in 1865. At this time he made a trip to Munich expressly to hear the first performance of Wagner's *Tristan und Isolde*. While there, he was formally introduced to the master. Wagner invited Bruckner to his home, and from that time on there developed a friendship between them which persisted until the death of Wagner. It is well known that, thruout his entire life, Bruckner adored Wagner, that (to cite merely one example) after the first performance of *Parsifal* in Bayreuth, Bruckner fell on his knees in front of Wagner and said reverently: "Master, I worship you!"

On July 6, 1868, Bruckner was appointed professor at the Conservatory of Vienna. The period that followed was filled with misery and frustration. The première of the *First symphony* in Linz, in 1868, was a fiasco, both because it was years ahead of its time and because of an execrable performance. The *Mass in F-minor* was refused a performance in Vienna because of its difficulty. Bruckner was to know disappointment in love as well. She was Josephine Lang, a girl of seventeen, whom Bruckner entertained dreams of marrying. He was finally rejected by the girl's parents because of the discrepancy in age between the lovers.

It was to escape from these disappointments that Bruckner decided to neglect composition momentarily and to set out upon a concert tour as organist. His successes in London and France exhilarated and encouraged him, and he returned to Vienna considerably vitalized in spirit. In June, 1872, he hired the Philharmonic orchestra for 300 gulden (eight months of his wages!) to introduce his *Mass in F-minor* to Vienna. It cannot be said that he was compensated for this extravagance by the appreciation of his audience, even though no less a critic than Eduard Hanslick was impressed with some pages of the music. A few months later, Bruckner expended another 400 gulden to introduce his *Mass in F-minor* to one critic found this work important— Spiedel, who wrote in the following

glowing terms: "It is no common mortal who speaks to us in this music. There is introduced to us in this symphony a composer whose very shoe-laces his numerous enemies are not fit to tie."

Bruckner, at this time, was in a pitiable plight. "I have only my place at the Conservatory," he wrote a letter, dated 1875, "on the income of which it is impossible to exist. I have been compelled to borrow money over and over again or accept the alternative of starvation. No one offers me any help." But finance was one of the smaller of Bruckner's problems. One of the officials at the Conservatory told him: "It is time for you to throw your symphonies in a trash-basket"; and Bruckner, who was always sensitive to criticism, suffered unspeakably as a result of this acrid remark. His *Third symphony*— dedicated to and praised by Richard Wagner—was accepted for performance by the Vienna Philharmonic, only to be discarded after one rehearsal because of its difficulty. In 1877, Bruckner himself conducted this "Wagner" symphony, to be greeted by jeers, hissing and laughter. When the symphony was over only a dozen people were left in the audience: one of these was Gustav Mahler, who rushed to congratulate the composer for a masterpiece; another was Rättig, the publisher, who admired the work so sincerely that he decided to publish it, irrespective of financial losses.

It was, therefore, perhaps no coincidence that, at this time, Bruckner was composing a symphony which he entitled, *Tragic*.

Abuse, financial troubles, severe criticisms all combined to undermine Bruckner's health. In 1880 he suffered a severe attack of nerves. He left for Switzerland for a holiday. From there he went to Oberammergau for the Passion Play. In Oberammergau he fell in love once again, this time with Marie Bartl, also seventeen years of age. For a time, Bruckner and his beloved exchanged tender phrases thru letters. But it was not long before the girl tired of this relationship and Bruckner's yearning letters found no answer.

Upon his return to Vienna, Bruckner found a complete reversal of fortune.

Hans Richter, the great conductor, saw the score of the *Romantic symphony* and was so moved by the work that he decided to perform it without delay at the concerts of the Vienna Philharmonic. The praise which greeted this work at its performance was no longer single-voiced. In 1884, Artur Nikisch conducted the *Seventh symphony*, which soon afterwards was also performed by Hermann Levi in Munich and Felix Mottl in Karlsruhe. There followed other performances of Bruckner's symphonies in America, by Anton Seidl, and in Graz, by Karl Muck. Obviously, Bruckner's star was soaring. Further recognition came in 1891 when he was created Honorary Doctor of the University of Vienna. Shortly after this, an insignia was bestowed upon him by Emperor Franz Joseph of Vienna who also invited the composer to live in an apartment in the wing of the Belvedere palace.

In 1894, on the occasion of his seventieth birthday, Bruckner found himself generally recognized as one of the foremost composers in Vienna. His birthday was celebrated with festivity. There were telegrams from half the music-world, elaborate articles of praise in the Viennese press, honorary concerts. Linz gave him the key to the city. Many musical organizations bestowed upon him official honorary titles.

But he was, unfortunately, not fated to taste this sweetness much longer. On January 12, 1896, he attended a performance of his *Te Deum*; it was the last of his works he was to hear performed. During the summer he fell ill. On October 11—it was Sunday—he was working upon the final sketches of his *Ninth symphony* when he complained of a chill and asked for a cup of tea. A friend helped him to bed. No sooner did he straighten himself in it than he breathed his last.

At the funeral services, Ferdinand Löwe conducted the adagio movement of Bruckner's *Seventh symphony*. As Bruckner himself had requested, he was buried under the organ of St. Florian.

Gabriel Engel, the author of a monograph on Bruckner, has given us the following verbal portrait of the composer: "He was a little above the average in height; but an inclination to corpulency made him appear shorter. His physiognomy, huge-nosed and smooth-shaven as he was, was that of a Roman emperor; but from his blue eyes beamed only kindness and childish faith. He wore unusually wide white collars, in order to leave his neck perfectly free; and his black loose-hanging clothes were obviously intended to be, above all, comfortable. He had even left instructions for a roomy coffin. The only thing about his attire suggestive of the artist was the loosely arranged bow-tie he always wore. About the fit and shape of his shoes he was, according to his shoe-maker, more particular than the most exactingly elegant member of the fair sex. As he would hurry along the street swinging a soft black hat, which he hardly ever put on, a colored handkerchief could always be seen protruding from his coat-pocket."

He was not a man of social graces; frequently his appearance and awkward behaviour aroused mild amusement among those with whom he came into contact. He was very modest and unassuming, asked little of his friends and expected little; and whenever a favor was done to him he was so effusive in his gratitude that he frequently proved to be embarrassing. He enjoyed most a glass of Pilsen beer in the company of pleasant friends.

Where Bruckner's music is concerned, the music world has been definitely divided into two opposing camps. There are those who believe that Bruckner is one of the greatest symphonic composers of all time, the inevitable successor of Johannes Brahms. On the other hand there are those who esteem him a mediocrity, a pompous, pretentious, loud-voiced, self-appointed prophet. Music history has few examples in which a composer, four decades after his death, is still the subject of such extravagant and hysterical dispute.

Wherein does the truth lie? It is quite true that Bruckner's music shrieks with faults. His symphonies are frequently full of bombast, frequently inflated with musical wind. Too often is he prolix, and too often arid and dull. And yet, to dismiss Bruckner because of these shortcomings is a sad injustice.

.At his best—the *Agnus Dei* of the *Mass in F-minor*, the slow movement of the *Fourth symphony*, the superb opening of the *Seventh*, as well as its other-worldly *Adagio*—Bruckner has given voice to a music whose poignancy and deathlessness must ultimately be accepted. At such moments "he is both the poet and the seer," as Lawrence Gilman has written, "looking at us with fathomless, grave eyes, speaking soberly of incredible things; or uttering magnificence like a Hebrew prophet; or rolling up heavens like a scroll. This is the treasurable Bruckner—the mystic, rhapsodist, prophet, whose speech was transfigured, whose imaginings were penetrated (as Swinburne said of Baudelaire) with the suggestion of indescribable wonders, echoing with a strange murmur of revelation."

"Bruckner's particular significance" wrote Paul Bekker, "lies in his having made use of the most subjective elements of romanticism in the expression of popular feeling and naïvely religious faith. For this reason also his music seems to many of us to possess a calm and tranquil beauty. He differs from Brahms in the first place by the inevitable grandeur of his form, for as a composer of the expansive type he strove for symphonic structure, while the concentration of chamber-music forms was foreign to his nature. The intellectual and psychological factors in romanticism were equally alien to him. Here again he differs significantly from Brahms. Thru the simplicity of his feeling, Bruckner is the first to return to the expression of an impersonal, a universal attitude. That it is which gives him his religious trend and gives his music its tranquility."

Principal works by Anton Bruckner:

CHORAL: *Requiem*; Three masses; *Te Deum*; *Psalm 150*; *Helgoland*; *Abendzauber*.
ORCHESTRA: Nine symphonies.
CHAMBER MUSIC: *String quintet*.

About Anton Bruckner:

Bekker, Paul. *The Story of Music*; Engel, Gabriel. *The Life of Anton Bruckner*; Fuller-Maitland, J. A. *Masters of German Music*; Goellerich, August. *Anton Bruckner: Ein Lebens- und Schaffens-Bild*; Gräflinger, Franz. *Anton Bruckner: Bausteine zu einer Lebens Geschichte*; Grüninger, Fritz. *Der Ehrfürch-*tige; *Anton Bruckner's Leben dem Volk*; Kurth, Ernst. *Bruckner*; Tessmer, Hans. *Anton Bruckner*.

Important recordings of music by Anton Bruckner:

CHORAL: *Mass in E-minor* (CHRISTSCHALL).
ORCHESTRA: *Symphony No. 7 in E-major* (VICTOR-Ormandy).

Alfred Bruneau *1857-1934*

(See *Composers of Today*)

John Bull *1562-1628*

JOHN BULL, distinguished contemporary of William Byrd, was born in England in 1562; both the exact place and date of his birth are unknown.

Between 1572 and 1578, Bull was brought up at the Chapel Royal under the tutelage of William Blitheman. When he completed his studies, he turned to the composition of vocal works. After serving his creative apprenticeship in this field, he abandoned vocal music and devoted himself to the creation of instrumental works.

He acquired an imposing reputation as a virtuoso of the virginal and the organ. On December 24, 1582 he was appointed organist at the Hereford Cathedral. After three years at this post, he was admitted as a Gentleman of the Chapel Royal. In the meanwhile, he did not abandon his studies, receiving his musical baccalaureate from Oxford in 1586, and his doctorate from Cambridge four years later.

By this time, his important position in English music was generally accepted by his compatriots. He came into high favor with English royalty, honored by the Queen with a lease upon several lands and a sinecureship consisting of the Keepership of Enfield Chase.

In 1601, John Bull began an extensive continental tour as virtuoso of the virginal and the organ, achieving great success wherever he performed. The tour was abruptly discontinued because of Bull's failing health. It was on this trip that there took place an event most frequently related about this composer. He had come incognito to the Cathedral of St. Omer. Conducted by one of the musicians into the vestry and being shown a song of forty parts, he was told that there was not a musician in the world who could add an additional part. Bull quietly accepted the challenge, locked himself in the vestry and composed forty more, each more original than the preceeding one. When the musician noticed the ingenuity and talent of the forty additional parts, he cried out: "Only the devil could have accomplished this!" "Not the devil," answered the composer, "but your humble servant, John Bull."

In 1607, John Bull married "Elizabeth Walter of the Strand, aged about twenty-four, daughter of Walter, citizen of London." Three years later, Bull entered the service of Prince Henry, but in 1613 suddenly deserted England to enter the service of the Archduke of Brussels. This departure, the cause of which was veiled in mystery, created a sensation. Bull was greatly admired in England (there were many who esteemed him the greatest musician of the day), and it was a source of amazement that his services should be removed from England. King James dispatched a note to the British Minister in Brussels expressing his indignation that the Archduke of Brussels should show such lack of courtesy in engaging Bull. The reply which the British Minister returned to King James is a bewildering one, and has never been fully explained. He wrote that Bull did "steal out of England thru the guilt of a corrupt conscience in order to escape punishment which notoriously he had deserved and was designed to have been inflicted on him by the hand of justice for his . . . grievous crimes."

John Bull spent the remainder of his life in Belgium. In 1617 he became organist of the Antwerp Cathedral, holding this post with honor until his death. He died in Antwerp on March 13, 1628. Two days after his death he was buried in the Notre Dame Cathedral of Antwerp.

John Bull's importance as a composer rests principally with his works for keyboard instruments, particularly those for the virginal, many of which appear in the monumental *Fitzwilliam Virginal Book*. "Bull's keyboard music . . . is not of equal interest," we are informed by Margaret H. Glyn, "and some of it suggests an excursion in counterpoint, but it is all extremely playable, lying well under the hands. His greatest work in the pianoforte style . . . is his *Walsingham variations,* a big virtuoso piece, containing nearly all present piano technique, if allowance be made for the limited treble compass and the absence of octave passages."

Wanda Landowska, who has brought prominence to the virginal music of John Bull in our day thru her periodic performances, considers these keyboard pieces of William Byrd and John Bull as the most important instrumental music of the entire period. "Something like twenty years separate these two composers, Byrd being the older of the two. . . . Each one of them brings popular music to the same destination. The prowess of augmentation and diminution is as familiar to the one as to the other. And both are intoxicated with perpetual movement, with a harsh and robust rhythm. Notice these clusters of semiquavers which, with Byrd and Bull, roll, overflow and spread out the exuberance of life over the measure-bars."

Principal works by John Bull:

VOCAL: *Almighty God*; *Attend unto my tears*; *Deliver me, O God*; *How joyful and how good*; *In the departure of the Lord*; *In Thee, O Lord*, etc.

INSTRUMENTAL: About 150 pieces for the gan, virginal, viols, etc.

JOHN BULL

About John Bull:

Bridge, Frederick. *Twelve Good Musicians*; Glyn, Margaret H. *About Elizabethan Virginal Music.*
Musical Times 69:127 February 1928.

Important recordings of music by John Bull:

INSTRUMENTAL: *Gigge* (PARLAPHONE); *The King's hunt* (COLUMBIA-Dolmetsch).

Ferruccio Busoni *1866-1924*

FERRUCCIO BENVENUTO BUSONI was born in Empoli, Tuscany, on April 1, 1866, the son of excellent musicians. His father was a professional clarinet-player, and his mother was a pianist of considerable talent.

It was the piano, rather than the clarinet, that attracted Ferruccio Busoni from the first. At the age of four he already could perform upon it any melody that was played for him. Intensive study enabled him to make his debut as concert pianist in his ninth year in Vienna, a performance which aroused the admiration of Eduard Hanslick. One year later, Busoni was to make his bow as a composer, when he himself directed his own *Stabat Mater*.

Busoni now made an extensive tour as child-prodigy thru Italy, Austria and Germany with great success. In Italy, he was honored by being offered a membership in the Philharmonic Academy of Bologna, the youngest musician since Mozart to receive this distinction. His travels, finally, brought him to Leipzig. Here he settled temporarily to absorb its musical life. He came into contact with such musicians as Delius, Mahler, Tschaikovsky and Greig, and in their company acquired a maturer conception of his art. At this time, he composed his first string quartet, a work of adult maturity, and made the first of his distinguished transcriptions, for piano, of the organ works of Johann Sebastian Bach, the *D-major fugue*.

In 1889, he was called to Helsingfors to become professor at the Conservatory. He remainded here only a brief period. The following year, the Rubinstein award brought him to Russia, where he taught at the Moscow Conservatory, and where he met Rimsky-Korsakoff and Glazunov. One year later found Busoni in still an-

other continent, America, whither he had come to teach at the New England Conservatory in Boston. Simultaneously, he gave concerts on the piano, rapidly acquiring a reputation as one of the greatest interpreters of piano literature of his time.

He was, however, so keenly dissatisfied with his piano performances that he decided at this time to go into retirement in order to take up the study of the piano from the very beginning, based upon an entirely new method. For this purpose, he established himself in Berlin in 1894. For several years he devoted himself completely to studying piano technique intensively, varying this routine with composition and direction of symphony concerts. Then, feeling satisfied with his progress, he embarked upon a new concert tour. From this time on he was acclaimed as one of the preeminent pianists of the generation.

In 1912, Bustoni's first opera, *Die Brautwahl,* was given its première in Hamburg with negligible success.

1913 found Busoni in Bologna, where he served as director of the Liceo Musicale. The war broke out during his activities as teacher and director, and— disgusted and horrified by the direction in which his country was heading— Busoni fled to Zürich to seclude himself from a world gone mad. Here, he found escape in feverish composition and in the direction of the *Concerts d'abonnement.*

When the war ended, Busoni returned to the concert stage and made a triumphant tour of Paris, Italy and Germany. There followed once again choruses of praise for his performances. His activity as concert pianist did not, however, curtail his composition. In 1921, the Berlin State Opera presented *Turandot* and *Arlecchino,* both of which enjoyed considerable prestige and honor.

The collapse of the German mark brought Busoni to Paris where he hoped to settle permanently. Here, on October of 1923, his frend, Isidor Philipp, noticed that Busoni appeared ill, and urged him to visit a specialist. The physician told him that his days were limited, that if he would give up all drinking and smoking he might live another six months.

Ferruccio Busoni died in Berlin on July 27, 1924. He had suffered from chronic inflammation of the kidneys, together with inflammation of the muscles of the heart. His greatest work, an opera—*Doktor Faust*—lay uncompleted upon his desk. *Doktor Faust,* put into final shape by Philipp Jarnach, was given its first performance in Dresden on May 21, 1925.

Ferruccio Busoni, who was known to be a very eccentric personality, was genial and lovable. He was famous for his sense of humor, which frequently could be stingingly malicious; his conversation was always spiced with wit and mellowed with wisdom. His preferences included cigars, liquor and cheerful company. He loathed the music of Wagner, admired Bach and Beethoven, but adored Mozart. "Mozart," he once wrote, "is up to the present the most perfect manifestation of musical talent."

Edward J. Dent has written that the "real Busoni" was never known or understood by the public at large. "He knew himself inwardly to be a composer and perhaps something more; it is not too much to say that he knew himself to be a philosopher and prophet. It was not merely personal vanity or ambition that dominated his thoughts; any weakness of that kind he had shaken off years ago. What made it impossible for the world to understand him was that he felt himself to be a man with a mission. The ordinary artistic world can understand easily enough a man whose motives are purely commercial; it can even extend a certain tolerance to mere vanity; but a man who regards his art as if it were a religion which he has been called by heaven both to preach and to practise, regardless of worldly conventions and understandings, finds himself in an impossible position."

Busoni was a prolific composer, producing a quantity of works in almost every field of musical endeavor. As to this output, Cecil Gray has written, "one finds great qualities—striking and original conceptions, gigantic technical resource— yet one is never wholly satisfied with any single work. It is in the mental process which intervenes between the conception and execution of a work that Busoni would seem to fail—in the em-

FERRUCCIO BUSONI

bodiment of the abstract idea in musical flesh, as it were. There is a lack of distinction about the musical material of his buildings; one does not feel that any discrimination has been exercised by the composer in its choice. . . . It is at least certain that his most impressive works, and those which come nearest to being successful, are those which are built out of the musical material of others. . . . He is a master builder to whom could be confided the execution of the most difficult tasks and gigantic conceptions, provided that they have already been put on paper by the architect. . . . He is like the Cyclops, the workman of the Gods, but not themselves gods, nor yet mere mortals."

The above criticism was penned before *Doktor Faust* was introduced to the world, a work that is generally accepted as Busoni's crowning artistic achievement. "There is in Faustus," wrote Lazare Saminsky, "a mellowness and warmth which is granted only to creators with a feeling for the human voice. . . . In this work his inbred eclecticism is much less manifest than in any other work—the *Piano concerto* or the *Clarinet concertino,* for example. He has contrived to give his opera a unity, a style and a flexibility of musical action that might serve as a challenge to any creator. His fastidious speech and pure, exalted musicianship usher Busoni into the sublime circle of Liszt, Scriabin, Debussy and Schönberg. Busoni is one of the few embodiments of that elevated artistry surviving into our own busy time.

"As an operatic conception *Doktor Faust* is a relief from the stodgy and artificial continuity of the Wagnerian drama. The return to the fantastic and picturesque, to whim and episode, to the elegent adventure in art sought by Berlioz and Delacroix, is more relevant to our time and to the new opera than the tedious consequentialism of Wagner.

"Another feeling that remains after hearing *Faust* is one of profound admiration for a race that still gives us masters who are, much more than Titus was, the 'consolation of humanity.'"

Ferruccio Busoni was also a distinguished theoretician. The bulk of his theories on music appear in a book which has been translated into English, *A New Aesthetic of Music*.

Principal works by Ferruccio Busoni:

OPERA: *Die Brautwahl*; *Turandot*; *Arlecchino*; *Doktor Faust*.

ORCHESTRA: *Symphonic suite*; *Concerto for violin and orchestra*; *Lustspiel overture*; *Nocturne symphonique*; *Concertino for clarinet and small orchestra*; *Divertimento*; *Tanzwalzer*; *Concerto for piano and orchestra*.

CHAMBER MUSIC: Two string quartets.
Songs, Pieces for the piano, etc.

About Ferruccio Busoni:

Dent, Edward J. *Ferruccio Busoni*; Gray, Cecil. *Survey of Contemporary Music*; Leichentritt, Hugo. *Busoni*; Pannain, Guido. *Modern Composers*; Saminsky, Lazare. *Music of Our Day*.
Musical Quarterly 7:331 July 1921; *Sackbut* 2:33 June 1921.

Important recordings of music by Ferruccio Busoni:

PIANO: *Ballettszene in D-major* (ODEON); *Elegie* (POLYDOR).

Dietrich Buxtehude *1637-1707*

"As John the Baptist was to Christ so was. . . . Buxtehude to Bach"
—A. EAGLEFIELD HULL

DIETRICH BUXTEHUDE, distinguished contemporary of Bach and Handel, was born in Helsingborg, Sweden, in 1637. His father, Johann Buxtehude, who for almost thirty years

was the organist of the St. Olaf Church in Helsingör, Denmark, was his only teacher, introducing him at an early age to the library of great organ music. Young Buxtehude was an apt pupil. Upon completing his studies, he held several minor organ posts in Helsingör (between 1657 and 1660) attracting attention to his virtuosity.

At the age of thirty, Buxtehude migrated to Lübeck where he became organist at St. Mary's, marrying the daughter of his predecessor, Tunder, as was prescribed by the rules of this position. For forty years he remained here, acquiring a reputation as organist which spanned the continent. "There is no doubting that Buxtehude was a remarkable player who exploited all the possible effects of his magnificent, probably unique, instrument," wrote A. Eaglefield Hull. "His works prove it. To mention one point only, his music contains many more directions than Bach's for rapid changes of keyboard; and whereas it is possible to play thru Bach's pieces without changing manua's, it is not possible to do so with Buxtehude's organ music."

Especially famous were Buxtehude's regular *Abendmusik* concerts, which took place for five consecutive Sundays, prior to Christmas. These concerts, which featured great organ and choral music, were so famous that both Handel and Bach made pilgrimages to attend them, the former coming in 1703, and the latter two years later.

Dietrich Buxtehude died in Lübeck on the ninth of May, 1707.

It is not possible to overestimate his influence. Johann Sebastian Bach was a pupil of Buxtehude and was vitally affected by his teaching. Buxtehude solidified those forms later brought to their highest peaks of sublimity by Bach, and first suggested their marvelous artistic potentialities: the passacaglia, the chaconne, the prelude and fugue, the fantasia, and the choral prelude. Of these forms, the choral prelude seemed to be Buxtehude's most felicitous vehicle of expression. "The choral prelude," wrote Cecil Gray, "was raised to an unexampled pitch of elaboration, and enriched with every conceivable device of contrapuntal and decorative resource at his disposal. In his hands, indeed, the theme is frequently so varied and adorned with arabesques as to become totally unrecognizable, and even when presented textually it is often hidden from sight altogether under the exuberant welter of ornamentation with which it is surrounded."

In commenting upon the nature of Buxtehude's music, Romain Rolland has explained: "Writing for a concert public, and not for religious service, he felt the need of making his music of a kind which would appeal to everyone. . . . Buxtehude avoided in his music the ornate and clustering polyphony which was really his *métier*. He sought nothing but clear, pleasing and striking designs, and even aimed at descriptive music. He willingly sacrified himself by intensifying his expression, and what he lost in abundance he gained in power. The homophonic character of his writing, the neatness of his beautiful melodic designs of a popular clarity, the insistence of the rhythmic and repetition of phrases which sink down into the heart in so obsessive a manner are all essentially Handelian traits. No less is the magnificent triumph of the ensembles, his manner of painting in bold masses of light and shade."

Principal works by Dietrich Buxtehude:

ORGAN: Choral preludes, fantasias, passacaglias, chaconnes, fugues, etc.
CHAMBER MUSIC: Sonatas for strings, etc.

About Dietrich Buxtehude:

Gray, Cecil. *A History of Music*; Pirro, André. *Dietrich Buxtehude*; Seiffert, Max. *Buxtehude, Handel, Bach*.
Chesterian 14:72 January-February 1933; *Monthly Musical Record* 50:147 July 1920.

Important recordings of music by Dietrich Buxtehude:

ORGAN: *Fugue in F-major* (GRAMOPHONE); *In dulci jubilo* (ULTRAPHONE); *Komm heiliger geist* (KANTOREI); *Prelude and fugue in E-major* (ARTIPHONE); *Prelude and fugue in G-minor* (BRUNSWICK); *Prelude, fugue and chaconne* (ODEON).
CHAMBER MUSIC: *Sonata in D-major,* for violin, violoncello and harpsichord (ARTIPHONE).

William Byrd *1543-1623*

WILLIAM BYRD, the father of the Elizabethan school of music, was said to have been born in Lincolnshire in 1543. It is not known who his parents were, or from what sources they stemmed. It is known only that, as a boy, William Byrd studied at the St. Paul's School where his education was comprehensive; in later life, he revealed a thorough knowledge of mathematics and Latin.

The first tangible fact connected with Byrd's life which is in our possession is his appointment as organist of Lincoln Cathedral, which came to him on February 27, 1563. Six years later he was sworn in as Gentleman of the Chapel Royal, sharing with Thomas Tallis— another eminent composer of the period —the honorary post of organist. On January 22, 1575, both Byrd and Tallis received from the Queen a patent for the printing and selling of music-paper, which, upon the death of Tallis, passed on exclusively to Byrd. This venture was unsuccessful, for, unfortunately, the business acumen of both Tallis and Byrd was not equal to their musical gifts.

Byrd, who was in high favor with the Queen, was granted by her leases to two manors. In 1572, he went south with his wife and children, and after a short stay at Harlington, settled in his second manor at Stondon Place, in Essex, where he was to remain the greater part of his life. In 1575, he first enjoyed prestige as a composer by publishing, together with Tallis, a volume of *Cantiones* that contained sixteen motets by Tallis and eighteen by Byrd.

With the death of Thomas Tallis in 1585, William Byrd became the undisputed monarch of English music. His creative force was, henceforth, to be fertile and versatile. In 1588, he published his first volume of madrigals, thereby introducing and establishing a form in English music which was soon thereafter to become one of the most famous expressions of the Elizabethan era. The madrigal was first introduced to England by an amateur-musician, Nicolas Yonge, who, intimately acquainted with Italian and Netherland madrigals, had frequent performances

WILLIAM BYRD

of them at his home. In the early part of 1588, Yonge published a volume of fifty-seven of the best specimens of foreign madrigals; it was in this volume that there appeared two additional madrigals by William Byrd, the first examples of English madrigal-writing.

In 1590, Byrd once again was the innovator by composing extensively for the virginal, becoming the first great composer to turn his talents towards a keyboard instrument.

In 1610, he composed the first of his monumental Masses, which was—wrote W. H. Hadow—"the finest of their kind ever written by an English composer, and of the highest rank the world over. Not Lassus or Palestrina ever rose to a loftier and more serene eminence."

It is believed that William Byrd died at Stondon Place in Essex on July 4, 1623. Upon his death, he was reverently referred to by the Chapel Royal Check Book as "Father of Musicke."

There can be no question but that Byrd is one of the great names in the history of English music. He was a composer of originality, inspiration and inexhaustible inventiveness. He enjoys greatness particularly because of "the splendid range and opulence of his melody," to quote W. H. Hadow once more, "the audacities of his harmonic color which so shocked the pedants of

the nineteenth century and which have proved to be so certainly and triumphantly right; the depth and sensitiveness of his emotion; his variety of structure, always adventurous and always suitable to the subject proposed."

His influence upon the history of musical art has been far-reaching. First and foremost, he was the parent of English madrigal, the first composer in England to bring prominence to this form and, consequently, to pave the way for the great line of madrigal composers who were to enrich Elizabethan music immeasurably. The madrigal specimens which William Byrd composed for Nicolas Yonge's collection aroused so great an enthusiasm that thruout England composers began to create works in the new form. It was not long before a volume containing the most representative examples of English madrigals was published, *The Triumphs of Oriana* in 1603.

The madrigal is a secular song in three or more independent parts, usually of a light and delicate nature. Many of these madrigals were love-songs; others were meditative, satiric or humorous. It was essentially a domestic form of art, not intended for concert performance. After dinner, the company would receive booklets of madrigals and would join in singing them as naturally as they might play cards or dice.

Equally significant was Byrd's influence upon instrumental music. Up to this time, the emphasis had been placed entirely upon vocal music. With a remarkable library of virginal pieces, about one hundred and twenty of which have survived (some of which appear in the *Fitzwilliam Virginal Book*), William Byrd proved emphatically what a remarkable medium for artistic expression this keyboard instrument could become. "If we consider all this keyboard music as a whole," we learn from Frank Howes, "that it is not great music even in a small form, as the Church music is great or as the secular madrigals are great. It is not so profound as the one or so vigorous and assured as the other. Much of it is tentative and hardly interesting to play or to listen to. But much of it . . . is charming, some of it is gay, a good deal has the grave wistfulness so characteristic of the composer, a little of it is deliciously fanciful and a little is playful. Some of it is brilliant technically and some brilliant in sound."

William Byrd was (to conclude with a few lines of Wanda Landowska) "a poet. The curve of his melodic line, which is both sinuous and ornamental, is full of sweetness, with a content fresh and savoury." Iconoclast and innovator, as he was in his madrigal and virginal pieces, dreamer and artist, as he was in his church music, he was the brightest light of the Elizabethan era, and one of the glories of English music.

Principal works by William Byrd:

VOCAL: Masses; motets; madrigals; psalms; songs; sonnets, etc.

INSTRUMENTAL: Fantasias; preludes; pieces for the virginal, etc.

About William Byrd:

Hadow, W. H. *Collected Essays*; Hadow, W. H. *English Music*; Howes, Frank. *William Byrd.*

Important recordings of music by William Byrd:

VOCAL: *Agnus Dei* (COLUMBIA); *Lullaby, my sweet little baby* (COLUMBIA); *Though Amaryllis dance in green* (ROYCROFT-English Singers); Madrigals, *Come to me grief forever, This sweet and merry month of May, Turn our captivity, etc.* (GRAMOPHONE-English Singers).

INSTRUMENTAL: *The Bells* (ANTHOLOGIE SONORE); *Pavan* and *Galliard* (COLUMBIA); *Sellinger's round* (PARLAPHONE); *Variations on O mistresse mine* (COLUMBIA); *Wolsey's wilde* (VICTOR-Landowska).

Giulio Caccini *1550-1618*

GIULIO DI MICHAELANGELO CACCINI, one of the founders of the Italian opera, was born in Rome; modern research has placed the year as 1550.

Possessing a voice of beautiful quality, as well as an unusual talent for music, Caccini was trained in voice and lute at an early age by Scipione della Palla. In 1564, Caccini came to Florence where he procured a position as court-singer and lutist to the Grand Duke of Tuscany. He remained in Florence until the end of his life, except for a brief intermission in 1604 when he visited Paris.

In 1580, Caccini came into contact with a group of art-lovers who gathered regularly at the home of Giovanni Bardi, a cultured dilettante. These art-lovers included Vincenzo Galilei, a talented performer on the lute and viol and an amateur composer (the father of the world-famous scientist Galileo), Ottavio Rinuccini, a poet, Jacopo Peri, a famous composer. These artists, who today are known as the "camerata," were inspired by the Renaissance to turn to Greek models for the creation of a new musical art. Weary of polyphonic music and the manner in which it was suffering abuse at the hands of contemporary composers, they fed upon Aristoxenus' treatise on music and from it drew the idea of making music use speech as a model for its form. In this way, they evolved the recitative.

The recitative was brought to the attention of the music world in a series of "monodies" by Caccini, published in 1602 under the title of *Nuove musiche*. In his preface, Caccini explained the aim of this "new mission." "These wise and noble personages have constantly strengthened me and with the most lucid reasons determined me to place no value upon that music which makes it impossible to understand the words and thus to destroy the unity and meter, sometimes lengthening them in order to suit the counterpoint—a real mangling of the poetry; but they have influenced me to hold to the principle so greatly extolled by Plato and other philosophers: 'Let music be, first of all, language and rhythm, and secondly tone, but not vice-versa.'"

It may be true, as Pietro della Valle emphasized strongly, that Caccini was brought to the composition of "monodies" only because he was a poor contrapuntist. If this is so, his weakness was proved to be a boon to the development of the musical art. Without a doubt, Caccini's *Nuove musiche* was an epoch-making work, definitely making a break from polyphony—to which music had been enslaved for so long a time—and pointing a finger in that direction which, in later centuries, was to bring opera and the song-form to their inevitable destinations. "It must be confessed," wrote Giovanni Battista

Doni, "that we owe to him, in a great measure, the new and graceful manner of singing, which at that time spread itself all over Italy; for he composed a great number of airs which he taught to innumerable scholars."

But the recitative was not the only important invention of the "camerata." Imbued with the Greek ideals of art, they determined to bring music back to the secular theatre. The first work in this new form was produced by Jacopo Peri.

Jacopo Peri was born in Florence on August 20, 1561. He was a pupil of Cristoforo Malvezzi, the well-known canon and chapel-master in Florence. Being a member of the "camerata," Peri was in the centre of the musical discussions, and he was urged to compose a work in the new style. On a libretto by Rinuccini, he composed *Dafne,* credited as being the first opera in musical history, performed in 1597 at the Palazzo Corsi. In 1600, Peri composed his second and last opera, *Euridice,* commissioned to do so for the festivities attending the marriage of Henry IV of France to Maria de Medici. Jacopo Peri died in Florence on August 12, 1633.

Caccini was not slow in following Peri's lead. In 1600, Caccini published his own opera, *Euridice.* From that time on he wrote a series of operas which for the first time definitely established the opera as an important art form. Combarieu speaks, in his history of music, of the "monotony," the "gaps" and the "false vocal ornaments" of Caccini's *Euridice.* Its historical importance, however, cannot be doubted.

Carl Engel has commented upon the singular importance of the "camerata" in the history of music. "The Florentine experimenters rendered musical art one service which cannot be too highly valued. With their demand that music pay greater heed to the words and express more accurately the *sentiments* of the words, they stressed the quality of feeling, of emotion in music. Music should come from the heart as well as from the brain. Musical painting, even program music, can be found in some of the madrigals. The only

actual invention of the Florentine musicians was their musico-dramatic speech—the so-called *stilo recitativo,* or *stilo rappresantativo.* What they aimed at—even if they did not perfect it at once—was musical eloquence, moulded over the prosody of the text. Their new style was intended to be "representative" indeed; that is, expressive of sentiments which move the human breast, of different states of mind, of varying moods of the soul."

Caccini was not, creatively, a great composer; his music would today afford very little aesthetic pleasure. "A curious and ingenious spirit, he lacked power," wrote Robert Marchal. "He is not one of the great musical forces in the collective spirit of a people who drain their silent aspirations to pour them into tones. . . . Like the poets who were his collaborators, he is lovable and superficial. With a strong conscience he worked at the foundation of a structure which greater talents have built up. . . . But he indicated at the same time the new possibilities. . . . Let us permit the *Nuove musiche* and *Euridice* to rest quietly in their eternal sleep, and let us not do Caccini the evil service of awakening them. But let us remember that their author was a workman of first importance, and that he pointed out a direction, to those who followed him— the realm of Song—which worthier and stronger souls than he were to enrich and ennoble."

How operas were performed for the general public in Caccini's day and shortly afterwards, has been described by Pietro della Valle. A cart brought an opera company to the public square where the opera was performed several times a day. And the appeal of these operas was so great that "there were some who even continued following our cart to ten or twelve different places where it stopped, and who never quitted us as long as we remained in the street, which was from four o'clock in the evening until after midnight."

Principal works by Giulio Caccini:

OPERA: *Euridice; Combattimento d'Apolline col serpente; Il Ratto di Cefale* (with Peri).
VOCAL: *Nuove musiche;* Madrigals, etc.

About Giulio Caccini:

Combarieu, J. *Histoire de la Musique*; Ehrichs, A. *Giulio Caccini*; Ewen, David (editor). *From Bach to Stravinsky*; Gérold, Théodor. *L'Art du Chant*; Henderson, W. J. *Some Forerunners of the Italian Opera.*

Important recordings of music by Giulio Caccini:

SELECTIONS FROM OPERA: *Euridice*, "Non piango e non sospiro" (VICTOR).

VOCAL: *Amarilli,* solo madrigal, and *Fere selvagge,* madrigal (MIA).

Giacomo Carissimi *1604-1674*

GIACOMO CARISSIMI, father of the oratorio, was born in a small town near Rome, Marino by name, in 1604. The biographical material available on Carissimi is so meagre that it can be summarized in a few lines. In his twentieth year, he served as an organist at the Cathedral of Tivoli, a position which brought him a measure of fame. In 1628, he went to Rome, procuring there a post which he held until the end of his life, that of chapel-master at St. Apollinaris. His music career from that time on, though uneventful, was rich in achievement. Thru his composition and thru his teaching (his pupils included such eminent musicians of the age as Alessandro Scarlatti, Bassani and Buononcini), his influence was widely felt in the Italian music of his time. He died in Rome in 1674.

While most Italian composers of this period devoted themselves almost exclusively to the newly developed operatic form, Carissimi turned his enormous gifts to Church music. Not the least of his accomplishments was the enrichment and plasticity of form which he brought to the cantata, thereby paving the road for Johann Sebastian Bach. Equally important was his influence upon the oratorio. He took the crude form of Cavaliere's *La Rappresentazione di anima e di corpo* (often referred to as the first oratorio in musical history) and brought it such technical and artistic distinction that he is generally recognized by the musical historian as the father of the oratorio.

Carissimi's significance as a composer branches in several directions.

He brought to further development the recitative form of Caccini. "He deprived it in a great measure of the formal closes and cadences," explains George Hogarth, "which it had in common with the airs of that time and rendered it more articulate and expressive by adopting the accents and inflections of speech." He established, for the first time, new technical resources which were later to become integral parts of the musical art. "In his music," writes Theodore M. Finney, "the tonality of key, at least in its diatonic implications, became a realized fact, and the doom of the old ecclesiastic modes was sealed. The principle which is fundamental to all monophonic form—repetition after contrast . . . finally became the accepted basis for structure."

Most important of all, Carissimi stands in musical history as the mighty Colossus who spanned the period between the "old art" of polyphony and the "new art," fusing the two styles into one, so to speak. "The impetuous reformers in the style of Galilei," to quote Karl Nef, "quite unreasonably desired to forget completely the old choral art. However, they soon found themselves compelled to borrow from it, and a complete amalgamation took place in the case of Carissimi, who treated the chorus in his oratorios in as masterly a manner as he did the solo, and with consummate skill allowed them to relieve and supplement one another. He stripped off the realistic elements which had long cleaved to the new music. In his compositions, the new style confronts us in perfect clarity. Carissimi advances to a classical purity, and he was fully conscious of this fact, for he had achieved it only thru struggle."

The essential characteristics of Carissimi's music are, in the estimation of Cecil Gray, "pathos and a sweetness which sometimes hover perilously on the verge of sentimentality and effeminacy." "In his arias, too," wrote George Hogarth, "a simplicity . . . and a flow of melody, which are still, and we apprehend will always be, sufficient to give delight to unperverted taste."

Carissimi's style was facile, unpretentious and unacademic. He always made a conscious effort to avoid complexity. "Oh, how difficult it is to be simple!" he once told a friend; simplicity of structure and development is one of the most distinguishing traits of all his compositions.

Principal works by Giacomo Carissimi:

ORATORIO: *Felicitas beatorum*; *Lucifer*; *Job*; *Jonas*; *The Last judgment*; *Abraham and Isaac*; *David and Jonathan*; *Daniel*; *Jephtha,* etc.

About Giacomo Carissimi:

Hiller, Ferdinand. *Musikalisches und Personliches*; Hogarth, George. *Musical History, Biography and Criticism*; Nef, Karl. *An Outline of the History of Music*; Schmitz, E. *Beitrage zur Geschichte der Italienischen Kammerkantate im 17 Jahrhundert*; Vogel, E. *Die Oratorientechnik G. Carissimis.*

Important recordings of music by Giacomo Carissimi:

SELECTIONS FROM ORATORIO: *Ezechias,* "Air" (COLUMBIA).

VOCAL: *Vittorio, mio core* (VICTOR).

Francesco Cavalli *1602-1676*

"Cavalli's musical genius. . . . dominated the whole of Italian opera writers in the 17th century."—ROMAIN ROLLAND

PIETRO FRANCESCO CAVALLI was born in Crema on February 14, 1602. His father—whose name was not Cavalli but Gian Battista Caletti-Bruni —was the choirmaster of the town. It was from him that young Cavalli learned his first lessons in music.

Blessed with a beautiful voice, Cavalli soon joined his father's choir where he attracted the attention of Fredrico Cavalli, the Podestá of Crema, who was so impressed with the tender quality of the boy's voice and his acute musical intelligence that he begged the father for permission to adopt the boy. Gian Caletti-Bruni, whose meagre income as choirmaster converted everyday existence into a perpetual struggle, finally assented. Thus, in 1616, the young musician was brought by his patron to Venice where he became a singer in the choir of St. Mark and a pupil of the great Monteverdi.

His life henceforth was closely associated with Venice. In 1627, he was registered as a tenor in St. Mark's under the name of Francesco Caletto. When, in 1640, he was appointed organist of the Cathedral, he had already assumed the name of his patron. In 1665, he rose to the position of head organist, and three years later he became chapel master.

Meanwhile, he had made several trips to Paris. In 1660, he was invited to the French capital to produce his opera *Xerse* in connection with the marriage ceremonies of Louis XIV. He was so successful that, in 1662, he was once again called to Paris, this time to present his *Ercole amante* in celebration of the Peace of the Pyrenees.

Francesco Cavalli died in Venice on January 14, 1676. At his funeral a Requiem was performed which he had composed shortly before his death expressly for this occasion. His ashes rest in the Church of San Lorenzo in Venice.

Cavalli's name is prominent in the early history of Italian opera. During his lifetime, the popularity of the opera as an art-form grew prodigiously. In 1637, the first public opera house was opened in Venice, proving so successful that German princes retained theatre boxes for themselves, keeping constantly in close touch with the new works. Between 1641 and 1749 no less than thirty different operas were produced successfully. Cavalli, therefore, found the time uniquely propitious for the production of his art.

Altho Cavalli began the composition of operas as early as 1639, he did not gain prominence until several years later when the first of his successful operas, *Le Nozze di Teti e di Peleo,* was produced in Venice. This 'work is of importance to us particularly in view of the fact that this is the first work in this new dramatic form which was officially termed an "opera," or—to be more accurate—"opera scenica." The success of *Le Nozze* encouraged Cavalli, who realized that he was on the right path. From that time on, he produced no less than thirty-eight operas which were eminently successful, and which were instrumental in bringing the form of the opera to new phases of development.

In the history of early Italian opera, Cavalli—who followed Monteverdi and continued his work—is significant for several reasons. First and foremost is the fact that it was he who introduced the "aria"—as distinct from the recitative—into opera (in *Giasone*). Equally important was Cavalli's adroitness in the use of the orchestra. Like Monteverdi, he did not use the orchestra merely as a feeble accompaniment, but rather depended upon it as the vital spine of his music. "In his hands," wrote R. A. Streatfeild, "the orchestra began to assume new importance. His attempts to give musical expression to the sights and sounds of nature—the murmur of the sea, the rippling of the brook and the tempestuous fury of the winds—mark an interesting step in the history of orchestral development."

Finally, Cavalli enriched melodic treatment immeasurably. His operas were distinguished, as Combarieu points out, "in the manner in which he treats the voices: the aria, the duet (which he liked particularly) and the choruses. . . . With a very neat rhythm, he has given a more agreeable allure to the melody, and sometimes made it very popular. He is most near to modern tonality."

"Cavalli speaks the language of his time and borrowed from his master, Monteverdi, a part of his vocabulary," wrote Henri Prunières in summing up the composer's artistic significance. "It is thru the vigor, the freedom, the sparkle of his style as well as by the richness of his speech that he intrigues us. . . . If he is simple, if he pleases himself with consonant harmonies, it is not because of his incapacity to write a more complicated music . . . but because he has expressly chosen to do so."

"Cavalli is at his best in recitative and dramatic expression; and he is fresh and original in melody," to quote Taddo Wiel. "He may perhaps be blamed for certain concessions when, stooping to the popular element in his solo songs and in comic scenes, he gives free course to his facile vein. They are, however, concessions to the taste of the country and to the times. . . . He revealed himself in truth superior in great dramatic and passionate scenes, and in scenes of enchantment, frequently found in the melodrama of that day."

Principal works by Francesco Cavalli:

OPERA: *Le Nozze di Teti e di Peleo*; *Didone*; *Giasone*; *Xerse*; *Ercole amante*; *Erismena*; *Cro*; *Coriolano,* etc.

CHORAL: *Requiem*; motets. etc.

About Francesco Cavalli:

Combarieu, J. *Histoire de la Musique*; Laurencie, Lionel de la. *Les Créateurs de L'opéra Français*; Prunières, Henri. *Cavalli et L'opéra Venetien au 17e Siècle*; Streatfeild, R. A. *The Opera*.

Important recordings of music by Francesco Cavalli:

SELECTIONS FROM OPERA: *Ercole amante,* "Scène de sommeil" and *Giasone,* "Invocation de Médée" (COLUMBIA); *Xerse,* "Beato chu puo" (MIA).

Marcantonio Cesti   *1620-1669*

MARCANTONIO CESTI, distinguished contemporary of Cavalli and Carissimi, was born in Arezzo between 1618 and 1623, modern research placing the year as 1620.

Coming to Florence, the seat of Italian culture at the time, Cesti became a pupil of Carissimi. When his studies were completed, he was appointed chapelmaster (1646). In 1660, he became a member of the papal choir. During the last three years of his life, he served as vice chapel-master in Vienna. Shortly before his death he returned to Italy, dying in Venice in 1669.

Cesti, while less significant than his eminent contemporaries—Cavalli, Monteverdi and Carissimi—was, nevertheless, a popular opera composer during his day who contributed greatly towards the development of operatic form. His principal distinction lies in the fact that he applied the progress made by Carissimi in the oratorio to opera. "In Cesti's operas," explains Theodore M. Finney, "the most famous of which was *L'Orontea*, the tendency towards lyricism—towards placing the importance on pleasing, smooth-flowing melody, at the expense of intensity of expression—is even more perceptible than in the works of Cavalli and Carissimi."

Something of the enormous popularity that Cesti's most famous opera, *L'Orontea,* enjoyed might be suggested by the fact that it was produced in Venice in 1649, 1666 and 1683; in Milan in 1662, and in Bologna in 1669.

Comparing Cesti with his distinguished contemporaries, Cavalli and Monteverdi, R. A. Streatfeild wrote: "Those of his operas which remain to us show a far greater command of orchestral and vocal resource than Monteverdi or Cavalli could boast, but so far as real expression or sincerity are concerned, they are inferior to the less cultured efforts of the earlier musicians."

Continuing the comparison, Cecil Gray wrote: "In Cavalli's work the balance between aria and recitative is more or less equal; in that of Cesti the arias definitely predominate in number, length and significance. In the operas of the former the musical treatment generally coincides with the dramatic interest; in those of the latter the situation is unfolded in dry and perfunctory recitative, and the musical development reserved for moments of dramatic repose. . . . In fact, he continually tends to sacrifice dramatic to lyrical expressiveness, and. . . . one finds in his work, to a far greater extent than in that of Cavalli, an attempt to effect a compromise between the conflicting claims of monodony and polyphony."

Principal works by Marcantonio Cesti:

OPERA: *L'Orontea*; *Cesare amante*; *La Dori*; *Tito*; *Semiramide*; *Il Pomo d'oro*; *L'Argia*; *La Schiava fortunata*, etc.

CHORAL: Motets, canzonets, cantatas, etc.

About Marcantonio Cesti:

Burney, Charles. *A General History of Music*; Finney, Theodore M. *A History of Music*; Streatfeild, R. A. *The Opera*. *La Revue Musicale* 9:169 June 1928.

Important recordings of music by Marcantonio Cesti:

SELECTIONS FROM OPERA: *L'Orontea*, "Intorno all'idol mio" (VICTOR).

Emmanuel Chabrier *1841-1894*

"Chabrier is not only a great musician; he is one of our greatest."—CHARLES KOECHLIN

A LEXIS EMMANUEL CHABRIER was born in Ambert, in Auvergne, on January 18, 1841. As a child, he be-

gan the study of music with a Spanish refugee, Saporta by name, who accompanied each lesson with lusty blows of the hand.

It was not at first intended that Chabrier turn towards music as a profession. His father, a lawyer, was determined to have his son follow in his footsteps. For this purpose, Chabrier was sent to Paris, where he completed his legal studies. Following this, he was appointed to a position in the Ministère de l'Intérieur. He did not, however, neglect music. During this period in the ministry, Chabrier followed the study of the piano under Edouard Wolf, and harmony, counterpoint and fugue under Richard Hammer and Semet.

After devoting more than a score of years to law, he suddenly turned more seriously to musical composition. His earliest creations were two operettas, *L'Étoile* (produced by the Bouffes Parisiens in 1877) and *L'Éducation manquée* (presented at the Cercle de la Presse in 1879), both of which revealed considerable talent. Music, however, was still to Chabrier only a pastime to which he devoted himself in hours free from his work.

In 1880, Chabrier took a short leave of absence from the ministry for the purpose of attending a performance of Wagner's *Tristan* in Munich. That performance changed the entire course of his life. Vincent D'Indy has left us a description of how deeply Chabrier was moved by the music, of how in the very opening prelude the tears coursed down his cheeks as he said: "I have waited ten years to hear that 'A' in the violoncello!" It was this performance of *Tristan* that brought a vow to Chabrier's lips: He would henceforth devote himself completely to music.

In 1882, he took the final steps to bring this vow to fulfillment. Resigning from the ministry, he affiliated himself with the Lamoureux orchestra as assistant conductor. Here, he was a vital factor in bringing about a concert performance of the first two acts of *Tristan*.

He, likewise, devoted himself assiduously to composition. His importance as a creative artist was to become apparent much sooner than even he dared to hope. In 1883, he left for a three-month vacation in Spain where, for the first time, he came into contact with Spanish folk-music. Spain fascinated him—its women, its dances and, most of all, its music. He took copious notes of musical themes and rhythms, autocthonously Spanish, which intrigued him.

Upon his return to France, Chabrier composed a work, utilizing Spanish rhythms and *motifs*, an expression of his own enthusiasm for that exotic country. Lamoureux, the conductor, heard Chabrier play piano sketches of this work, and was so delighted with it that he urged Chabrier to orchestrate it. On November 4, 1883, Lamoureux introduced Chabrier's *España* at his concerts —and, despite the fact that both composer and conductor had prophesied at the final rehearsals that the work would be a failure because of its novel material, it was phenomenally successful, so successul, as a matter of fact, that Chabrier's reputation as a composer was firmly established after the first performance.

España has remained one of Chabrier's most popular works, a perennial favorite on symphony programs.

"*España* constitutes a musical tableau possessing an extraordinary intensity of life," wrote Julien Tiersot in analysis, "a brilliant color and a dazzling sonority. Across the seductive and intriguing rhythms of its themes one seems to perceive the contortions of Spanish dancers carried away as by some frenetic whirlwind. Strange associations of sounds . . . accumulations of harmonies which are so overcharged and so voluntarily incomplete, chords with free combinations, rhythms either broken or badly superimposed—this is what one perceives in this work which is so different from anything one has heard in France, Germany or anywhere else."

It was inevitable that Wagner's profound influence upon Chabrier should draw him into the theatre. Provided with an admirable libretto upon a mediaeval legend, written by Catulle Mendes, the poet, Chabrier turned to music-drama soon after the success of *España*. This music-drama—it was *Gwendoline*— had its first performance at the Théâtre de la Monnaie in Brussels in 1886, but because of the bankruptcy of the man-

EMMANUEL CHABRIER

agement was given only two performances. However, *Gwendoline* was to be given many performances in Germany between the years of 1889 and 1893 where it enjoyed a quiet but substantial success.

Chabrier's idiom, however, was not meant for serious music-drama. After the composition of *Gwendoline* (Chabrier's homage to Wagner), he returned to his first-love, comic opera. The result was what is generally accepted as his masterpiece, the *Le Roi malgré lui*, performed at the Opéra Comique in 1887. Once again misfortune dogged Chabrier's steps—this time in the guise of a fire which, after the third performance of *Le Roi*, demolished the opera house. *Le Roi malgré lui* was ultimately acclaimed not only in France but in Germany as well. It was Maurice Ravel, distinguished modern French composer, who once remarked that he would rather have composed Chabrier's *Le Roi* than Wagner's Niebelungen tetralogy.

Chabrier's last work was an uncompleted opera, *Briséis*—once again on a libretto by Catulle Mendes—which was composed in 1890 and performed for the first time at the Lamoureux concerts in 1897.

During the last two years of his life, Chabrier was a virtual prisoner in his home as a result of paralysis. Moreover, towards the closing days, his mind was beginning to give way. He died in Paris on September 13, 1894; three days later he was buried in the cemetery at Montparnasse.

Cécile Chaminade has described Chabrier as "caustic, full of animal spirits, brusque, and a 'good fellow.' This brilliant musician . . . had a very mercurial temperament. Ambitious, enthusiastic and good-hearted, he was a loyal friend to those whom he liked. . . . He was subject to fits of profound melancholy, irritability and nervousness, which were the forerunners of the terrible malady which later took him from our midst. In more exalted moments, he passed all bounds in his enthusiasm for artists and people with whom he was in sympathy."

One French critic has felicitously described Chabrier's musical style as *"le rire musical,"* the "musical laugh." Chabrier's idiom was essentially a light-handed one, latent with chuckles and good humor. "It has an air of mirth," describes G. Jean-Aubry, "a frank and somewhat boisterous manner of presenting itself. There are some who stop at that and say, 'How funny!' as one might of some artist's prank, and they seek no further. And yet—he is a man who endeavors to conceal his heart with a laugh, who loves life, and finds in it a manifold enjoyment. . . . He had . . . a sense of true life, a genius for comic music that none has surpassed, unremitting fancy in the handling of the orchestra, overflowing imagination, and above all these, a taste that remained surest in his most ardent mirth."

As his music, so the man. Chabrier was famous for his jovial personality and his fresh sense of humor. His bon mots were quoted and repeated in gatherings of music lovers. "There are three kinds of music," was one of his famous sayings, "the good, the bad, and that of Ambroise Thomas." Occasionally, his wit could be even more pungently stinging. Once when Benjamin Godard said to him: "What a pity you applied yourself to music so late in life," he answered, "And what a pity you applied yourself to music so early!"

Where musical composition was concerned, he had a severe conscience. "It will be performed," he said of his works, "when I am satisfied with it; when I shall have terminated it after a conscientious and unhurried labor—or else I'll send it flying to the devil and it will not be performed. It will be good or it will not be at all. Everything costs me a great deal of trouble. I haven't what is known as facility."

Concerning Chabrier's position in French music, Gilbert Chase has written: "He was the direct precursor of Ravel and Debussy, whose most daring effects he anticipated. By his harmonic sensitiveness and his extremely subtle, and at times, daring feeling for tonal relationships, he showed himself to be very much in advance of his times."

Principal works by Emmanuel Chabrier:

OPERA: *Gwendoline; Le Roi malgré lui; Briséis,* etc.

ORCHESTRA: *España; Bourrée fantasque* (orchestrated by Felix Mottl); *Habañera; Joyeuse marche.*

PIANO: *Dix pièces pittoresques; Trois valses romantiques; Bourrée fantasque,* etc.

Songs.

About Emmanuel Chabrier:

Desaymard, Joseph. *Chabrier D'après ses Lettres;* Jean-Aubry, Georges. *Modern French Music;* Martineau, R. *Emmanuel Chabrier;* Seré, Octave. *Musiciens Français d'aujourd'hui;* Servières, Georges. *Emmanuel Chabrier;* Tiersot, Julien. *Un Demi Siècle de Musique Française.*

Important recordings of music by Emmanel Chabrier:

SELECTIONS FROM OPERA: *Gwendoline,* "Ouverture" (GRAMOPHONE-Coppola). *Le Roi malgré lui,* "Ouverture" (DECCA); "Barcarolle" (ODEON); "Cérémonial" and "Romance du Roi" (DECCA); "Danse slave" (VICTOR); "Fête polonaise" (ODEON-Pierné).

ORCHESTRA: *España* (VICTOR-Gabrilowitsch); *Bouréee fantasque,* arranged for orchestra (ODEON-Pierné); *Habañera* (COLUMBIA-Gaubert); *Joyeuse marche* (GRAMOPHONE-Coppola).

PIANO: *Trois valses romantiques* (DECCA).

George Chadwick 1854-1931

GEORGE WHITEFIELD CHADWICK was born in Lowell, Massachusetts on November 13, 1854. He stemmed from American stock; his grandfather fought at the Battle of Bunker Hill.

In 1860, the Chadwick family changed its home to Lawrence, Massachusetts,

GEORGE CHADWICK

where George Chadwick's musical education was initiated. His older brother taught him piano and harmony; singing he learned from the director of the Lawrence Church choir of which he was a member. His musical education took broad strides; by 1869, he could not only play the organ competently but he could also compose agreeable melodies.

His musical talent marked him for an artistic career. In 1872, he was entered as a student at the New England Conservatory of Music, studying under Dudley Buck and George E. Whiting. Financial difficulties, however, soon compelled him to abandon his studies. From 1873 until 1876 he earned his livelihood as a clerk in his father's insurance office. Business was distasteful to him, and by 1876 he could keep himself from music no longer. He returned to his studies with renewed enthusiasm which prepared him for the profession of music teacher in the small town of Olivet, Michigan.

His earnings from his teaching enabled him to bring a life-long dream to realization. In 1878 he set off for Europe to complete his study of music. In Leipzig, he worked under Reinecke and Jadassohn; in Munich, under Rheinberger. When he returned to America, in 1880, he was already the mature musician. In that year, the Handel and Haydn Society performed, under his own baton, his American Overture, *Rip Van Winkle*, which officially introduced him as a composer of talent.

For a living, Chadwick turned to pedagogy, a field in which he soon proved himself to be a uniquely distinguished force in American music. In 1880, he became a member of the faculty of the New England Conservatory of Music, rising to its directorship in 1887. Sympathetic, understanding, clear-minded and keenly analytical, he was one of the significant musical teachers of his time, who exerted a potent influence upon an entire generation of young American composers who studied under him.

In 1885, Chadwick was married to Ida May Brooks, and two sons were born to them. From that time on, the major part of his life Chadwick spent in Boston, where his time was divided between his pedagogic and creative duties. He composed prolifically, his works having been widely performed in America. At one time, Chadwick was esteemed the foremost American composer of his day. Towards the end of his life, however, his reputation drooped, and while the charm of some of his music still held a particular appeal, it had ceased to exert an important influence in our musical development.

Chadwick was most effective in composing for orchestra and chamber groups. Concerning his music for the orchestra, Henry Hadley has written: "He had a fine taste and sure judgment, and always chose the richest, the most expressive colors from his musical palette. . . . In all his works, he constantly achieves startling effects thru peculiarly skilful instrumentation, and his profound knowledge of the possibilities of the orchestra."

In analyzing Chadwick's chamber works, Carl Engel found that they "occupy an important and distinguished place in American music on account of the presence of traits peculiar to American folk-music or what has been accepted as such. . . . Their chief merit is their adroit handling of the instruments and the scholarly treatment of the musical fabric, to which may be added the quality, alluded to, of being more recognizably native, in certain ways, than any music written previously; indeed, Chadwick deserves to rank as a pioneer in the musical development of America."

Chadwick has been described as a lovable, warm-hearted, good-humored person, fond of the society of good friends and keenly alive to the world about him. He was a voracious reader of history, a lover of the arts—particularly of painting and sculpture. He was fond of the open country and peaceful surroundings; some of his happiest months were spent in his vacation home at Martha's Vineyard each summer, where, he composed the bulk of his music.

George Whitefield Chadwick died in Boston on April 4, 1931.

Principal works by George Whitefield Chadwick:

ORCHESTRA: *Angel of death*; *Aphrodite*; *Symphonic sketches*; Three symphonies; *Tam O'Shanter*; *Overture Melpomene*, etc.

CHAMBER MUSIC: Five string quartets; *Piano quintet.*

OPERA: *The Quiet lodging*; *Tabasco*; *Judith*; *The Padrone*; *Love's sacrifice.*

CHORAL: *The Song of the Viking*; *Noël*; *Lovely Rosabel*; *The Lily nymph*; *Land of our hearts.*

Songs, Pieces for the piano, for the organ, etc.

About George Whitefield Chadwick:

Cobbett, Walter Willson. *Cyclopedic Survey of Chamber Music*; Howard, John Tasker. *Our American Music*; Hughes, Rupert. *Famous American Composers.*
American Academy of Arts and Letters 77: 99 March 1932; *Musician* 10:505 December 1905.

Ernest Chausson *1855-1899*

ERNEST CHAUSSON was born in Paris on January 21, 1855. His life was not particularly eventful and can be summed up in a few lines. His parents were wealthy. In spite of the fact that they hoped to train him for law, they were influenced by obvious signs of musical talent into permitting him to adopt a musical career.

In his twenty-fifth year, Chausson was entered at the Paris Conservatory where, for a short while, he studied composition under Massenet. In 1880, he became a pupil of César Franck, whose influence upon his artistic development cannot be overestimated. It was Franck who turned Chausson towards abstract musical forms, and who aroused in him the ideal of creating a pure music. Before

long, Chausson abandoned the Conservatory in order to study privately under the great composer. For the remainder of his life, Chausson remained Franck's most devoted disciple and closest friend; and in his creative work was continually guided by the examples set for him by his master.

Chausson was slow in revealing himself as an important creative voice. In 1878, he published his first work—two songs—which failed to attract any notice. His development after that was a gradual one. It was not until the closing years of his life that he attained full stature as a creative genius.

In 1888, Chausson was appointed secretary of the Société Nationale de Musique, whose mission was to bring important music of younger composers to the attention of the Parisian music public. For ten years, Chausson was one of its most enthusiastic and conscientious workers.

Ernest Chausson died at his home in Limay, Seine-et-Oise, on June 10, 1899. He was riding a bicycle down a hill when he lost control of the wheel and smashed his head against a rock. Critics are generally agreed that Chausson died at the height of his creative power, with a great future still before him. There can be little doubt that his untimely death robbed us of a composer whose genius was flowering and developing with each succeeding work.

In a discerning memorial article written shortly after Chausson's death, Pierre de Breville wrote: "Chausson, like César Franck, was unknown during his life. He did not occupy publicly the place to which he had a right. Directors of concerts thought little about him, managers of theatres were not curious about his operas, and the newspapers were, as a rule, unkind or silent. . . . He himself was interested in the music of his colleagues; their success brought him joy. . . . He was ingenious in his methods of bringing the young before the public; he was always ready to render them, in a delicate manner, any service. If he met with ingratitude, he did not mind it, for kindness was natural to him, and he was generous because he was in love with generosity. His library showed the breadth of his intelligence, the various subjects in which he was interested. He had collected memoirs, legends, the literature of all folk, poets, philosophers. He had read these books, so that one could not see how in so short a time he had accomplished so much in so many ways."

Chausson is probably best known for his *Symphony in B-flat* (first performed at the concerts of the Société Nationale de Paris on April 18, 1891, and then introduced to Germany by Arthur Nikisch in 1892), the *Poème,* for violin and orchestra, and the later chamber works. These last works of Chausson reveal, as Julien Tiersot commented, "a greater sureness of touch, greater authority and mastery; they are luminous, airy, full of joyous and vibrant power. . . . Here, he had the soul of a poet; his melodies . . . are exquisite."

It is quite true that in his work Chausson revealed what a strong power the music of César Franck imposed upon his own creation. And yet, though the idiom he employed was frequently modeled after that of his master, Chausson could be himself in his music, a unique and strong personality, speaking a beauty that was his own personal speech. "When he is himself," as G. Jean-Aubry has written, "Chausson is nearly unequalled. Others have more charm, more power, more refinement; others succeed better in investing our minds by all the avenues of our curiosity, but none has greater purity than he. . . . Chausson's scrupulous soul is incapable of evasion. At every moment, we see it face to face in its entirety. . . . Where he is himself, his emotion is pure and noble, with nothing to make us feel that it claims to outrange us. On the contrary, it is there, at our side, in a discreet attitude, waiting gently meditative for us to pay attention to the simple, lasting words it utters. . . . Chausson's soul is revealed . . . diverse in its constant purity, passing from juvenile and serious freshness to the melancholy to which his mature mood was more conducive. . . . Where he is himself, one can only cherish him; and even when he is not himself, as in the symphony, where the figures of Wagner and Franck are too closely indicated, he still succeeds in infusing a charm that is

ERNEST CHAUSSON

his only, and which makes bearable the avowal of discernible influences."

To Vincent D'Indy, Chausson's chamber-works represent the highest achievements of this composer. Here, his "art is revealed more completely than even in his dramatic or symphonic works. It is in this branch, especially, that his ascent towards the highest becomes assured, and it is here that the transformation is seen in continuous—one might almost say in gradual fashion—of the richly endowed scholar unto the master called to tread the loftiest summits of music."

Principal works by Ernest Chausson:

OPERA: *Hélène; Le Roi Arthur.*

SCENAS: *Le Poème de l'amour et de la mer; Chanson perpétuelle; Jeanne D'Arc.*

CHORAL: *Hymne védique.*

ORCHESTRA: *Viviane; Un Soir de fête; Symphony in B-flat; Poème* (for violin and orchestra); *Solitude dans les bois;* Incidental music to *The tempest, Les Caprices de Marianne,* etc.

CHAMBER MUSIC: *Concerto for piano, violin and string quartet; Piano quartet in A; Trio.*

Pieces for the piano, songs, etc.

About Ernest Chausson:

Cobbett, Walter Willson. *Cyclopedic Survey of Chamber Music;* Jean-Aubry, Georges. *French Music of Today;* Seré, Octave. *Musiciens Français d'aujourd'hui;* Tiersot, Julien. *Un Demi Siècle de la Musique Française.*

Important recordings of music by Ernest Chausson:

ORCHESTRA: *Poème,* for violin and orchestra (VICTOR-Menuhin); *Symphony in B-flat Major* (VICTOR-Coppola).

CHAMBER MUSIC: *String quartet in A-major* (TRI-ERGON); *Concerto for piano, violin and string quartet* (VICTOR-Thibaud, Cortot).

Luigi Cherubini *1760-1842*

"One of the two art-heroes of our time who, as a classical master and creator of new paths of his own, will forever shine brilliantly in the history of art."—KARL MARIA VON WEBER

MARIA LUIGI CARLO ZENOBIO SALVATORE CHERUBINI was born in Florence on September 14, 1760. His musical career was clearly subdivided into three distinct periods. The first of these—the Italian period—extended from 1760 to 1784. At the age of six he studied music with his father, a cembalist, and three years later he turned to composition. He showed amazing creative talent. Between 1773 and 1777 he composed several masses and an oratorio, which were performed and praised. His ability attracted the enthusiasm of the Duke of Tuscany who enabled Cherubini to study under Giuseppe Sarti, a popular composer and theoretician of the time. For four years, Cherubini was Sarti's pupil, acquiring from his master a technical equipment that was thorough and adroit.

In his nineteenth year, Cherubini composed his first opera, *Il Quinto Fabio,* which was performed shortly afterwards in Alessandria. The opera form intrigued him to such an extent that before 1784 he had composed seven more operas. All of these works followed the accepted tradition of Italian opera closely. They were so deftly constructed and so melodious that they brought to the composer an imposing reputation. Charles Burney who first published his history in 1789 commented upon Cherubini at that time as "a young man of genius . . . who . . . is now travelling fast to the temple of Fame."

In 1784 began the second, or transitionary, period in Cherubini's career. Leaving Italy, he came to London where he was greatly admired by the Prince of Wales, and where, for one year, he filled the honorary office of composer to the King of England. The importance of his stay in London, however, rested principally in the fact that he was enabled to come into contact with many of Handel's works, whose high dramatic qualities influenced Cherubini excessively.

After two years in London, Cherubini crossed the Channel and, in July of 1786, settled permanently in Paris. It was in Paris that he reached the third, and final, stage of his artistic development.

In Paris, Cherubini was introduced to the operas of Gluck which brought him the forceful realization that he had been travelling in a wrong direction in his own operatic creation. It was because of Gluck that Cherubini discarded his former trivial style of operatic composition and, with *Démophon* (1788), adopted a more complex and grander style in which greater emphasis was placed upon dramatic content. In Paris, too, Cherubini was enabled to hear great German symphonic music with which he had until now been completely unfamiliar; J. P. Reichart relates how spellbound Cherubini was upon hearing a Haydn symphony at the *Concert Spirituel* for the first time.

When Cherubini first came to Paris, he came in touch with his countryman, Viotti—the celebrated violinist, who was at that time very much in vogue. For a short period, Cherubini made his home with Viotti. Viotti introduced the young musician to high society, opening for him the most exclusive doors and giving him his first valuable contacts. Thus, entirely thru Viotti's influence, Cherubini secured his first important positions. In 1789, when Viotti became director of the Théâtre de Monsieur, Cherubini was added to the staff. From 1789 to 1792, Cherubini was conductor of the "bouffons"—light Italian opera—at the Théâtre de la Foire, in St. Germain. When the Conservatory of Paris was founded in 1795, Cherubini was made Inspecteur. For the next forty-seven years, Cherubini retained his association with the Conservatory, serving as its director for almost two decades.

During the years of the French Revolution, Cherubini's creative genius ripened; in this period, and in the few years which followed it, he produced those works which posterity has associated with his name: the two operas, *Anacréon* and *Les Deux journées* (the latter, better known as *The Water carrier*), *the Requiem,* and the *Symphony in D* (composed as a result of a commission from England). In 1805, Cherubini visited Vienna to attend the first performance of *The Water carrier*. While there, he met Beethoven for the first time. Beethoven considered Cherubini the foremost composer of the time, but, strange to say, Cherubini did not return the compliment.

Honor and fame were generously accorded to Cherubini in Paris during the height of his career. There were few to deny that he was the most influential musician of his time, and one of the distinguished composers of his generation. His important position in the world of music was recognized. He was made a member of the Legion of Honor, appointed musician and superintendent of the King's Chapel (at a salary of some 3000 francs a year) and, in 1822, was raised to the post of director of the Paris Conservatory.

The final years of Cherubini's life were spent in comparative retirement and seclusion, in the company of a beloved family consisting of his wife, one son and two daughters. He died in Paris on March 15, 1842. He was buried in Père Lachaise with the pomp and ceremony befitting a world-famous musician.

His personality was a curious blend of irritability and warm affection, of brusqueness and amiability. It is true that to his pupils at the Conservatory, and to his fellow-musicians, he often appeared inordinately severe and callous. His was a blistering tongue. At one time, for example, he attended the rehearsal of a new Halévy opera. At the conclusion of the work, the composer eagerly asked Cherubini for his opinion. Cherubini did not answer. Halévy, believing that the master had not heard his question, once again inquired for a critical opinion. And once again Cherubini failed to answer. Finally, Halévy exclaimed impatiently: "But master, you do not answer me!" "Why should I answer you?" Cherubini asked sharply, "if after having spoken to me for two

LUIGI CHERUBINI

full hours you have said absolutely nothing!" Another anecdote concerns Napoleon, who once confided to Cherubini that he did not like his music which was far too loud and complex, not half so ingratiating or pleasing as that, for example, of Paisiello. "I see that Your Excellency prefers music that does not prevent him from thinking of matters of State!" was Cherubini's answer.

Cherubini had a severe conscience where art was concerned, an unquestioned integrity. At the funeral of a friend who was an oboe-player he derided all the eulogies that were heaped upon the deceased and reminded those near him that, after all, the man was a poor musician with a "small tone."

His passion for system and order, which characterized his régime as director of the Conservatory, likewise governed his everyday life. He routinized his day so meticulously that, for decades, each day was a photostatic copy of the preceding. He always had his pocket handkerchiefs numbered, using them only in strict order. It was said that on his death-bed, a handkerchief with the wrong number was given to him, which he promptly refused.

As a composer, Cherubini was strongly influenced by many of his predecessors and contemporaries. J. Combarieu informs us that "he owes something to Gluck to Haydn for his instrumentation, to Mozart for his treatment of voices. . . . He belongs between the old tradition of Italian music and the brilliant works of the nineteenth century, but more to the former than to the latter."

"Cherubini's finest works," in the opinion of R. A. Streatfeild, "suffer from a frigidity and formality strangely in contrast with the grace of Grétry or the melody of Méhul, but the infinite resources of his musicianship make amends for the lack of inspiration, and *Les Deux journées* (*The Water carrier*) may still be listened to with pleasure, if not with enthusiasm. . . . The solidity of his concerted pieces and the picturesqueness of his orchestration go far to explain the enthusiasm which his works aroused in a society which as yet knew little, if anything, of Mozart."

To Frederick Niecks, neither *Anacréon* nor *The Water carrier* represents Cherubini's "highest flight" in opera, but rather *Medée*, composed in 1797. This opera, to Niecks, is a "work, overwhelming in tragic passion and immense in constructive musicianship. As to the overwhelming nature of the tragedy, *Medée* has reminded more than one musician of the two most powerful of Wagner's dramas: *The Dusk of the Gods*, and *Tristan*." Johannes Brahms was likewise most enthusiastic about this opera. "*Medée*—this is what we musicians among ourselves recognize as the highest dramatic music!"

A painting of Cherubini by Ingress is on exhibition at the Louvre Museum in Paris.

Principal works by Luigi Cherubini:

OPERA: *Lodoïska*; *Medée*; *La Prisonnière*; *Les Deux journées* (*The Water carrier*); *Anacréon*; *Faniska*, etc.

CHORAL: Two requiems; Four masses; Two kyries, etc.

ORCHESTRA: *Funeral march*; *Symphony in D*; *Overture*, etc.

CHAMBER MUSIC: *String quintet*; Six string quartets.

About Luigi Cherubini:

Bellasis, Edward. *Cherubini*; Crowest, Frederick J. *Cherubini*; Schemann, Ludwig. *Cherubini*; Streatfeild, R. A. *The Opera*.

Monthly Musical Record 46:4, 34, 65, 131, 163 January-June 1916; *Music and Letters* 5:223 July 1924.

Important recordings of music by Luigi Cherubini:

SELECTIONS FROM OPERA: *Anacréon*, "Ouverture" (COLUMBIA-Mengelberg). *Les Deux journées*, "Ouverture" (POLYDOR-Walter). *Medée*, "Ouverture" (COLUMBIA).

Frédéric Chopin *1810-1849*

"Chopin is less a musician, than a soul who made himself felt."—BALZAC

"If Chopin was small in great things, he was great in small things."—J. CUTHBERT HADDEN

FRÉDÉRIC FRANÇOIS CHOPIN, perhaps the greatest composer that the pianoforte produced, was born in a village near Warsaw, Zelazowa Wola, on February 22, 1810. His ancestry was mixed: French on his father's side, and Polish on his mother's, his personality seemed to assimilate the characteristic traits of both nationalities.

His childhood was known to have been idyllically happy. At home, he found both understanding and love, sympathy and freedom. His happiest hours as a child were spent in wandering the countryside near his home, listening to the fiddling and singing of peasants. As he grew older, he found equal delight in brooding over the keyboard of a piano, and in drawing from it melodies of his own invention. He would spend so many hours, often late at night, in playing the piano, that his parents realized that he was strongly endowed with musical talent. They engaged a music teacher—Adalbert Zywny from Warsaw to teach the boy the piano—Chopin made such rapid progress, that at the age of nine he was enlisted to play the piano at a charity concert. The reception his performance received was tremendous. It made Frédéric the pampered pet of his neighbors, and the pride and hope of his family.

In 1824, Chopin was sent to the Lyceum in Warsaw, where he was placed under the instruction of a particularly sympathetic and understanding musician, Joseph Elsner. Elsner realized almost immediately that in Chopin he had a peculiarly sensitive and talented pupil. Rather than hem in the unbridled spirit of the gifted boy with ponderous rules and sterile exercises, he permitted Chopin to express himself romantically in music without considering constricting laws and principles. Under such freedom, Chopin thrived artistically. "Frédéric Chopin, third year student," was the report he received in composition, "reveals amazing capabilities and musical genius."

When Frédéric Chopin graduated from the Lyceum, he left Warsaw to visit Berlin and Vienna. He gave several concerts on the piano, introducing at the same time a few of his early pieces which made a striking impression. The *Allgemeine Musikalische Zeitung* of November 18, 1829 spoke of the "indescribable dexterity of his technique, the subtle finish of his gradations of tone, reflecting a profoundly sensitive nature, the clearness of his interpretation and of his compositions which bear the mark of great genius."

After this short trip, Chopin returned to Warsaw where he remained a full year. However, having had a glimpse of glorious Vienna, he felt himself ineluctably drawn back to this city of music. On November 1, 1830, his friends at Wola gave him a rousing farewell party, on the occasion of his departure for Vienna, giving him as a momento a silver goblet filled with Polish earth. "May you never forget your native land wherever you go," he was told. Chopin wept, as though he had a presentiment that he would never again see his native country.

He came to Vienna where, after a few weeks, he heard the tidings that Poland was in revolution. His first impulse was to rush back and fight for the honor of his country. His parents, however, urged him to remain in Vienna, reminding him that he was too delicate in constitution to assume a soldier's life. Somewhat regretfully, he did so. Then— partially out of loneliness—he embarked upon a concert tour thru Germany. In Stuttgart, in July of 1831, he heard the news that Warsaw had fallen into the hands of the Russians. This news moved him profoundly. Seeking expression for his emotion, he composed a piece for the piano which was to become famous the world-over as the *Revolutionary Étude*.

On September 1, he visited Paris. He intended to make his stay brief (his passport said "passing thru Paris to London") ; but Paris was to remain his home for the remainder of his life. He rented an apartment at 27 Boulevard Poissonière. Almost immediately he sought out Cherubini, director of the Conservatory, to whom he presented a letter of introduction. Cherubini introduced Chopin to the leading musicians of Paris, paving the way for his first appearance.

The début took place at the Salle Pleyel on January 26, 1832, and, strange to say, was discouragingly unsuccessful. Only one critic recognized the spark of genius in Chopin—the eminent Fétis, who wrote in *La Revue Musicale*: "Here is a young man who, by giving himself up to his natural impressions, and following no model, has discovered, if not an absolute revolution in piano music, at least something of what composers have been seeking in vain for a long time past, namely, an abundance of original ideas whose type is nowhere to be found." But like that of all prophets, the voice of Fétis was not listened to seriously. For the most part, both audience and critics dismissed Chopin.

During the next few years, Chopin's concerts were few and far between; during this period he knew, for a while, want and spiritual depression. A series of fortuitous accidents, however, brought him back to high society, where his suave manner, his gentle personality and

FRÉDÉRIC CHOPIN

his great musical talent made him particularly appealing in the *salon*. He succeeded in procuring high-priced pupils, and for the first time luxury and soft-living became his. "I move in the highest circles," he wrote at this time, "and know not how I got there. . . . You will imagine that I must have a fortune by this time; but the cabriolet and the white gloves eat the earnings almost entirely, and without these things people would deny my good form."

We possess several vivid word-descriptions of Chopin, as he appeared at this time. "I found myself face to face with a pale, melancholy, elegant young man with a slight foreign accent, brown eyes of incomparable softness and limpidity, chestnut hair almost as long as that of Berlioz, and falling in a wisp on to his brow," wrote Legouvé. And Franz Liszt: "His whole person is harmonious. His glance was intelligent rather than dreamy; his soft, shrewd smile had no touch of bitterness. The fineness and transparency of his complexion charmed the eye, his fair hair was silky, his nose slightly aquiline, his movements well-bred, and his manners bore such an aristocratic stamp that one involuntarily treated him like a prince. His gestures were frequent and graceful. His voice was always toneless, and often indistinct; he was not very tall, and was slightly built."

Late in 1837, Chopin met the "incomparable" George Sand, that amazing character whose brusque masculinity, unbridled independence of the conventions of society, and innumerable love-affairs nursed and fed so many of the conversations of the French *salon*. Chopin was twenty-eight; George Sand, thirty-four. It cannot be said that George Sand, at first, made a vividly agreeable impression upon the composer. "How repellent that woman is!" he said to a friend after the first meeting. "Is she really a woman?"

In 1838, when George Sand settled in Paris to consummate divorce proceedings against her husband, she was to meet Chopin a second time, and the first disagreeable impression on the part of Chopin was to yield to a pleasanter one. George Sand's keen and electric mind, her strength of character, her vibrant personality impressed him greatly. She attracted Chopin because she was essentially his opposite. Their acquaintanceship soon developed into a bond of close friendship. And from close friendship to love was only a step.

The illness of George Sand's son, Maurice, necessitated her departure from Paris for the warmer climate of Majorca. Chopin, now hopelessly involved, begged permission to accompany her, finding his own delicate health an excuse for seeking Majorca's warm climate. George Sand, however, feared that Chopin could not be happy away from Paris, and refused to grant his request. Shortly after her departure, Chopin left Paris suddenly and mysteriously. He caught up with his beloved in Perpignan. Together, they arrived in Palma, where they rented a country villa, *Son Vent,* for fifty francs a month.

Unfortunately, Majorca was not half so idyllic as Chopin and Sand hoped. They had arrived in the rainy season; the chill and damp weather played havoc with Chopin's delicate constitution. Ill, exhausted, frequently in pain, his mind soon became a victim to strange fantasies and nightmares, inspired, no doubt, by his bleak surroundings. "He became utterly demoralized," wrote George Sand in later years. "He could bear pain with a fair amount of courage, but he could not control his uneasy imagination. Even when he was well, the cloister was filled for him with terror and phantoms. He did not say so, and one had to divine it. On returning from my nocturnal explorations with the children, I would find him at ten o'clock at night sitting at the piano, pale and with haggard eyes, and his hair almost standing on end. It took him some moments to recognize us. . . . Then, he would make an effort to laugh, and play us sublime things which he had just composed, or rather, terrible and heartening ideas which had just taken possession of him. . . . It was here that he published the finest of those short pages which he modestly called preludes."

Chopin's health went from bad to worse. He was growing irritably impatient with Majorca. His spirit was enmeshed in melancholy. He was yearning for Paris. With the return of good weather, it was decided to return to Paris. The warm climate of southern France and the prolonged rest that Chopin was then to enjoy for a few months at Marseilles and Nohant magically revived his strength. He returned to Paris rejuvenated in spirit and health.

For the next seven years, Chopin spent a comparatively uneventful life, devoting his winter time to Paris, and his summers to Nohant. In 1841, Chopin gave a piano recital at the Salle Pleyel, his first in nine years, which was phenomenally successful. He was recognized at this time as one of the greatest pianists of his generation.

The last years of Chopin's life were absorbed in concert-work and composition. In 1847-1848 there occurred the rupture between him and George Sand which affected his spirit so vitally. The precise cause for this rupture is not known, but there are many suggestive clues. For one thing, George Sand's contempt of Chopin's Catholicism was always a source of poignant pain to the composer. Secondly, Chopin was—as Sand frequently complained—"foreign to my studies, my enquiries and hence to my convictions." But perhaps the most important explanation lurks in a sentence which appears in a letter of hers, dated May 12, 1847. "He complains to me that I have killed him by refusing sexual relations, whereas I knew for certain that I should kill him if I acted otherwise."

In any case, by 1848 they were living separate lives. This separation affected Chopin intensely. "In spite of the arts employed by his friends to keep this subject out of his memory," wrote Liszt, "in order to prevent the dangerous emotion which it caused, he loved to revert to it, as if he wished to stupefy himself with this fatal balm. . . . Chopin felt and often repeated that in breaking this long affection, this powerful bond, he had broken his life."

In the meanwhile, his health was suffering rapid disintegration. We are told that by 1848 he could hardly walk without suffering pain, and as early as 1847 he was so ill that it was thought his death was near at hand. Death, however, was still at a distance. Chopin recovered sufficiently to make a trip to England. When he returned to Paris, in 1849, his spirits were at low ebb. He deserted composition and refused to play the piano. He scrupulously avoided the society of friends.

He died at his home in Rue de Chaillot on October 17, 1849. His face in death was said to have been "radiant in its beauty." Following a performance of Mozart's *Requiem*, the body was accompanied by the music of Chopin's own funeral march to Père Lachaise, where it was buried near the graves of Cherubini and Bellini.

Chopin's personality was characterized by softness and effeminacy. He was full of the spirit of mockery, delighting in acting the clown. Berlioz has written about his sparkling good humor which brought "an irresistible attraction to his friends for him." He had an unusual gift at mimicry, often delighting his friends by imitating a Polish Jew, a sentimental Englishman or a pompous French nobleman. Yet, though good humor was an integral part of Chopin's character, he could also be broodingly melancholy. His life consisted, for the most part, in this strange alternation between frivolity and despondency.

Chopin is probably the foremost genius that the pianoforte has produced. With a few solitary and negligible exceptions, he devoted his genius entirely to this instrument. He increased its technical resources, found for it qualities it had never before expressed, and opened up for it entirely new vistas of beauty. What Beethoven has been to the symphony, Bach to the cantata, and Wagner to the music-drama, Chopin has been to the pianoforte.

In analyzing his amazing output of études, preludes, nocturnes, mazurkas, ballades, fantasias etc., we discover that the outstanding influence in his art was the Polish folk-song. "It was an aspiration with him from the first to put Poland, as it were, into his music," wrote J. Cuthbert Hadden. " 'I should like,' he said, 'to be to my people what Uhland is to the Germans.' To be sure, the external qualities of his music are all his own. But the texture is essentially of native growth and native substance. Mr. Hadow brings this out more clearly and with more detail than any other writer who has touched on the subject. He shows that there are three separate ways in which the national influence affected Chopin's work. In the first place, it determined the main forms of his art-product. The popular music of Poland is almost invariably founded on dance forms and dance rhythms: more than a quarter of Chopin's entire composition is devoted ostensibly to dance forms, and thruout the rest of it their effect may be seen in a hundred phrases and episodes. A second point of resemblance is Chopin's habit of 'founding a who!e paragraph either on a single repeated phrase in similar shapes, or on two phrases in alternation.' This is a very primitive practise, for which no artistic value can be claimed when standing by itself. But 'when it is confined to an episodical passage, especially in a composition founded on a striking or important melody, it may serve as a very justifiable point of rest, a background of which the interest is purposely toned down to provide a more striking contrast with the central figure.' It is in the mazurkas that we find this practise most successfuly employed. . . . Thirdly, Chopin was to a considerable extent affected by the tonality of his native music. The larger number of the Polish folk-songs are written, not in our modern scale, but in one or other of the mediaeval Church modes—the Dorian, the Lydian and the rest. . . . Of this tonal system, as Mr. Hadow shows, some positive traces may be found in the mazurkas."

Who is more competent to judge the greatness of Chopin's piano music than that other genius of the pianoforte, Franz Liszt? "In it," wrote the master, "we meet with beauties of the highest kind, expressions entirely new, and harmonic material as original as it is thoughtful. In his compositions boldness is always justified; richness, often exuberance, never interferes with clearness; singularity never degenerates into the uncouth and the fantastic; the sculpturing is never disordered; the luxury of ornament never overloads the chaste tenderness of the principal lines. . . . Daring, brilliant, and attractive, they disguise their profundity under so much grace, their science under so many charms, that it is with difficulty we free ourselves sufficiently from their magical enthrallment to judge coldly their theoretical value."

Summing up Chopin's place in musical history, Daniel Gregory Mason wrote: "Chopin may not be a giant like Bach, or Mozart, or Handel, or Beethoven, but he is a sincere and earnest artist, who feels vividly and spares no pains to give his feelings worthy expression, and to attain a supreme plastic beauty. Above all, he is a man of the most delicate sensibility, the most discriminating taste, the most exacting ideal of artistic perfection. . . . In that firmament of music he will continue to shine, a fixed star, not perhaps of the first magnitude, but giving a wondrously clear, white light, and, as he would have wished, in peerless solitude."

Principal works by Frédéric Chopin:
ORCHESTRA: Two concertos for piano and orchestra.
CHAMBER MUSIC: *Piano trio; Sonata for violoncello and piano.*
PIANO: Two sonatas; Four ballades; Two series of études; Nineteen nocturnes; Eleven polonaises; Twenty-four preludes; Thirteen waltzes; Four fantasias; Fifty-four mazurkas; Impromptus, Scherzos, Variations, etc. Songs.

About Frédéric Chopin:
Bidou, Henri. *Chopin*; Hadden, J. Cuthbert. *Chopin*; Maine, Basil. *Chopin*; Mason, Daniel Gregory. *The Romantic Composers*; Murdoch, William. *Chopin: His Life*; Niecks, Frederick. *The Life of Chopin.*

Important recordings of music by Frédéric Chopin:
ORCHESTRA: *Concerto in E-minor,* for piano and orchestra (BRUNSWICK-Brailowsky); *Concerto in F-minor,* for piano and orchestra (VICTOR-Rubinstein).
PIANO: *Études,* complete (VICTOR-Bachaus); *Ballades,* complete (COLUMBIA-Casadesus); *Twelve mazurkas* (COLUMBIA-Friedman); *Twelve nocturnes* (COLUMBIA-Godowsky); *Seven polonaises* (GRAMOPHONE-Rubinstein); *Twenty-four preludes,* complete (VICTOR-Cortot); *Fourteen waltzes* (GRAMOPHONE-Cortot).
CHAMBER MUSIC: *Sonata for violoncello and piano,* "Largo" (COLUMBIA).

Domenico Cimarosa *1749-1801*

DOMENICO CIMAROSA was born in Aversa, Naples, on December 17, 1749. His parents were humble folk: his father was a stone mason who was killed by falling from a high scaffold when Domenico was still a child; his mother was a washerwoman.

As a child, Cimarosa was sent by his mother to a free school maintained by the Franciscan monks, where he studied Latin and music. His talent for the latter soon urged his teachers to send him to the Conservatory of Holy Maria of Loreto, where his teachers were Sacchini, Fenaroli, and that eminent composer of Italian opera, Piccinni. He remained at the Conservatory for eleven years, and was particularly influenced by the teachings of Piccinni.

Upon leaving the Conservatory, Cimarosa turned to composition. In 1772, came his first opera, *Le Stravaganze del conte*, produced at the Fiorentini Theatre in Naples where it enjoyed so great a success that, overnight, Cimarosa became a famous composer.

For the next twenty years, Cimarosa lived alternately at Rome and at Naples, composing one opera after another that enjoyed popularity wherever opera was performed in Europe. His contemporaries esteemed him as the foremost dramatic composer of his time, placing him on an even higher pedestal than the much-loved Paisiello.

In 1787, Cimarosa went to Russia as court composer of Catherine II. Shortly after this, Leopold II invited him to come to Vienna to succeed Salieri as chapel-master, at a substantial salary —12,000 florins a year. It was in Vienna that, in 1792, Cimarosa composed a comic opera which historians agree unanimously is his masterpiece, *Il Matrimonio segreto*. *Il Matrimonio segreto* was acclaimed by the Viennese. The Emperor, who attended the second performance, was so delighted with the work that he ordered the entire opera to be encored then and there.

Several months after the composition of *Il Matrimonio*, Cimarosa returned to Naples where great honor awaited him. He was appointed chapel-master to the

DOMENICO CIMAROSA

King, and instructor to the royal children. He was also to see many of his operas—particularly his Viennese gem, *Il Matrimonio*—accepted by the populace as masterpieces.

Towards the close of his life, Cimarosa came upon unfortunate days. He became involved in revolutionary movements which resulted, in 1798, in his imprisonment. Only his great fame as a composer saved him from death. He was set free by King Ferdinand but on the express condition that he leave Naples never to return.

Exile broke Cimarosa's heart and spirit. Bound for Russia, he went as far as Venice where his health collapsed completely. He died in Venice on January 11, 1801. His sudden death inspired the rumor that he had been poisoned by Queen Caroline. This rumor gained so much credence among Italians that it was necessary for the Court to issue an official denial; and the physician, who attended Cimarosa during his last hours, was forced to give a signed statement to the effect that Cimarosa's death was the result of broken health.

Cimarosa had been married twice. His first wife died while bearing him a son; his second wife died one day after she gave birth to twins.

He was a jovial, charming and lovable personality, extremely cultured and well-poised, possessing a pungent and delectable wit. He was almost as gifted in the fashioning of verse as in the composition of music. Extremely social, he always sought the company of agreeable friends; he even liked to be surrounded by boisterous company when he was composing. Yet, he was acutely sensitive to noise; even the sound of church bells frequently caused him excessive pain.

Thruout his entire life he was convinced of his genius (he frequently referred to himself as the greatest Italian composer of his time), but he did not overestimate his greatness. At one time, a painter disparaged the music of Mozart in comparing it with that of Cimarosa. "What would you say," was Cimarosa's answer, "if I were to attempt to convince you that you are greater than Raphael?"

Cimarosa was a prolific composer. His output of operas, oratorios, cantatas and masses was voluminous. These have for the most part, gone the way of all things. Cimarosa's name, as a matter of fact, would have hardly survived had it not been for his comic opera, *Il Matrimonio segreto*, which is still performed in Europe, and its popularity, because of the deftness and glittering sparkle of the score, seems deathless.

Cimarosa's touch was essentially a light one; he excelled when he was least pretentious. "He was the finest example of the school perfected by Piccinni," wrote George T. Ferris, "and was, indeed, the link between the old Italian opera and the new development." His operas were familiar to Mozart who, as Edward J. Dent points out, "took over all his conventions—his breathless back-chat in recitative, his charming tunes, his patter songs for the bass, his chattering ensembles—and added to them his own warmth of harmony and ingenuity of orchestration."

Domenico Cimarosa belonged, as R. A. Streatfeild has written, to the school of *opera-buffa* that preceded him, whose finest example was, of course, Pergolesi's *La Serva padrona*. "His talent is thoroughly Italian, untouched by German influence, and he excels in portraying the gay superficiality of the

Italian character without attempting to dive far below the surface."

In recent years, the eminent contemporary Italian composer, Francesco Malipiero, has collected into a suite and orchestrated five pieces of Cimarosa which he entitled *La Cimarosiana*, which has been performed by leading symphony orchestras everywhere.

Principal works by Domenico Cimarosa:

OPERA: *Le Stravaganze del conte*; *La Ballerina amante*; *Artaserse*; *L'Olimpiade*; *La Cleopatra*; *Il Matrimonio segreto*; *L'Amante disperato*; *L'Impegno superato*, etc. Oratorios, cantatas, masses, sonatas for harpsichord, etc.

About Domenico Cimarosa:

Bachrach, A. L. *The Musical Companion*; Ferris, George T. *Great Italian and French Masters*; Streatfeild, R. A. *The Opera*; Vitale, Roberto. *Domenico Cimarosa*.

Important recordings of music by Domenico Cimarosa:

SELECTIONS FROM OPERA: *Il Matrimonio segreto*, "Overture" (GRAMOPHONE-Blech); "Udite, tutti, udite" (PARLAPHONE).
ORCHESTRA: *La Cimarosiana*, a collection of Cimarosa melodies arranged for orchestra by Malipiero (REGAL).

Muzio Clementi *1752-1832*

MUZIO CLEMENTI, sometimes designated as the "father of modern pianoforte playing," was born in Rome in 1752. His father, a silversmith, became aware of his precocious musical talent and procured for him musical instruction when he was seven years old. Muzio Clementi was so apt a pupil that, two years later, he competed successfully for a position as organist.

A wealthy Englishman, Beckford by name, was struck with this boy's unusual gifts, and offered to adopt him and bring him to England, where he was given a thorough academic and musical education.

In 1770, Clementi made his first appearance as a pianist, electrifying his audience with the facility of his technique. That was the beginning of his career as concert pianist which continued for the next eleven years, bringing him to the front rank of the pianists of his day.

An extensive European tour began in 1781, carrying Clementi to France, Germany and Austria. Wherever he performed he was acclaimed. In Vienna, at the instigation of Emperor Joseph II, he entered into a "musical duel" with Mozart. Clementi performed his own *B-flat major sonata* and Mozart extemporized a series of variations. Each proved to be so phenomenal in his own way that the Emperor was reluctantly compelled to call this battle of giants a draw. It is interesting, in this connection, to note that ten years later Mozart borrowed the opening theme of Clementi's *B-flat major sonata* for his *Magic flute overture* a fact which so infuriated Clementi that in all future editions of the sonata he boldly printed the fact that he himself had performed that work before Mozart and Emperor Joseph II ten years before the composition of the *Magic flute overture.*

Between 1782 and 1802, Clementi remained in England where he was active as pianist, conductor and teacher. His importance as a pedagogue almost equalled his interpretative attainments; at least two of his pupils—J. B. Cramer and John Field—were recognized among the foremost pianists of the time. At the same time, Clementi turned his efforts towards manufacturing pianos. After many vicissitudes, he achieved great commercial success in this field. In 1807, almost $200,000 worth of property in Clementi's piano firm was destroyed by a fire.

By 1810, Clementi had given up all concert work to devote himself principally to composition and to his piano manufacturing business. From this time on, his life was to be comparatively uneventful. The last years of his life were spent quietly in Evesham, where he died on March 10, 1832. He was buried in Westminster Abbey.

Clementi had been married three times.

During his lifetime, Clementi had amassed a fortune which, thriftily, he preserved until his death. His thrift was frequently the subject of much derision among his friends and acquaintances. Even when he was excessively rich, Clementi guarded his every penny

MUZIO CLEMENTI

with scrupulous diligence. Spohr has written in his autobiography about Clementi's frugal nature. "One day, I found teacher and pupil [John Field] at the washtub with upturned sleeves engaged in washing out their stockings and other linen. . . . Clementi advised me to do the same, saying that washing in St. Petersburg was not only expensive, but also the linen suffered greatly from the method of laundry employed." He seemed to derive singular pleasure in merely amassing wealth. His only other pleasure, it seemed, was playing billiards.

Muzio Clementi composed one hundred and six sonatas for the piano, which have elicited the praise of all students of piano music. Waldo Pratt has spoken of them as "resourceful and full of nervous energy." To Frederick Niecks they represent Clementi's "most important poetic achievements, the works in which he has incorporated the greatest emotional intensity possible to him, and where the virtuoso contents himself with being the servant of the idea." "His divination of the treatment most appropriate to the instrument," wrote Hubert Parry, "marks his sonatas as among the very first in which the genuine qualities of modern pianoforte music on a large scale are shown." Today, Clementi's piano sonatas are played principally by music students, and are never featured on piano recital programs. Their importance is essentially a historic and pedagogic one.

Even more important, however, than these piano sonatas is the *Gradus ad Parnassum*, one hundred studies for the piano composed in 1817, upon which, it is said, the art of modern piano playing rests. To this day, piano students utilize the *Gradus ad Parnassum* for the development of their technique. No less a pianist than Tausig has said that the *Études* of Chopin and the studies of Clementi are the "only two works in musical literature which are entirely indispensible to the pianist."

It is not generally known that Clementi composed a series of symphonies for orchestra, upon which he worked for more than fifteen years during the closing period of his life, intending them as his "testament to posterity." These symphonies disappeared mysteriously after his death. In 1917, they came to light when, on the death of the English musicologist, Dr. William H. Cumming, his manuscript library was auctioned. This library contained manuscript copies of Clementi's symphonies, which were promptly bought by Carl Engel for the Library of Congress in Washington, D.C.

Recently, the well-known modern Italian composer, Alfredo Casella, reconstructed from these scattered manuscripts the *C-Major symphony* of Clementi, in which form the work—after a century of silence—was heard again in Turin under Casella's baton. It is the intention of Mr. Casella to reconstruct as many of Clementi's symphonies as possible and to reintroduce them to the music world.

Concerning Clementi's symphonies, Alfredo Case la has written. "The style is that of a musician whose life spans the gap from the death of John Sebastian Bach to the bloom of romanticism. A fundamentally classic spirit, severely trained and the possessor of a truly exceptional constructive technique, Clementi in these symphonies aims visibly to renew the great classic heredity with the new aspirations of the century. And his profoundly Italian genius happily achieves this synthesis. In these works we find a new and more potent assertion of the music, at once grandiose and witty, tragic but more often serene, of his best piano sonatas."

Principal works by Muzio Clementi:
ORCHESTRA: Symphonies.
PIANO: 106 sonatas; *Gradus ad Parnassum*.

About Muzio Clementi:
Unger, Max. *Muzio Clementis Leben.*
Music and Letters 13:286 July 1932; *Musician* 8:289 August 1903.

Important recordings of music by Muzio Clementi:
PIANO: *Sonatina in C-major* (VICTOR); *Sonatina in E-flat major* (COLUMBIA-Samuel).

Samuel Coleridge-Taylor *1875-1912*

SAMUEL COLERIDGE-TAYLOR, Negro composer, was born in London on August 15, 1875. His father, a full-blooded Negro, was a medical man who, a few years after the boy's birth, deserted his family to return to his native Sierra Leone. "Neither of my parents was particularly musical," Coleridge-Taylor wrote in later years, "but my father interested himself in an instrument named colangee, known on the West coast of Africa."

After acquiring the elements of music from Benjamin Holman, Coleridge-Taylor became a pupil of Joseph Beckwith who remained his teacher for seven years. It was Beckwith who first recognized unmistakable musical talent in the boy, and who was the first to urge him to devote his undivided energy to the art.

As a boy, Coleridge-Taylor served in the choir of St. George's Presbyterian Church in Croydon. "He was a most delightful pupil," commented Herbert Walters, the choirmaster, "quick, eager, and with a wonderful ear." Coleridge-Taylor made so marked an impression upon his choirmaster that Herbert Walters decided to adopt him. It was Walters who enrolled the young musician in the Royal College of Music where his teachers were Charles Villiers Standford, in composition, and J. F. Bridge, in violin.

Coleridge-Taylor soon proved his extraordinary musical gifts. In 1896, his symphony, based on Negro themes, was performed by the College orchestra, proving that his was no ordinary talent. Two years later came a performance of *Hiawatha's wedding feast*, the first part of the *Songs*, which was enormously successful, eliciting the high praise of even so authoritative a musician as Sir Arthur Sullivan. Shortly after this, the Three Choirs Festival presented the orchestral *Ballade in A-minor*, a work that definitely brought Coleridge-Taylor to artistic maturity.

The opinion of critics concerning the *Ballade*, when it was first introduced, was that, though charged with genius, its style was "barbaric." This is a strange verdict, indeed, for the *Ballade* possesses a unique simplicity of structure and content. "There probably never has been an orchestral work of such importance intrinsically and in its relation to the world of music that has been constructed on so simple a theme of tonality, theme or orchestration," writes Herbert Antcliffe today.

From 1900 until 1907 Coleridge-Taylor extended his musical activities by becoming the conductor of the Rochester Choral Society. During this period he made two visits to the United States—in 1904 and 1906—where he was welcomed with pomp and ceremony, with festival concerts devoted to his works. Returning to England, he led an uneventful life which was devoted principally to composition, to conducting and to the teaching of music in Croydon. In 1910, he made his third and last visit to the United States, where the première of his Violin concerto took place (Norfolk, Connecticut).

Samuel Coleridge-Taylor died at his home in Croydon on September 1, 1912. His biographer, W. C. Berwick Sayers, has given us a touching picture of the last hours. "Propped up by pillows, he seemed to imagine an orchestra before him. With complete absorption, and perhaps unconscious of his surroundings, he conducted his violin concerto, beating time with both arms and smiling his approval here and there. The smile never left his face, and the performance was never completed on earth. Still smiling and conducting, he sank back on his pillows."

Coleridge-Taylor was a methodical worker as a composer, devoting a

SAMUEL COLERIDGE-TAYLOR

specified number of hours each day to his creative work, never permitting concert engagements to interfere with it. He wrote quickly and fluently, but was a severe self-critic.

It was Booker T. Washington who has given us a clear resumé of Coleridge-Taylor's style of composition. "His work possesses . . . not only charm and power but distinction, the individual note. The genuineness, depth and intensity of his feeling, coupled with his masterly technique, spontaneity and ability to think in his own way, explain the force of the appeal that his compositions make. Another element in the persuasiveness of his music lies in the naturalness the directness of its appeal, the use of simple and expressive melodic themes, a happy freedom from the artificial."

"Like his half-brothers of primitive race," commented Hubert Parry, "he loved plenty of sound, plenty of color, simple and definite rhythms, and, above all things, plenty of tune. Tune pours out in passage after passage, genial and kindly and apt to the subject, and in an emotional way often warmly and touchingly expressive."

Samuel Coleridge-Taylor had two children, both of whom are musicians. His son, Hiawatha, conducted his father's *Hiawatha* in London in 1924.

His daughter, Gwendolen, is the composer of many songs that have been published and performed.

Principal works by Samuel Coleridge-Taylor:

ORCHESTRA: *Symphony in A-minor*; *Ballade in A-minor*; *Idyll*; *African suite*; *Solemn prelude*; *Toussaint l'Ouverture*; *Symphonic suite on an African air*; *Bamboula*; *Concerto for violin and orchestra*; *Characteristic waltzes*; *Christmas overture*; *Petite suite de concert*; Incidental music to Ulysses, Herod, Nero, Faust, Othello, etc.

CHORAL: *Songs of Hiawatha*; *The Blind girl of Castél-Cuillé*; *The Atonement*; *Five choral ballads*; *Kubla Khan*; *Endymion's dream*; *Bon-Bon suite*; *A Tale of old Japan*; *Two songs* (with orchestra); *The Gitanos*.

OPERA: *Thelma*.

CHAMBER MUSIC: *Quintet in A*; *Quartet in D-minor*; *Fantasie-stücke*.

Songs, pieces for the violin, pieces for the piano, pieces for the organ, etc.

About Samuel Coleridge-Taylor:

Sayers, W. C. Berwick. *Samuel Coleridge-Taylor*.

Musical Quarterly 8:180 April 1922; *Musical Times* 50:153 March 1, 1909.

Important recordings of music by Coleridge-Taylor:

ORCHESTRA: *Characteristic waltzes* (GRAMOPHONE); *Christmas overture* (COLUMBIA-Pitt); *Othello suite* (GRAMOPHONE); *Petite suite de concert* (COLUMBIA).

CHORAL: *Songs of Hiawatha* (GRAMOPHONE).

Arcangelo Corelli *1653-1713*

"The prince of all musicians."—MATTHESON

ARCANGELO CORELLI was born in Fusignano, in the vicinity of Bologna, on February 12, 1653. His first teacher in music was Matteo Simonelli, a singer in the pontifical choir. Church music, appealing little to Corelli, was soon deserted for secular music. Corelli turned from Simonelli to Bassani for instruction, and the latter gave him an intensive training in the playing of the violin. Corelli proved his aptitude for the instrument almost from the beginning, becoming a reputable virtuoso in a short period. By 1672, his musical talent as a violinist was so pronounced that when he visited Paris, he was forced back to Rome by the envious Lully (according to the testimony of John Hawkins, which is put to question by Charles Burney), who was afraid that the enormous musical abilities of his compatriot might succeed in obscuring his own great popularity.

In 1680, Corelli toured Germany where he was royally received by German princes, particularly the Elector of Bavaria, in whose service he was retained. Returning to Rome, two years later, he published his first work, *Twelve sonatas*, for two violins and a bass.

About 1700, Corelli became the leader of the opera band in Rome, a position which brought him into contact with Handel. Their meeting, as described by Hawkins, was not a happy one. Handel was in Italy assisting at the rehearsal of his cantatas, and Corelli—who was unaccustomed to the complexity of Handel's style—found great difficulty in understanding the desires of the great composer. Finally, his patience exhausted, Handel snatched the violin from Corelli's hand and showed him exactly how the passage was to be played.

Notwithstanding this unfortunate episode, Handel had a high opinion of Corelli. For, in truth, Corelli was at that time esteemed the foremost musician in Italy. He was generally recognized as the greatest violinist of his time. Contemporary critics spoke effusively about his beautiful singing tone, his incredibly supple technique and the fire and brilliance of his interpretations. When Corelli played, we are informed by eye-witnesses, his "countenance was distorted," his eyes were "red as fire" and his "eyeballs rolled in agony." This intensity of emotion found expression in his interpretation. No less a musician than Alessandro Scarlatti sang paeans of praise to Corelli's interpretative genius.

He was almost equally celebrated as a composer. A contemporary writer, Adami, refers to Corelli as the "chief glory of the age, with the fame of whose five works, already published, the world is filled; and the sixth, consisting of concertos, which he is now (1711) preparing for the press, will complete his immortality."

ARCANGELO CORELLI

Corelli was, therefore, the favorite son of high society in Rome, greatly fêted and honored. He was particularly esteemed by Cardinal Pietro Ottoboni who, until the end of Corelli's life, was his closest friend and patron. Corelli made the palace of the Cardinal his home until the very end of his life, there conducting every Monday concerts which became the outstanding musical events in Rome of the time.

The last years of Corelli's life were bathed with melancholy. He was to see violinists younger than he, with more facile technique and more spectacular style, gain the fancy of the public; and he was to witness the popularity of his own works succeeded by the less important music of Valentini, for example, whom Corelli esteemed lightly. To have passed out of the limelight caused Corelli no end of mortification. When an oboe player received the tremendous ovation which had, in former years, been accorded to him, he became so bitter that he swore never again to appear in public.

Thus he died a bitter and unhappy man on January 10, 1713. He died comparatively rich, with almost $30,000 in cash and a number of precious art-works of enormous value. All his wealth he bequeathed to Cardinal Ottoboni, who refused the cash—passing it on to Corelli's distant relatives—but

accepted the masterpieces. Corelli was buried in the Pantheon; for many years after his death, its anniversary was commemorated by solemn musical performances at his grave.

Corelli has been described as a mild, lovable and modest personality. He was a passionate admirer of pictures, his favorite hobby being the collection of art-works of which he possessed a valuable number. Thrifty to the point of being parsimonious, he dressed shabbily, was very careful about his expenditures and led a life of simplicity devoid of ostentation. Handel has laughingly commented upon Corelli's passion for visiting picture galleries "when there was no admission charge."

Corelli possessed a sense of humor that was warm but pointed: Once at the home of the Cardinal, he was performing a violin solo when, in the middle of a passage, he came to an abrupt stop. Asked by the Cardinal why he had stopped, he answered, "I was afraid my music might interrupt your conversation."

His name is all important in musical history by virtue of the fact that he was the father of the violin sonata (the founder of that school of composers for the violin which included Viotti, Veracini, Geminiani, etc.), one of the pioneers of the concerto grosso—as a matter of fact, one of the earliest instrumental composers in the history of music whose works still afford us aesthetic pleasure.

C. Hubert Parry has analyzed Corelli's style: "Corelli's methods are ostensibly contrapuntal, but it is noteworthy that his is not the old kind of counterpoint, but rather an artistic treatment of part-writing, which is assimilated into chords whose progressions are adapted to the principles of modern tonality. He uses sequences for the purposes of form, and modulations for the purposes of contrast and balance, and cadences to define periods and sections, and other characteristic devices of modern art; and though the traces of the old church modes are occasionally apparent, they are felt to be getting more and more slight. There is more of art than human feeling in his work, as is inevitable at such a stage of development; but his art as far as it goes is very good, and the style of expression refined and pleasant."

"The importance of Corelli," wrote J. Combarieu in his *Histoire*, "rests in the fact that he brought progress to style, that is to say the art of constructing the period, the logic and the phrase of musical discourse. One has frequently praised the expressive character and the nobility of his adagios. In his sonatas for violin solo, he owns a personal language."

One of the most famous of Corelli's works for violin—the *La Follia* variations, still featured prominently on programs of violin-recitals—has been orchestrated by Max Reger.

Principal works by Arcangelo Corelli:

CHAMBER MUSIC: *24 Suonate da camera a tre*; *12 Suonate da chiesa a tre*, etc.

ORCHESTRA: Twelve concerti grossi.

Solo sonatas for violin, etc.

About Arcangelo Corelli:

Combarieu, J. *Histoire de la Musique;* Hawkins, John. *History of Music*; Parry, C. Hubert. *The Evolution of the Art of Music*; Pincherle, Marc. *Corelli*.

Important recordings of music by Arcangelo Corelli:

ORCHESTRA: *Concerto grosso, no. 8* (COLUMBIA); *Suite*, for string orchestra (COLUMBIA).

CHAMBER MUSIC: *Sonata for two violins, viola and organ* (KANTOREI); *Sonata da camera in B-flat major* (PRO MUSICA).

Peter Cornelius *1824-1874*

PETER CORNELIUS was born in Mayence on December 24, 1824. He was the son of an actor, and the godson of the famous painter, Cornelius (a distant relative) for whom Felix Mendelssohn composed his *Cornelius march*.

His father wished him to become an actor, and as a child he made several appearances on the stage. His failure to create a favorable impression finally decided him to turn to his second great love, music. He began the study of the violin under haphazard instruction. In 1841, he came to London where he procured a post as second violinist of

the German Opera Company in the Drury Lane Theatre. He accompanied this work with intensive study of composition under Heinrich Esser.

After the death of his father, which took place in 1844, Cornelius devoted himself completely to the study of music. One year later he came to Berlin, where he was a guest at the home of his famous relative, the painter. Thru his kinsman, Cornelius was introduced to many distinguished people, some of whom gave him advice and encouragement. In Berlin, Cornelius continued his studies under W. S. Dehn. The first of his compositions was created at this time—an overture for grand orchestra, a *Stabat mater*, and a march, none of which have been preserved.

These early compositions—together with the outlines of a musical tragedy—Cornelius brought to the notice of two celebrated musicians in Berlin, Taubert (the conductor of the Berlin opera) and Nicolai (famous composer of *The Merry wives of Windsor*). Their verdict on the quality of his music would have depressed stronger spirits than that of Cornelius. "I had brought a tragedy, and he [Taubert] said 'write songs!' I had come with plans for palaces, and he said, 'Go build pig-sties!'" Nicolai was even more cruel. "He says I know nothing, can't write a note correctly. . . . In fact, he kicked me!"

PETER CORNELIUS

From Berlin, Cornelius came to Dessau with the hope of studying under Friedrich Schneider, who, however, was too old and sick to accept pupils. From here, Cornelius' road stretched to Weimar, where he knocked at the door of Franz Liszt. "He shook hands with me in a friendly manner," recorded Cornelius. As a matter of fact, Cornelius soon became a frequent visitor at Liszt's home, a personal friend of the great composer. In Liszt's salon, Cornelius met such musicians as Raff, Joachim and Berlioz. Berlioz, interesting himself in the young musician and moved by his poverty, gave him a commission to translate his own *Flight into Egypt* into German, paying him twenty dollars for the job. Berlioz gave Cornelius several other occupations, from time to time, enabling the young composer to keep body and soul together.

Liszt felt strongly that Cornelius possessed talent. Guided by his own religious preoccupations, Liszt urged the young composer to turn his hand to religious music. Under Liszt's personal guidance, Cornelius composed Masses and a *Salve Regina*. However, he soon felt that he was not meant for the composition of church music. Feeling at the same time that he was suffering from Liszt's influence, he left Weimar and came to the Thuringian forests "to find himself." Emancipated from Liszt's influence, Cornelius composed at this time many songs of great distinction.

He was back in Weimar in 1854, doing little jobs for Liszt. It was at this time that an idea came to him for a sprightly comic opera. Liszt did not like the subject and tried to dissuade Cornelius from the venture. Cornelius, however, was too intrigued by his plans to listen to advice. He prepared his own libretto, and when his score was completed he played portions of it to Liszt. The master realized that, in spite of the questionable subject, Cornelius had succeeded in composing sparkling, deft and charming music. As a result, Liszt accepted this comic opera (it was the *Barber of Bagdad*) for production. It was given its first performance under Liszt's baton on December 15, 1858.

[1] See sketch on Franz Liszt.

It is well known that, at this time, there was a well-planned cabal against Liszt.[1] The first performance of Cornelius' comic opera was greeted with hissing and derision by the audience not because the work failed to please but rather as a concerted attack against the conductor. It was as a result of this demonstration that Franz Liszt resigned his post as chapel-master at Weimar.

Thus, entirely thru extraneous circumstances, *The Barber of Bagdad* was a depressing failure. It was never again performed during Cornelius' lifetime. After his death, however, the opera emerged from neglect. In 1885 it was produced with great success in Munich. Five years later, Anton Seidl introduced this work at the Metropolitan Opera House in New York.

Commenting upon *The Barber of Bagdad*, R. A. Streatfeild wrote: "The beauties of the score are doubly astonishing when it is remembered that when it was written *Die Meistersinger* had not been composed. The germ of much that delights us in Wagner's comic-opera may be found in *The Barber*. . . . The plot of *The Barber* is long-winded and puerile, and the interest is entirely centered in the music. . . . Cornelius had a pretty gift for humorous orchestration, and his accompaniments often anticipate the dainty effects of *Die Meistersinger*."

With Liszt's retirement from Weimar, Cornelius went to Vienna and settled there in 1859. He met Richard Wagner who induced him to come to Munich. In Munich, in 1865, Cornelius received his first permanent employment in the faculty of the Conservatory.

The remainder of his life, Cornelius lived in obscurity and poverty, composing only one more opera (*Le Cid*) but many songs of deathless beauty. He never succeeded in attracting the notice of the music world to his work. He died in the city of his birth on October 26, 1874.

A great measure of Cornelius' obscurity may be traced to his unenergetic and apathetic temperament. He seems to have been singularly indifferent to beating a path for himself in the music world, making little effort to secure performances or publishers. He was altogether incapable of taking advantage of such opportunities as presented themselves to him during his life.

"Who could approach Peter Cornelius without at once loving him?" once wrote Karl Goldmark. "His spirit was of such childlike naivete, and yet such depth; his true, warm-hearted open nature, his highly cultivated, clear mind could not fail to take every one captive at once. . . . I often went to his room, we drank black coffee, and over our cigars chatted agreeably on music and musical development; and naturally we spoke much about Richard Wagner. . . . One day, Cornelius sent me a note inviting me to an important event. Richard Wagner had sent him the proof sheets of his *Tristan* piano score. We were to go thru them together with Tausig. The impression of this performance will remain unforgettable to me. . . ."

Cornelius was a person of excessive generosity. The first sum of money he received (the twenty dol'ars from Berlioz for the translation of *Flight into Egypt*) he sent in its entirety to his mother, even though he was starving at the time. Upon another occasion, in Vienna, he was known to have dropped his last coin into the hat of a beggar. Intensely superstitious, he was frequently prevented from making important moves merely because he recognized evil omens; as a matter of fact, he was almost kept from visiting Liszt for the first time because there were thirteen steps extending to Liszt's door.

Lawrence Gilman has commented upon Cornelius' great talent as a composer of song, particularly of Christmas songs. Here, "his world . . . is a world of ineffable and melancholy twilight, remote, mysterious, dream-haunted. There are moments when he seems immeasurably distant, wrapped in a shimmering, impenetrable mist of dreams, but even as you would strain your senses to follow him, he is standing beside you again, smiling that infinitely winsome smile of his and talking to you. . . . Those songs which most justly represent him—such as *Angedenken, Trauer, Ein Ton, An der traum, Nachts, Auftrag* . . . are the articulate and surviving documents of

one to whom 'upon the public ways life came.' He has not told us all that, perhaps, he might have told us; but it is something to have borne witness, as he indubitab.y has, to so much that is of enduring validity and beauty."

Principal works by Peter Cornelius:

OPERA: *The Barber of Bagdad*; *Le Cid*; *Gunlöd* (fragment).

VOCAL: *Lieder und gesänge* (solo); *Lieder und gesänge* (concerted).

CHORAL: Masses, *Salve Regina*, etc.

About Peter Cornelius:

Gilman, Lawrence. *Phases of Modern Music*; Streatfeild, R. A. *The Opera*. *Musical America* 41:3 December 20, 1924; *Musical Times* 47:609 September 1906.

Important recordings of music by Peter Cornelius:

SELECTIONS FROM OPERA: *The Barber of Bagdad*, "Overture" (GRAMOPHONE-Blech); "O holdes bild" (PARLAPHONE); "Sanfter schlummer wieght ihn ein" (PARLAPHONE); "Vor deinem fenster" (GRAMOPHONE).

SONGS: *Ave Maria* (GRAMOPHONE-McCormack); *Die Hirten* and *Die Könige* (CHRISTSCHALL); *Weihnachtsliedern* (GRAMOPHONE).

François Couperin-le-Grand
1668-1733

FRANÇOIS COUPERIN—designated by the historian as "Couperin-the-Great" to single him out from the long line of Couperins who, for two centuries, were influential in French music —was born in Paris, in one of the annexes of the Church of St. Gervais, on November 10, 1668. His father, the organist of St. Gervais, was his first teacher, from whom young Couperin acquired not merely the rudiments of organ playing but a sound and comprehensive musical education as well. His next teacher was Jacques Denis Thomelin, organist of the King's Chapel. While still Thomelin's pupil, Couperin revealed a rapidly growing creative talent by composing several organ pieces and motets of great originality.

In his twenty-fifth year, Couperin entered the King's service. Shortly afterwards, the position of organist to the Chapel Royal was open, and it was decided to hold open competition among all the applicants for the post, with Louis XIV himself as judge. François

Couperin easily surpassed the efforts of his competitors, winning the vote of the King. In this position, Couperin was introduced to the brilliant social life of the court in Paris.

His great musical talent at the organ, and especially at the harpsichord, brought him many honors and royal favors. He was appointed *"joueur de clavecin de la musique de la chambre du roi,"* and was selected as the music teacher of those princes closest to the throne. Before long, he became personal music-master to Louis XIV, for whom he composed the *Concerts royaux* which, during the last years of the King's life, were performed every Sunday in Versailles with Couperin at the harpsichord.

After the death of Louis XIV, Couperin's association with Versailles became less significant. During his last years, he lived in comfort in the Palais Royale section of Paris, where he devoted himself to his family and to music. His was now a quiet and unobtrusive existence in which the making of music was the principal pleasure. Together with his two sons, he gave regular concerts at his home for the delectation of personal friends.

François Couperin died in Paris on September 12, 1733. "I thank the public for the applause it has so generously bestowed on my works," he wrote several years before his death. "I trust that I have left something to make my loss regretted, if regrets may avail us in aught after this life."

In the development of instrumental music, Couperin was a powerful force. He was not only the first Frenchman to compose violin sonatas in imitation of Corelli, but he was virtually the father of piano music. With his *Pièces de clavecin*, which were published in 1713, 1716, 1722 and 1730, he showed his contemporaries how effective the harpsichord could become as a solo instrument.

"I confess," wrote Couperin, in explaining his method of composition, "that I love that which stimulates me much more than that which overwhelms me." In his *Pièces de clavecin* there are no powerful emotions or driving forces, but a quiet, subdued beauty which is

FRANÇOIS COUPERIN-LE-GRAND

more intellectual than emotional. In these pieces, the harpsichord assumes, as G. Jean-Aubry points out "every variety of accent in turn . . . fastidious, enchanting, observant, witty, mocking, slily malicious, ironic, biting." They are, in the words of Karl Nef, a "veritable world picture-book, an *orbus pictus*," in which he "has presented with a delightful charm and sureness, with an amazing precision, everything that can in any way be expressed in tone. As a color genius, he draws forth every tonal charm that slumbers in the harpsichord."

Principal works by François Couperin-le-Grand:

CHAMBER MUSIC: *Les Nations*; *L'Apothéose*; *Concerts royaux*. Four books of *Pièces de clavecin*, airs, sonatas for violin, etc.

About François Couperin-le-Grand:

Tessier, André. *Couperin*; Tiersot, Julien. *Couperin*.

Monthly Musical Record 19:25, 49, 77, 99, 124, 174 February-August 1889; *Musical Quarterly* 12:406 July 1926.

Important recordings of music by François Couperin-le-Grand:

CHAMBER MUSIC: *Concert dans le gout théâtral*, arranged by Cortot for chamber orchestra (GRAMOPHONE); *Concert royal no. 2* (ANTHOLOGIE SONORE).

HARPSICHORD: Collection of some of the most famous of Couperin's morsels for harpsichord, *Couperin Society album* (HIS MASTERS VOICE-Landowska).

Sir Frederic H. Cowen *1852-1935*

(See *Composers Of Today*)

Johann Baptist Cramer *1771-1858*

JOHANN BAPTIST CRAMER, who was born in Mannheim on February 24, 1771, stemmed from a family of musicians. His grandfather was a flautist in the then world-famous Mannheim orchestra; his uncle was a drummer in the court band; and his father was a violinist of repute.

When he was still an infant in arms, Cramer was brought to England, and from that time on England remained his home. It is for this reason that, altho Cramer was born in Germany, he is frequently referred to as an English composer.

His father had aspirations of making him a violinist. When Johann was four years old, therefore, he began systematic study of the violin. One day, he was sent by his father to the attic to practise his lessons there. An old and neglected piano was stored in that attic, and Johann abandoned his violin to toy with the keys of the piano. From that time on, he was frequently found in the attic, drawing music from the old piano. His parents were wise enough to realize that it was foolish to discourage so spontaneous a reaction. They placed Johann under J. D. Benser for piano instruction. Three years later, Cramer became a pupil of J. S. Schroeter. On April 5, 1781, he made his first public appearance as pianist.

When he was twelve years old, Cramer became a pupil of the celebrated Clementi. Though he studied under the master only two years, the course of study was a revelation to the young musician. Clementi broadened Cramer's musical horizon limitlessly, developing his technique and interpretative faculty. After these valuable years, Cramer relied almost exclusively on his own resources for the development of his technique.

On March 10, 1784, Cramer performed a duet with Clementi at the Hanover Square Grand Concerts, attracting considerable attention. There followed other appearances in which Cramer's reputation grew. In 1788, he went abroad, playing in France and Germany with great success.

He was in Paris during the revolution of 1789, when a curious and all-important incident took place. A Russian in Paris came into his debt. Unable to repay Cramer, he offered instead some musical manuscripts which he had in his possession. These manuscripts were some choral works of Johann Sebastian Bach, and it was the first time that Cramer became intimately acquainted with the music of the master. The profundity of this music struck Cramer so forcefully that, after this, he became a devoted disciple of the Leipzig musician.

In 1791, Cramer was back in England where he gave many performances—including one with Hummel, aged twelve. At this time, he made the acquaintance of Josef Haydn who took a great fancy to him. This friendship between Haydn and Cramer was further cemented in 1799, when Cramer visited Vienna. Haydn introduced Cramer to many great musicians in Vienna of that time. It is interesting to note that Cramer went in the company of Beethoven to a performance of Mozart's *Don Giovanni*.

By this time, Cramer's career as a piano virtuoso was fully launched. He was unquestionably one of the great

JOHANN BAPTIST CRAMER

pianists of his time; his extensive tours brought him great fame everywhere. Cramer was equally distinguished as a teacher of the piano; for many years it was the ambition of every aspiring virtuoso to study under Cramer in England.

Cramer's famous studies for the piano, which brought him immortal fame, were composed in 1804. These studies have proved to be of incalculable importance to music students in the attainment of piano technique. Beethoven thought highly of them. "Our master," Schindler has recorded, "declared that these études were the chief basis of all genuine playing." But these études are not only of pedagogic importance, but contain artistic value as well. Dannreuther has pointed out that many of them are "poems, like Mendelssohn's *Songs without words.*"

In 1813, Cramer was one of the founders of the famous Royal Philharmonic Orchestra of London. For a few years he was not only one of its conductors, but also a featured piano soloist. In the latter capacity he introduced for the first time to London audiences not only his own concertos but also many of the concertos of Mozart.

Cramer's musical importance was felt in other directions. For many years, he was one of the professors at the Royal Academy of Music. In 1812 he became a publisher of repute when he became an official partner of Chappell and Company; ten years later, he established his own publishing firm.

Johann Baptist Cramer died at his home in Kensington on April 16, 1858. He was buried in the Brompton cemetery.

It is quite true that Cramer's piano music never makes its appearance on concert programs in our time, being known only to piano students. But critics have, periodically, pointed out that there is much of artistic importance in Cramer's piano works which, in consequence, are well deserving of exploration. "In pianoforte music," wrote Alexander Brent-Smith, "there is a beautiful district unknown to concertgoers but highly appreciated by all pianists—the district of Johann Baptist Cramer. Of his many compositions (he wrote 105 sonatas) little remains in constant use except his studies. All of these have a great technical value, and many have, in addition, considerable musical beauty. We might even go so far as to say that one or two are not unworthy to stand in the company of the preludes of Bach, such as the study in D-major, with its rippling demi semiquavers; the vigorous two-part study in C-minor; and, loveliest of all, the study in A-minor. Each of these is so essentially pianistic that it would perish if dissociated from the pianoforte."

Principal works by Johann Baptist Cramer:

ORCHESTRA: Seven concertos for piano and orchestra.

CHAMBER MUSIC: *Quintet*; *Piano quartet.*

PIANO: 105 sonatas; studies; fantasias; rondos; variations, etc.

About Johann Baptist Cramer:

Musical Times 43:641 October 1, 1902; *Musical Times* 72:405 March 1931.

César Cui *1835-1918*

CÉSAR ANTONOVITCH CUI, one of the members of that distinguished group of Russian nationalist composers known as the "Five," was born in Vilna on January 18, 1835. His father, Antoine Cui, was a Frenchman who had come to Russia in 1812 with Napoleon's army. He was wounded in Smolensk, left on the battle-field, half-frozen, as dead. When he recovered, he decided to settle permanently in Russia. He married a Lithuanian woman, and turned towards pedagogy as a profession, becoming professor of French at the High School of Vilna.

It was at this high school that César Cui received his early education. Both in his studies at school and in his private lessons in music (one of his early music teachers was Moniuszko, the celebrated Polish composer) he proved to be in possession of an alert intelligence, so alert that his father decided to direct him towards engineering.

In 1850, Cui was entered in the School of Military Engineering at St. Petersburg where his competence in his studies was so marked that, upon his graduation seven years later, he was appointed sub-professor. He specialized

Cui: Kwē

in the subject of military fortifications, becoming an authority in this field. He held the rank of Major General, wrote several books in his subject—including the *Abridged History of Permanent Fortification* and *A Manual of Flying Fortification*—and was the teacher of eight members of the Imperial family, including Nicholas II.

During this period, Cui had turned sharply away from music. In 1857, however, he met Balakirev, whose theories on national music awakened Cui's dormant love for the art. Cui immediately joined forces with Balakirev. Together they evolved a new school of composition whose influence was to be all-important in the history of Russian music.[1]

In 1859 came Cui's first important work, the opera *The Captive in the Caucasus,* based upon a poem of Pushkin, which, however, was not performed until twenty-four years later. This whetted his appetite in composition, and from this time on Cui was uniquely productive, particularly in the field of the opera where he attempted to embody the principles of the "Five."

The most famous of his operas proved to be *William Ratcliff,* introduced at St. Petersburg on February 26, 1869. *William Ratcliff* elicited the high praise of some musicians, Rimsky-Korsakoff going so far as to write in the *St. Peters-*

burg Gazette that the love-duet in Act III was "the finest . . . in all contemporary musical literature." Other critics, however, were denunciatory and the public for the most part was indifferent. After seven performances it was removed from the repertoire. In 1900, *William Ratcliffe* was revived in Moscow when it was more favorably received.

César Cui was, probably, as fertile in the field of music criticism as in composition. Beginning with 1864, he wrote prolifically for Russian, French and Belgian publications, spreading the gospel of the new Russian school. Russian composers of the late nineteenth century, who followed the nationalist banner, found in his pen a vigorous protagonist and a faithful ally. Cui was also the author of *La Musique en Russie,* which attempted to spread propaganda for Russian national music to French-speaking nations.

César Cui died in St. Petersburg on March 14, 1918. He died seeing his work completed: Russian music was now accepted thruout the entire world of music, and the Russian national idiom was firmly established.

In analyzing Cui's style of composition, Hermann Laroche has pointed out Cui's lack of originality even in his best works. "Cui's gift for melody is not abundant. His tunes cannot exactly be called common; one merely feels that they lack individuality. One cannot point at any particular place to plagiarism, or indicate the source from which such and such a motive has been taken, for they have not been stolen from anywhere; they have simply been suggested; and these suggested ideas, which are adapted with such taste and sense of beauty in Cui's writing, take the place, in Cui's music, as in that of so many others, of original melodic invention."

The truth, no doubt, is that—as M. D. Calvocoressi recently wrote—Cui, as a composer, "has sunk almost into complete oblivion. His operas are no longer produced and, though he possessed creative talent, his music no longer affords aesthetic pleasure or exerts an influence. Cui's name is kept alive in musical history not because of his compositions, which are practically dead,

CÉSAR CUI

[1] For the origin and ideals of the "Russian five," see sketch of Balakirev.

but by virtue of the fact that he was a leader in an all-important musical movement."

Principal works by César Cui:

ORCHESTRA: *Marche solennelle*; *Tarantella*; *Petite suite*; Three suites; *Suite concertante* (for violin and orchestra).

OPERA: *The Captive in the Caucasus*; *The Mandarin's son*; *William Ratcliff*; *Angelo*; *A Feast in time of plague*; *The Captain's daughter*, etc.

CHAMBER MUSIC: *String quartet in C-minor.*

CHORAL: *Mystic chorus*; *Les Oiseaux d'Argenteau*; Two choruses for male voices; Seven a cappella choruses.

Songs, pieces for the piano, etc.

About César Cui:

Calvocoressi, M. D. and Abraham, Gerald. *Masters of Russian Music*; Montagu-Nathan, Montagu. *Contemporary Russian Composers*; Pougin, Arthur. *A Short History of Russian Music*; Rimsky-Korsakoff, Nicolas. *My Musical Life.*

Important recordings of music by César Cui:

ORCHESTRA: *Tarantella* (POLYDOR-WOLFF).

VIOLIN AND PIANO: *Berceuse russe* (POLYDOR); *Orientale* (VICTOR-Elman).

SONGS: *Hunger* (PARLAPHONE-Rosing); *Romance* (PARLAPHONE-Rosing).

Karl Czerny *1791-1857*

KARL CZERNY was born in Vienna on February 20, 1791. His father was his first teacher in music.

An intimate friend of the Czerny family was attracted by young Karl's phenomenal musical memory, which had absorbed a rich library of piano music, and brought the prodigy to Beethoven. Beethoven, in turn, was so impressed by Czerny's performance that he offered to become his teacher. For three years, Czerny was Beethoven's pupil; at the same time, he coupled his piano studies with private excursions into the harmony treatises of Fux and Albrechtsberger. During this period, Beethoven introduced Czerny to Prince Karl Lichnowski and Archduke Rudolph, both of whom took the young musician under their wing, became his patrons, and were powerfully instrumental in furthering his career.

Czerny's importance as a musician became discernible at an early age. In his fourteenth year his first public work,

Czerny: Chĕr'nē

KARL CZERNY

a *Theme and variations* appeared, whose popularity became so great that, at one time, the publishers could not cope with the demand. One year later, Czerny had acquired such a technical mastery of the piano that his services were widely sought as teacher. The demand for his instruction frequently compelled him to work more than ten hours a day.

In 1804, Czerny planned an extensive concert tour as pianist. Political unrest in Europe prevented the realization of this project. After a few appearances in recital, Czerny definitely decided that pedagogy, rather than concert work, would be his major occupation. He became one of the greatest of all European teachers of the piano. His Sunday afternoon musicales at his home, devoted to pupil performances (at which such celebrities as Beethoven, Clementi and Hummel were present) were famous thruout the world of music. It is indicative of Czerny's importance as a teacher that his pupils included such world-famous virtuosi as Franz Liszt, Thalberg and Leschetizky.

This intense pedagogical activity did not interfere with Czerny's creative work. Czerny's music sold well, so well, in fact, that he was flooded with commissions from his publishers. The fulfillment of this demand cost him many nights of hard work. Czerny's popularity as a composer rivalled his prestige as a teacher; his publishers—Cappi and Diabelli—earned handsome profits from his works.

A lifetime of intense activity brought with it ill health and nervous disorders prematurely. About 1850, Czerny was compelled to give up his indefatigable composition. It was not long before even teaching was impossible for his declining strength.

Karl Czerny died in Vienna on July 15, 1857. He had never married, and was survived by no near relatives. His entire fortune, therefore, was divided among numerous charities, as Czerny had specified shortly before his death.

C. F. Pohl describes Czerny as "modest and simple in manner of life, courteous and friendly in his behaviour, just and kindly in his judgment on matters of art, and helpful to all young artists who came in his way. His disposition was so gentle that he shrank from a harsh or coarse word even spoken in jest."

He had a pleasant face with bright, expressive eyes that glistened behind spectacles, sensitive lips, an effeminate chin and rather short, woolly hair. He was a student of politics, and well-versed in many cultural subjects. His unique passion was cats; he frequently had as many as six near him. He was extremely stingy. It was said that he never used his fees as a teacher but stored them in a bag. After his death, the bag was discovered with more than $50,000 in cash in it.

Karl Czerny was a productive composer, his output including many examples of almost every form of musical compositions. His best known works, however, are for the piano. "His writings lack depth," wrote Leschetizky, "but no one can deny that they show a great knowledge of form, of the resources of the instrument and of all the pianistic effects."

The work by which Karl Czerny is best remembered today is his remarkable series of studies for the piano, with which every piano student becomes intimately acquainted. Discussing this work, Hugo Riemann wrote: "Czerny understood better than anyone else the simple, primitive form from which all

pianoforte passage writing is evolved: his studies, therefore, are of immense help in the earlier stages of development."

Principal works by Karl Czerny:

CHORAL: Masses; requiems; offertories; choruses, etc.

ORCHESTRA: Symphonies; overtures; concertos for piano and orchestra.

CHAMBER MUSIC: Quartets; string trios, etc.

Pieces for the piano, arrangements for two and four hands of famous symphonies, overtures, operas and oratorios, etc., studies for the piano, songs, etc.

About Karl Czerny:

Etude 27:375 June 1909; *Musical Record* 6: 260 June 1900; *Musician* 20:504 August 1915.

Important recordings of music by Karl Czerny:

PIANO: *Étude,* Op. 740, no. 13 (VICTOR); *Scherzo fantasque* (PATHE).

Claude Daquin *1694-1772*

LOUIS CLAUDE DAQUIN (sometimes known as D'Aquin) was born in Paris on July 4, 1694. His first lessons on the organ and harpsichord were given him by an uncle. At the age of six, he was taken to court where he performed upon the harpsichord before Louis XIV who was so delighted with the performance that he took the little musician upon his knees and said: "Some day you will be one of our most celebrated artists."

After taking some lessons in composition from Bernier, he began creative work at the age of eight, producing a symphony and a choral composition. At twelve, he was already a professional musician, becoming the organist of the chapel of St. Antoine, to which crowds came, expressly to hear his performance.

In 1727, he entered a competition for the post of organist of Saint Paul. Despite the fact that one of the competitors was no one less than Rameau, Daquin came out triumphant, receiving the position. This he held with considerable honor. It was at this time that Louis Marchand, the great organist, heard him perform and was sufficiently convinced of the genius of the young

CLAUDE DAQUIN

harpsichord, but—as the score specifically points out—capable of being performed by violins, flutes and oboes.

Principal works by Claude Daquin:

CHORAL: *La Rose*; motets, etc.

INSTRUMENTAL: Pieces for the harpsichord; pieces for the organ; *Noëls*; fugues; trios, etc.

About Claude Daquin:

Allgemeine Musikzeitung 38:531 September 1911; *Le Guide du Concert* 17:16 January 23, 1931; *Le Monde musical* 37:275 July 31, 1926.

Important recordings of music by Claude Daquin:

ORCHESTRA: *Musette, Rigaudon and Tambourin*, arranged from harpsichord (GRAMOPHONE).

HARPSICHORD: *Le Coucou* (VICTOR-Landowska); *L'Hirondelle* (GRAMOPHONE-Landowska).

musician to offer to become his teacher. As result of this valuable instruction, Daquin emerged one of the great organists of France.

Upon Marchand's death, in 1732, Daquin was appointed organist of the convent of the Cordeliers. In 1739, he became the organist of the Chapel Royal. In these posts he gave continued evidence of his great ability, and the foremost musicians of the time—including Handel himself—did him honor.

The closing years of Daquin's life were unhappy ones. Always negligent about finances, he had squandered a fortune until, at the end of his life, he found himself completely destitute. Poverty—a striking contrast to the magnificence he had formerly known—caused him no end of humiliation and suffering.

He died in Paris on June 15, 1772.

As a composer, Daquin created many brilliant pieces for the organ. He is, perhaps, best known for his charming morsels for the harpsichord, of which the famous *Le Coucou* is an example. The first volume of these harpsichord pieces appeared in 1735, and succeeded in increasing the resources of the instrument. These pieces are witty, bright and fresh. Even today they have lost none of their original appeal.

Equally distinguished is Daquin's volume of *Noëls*, composed for organ and

Alexander Dargomijsky *1813-1869*

ALEXANDER SERGEIVICH DARGOMIJSKY, recognized as Glinka's successor in the field of national Russian opera, was born in the government of Toula on February 14, 1813. His parents were prosperous land proprietors who had vacated their ancestral home in Smolensk during Napoleon's invasion.

It was thought, at first, that Alexander had been born a mute. Until his fifth birthday he failed to speak a word. However, his parents could not question his mental alertness or his sensitivity to art. As a mere child, he built his own marionette theatre on which he enacted little plays of his own creation. Shortly after his sixth birthday, he began the study of the piano, paying scant attention to technical studies but interesting himself much more in his musical discussions with his teacher. Two years later he began the study of the violin, and soon afterwards he became a member of a string quartet.

His parents, conscious of his great love for music, placed him under competent instruction. From Schoberlechner, Dargomijsky acquired a thoro knowledge of harmony and counterpoint which enabled him to pursue composition with greater self-assurance.

In 1831, he was a successful candidate for a government post in the ministry of the Imperial household. His governmental duties, however, did not interfere with his musical study. During these years, he perfected his piano technique until he became a pianist of great skill, and continued his composition, producing several cantatas and songs.

Accident brought him into contact with Glinka in 1833, changing the entire course of his life. Glinka's ideals not only turned Dargomijsky towards the theatre, but also imbued him with the ideal of becoming a true Russian voice. Relinquishing his government post, Dargomijsky turned more devotedly to his studies. He memorized harmony and counterpoint texts from books which Glinka lent him; he spent tireless hours studying musical scores. Then, when he felt that his grip had become sure, he plunged more feverishly than before into composition.

It was inevitable—in view of Glinka's influence upon him—that at this time he should turn to the composition of operas. His first work in this field was *Esmeralda,* based upon Victor Hugo's *Notre Dame de Paris,* which was presented at the Paris Opéra in 1836. *Esmeralda* was a failure. Undismayed, Dargomijsky presented the opera in a Russian version to the management of the Imperial Opera House. He waited eight years for an answer which, finally, was a favorable one. *Esmeralda* was produced in Moscow on December 5, 1847, and was so warmly received that it was repeated in St. Petersburg.

"There is hardly a trace of originality in this work," wrote Arthur Pougin. "Certain pages in it, however, are very vivid and happily contrived. . . . One may also notice the remarkable skill which Dargomijsky showed even at this time in his method of writing for voices."

Dargomijsky's next work was a cantata, *The Triumph of Bacchus,* which was refused a performance. For the next few years—partially thru discouragement at the failure of his cantata to receive a hearing—the composer devoted himself almost exclusively to the creation of songs and small pieces. This was only a transitory period, however.

Eventually, the lure of the opera proved irresistible for him, and he began to hunt for a libretto which he might develop into a second opera.

This second opera brought Dargomijsky fame. It was *Roussalka,* based on a poem by Pushkin, which was performed at St. Petersburg on May 4, 1856. It was this opera which brought Dargomijsky the distinction of being esteemed as Glinka's successor. César Cui has condemned the opera for its many individual numbers—arias, duets, trios, etc.—but confesses that its dramatic qualities are of unquestionable effectiveness and its recitatives are expertly written. "In this work, Dargomijsky was endowed with the very special gift of knowing how to fit each period or sentence with the musical phrase best adapted to it, and how to discover a melodic style best suited to each character. With him, all the words of the text and all the details of the drama seem to be of a piece with the music."

In 1864, Dargomijsky left Russia to visit Europe, in order to introduce his music to foreign musicians. He made little impression in France and Germany, but Belgium welcomed him cordially. Upon his return to Russia, he allied himself with that young group of national composers, the "Russian-five." Inspired by their ideals, he determined to write a new opera which would express

ALEXANDER DARGOMIJSKY

the lofty principles of the new school. "It is my intention," he wrote at this time, "that the music should interpret the words. I have not the slightest intention of reducing music to a mere pastime for the benefit of dilettanti. For me, the truth is indispensable."

With his goal vividly before him, Dargomijsky composed his last, and greatest, opera—*The Stone guest*, a version of the Don Giovanni legend utilized by Pushkin. This opera, which was not produced until four years after the composer's death, was at first received coldly. It lacked warmth and lingering melodies. In Dargomijsky's preoccupation with the dramatic elements of his text, he had given great importance to recitative. A contemporary of Dargomijsky, Wilhelm von Lenz, summed up the attitude of the audience which first witnessed *The Stone guest* when he wrote that this opera was "a recitative in three acts."

Since that time, however, *The Stone guest* has won the esteem it deserves. Today it is recognized (in the words of César Cui) as "the cornerstone of the new school of Russian opera."

Alexander Dargomijsky succumbed to aneurism on January 17, 1869 in St. Petersburg. He died leaving *The Stone guest* unfinished, and he assigned its completion to César Cui and its orchestration to Rimsky-Korsakoff.

A friend of Dargomijsky, Youri Arnold, described him as follows: "He was of small stature—no taller than Glinka; and his head was remarkably big in proportion to the rest of him, especially on account of its great breadth at the top. He had chestnut hair, high cheek bones, a slightly flat snub nose, rather thick lips, and small eyes that continually blinked. A tiny scrap of a moustache imparted a highly original character to his pale, sickly looking face —a mobile and expressive face which betokened thoughtfulness and will-power. His carriage and manner bore the stamp of perfect breeding."

It should be pointed out that Dargomijsky was one of the first composers to utilize extensively the whole-tone scale, which was brought to its highest expressiveness by Debussy. It is more than likely that Debussy was introduced to the whole-tone scale thru Dargomijsky's

music, which he must have heard when he visited Russia during his student days.

Principal works by Alexander Sergeivich Dargomijsky:

OPERA: *Esmeralda*; *Roussalka*; *The Stone guest*.

ORCHESTRA: *The Little Russian kazachok*; *Baba-Yaga*; *The Dance of mummers*; *Finnish fantasia*.

Pieces for the piano, songs, choral works, etc.

About Alexander Sergeivich Dargomijsky:

Calvocoressi, M. D. and Abraham, Gerald. *Masters of Russian Music*; Montagu-Nathan, Montagu. *A History of Russian Music*; Newmarch, Rosa. *The Russian Opera*; Pougin, Arthur. *A Short History of Russian Music*.

Important recordings of music by Alexander Sergeivich Dargomijsky:

SELECTIONS FROM OPERA: *Roussalka*, "Mad scene" and "Death of the Miller" (GRAMOPHONE-Chaliapin); "Miller's aria" (VICTOR-Chaliapin); "Olga's aria" (GRAMOPHONE).

SONGS: *Darling girl* (GRAMOPHONE); *The Old corporal* (GRAMOPHONE-Chaliapin); *Vanka Tanka* (GRAMOPHONE).

Félicien David *1810-1876*

FÉLICIEN CÉSAR DAVID was born in Cadenet, France, on May 13, 1810. The son of musical parents, he evinced an extraordinary precocity for the art. At the age of six, he possessed a flexible and attractive voice and a discerning ear, attracting the notice of the first oboe player of the Paris Opéra, who urged Félicien's father to permit the boy's talent to be developed. Shortly afterwards, the family transferred its home to Aix, where Félicien became a member of the cathedral choir. It was here that he turned to musical composition for the first time, producing hymns, songs and motets.

In 1825, David was entered as a student at the Jesuit college at Aix. Here he continued with his music studies. Four years later, he undertook his first musical assignment—second conductor of a theatre orchestra. He held this position for three years, resigning to become chapel master of the cathedral.

Dissatisfaction with the limited musical sphere of Aix brought David to Paris, in 1830, to complete his musical studies

FÉLICIEN DAVID

the remainder of his life, influencing his musical creation vitally.

Shortly after his return to Paris from these travels, David composed his most famous work, a symphonic ode, *Le Désert,* in which he attempted to speak of the Far East in tones and reproduce musically its exotic charm. This work was given a first performance on December 8, 1844, creating a vivid impression upon the audience which found the music full of colorful appeal.

"The great charm of *Le Désert,*" wrote Arthur Hervey, "lies in the poetry of its conception, the picturesqueness of the music. David was rather a tone-painter than a symphonist; he made little or no attempt to develop his ideas, satisfied to record his impressions as they occurred to him. The musical tableau of sunrise in the desert is really wonderfully descriptive and quite modern in style."

While David's productivity continued, he never equalled the artistic success of *Le Désert.* In 1846, he composed an oratorio, *Moïse au Sinaï,* which was given its first performance in Germany, to which country David had come upon a concert tour. This was followed by a symphony, *Christophe Colomb,* and a "mystery," *L'Éden.* None of these works impressed their audience. It was only with an *opéra-comique, La Perle du Brésil,* which came in 1851, and a serious opera, *Lalla Roukh* (1862), that David succeeded, after several years, in achieving something of the acclaim that had been accorded to *Le Désert.*

Towards the end of his life, Félicien David—sick in body and spirit—was offered the hospitality of an affluent widow, Mme. Tastet, in St. Germain-en-Laye, where he knew comfort and seclusion. One day, the servant, in bringing him his mail, told him of a bird that had a few moments before flown in thru the window, alighted upon the piano, and regarded her with stark eyes. "It is the announcement of my death," the composer told her.

A few days later—on August 29, 1876—Félicien David was dead.

"Every artist has a masterly quality which gives his work its principal character," Camille Saint-Saëns once wrote. "David possessed the rarest of all:

under more competent instruction. He presented himself to Cherubini who, after glancing cursorily over the mass of manuscripts, shouted impatiently at the young composer: "You know nothing. You write nothing but mistakes. This is no music!" Undismayed by this brutal criticism, David entered the Conservatory, studying harmony under Millot, and counterpoint and fugue under Fétis. During this period, he knew appalling poverty. "I go from bad to worse," he wrote in a letter at this time. "I was sick three weeks . . . my illness provoked by the poor nourishment in the restaurants of Paris." But not even starvation and sickness could smother his enthusiasm and aspirations.

In 1831 occurred the most important event in Félicien David's life. In that year, he joined a religious brotherhood known as the Saint-Simonians. David embraced the religious doctrines of this brotherhood with fervor and enthusiasm. For a long while he lived in monastic seclusion with the brothers, devoting himself to religious meditation and prayer. When the brotherhood was dissolved in 1833, David travelled with several members of the sect to the south of France, and from there to the Far East. For several years, Félicien David wandered thru Constantinople, Egypt and the Holy Land, gathering impressions which were to linger with him for naïvete. It is this quality which brought the astonishing success to *Lalla-Roukh* and *Le Désert*. The public did not expect it; it is at all times prepared for great and small effects, for piquant melodies, for noisy orchestration, for distinguished harmonies. But it is defenseless against a soul which opens itself, and says simply whatever it chooses to say."

"To his feeling for color and to the melodic charm of his inspiration," commented Ernest Reyer, "Félicien David added a great purity of style, and an exceptional suppleness in the art of handling the orchestra and making the voice sing."

Principal works by Félicien David:

OPERA: *La Perle du Brésil*; *Herculanum*; *Lalla-Roukh*; *Le Saphir*; *La Captive*.

CHORAL: *Moïse au Sinai*.

ORCHESTRA: *Two symphonies*; *Le Désert*; *Christophe Colomb*.

CHAMBER MUSIC: Twenty-four quintets; Two nonets for wind.

About Félicien David:

Azevedo, Alexis. *Félicien David*; Brancour, René. *Félicien David*.

Important recordings of music by Félicien David:

SELECTIONS FROM OPERA: *Lalla Roukh*, "Ma maitresse a quitté la tante" and "Si vous ne savez plus charmer" (PATHE). *La Perle du Brésil*, "Charmant oiseau" (VICTOR).

Claude Debussy *1862-1918*
(See *Composers Of Today*)

Reginald De Koven *1859-1920*

HENRY LOUIS REGINALD DE KOVEN, beloved American composer of operetta, was born in Middletown, Connecticut, on April 3, 1859. When he was thirteen years old, his father, a clergyman, moved to England. Thus, Reginald's education took place principally in England, where he received his degree from St. John's College at Oxford in 1879.

As a child he rebelled strongly against the study of music, showing far greater aptitude for languages (he could read Latin at sight at the age of six). His mother, a music lover, insisted that he study music. It was only after several years of association with music that de Koven became strongly attached to it.

By the time he graduated from St. John's College, he knew that he would be a musician by profession. For this purpose, he went to Germany to study piano under Lebert and Spiedel, and harmony under Pruckner. From Stuttgart, he went to Frankfort-on-the-Main, where he received intensive training in composition under Dr. Hauff. After several months of the study of the voice under Vanuccini, in Florence, Reginald De Koven came to Paris where he brought his study of music to a close under Léo Delibes.

In 1882, De Koven returned to America, settling in Chicago. At first he earned his living as a bank teller, then by working in the office of a stockbrokerage house. Shortly after his return to Chicago, he met Anna Farwell, the daughter of a millionaire. The two fell in love almost immediately, and were married. Reginald De Koven's father-in-law took the young musician into his own enormous dry-goods establishment.

It was at this time that Reginald De Koven's wife became engaged in a real estate transaction which brought fabulous wealth to the composer. The state of Texas, eager to raise funds for a new capital, offered to sell 3,000,000 acres of land at a nominal price. De Koven's father-in-law was shrewd enough to

REGINALD DE KOVEN

recognize the value of the land, and bought a considerable parcel for his daughter as a gift. The land soared in value. Before long, the De Kovens were financially firmly established.

Fortune, never coming single-handed, likewise established De Koven as a composer at the same time. Until now, De Koven had composed several operettas, none of which attracted much notice. Upon a visit to Minneapolis, De Koven met Harry B. Smith, librettist. After several conversations, the composer and librettist decided to join forces. It was this union that succeeded in bringing about one of the most successful operetta teams in America.

Their first collaborative effort was *Robin Hood*, composed in ninety days, which was given its first performance in Chicago by the Bostonians on June 9, 1890. At first only moderately successful, *Robin Hood* eventually increased in popularity until it firmly established itself—particularly in New York—as a classic of American operetta. De Koven's light touch, his fertile melodic vein, his ability to etch witty strokes with the pen made his score contagiously popular. One of the songs of *Robin Hood*—the perenially famous *Oh, promise me!*—took America by storm, and to this day has maintained its important rôle—together with the wedding marches of Wagner and Mendelssohn—in American wedding ceremonies.

Robin Hood retained its great popularity for several decades. The Bostonians performed this work more than 4,500 times. It has likewise been introduced thruout the world with equal success.

It is not generally known that the success of *Robin Hood* almost made de Koven a collaborator of the great William S. Gilbert, of Gilbert and Sullivan fame. At this time, Gilbert and Sullivan were involved in one of their bitter disputes. Gilbert, searching the horizon for a new collaborator, asked De Koven to come to see him. De Koven's extreme youth, however, prejudiced Gilbert, and made him reluctant to accept the young composer.

Altho De Koven was financially independent, he worked for many years as a music critic. In 1889, he accepted a position as music editor on the *Chicago Evening Post*, because he felt strongly that his great fortune was bringing with it mental stagnancy. One year later, De Koven joined the force of the *New York World*. From 1897 until 1899, the *New York Journal* published De Koven's discerning criticisms. Between 1902 and 1905, De Koven officiated as conductor of the Washington Philharmonic, which he himself had brought into being. And from 1907 until 1912, he was back at his critic's desk with the *New York World*.

During these busy years of criticism, De Koven, the composer, was not idle. He produced many popular operettas, each of effervescent zest and freshness, finding a large and appreciative following. These included *The Knickerbockers* (1903) *The Golden butterfly* (1907) and *Her little highness* (1913).

In 1917, De Koven's musical talent was recognized when the Metropolitan Opera House of New York engaged him to compose a grand opera to a poetical drama by Percy Mackaye. It cannot be said that the *Canterbury pilgrims* was even a moderate artistic success, nor that it deserved the painstaking and lavish performance it received. Herbert F. Peyser pointed out that De Koven failed completely to catch the spirit or atmosphere of the background in his music; and other critics lamented De Koven's light hand which was little suited to so dignified a subject as Mackaye's poetical drama. Reginald De Koven produced one more grand opera after the *Canterbury pilgrims*, *Rip Van Winkle,* produced in Chicago in 1920.

Reginald De Koven died in New York City on January 15, 1920. During the last years of his life he suffered intensely from gout.

De Koven lived in palatial splendor on Park Avenue, New York. His home was, for many years, one of the attractions of the city, furnished as it was, with glassware, tapestries and furnishings secured from medieval European palaces and cathedrals. In such sumptuous surroundings, De Koven moved with grace. He was a gentleman, in the finest sense of the word. He dressed magnificently; it was said that he wore many of his outfits only once. He was a gourmet, passionately fond of Moselle wine and pheasant; delicacies from all over the world were imported for his table. He smoked excessively.

He was uniquely sensitive about his girth. He could never pass a mirror without directing a hurried glance towards his waistline. He kept a scale in his studios, watching his weight with meticulous fastidiousness. At one time, his manager played a trick upon him by adjusting the scales so that it registered two pounds more. A few hours later, the manager found De Koven in bed, restricting himself to a diet of hot water and dry bread.

De Koven was enormously superstitious. He was convinced that thirteen was a lucky number for him, and he made every effort to have his productions open on the thirteenth of the month.

Today, of course, De Koven no longer enjoys the high position in American music that was once his. His operettas have aged considerably. Upon occasional revival, they fail to give the pleasure that they once imparted. Some of De Koven's melodies, however, still appeal strongly by virtue of their sentiment and charm.

Principal works of Reginald De Koven:

OPERA: *Robin Hood*; *The Knickerbockers*; *The Mandarin*; *Red feather*; *The Golden butterfly*; *Her little highness*; *The Canterbury pilgrims*; *Rip van Winkle*, etc.

ORCHESTRA: *Suite*.

More than 400 songs, pieces for the piano, etc.

About Reginald De Koven:

Cooke, James Francis. *Great Men and Famous Music*; De Koven, Anna. *A Musician and His Wife*; Howard, John Tasker. *Our American Music*; Hughes, Rupert. *Contemporary American Music*.

Important recordings of music by Reginald De Koven·

SELECTIONS FROM OPERA: *Robin Hood*, "Medley of selections" (VICTOR); "Oh, promise me" (VICTOR-Homer)

SONGS: *Marching song* (VICTOR).

Léo Delibes *1836-1891*

CLÉMENT PHILIBERT LÉO DE-LIBES was born in St. Germain du Val on February 21, 1836. His father died while he was still a child.

Brought to Paris at an early age, Léo Delibes sang for a period in the choir of the Madeleine church. It was not only his pleasing voice but his musical intelligence as well that urged his mother to encourage him to begin the study of music seriously. In 1849, he was entered in the Paris Conservatory, where his instructors included Bazin, Benoist, Le Couppey and Adolph Adam.

Thru the influence of Adam, Delibes procured a position as accompanist at the Théâtre Lyrique, and as an organist at the Church St. Pierre de Chaillot, in 1853. Self-sufficient financially, he could turn to composition. From the very first, the theatre attracted him strongly. His apprentice works included *Deux sous de charbon,* produced in 1855, and *Maître Griffard,* presented in 1857—neither work of sufficient distinction to attract attention.

In 1862, Delibes was appointed organist of the church of St. Jean-et-St. François, retaining this position for nine full years. Three years later, an opening was found for him at the Paris Opéra as assistant chorusmaster, a post which proved to be providential. Before long, he attracted the notice of Monsieur Perrin who asked him to compose music for a two-scene ballet, *La Source. La Source,* produced at the Opéra on November 12, 1866, first brought Delibes fame. "One easily recognized here originality and distinction of style," wrote Ernest Guiraud concerning this early work.

From this time on, Delibes's rise to importance was swift. In 1870, he was commissioned to compose an entire ballet. The result was *Coppélia,* often regarded the most felicitous of Delibes' scores. In 1873, he produced a three-act opera, *Le Roi l'a dit,* at the Opéra Comique, greatly increasing his prestige as a composer. *Sylvia* came in 1876; the opera, *Lakmé,* in 1883.

Delibes now enjoyed an all-important position in French music. After becoming an officer of the Legion of Honor in 1877, he was made a member of the Institut in 1884. Three years prior to that, he had been appointed professor of composition at the Conservatory.

Léo Delibes died of congestion of the lungs in Paris on January 16, 1891.

LÉO DELIBES

"Without doubt," wrote Alfred Bruneau, "there are many pages of picturesque and delicate poetry in *Lakmé* which should not be under-estimated. But it is in the charming class of ballet that he was truly an original creator." Elaborating upon this very same opinion, Jean Poueigh wrote: "It is especially because he wrote *Coppélia*, and even more, *Sylvia* that Léo Delibes deserves to figure among the precursors of the modern school. In a class of composition which, until then, had been neglected, he brought an elevation and vigor of style, a fullness of forms and a richness of instrumentation unknown before him. . . . He introduced symphonic music into the ballet, at the same time remaining truly French and preserving in choreographic music that nimble elegance, that caressing grace, that spiritual vivacity which are like wings of the dance."

Delibes' last opera, *Kassya*—left unfinished by his death—was brought to completion by Jules Massenet.

Principal works by Léo Delibes:

OPERA: *Le Roi l'a dit*; *Jean de Nivelle*; *Lakmé*; *Kassya*.
BALLET: *La Source*; *Coppélia*; *Sylvia*.
CHORAL: *Alger*.
Songs.

About Léo Delibes:

Bruneau, Alfred. *La Musique Française*; Guiraud, Ernest. *Notice sur la Vie et les Oeuvres de Léo Delibes*; Jullien, Adolphe.

Musiciens d'aujourd'hui; Lavignac, Albert. *La Musique et les Musiciens*; Pougin, Arthur. *Musiciens de 19e Siècle*.
Musical Quarterly 8:605 October 1922.

Important recordings of music by Léo Delibes:

BALLET: *Coppélia* (PATHE); *Sylvia* (GRAMOPHONE-Barbirolli).

SELECTIONS FROM OPERA: *Lakmé*, "Prélude" (ODEON); "Prière et choeur d'entrée" (ODEON); "Fantasie aux divins mensonges" (COLUMBIA-Thill); "Pourquoi dans les grands bois" (PARLAPHONE-Pons); "Ballet music" (PATHE); "Là bas, dans la forêt" (VICTOR-Pons); "Entr'acte, Act III" (ODEON); "Ah, viens dans cette paix profonde" (POLYDOR).

Frederick Delius *1863-1935*
(See *Composers Of Today*)

Karl von Dittersdorf *1739-1799*

KARL VON DITTERSDORF—who enjoyed, in his time, a reputation as composer eclipsing that of his contemporaries, Haydn and Mozart—was born as Karl Ditters in Vienna on November 2, 1739. His father, a humble embroiderer at the court, was sufficiently sensitive to art to train his son musically. As a boy, Karl played the violin in the orchestra of St. Stephen, where a horn player noticed him and recommended him to Prince Joseph von Hildburghausen. Thus, in his eleventh year, Karl Ditters was employed as page and musician to the Prince, who took a paternal interest in him and saw to it that he was fully instructed in music, languages and the social graces.

In 1761, financial difficulties compelled the Prince to disband his orchestra. However, he provided for each one of the musicians by procuring for him a three-year contract at the Imperial Chapel. The work there was difficult and unremunerative; for a period, Karl Ditters knew a trying existence. Fortunately, at this time, he became a friend of Gluck, the composer, whose influence resulted in relieving Ditters of some of his strenuous work at the Chapel and in procuring for him some additional private pupils.

At this time, Gluck proposed to Ditters that he accompany him on a trip that he was about to make to Italy.

Count Durazzo, who had interested himself deeply in Ditters, supplied the necessary funds. In Italy, Ditters gave several successful concerts on the violin.

In 1764, Ditters was employed by the Bishop of Grosswardein in Hungary as chapel-master. For the new few years, Ditters' life was idyllic. The work was pleasant, and the comforts numerous. Here, Ditters directed weekly concerts, for which he composed some of the oratorios that were first to bring him to fame.

Unfortunately, this position soon came to an end. The Bishop had received severe criticism from Maria Theresa for the scandalous life which he was reputed to lead at Grosswardein. In partial repentance, the Bishop decided to dismiss his entire chapel. This was in 1769. The popular and ingratiating chapel-master was not long without a post. He soon received an even more attractive situation with Count Schaffgotsch, who brought him to the castle at Johannisberg.

Between the Count and Karl Ditters there developed a bond of friendship which resulted in many flattering honors for the musician. The Count conferred on him the Order of the Golden Spur. Then—in order to keep him permanently in Johannisberg—he appointed him Overseer of Forests, and finally Chief Magistrate, the latter post bringing with it nobility.

Now a nobleman, the composer—from this time on called Karl von Dittersdorf —visited Vienna in 1773 to assist at a performance of his oratorio, *Esther*. Emperor Joseph II offered him the important post of chapel-master, but Dittersdorf had become too attached to the pomp, splendor and leisure of his life in Johannisberg to consider a change.

Meanwhile, his fame as a composer had reached prodigious proportions in Vienna. The success of *Esther* was followed by an even more auspicious reception of another oratorio, *Job*. An opera, *The Doctor and the apothecary* enjoyed sensational acclaim, bringing its composer a commission for three more operas, all of which, in turn, achieved contagious popularity. By this time, Karl von Dittersdorf had become the

KARL VON DITTERSDORF

favorite composer of his period; his music was in vogue everywhere. His symphonies, overtures, concertos for the violin, cantatas, masses, oratorios and operas were performed frequently. In 1789, Dittersdorf came to Berlin, as a personal guest of Frederick William II, to conduct *The Doctor*.

Karl von Dittersdorf's reputation soared like a comet—and sank like one. Upon the death of his friend, the Count, Dittersdorf was removed from his important position and given a meagre pension. For a long time, he knew actual want. Finally, Count Still, aware of the composer's distressing circumstances, took Dittersdorf and his family to his home in Bohemia, where the composer remained until his death.

During the last years of his life, Dittersdorf realized forcefully that his day of triumph was over. The performances of his music had become increasingly rare until it was almost impossible to find an orchestra or an opera house willing to present his works. His reputation drooped to such an extent that the publishers, Breitkopf and Härtel, refused to publish any more of his works, on the ground that there no longer existed, among musicians, an interest in them.

There is no doubt that this sudden return to obscurity broke his heart, and brought on the illness that terminated his life. Karl von Dittersdorf died in Bohemia on October 24, 1799. Three days before his death, he completed his autobiography.

As a personality, Dittersdorf was fond of outward display, of pomp and ceremony. Luxury was indispensable to his happiness. He loved to dress well and to live in sumptuous surroundings.

His musical perception was not keen. He confessed that he did not understand Gluck, that Mozart bored him, and that he did not esteem Haydn very highly.

In his symphonies, wrote Frederick Niecks, "there is a great deal of tone-painting, and really exce.lent tone-painting, but extremely little of what is popularly so-called, namely, imitation of nature. The object of the composer's painting is moods and feelings, and scenes and actions in their brightness or darkness, their rest or movement, their swiftness or slowness, their precipitance or reluctance, their vigor or languor, their roughness or smoothness, etc. . . . The style of the symphonies is that of a facile, but not of a careless or insipid, writer. Dittersdorf had not the powerful genius of a Haydn, a Mozart or a Beethoven, but the freshness and abundance of his ideas and his dexterous handling of the form prove that he was more than a mere man of talent; that, in fact, he too was a genius, only much less exalted than the three sublimities."

Discussing Karl von Dittersdorf's operas, Frances O. Souper wrote that it is here that the composer is at his best, "speaking with a voice which might even yet be heard had he something more human than mere lightness and humor to offer. Combined with his fresh flow of easy melody, humor and sense of color, he produced a living thing. His crescendos and his finales are two devices in which he shows his dramatic power most markedly."

Principal works by Karl von Dittersdorf:

OPERA: *The Doctor and the apothecary*; *Betrug durch Aberglauben*; *Die Liebe im Narrenhaus*; *Orpheus der Zweite*; *Hocus pocus*.

CHORAL: Oratorios; masses; motets, etc.

ORCHESTRA: Symphonies; concertos for violin and orchestra; overtures; divertimenti, etc.

CHAMBER MUSIC: Twelve string quartets.

About Karl von Dittersdorf:

Kilburn, Nicholas. *The Story of Chamber Music*; Krebs, K. *Dittersdorfiana*. *Monthly Musical Record* 59:43 February 1929.

Important recordings of music by Karl von Dittersdorf:

CHAMBER MUSIC: *Quartet in D-major*, "Finale" (GRAMOPHONE-Budapest); *Quartet in E-flat major* (POLYDOR); Quartet in A-major, "Minuet" (VICTOR-Budapest).

Gaetano Donizetti *1797-1848*

"He is the man who will shine."—GIU-SEPPE VERDI

GAETANO DONIZETTI was born in Bergamo, northern Italy, on November 29, 1797, the fourth son of Andrea Donizetti, a weaver. There has been created a legend, palpably false, that his father was originally a Scotchman, Donald Izett by name, who, when he settled permanently in Italy, changed his name to Donizetti.

As a boy, Gaetano Donizetti was apprenticed to an architect. He was, however, more sensitive to poetry and music than to architecture, and was, for the most part, a dull apprentice. His father, realizing the futility of imposing upon his son a life-work for which he showed little aptitude, finally decided to send him to the Conservatory of Naples. Here, Donizetti first came into contact with the printed scores of Rossini's operas which were forbidden to the students of the Conservatory because they violated operatic traditions. Donizetti, however, had become a friend to the librarian, upon whom he prevailed to smuggle the forbidden operas into his bedroom. These operas opened a new world for Donizetti, one into which he, too, hoped to enter. It was probably to bring this goal to realization that, when his Conservatory days were over, Donizetti went to Bologna to study under Padre Mattei, who had also been Rossini's master.

Donizetti's father, however, was still not convinced that music was a suitable profession, and urged his son to adopt

GAETANO DONIZETTI

teaching. This was such an unpleasant prospect to young Donizetti that, in preference, he joined the army. He combined military exercises with musical composition, and while quartered in Venice in 1818, composed his first opera, *Enrico di Borgogna*, in which he slavishly imitated Rossini's style.

Success came to Donizetti as early as 1822. In that year, his opera, *Zoraïde*, was given a first performance in Rome, creating such a furor that after the first performance the composer was carried in triumph to the Capitol to be crowned. The success of this opera brought with it Donizetti's exemption from military duty.

From this time on, Donizetti applied himself with indefatigable industry to the composition of operas. In 1830, came *Anna Bolena*, the opera that carried Donizetti's rising reputation out of Italy to half of Europe. In 1832, he composed *L'Elisir d'amore*. Three years later, he produced what many critics have designated as his masterpiece, *Lucia di Lammermoor*.

With the composition of *Lucia*, Donizetti's fame thruout Europe became so great that he was universally accepted as one of the eminent operatic composers of the time. In 1839, Donizetti visited Paris to assist in the production of several of his operas. It was at this time that a starving composer in

Paris—Richard Wagner, by name—copied the entire score of Donizetti's *La Favorite* because it had impressed him so strongly. From Paris, Donizetti came to Vienna, receiving the honorary titles of Hofcompositeur and Kapellmeister. In 1844, the last of Donizetti's operas—his sixty-third—*Catarina Cornaro*—was produced in Naples.

The last years of Donizetti's life were marked by sombre tragedy. Late in 1844, he became subject to fits of depression and mental hallucinations which became so intense that, before long, he collapsed mentally. He was confined to an insane asylum where, for long periods, he would sit in almost complete silence, muttering to himself "Dom Sebastino. . . Dom Sebastino. . . ." At one time, when a visitor called to see him, he took his visitor's face in his hands, and peering at it with half-insane eyes, cried out: "I am mad, my friend, hopelessly mad!" However, even such moments of clarity were few and far between. For the most part, Donizetti's mind was completely confused.

In 1847, he was released from the asylum so that he might return to the city of his birth, to be cared for by his brother. The voyage to Bergamo was an arduous one. On the way, Donizetti became completely paralyzed. He died soon after his return to his native city, on April 8, 1848, and was buried a short distance from the town.

"More than four thousand persons were present at the funeral," wrote Donizetti's valet, Antoine. "The procession was composed of the numerous clergy of Bergamo, the most illustrious members of the community and its environs and of the civic guard of the town and the suburbs. The discharge of musketry, mingled with the light of three or four thousand torches, presented a fine effect; the whole was enhanced by the presence of three military bands. The young gentlemen of Bergamo insisted on bearing the remains of their illustrious fellow townsman, altho the cemetery was a league and a half from the town. Never hitherto had such great honors been bestowed on any member of that city."

On April 26, 1875 the remains of Donizetti were disinterred and removed to the church of Santa Maria Maggiore, in Bergamo, where they rest at the present time.

Donizetti bequeathed his piano to his brother. "Do not sell at any price the pianoforte which holds within it all my artistic life," was Donizetti's last plea. "From 1822, it has rung in my ears; there whisper all the Annas, the Marias, the Lucias, the Marines. Oh, let it live as long as I live! In its company, I spent the hopeful years—married life—loneliness. It heard my joys, my sorrows, my vain hopes, honors; it shared with me toil and stress—it holds every epoch of my career; within it lives my inspiration."

In his composition, Donizetti was amazingly facile and spontaneous. Writing came to him easily, and he almost never made corrections. He was unable to compose if he did not have at his side a small ivory scraper, a gift from his father, which, incidentally, he never used. Donizetti always worked quickly. *Don Pasquale* was composed in eleven days; *Lucia di Lammermoor* in six weeks. Between 1831 and 1834 he composed eight operas, including *L'Elisir d'amore* and *Lucrezia Borgia.*

It was probably this spontaneity and swiftness that brought with them so much superficiality in Donizetti's music. Certainly, the bulk of his works has been forgotten; many of the operas which were sensational in their day grew old overnight.

However, as Cecil Gray took pains to point out, "the fact remains that when he chose to take trouble he was capable of attaining remarkable heights, as in *Lucia di Lammermoor*—undoubtedly his best work as a whole—and particularly in the justly celebrated Sextet which is one of the very finest examples of concerted vocal writing in the whole range of opera. . . . His delightful comic-operas . . . . such as *Don Pasquale* and *L'Elisir d'amore,* which reveal an entirely different aspect of his talents, have recently begun to receive the attention they richly deserve. In sparkle, brilliance and comic verve they are scarcely, if at all, inferior to the *Barber* of Rossini, on which they are obviously modelled."

Donizetti once remarked that his brain was divided into two cells, one of which produced his serious grand opera, and the other, comic operas. While it is quite true that in grand opera he produced a masterpiece like *Lucia*, it is in his comic operas that Donizetti revealed his greatest powers as a composer. These comic operas, as R. A. Streatfeild pointed out, "are totally free from the ponderous affectations of the composer's serious operas. Here we find Donizetti at his best, because here he writes according to the natural dictates of his imagination, not in accordance with the foolish or depraved taste of fashionable connoisseurs."

Principal works by Gaetano Donizetti:

OPERA: *Zoraïde; L'Elisir d'amore; Lucrezia Borgia; Lucia di Lammermoor; La Fille du régiment; La Favorite; Linda di Chamounix; Don Pasquale; Don Sebastiano,* etc.

About Gaetano Donizetti:

Cametti, Alberto. *Donizetti;* Gray, Cecil. *History of Music;* Streatfeild, R. A. *The Opera.*

Important recordings of music by Gaetano Donizetti:

OPERA: *Don Pasquale,* complete (VICTOR-La Scala); *L'Elisir D'amore,* abridged (COLUMBIA-La Scala); *La Favorite,* abridged (COLUMBIA-La Scala); *Lucia di Lammermoor,* complete (COLUMBIA-La Scala).

John Dowland *1563-1626*

"Dowland, whose heavenly touch on the lute ravishes men's souls."—RICHARD BARNFIELD

"He is unquestionably the greatest of all English song-writers."—PHILIP HESELTINE

JOHN DOWLAND, eminent Elizabethan composer, was born near Dublin early in January of 1563. At the age of fifteen, he came to London, where he became a page to Sir Henry Cobham. When, in 1579, Sir Henry was appointed English ambassador to France, he took Dowland with him to Paris. It was here that, in 1582, Dowland became a Roman Catholic. Until 1583, he remained in Cobham's employ. Then he was engaged by Cobham's successor, Sir Edward Stafford, who took Dowland frequently with him upon tours thru France.

His musical career began when he was employed by Sir George Carey as a household musician. Meanwhile, Dowland continued his musical education. In 1588, he graduated from Oxford University, celebrating the occasion by publishing his first serious composition, *Galliard.*

He was aspiring to a court appointment. On the death of John Johnson, distinguished lutist of the court, Dowland made a formal bid for the post. He was rejected, possibly because he was known to have been a Catholic. As solace for his disappointment, he undertook in 1594 a trip to the Continent. He visited Cassel, where he was well received by the Duke of Brunswick, who greatly appreciated Dowland's great gifts for the lute. From Germany he went to Italy, where for a short period he studied under Marenzio.

In 1597, Dowland published the first of his monumental volume of *Ayres,* with lute accompaniment. This work was successful, going into five editions within the next twenty years. It was probably the success of these *Ayres* which earned for Dowland, in 1598, an appointment as lutist to the court of Denmark, at the substantial salary of 500 dalers a year. In this position, Dowland remained for several years, amassing a comfortable fortune. In 1601, his second volume of *Ayres* reached publication. In 1603, it was succeeded by a third volume. Soon afterwards, Dowland's most famous instrumental work—the *Lachrymae, or Seven teares*—made an appearance.

In 1605, Dowland was given a brief holiday from his court duties in Denmark, enabling him to visit his birthplace near Dublin. He found recognition awaiting him, in the form of an honorary degree from the University of Dublin. Upon his return to Denmark, Dowland was suddenly and unexpectedly dismissed from his post. He returned to London, settling there permanently.

The remaining years of Dowland's life were not particularly eventful. He never succeeded in gaining recognition commensurate to his great importance as a lute-player and as composer. In 1609, he was employed as lutist to Lord Walden, son of the Earl of Suffolk.

Three years later, he was, at last, appointed musician in the court of King James. It was in 1612, too, that his last book of *Ayres*—subtitled, *A Pilgrimes solace*—saw the light of day.

John Dowland died on January 21, 1626. He had spent the money he had earned abroad liberally, and he died a poor and bitter man. Neither the place of his death or burial are known today.

There is some existing evidence to the effect that John Dowland, upon his return from Denmark, gave Shakespeare the threads of a play which was later to be woven into *Hamlet.*

As Wanda Landowska has pointed out, John Dowland's prolonged sojourns in foreign countries "placed him in contact with Italian and French masters; a contact which brought his genius to fertility in magnificent fashion. His learned music, conceived with a perfect knowledge of the vocal and instrumental art, attracts, above all, by the intensity of its expression and its dramatic power."

Altho John Dowland was by no means the first English composer to create songs, he was most certainly the first of England's great song composers. Ernest Newman places him among the half-dozen of the world's greatest song writers. Whether he wrote part-songs, such as *Awake, sweet love* and *Now, oh, now,* or songs for solo voice such as *I saw my lady weep* and *Come, heavy sleep,* he was always the superb craftsman, always the fine and sensitive artist who could pen variety, poignancy and an unforgettable beauty.

It is the opinion of Philip Heseltine that, of the four books of *Ayres* that Dowland composed, the last—*A Pilgrimes solace*—is the greatest. "Taken as a whole, *A Pilgrimes solace* must be regarded as his masterpiece, and the crown of his life and achievement. In every number in this amazing book we see his genius displayed in full maturity. It is a remarkable fact that this book, appearing at a time when polyphonic tradition was fast giving way before the figured bass and its attendant harmonic developments, is at once the most contrapuntal of Dowland's works and the one in which the widest range of purely harmonic combinations may be found.

This was, indeed, 'new music,' but it bore little resemblance to the 'new music' of the Italians who were bent on making music subservient to diction. Careful as he was in setting words with the just note and accent. . . . Dowland was not the man to sacrifice any element of musical expression to mere verbal exigencies."

Principal works by John Dowland:

VOCAL: Four Books of *Ayres* (including *A Pilgrimes solace*).

INSTRUMENTAL: *Lachrymae, or Seven teares*.

About John Dowland:

Fellowes, Edmund Horace. *English Madrigal Composers*; Flood, W. H. Grattan. *Late Tudor Composers*; Heseltine, Philip. *The English Ayre*.
Proceedings of the Musical Association 56:1 (1930-1931).

Important recordings of music by John Dowland:

VOCAL: *Ayres*, "Awake, sweet love" (COLUMBIA); "Come heavy sleep" (ODEON); "Fine knacks for ladies" (COLUMBIA).

INSTRUMENTAL: *Lachrymae, or Seven tears,* "Pavane," arranged for piano (COLUMBIA).

Guillermus Dufay *1400-1474*

ONE of the pioneer schools of polyphonic music was the school of the Netherlands, of which Guillermus Dufay was leader.

Guillermus Dufay (whose name is less frequently spelled as du Fay, or Dufais, or Duffai) was born in Hainault, in the Netherlands, about 1400. It is known that as a boy he was a chorister in the Cathedral of Cambrai, that in 1416 he composed a song to celebrate the marriage of Charles Malatesti and Vittoria di Lorenzo Colonna (niece of Pope Martin V), and that in 1428 he was a singer in the Papal choir.

From 1433 to 1435, he visited Pisa and Florence in the company of Eugene IV. Then, returning to his homeland, he entered the priesthood, receiving the canonicate of Cambrai on March 21, 1437. Shortly afterwards, he went to Paris, where he studied at the Sorbonne, receiving the degree of Master of Arts. He was also, during this period, in the employ of Philip the Good, the Duke of Burgundy.

The last thirty years of his life he spent in Cambrai. Here he was active musically, his importance being widely recognized. In 1450, he was given sixty gold pieces as an honorarium "because of the quality and merit of our master, G. Dufay, who has enriched our church with musical songs."

Guillermus Dufay died in Cambrai on November 27, 1474. A few months before his death—on July 8, 1474—he wrote his will in which he asked that in his dying hour a group of choristers of the Cathedral should come and sing for him first the hymn, *Magno salutis gaudio,* and then his own motet, *Ave Regina,* which he had composed expressly for this purpose. Thus Dufay died, with the notes of his own motet in his ears.

Dufay composed a considerable quantity of motets, masses, and secular songs. In his greatest work he showed the unmistakable influence of Dunstable, English genius of counterpoint. "There can be no doubt that Dufay would not have been what he was if the English master had not shown him the way," wrote no less an authority than Charles van den Borren. "He owes much to Dunstable . . . [but] it is precisely because he knew how to emancipate himself from this influence that he won the eminent position which he occupies in the history of music."

Dufay's name is prominent in musical history because he brought the canon form to a high degree of technical development, and by his supple use of imitation paved the way for the fugue form.

In his early years as a composer, Dufay was, of course, the experimenter in the polyphonic style; his music of this period was often dry and pedantic. But, after 1437, when the influence of Dunstable began to assert itself more strongly, his style underwent a marked change. "We recognize unmistakably the suave and flowing melody in the separate parts," wrote H. E. Wooldridge in the *Oxford history of music,* "the pure harmony of the whole, the agreeable phrasing, the propriety in the sequence of combined sounds."

It is the opinion of Julien Tiersot that the "masses of Dufay are his most important compositions. Are they his most beautiful works? One is reluctant to say so. Their exterior appearance leaves uncertain impressions. . . . They are not, in any case, the vast and complete monuments like those which Palestrina, Bach and Beethoven erected later on. This inferiority explains itself: the material, in the time of Dufay, was hardly assembled. . . . After all, the architect does not create the stone; he merely assembles it and gives it shape."

Dufay's influence over his contemporaries was so great that an entire school of contrapuntal music was influenced by his works. Among the other outstanding composers in this Netherland school were Jacob Arcadelt (1514?-1575?), Egide Binchois (1400?-1465), Anton Busnois (died 1492), Jean de Okeghem (1430?-1495), Jakob Obrecht (1430?-1505), Josquin des Prés and Orlando de Lasso.[1] With their output of masses, motets, hymns and part-songs they brought greater fluency and plasticity to contrapuntal writing, introduced an original note in their music, and prepared the ground for such contrapuntal giants as Palestrina. What Ambros said of Okeghem (who, upon Dufay's death, assumed the leadership of the Netherland school) might very well apply to the composers of the entire school. "Okeghem is original and interesting; his intricacies of counterpoint, his canon movements, however strict and skilful, have had breathed into them his singing soul. There are found in his works whole periods, often in the middle voices, of most wonderful melodic leading, and of extraordinary tenderness of expression."

Commenting upon the contribution of the Netherland school, Emil Naumann has written: "Almost at the beginning of the Netherland school, mechanical invention was made subservient to idea. It was no longer contrapuntal writing for counterpoint's sake. Excesses were toned down, and the unquestionable desire was that the contrapuntist's art should occupy its proper position as a means to an end. Euphony and beauty

of expression were the objects of the composer."

Principal works by Guillermus Dufay:

Masses, motets, hymns, part-songs, secular songs, etc.

About Guillermus Dufay:

Ambros, August Wilhelm. *Geschichte der Musik*; Borren, Charles van den. *Guillaume Dufay, son Importance dans l'évolution de la Musique du 15e Siècle*; Menil, Félicien de. *L'école Flamande du 15e Siècle*; Sollitt, Edna Nicholson. *From Dufay to Sweelinck*; Stainer, John F. R. *Dufay and his Contemporaries* (foreword).

Important recordings of music by Guillermus Dufay:

CHORAL: *Alma redemptoris mater* (LUMEN); *Christe redemptor* and *Conditor alme siderum* (COLUMBIA); *Gloria in excelsis* (PARLAPHONE); *Vergine bella* (LUMEN).

Paul Dukas *1865-1935*

(See *Composers Of Today*)

John Dunstable *1370-1453*

"Dunstable. . . . was as preeminent in his generation as Bach or Handel in theirs."
—W. H. HADOW

JOHN DUNSTABLE is frequently designated as the first important composer in musical history. Certainly, he was the first composer great enough to create a school, and the first to influence not only his own generation but succeeding ones as well.

The biographical material about Dunstable is scanty. The existing facts can be summed up in a few lines. He was born about 1370, possibly in Dunstable, in Bedfordshire, England. Legend would have us believe that his ancestor was Dunstan, the celebrated ecclesiastical statesman of the tenth century.

John Dunstable traveled extensively during his lifetime. At one time in his career he taught music to Dufay and Binchois of the Netherland school, influencing them vitally. He died on December 24, 1453 and was buried in St. Stephen's church, Walbrook, London. His gravestone refers to him as an "astrologer, mathematician and musician."

About fifty of Dunstable's compositions are to be found in collections on the Continent, principally in Trent and Modena, and in the British Museum.

---

[1] Josquin des Prés and Orlando de Lasso are discussed in this book.

"Dunstable presents himself to us as the earliest composer of any nationality who can really be said, archaic though his method inevitably is, to have something like artistic style," wrote Ernest Walker. "His feeling for melodiousness of parts is often very remarkable, and occasionally he rises to sheer beauty, as in the delicate little *Alleluia* at the end of his motet, *Quam pulcra es.*"

Martin le Franc ascribes two qualities to Dunstable's music: "sweetness of tone, and firmness of outline." Elaborating upon this characterization, H. E. Wooldridge wrote in the *Oxford History of Music*: "In beauty, in sweetness and purity of sound . . . it by far exceeded that of the foreign schools, to whom, indeed, as they themselves confessed, it came as a revelation, and the prospect of a new art; but its texture was equal with that of the foreign music lacking in respect of variety, and was not at all adaptable to the special sentiment of words. The eminence of Dunstable . . . consisted not so much in a finer and more expressive style than theirs, as in more effective varieties of plan and contrivance in the presentation of this somewhat monotonously beautiful material."

And yet, expressiveness is essentially the quality which Charles van den Borren finds in all of Dunstable's music. "Expression—that is the right term to use in speaking of Dunstable. . . . There can be no doubt that in this respect, Dunstable has realized works which are more and better than beautiful sonorous compositions. The sacred motets have not only a character essentially different from the secular chansons of the time, but one may go so far as to say that the English master often inspired the generalized expression of his melody with a romantic subjectivity, of which no trace is to be found in his Franco-Netherlandish successors of the second half of the fifteenth century."

Technically, Dunstable's music was characterized by a bold and revolutionary use of discords, by the supple use of the third and sixth intervals in harmony, and by a pioneer attempt at the variation form. His influence over the Netherland school of counterpoint that succeeded him was so great that no less a

critic than Johannes Tinctoris, refers to Dunstable as their "head."

Principal works by John Dunstable:
Masses, motets, part-songs, hymns, etc.

About John Dunstable:
Hadow, W. H. *English Music*; Walker, Ernest. *A History of Music in England*; Wooldridge, H. E. *Oxford History of Music*, vol. 2.
Proceedings of the Musical Association 47: 79 (1920-1921).

Important recordings of music by John Dunstable:
CHORAL: *Hymn after Agincourt* (COLUMBIA).

Henri Duparc   *1848-1933*

MARIE EUGÈNE HENRI FOUQUES DUPARC, one of the foremost of French song-composers, was born in Paris on January 21, 1848. As a child, he disclosed sensitivity toward music, but no unusual talent. He was, therefore, sent to the Jesuit college at Vaugirard to study law. Here, his teacher at the piano was César Franck, who aroused Duparc's great love for music. Franck introduced Duparc to the classics of musical literature, particularly to Gluck, and with his penetrating analysis opened up for the young student the world of music. It was not long before Duparc began attending symphony concerts. The next step was to study harmony assiduously.

In 1870, the first fruits of his creative talent made their appearance, six little pieces for the piano, *Feuilles volantes,* published by Flaxland. This was not particularly striking music, giving little indication of the talent and power that Duparc was soon to disclose. At the close of the year, Duparc fulfilled his military service in the eighteenth battalion of the Garde Mobile. Upon discarding his uniform, he returned with greater enthusiasm to composition. In 1873, came his *Ländler* for orchestra, performed by the Société Nationale on June 24, 1874. Three years later, *Lénore,* a symphonic poem, was introduced by the Pasdeloup Concert Populaire. With these two works, Duparc's reputation as a composer was established.

Between 1875 and 1886, Henri Duparc was active in the musical life of Paris.

Together with Vincent D'Indy, he was the founder of the *Société Nationale de Musique,* whose mission it was to fight the battle for the unknown composer. In the meanwhile, his pen was intermittently producing a series of songs which comprised his most important contribution to music.

In 1885, ill-health compelled Duparc to abandon all musical activity. He left for Pau for a rest cure. Failing to regain his former strength, he settled permanently in Switzerland. From that time on, his creation came to a standstill. It is quite true that at this time his most important songs made their appearance in print, but they had been composed before 1885.

Henri Duparc died on February 13, 1933 at Monte de Marson. At his death it was generally conceded that he was one of the foremost song-composers France had produced.

Analyzing Duparc's art, Georges Jean-Aubry wrote: "There is perhaps no expression more apt to throw light on the nature of Henri Duparc's work than the sentence in which Baudelaire says: 'I have found the definition of the beautiful, of that which, to me, is beauty; it is something ardent and sad, something a little vague, leaving scope for conjecture.' For Henri Duparc, beauty is of the same nature. It is something ardent and sad, but this ardor is not set free, this sadness is not spoken, but is exhaled with poignant simplicity. The art of these works is not complex, altho the substance of the musical dream contained in them is rich. This art is not complex if the writing is considered in general. From the first moment, a line is revealed that is noble and of wholly classical purity. It is not until afterwards that we are struck with the delicate undulation of this line, in which is discovered a power of expression that cannot be surpassed by methods of refinement. . . . It is nearly always . . . by means of nuances that Henri Duparc gives accents to his dreams. Nothing is further from romanticism and from verbal lyricism, but perhaps nothing is nearer to the modern soul, whose deepest anxieties are betrayed, outwardly, only by almost imperceptible waves."

HENRI DUPARC

In all of his music, Duparc revealed the unmistakable influence that his great teacher, César Franck, exerted upon him. Sydney Northcote has carefully analyzed the resemblances and differences in the style of these two composers: "Duparc's pupilage is unmistakable. It may be discerned in such general tendencies as enharmonic modulations and characteristic chromaticisms, a fondness for the two bar phrase unit, and here and there a typical melodic motive. But there is a manifest a subtle and sure sense of dramatic expression, and a more postive melodic eloquence than the master ever achieved. His harmonic texture lacks the depth and infallibility of Franck, and now and then it succumbs to the limitations of the idiom. But it is always fluid and expressive, with a sincere impressionism that is at once restrained and natural. There is a quality of originality in the flexibility and amplitude of phrases and development, and the sincerity and balance of the declamation are undeniable."

César Franck's celebrated *Symphony in D-minor* is dedicated to Henri Duparc.

Principal works by Henri Duparc:

ORCHESTRA: *Poème nocturne; Ländler; Lénore; Nocturne: Aux étoiles.*

CHORAL: *Benedicat vobis Domine.*
An entire library of songs.

About Henri Duparc:

Coeuroy, André. *La Musique Française Moderne*; Jean-Aubry, Georges. *French Music Today*; Seré, Octave. *Musiciens Français d'aujourd'hui.*

Le Courrier Musicale 35:108 March 1, 1933; *Le Monde Musicale* 44:35 February 28, 1933; *Music and Letters* 13:401 October 1932.

Important recordings of music by Henri Duparc:

ORCHESTRA: *Aux étoiles* (COLUMBIA-Gaubert).

SONGS: *Chanson triste* (GRAMOPHONE); *L'Invitation au voyage* (VICTOR); *Le Manoir de Rosemonde* (GRAMOPHONE); *Soupir* (GRAMOPHONE); *La Vague et la cloche* (VICTOR); *La Vie antérieure* (VICTOR).

Johann Dussek *1761-1812*

JOHANN LUDWIG DUSSEK was born in Časlav, Bohemia, on February 9, 1761, the son of the town organist. At the age of five he began the study of the piano, making such remarkable progress that four years later his father decided to give him intensive training in the organ as well. Shortly after this, he was entered as a chorister in the Minorite church of Iglau. His schooling took place at the Jesuit College in Iglau, and was completed at Kutenberg, where he received—despite his youth— an appointment as organist of the Jesuit church.

Removing to Prague, Dussek entered the University, and was finally graduated from it. For a period he contemplated seriously entering the Church. At this time, however, he met an Austrian officer, Count Männer, who recognized his musical talents. Count Männer took the boy with him to Mechlin, where he gave his first piano recital.

Weary of Mechlin, Dussek came to Berg-op-Zoom, accepting there a post as organist. In 1782 he reached Amsterdam, where—giving up his career at the organ—he turned to the teaching of the piano and to composition, achieving a great reputation. He attracted the notice of the Stadtholder of The Hague, who brought Dussek into the latter city as a teacher of music for his children. It was at this time that Dussek composed important compositions for the piano, including twelve sonatas.

By his twenty-second birthday, Dussek boasted an enviable prestige as composer, teacher and pianist. However he was still dissatisfied with his abilities, and decided to go to Hamburg and study under Carl Philipp Emanuel Bach. One year of intensive work brought Dussek to high technical and interpretative attainments. Coming to Berlin, he gave a recital which definitely placed him in the front rank of concert pianists.

For the next few years, Dussek toured Europe, giving performances not only on the piano, but on the harmonica as well! He visited the principal cities of northern Germany, Russia, Poland, France (performing before Marie Antoinette in 1786) and, finally, Italy. It was in the last-named country that he became so disgusted with his audiences, which preferred his harmonica to his piano, that he decided to terminate the tour. He was back in Paris in 1788. When political disturbances made Paris an unhealthful place, he crossed the channel.

In London, Dussek married. For the next twelve years he made the English capital his home, establishing himself there as a musician of first importance. Shortly after his marriage he entered into a business partnership with his father-in-law. The venture was at first successful, but after a period of years, Dussek's unbusinesslike habits and lack of practical insight brought it to ruin. In 1800, Dussek was forced to flee from London to avoid imprisonment for debt.

He went to Germany, and from there to Prague. In 1803, Dussek met Prince Louis Ferdinand of Prussia, a devoted music-lover. Before long, the two became so attached to one another that the Prince urged the composer to live with him. For three years, Dussek lived with the Prince in Berlin and in Magdeburg. It has been recorded that more than one night did the Prince, in undershirt, drag Dussek from his bed to have him perform for him on the piano.

The Prince lost his life in the battle of Saalfeld. To his memory, Dussek composed the *Élégie harmonique* for piano, "not only one of Dussek's finest works," comments James W. Davison, "but one

Dussek: Doo-shĕk'

of the most pathetic and beautiful in the repertory of the piano."

In 1807, Dussek was back in Paris, officiating as pianist to Talleyrand. He enjoyed great honor in Paris at this time, being esteemed one of the outstanding musicians of the day.

Gout, which troubled Dussek considerably during the last years of his life, compelled him finally to withdraw from all musical activity. He settled in a country house in St. Germain-en-Laye, on the outskirts of Paris, where during the final years of his life he lived in complete retirement. Johann Dussek died in this country home on March 20, 1812.

Josef Haydn referred to Dussek as a "most upright and moral man." To this description, A. W. Thayer adds that Dussek was "good, noble and just, impartial and kindly, a real friend; sympathizing with all that was true and beautiful in those he knew. . . while his joyous disposition, liberal sentiments and freedom from prejudice of any kind endeared him especially to musicians."

Altho Dussek composed abundantly in many forms, he is most famous for his works for the piano. Unfortunately, coming as he did between two such giants as Haydn and Beethoven, his stature has become considerably dwarfed in musical history by contrast. Yet, as C. Hubert Parry pointed out, this proximity to the two great musical geniuses of the period, did not "suppress Dussek's personality or extinguish his individuality, which is still clear in his own line, and has exerted some influence both upon the modern style of playing, and also upon the style of musical thought of a few modern composers to whom the giants did not appeal strongly."

Albert Soubies has asserted, in the *Histoire de la Musique en Bohème*, that Dussek did not belong to any school of Bohemian composers, that there is nothing in his music that suggests national influences. In spite of this fact, Dussek is often regarded as one of the pioneers in the Bohemian school of music, principally because he was the

JOHANN DUSSEK

first Bohemian composer to attain international reputation.

"If this artist," Henri Curzon sums up, "with his numerous and rich melodic ideas had taken the pain of deepening and developing them musically, his compositions would have assumed a much stronger and more original character. They possessed improvisations of great beauty, amplitude and unrivalled poetry, and certain of his 'organ points' are celebrated."

Principal works by Johann Dussek:

OPERA: *The Captive of Spillburg.*

ORCHESTRA: *Serenade in E-flat*; *Feudal times overture*; *Pizarro*; Fifteen concertos for piano and orchestra.

CHORAL: *Mass*; *Easter cantata*; canons.

CHAMBER MUSIC: *Piano quintet*; Three string quartets; Two piano quartets; Eighteen piano trios; Two trios for harp, violin and violoncello; Two trios for piano, flute and violoncello; Three sonatas for flute and violoncello; Thirty-eight sonatas for violin and piano; Sixteen sonatas for flute and piano.

PIANO: Twenty-eight sonatas; fantasias; sonatinas; rondos; variations; waltzes; etudes; exercises, etc.

Songs, music for four hands and for two pianos, etc.

About Johann Dussek:

Soubies, Albert. *Histoire de la Musique en Bohème.*

Guide Musicale 58:227 March 24, 1912; *Musical Opinion* 51:271 December 1927; *New Music Review* 26:9 December 1926.

Antonín Dvořák   *1841-1904*

ANTONÍN DVOŘÁK, probably the foremost of Bohemian composers, was born in a small town near Prague, Nelahozevec, on September 8, 1841. He came from humble stock—the oldest of eight children whose father was a butcher and inn-keeper. Antonín's father, however, was a man not without ambition for his children. He had aspirations of making his first born a lawyer. For this reason, Dvořák was given an intensive education, first at the village school, then in Zolnitz, and finally in Kamnitz. Music were merely an incidental study to round out a cultural background. After acquiring the elements of violin playing from the village schoolmaster, Antonín studied theory, the piano and the organ from private instructors in Zolnitz.

In Antonín's life, however, music refused to occupy that incidental position which father Dvořák had intended for it. By the time Antonín returned from Kamnitz, he was fully determined to study music in all seriousness. At first, his father was deaf to all entreaties. He would have preferred, by far, that his son become a respectable butcher like himself than a professional musician. But Antonín's obstinancy knew no refusal. Finally, in 1857, his father reluctantly sent him to Prague to study at the Organ School.

During his first few months of study in Prague, Antonín was supported by his father. The income, however, soon stopped. There followed several years of intense poverty for the young music student. Antonín played the viola in the streets during free hours of the day, and at cafés during long evenings—hardly succeeding, with all these efforts, in procuring enough money to pay for his drab room and an occasional loaf of bread. Life was difficult but, as Dvořák later confessed, it was not starvation nor hard work nor the cold that tried his soul in those years half so much as the fact that he was too poor to hear a concert or to buy an orchestral score for home study.

In 1860, he graduated from the organ school, attracting the attention of that distinguished Bohemian composer, Smetana, who was sufficiently interested in Dvořák to lend him some scores for study and to procure for him a position in the National Theatre in Prague. The next ten years were not particularly eventful. They were devoted principally to "hard study, occasional composing much revision, a great deal of thinking, and very little eating," as Dvořák himself wrote later on. As for his teachers during this period: "I studied with God, with the birds, and the trees, rivers and myself."

In 1873, Dvořák became organist at the St. Adelbert's Church, where he organized classes in composition. Sufficiently encouraged by his first financial stability, Dvořák entered upon matrimony, with the result that "I ate less, and gave more lessons than ever." However, success was at his elbow. In that year, he composed a cantata, *The Heirs of the White Mountain,* which was performed in Prague with enormous success. This cantata brought Dvořák a commission from the National Theatre in Prague to compose an opera on national lines. Strange to say, Dvořák—who was always heart and soul interested in Bohemian music—decided to write an opera according to Wagnerian formula. The result was a stilted and pathetic failure. Dvořák then radically revised the score. Once again, his opera was a failure, this time because of its stereotyped libretto. Still undismayed, Dvořák changed the libretto. Finally, the opera (its only similarity to the original being its title, *The King and the collier*) became a success. In Vienna it was instrumental in bringing its composer a government stipend of almost two hundred and fifty dollars a year.

By this time, Dvořák's name was gaining in importance. He was introduced to Johannes Brahms who became so interested in him—esteeming him a talent of first importance—that he decided to further his career by giving him an enthusiastic introduction to the publisher, Simrock. Simrock commissioned Dvořák to compose an orchestral work based upon authentic Bohemian themes. In 1878 the *Slavonic dances* made their appearance. From that time on, Dvořák was on his way to fame.

Dvořák: Dvaw'jak

Dvořák now attracted the attention of such eminent musicians as Hans von Bülow, Franz Liszt and Joseph Joachim, all of whom were so convinced of his genius that they spread his name thruout Europe. The result was that, in 1879, the *Slavonic dances* were introduced at the Crystal Palace in London, followed by a performance of *Stabat Mater.* Dvořák's popularity as a composer so gained ground in England that, in 1884, he was invited there to conduct performances of his music. His visit was a great personal triumph. He was engaged to compose a special cantata for the Birmingham Festival, *The Spectre's bride,* which likewise enjoyed a great vogue. The result of this prolonged success in England was that, in 1890, Dvořák was given an honorary degree from Cambridge.

It was not long before Dvořák's growing reputation spanned the Atlantic. In 1892, he was invited to become director of the National Conservatory of Music in New York. Upon his arrival in America, a monster concert was given in his honor, at which the composer was accorded a warm welcome.

Late in 1892, the American music-critic, Henry E. Krehbiel, brought to Dvořák's attention several Negro melodies which made a strong impression on him. Dvořák decided to compose a large work which would give expression to these poignant Negro melodies and vital Negro rhythms. He left for Spillville, Iowa, worked feverishly on his sketches for a symphony, and in the Spring of 1893 completed it. This new symphony based on American themes, the *Symphony from the New World,* was given its first performance on December 15, 1893 by Anton Seidl at the concerts of the New York Philharmonic Society. The composer was in the audience.

The symphony aroused bitter controversy. The title of the work itself inspired battle: *Symphony from the New World*—did that denote that the composer had intended the work to spring from the very soil of the new world? Or did the title designate that it was merely the nostalgic expression of a Bohemian composer written in the new world? Musical New York was divided into two camps. There were those who

ANTONÍN DVOŘÁK

felt strongly that this work was a masterpiece. And there were those who bitterly maintained that it was neither flesh, fish nor fowl—neither American music nor Bohemian—but a strange mixture of the two.

This controversy has long ago been forgotten. But the symphony remains, one of the beloved classics in symphonic literature. It is true that, occasionally, Dvořák mingles indigenous Negro melodies with characteristic Bohemian phrases, but it was blended by the sure hand of an artist into a truly personal expression. Today, no one questions whether it is American music or Bohemian music. One is conscious only of the fact that it is music flushed with beauty, imagination and poetry, one of the most personal utterances of this eminent composer.

Antonín Dvořák did not remain in America a long time. He was painfully homesick. Before long the attractions of the new world began to pall. He felt that with his Symphony, his *American quartet* and *Quintet* he had exhausted the artistic possibilities of Negro music. He began to yearn for Bohemia. He therefore suddenly returned to Prague in 1895. In 1901, he was appointed director of the Prague Conservatory, a position he held until the end of his life.

In 1904, his last opera, *Armida,* was given at the National Theatre, and was so dismal a failure that it broke the composer's heart. It is quite certain that the ill-health that followed was the direct result of his brooding and disappointment at the reception accorded *Armida.* Not even his most immediate relatives realized how sick a man he was.

He died suddenly of apoplexy at the dinner-table, on May 1, 1904. His funeral was magnificent. There could no longer be a doubt that, notwithstanding the reception his last work received, he was considered by Bohemia its greatest composer.

Antonín Dvořák was striking both in appearance and in personality. He was a man of the utmost simplicity, with an abhorrence for outward show or affectation. A man of the greatest generosity and warmth of heart, he could, suddenly, become ferociously vituperative in the face of dishonesty or pretentiousness. He was notoriously absent-minded, he would forget to perform the most perfunctory of social formalities. He drank strong coffee in great quantities, and smoked cigars profusely. After dinner, his greatest enjoyment consisted in relaxing upon a couch and having his daughter perform for him on the piano.

His weakness was an intense fear of thunderstorms. When one occurred, he refused to teach, and—pale as a ghost— he would sit at a piano, attempting to drown the din of the storm with loud chords. He loved shop-windows and long walks. In his dress, his only peculiarity was that he always wore a top-hat.

Of all the composers of the past, he adored Beethoven the most. At one time, a group of Prague citizens brought him a laurel wreath with the inscription: "To the greatest composer in the world." The next time they visited him, they found the wreath encircling the brow of a bust of Beethoven.

In his music, Dvořák was not interested in uncovering a new speech, nor in striking new paths. He was intent only upon creating music of simplicity and beauty, music which came from the heart. His music is generally characterized by Slavic traits. Its often religious feeling, its color and temperament, its vital rhythms, its feeling for the soil are all distinguishable Slavic qualities. Certainly, the greatest strength of his music lies in its rich melodic gift.

Discussing Dvořák's creative characteristics, W. H. Hadow has written: "His melody is often as simple and ingenuous as a folk-song, but in polyphony, in thematic development, in all details of contrast and elaboration, his ideal is to organize the rudimentary life and to advance it into a fuller and more adult maturity. . . . He has little sense of economy, little of that fine reticence and control which underly the most lavish moments of Brahms and Beethoven; his use of wealth is so prodigal that his generosity is sometimes left with inadequate resources. . . . But for all this, he is a great genius, true in thought, fertile in imagination, warm and sympathetic in temper of mind."

Philip Hale neatly summed up the strength and weakness of Dvořák's music when he wrote: "His music was best when it smacked of the soil, when he remembered his early days, the strains of vagabond musicians, the dances dear to his folk. One of a happily primitive folk, he delighted in rhythm and color. He was not a man to translate pictures, statues, poems, a system of metaphysics, a gospel of pessimism into music. He was least successful when he would be heroic, mystical, profound. . . . Dvořák had his faults, and they were tiresome and exasperating. His naïvete became a mannerism. Like a child, he delighted in vain repetitions; he was at times too much pleased with rhythms and colors, so that he mistook the exterior dress for the substance and forgot that after all there was little or no substance behind the brilliant trappings. We believe that he will ultimately be ranked among the minor poets of music. His complete works may gather dust in libraries; but no carefully chosen anthology will be without examples of his piquancy, strength, and beauty in thought and expression."

In conclusion, it might be of interest to contrast Dvořák with his important forerunner in Bohemian music,

Smetana. Karel Hoffmeister notes: "Both are melodists with a highly developed feeling for characteristic rhythm. But Smetana's melody and rhythm are restricted to his own personality and to the Czech character, whereas Dvořák with his wider outlook showed greater diversity in these respects. His music shows a more general Slavonic coloring, and an exclusively Czech style appears only from time to time, while here and there we discern his close affinity to his models, Beethoven and Schubert. Smetana works in more restricted area, but his outline is always firm and original. Dvořák covers a wider ground, but his lines of demarcation are less definite, and occasionally admit an outside influence. . . . Smetana pays comparatively little attention to the externals of his art. . . Smetana planned for himself a lifetask: to depict in music the soul of the Czech people in all its most significant features. . . . Not so with Dvořák. The guiding factor in his creative work was not intellectual power but the gift of intuition. Intellect, which in Smetana balanced intuition, was of far less importance in the case of Dvořák."

Principal works by Antonín Dvořák:

OPERA: *Vanda*; *Selma sedlák*; *Rusalka*; *Dimitrij*; *The Jacobin*; *Armida*.

CHORAL: *St. Ludmilla*; *Requiem*; *The Spectre's bride*; *The American flag*; *Hymn* (for mixed chorus and orchestra); *Stabat Mater*.

ORCHESTRA: *Five symphonies*; *Mein heim overture*; *Husitská*; *With nature*; *Othello*; *Carnival overture*; *Concerto for piano and orchestra*; *Concerto for violin and orchestra*; *Concerto for violoncello and orchestra*; *Slavonic dances*; *Slavonic rhapsodies*; *The Noonwitch*; *Heldenlied*, etc.

CHAMBER MUSIC: Two string quintets; *Sextet*; Five string quartets; Two piano quartets; *Dumsky trio*.

About Antonín Dvořák:

Hadow, W. H. *Studies in Modern Music* (2d series); Hoffmeister, Karel. *Antonín Dvořák*; Mason, Daniel Gregory. *From Grieg to Brahms*.

Important recordings of music by Antonín Dvořák:

SELECTIONS FROM OPERA: *The Jacobin*, "Orchestral selections" (PARLAPHONE); "Burgrave's air" (GRAMOPHONE); *Rusalka*, "Air of the water fay" (GRAMOPHONE); "I have golden hair" (GRAMOPHONE); "O, lovely moon" (GRAMOPHONE).

ORCHESTRA: *Symphony in G-major* (VICTOR); *From the New World symphony* (VICTOR-Stokowski); *Sixteen Slavonic dances* (VICTOR); *Concerto for violoncello and orchestra* (COLUMBIA-Feuermann); *Carnaval overture* (VICTOR-Goossens); *Slavonic rhapsody in A-major* (COLUMBIA-Beecham).

CHAMBER MUSIC: *Quintet in A-major* (VICTOR-Pro-Arte, Schnabel); *Quartet in F-major* (COLUMBIA); *Quartet in A-flat major* (GRAMOPHONE); *Quartet in G-major* (VICTOR); *Dumsky trio* (DECCA)

Sir Edward Elgar *1857-1934*
(See *Composers Of Today*)

Heinrich Ernst *1814-1865*

HEINRICH WILHELM ERNST was born in Brünn, in the province of Moravia, Austria, on May 6, 1814. He studied at the Vienna Conservatory under Böhm, Mayseder and Seyfried. His progress with the violin was phenomenal. At the age of sixteen his studies came to an end, and he toured Germany with great success. At this time he heard Paganini play, a performance which thrilled him so greatly that he followed the great violinist from city to city, listening to all of his concerts and studying his style.

In 1832, Ernst came to Paris, settling there for six years. Here he gave further public concerts, at the same time studying under Charles de Bériot. His first important composition for violin was produced here, a series of pyrotechnical variations on Paganini's *Carnival of Venice*, which revealed Paganini's great influence upon him. In 1834, Ernst set out on an extensive concert tour of Europe.

There is a pathetic story connected with the composition of the *Élégie*, one of the best known of Ernst's smaller pieces for the violin. When Ernst left Vienna in 1831, he parted from his sweetheart, who swore that she would wait for him until he made his mark in the world. Six years later, Ernst—after the consummation of several successful tours which brought a European fame to his name—returned to Vienna to claim his bride. He found, instead, that his beloved had died a day previous to his return. As an expression of his grief, Ernst composed the *Élégie*.

HEINRICH ERNST

In 1843, Ernst went to England which, except for brief excursions, remained his home for the remainder of his life. He concertized extensively, and there were many critics who felt that Ernst had acquired a technique comparable to that of Paganini.

In 1859 a spinal complaint began to manifest itself. By 1862, complete paralysis set in. Having been financially extravagant thruout his life, Ernst was forced to face his severe illness completely destitute. Fortunately, several close friends came to his aid, sponsoring a series of benefit concerts for him, the proceeds of which assured him of financial independence.

During the last three years of his life, Ernst suffered intensely. In the fall of 1865, he left for Nice to avoid a difficult London winter. He died there on October 8, 1865.

The London *Athenaeum* published the following obituary paragraph: "A more amiable man never breathed than Ernst; nor one of better heart, a finer intelligence and a more generous and unenvying nature. A certain languor of temperament, approaching to indolence, and of later years aggravated by illness, prevented him from doing full justice to his powers, either as a creative musician or as a member of society; but his friends will recollect him not merely by his nobility of nature, incapable of intrigue, jealousy and suspicion, but also by his quiet and delicate sense of humor. As an artist, he cannot be overrated among violinists."

Heinrich Ernst's best compositions are those which he wrote for his own instrument, exploiting its technical resources. They show, wrote Edmund Sebastian van der Straeten, "deeper poetical feeling than those of his contemporary virtuoso composers, but most of them show the wear of time. . . . His *Concerto in F-sharp minor,* however, is genuinely inspired work, and like the fine *Othello fantasia* contains so many features of technical violinistic interest . . . that they will always be welcome to the few who can effectively master their enormous difficulties."

Principal works by Heinrich Ernst:

ORCHESTRA: *Concerto in F-sharp minor* (for violin and orchestra).
CHAMBER MUSIC: Two string quartets.
VIOLIN: *Fantasy on Hungarian airs; Othello fantasy; Fantasy on Paganini themes; Variations on Carnival of Venice; Élégie, etc.*

About Heinrich Ernst:

Hart, George. *The Violin and Its Music;* Straeten, Edmund Sebastian van der. *The History of the Violin.*

Giles Farnaby *1560-1600*

"Those who love the grace and wit of Couperin-the-Great, the delightful melodiousness of Haydn, the romanticism of Schumann will be glad to recognize all these qualities in the sixteenth century English musician, Giles Farnaby."—A. EAGLEFIELD HULL

ONE of the lesser figures in the Elizabethan school of music was Giles Farnaby, concerning whom little material exists. He was of Celtic origin, and it is believed that he was born in or about 1560. A comprehensive study of music was undertaken by him in 1580. He came to London in 1586, making it his home. His musical studies were completed at Oxford in 1592.

He first came to notice as a composer with a series of psalms which he contributed to Este's *Psalter,* published in 1592. Six years later, he published his celebrated *Canzonets to foure voyces with a song of eight parts,* a publication which contained commendatory verses by his friends Anthony Holborne and

John Dowland. These canzonets were recently edited and republished by Dr. E. H. Fellowes in his monumental *English Madrigal School,* volume twenty, (1922).

However, it is not to these canzonets that Farnaby owes his place in musical history, but rather to his significant pieces for the virginal in which, together with his great contemporary, John Bull, he laid the foundation of keyboard technique and clavier figuration. His most important pieces for the virginal—galliards, preludes, almans, fantasias, pavanes, etc.—appear in the *Fitzwilliam Virginal Book.*

It is quite true that Giles Farnaby was not of the artistic stature of his distinguished compatriots, William Byrd, John Bull or Orlando Gibbons, but his important contribution to music cannot be questioned. "Though he had neither the depth and pathos of Gibbons, the scope of Bull, nor the rugged strength of Byrd," wrote Margaret H. Glyn, "he has at his best something that is different from all these and is sufficient unto himself. . . . At the same time, the extraordinary charm of much of his writing places him far above the level of the ordinary minor composer and in a niche of his own."

Charles van den Borren has analyzed Farnaby's music as follows: "He is one of the most graceful musicians possible. He is also one of the most spontaneous, even in his audacities, and of these he has as many as Bull, whether in the realm of harmony or in that of melody, of an abundant and easy fancy like Schubert, whose qualities and effects he shares. He is so great a lover of melody that when he adorns it with figurations it is often to create new melodies more delightful and more characteristic than the one that formed his starting point. He is fanciful even to singularity. He is simple, sportive, popular, witty, mocking, even 'clownish.' He loves piquant detail, and at times carries it even to precocity. He is the most original of all the virginalists, and at the same time the one who best represents the spirit of 'Merry England.' Like Byrd, he is profoundly English; but while the elder master embodies the dreamy side of the

British character, Farnaby expresses rather the humorous side of it."

Giles Farnaby died about 1600 in England. His son, Richard Farnaby, also a composer for the virginal, is represented in the *Fitzwilliam Virginal Book* by four pieces.

Principal works by Giles Farnaby:
VOCAL: Psalms; canzonets, etc.
INSTRUMENTAL: Pieces for the virginal.

About Giles Farnaby:
Borren, Charles van den. *Sources of Keyboard Music*; Flood, W. H. Grattan. *Late Tudor Composers*; Glyn, Margaret H. *About Elizabethan Virginal Music and Its Composers.*

Important recordings of music by Giles Farnaby:
Virginal (HARPSICHORD): *His dreame* (COLUMBIA); *His humour* (COLUMBIA); *His rest* (COLUMBIA); *The New Sa-Hoo* (ANTHOLOGIE SONORE); *A toye* (COLUMBIA).

Gabriel Fauré *1845-1924*
(See *Composers Of Today*)

Zdĕnek Fibich *1850-1900*

ZDĚNEK FIBICH, a significant member of the national school of Bohemian composers, was born in Vseboric, near Czaslau, Bohemia, on December 21, 1850. His father was a forester on the estate of Count Auersburg. Fibich's childhood, therefore, was spent in the beautiful setting of Bohemian woods.

His early interests were poetry and music—particularly music. As a child, Fibich composed a song which disclosed much talent. The study of the piano came soon thereafter. In his tenth year, Fibich was sent to the Vienna Gymnasium for more intensive musical training. In 1862, he was a student at Smetana's musical institute in Prague. Two years later he composed a symphony, one movement of which he himself conducted at a public performance.

When he reached his fifteenth birthday, Fibich was sent to the Leipzig Conservatory where his uncle was a professor of music. There followed two years of comprehensive music-study, with Moscheles, Richter and Jadassohn. From here, Fibich went to Paris, equipped with important letters of intro-

ZDĚNEK FIBICH

duction. These gained him access to important artistic circles, where he soon became a favorite. Fibich's first outstanding work dates from this Paris sojourn—the *Studies in painting*, for piano, consisting of musical impressions of paintings by Ruysdael, Breughel, Correggio and Watteau.

Following a brief stay in Mannheim, where he studied under Vincenz Lachner, and heard many performances of Wagnerian music-dramas which stirred him, Fibich returned to Prague in 1870, marrying, and becoming a teacher of the piano. Three years later, he was brought to Poland by an appointment as teacher of the pianoforte. The social life of Vilna was not congenial, and this, coupled with the severe illness of his wife, caused Fibich to surrender his position and return to Prague. His wife died shortly after his return.

In 1875, Fibich was appointed assistant music director of the National Opera, resigning this post three years later to become choirmaster of the Russian Church in Prague. Meanwhile, he had married a second time—a marriage more of convenience than of love.

After three years as choirmaster, Fibich suddenly decided to withdraw from all public activity and to devote himself almost entirely to composition. For an extended period, he lived the life of a recluse, avoiding all social contacts.

About 1890, he deserted his wife to live with the celebrated actress, Anezka Schulzova. She had a revivifying influence upon his spirits. As a result of her influence, he emerged from retirement and his monastic existence, and once again interested himself in social and public affairs.

The closing years of his life were marked by ill-health. A severe cold brought him to his deathbed. He passed away in Prague on October 10, 1900.

Zděnek Fibich composed more than six hundred works. "Like Tschaikovsky," wrote Ralph Hill, "Fibich's idiom is more western than national in style; he used folk-song only when a particular tune interested him as such or when his literary text demanded an essentially national treatment. In this way, his musical outlook was the antithesis of his famous contemporaries, Smetana and Dvořák. . . . Most of Fibich's music was directly inspired by poetry and fairy-tales of a fantastic nature. His love for poetry and mythology was second only to music. . . . The most interesting and individual part of his output is the pianoforte music and the melodramas."

In his melodramas, Fibich was strongly influenced by Wagnerian principles, to which he always remained faithful. However, notwithstanding his allegiance to Wagner, Fibich beat a new path for music-drama, principally thru his use of spoken recitatives. "He completely subjected the music to the poetry," pointed out Henri Hantich. "The spoken voice dominates the symphonic tonality of the orchestra, which makes abundant use of the leit-motif, and is bound by no other rules except those which the dramatic accent imposes. In this way, he went further than Wagner. . . The ideal type of this new form created by Fibich is the trilogy *Hippodameia*. This work, composed of three dramas. . . abounds with dramatic scenes full of captivating effects, and assures for Fibich a prominent place among recent composers."

"The importance of Fibich's operas," in the opinion of Vladimir Helfert, "lies in the fact that they represent the most faithful application of Wagner's theories in Czech opera. . . . Fibich may be called the creator of modern Czech melodrama. Following in the footsteps of. . . . Schumann and Liszt, Fibich created a new form of melodrama on the basis of the Wagnerian leit-motif idea. . . . Thereupon he made the bold attempt at creating a great scenic melodrama by means of a continuous musical accompaniment to the spoken drama."

Principal works by Zdeněk Fibich:

OPERA: *Bukovin*; *Blaník*; *The Bride of Messina*; *The Tempest*; *Hédy*; *Šárka*.

MELODRAMA: *Christmas Eve*; *Eternity*; *The Water sprite*; *Queen Emma*; *Hakon*; *Hippodameia* (trilogy including *Pelop's wooing, The Atonement of Tantalus,* and the *Death of Hippodameia*).

ORCHESTRA: *The Jew of Prague*; *Overture in E-major*; *Comedy overture*; *Komensky Festival overture*; Three symphonies; *Othello*; *Toman and the wood-nymph*; *The Tempest*; *Spring*; *Vigiliae*.

CHAMBER MUSIC: *Quintet* (for violin, violoncello, clarinet, horn and piano); *Piano quartet*; Two string quartets; *Trio*.

Songs, ballads, duets, pieces for the piano, etc.

About Zdeněk Fibich:

Hantich, Henri. *La Musique Tchèque*; Richter, Carl Ludwig. *Zděnko Fibich: Eine Musikalische Silhouette.*
Musical Opinion 54:497 March 1931.

Important recordings of music by Zdeněk Fibich:

ORCHESTRA: *Poème*, arranged for violin and orchestra (COLUMBIA).
CHORAL: *Silent night* (GRAMOPHONE).

John Field *1782-1837*

"Field may justly be described as one of the most original pianistic phenomena."—
HUGO RIEMANN

JOHN FIELD—who has earned a permanent place in musical history by virtue of his nocturnes, a form which he was the first to bring into being—was born in Dublin, Ireland, on July 26, 1782. His father, Robert Field, was a violinist in the Theatre Royal of Dublin. Recognizing signs of musical talent in his son, father Field soon brought him into contact with musical instruction. John Field's first teacher was his grandfather, who taught him the piano with iron discipline and a merciless rod. Thus, with blows, Field was introduced to music.

Acquiring the fundamentals of music, John Field was sent to Tommaso Giordani, a celebrated music teacher in Dublin, for further lessons. Giordani proved to be a uniquely sympathetic and understanding teacher. Under his warm praise and encouragement, young Field made prodigious strides. At the age of ten, he made his first public appearance in a benefit concert. Shortly afterwards, he appeared as soloist in Giordani's Spiritual Concerts in Dublin, where he was so enthusiastically received that he made two further appearances; it was at these concerts that John Field first made his bow as a composer, with a rondo for piano.

In December of 1793, John Field's father received an appointment as leader of the orchestra at Haymarket Theatre in London. Thus, young Field, trailing an imposing reputation as à child prodigy, came to the English capital. Here, early in 1794, he was apprenticed by his father to Clementi, the famous pianist and manufacturer of pianos, and in return for working in the warehouse, Field received regular instruction from the great artist.

In the meanwhile, concert work was not neglected. In May of 1794, Field made a public appearance, playing a Clementi sonata. Shortly afterwards, he appeared once again, this time at the Barthelemon concerts. His success was encouraging, and he began to enjoy a growing popularity as piano virtuoso. His first important success came in 1799 when, at the Pinto concerts, he performed his own concerto.

John Field remained in the employ of Clementi for many years, remaining faithful to his employer thru all the startling vicissitudes of fortune which the piano establishment experienced. There followed a great attachment between teacher and pupil, employer and apprentice. Clementi recognized Field's great talent and was always at hand to give it encouragement. In 1801, he published at his own expense *Three sonatas* of Field, the first works of this composer to reach publication. In 1802, he took Field with him to Paris, to enable him to concertize in the French capital—concerts which were sensational. From Paris, Clementi took Field to Vienna, where once again he concertized with great success. Towards the end of 1802, the two musicians arrived in St. Petersburg.

Russia appealed so strongly to Field that he remained there when, in 1802, Clementi decided to return to England. It was a wise move for, in a short while, he enjoyed a meteoric success in Russia which made his name a household word to every music lover. He became the fashionable piano teacher. In consequence, he amassed a sizable fortune. During this period, he wrote some of his larger works, including a new piano concerto and the *Piano quintet*.

Unfortunately, wealth, luxury and fame turned Field's head. He became indolent, and reluctant to work at his composition. He took to drink and dissipation. His life became waste and idleness. In 1808, he married a French actress, Mademoiselle Percheron, a marriage that was ill-fated from the first; they were separated in 1813.

In 1814, Field composed the first of his nocturnes, a form in which he was most successful in expressing his musical thoughts, and in which he exerted so powerful an influence over another pianistic genius, Chopin. In his edition of Field's *Nocturnes*, Franz Liszt wrote as follows: "Their first tones, already, transport us into those hours when the soul, freed from the burdens of the day and resting only in itself, soars upward to the mysterious regions of the starry heights. Here we see it, like Philomel of the ancients, ethereal and winged, hovering among the flowers and scents of the garden of a nature with whose essence it is lovingly permeated."

This same year was also distinguished by the fact that Field became the teacher of a young musician who was later to become Russia's greatest composer, Glinka.

In 1822, Field transferred his home from St. Petersburg to Moscow. Here, he went from bad to worse. He was becoming a habitual drunkard; he was spending his energies in wasteful living; he indulged extravagantly in carnal diversions. He became less and less interested in music, neglected his teaching appointments, and completely abandoned composition. His former fortune melted away. Before long, not only poverty but ill-health faced him.

For many years, Field lived this empty, extravagant existence. Finally, in an effort to recapture his fame and fortune, he revisited London in 1832, after thirty years of absence. He was given a royal welcome. He performed his own *Concerto in E-flat* at the concerts of the Philharmonic amid triumphant acclaim. One month later, his teacher and friend, Muzio Clementi, passed away; Field was one of his chief mourners at Westminster Abbey.

Field now undertook an extensive concert tour. He went to Paris where he heard Chopin for the first time, strangely enough esteeming the great composer and pianist as a "sick-room talent." Then to Brussels and the French provinces; from there to Switzerland and Italy. Wherever he came, he triumphed. It seemed that, magically, Field had taken a new hold upon life. In Naples, however, he fell gravely ill, in May of 1834. He entered the hospital for a serious operation, and when, after many months of severe illness, he left the hospital, he was completely impoverished. By a stroke of good fortune, he stumbled across a Russian family who had been his friends in St. Petersburg, and who now took him with them to a cure in Ischia.

But health never fully returned to Field. After giving three magnificent concerts in Vienna, he returned to Moscow, broken in physique and spirits. He was once again confined to bed. On January 11, 1837 he passed away.

Despite his indulgence in dissipation, Field was not without appeal as a personality. His generosity was famous. Each Sunday morning he held open house for all those who were in need, to each one of whom he gave five rubles. He was sublimely impractical about money matters, never really knew how much he earned or had, and misplaced large bank notes with surprising absent-mindedness.

He was clean-shaven, with soft expressive lines of face, an arched nose and fair hair. His smile had warmth and expressiveness. He was a man of understanding and sympathy, qualities

JOHN FIELD

which made him an extraordinary teacher.

He owned four dogs, each of whom he called by a classical name. His favorite pastime was to take long rides in his carriage and to drop off at a tavern at intervals for food and drink.

He was notoriously irreligious. He acknowledged no faith, and refused to believe in the existence of a supreme being. At one time, shortly before his death, a priest engaged him in conversation. "Are you a Protestant?" the priest asked. John Field smiled a polite denial. "A Catholic?" Once again Field smiled and shook his head. "Then, perhaps, a Calvinist?" "No, not a Calvinist," Field answered. "Only a clavecinist."

As a pianist, John Field was an acknowledged artist of first importance. "Field's playing," in the words of Glinka, "was at once sweet and strong and characterized by admirable precision. His fingers fell on the keys as large drops of rain that spread themselves like iridescent pearls."

Discussing his compositions, Ernest Walker wrote: "Field's instrument has only one string—his notions of structure are as a rule elementary, and outside of the nocturnes his music is totally negligible; but the best of these exquisitely polished miniatures, with their delicate melodies and their shy fugitive gracefulness, will long serve to keep their name fragrant."

It was the celebrated German critic, Rellstab, who placed Field's nocturnes on a higher artistic level than Chopin's. This may be excessive praise. In any case, in his nocturnes Field not only influenced the future pianistic style of Chopin, but also proved himself to be a distinguished composer. In the nocturnes, commented Eric Blom, "Field is unique. . . . There is nothing else to take their place, not even Chopin's similarly named pieces. Here, he sings his heart out, and it is because he has learnt to sing that he becomes so entirely himself. . . . His range of mood within the species of the Nocturne is extraordinary—far greater than Chopin's. . . . [Here] John Field gave something to the world of music without which it would be as the world of flowers without the daisy; no worse for those who do not know what they miss, but not free from wistful regret for those who had once beheld the modest blossom."

Principal works by John Field:

ORCHESTRA: Seven concertos for piano and orchestra.

CHAMBER MUSIC: *Piano quintet.*

PIANO: Nocturnes; sonatas; miscellaneous pieces.

About John Field:

Flood, William Henry Grattan. *John Field of Dublin*; Walker, Ernest. *A History of Music in England.*

Important recordings of music by John Field:

PIANO: *Nocturne in A-major* (COLUMBIA-Hess).

Friedrich von Flotow   *1812-1883*

WILHELM FRIEDRICH FREIHERR von FLOTOW was born on the family estate of Teutendorf in Mecklenburg on April 27, 1812. He sprang from an old noble family that derived its name from the town of Vlotha, near Westphalia, and which had come to Mecklenburg with Duke Henry, the Lion-Hearted.

Although both parents were music lovers, Flotow's father—a captain of the cavalry—objected to a musical career for his son, preferring the more dignified calling of diplomatic service. A clarinet player, Ivan Müller, interceded for Wilhelm Friedrich until Captain von Flotow gave his consent. Having finally decided to give his son a musical education, Captain von Flotow determined to make it an intensive one. For this purpose, Friedrich was sent to Paris. This move horrified the other members of the family, some of whom vowed that if young Friedrich ever became a musician he would no longer be recognized as a member of the venerable family.

Friedrich, now in Paris, became a pupil of Anton Reicha, an excellent theorist, under whom he made rapid progress. The revolution of 1830 abruptly terminated his studies, and for a brief period he returned home. When the news arrived that Parisian life had again become normal, Flotow hurried back to continue his musical activities. At this time, he became acquainted with a group of opera composers in Paris, including Offenbach, Halévy, Meyerbeer, Rossini and Auber, who succeeded in directing Flotow's musical interest towards the theatre.

At first, Flotow turned his hand to the composition of operettas. Then, feeling greater self-assurance, he turned to more ambitious ventures. In 1839, he achieved his first definite success with *Le Naufrage de la Méduse* (composed in collaboration with Albert Grisar, a favorite composer of the day) which achieved fifty-four performances at the Théâtre de la Renaissance. From that moment on, Flotow's rise to fame was rapid. *Lady Harriet* was presented at the Opéra; *L'Esclave de Camoëns* at the Opéra Comique. With these two works, Flotow's position in the operatic world of Paris was assured.

The two operas by which Flotow is today remembered came between the years of 1844 and 1847. In the former year, he converted early sketches of a lyrical piece into a German opera. The final result—*Stradella*—was given its first performance at Hamburg on December 30. Three years later, Vienna introduced *Martha* to the world, an opera remodelled after the earlier *Lady Harriet* and which Flotow revamped completely four times before he was finally satisfied with it. *Martha* spread the name of Flotow thruout the entire world of music. By 1882 it was given its five hundredth performance in Vienna, and had been introduced into the repertory of virtually every leading opera house.

Martha deserved its success because, as one French critic pointed out, it was full of "grace and emotion, a charm that is often distinguished, an adroit verve and, upon occasion, felicitous, lively rhythms as well as distinguished melodies." One of the arias of Martha, *The Last rose of summer*, is world-famous.

Notwithstanding this great · success, Flotow suffered ostracism from high society. Many years before this, when he was scarcely old enough to realize what he was doing, he was induced to marry a girl whom he did not love and who did not love him. Their married life was wretched, and they finally parted by mutual consent. After the divorce, Flotow married the sister of his former wife, whom he adored and who idolized him. That Flotow should marry the sister of his wife, shocked his closest friends. From that time on, aristocratic circles refused to have him as a guest in their homes. He became something of a pariah, scrupulously avoided by his neighbors. This ostracism brought Flotow considerable pain and humiliation. During these years, he aged rapidly.

FRIEDRICH VON FLOTOW

When he was only fifty years old, "his hair was white and he was bent down like an octogenerian," wrote an interviewer in *Appleton's Journal*. "He looked like an old broken-down man."

From 1856 until 1863, Flotow was Intendant of the court theatre in Schwerin. The remainder of his life he spent partially in Paris and principally in Vienna. He died in Darmstadt on January 14, 1883.

Altho Flotow's pen continued to be productive after the composition of *Martha* it failed to produce any work of first importance. Such operas as *Indra*, *La Veuve Grapin*, and *L'Ombre* were successful enough in their time, but the success was ephemeral and failed to survive their composer.

Today, Flotow is known to us only because of *Stradella* and *Martha*. In both of these operas, Flotow achieved a superficial type of musical beauty whose appeal to operatic audiences never seems to have palled. No one will attempt to say that, even in their best pages, these works touch depth or profundity. They are graceful, light-hearted and gay with melodies that sparkle like champagne.

To some critics, the importance of *Martha* has been greatly overestimated. R. A. Streatfeild, for example, has written: "Flotow had a certain gift of melody, and the music of *Martha* has the merit of a rather trivial tunefulness, but the score is absolutely devoid of any real musical interest." Other critics, however, appreciate the fact that, altho *Martha* did not open new worlds, its ingenuous and charming appeal should not be dismissed. For Flotow, in the words of Edgar Istel, "understood without subtlety and parade of learning how to spread over the two text-books, melodies which take hold of one, less owing to their sincerity than to their pleasantness and rhythmical life."

With the exception of *Martha*, which was the product of careful and assiduous labor, Flotow worked with lightning rapidity, frequently making special effort in his works to produce melodies that might have contagious appeal. At one time, we are told, he encountered one of his infrequent obstacles in composition.

He was searching for a bright and lilting melody, and no fresh idea would come to him. Suddenly, he heard his cook hum a tune that was precisely the melody for which he was groping. He hurriedly put it on paper. Flotow never disclosed which of his tunes this was, but he confessed that it made its appearance in one of his best operas and enjoyed considerable vogue.

Principal works by Friedrich von Flotow:

Opera: *Stradella*; *Martha*; *Indra*; *La Veuve Grapin*; *Zilda*; *L'Ombre*; *Naïda*; *Il Fior d'Harlem*, etc.

About Friedrich von Flotow:

Flotow, Rosa Rosine von. *Friedrich von Flotow's Leben.*
Neue Zeitschrift für Musik 79:233 April 25, 1912.

Important recordings of music by Friedrich von Flotow:

Selections from Opera: *Martha*, "Overture" (Columbia); "The Last rose of summer" (Victor-Galli-Curci); "Canzone del Porter" (Victor-Journet); "M'Appari" (Victor-Gigli). *Stradella*, "Overture" (Columbia); "Alles teile unser glück" (Polydor); "Hymnus: Jungfrau Maria" (Parlaphone); "Tief in den Abruzzen" (Gramophone).

Stephen Foster *1826-1864*

"He was like Burns, a man who sang the purest poetry of humble life."—Louis C. Elson

IT is a particularly curious paradox that Stephen Foster, eloquent singer of America's South, never once went below the Mason and Dixon Line.

In Spring of 1817, Colonel William Barclay Foster, father of the composer, took his bride on horseback from Chambersberg, Pa. to Pittsburgh, where he built the "White Cottage." Here, Stephen, the youngest of seven children, was born on July 4, 1826.

He was not a bright child, but he showed an instinct for music. He liked to attend the church of the colored people and listen to their singing. In play-time, he would pluck at the strings of a guitar that belonged to his sister. There is a story to the effect that his mother bought him a flageolet, when he was seven years old, upon which he played flawlessly after a few moments of experimentation.

STEPHEN FOSTER

In 1839, he entered the Athens Academy at Tioga Point, where, as his classmates later remembered, he practised indefatigably on the flute. Here he composed the first of his pieces to receive performance, the *Tioga waltz*. In 1841, Foster went on to Jefferson College at Canonsburg. Three years later, his first publication made an appearance—a song, *Open thy lattice window*.

For a while, Foster entertained the idea of joining the navy. Finally, rejecting this plan, he became a bookkeeper in Cincinnati. In 1845, he formed a club which met twice a week for the purpose of singing the favorite songs of the day. It was Foster's idea that the club try new songs as well. For this club, Foster composed *Louisiana Belle* and *Old Uncle Ned*. Both of these songs impressed a Cincinnati publisher, Mr. Peters, who offered to publish them if Foster were willing to forego royalties. Foster, always impractical about money matters, agreed eagerly. In a few years' time, Mr. Peters earned more than ten thousand dollars, of which not one cent was returned to the composer.

These early songs were followed by *O Susanna!* and *Away down south* which enjoyed such widespread popularity that they were sung and heard everywhere. The success that his songs were now enjoying tempted Foster to give up bookkeeping. In 1850, he re-turned to Allegheny City to devote himself entirely to musical composition. In that year, he married Jane McDowell, a union which was not happy for either one. But an even more significant event took place in 1850: shortly after his marriage, Foster composed *Old folks at home*.

There now came that series of immortal songs which made Foster the best loved composer America produced. *Massa's in de cold, cold ground* came in 1852; *My old Kentucky home* in 1853; *Old Black Joe* in 1860. Stephen Foster's fame had by this time grown to phenomenal proportions. He was earning a yearly royalty of $1300, not a small figure when one considers the time.

In July of 1860, Stephen Foster, separated from his wife and family, came to New York to open a grocery store. There followed the most pathetic years of his life. He yielded more and more to the desire for alcohol, becoming before long a habitual drunkard. Pathetically enough, he took any remedy suggested to him to cure him, but all his efforts were futile. Poverty, squalor and ill-hea'th followed.

He was found lying in the hall of his Bowery lodging house on January 10, 1864, blood dripping from the corners of his mouth. He was taken to the Bellevue Hospital. Three days later he died in a charity-ward.

Few song composers have enjoyed the fame of Stephen Foster. His *Old folks at home* is frequently spoken of as the most famous song in the world, with the possible exception of *La Marseillaise*. Five years after it made its appearance, more than 400,000 copies were sold. Today, it has been translated into virtually every European and Asiatic language.

Certainly, a great measure of Foster's fame was the simplicity and unpretentiousness of his musical idiom. His was not a learned speech. It was sentimental, ingenuous, emotional. Foster's chief concern was to express what others about him felt. In their almost homely simplicity, in their undecorated emotions, in their indigenous qualities, the songs of Stephen Foster have been regarded almost as folk-music of America. They seem an inextricable part of our heritage.

"Stephen Foster," wrote Harold Vincent Milligan, "is a solitary figure in the history of music, occupying a unique position. Limited as his genius was, it was of the purest quality and exactly suited to the expression of those simple but profound emotions, common to all humanity, embodied in his songs. His immortal melodies are a distinct contribution to the world's music."

There are many anecdotes told in connection with Stephen Foster's songs. The best of these tells of the time, during the Civil War, when a group of Southern officers was sent home on leave with pay. They dropped into a tavern on the road, began to drink heavily, spent their money recklessly. Brawls ensued. Every attempt to pacify these inebriated soldiers seemed futile. Finally, an inspired thought came to the musician of the tavern. Suddenly, the small tavern band struck up *Old folks at home*. The melody proved to be more sobering than the strongest of coffees. In half an hour, the soldiers were completely mollified, and were on their way—èager to see their homes again.

Principal works by Stephen Foster:
An entire library of famous songs including *Old folks at home, Oh Susanna, My old Kentucky home, Old Black Joe, Massa's in de cold, cold ground, Old Dog Tray,* etc.

About Stephen Foster:
Howard, John Tasker. *Stephen Foster: American troubador*; Milligan, Harold Vincent. *Stephen Foster: a biography.*

Important recordings of music by Stephen Foster:
SONGS: *Stephen Foster melodies*, a collection of the best-known songs of Stephen Foster arranged by Shilkret (VICTOR).

César Franck *1822-1890*

"His music leads us from egoism to love by the path of the true mysticism of Christianity; from the world to the soul, from the soul to God."—GUSTAVE DEREPAS

"Franck's place in the history of music is beside Bach."—ARTHUR COQUARD

CÉSAR AUGUSTE FRANCK, a Belgian by birth, is recognized as one of the greatest composers that France has produced. He was born in Liège on December 10, 1822, where several of his ancestors had been famous Walloon painters.

Reversing the fate that met most composers in their youth, Franck was strongly encouraged by his father, a banker, to become a musician. Even before he could walk, César Franck was given musical instruction on the piano. He was entered as a student at the Liège school of music. In his eleventh year, his father took him on a concert tour as pianist thru Belgium, a tour that was only moderately successful.

César Franck, having finished his studies at the Liège school, was now enrolled at the Paris Conservatory (1837). He was a superior student from the first, and it was only the perversity of his nature which prevented him from winning every prize within reach. Late in 1837, for example, he was entered in the piano competition where he shocked Cherubini, director of the Conservatory, by impudently transposing the Hummel *Concerto in A-major* placed before him one-third below, and playing it flawlessly in the new key. This impudence robbed Franck of the first prize, but his performance had been too striking to be altogether ignored; he was given a special honorary mention. In 1840, Franck received first prize in fugue; one year later, a second prize in organ-playing.

By this time, father Franck was becoming impatient with his son's slow progress towards musical fame. He removed him from the Conservatory, took him back to Belgium where César gave several piano recitals and exhibited his first creative fruits—some trios, and some exhibitionistic piano pieces—before the King of Belgium. For two years, the Franck family remained in Belgium, but César failed to make any visible impression either on his audiences or on the King. In 1844, therefore, the Francks were back in Paris.

It was at this time that Franck began work upon his first major creation, his Biblical eclogue, *Ruth*. *Ruth* was given its première in the concert rooms of the Conservatory in 1846. This work, which Arthur Hervey terms "a simple work full of delicacy and charm," was considered by the critics a poor imitation of the then popular *Le Désert* of Félicien David.

On February 22, 1848—in the very midst of the revolution—Franck was married to a young actress, Mademoiselle Desmousseaux, at the Notre Dame de Lorette church. We are told that the young couple had to climb over barricades to reach the church.

Perhaps the most important result of this marriage was that it freed Franck from his paternal yoke. He set up an independent home in which he was finally released from his father's influence. Henceforth, he was no longer to be motivated by the desire for financial success, but only by the need to express himself honestly and artistically in his music.

Three years after his marriage, Franck began work upon an opera, *Le Valet de ferme*. His daytime belonged to teaching, so that only during the night could he turn to composition. For two years, he worked so industriously upon his opera that he finally collapsed with nervous prostration. He was so ill that work and composition, for a period, were out of the question. Unfortunately, his colossal labor on the opera had been in vain. Not only was it never produced but when the opera was completed Franck himself confessed that "it was not worth printing."

With the restoration of health, Franck became organist of the Notre Dame de Lorette. This was merely the apprenticeship to a more significant position which came in 1858 when he was appointed organist at Ste. Clotilde. It was here that the composer spent the best years of his life, in the organ chamber of the church, playing the organ, composing his music, improvising. It was here, too, that Franz Liszt came to hear him play in 1866, leaving the church in a daze and muttering under his breath a sentence in which he coupled the name of Franck with that of Johann Sebastian Bach.

In 1872, Franck was appointed professor of organ at the Conservatory. At the same time, he was putting final touches on his oratorio, the *Rédemption*. The *Rédemption* was introduced by Co-

lonne at the *Concert Spirituel* in 1873. Principally because of the inadequate performance it received, the work was a failure. Franck, however, was too absorbed with his creative work to permit this disappointment to wound him seriously. He was working industriously upon his *Les Béatitudes,* which he did not complete until six years later.

Feeling strongly that *Les Béatitudes* was his greatest work up to that time, Franck was eager to introduce it to the leading musicians of Paris. He arranged a special performance of several of its principal sections at his own home, himself officiating at the piano. To this private performance were invited the Minister of Fine Arts, the directors of the Conservatory and the Opéra, and all of the leading critics. The day before this concert, Franck sprained his hand in opening a carriage door. Regretfully, he had to assign the work of accompanying *Les Béatitudes* to his pupil, Vincent D'Indy. But this was merely the first of Franck's disappointments. At eight o'clock on the evening of the concert, the Minister of Fine Arts sent word that he was unable to come. A half hour later came word from the directors of the Conservatory and the Opéra that they, too, were unable to be present. Some of the critics came, but they slipped out of the room while the music was in progress. The première of *Les Béatitudes* was, therefore, a fiasco, and almost broke its composer's heart.

About fifteen years later, *Les Béatitudes* was given in its entirety by Édouard Colonne, greeted with great applause and warm praise. Today, there are some critics who consider this the greatest music César Franck created, greater than the symphony, the sonata, the quintet or the quartet. These critics believe with Ernest Chausson that it "certainly surpassed all other French music in sublimity. One would be obliged indeed to go back to the very first classical masters to find so powerful an expression of the soul's despair, its appeal to divine justice, its striving after the ideal, after holiness."

Meanwhile, the many pupils and admirers of César Franck, appalled by the neglect that their master was suffering, raised a fund for the purpose of arranging a concert devoted entirely to his music. This concert took place on January 30, 1887 at the Cirque Hiver, the program including the symphonic-poem *Le Chasseur maudit*, the *Variations symphoniques* for the piano and orchestra, and portions from *Ruth* and *Les Béatitudes*. The fates were once more against Franck. The performance was shabby, and the music suffered intensely.

Neglect, however, did not poison Franck's inspiration. During the years that followed he produced four masterpieces which strengthened his already formidable position in French music. On February 17, 1889, his *Symphony in D-minor* was introduced by the *Société des Concerts du Conservatoire*. The musicians of the orchestra during the rehearsal objected violently to playing such outlandish music. It was only the insistence of the conductor, Jules Garcin, that enabled this work to reach performance.

The apathy which greeted this masterpiece is amazing. Not only the audience, but the outstanding musicians of Paris as well, were deaf to its greatness. When the director of the Conservatory was asked for his opinion, he answered: "This is no symphony! Who ever heard of a symphony with an English horn?" Gounod found the work an "affirmation of impotence pushed to dogma." The critics were vitriolic.

There will be few in our time to deny that the César Franck *Symphony* is one of the few great symphonies since the Beethoven *Ninth*. H. C. Colles has spoken of it as "noble." Vincent D'Indy describes it as "the majestic, plastic and perfectly beautiful *Symphony in D-minor*." It has deservingly earned an important place in the repertoire of every major symphony orchestra.

In 1890, came one of the few successes that César Franck knew during his lifetime. On April 19, the *Société Nationale de Musique* introduced his *String quartet* with such honest enthusiasm among audience and critics that Franck was tempted to say: "The public is beginning to understand me."

In May of 1890, Franck was on his way to visit a pupil, Paul Brand, when he was struck by an omnibus. He succeeded in reaching the home of his pupil where he fainted. This was the

CÉSAR FRANCK

beginning of his ill-health which terminated with death. The following Autumn, he was confined to his bed with pleurisy. Complications—the result of his accident, which had not been properly treated—set in.

He died on November 8, 1890 in Paris. His last work, the *Chorales* for organ, was at his side. Dying, he attempted to leave his bed and reach his organ-loft so that he might put the final strokes of the pen on his last composition, but his strength failed him.

The funeral was modest. Only a handful of sincere disciples followed his body to the cemetery of Montrouge where it was buried. A few years later, the remains were exhumed and brought to the Montparnasse cemetery where they rest today.

"César Franck was short, with a fine forehead and a vivacious honest expression, altho his eyes were almost concealed under his bushy eyebrows," described Vincent D'Indy. "His nose was rather large, and his chin receded below a wide and extraordinarily expressive mouth. His face was round, and thick, grey side-whiskers added to its width. . . . There was nothing in his appearance to reveal the conventional artist type. . . . Anyone who happened to meet this man in the street, invariably in a hurry, invariably absent-minded, and making grimaces, running rather than walking, dressed in an overcoat a size too large for him and in trousers a size too short, would have never suspected the transformation that took place when, placed at the piano, he explained or commented upon some fine composition."

César Franck's personality—his humility, his simplicity of character, his modesty, his devout reverence—has frequently been described. "Franck," wrote Claude Debussy, "was a man without guile. The discovery of a beautiful harmony was sufficient to make him as happy as the day was long. . . . A great deal has been said about his genius without ever mentioning the unique quality of his ingenuousness. This man, who was unfortunate, unrecognized, possessed the soul of a child, and one so irradicably good that neither contradictory circumstances nor wickedness of others could ever make him feel bitter. . . . He wrote . . . so to speak, face to face with the spirit of music, before whom he would kneel, uttering at the same time the most profoundly touching prayer that ever fell from human lips. César Franck served his art with steadfast devotion. . . . He served music without ever asking it for renown."

In César Franck's principal works there appears a technical device known as the "cyclical form," in which, striving at greater unity, he repeats, in his final movement, the principal themes of the preceding movements.

Leland Hall has summed up other characteristics of Franck's music: "With the exception of a few early pieces for piano, all his work bears the stamp of his personality. Like Brahms, he has pronounced idiosyncrasies, among which his fondness for shifting harmonies is the most constantly obvious. The ceaseless alteration of chords, the almost unbroken gliding by half-steps, the lithe sinuousness of all the inner voices seem to wrap his music in a veil, to render it intangible and mystical. Diatonic passages are rare, all is chromatic. Parallel to this is his use of short phrases, which alone are capable of being treated in this shifting manner. His melodies are almost invariably dissected, they seldom are built up in broad design. They are resolved into their finest motifs, and as such are woven and twisted into the close

iridiscent harmonic fabric with bewildering skill. All is in subtle movement. Yet there is a complete absence of sensuousness, even, for the most part, of dramatic fire. The overpowering climaxes to which he builds are never a frenzy of emotion; they are superbly calm and exalted. The structure of his music is strangely inorganic. His material does not develop. He adds phrase upon phrase, detail upon detail, with astonishing power to knit and weave closely what comes with what went before. His extraordinary polyphonic skill seems inborn, native to the man. Arthur Coquard said of him that he thought the most complicated things in music quite naturally."

César Franck's influence both as a teacher and as a composer upon an entire generation of French musicians has been considerable. He left behind him a group of disciples who esteemed him one of the greatest masters that music has produced, and who attempted to write in his idiom. What one of these disciples, Guy de Ropartz, wrote about Franck might well have been voiced by all other Franckists. "He stands out from among his contemporaries like a man of some other age; they are skeptics, he was a believer; they are self-advertising, he worked in silence; they seek glory, he was content to await it; they aim at easily acquired reputations by daring improvisations, he built enduring monuments amid the calm of a retired life."

Franck's most devoted disciples, together with Guy de Ropartz, included such distinguished composers as Vincent D'Indy, Ernest Chausson and Henri Duparc.

Principal works by César Franck:

OPERA: *Le Valet de ferme*; *Ghisèle*.
CHORAL: *Ruth*; *Rédemption*; *Les Béatitudes*; masses; motets; hymns.
ORCHESTRA: *The Sermon on the Mount*; *Les Éolides*; *Le Chasseur maudit*; *Symphony in D-minor*; *Variations symphoniques* (for piano and orchestra); *Les Djinns*.
CHAMBER MUSIC: *Piano quintet*; *Quartet*; *Trio*; *Sonata for violin and piano*.
PIANO: *Prelude, chorale and fugue*; *Prelude, aria and finale*, etc.
Works for the organ.

About César Franck:

D'Indy, Vincent. *César Franck*; Emmanuel, M. *César Franck*; Ewen, David (editor).

From Bach to Stravinsky; Robin, Grey (editor). *Studies in Music.*

Important recordings of music by César Franck:

CHORAL: *Rédemption,* "Symphonic Interlude, Part II" (COLUMBIA). *Les Béatitudes,* "Heureux les coeurs" (COLUMBIA-Thill); "Mater Dolorosa" (POLYDOR); Psalm 150 (COLUMBIA).

ORCHESTRA: *Symphony in D-minor* (VICTOR-Stokowski); *Variations symphoniques* (VICTOR-Cortot, Ronald); *Symphonic suite from Psyché* (COLUMBIA).

CHAMBER MUSIC: *Piano quintet* (VICTOR-Cortot, International); *Quartet* (VICTOR-Pro Arte); *Trio in F-sharp minor* (COLUMBIA); *Sonata for violin and piano* (VICTOR-Menuhin).

PIANO: *Prelude, choral and fugue* (COLUMBIA-Maas); *Prelude, aria and finale* (VICTOR-Cortot).

ORGAN: *Prelude, fugue and variations* (GRAMOPHONE); *Chorale in A-minor* (GRAMOPHONE).

Robert Franz *1815-1892*

ROBERT FRANZ, genius of the *Lied,* was born in Halle on June 28, 1815. He was descended from a tribe of Celtic origin called the "Halloren," said to have been pioneers in working the salt-mines of Halle, remaining strictly apart from the Teutons of Halle and maintaining rigidly their family traditions which permitted no intermarriage.

Robert Franz's father was a business man whose name originally was Knauth. He changed his name to Franz only because his brother was in a competitive business, the identity of the names leading to considerable confusion. During the latter part of his life, Robert Franz was often maliciously accused of having himself changed his name from Knauth to Franz only to encourage comparison with that other Franz, genius of the *Lied,* namely, Franz Schubert.

Christoph Franz, father of Robert, was a simple man who was very fond of music. When he came home from work, he derived his sincerest pleasure from singing hymns. This love for music passed on to Robert, who, as long as he could remember, was sensitive to the art. He was enormously fond of the chorales he heard in church and the hymns at home. One of the most vivid impressions he received as a child

dates from the celebration of the Reformation in 1817, when he was enchanted by Luther's *Ein Feste Burg.* "As if in a dream I still hear the tones of the trombone choirs, wafted down upon us from the Hausmanns towers," he wrote in later years.

At school, he frequently delighted himself in the singing class by attempting to create harmonizations to the unison singing, for which he was rewarded by severe cuffings from the singing-teacher. At home, however, his love for music found sympathetic understanding. Thru the efforts of his mother, a spinet was brought into the house. From that moment on, Franz entered a new world, spending endless hours drawing melodies from the keyboard.

Robert Franz became a student at the Gymnasium in Halle, where his singing teacher, Cantor Karl Gottlieb Abela, a uniquely endowed musician, recognized his talent. Abela gave Franz piano instruction, at the same time introducing the young musician to the great oratorios of Handel and Haydn.

Robert Franz, at this time, was devoting so much time to music, and so little to other studies, that he incurred the disfavor of his father. There followed disputes between father and son, in which the son vehemently swore that he would never give up the study of music. Fortunately, a distant relative, Dr. Erich, was a spectator at one of these quarrels, and interceded for young Robert. The result was that Christoph Franz grumblingly gave his consent to a musical career for his son, sending Robert to Dessau to study under Friedrich Schneider, a famous musician of the time.

The formulary studies to which Robert Franz was subjected under Schneider so irritated him that, in less than two years, he gave up his studies and returned to his home in Halle. To Christoph Franz this was a definite sign that his son had failed as a musician. He now insisted that Robert turn to business.

Fortunately, Robert Franz was unable to procure remunerative employment during the years that followed. He, therefore, devoted himself to study—philosophy, literature, music. These

ROBERT FRANZ

years brought intellectual maturity to the young man, preparing him for the creative life that was awaiting him.

An adolescent love-affair turned him to composition. To express his great love, he composed a group of songs. These, somewhat timidly, he sent to Leipzig, to the eminent Robert Schumann, for criticism. Schumann was so impressed with the talent of these songs that not only did he write an article on Franz in the *Neue Zeitschrift,* but he procured a publisher for his music. Mendelssohn, too, saw these songs, and wrote a long and effusive letter to the composer, praising him for his achievement.

In 1841, Franz became organist of St. Ulrich. Shortly after this, he was appointed teacher of music at the University, and head of the Singakademie of Halle (which is still in existence and which, today, is called the Robert Franz Singakademie). He was now economically independent, able to devote himself more freely than ever before to his composition of songs. Economic independence also enabled Franz, in 1846 to make a visit to Vienna, where he met Franz Liszt who was profoundly impressed by the talent of the young composer.

In 1848, Franz married Maria Hinrichs, the daughter of a philosopher, and a musician and song-composer in

her own right. It was shortly after this marriage (one of the few sources of comfort to the unhappy composer) that there occurred the tragedy that darkened his entire life. A shrill whistle of an engine affected his eardrums. For a long period, he was completely deaf. When hearing was, at last, partially restored, it was discovered that his ear could no longer catch high notes; and that it was only a matter of time before complete deafness would return.

Robert Franz, however, did not permit this impending tragedy to affect his musical labors. He undertook a colossal editorial assignment—new editions of the music of Bach and Handel. With this he achieved such success that his name became well known to musicians outside of Germany. In recognition of this achievement, the King awarded Franz in 1856, an annual stipend of two hundred thalers.

By 1867, total deafness removed Franz from all musical activity. His income thus terminated, he knew the pinch of poverty for a long period. A committee was formed to find means with which to support the composer. There followed Robert Franz concerts thruout Europe. On June 28, 1873, Franz was given a gift of 30,000 thalers —the gift of an entire music-world to a genius of song—which insured him economic independence for the remainder of his life.

During his final years, Franz knew honor and recognition. Halle made him an honorary citizen. On his seventieth birthday, messages poured in upon him from the four corners of the world.

Robert Franz died in Halle on October 24, 1892.

His last year he lived entirely alone (his wife died in the Spring of 1891). His hands were almost completely paralyzed, his voice so thin that it was almost inaudible, his ears dead to the outside world. "It was most pathetic," wrote the American critic, Henry T. Finck, who visited the composer in the summer of 1891, "to see the deaf old master, shut from the tone-world he had helped to create, dwelling for fifteen minutes on the songs of his wife (of his own he seemed to have no thought) with tears repeatedly rolling down his cheeks. 'Her picture is in the other room—did you see it? No? Then I must get it!' Placing it in my wife's hands, he exclaimed: 'There, take a good look at that! Such a face you will never see again!' "

A contemporary of Robert Franz has left us a vivid description of the composer. "Lean, fairly tall and sinewy, he moved forward with a stoop and with nervous restlessness as if otherwise he might not reach his goal," wrote Theodor Held. "His free and slightly receding forehead, his prominent eyebrows and his long, pointed nose made an impressive combination. His blue eyes had a kindly and arched expression. The whole picture was framed by dark, closely brushed hair which did not turn grey until his very last years. Beardless he went thru the world. He spoke rapidly, but clearly, with a slight lisp."

Robert Franz was a man of profound scholarship, well versed in literature, philosophy and politics. By temperament, he was retiring and diffident. He was highly introspective, a dreamer and a recluse. Smoking was one of the few pleasures in which he indulged.

Robert Franz left almost three hundred songs. Thruout his entire life he worked and reworked on his songs so that even his earliest specimens are mature fruits of his genius. "My Opus 1," he once said, "I consider no better and no worse than my Opus 53."

"In examining Franz's songs," wrote Henry T. Finck, "one is first of all impressed by the reticence, dignity and purity of their style. They are true lyrics—expressions of personal feeling in simple, well-balanced, musical forms, undisfigured by dramatic episodes, obtrusive climaxes, or any of those other devices of less fastidious song-writers which are as abhorrent to true artistic feeling as they are grateful to the egotism of singers and the sentimentality of listeners. . . . He cared primarily, not for the luxuriance of decoration, but for structural symmetry and harmony; not for an emotionality bordering on hysteria, but for the calm expression of sincere, simple feeling; not for utter self-revelation but for a dignified presentation of what was artistically worth presentation, against a background of reticence and reserve. . . . In simplicity, and graciousness of melody, in musicianly part-writing, and in legitimately expressive harmony, Franz is preeminent."

In the history of the *Lied*, Franz's position is an all-important one. As W. F. Apthorp wrote: "He carried the German *Lied* to its highest known pitch of perfection. Uniting the purely lyric element one finds in such splendor in Schubert with the wondrously subtle and mobile expressiveness of every varying shade of emotion that characterized Schumann, fusing these two elements so that their union was absolutely . . . complete, Franz gave the finishing master touch to the plastic form of the *Lied*. Franz's songs are as truly lyrical, in the most exact sense of the word, as Schubert's; at the same time, they are to the full as emotionally expressive, as picturesquely and poetically suggestive, as vivid pieces of tone-painting, as Schumann's. And more than this, he has given them the most stoutly-organized, pure and concise form known in songwriting. To what Schubert and Schumann did before him, Franz brought the natural and logical completion; he crowned the edifice."

Principal works by Robert Franz:

Choral: *Psalm 117*; *Choral liturgy*; chorals; part-songs, etc.

An entire library of great songs including such famous *lieder* as *Die Lotosblume, Mutter, O sing mich zur rüh, Im Rhein, im heiligen strom, Stille sicherheit, Die Widmung, Marie am fenster, In meinem auge.*

About Robert Franz:

Apthorp, W. F. *Musicians and Music Lovers*; Barbak, S. E. *Die Lieder von Robert Franz*; Finck, Henry T. *Songs and Song Writers*; Pfordten, Hermann von der. *Robert Franz.*

Monthly Musical Record 39:98 May 1, 1909; *Musical Quarterly* 1:497 October 1915.

Important recordings of music by Robert Franz:

Songs: *Robert Franz Album*, a collection of twenty-four celebrated *Lieder* (Columbia-Wolff).

Girolamo Frescobaldi *1583-1643*

GIROLAMO FRESCOBALDI, whose contrapuntal genius and ability at the organ have caused more than one critic to refer to him as the "Italian Bach," was born in Ferrara in September of 1583, and baptized on the ninth of that month.

As a boy, studying under Luzzasco Luzzaschi (an eminent organist of the time) he disclosed unusual talent for music. He possessed a striking voice and an unusual adaptability for the organ. As a result, while still a boy, he was conducted thru the cities of Italy as a musical progidy, being greeted with great acclaim.

In 1608, he visited the Netherlands where he published his first major work, a book of five-part madrigals which increased his prestige greatly. Before long, he was back in Italy, occupying the post of organist at St. Peter's in Rome. Altho he was only twenty-five years old at the time, his fame was so great that, at his first appearance as organist, more than thirty thousand people were said to have come to the church to hear him perform.

Dissatisfied with the meagre compensation he received at St. Peter's, Frescobaldi took an extended leave of absence, in 1628. He came to Florence, on an invitation of the Grand Duke of Tuscany, Ferdinand II, and for five years was his private organist. He would probably have remained in Florence permanently but for the fact that a plague and war struck Florence, forcing him back to Rome.

He was reengaged as organist of St. Peter's, holding this post for the remainder of his life. He acquired the reputation of being the greatest organist of his generation. It was said of him that he could play better with his hands crossed than other organists could with hands in their natural position. One of his contemporaries referred to him as "the marvel of the age."

That eminent historian, Ambros, wrote that with Frescobaldi began that great classical period of organ-playing which was to reach its culmination one century later with Johann Sebastian Bach.

GIROLAMO FRESCOBALDI

Girolamo Frescobaldi died in Rome on March 1, 1643.

He composed prolifically for the organ —ricercari, caprices, toccatas, fugues, etc. "Both his subjects and the manner in which they are treated are more pronouncedly instrumental in character than those of any of his predecessors," wrote Cecil Gray. "His genius was essentially diatonic, the natural bent of his mind strongly traditional and averse to innovations which, when they appear in his music, lack spontaneity and inevitability."

Frescobaldi was one of the first great composers of the fugue, a form which he brought to a high degree of technical perfection. "Many of these fugues are upon two, three and even four subjects," Charles Burney informs us, "and every learned artifice of inversion, augmentation, diminution and *moto contrario* is used."

Frescobaldi likewise composed music for the harpsichord and for voice. His printed works were so well known in his time that they were considered indispensible to every professional musician not only in Italy but in Germany and France as well.

What distinguished Frescobaldi from his contemporaries, according to Alfredo Casella, was, first, the fact that he produced "a truly instrumental music already free from vocal tyranny," and, second, that "the music of these other musicians, beautiful though it be, never offers a real human interest, whereas with Frescobaldi one feels music vitalized by the breath of love—humble, but already like a vision of serenity."

One of Frescobaldi's most distinguished pupils was the composer Johann Jakob Froberger, who was sent by Ferdinand III to Rome expressly to study organ and composition under this master. Froberger spread Frescobaldi's influence thru England, France, Germany and Austria.

Principal works by Girolamo Frescobaldi:

INSTRUMENTAL: Toccatas, ricercari, partitas, correnti, fugues, caprices, etc. for organ, and for harpsichord.

VOCAL: Madrigals, canzoni, etc.

About Girolamo Frescobaldi:

Ambros, August Wilhelm. *Geschichte der Musik*; Burney, Charles. *A General History of Music*; Nef, Karl. *An Outline of the History of Music*; Ronga, Luigi. *Girolamo Frescobaldi*.

Important recordings of music by Girolamo Frescobaldi:

VOCAL: *Mia pallida faccia* and *Non mi negate* (MIA).

ORGAN: *Toccata for the Elevation* (ANTHOLOGIE SONORE).

Johann Froberger *1616-1667*

JOHANN JAKOB FROBERGER, a pioneer in the development of clavier music, was born in Halle, Saxony, on May 19, 1616. His father, who was chapel-master in Halle from 1599, gave him his first musical education. Young Froberger made sufficient progress to receive an appointment as court organist in Vienna in 1637.

During this period, a grant of two hundred florins from the Vienna court enabled Froberger to make a trip to Rome and study, for four years, under the great Frescobaldi, the most distinguished organist and contrapunist of his time. Frescobaldi's influence upon Froberger was so great that, in all of his future organ composition, Froberger never succeeded in freeing himself from the style of his master.

Froberger remained in Vienna until 1657, attaining a formidable reputation as organist. Upon his resignation from his Vienna post, Froberger came to France, where he was greatly impressed by the lute playing of Galot and Gautier. It was these lute performances which decided Froberger to apply lute technique to harpsichord performance, thereby being one of the first to free the technique of harpsichord playing from its bondage to organ-style, and evolving a new type of harpsichord performance destined to bring the history of keyboard playing to new development.

In 1662, Froberger left for England, a journey which was singularly adventurous. En route to Calais, he was attacked by highwaymen, who robbed him of all his possessions. He arrived at Calais in ragged condition. Near the English coast, the vessel upon which he was sailing was attacked by pirates. Froberger, who was an excellent swimmer, evaded capture by jumping overboard and swimming towards the coast. He was picked up by a fisherman, who gave him some dry clothes and a few pence. The remainder of the journey to London, Froberger made on foot, begging for bread and water on the way. He arrived, half-starved, shabby and footsore, without home or friends. Passing by Westminster Abbey, he decided to enter and give thanks to God for his safety. Being very pious, Froberger was so absorbed in prayer that he did not realize how rapidly time was passing. Before long, Christopher Gibbons, the chapel-master of the Abbey (son of the great composer, Orlando Gibbons), approached him and told him that it was time for him to go. To Froberger's delight, he discovered that Gibbons understood French, and he explained his pathetic plight to the chapel-master. Sympathetic, Gibbons offered Froberger employment as a bellows-treader.

At the marriage of Catherine of Braganza to Charles II, Gibbons was invited to officiate at the organ. Froberger was so lost in the music of the organ that he completely forgot, at one passage, to blow the wind, and the music was lost in mid-stream. Gibbons, infuriated, cuffed his apprentice vigorously, and stamped angrily out of the organ-chamber. Driven by a force too potent for him, Froberger passed his fingers lovingly over the keys of the organ.

Before long, he forgot completely where or who he was. His magnificent improvisation struck the admiration of those below. One of the ladies, who had been in Vienna, recognized Froberger's individual style. The news came to the king that none other than Johann Jakob Froberger, eminent organist and harpsichordist from Vienna, was performing. A harpsichord was hurriedly summoned, and Froberger was asked to give a performance. He enchanted his audience so completely that the King took off a gold chain he was wearing and hung in about Froberger's neck.

For the next few years, Froberger was the official harpsichordist of the court, a favorite of royalty, one of the most prominent musicians in England. He became fabulously rich, finally able to return to the Continent in gallant style.

The remaining years of his life Froberger spent at the chateau Héricourt of Sibylla, Duchess Dowager of Würtemberg, who was his patron and admirer. Here he died on May 7, 1667, attacked by apoplexy while saying his vesper prayers. The day before his death, we are informed by a letter of the Duchess, he gave his patron "a piece of gold wrapped up and sealed, and written on the envelope that it should be given to the pastor (of the parish) where he had chosen a burial place, asking me to deliver it, and let him be buried in the church of Bavilliers; also to distribute alms among the poor, and to give presents of money to the lower menials of the chateau."

Johann Froberger composed both for the organ and the harpsichord. It was in his compositions for the latter instrument that he proved his particular importance. "If in style, generally, his organ music shows him to be a follower of Frescobaldi," commented Cecil Gray, "his compositions for harpsichord, on the other hand, show him in the rôle of an innovator and pioneer. If not actually the inventor of the Suite . . . he was nevertheless the first to raise it to a high standard of artistic excellence and even occasionally to make it the vehicle for the expression of profound emotions."

"As a composer," summed up Edmund van der Straeten, "Froberger combined originality of thought with a perfect mastery over all the resources of his art, and daring spirit of innovation, particularly with regard to the use and treatment of discords."

Principal works by Johann Jakob Froberger:

INSTRUMENTAL: Toccatas, suites, caprices, canzones, ricerari, etc. for the organ, and for the harpsichord.

About Johann Jakob Froberger:

Bauer, Harold. *Great Composers of the Past* (introduction by Richard Aldrich); Beier, F. *Über Johann Jakob Frobergers Leben.*
Monthly Musical Record 46:11 January 1, 1916.

Giovanni Gabrieli *1557-1612*

"The Church music of Gabrieli, with its answering choirs and its accompanying strings and trombones, is to music what an Assumption of Titian is to painting."— AMBROS

GIOVANNI GABRIELI, one of the outstanding composers of the Venetian school of music, was born in Venice in or about 1557. His early lessons in music were derived from his celebrated uncle, Andrea Gabrieli, organist at St Mark's Cathedral. From 1575 until 1579, Gabrieli remained at the court of Munich where he was a pupil of the great contrapuntist, Orlando di Lasso.

On January 1, 1585, Giovanni Gabrieli became first organist at St. Mark's Cathedral, where he gained a reputation, both as organist and as composer, which spanned the musical world of the time. Between 1587 and 1597, Gabrieli published his first works, disclosing his amazing contrapuntal technique. In 1597, the first part of his *Sacrae symphoniae*—containing vocal motets for as many as sixteen voices—made an appearance.

Something of Gabrieli's enormous prestige as composer may be drawn from the opinion which some of his more celebrated pupils held of him. Michael Praetorius, one of the most learned masters of music of the period, speaks in his *Syntagma musicum* (third chapter) of Gabrieli as "the most eminent and most famous of all musicians," frequently using him as a model for composition. Heinrich Schütz, great German composer, was impelled to write of him: "What a man is Gabrieli! If antiquity had known him it would have preferred him to Amphion; if the Muses would wish a spouse, Melpomene could not have chosen anyone but him, so great was his mastery in song. All this is confirmed by his certain reputation. As for me, I am the first witness of his reputation; for four years I enjoyed his instruction—to my great advantage." Incidentally, it was thru Heinrich Schütz that Gabrieli's influence spread to Germany.

Discussing Gabrieli's contrapuntal art, L. Finzenhagen has written: "One recognized in his work the richest, the fullest development of the Venetian school. This music possesses the fullness of harmonic colors and it also owns that sweet, and at the same time, lively play of nuances, which is the singular characteristic of the Venetian school of painting."

Giovanni Gabrieli died in Venice in or about 1612.

Almost as significant in the Venetian school of composers was Giovanni Gabrieli's uncle, Andrea, who was born in Venice in 1510, and died there in 1586. After being a pupil of Andreas Willaert, father of the Venetian school, Andrea Gabrieli became a singer in the chapel of St. Mark in 1536, rising finally to the post of first organist. He composed many distinguished madrigals, ricercare, motets, *Sacrae cantiones, Cantiones ecclesiasticae,* and *Canti concerti* for six, seven, eight, ten and sixteen voices.

Principal works by Giovanni Gabrieli:

VOCAL: *Sacrae symphoniae*; madrigals, motets, etc.
INSTRUMENTAL: Sonatas for various combinations, pieces for organ.

About Giovanni Gabrieli:

Winterfeld, Karl Georg August. *Johannes Gabrieli und sein Zeitalter.*
Le Guide Musical 59:273 March 30, 1913.

Important recordings of music by Giovanni Gabrieli:

CHORAL: *Benedictus* (GRAMOPHONE); *Benedixisti,* motet (PARLAPHONE).

INSTRUMENTAL: *Sonata pian e forte* (ANTHOLOGIE SONORE); *Ricercare in the tenth tone,* for organ (ANTHOLOGIE SONORE); *Canzon* (ANTHOLOGIE SONORE).

Niels Gade *1817-1890*

NIELS WILHELM GADE was born in Copenhagen on February 22, 1817. He was the son of a maker of musical instruments.

"He received his first instruction in music," wrote Robert Schuman, "from one of those ordinary teachers who everywhere pay regard to mechanical industry, not to talent, and it is said that the mentor was not particularly satisfied with the progress of his pupil." At fifteen, however, Gade received more professional instruction from Wexschall and Weyse. One year later, he became a member of the orchestra of the Royal Opera House where he soon made his mark as solo violinist.

In 1841, he was awarded a prize by the Copenhagen Musical Union for an overture entitled *Nachklänge aus Ossian,* the judges being Louis Spohr and Friedrich Schneider. Encouraged, Gade set to work upon a symphony which, upon its completion, he sent to Mendelssohn for criticism. "I cannot resist the wish to address you in order to tell you what an extraordinary pleasure you have given me by your excellent work," Mendelssohn wrote the young composer on January 13, 1843. "For a long time past no work has made a more vivid and beautiful impression upon me." Two months later, Mendelssohn wrote Gade another note. "Yesterday, your *Symphony in C-minor* was performed here for the first time . . . to the lively and unalloyed pleasure of the whole public who, after every one of the four movements, broke out into the loudest applause. After the *scherzo,* the people were in a state of real excitement, and there was no end to the rejoicing and clapping of hands."

As a result of this success, Gade received a royal stipend which enabled him to visit Leipzig, and to come into personal contact with Mendelssohn and Schumann, both of whom influenced him strongly. In Leipzig, he became assistant conductor to Mendelssohn of

NIELS GADE

the Gewandhaus orchestra, as well as a member of the faculty of the Royal Conservatory of Music. Upon Mendelssohn's death, Gade became permanent conductor of the Leipzig Gewandhaus, retaining this post until 1848.

He returned to his native city to become the conductor of the Copenhagen Musical Union, which had been founded in 1836. From this time on, he was intensely active in the musical life of his country. He directed performances at the Royal Opera House. In 1865, he was given full charge of the Copenhagen Conservatory of Music. His work as conductor, teacher and composer was fully appreciated by the government. In 1872, he was appointed Commander of the Daneborg; four years later, the parliament voted him a yearly pension of 3000 kronen.

Between 1862 and 1882, Gade was a frequent guest-conductor to the important orchestras in Germany, Austria, Holland, France and England. His eminence with the baton was recognized by Germany in 1882 when he received the Prussian order *Pour le mérite*.

Niels Wilhelm Gade died in Copenhagen on December 21, 1890.

"Gade's musical activities," wrote Cornelius Rybner, "may be divided into two periods, the first of which may be called the weightier of the two. During the *Ossian* period, he composed those

of his works that have contributed most to the national element in Scandinavian music, and have for all times secured him a place in the hearts of his own people and by his treatment of that very element shown the world the beauty of that folk-lore of the north at the hands of a great sculptor.

"The splendid means of instrumentation at his command gives to his orchestral works a certain elusive beauty of coloring that seems to have its roots in the very heart of his country and which has ever since haunted the music of all Scandinavians. Thru his friendship for both Mendelssohn and Schumann, a new element creeps into his music, that of the German school of Romanticism, and he now reaches his second period."

Because of the strong influence which Mendelssohn and Schumann exerted upon him, many critics have failed to perceive the national qualities of Gade's music. It would be a great mistake, however, to call Gade a "decided Germanist," as Sir Charles Villiers Stanford and Cecil Forsyth have done in their history of music. Gade was, indeed, strongly affected by Scandinavian folk-song and poetry, and his music reveals marked Scandinavian tendencies. "The beautiful bizarries of his orchestration give one many a passing mental glimpse of the fjeld and the fjord," wrote William Saunders, "while with the charm and delicacy of line and color, so characteristic of his larger works, there is much that is reminiscent of the calm yet not unjoyous life of the villagers and peasantry of these northern climes."

Principal works by Niels Gade:

OPERA: *Mariotta.*

CHORAL: *Comala*; *Frühlingsfantasie*; *Elverskud*; *Die heilige Nacht*; *Kalanus*; *Zion*; *Die Kreuzfahrer*; *Gefion*; *Psyche*; *Der Strom*; part songs, etc.

ORCHESTRA: *Nachklänge aus Ossian*; Eight symphonies; *Im Hochland*; *Hamlet*; *Michaelangelo*; Two suites; Four novelletten (for strings); *Concerto for violin and orchestra.*

CHAMBER MUSIC: *String octet*; *String sextet*; *String quintet*; *Piano trio*; Four sonatas for violin and piano, etc.

Songs, pieces for the piano, etc.

About Niels Gade:

Behrend, William. *Niels Wilhelm Gade*; Blaze de Bury, Angé Henri. *La Musique dans le Nord*; Ferris, George F. *Great German Composers.*

Monthly Musical Record 13:3 January 1, 1883; *Music Teacher* 8:399 July 1930; *Musical Quarterly* 3:115 April 1917.

Important recordings of music by Niels Gade:

CHAMBER MUSIC: *Trio* (COLUMBIA).

SONGS: *Agnete og Havmanden* (GRAMOPHONE); *Agnetes Vuggvise* (GRAMOPHONE); *Knud Lavard* (GRAMOPHONE).

Baldassare Galuppi *1706-1785*

"Brave Galuppi! That was music! good alike at grave and gay!
"I can always leave off talking when I hear a master play."—ROBERT BROWNING

BALDASSARE GALUPPI was born on the island of Burano, on October 18, 1706. His father, a barber, played the violin sufficiently well to enable him to procure engagements in theatre orchestras; it was he who gave Baldassare Galuppi his first instruction in music.

In 1722, Galuppi went to Venice, where he earned his living by playing the organ in several small churches. At the same time—altho he was still unschooled in the technique of composition—he produced his first opera, *La Fede nell'incostanza,* which was greeted with hissing and malicious jeers. This reception of his first work so disappointed him that he firmly determined to give up all thought of music and to become a barber.

Fortunately, at this time he met the celebrated Venetian musician, Marcello, who felt confident of Galuppi's talent and urged him to continue his music studies at the Conservatory degli Incurabili. For three years Galuppi studied under Lotti, becoming one of the master's most highly esteemed pupils. The schooling completed, Galuppi composed a second opera, *Dorinda,* which was performed at Saint-Angelo Theatre in 1729. This time his work was greeted with enthusiasm and ovations.

From 1729 on, Galuppi composed a long series of operas (some of them on librettos by Goldoni) which were performed in the principal theatres of Italy, bringing him great fame. Such operas as *Scipione in Cartagine* and *Enrico* were presented in England where their appeal was no less marked, and where—as Charles Burney pointed out—they influenced an entire school of English operatic composers.

In 1748, Galuppi became assistant chapel-master at St. Mark's Cathedral in Venice, rising to full chapel-mastership in 1762. Four years later, Catherine II invited Galuppi to Russia to present his operas there, offering him the substantial salary of 4,000 rubles and free lodging and carriage. Galuppi's first opera in Russia, *Didone,* pleased Catherine so intensely that the following morning she sent the composer a gift of a golden snuffbox studded with diamonds.

Galuppi was back in Venice in 1768. For the remainder of his life he was active both as a composer of operas and church music, and as a director of the Conservatory degli Incurabili (to which post he had been appointed in 1762), bringing that institution to great prominence.

Baldassare Galuppi died in Venice on January 3, 1785. He has been described by one critic as follows: "He was very slender, with small face full of intelligence. His conversation sparkled with wit. His manners were distinguished, and he had a love of all the arts; he owned some magnificent canvases by Veronese. His character was esteemed no less than his talents; he had a

BALDASSARE GALUPPI

numerous family and lived a quiet, and respectable life."

To Charles Burney, Galuppi once defined good music as "beauty, limpidity and good modulation."

Galuppi's fame rests principally with his comic operas (the most popular of which was *Il Filosofo di campagna*) which, for a long time, enjoyed great vogue thruout Europe, and exerted a strong influence on the development of German comic opera. The music of Galuppi, Fétis wrote, "does not glisten with harmonic color; but with a sustained gaiety, an indefatigable verve. The graceful forms of his song have brought him a fame which, for a long time, resisted the caprices of fashion."

It has never been ascertained precisely which toccata of Galuppi Browning had in mind when he wrote his poem, entitled *To a Toccata of Galuppi*.

Principal works by Baldassare Galuppi:

OPERA: *Scipione in Cartagine*; *Enrico*; *Didone*; *Ifigenia in Tauride*; *Il Filosofo di campagna*, etc.

CHORAL: Three dramatic cantatas; Twenty oratorios, etc.
Works for the harpsichord, for organ, for violoncello, etc.

About Baldassare Galuppi:

Fétis, F. J. *Biographie Universelle des musiciens*.

Important recordings of music by Baldassare Galuppi:

INSTRUMENTAL: *Sonata*, "Gigue" (COLUMBIA); *Harpsichord sonata*, "Allegro" (GRAMOPHONE).

Francesco Geminiani *1674-1762*

FRANCESCO XAVIER GEMINIANI, one of the important disciples of Corelli both as composer and as violinist, was born in Lucca in or about 1674. His first teacher in music was Carlo Ambrogio Lunati (known as "The Hunchback"), who gave him a competent introduction to violin-playing. Further instruction followed in Rome under Corelli.

In 1706, Geminiani returned to Lucca, and for three years he held the position of violinist in the Signoria orchestra. In 1711, he came to Naples to become leader of an orchestra, a position in which he was not successful. Burney informs us "he was soon discovered to be so wild and unsteady a timist that instead of regulating and conducting the band, he threw it into confusion." Here, he was a pupil of Alessandro Scarlatti in composition.

Geminiani went to England in 1714, where he succeeded in gaining several powerful patrons whose influence brought him great prestige and popularity. He was invited to play in Court, and consented to do so only when Handel agreed to accompany him.

For the next few years, Geminiani was a fashionable teacher of the violin and a favorite virtuoso, though his appearances on the concert stage were few and far between. It was at this time that he first turned seriously to composition, publishing, in 1716, *Twelve solos for violin, bass and harpsichord*. Concerning this work, Burney wrote: "Though few could play them, yet all the professors allowed them to be still more masterful and elaborate than those of Corelli."

For the next nine years, Geminiani was occupied in various endeavors. He was not only an industrious teacher and composer, but he also prepared a standard book on violin playing and arranged and edited several Corelli concertos, published by subscription. But music alone did not absorb his efforts. At this time he likewise became a picture-dealer (Geminiani frequently said that he loved painting far more than music)—with disastrous results. He suffered such financial losses that he incurred bankruptcy and was incarcerated. His pupil and patron, Lord Essex, extricated him from prison.

In 1727, Geminiani was offered an important position as Master of Music of the State of Ireland, which he refused perfunctorily when he learned that, to gain it, he would have to renounce his Roman Catholicism. Instead, he turned with renewed industry to the playing of the violin and to composition. In 1731, he gave a series of twenty concerts which were highly successful; in 1733 he went to Dublin where he opened up his own concert-hall—"The Geminiani Great Room"—where he gave concerts that attracted large audiences. During this period, too, he published two sets of Concerti grossi in which he brought the form, first integrated and solidified by his master Corelli, to more plastic development. This publication, wrote Burney, placed Geminiani "at the head of all masters then working in this species of composition."

Between 1737 and 1740, Geminiani concertized extensively in Dublin. Three years later, his *Six concertos* and the *Pièces de clavecin* saw publication.

In 1748, Geminiani produced his monumental *Art of violin playing*. This was the first book of its kind ever written, preceding a similar thesis published by Leopold Mozart (the father of the great composer) by several years. This pedagogical treatise handed down to posterity the principles of violin playing as established by Corelli. In many respects, this work is surprisingly modern in technique.

The remaining years of Geminiani's life were active. For a short period, he lived in Paris where he brought out a new edition of solo violin sonatas. Then he went to Ireland as violin teacher. During these years, his energy was absorbed by his creative work, pedagogy and the writing of treatises on violin playing.

Francesco Geminiani died in Dublin on September 17, 1762. It has been said that his death was brought about prematurely by the grief caused by the loss of one of his manuscripts on playing the violin, stolen from his home.

"Though he had more variety of modulation and more skill in diversifying his parts than Corelli, his melody was even inferior, and there is frequently an irregularity in his measures and phraseology, and a confusion in the effects of the whole," was Charles Burney's comment on Geminiani's music.

There could be no doubt that Geminiani's influence upon the history of violin playing, and upon the development of the concerto form, was far-reaching. Wrote Edmund van der Straeten: "He was undoubtedly one of the greatest, if not *the* greatest violinist of his time, who had enlarged in many ways the resources of his instrument,

FRANCESCO GEMINIANI

as his concertos and sonatas clearly show. He also extended the sonata form which is more developed and freer in form, even if that often lacks the clearness and beautiful symmetry of the work of his master Corelli. Burney and many great musicians have pointed out his want of originality and weakness in harmonic treatment, but those who have the courage to judge for themselves will find many beautiful melodies in his slow movements, and the most delightful dance movements, while some of his allegros are likewise attractive. He was a master of the instrumental fugue."

Geminiani's theoretical works included: *Rules for playing in a true taste on the violin, Guida armonica, The Art of accompaniment, The Art of playing the guitar, Treatise on good taste,* and *The Art of violin playing.*

Principal works by Francesco Geminiani:

ORCHESTRA: Concerti grossi.

Solos for violin; solos for violoncello; sonatas for violin; trios; pieces for the harpsichord, etc.

About Francesco Geminiani:

Burney, Charles. *A General History of Music*; Straeten, Edmund van der. *The History of the Violin.*
Strad 40:348 November 1929; *Westminster Magazine* 5:174 April 1777.

Important recordings of music by Francesco Geminiani:

INSTRUMENTAL: *Sicilano* (GRAMOPHONE-Busch); *Gavotte* (COLUMBIA); *Andante* (COLUMBIA).

Edward German *1862-1936*
(See *Composers Of Today*)

Carlo Gesualdo *1560-1614*

ONE of the foremost madrigalists of the Renaissance was Carlo Gesualdo, Prince of Venosa, born in Naples in or about 1560. The descendant of one of the oldest and most distinguished princely houses of Naples, Carlo Gesualdo moved in surroundings of splendor from earliest childhood.

He was permitted by his parents to indulge in musical diversions. He became a pupil of Pomponio Nenna of Bari, a famous teacher and madrigalist, who gave him a thorough training in composition and in the playing of the lute.

As a young man, Gesualdo became chapel-master of Scuola Napoletana, where he gained great recognition for his musical talent. At the same time, he was known to have been one of the most influential musical patrons in Naples: He maintained large staffs of composers, singers and instrumentalists at his court.

During Easter of 1588, Carlo Gesualdo became acquainted with the great poet, Torquato Tasso. Tasso soon became one of his closest friends, and wrote many of the poems which Gesualdo set to music.

At the age of twenty-five, the Prince married the beautiful Donna Maria d'Avalos, also a member of a powerful Neapolitan family, who, despite her youth, had already been married twice, both of her husbands having died mysteriously. Two years later, Gesualdo's uncle tried to have an affair with the beautiful Maria. Frustrated, he brought the Prince the news that Maria was an unfaithful wife who, at that very time, was having an affair with a young Duke. Prince Gesualdo was skeptical until incontrovertible evidence removed all possible doubt. He had both his wife and her lover killed, and ordered that their

CARLO GESUALDO

naked bodies be flung upon the steps of the palace, not to be removed—upon the penalty of death—for several days.

This incident has been frequently borrowed by story-writers. It makes its appearance in Anatole France's *Le Puits de Sainte-Claire,* and in Brantôme's celebrated *Les Vies des Dames Galantes.*

It may have been that the Prince was eager to escape from the scene of this sordid tragedy or, as so many other historians maintain, from the avenging hands of Maria's family. At any rate, shortly following this incident, the Prince undertook a long journey. He settled finally, in 1594, in Ferrara (which boasted of one of the most musical courts in all of Italy) where he rented a spacious palace, and married once again. It was at this time that, partially to express some of the misery he felt, he turned to the composition of madrigals.

Gesualdo did not return to Naples until the end of the century, when he established there a musical academy. He died in the city of his birth in 1614.

Gesualdo's fame as a composer rests upon six books of madrigals which were published between 1594 and 1626. "The distinguishing excellences of the composition of this admirable author," wrote Sir John Hawkins, "are fine contrivances, original harmony and the sweetest modulations conceivable."

What specifically characterized Gesualdo's madrigals was their harmonic independence (Gesualdo emancipated himself completely from modal harmonies), their sense of balance of form, their brilliant contrapuntal writing and particular felicitousness in giving tonal expression to every shade, emotion and sentiment of the words.

"Gesualdo was a composer of extraordinary genius," wrote Philip Heseltine, "whose works . . . still *live* in the fullest sense of the word as vivid and passionate exclamations of the human soul.

"While Peri and Monteverdi were bringing to birth that new vehicle of expression which was to become opera, Gesualdo, without the aid of action and a theatre, was dramatizing the emotions themselves—and his contribution to the first period of dramatic music was no less important than theirs."

Principal works by Carlo Gesualdo:

VOCAL: Six books of madrigals; *Sacrae cantiones* (for 5, 6 and 7 voices).

About Carlo Gesualdo:

Gray, Cecil and Heseltine, Philip. *Carlo Gesualdo, Prince of Venosa, Musician and Murderer*; Keiner, Ferdinand. *Die Madrigale Gesualdos von Venosa.*

Important recordings of music by Carlo Gesualdo:

VOCAL: *Io. Tacero* (BRUNSWICK); *Resti di darmi noia* (PARLAPHONE).

Orlando Gibbons *1583-1625*

ORLANDO GIBBONS, one of the most distinguished composers of the Elizabethan period, was born in Cambridge, in or about 1583. His ancestors were of yeoman stock. His father, who was a musician, introduced him to music.

In February of 1596, Gibbons became a chorister at King's College. He was highly talented, acquiring a great reputation as organist. In 1604, he received an appointment as organist of Chapel Royal, a remarkable achievement for one so young. He held this position until the end of his life, and was recognized as one of the greatest organists in England.

In 1606, Gibbons received his baccalaureate from Oxford. In the same year, he was married to Elizabeth Patten.

In 1611, he made his first appearance as a composer, when six of his virginal pieces appeared in the collection, entitled *Parthenia,* together with compositions by Byrd and Bull. Of these virginal pieces, the most remarkable was the *Fantasia of four parts.* One year later, Gibbons published his book of madrigals. "Among these madrigals . . . are many of the finest specimens of that beautiful form in which the art of polyphonic vocal music seems to have reached its highest point," wrote J. A. Fuller-Maitland. These included *The Silver swan, What is our life, Ah! Dear Heart, Fair is the rose,* etc.

In 1622, Gibbons received his doctorate from Oxford. Three years later, he was invited by Charles I to Canterbury to prepare the music for the festivities held in honor of Henrietta Maria. Here he suffered an apopleptic stroke. He died on June 5 of 1625, and was buried in Canterbury Cathedral.

Perhaps the most distinguishing trait of Gibbons' music is its variety of style. "There is in Gibbons," we are informed by E. H. Fellowes, "a diversity of character, a variableness of intention which distinguishes him from his forerunners."

"Though he never reaches the same depths of etherealized tenderness and mystic sublimity as Byrd," wrote Ernest Walker, "he has perhaps more variety of style; and his easy mastery over all

ORLANDO GIBBONS

his material enabled him to succeed brilliantly in anything he touched."

Gibbons not only composed madrigals and music for the virginal, but he was also a great composer of Church Music (psalms, preces, services, anthems, hymns, etc.). His output likewise included instrumental works for trio, quartet and six instruments. Casting a critical glance over Gibbons' entire production, W. H. Hadow generalized as follows: "His prevailing tone is grave and solemn, as though with him the madrigal caught some echo from the Church service; he has keen feeling for expressive melody and harmonic beauty of sound."

Orlando Gibbons had three sons and four daughters. Of these the most celebrated was Christopher Gibbons, later organist of Westminster Abbey, who featured in a famous anecdote connected with the life of Johann Froberger.

Principal works by Orlando Gibbons:

CHORAL: Madrigals; psalms; anthems; hymns; preces; services, etc.

INSTRUMENTAL: Pieces for the virginal; Fantasias for string trio; *Galliard*; Fantasias for string quartet; Fantasias for six strings, etc.

About Orlando Gibbons:

Fellowes, Edmund Horace. *Orlando Gibbons*; *A Short Account of His Life and Works*; Glyn, Margaret H. *About Elizabethan Virginal Music and Its Composers*. *Chesterian* 6:177 May 1925.

Important recordings of music by Orlando Gibbons:

CHORAL: *The Silver swan* (ROYCROFT-English Singers); *Ah! Dear heart* (COLUMBIA); *Hosanna to the Son of David* (COLUMBIA); *Nunc dimittis* (COLUMBIA).

Henry F. Gilbert   *1868-1928*

HENRY FRANKLIN BELKNAP GILBERT, one of the most significant of native American composers, was born in Somerville, Massachusetts, on September 26, 1868. Both his parents were musical. His father played the organ and, in Gilbert's own words, "manufactured hymns"; his mother sang solos in church.

As a child, Gilbert heard Ole Bull, the famous violinist, in a concert. He was so touched by the music that he determined to become a violinist. His grandfather manufactured a violin for him from a cigar-box. Upon this, young Gilbert practised indefatigably until he acquired an almost supple technique. Other instruction was procured from local tutors. On reaching early manhood, his ambition reached partial fulfillment when he secured a position playing the violin in hotel orchestras and theatres in Massachusetts and Florida.

In 1888, Edward Macdowell, the celebrated American composer, returned from his musical triumphs in Europe to join the faculty of the New England Conservatory of Music. By this time, Gilbert had fully determined to pursue the study of music industriously. He became Macdowell's first pupil in composition. For three years, Gilbert studied under Macdowell, acquiring solidity in his technique. At the same time, the study of the violin was pursued under Emil Mollenhauer.

Financial difficulties compelled him to surrender all thoughts of music, in 1892, for the sake of business. For the next ten years, he was employed first in the printing firm of his uncle, F. H. Gilson, then in the music-publishing house of C. C. Birchard. Only his leisure hours could be devoted to music.

During this time, Gilbert first became a devoted enthusiast of American folk music, which he was later to attempt to embody in his creative work. In 1901, he was a vital figure in the movement sponsored by the Wa-Wan Press to spread propaganda for Indian and Negro folk music.

Late in 1901, Gilbert—who, thruout his life, had been an idealistic democrat —heard that Gustav Charpentier, the French composer, had composed a proletarian opera entitled *Louise*. Without hesitation, Gilbert gathered his meagre savings, resigned from his position, and boarded a cattle-boat for France. His first hearing of *Louise* convinced him of one truth: He would henceforth devote himself completely to musical composition.

Typhoid struck Gilbert in Paris. Broken in health, he returned to America to begin creative work. He rented a barn near Cambridge, and— refusing to be dismayed by the stinging poverty that was facing him—he hurled himself into the work of composition with passionate abandon.

From the very first, he attempted to compose indigenous American music. He believed strongly in American folk songs, and felt that they deserved artistic treatment. Thus, thruout his life, he built his most famous works on native Negro melodies, Indian themes or popular folk music drawn from the storehouse of America's past.

His very first major symphonic work, *Americanesque,* was based upon three minstrel tunes. "Without inquiring too closely into their origin," explained Gilbert at the time, "I have tried to bind together a few scraps into an art form very much in the manner of Edvard Grieg and the folk music of Norway."

In 1906, his declining health compelled him to summon physicians. They found that, as a result of his former typhoid, he had a heart condition which no one had been known to survive beyond the thirty-sixth year. The physicians strongly urged Gilbert to give up all work, expressing the hope that, with sufficient quiet, rest and leisure, he might live for another few, counted years.

However, he defied not only the advice of his physicians, but their prediction as well. Notwithstanding the fact that he plunged himself more deeply than ever before in work, he did not die in a few years but—to the amazement of the medical world—lingered on for more than two decades longer.

In 1911, Gilbert produced the first work to bring him fame as a composer, the *Comedy overture on Negro themes,* performed in Boston and New York with great acclaim. This, in many respects, is one of his strongest works. "It is characteristic in every measure of the composer," wrote Olin Downes, "and it is a substantial justification of his theories and practices. . . . Those who analyze the thematic material of the *Comedy overture* will find that the thematic material as well as its development appears as the very fabric of the composer's thought. . . . In its rhythmical impulse born of the fragment of the Spiritual, its shrewd wit, its infectious

HENRY F. GILBERT

laughter, it announces itself as a piece of craft which could have come from nowhere but America."

Gilbert solidified his position as one of the most important of native American composers with the *Negro rhapsody* (given its first performance at the Norfolk Festival in 1913) and the symphonic prologue *Riders to the sea* (introduced at the Peterboro Festival in 1915). In 1918, he attained new importance when the Metropolitan Opera House gave the première of his *The Dance in Place Congo,* a symphonic ballet based on Creole themes from Louisiana.

In 1927, Henry F. Gilbert was selected as one of two American composers to represent this country at the International Music Festival in Frankfurt. Altho his health was so broken that it was believed he was on death's threshhold, Gilbert insisted upon going to Europe. He had to be carried aboard ship. But he lived not only to fulfill his commission but to return to America.

Gilbert died at his home near Cambridge on May 19, 1928. His last works, *Nocturne* and *Symphonic piece,* had been performed by the Boston Symphony Orchestra before his death.

Henry F. Gilbert, who looked very much the Bohemian, was a familiar figure at symphony concerts in Boston. He was easily recognizable by his long, flowing hair, his bronze complexion, his Indian profile, and his ever-present pipe. "His eyes had a glint of humor," Isaac Goldberg has written in description. "They were watery blue, as bland as his voice. There was no compromise in his nose; it came down straight over a strange, wide mouth. His lips, from their lines alone, should have made a scowl, yet despite their droop they usually produced the effect of a genial but watchful smile."

Although Gilbert's music is only infrequently performed in our symphony concerts today, its importance in the history of our cultural development was formidable. However it is the opinion of Isaac Goldberg that "greater than the legacy of scores will be the rare example of this man's integrity. He was one of the last true New Englanders, in whom the rebel, the philosophic anarchist, the spiritual aristocrat, burned brightly amid the damp darkness of a vanished leadership. He was a Thoreau in tone. Historically, he appeared to have come too late. . . . A genuinely national composer, indeed, may have to retrace some of the ground that Gilbert covered, and may discover that Gilbert came early after all. His Americanism was an organic phase of his sincerity, his independence, his wholeness; these qualities represent, perhaps, his chief meaning for those who are to follow."

Henry F. Gilbert has likewise distinguished himself for his critical writings on music which were featured, during the later years of his life, in outstanding musical journals. He was also a lecturer at Harvard in 1917-1918.

Principal works by Henry F. Gilbert:

ORCHESTRA: *Americanesque*; *Comedy overture on Negro themes*; *Three American dances*; *Negro rhapsody*; *Riders to the sea*; *Suite for chamber orchestra*; *Symphonic piece*; *Nocturne*.

BALLET: *The Dance in Place Congo*.

CHORAL: *To America*; *Six Indian sketches* (for chorus and orchestra); *Salammbô's invocation to Tanith* (for soprano and orchestra).

Songs, pieces for the piano, etc.

About Henry F. Gilbert:

Howard, John Tasker. *Our American Music.*
American Mercury 15:331 November 1928; *Musical Quarterly* 4:23 January 1918.

Alexander Glazunov   *1865-1935*
(See *Composers Of Today*)

Michael Glinka   *1804-1857*

THE history of Russian music may be said to have begun officially with Michael Glinka, its first great composer.

Michael Ivanovich Glinka was born in Novospasskoï, in the government of Smolensk, on June 1, 1804. His father, a prosperous landed proprietor, was a retired army captain.

The two qualities which distinguished Glinka from other children were his unusual nervousness (which frequently made him violently ill) and his extraordinary love for music. Everything musical had a particular appeal for him. He delighted in the sounds of bells, whose music he attempted to reproduce by beating together two copper bowls. The musical services at the church were a source of endless fascination to him. He would also sit spellbound whenever he heard his uncle's private orchestra perform. It is illuminating to point out that, even as a child, Glinka manifested an exceptional love for folk-music.

In 1817, Glinka was enrolled in a school at St. Petersburg which was attended only by children of nobility. Here he revealed himself to be an extraordinary student. He made rapid progress in languages, acquiring a mastery of Latin, French, German, English and Persian, and showed equal adaptability for the sciences. In music, of course, he made even more sweeping progress. He developed his piano technique under John Field, and acquired the rudiments of violin playing from Böhm. In 1822, he penetrated more deeply into musical activity by beginning composition for the first time, producing a set of five waltzes for the piano.

His intense concentration on study brought about a nervous breakdown. In 1823, Glinka went to the Caucasus to take the cure of the waters. On returning to his father's home from his vacation, he indulged in the study of music more industriously than before. Harmony and orchestration he acquired from text-books. He would frequently borrow his uncle's orchestra and rehearse with them masterpieces of orchestral music with which he was unfamiliar.

However, he had not as yet determined to adopt music as a life profession. In 1824, he entered the Civil Service, in the department of the Minister of Ways and Communications. For several years, Glinka was a slave to his desk. Then, feeling with increasing conviction that he was meant to be a musician, he suddenly resigned his post. He became affiliated with a group of young dilettantes who instilled into him further enthusiasm and zest for art. He was now convinced that he had found his proper sphere.

He was too dissatisfied with his technical equipment to indulge in intensive composition. In 1830, therefore, he traveled to Italy to continue studying. For one year, he remained in Milan, studying under Basili, director of the Conservatory. From Milan he went to Naples, and from there to Berlin. It was in Berlin that it first occurred to him to devote his art to the expression of his country's temperament. "Homesickness," he later wrote in his *Memoirs*, "led me little by little to write Russian music." And, in a letter which he wrote to a friend at this time, Glinka further elaborated upon his ideal. "My most earnest desire is to compose music which would make all my beloved fellow-countrymen feel quite at home, and lead no one to allege that I strutted about in borrowed plumes."

Returning to St. Petersburg, Glinka associated himself with prominent poets and men of letters of the time (including Pushkin and Gogol). In listening to their discussions on national poetry, he clarified his own views on national music. For a long time, he yearned to compose an opera, an opera that would speak of Russia. He found a suitable libretto in *A Life for the Tsar*. Plunging into the task of composing his first opera, he worked with industry and zest. It was finally presented in the Imperial Theatre at St. Petersburg on November 27, 1836.

"There appears to be very little in the score of *A Life for the Tsar*," comments M. D. Calvocoressi, "which differs in any particular from the conventionalities of grand opera. Some of the music is fine in spirit as well as workmanship, and a few passages are of epic grandeur. Yet it is in vain that one seeks in it evidences of prophetic originality and highly imaginative beauty of Glinka's second opera, *Russlan und Ludmilla*. What remains a subject for wonder is Glinka's consummate skill, the purity and ease that characterize his utterances. He was . . . a born orchestrator; but the extent of experience which *A Life for the Tsar*, the first attempt of a practically self-taught composer reveals is marvelous."

A Life for the Tsar enjoyed only a moderate success. There were many who misunderstood Glinka's ideal and who called it "coachmen music" because it utilized popular folk-material. To others, however, it appeared to be a full and rich voice of Russia. Prosper Mérimée wrote of this opera, in 1840: "Poetically as well as musically, it is a faithful account of all that Russia has suffered and sung. In it are to be discovered her love and her hate, her lamentations and rejoicing, her gloomy nights and her radiant dawns. It is more than opera; it is a national epic."

Shortly after the production of *A Life for the Tsar*, Glinka was appointed choral director of the Imperial Chapel. In this capacity, he took frequent trips to Finland and Little Russia to find new singers for his chorus. During this time, his mind was busily revolving plans for a new opera, an opera even more Russian in spirit and message than *A Life for the Tsar*; an opera that would bring his national ideals to an even more successful consummation than his first opera had done.

Utilizing a poem of Pushkin for his text, Glinka composed *Russlan und Ludmilla*, first performed in St. Petersburg on November 27, 1842.

"*Russlan und Ludmilla*," wrote César Cui, "is the product of a mature talent that has reached the final stages of development. Regarded as absolute music, *Russlan* is a work of the first rank; and from this point of view it will bear comparison with the great operatic masterpieces. In it, Glinka marked out new paths and opened up horizons undreamed of before his time."

It cannot be said that *Russlan und Ludmilla* realized at first the success it

MICHAEL GLINKA

play. His sister, Mme. Ludmilla Shesta-kov, has given us a personal glimpse of the composer in her *Memoirs*. "My brother," she wrote, "had an innocently childlike, tender, delicate, affectionate nature. He was certainly a little capricious, and was spoilt; he had to have everything his own way. Still if he had his faults, he made haste to recognize them and redress them. He never forgot a good turn or a good action. Nothing disturbed his good nature: neither family disputes nor the conversations at the clubs where he happened to be. One cannot exactly say that he was unmethodical, but he was unable to conduct his own affairs; anything in the nature of household matters was particularly distasteful to him. His faults were excessive susceptibility and distrust. He dreaded death to such an extent that he took the most ridiculous precautions against it, and avoided everything, no matter how trivial, which he thought might possibly be harmful. The slightest indisposition terrified him, as though it were a disaster. He treated himself on homeopathic lines, and always kept in the house a small medicine chest containing the most necessary remedies. He followed von Hahnemann's principles in avoiding scents and smells, more especially camphor, which he looked upon as a poison. Spices and aromatic articles were banished from the table; at least he imagined they were. As a matter of fact, the cook did not hesitate to use them in dishes which she sent up for family consumption. One day, Glinka found a leaf of bay in his soup. Putting it on to the edge of the plate, he remarked: 'I dislike bay-leaves, either on my head or in my soup.'"

Hector Berlioz has analyzed Glinka's style of composition as follows: "Glinka's talent is essentially supple and varied. His style has the rare advantage of being able to adapt itself, at the desire of the composer, to the exigencies and character of the subject treated. Glinka can be simple and even naïve without ever condescending to employ a vulgar phrase. His melodies take unexpected turns, and are built on periods which charm by their very strangeness. He is a great harmonist, and uses the instruments with a care and an acquaint-

deserved. It peered too fearlessly into the future, was too much ahead of its time to be fully comprehended by its contemporaries. However, when *Russlan* was revived in 1859, it achieved an almost unprecedented acclaim. Since that time it has been generally recognized as one of the greatest operas created in Russia, the father of all Russian operas.

The last years of Glinka's life were spent in extensive travel. He visited France, Spain, Poland and Germany, coming into close contact with their musical life, and spreading in these countries propaganda for native Russian music. The outbreak of the Crimean War brought him back to St. Petersburg, where he attempted to compose a third opera. Finding his former enthusiasm gone, he turned instead to Church music.

In 1856, he went for a short trip to Berlin for the purpose of studying Western Church music. On February 15, on returning from a concert, he had a sudden seizure and died early the following morning. He was buried in Berlin, but a few months later his body was disinterred and taken to St. Petersburg. It rests today in the cemetery of the Alexander Nevesky Monastery.

As a personality, Glinka—true to the tradition of the Russian aristocrat—was vain, intolerant, self-centered, impatient of criticism and fond of pomp and disance with their most intimate resources, which make his orchestra one of the most novel and vivacious modern orchestras that one can hear."

"His claim to immortality," summed up M. Montagu-Nathan, "must rest upon his having unified the experience and aims of earlier and lesser composers in the accomplishment of his single purpose, that of placing Russian musical nationality on a firm basis."

Principal works by Michael Ivanovich Glinka :

OPERA : *A Life for the Tsar; Russlan und Ludmilla.*

ORCHESTRA : *Tarantella; Kamarinskaya; Jota Aragonese; A Summer night in Madrid;* music for *Prince Kholmsky.*
Songs, pieces for the piano, etc.

About Michael Ivanovich Glinka :

Cui, César. *La Musique en Russie;* Fouque, Octave. *Michael Ivanovich Glinka;* Montagu-Nathan, Montagu. *A History of Russian Music.*

Important recordings of music by Michael Ivanovich Glinka :

ORCHESTRA : *Kamarinskaya* (VICTOR-Coates).

EXCERPTS FROM OPERA : *A Life for the Tsar,* "March and mazurka" (GRAMOPHONE) ; "They guess the truth" and "Now I am far from all" (GRAMOPHONE-Chaliapin).
Russlan und Ludmilla, "Overture" (VICTOR-Stock) ; *"Farlaf's rondo* (VICTOR-Chaliapin) ; "Oh, my Ratmir!" (VICTOR)

SONGS : *Doubt* (GRAMOPHONE-Chaliapin *Midnight review* (VICTOR-Chaliapin) ; *The North star* (GRAMOPHONE)

Christoph Willibald Gluck *1714-1787*

"The truth of expression which brings with it purity of style and grandeur of form is of all time, and the beautiful pages of Gluck will forever remain beautiful."—BERLIOZ

CHRISTOPH WILLIBALD GLUCK (later called Christoph Willibald Ritter von Gluck) was born in Neumarkt, Germany, on July 2, 1714. The son of a forester (father Gluck was in the employ of Prince Lobkowitz), little Christoph frequently accompanied his father to the forests in mid-winter, carrying a heavy bundle of tools on his back, going barefoot thru snow and ice.

His education was for a long time negligible. He received his earliest schooling in the Catholic schools of Kamitz and Eisenberg, the only importance of which rested in the fact that it first introduced Gluck to music thru the violin and violoncello. Not until 1726, was Gluck to be given an intensive education. In that year he was sent to the Jesuit school at Komotau, in Bohemia, where his genius for music first flowered with studies of the piano and the organ.

In 1732, he set off for Prague, where he earned a miserable living teaching music, singing in churches and performing the violin at village dances. For a few years, he was a wandering minstrel, traveling from one town to another, performing music. It was a trying existence. In 1736, his roamings brought him to Vienna, the home of his father's employer, Prince Lobkowitz. Gluck gave one trial performance at the home of the Prince which so impressed the patron that he decided to take the young genius under his wing. Before long, another prince took a personal interest in Gluck, Prince Melzi, who decided to take the young musician to Italy and place him under competent instructors. Thus, Gluck was taken to Milan where, for four years, he studied under Sammartini.

His studies completed, Gluck received his first commission to compose an opera —for the court theatre of Milan. From the very first, he possessed an uncanny ability to compose melodies of nimble grace ; his first opera, *Artaserse,* was successful beyond his own expectation. During the next five years, he composed seven operas, all of which were performed in principal Italian cities, establishing his reputation.

Even England had become familiar with the achievements of this young composer. In 1745, Gluck was engaged by Lord Middlesex to become principal composer for the King's Theatre in London. After stopping off at Paris (where he made the acquaintance of Rameau and Lully), he arrived at London. He had come at an inauspicious moment. The Scotch rebellion had turned the attention of the public from art to politics ; moreover, Handel was at this time at the very height of his popularity in England—much to the detriment of every other operatic composer. Gluck's stay in England was, therefore, brief and unsuccessful. It was not, however, without an influence on him, for it enabled him to come into personal contact with such eminent English composers as Thomas Arne and with the great Handel (who said of Gluck that "he knows as much counterpoint as my cook!").

From England, Gluck went to Germany. In Dresden, the Electoral Prince of Saxony offered him a post in the royal chapel. Gluck did not retain this position for long. By 1748, he was in Vienna again. Here he came into favor with the Prince of Hildburghausen, who commissioned him to compose an opera to be performed on the birthday of the Empress Maria Theresa. The opera, *Semiramide riconosciuta,* was so popular that it made its composer the most fashionable composer of his time. Two years later, Gluck married Marianna Pergin, with whom he lived a happily married life for more than thirty years.

In 1754, Maria Theresa visited the palace of the Prince of Hildburghausen. In her honor, the prince collected musicians and singers to entertain the Queen, calling upon Gluck to compose music especially for this occasion. Gluck's music to *Le Cinesi* found so much favor with the Empress that she gave him a gold snuffbox filled with ducats. Nor did the Empress forget the composer after his return to Vienna. That same year, Gluck was appointed chapel-master of the court opera with an annual salary of two thousand florins. He held this position with distinction for ten years.

Thus far, Gluck had composed more than three score Italian operas, but not one of these would have earned him immortality. In 1760, came the turning point in his career. He became acquainted with a famous dramatic author, Ranieri di Calzabigi. To Calzabigi, Gluck confided certain theories of the opera which he had entertained for a long time, expressing his complete dissatisfaction with the operatic form then in existence. Calzabigi not only interested himself in Gluck's theories but supported them stoutly, offering to write a libretto which would help bring these theories to realization. The libretto was *Orfeo ed Euridice,* and was the vehicle for the first of Gluck's masterpieces.

Gluck, himself, has clearly explained the nature of his revolt in opera in his introduction to the opera, *Alceste,* published five years after the composition of *Orfeo.* "I endeavored to restrict music to its proper function, that of seconding the poetry by enforcing the expression of the sentiment and the interest of the situations without interrupting the action or weakening it by superfluous ornament. . . . I have been very careful never to interrupt a singer in the heat of the dialogue in order to introduce a tedious *ritornelle,* nor to stop him in the middle of a word for the purpose of displaying the flexibility of his voice on some favorable vowel. . . . I have not thought it right to hurry thru the second part of a song, if the words happened to be the most important of the whole, in order to repeat the first part four times over; or to finish the air where the sense does not end in order to allow the singer to exhibit his power of varying the passage at pleasure.

"My idea was that the *Sinfonia* ought to indicate the subject, and prepare the spectators for the character of the piece they are about to see; that the instruments ought to be introduced in proportion to the degree of interest and passion in the words; and that it was necessary, above all, to avoid making too great a disparity between the recitative and the air in the dialogue, so as not to break the sense of a period or awkwardly interrupt the movement and animation of a scene.

"I also thought that my chief endeavor should be to attain a grand simplicity, and consequently I have avoided making a parade of difficulties at the cost of clearness; I have set no value on novelty as such, unless it was naturally suggested by the situation and suited to the expression; in short, there was no rule which I did not consider myself bound to sacrifice for the sake of effect."

These principles—forerunners of the Wagnerian doctrine of music-drama— Gluck attempted to apply to *Orfeo ed Euridice.* *Orfeo* was performed for the first time at the Vienna Burgtheatre on

October 5, 1762. In the eyes of its first audiences it was a complete failure. The critics thought the orchestration too noisy (Gluck had introduced such percussion instruments as cymbals and bass drums, as well as trombones and clarinets, into his orchestra), and there were some captious tongues to comment that Gluck had expressly made his musicians play loudly in order to drown out the bad music. The simplicity of the melodic line (robbed of the flourishes and ornaments of the Italian aria) struck the musicians in the audience as poverty-stricken. A few arias appealed to them, but for the most part *Orfeo* was considered Gluck's most dismal failure.

It is only too well known how time has reversed this early decision. We know now that *Orfeo* is a masterpiece, a work which brought opera in an altogether new direction, a work of incomparable majesty and beauty. "The opening scenes of the first and second acts of *Orfeo*—Euridice's funeral rites and Orfeo's entrance into Hades—are still unsurpassed masterpieces," wrote W. F. Apthorp. "He was equally great in impassioned or pathetic melody and in every form of recitative. His dramatic use of the chorus can scarcely be surpassed in mastery." And Henry Chorley, speaking of *Orfeo,* wrote: "There is no other opera in the world's long list which, with merely three female voices and a chorus, can return to the stage, in days like ours, to make the heart throb and the eyes water."

Gluck continued fearlessly upon the new path he had selected for himself in spite of the failure of *Orfeo.* In 1767, he produced *Alceste,* with which he definitely and completely brushed aside the existing operatic conventions and further developed his experiments in the "new opera." *Alceste,* so many years ahead of its time, was likewise received with cold apathy.

With his succeeding venture, *Paride ed Elena,* Gluck aroused so much hostility and antagonism among Viennese musicians that he decided, in 1773, to brush the dust of Vienna from his boots. He came to Paris, where on April 19, 1774, his latest opera, *Iphigénie en Aulide,* was given its first performance.

CHRISTOPH WILLIBALD GLUCK

Paris, always more modern than Vienna, responded enthusiastically to Gluck's innovations. There were many vigorous voices, among them Jean Jacques Rousseau, who defended Gluck's operatic theories and proclaimed his operas in the new style as distinguished artistic creations.

Gluck's principles, however, did not enjoy a permanent victory in Paris. In 1775, he left Paris temporarily to devote himself to the composition of a new opera, *Roland.* During his absence, he learned that his enemies had brought to Paris a famous Italian composer, Niccolò Piccinni (staunch disciple of the old school of opera) to compose a competitive opera to *Roland.* The news infuriated Gluck. After destroying his own manuscript, in a heat of rage, he wrote a vitriolic letter, published in *L'Année littéraire.* That letter was the first shot in an artistic war which, probably, has had no counterpart in musical history. It divided Paris into two camps. There were the "Piccinnists," who attacked what Marmontel called "Gluck's harsh and rugged harmony, the incoherent modulations and the incongruities contained in his airs," and who adhered strongly to the old type of Italian opera, with its florid arias, stilted and ingenuous harmonizations and innocuous librettos. Opposing them were the "Gluckists" who pronounced a new creed for opera, a creed which spoke of the marriage of drama and music into a new art form.

Summarizing the differences between these two opposing camps, Arthur Ware Lock wrote: "The struggle between Italian and French music was a struggle between two tendencies, the one striving merely to please the ear with sensuous melody and to avoid complexity by use of simple harmonic background, and the other, emphasizing dramatic expressiveness and the development of the instrumental accompaniment."

The battle was a long and bitter one. When performances of Gluck's *Alceste* were received coldly, while Piccinni's *Roland* was acclaimed, it seemed that victory belonged completely to the followers of the Italian composer. Finally, the director of the Opéra, deciding to capitalize on this much-publicized rivalry, commissioned both Piccinni and Gluck to compose an opera on the subject of *Iphigénie en Tauride*, so that a better opportunity might be had to gauge their respective methods and talents.

Royal favor being on Gluck's side, it was Gluck's opera that was given performance first. Gluck's *Iphigénie* was sensational. The audience agreed that Gluck had produced a masterpiece. "I know not," said Grimm after the first performance, "if what we have heard be melody. Perhaps it is something much better; I forget the opera, and find myself in a Greek tragedy." Piccinni, who attended the first performance, was astute enough to realize that he was in the presence of greatness, and he entreated the manager of the Opéra to release him from his contract. The manager, however, was determined to carry on his show. The result was, as had been expected, an appalling fiasco. Piccinni's music, in contrast to Gluck's, sounded sterile and machine-made. Moreover, at least one of the principal singers, Mlle. Laguerre, performed her part under the spell of drink, adding considerably to the failure of the evening.

After this, there was no longer a question as to who was the victor in this monumental battle. From this time on, Gluck was accepted as the champion of the opera.

The last years of Gluck's life were spent quietly in Vienna, amid luxury, honor and contentment. He had amassed a considerable fortune; and he was generally recognized as one of the greatest composers of the period.

He died of an apopleptic stroke on November 15, 1787. He was buried at the cemetery of Matzleinsdorf. A simple inscription appears on his tombstone: "Here lies an upright German man. A zealous Christian. A faithful spouse. Christoph Ritter Gluck. Of the Noble Art of Music a Great Master."

In describing the personality of Gluck, Ernest Newman has noted that his "personal character shows itself both in his music and in his physical structure. To the last he was a hardy, virile peasant, trained to rough and sturdy habits of life. In his face can be clearly seen those qualities that appear again in his music and in his correspondence: the head is thrown back proudly and confidently, the large and mobile mouth has an air of quick intelligence, and the eyes look straight and fearlessly upon the beholder."

"In society he often wore a stiff and solemn air," wrote Romain Rolland, "but he was very quickly roused to anger. . . Gluck lacked self control, and was irritable, and could not get used to the customs of society. He was plainspoken to the verge of coarseness. . . He was insensible to flattery, but was enthusiastic about his own works. . . . He liked few people—his wife, his niece, and a few friends. . . . He was a jolly fellow, nevertheless, especially after drinking. . . . There was no idealism about him; and he had no illusion about either men or things. He loved money and did not conceal the fact. He was also very selfish. . . . On the whole, he was a rough sort, and in no way a man of the world."

It might be added that he was not without eccentricities. Once, while conducting, he went on his hands and knees and crept under the feet of players in order to pinch the calf of a double-bass player who had made a mistake. Often, he would have his clavier brought into a field, so that he might compose in the open countryside.

Precisely what is Gluck's importance in the history of music? C. Hubert Parry has summarized Gluck's contribution. "Gluck, like every one else, was forced to accept the work of his predecessors as the basis of his own, and even to retain some of the most conspicuous features of the scheme which he aimed at destroying. The point which is of highest importance in Gluck's victory, as far as the development of the art is concerned, is the restoration of the element of genuine human expression to its place in the scheme of art."

"Gluck's reforms are more frequently mentioned than understood," to conclude with a paragraph by Lawrence Gilman. "He was not a revolutionary and he made no radical changes in the operatic form which he found in general favor. What he did was distinctly in line with the movement towards simplicity, begun while he was yet an explorer of new fields, in his own search after the path to artistic success. . . . To accomplish his ends, he stripped the opera of the pompous garb of artifice which had been gradually imposed upon it by a century of pseudo-classicism and a slavish adherence to accepted models. He sought to wed text to music plainly expressive of the thought and to abolish all vocal device and meretricious ornament introduced as mere decoration and without dramatic purpose. And he discerned with the swift comprehension of genius the rightful place of the ballet, which had long been almost intrusive in French opera despite the fact that it was the principal ancestor of the lyric drama of the country."

Principal works by Christoph Willibald Gluck:

OPERA: *Orfeo ed Euridice*; *Alceste*; *Paride ed Elena*; *Iphigénie en Aulide*; *Armide*; *Iphigénie en Tauride*, etc.

ORCHESTRA: Symphonies; *Concerto for flute and strings*; *Ballet-suite* (arranged by Felix Mottl), etc.

CHAMBER MUSIC: *Quartet*; Seven trios for two violins and bass.

About Christoph Willibald Gluck:

Cooper, Martin. *Gluck*; Desnoiresterres, Gustave. *Gluck et Piccinni*; Einstein, Alfred. *Gluck*; Newman, Ernest. *Gluck*; Parry, C.

Hubert. *Evolution of the Art of Music*; Rolland, Romain. *Some Musicians of Former Days*.

Important recordings of music by Christoph Willibald Gluck:

EXCERPTS FROM OPERA: *Alceste*, "Overture" (DECCA-Mengelberg); "Bannis la crainte" (COLUMBIA). *Armide*, "Ah, si la liberté" (GRAMOPHONE); *Musette* (VICTOR-Damrosch). *Iphigénie en Aulide*, "Overture" (BRUNSWICK-Strauss); "Ballet excerpts" (VICTOR-Damrosch); "Diane impitoyable" (GRAMOPHONE); "Gavotte" (PARLAPHONE). *Iphigénie en Tauride*, "Dieux! qui me poursuivez" and "La Calme rentre" (POLYDOR); "O malheureuse Iphigénie" (DECCA). *Orfeo ed Euridice*, almost complete (COLUMBIA).

Benjamin Godard *1849-1895*

BENJAMIN LOUIS PAUL GODARD was born in Paris on August 18, 1849. While still a child, he was enrolled in the Paris Conservatory. He made progress in the playing of the violin under Henri Vieuxtemps. Vieuxtemps took so great a personal interest in his precocious pupil that, on two different concert tours to Germany, he took Godard with him, so that the artistic training of his prodigy might not be neglected.

On his return to Paris, Godard entered the composition class of Reber at the Conservatory. From this time on, the creative, rather than the interpretative, field of music absorbed his energy. In his sixteenth year he had already published several sonatas, quartets and small pieces for the piano, whose graceful melodic line and instinctively tasteful harmonizations found an enthusiastic public. Godard, hardly grown out of boyhood, already knew fame; some of his admirers went to the extent of referring to him as another Mozart.

In 1878, Godard produced his outstanding work, an "operatic-symphony" entitled *Le Tasse*, which won first prize in a competition conducted by the city of Paris. "One senses here a talent not fully developed, perhaps, but nevertheless a strongly pronounced personality," ran the official report on the award. "However, the abundance of ideas, the sustained inspiration, a remarkable variety of color, some pages of exquisite zest, and others of a poignant and profound sentiment compensate largely for the faults."

"This dramatic symphony," wrote Alfred Bruneau, "built according to the plan of the *Damnation of Faust* contains some remarkable pages, and remains Godard's best work." There are in this work," commented Julien Tiersot, "qualities of poetry, of passion, of internal warmth which definitely heralded the arrival of a new master. Unfortunately, the works that followed did not live up to these promises."

Godard's most ambitious work, the opera *Jocelyn* (whose *Berceuse* is one of the few pieces by which Godard is today remembered) came in 1888. Adolphe Jullien pointed out that the book of *Jocelyn* is most unsuited for operatic purposes; it is hardly more than a series of picturesque tableaux, and certainly not an integrated drama. Musically, there are many moments of interest in *Jocelyn*. "Godard, who wrote some short and touching pieces for the voice, has likewise here given expression to some felicitous melodic ideas like the *Berceuse* . . . or Laurencie's prayer. . . . But in the important dramatic scenes . . . the composer becomes winded and finds only stereotyped phrases, vulgar harmonies, supported by a noisy and crass instrumentation. Obviously, sensitive sentiments, revery, gentle tenderness or even picturesque

passages are well at his command, but bursts of passion, poignant emotional scenes are beyond his reach."

Benjamin Godard died suddenly in Cannes on January 10, 1895, in his forty-sixth year. Paradoxically enough, his last opera, *La Vivandière* (which he never finished, but which was brought to completion by Paul Vidal) achieved the greatest success of any of his works.

During his entire life, Godard was an arch-conservative where music was concerned, a defiant enemy of any experimental tendencies. It was a point of honor with him not to hear anything of Wagner, and he frequently boasted of the fact that during his entire life he never opened the score of a living composer. To some critics, here lies the explanation why Godard, instead of developing and maturing as an artist, virtually stood still after his thirtieth year.

Principal works by Benjamin Godard:

OPERA: *Les Bijoux de Jeannette*; *Pedro de Zalamea*; *Jocelyn*; *Le Dante*; *La Vivandière*, etc.

ORCHESTRA: *Le Tasse* (for soli, chorus and orchestra); incidental music for *Much ado about nothing*; *Symphony in B-minor*; *Gothic symphony*; *Oriental symphony*, *Symphonie légendaire*; *Ouverture dramatique*; *Scènes poétiques*; *La Lanterne magique*; *Concerto for piano and orchestra*; *Concerto romantique* (for violin and orchestra).

CHAMBER MUSIC: Two string quartets; Two piano trios; Four sonatas for violin and piano.

Pieces for the piano; over 100 songs, etc.

About Benjamin Godard:

Bruneau, Alfred. *Les Musiques de Russie et Musiciens de France*; Claire, M. *Benjamin Godard*; Imbert, Hughes. *Medaillons Contemporains*; Jullien, Adolphe. *Musiciens d'aujourd'hui*; Tiersot, Julien. *Un Demi Siècle de Musique Française*.

Important recordings of music by Benjamin Godard:

SELECTIONS FROM OPERA: *Jocelyn*, "Berceuse" (PARLAPHONE-Lehmann). *La Vivandière*, "Mon p'tit, si nous t'ecrivons" (PATHE); "Viens avec nous" (COLUMBIA).

ORCHESTRA: *Le Tasse*, "Air de Leonore" (POLYDOR); *Scènes poétiques*, "Au village" (PARLAPHONE).

BENJAMIN GODARD

Karl Goldmark *1830-1915*

KARL GOLDMARK was born in Keszthely, a small town in Hungary, on May 18, 1830. As a child, he astonished his elders by singing bits of song which he himself composed. One day, the schoolmaster of the town heard him hum one of his original tunes, and was so impressed that he decided to teach the boy the elements of music and to enlist the services of a friend, a choir-singer, in teaching him the violin.

While still very young, Karl on a Sunday morning heard a church organ in a performance of the Holy Mass. "I had never heard anything like this before," he wrote in his memoirs in later years, "the church being quite a distance off. Besides, we were never allowed to enter it. For the first time in my life I heard and experienced the overpowering force of harmony and of music in general. . . . At this moment my fate and future were decided and my career settled. I was to be a musician, and strangely enough it came about thru the Catholic church."

In 1842, Goldmark was enrolled as a student of Ödenburger Musikverein in violin and composition. He made such rapid progress that he was prepared to give a violin recital the following year. After this, he was sent to Vienna to continue his studies of the violin under Jansa, and, in 1847, to enter the Conservatory. Unfortunately, the Conservatory closed its doors in 1848, because of the revolution. Karl was now thrown into the maelstrom of Vienna to earn his living as best he could.

Those were difficult years. He was compelled to accept a position as violinist at the Raab Theatre, playing cheap music. And he knew hunger and cold continually.

At this time there occurred the most curious experience of his life. One day, he was called from the Raab Theatre by a government official, and was conducted by him to the city prison where he received the astounding news that the following morning he was to be shot as a rebel to his country. This was the most terrible night in Goldmark's life, as he later testified. All night long, he sat stiff and tired on a stone bench knowing that—despite his innocence—he would face death the following morning. By a miracle, the mistake was dis-covered before Goldmark faced the firing squad.

The revolution over, and peace and normalcy restored in Vienna, Karl Goldmark could return to music. He procured a position at the Karl Theatre, at a monthly salary of twenty florins. At the same time, he devoted himself conscientiously to the study of harmony and counterpoint, and to creative work. In 1857, he gave up his position at the theatre to concentrate entirely on composition. Soon afterward, he gave a concert of his own works in Vienna which was sufficiently successful to encourage him in his labors.

He went for a short period to Budapest for further intensive study, not only of music, but of philosophy, literature and languages as well. It was at this time that a score of Wagner's *Lohengrin* came to his hands. The young composer, who until now had considered Mendelssohn the greatest composer of them all, found a new world to explore in this score. *Lohengrin* gave Karl Goldmark new impetus in his composition. At this time, he produced his first important works for orchestra, including the *Sakuntala overture* and the *Rustic wedding symphony*.

After giving a second concert of his works in Budapest, in 1859, Goldmark returned to Vienna with a new string quartet in his trunk. This quartet (it was the one in B-flat) came to the attention of Hellmesberger, eminent member of a great string quartet, who was so delighted with its charm and freshness that he promised Goldmark he would perform whatever chamber-works he cared to compose. Hellmesberger introduced the *Quartet in B-flat* to Vienna. One day after the performance, Karl Tausig, the pianist, and Peter Cornelius, the composer, came to Goldmark's humble lodging to tell him that, in their estimation, he was a genius. This Goldmark considered as the first triumph of his career.

In 1866, Goldmark met Richard Wagner in Vienna for the first and only time. They had been introduced by a friend. During the course of their conversation, Wagner complained bitterly about his poverty, and neglect at the hands of contemporary musicians. "But master,"

KARL GOLDMARK

Goldmark asked, "are you not satisfied with the knowledge that your name will be immortal?" "Never speak to me in that fashion," Wagner answered hotly. "People consoled Cherubini as he lay dying with hopes of immortality. Immortality, indeed. Please do not make any bad jokes!"

During the years that followed, Goldmark earned his living by teaching the piano and writing criticisms for the *Konstitutionnelle Zeitung,* where he fought bitterly to gain recognition for Wagner's music dramas. During these years he was working industriously on an opera which he considered to be his *meisterwerk, The Queen of Sheba,* a work which absorbed ten years of his energy. When he completed the opera, he sent the score to Eduard Hanslick, the powerful critic. Hanslick, whose judgment has by no means been distinguished by infallibility, wrote Goldmark that he considered the work very untalented, and that only the Grand March was worthy of being heard.

At any rate, the Vienna Opera accepted *The Queen of Sheba* for performance, and on March 10, 1875 the work was given a première. It was sensationally successful. The directors of the Opera were so pleased with it that they asked Goldmark to compose other operas expressly for their opera house. The critics were effusive in their praise; one of them found that the *Queen* "marks a new era in opera."

To a certain degree, *The Queen of Sheba* has maintained its popularity. By 1925, it enjoyed no less than two hundred and thirty five performances in Vienna. It was introduced in New York at the Metropolitan Opera House on December 2, 1885, for many years being a distinguished feature of the Metropolitan repertoire. There is hardly an opera house in Europe which has not produced *The Queen of Sheba* successfully. And for good reason. "It is," as R. A. Streatfeild points out, "a strong and effective opera. The local color is managed very skilfully, and the orchestration is novel and brilliant." "In Goldmark's melodies there was always a leaning towards an Oriental coloring; he had a decided preference for orchestrating heavily and brilliantly, and for writing music with flourishes and postures. These characteristics—now that they appeared in an opera with an Eastern background—made the subject-matter of this opera live more vividly."

To Richard Wagner, however, *The Queen of Sheba* was an intense disappointment. He said that this opera made him sad, for it brought before him a picture of what he had been fighting against all his life.

After *The Queen of Sheba,* Goldmark composed two other popular operas: *Merlin* was given its first performance in Vienna in 1886; and the *Cricket on the hearth* was introduced in Berlin ten years later.

Karl Goldmark died in Vienna on January 2, 1915. He lived long enough to see his music occupy an important position in the symphonic and operatic world of his day.

"Goldmark's main characteristics," J. A. Fuller-Maitland summed up pithily, "are his complete mastery over every kind of musical effect, his wealth of melodic invention and skill in manipulating themes. His orchestral works are always effective and often interesting, and his chamber composition, notably his two suites for violin and piano—made familiar to English audiences by Sarasate—tell of his early familiarity with the violin."

"I have frequently been in Goldmark's company," wrote the distinguished conductor, Felix von Weingartner, "but never without receiving a mental stimulus. He was of astonishing freshness, not knowing what fatigue was. In jolly company, he was sure to be the last one to go home. Infirmities of age and a conforming manner of living were strangers to him. His mind was as clear and as bright as his eye. Frequently I met him in the Prater, and we walked together for a while. The talk at once soared from the commonplace to higher regions. Ordinary conversation he would never indulge in. He usually spoke of poetry or music. His opinions were acute, but amiable and never malicious, even when they were negative."

Principal works by Karl Goldmark:

OPERA: *Götz von Berlichingen*; *The Queen of Sheba*; *Merlin*; *Cricket on the hearth*.

CHORAL: Two choruses for male voices; *Frühlingshymne*.

ORCHESTRA: *Sakuntala overture*; *Rustic wedding symphony*; *Scherzo in E-minor*; *Concerto for violin and orchestra*; *Penthesilea*; *Symphony in E-flat*; *Im Frühling*; *Der gefesselte Prometheus*; *Sappho*; *In Italien*; *Aus Jugendtagen*; *Second concerto for violin and orchestra*.

CHAMBER MUSIC: *Quintet in B-flat*; *Quartet in B-flat*; *Quartet in A-minor*; *Trio*, etc.

Pieces for the piano, songs, suites and sonatas for violin and piano, etc.

About Karl Goldmark:

Goldmark, Karl. *Notes from the Life of a Viennese Composer*; Fuller-Maitland, J. A. *Masters of German Music*; Korngold, Julius. *Deutsches Opernschaffen der Gegenwart*.

Der Merker 6:64 February 1915; *Monthly Musical Record* 46:138 May 1, 1916.

Important recordings of music by Karl Goldmark:

ORCHESTRA: *Im Frühling* (VICTOR-Stock); *Sakuntala overture* (VICTOR); *Rustic wedding symphony* (VICTOR-Heger).

SELECTIONS FROM OPERA: *The Queen of Sheba*, "Ballet Music" (VICTOR-Stock); "Air of Schulamite" (GRAMOPHONE); "Einzugsmarsch (GRAMOPHONE-Blech); "Der Freund ist dein" (GRAMOPHONE).

Nicholas Gombert
(16th century)

(See sketch on *Josquin des Prés*)

François Gossec   *1734-1829*

FRANÇOIS JOSEPH GOSSEC was born on January 17, 1734, in Vergnies, a small village in the Belgian Hainault. He disclosed an interest in music at an early age. It was said that, while herding the cows, he would spend his time playing a fiddle which he had constructed from a sabot.

Possessing a beautiful voice, he spent his boyhood years as a chorister—first in Walcourt, then in Mauberge, and finally at the Notre Dame of Antwerp. It was at the last-named place that he began the study of music intensively—harmony, composition, the violin and the harpsichord.

He went to Paris in 1751 with a letter of introduction to the celebrated Rameau, who placed him in the service of that eminent music-patron Le Riche de la Pouplinière. It was here that Gossec began his celebrated career as a conductor, which vitally influenced the development of conductorial technique. In 1752, Gossec likewise made his formal bow as a composer by publishing several sonatas for violin and bass. Two years later, he began the composition of symphony, expressly for the Pouplinière orchestra.

In 1760, his celebrated *Messe des morts* was performed in Paris. This work electrified the audience because of Gossec's bold experiments in sonority and tone-color. The *Tuba mirum,* for example, was scored for two orchestras, one of woodwinds (which was off the stage), and the other of strings (on the platform). In this work, Gossec introduced horns and trombones into the orchestra.

It was not long before Gossec—who, by this time, had composed chamber, orchestral and church music—began to throw envious looks in the direction of the theatre. After *Le Tonnelier* and *Le Faux lord*, both of which were failures, he produced *Les pêcheurs* at the Comédie Italienne (1766). This was so successful that he was besieged by requests for other operatic works. He complied graciously, and for the remainder of his life he was uniquely productive in this branch of composition.

FRANÇOIS GOSSEC

Meanwhile, he was continuing his distinguished career as a conductor. In 1770, he founded the *Concert des Amateurs,* whose principal distinction was that it introduced the symphonies of Haydn to the Parisian music public. In 1773, Gossec became director of the *Concert Spirituel,* and in 1780 he became first conductor of the Opéra.

In 1784, Gossec founded the *École royale de chant et de déclamation,* a school outstandingly important in developing operatic singers in Paris, which was later to become the nucleus of the Paris Conservatory.

The revolution found Gossec one of its strongest and most enthusiastic advocates. He now dedicated his musical activity to the proletarian cause. "He clung to new ideas without bigotry or self-seeking," wrote G. Jean-Aubry, "and found in them an opportunity for the exercise of his art. He saw in 'patriotic fêtes' a means of endowing music with a new and totally different meaning; he realized that music which, up to the present, had been the prerogative of a special class and in the service of religion, should now appeal to the public in general."

He became the conductor of the band of the National Guard, and composed a series of works in honor of the more important events in the revolutionary life in Paris. The more famous of his revolutionary works include a funeral march for Mirabeau, the stirring *Peuple, réveille-toi, Le Chant du 14 Juillet* and *Le Triomphe de la République.* Works such as these gave him the position of official composer of the Revolution.

When the Conservatory of Paris was founded in 1795, Gossec's preeminent position ·in the musical life of Paris was recognized by an appointment both as Inspector and as professor of counterpoint. The latter position he held until 1815, resigning it only because he was now seeking seclusion and quiet.

Until the end of his life, however, he was fertile as a composer. It is said that when he died—at Passy on February 16, 1829—it was with pen in hand.

A friend of Gossec's, who has remained anonymous, has given us the following description of the composer: "His figure was small, heavily-set and solid. His face, tinted with red, breathed forth calmness and human-goodness. His blue eyes became vividly animated when he spoke about his art, and were touched with gentle understanding when he praised his contemporaries. He carried his head slightly bent towards the left. He remained faithful to the dress and habits of former years. . . . He wore a highly powdered wig, a little three-cornered hat, a large, gray suit with a vest fringed in white, and trousers and stockings of black silk. Large silver buckles were attached to his slippers, and he held in his hand a large cane with an ivory head."

It might be added that Gossec was generous and honest; that he possessed poise and charm and a quiet sense of humor; that he was a formidable egoist, ever hungry for glory; that he was a man capable of very little affection—after he left his father's home he never troubled to learn the welfare of his family, and, in his marriage, he was sublimely aloof from his wife and son who interested him only slightly.

While his music is rarely performed in our present-day concert-halls, Gossec's is an imposing name in musical history. He was one of the pioneers in the symphony form, and, with Haydn, helped to give the form integration. He was an all-important pioneer in the art of instrumentation and sonority. His influence on French music was far-reaching: he was a great conductor who vitally influenced and gave shape to the new art of orchestral conducting; he was a great teacher who, both at his own École and at the Conservatory, exerted a potent force upon an entire generation of French musicians.

"Gossec," wrote Paul Landormy, "represents an important phase of our musical history. He is, in the eyes of his contemporaries, the first French symphonist at the end of the eighteenth century. Then, under the Revolution, he was significant in organizing great demonstrations of popular art and musical instruction at the Conservatory. In this domain—as well as animator of crowds and creator of open-air music—he was an innovator. He anticipated the development of choral art, as well as that of 'fanfares,' and tone-colors in which he was a pioneer."

Notwithstanding his great popularity in his own day, Gossec was considered by his contemporaries as a composer of very intellectual music which "had to be heard several times in order to be well understood and appreciated." Today, upon the few occasions when his music is performed, what appeals to us most is its lucidity, its faded charm and graceful poise.

The celebrated *Gavotte* of Gossec, frequently appearing in the violin repertoire, is an arrangement of an excerpt from the opera *Rosine*.

Principal works by François Gossec:

ORCHESTRA: More than thirty symphonies; overtures; serenades, etc.

OPERA: *Les pêcheurs*; *Sabinus*; *Berthe*; *Hylas et Sylvie*; *La Fête du village*; *Thésée*; *Rosine*; *Les Sabots et le cerisier*, etc.

BALLET: *Philémon et Baucis*; *Les Scythes enchaînés*; *Mirsa*; *Callisto*.

CHORAL: *Messe des morts*; *Messe des vivants*; *Saul*; *La Nativité*; *Te Deum*; motets, etc.

CHAMBER MUSIC: Quartets; trios; duets for strings, etc.

About François Gossec:

Cucuel, Georges. *La Pouplinière et la Musique de Chambre au 18e Siècle*; Dufrane, Louis. *Gossec: Sa Vie et ses Oeuvres.*

Chesterian 15:63 January 1934; *Courrier Musicale* 31:63 February 1, 1929; *Musique* 1:107 December 15, 1927.

Important recordings of music by François Gossec:

CHORAL: *Hymne à la nature* (COLUMBIA); *Hymne à la liberté* (COLUMBIA).

VIOLIN AND PIANO: *Gavotte,* arranged (POLYDOR); *Tambourin,* arranged (TELEFUNKEN).

Charles Gounod *1818-1893*

CHARLES FRANÇOIS GOUNOD, composer of *Faust,* was born in Paris, near the church of St. Germain des Prés, on June 17, 1818. As a child, he was given his first instruction in music by his mother, a gifted pianist. On the death of his father (a painter of some reputation), the boy was placed, at the age of five, in a nearby boarding school, impressing his teachers with his unusual musical aptitude. From here, Gounod was sent to the Lycée St. Louis.

By this time his musical appetite had grown formidably. He was taken to the opera by his mother, the first impressive experience in his life. "I felt as if I were in some temple," he wrote in later years, "as if a heavenly vision might shortly rise upon my sight. . . . Oh, that night! What rapture! What Elysium!" This experience, no doubt, convinced him that he must become a musician. One day, he quietly announced to his mother that he wished to study music, and music alone. His mother, terrified at the thought that her son might become an indigent musician, went to the principal of the Lycée for advice, who assured her that the school would do everything in its power to divert the boy's interests into channels other than music. The following morning, the principal called young Gounod into his office, and asked him kindly: "Why do you want to become a musician, my boy?" Gounod answered "Because I love music." "But do you not know how difficult a musician's life is?" The boy replied that he did but that made no difference. "Very well, then," the principal finally said. "Show me the extent of your talent by composing for me here and now a song to the following poem." In a few hours, Gounod had composed his song, and as the principal listened to it his face acquired an expression of tenderness.

CHARLES GOUNOD

"If you will let me use your piano," the boy continued, "I will sing you the song with piano accompaniment." Gounod did so. When he finished the principal put his arm about the boy's shoulder and said: "You are right. You will be a musician!"

In 1836, Gounod became a student of Halévy's at the Paris Conservatory. He had remarkable native capacities. He possessed perfect pitch, could tell the tone in which dogs barked in the street and which tones were uttered by street vendors. He had an alert intelligence which could absorb learning with ease. As a result, in 1839 Gounod distinguished himself by winning the Grand Prix de Rome with his cantata, *Fernand*.

He wrote in his autobiography that his first contact with Rome disappointed him. Instead of a majestic city of dreams he saw dirty, crowded, noisy streets. However, the subtle charm of the Eternal City soon cast its spell over him. Some of the happiest hours of his life were spent on the Palatine hill among the ruins of the Forum. In Italy, Gounod studied the music of Palestrina, who remained one of his favorite composers; and he frequently attended the choral services at the Sistine Chapel. He was creatively productive as well. The principal fruits of this period were two Masses, one of

which was performed at the Chiesa San Luigi dei Francesi in 1841, and the other one in Vienna the following year.

After his stay in Rome, Gounod returned to Paris in 1842, taking a circuitous route home which brought him to Vienna, Leipzig and Berlin. This was an important voyage. It not only brought him into personal contact with Felix Mendelssohn in Berlin, but it also introduced him for the first time to the music of Robert Schumann, which made a deep impression upon him.

Back in Paris, Gounod became the organist of *Les Missions Étrangères* on the Rue du Bac. His daily contact with the Church decided him to study theology and enter the priesthood. For two years he wore the clerical garb, and was calle Abbé Gounod. Then, music holding too important a place in his life, he reversed his decision, renounced the idea of priesthood, and adopted plans to compose operas.

In 1851, thru the influence of a close friend—the singer, Mme. Viardot—Gounod's first opera, *Sapho*, was presented at the Opéra. It was not an epoch-making work, but it contained enough passages of beauty to attract the admiration of many critics. Berlioz, as a matter of fact, referred to Gounod at this time as "a young man richly endowed with noble aspirations; one to whom every encouragement should be given at a time when musical taste is so vitiated." Encouragement for Gounod likewise came from across the channel. On January 15, 1851, four portions of his *Messe solennelle* were performed successfully at St. Martin's Hall in London.

Having made his first mark as a composer, Gounod decided to marry, taking as a bride Agnes Zimmerman, the daughter of a well-known musician. In the same year (1852) he became the conductor of the Orphéon, holding this position for eight successful years.

During the next few years, he composed several unsuccessful operas (including *Ulysse, La Nonne sanglante* and *Le Médecin malgré lui*), and two highly talented symphonies which were performed at the concerts of the *Association des jeunes artistes*. In 1855, his most famous religious work, the *Messe à Ste. Cécile,* was produced, disclosing his growing powers as a composer.

His masterpiece came in March of 1859, after two years of hard work. At that time, the Théâtre Lyrique gave the first performance of *Faust.* It is strange, indeed, that this work, which placed its composer among the great composers of his time, should have received so frigid a reception. One critic referred to it as a failure in an experiment; there was not one publisher who was willing to issue it in print. It is interesting to point out that the *Soldiers chorus*—which to our ears appears as one of the most commonplace passages in the work—was one of the few sections singled out for praise.

Finally, an enterprising publisher, Choudens, was attracted to some of the music of *Faust* and decided to publish it even at a loss. To his amazement, *Faust,* far from being a loss, earned within a few years more than three million francs profit. When *Faust* was revived on March 3, 1869 its success was firmly established.

No one will attempt to deny that *Faust* has many pages of third-rate music. At its best, however, it is one of the most important operas in the répertoire. "The dreamy languor which pervades the scene," wrote R. A. Streatfeild, "the cloying sweetness of the harmonies, the melting beauty of the orchestration, all combine to produce an effect which was at that time entirely new to opera. . . . With all its faults, *Faust* remains a work of a high order of beauty. Every page of the score tells of a striving after a lofty ideal, and though as regards actual form Gounod made no attempt to break new ground, the aim and atmosphere of *Faust,* no less than the details of its construction, contrast so strongly with the conventional Italianism of the day, that it may well be regarded as the inauguration of a new era in French Opera."

Altho Gounod reached his highest peak as artist in *Faust,* he produced at least two more operas that brought him additional fame: the charming *Mireille* (1864), an opera based on the Provençal poem of Mistral, and *Roméo et Juliette* (1867).

The Franco Prussian War drove Gounod to seek refuge in England in 1870, where he became an important musical figure. At the opening of Albert Hall, his biblical elegy, *Gallia* was performed. Shortly afterwards, Gounod made personal appearances at the Crystal Palace with the Royal Philharmonic. He also formed a choir which is today known as the Albert Hall Choral Society.

Gounod returned to Paris in 1875. During the last years of his life, he reverted to his early absorption in religion. Composition was now devoted principally to sacred music, including the *Rédemption* and *Mors et vita,* both of which were performed at the Birmingham festivals, and the *Messe à Jeanne d'Arc,* which he had intended to compose on bended knees on the very stones, in the Cathedral of Rheims, on which Joan of Arc knelt when she crowned Charles VII.

Charles Gounod died in Paris on October 17, 1893, of a stroke. His wife found him lifeless in his study, bent over his work; he was in the midst of composing a *Requiem,* in memory of one of his grandchildren who had recently died.

After the ceremonies were completed at the Madeleine church, Gounod was buried in the cemetery of Auteuil. A tablet was erected in his honor in Parc Monceau in Paris.

Gounod has been described by Ernest Newman as an amiable man to the point of effusiveness, a flatterer whose soft words frequently became cloying, a gushing sentimentalist, a man whose insincerity made him distrusted even by his best friends. Wagner spoke derisively of his "unflagging and nauseous garrulity."

Discussing Gounod's musical style, Arthur Hervey wrote: "Gounod created a musical language of his own, one of extraordinary sweetness, of wondrous fascination, the soft eloquence of which seemed to penetrate into the innermost recesses of the heart. No asperities of style, no startling outbursts of ill-repressed passion were there to mar the exquisite suavity of melodies floating in a troublous atmosphere of intoxicating harmonies."

The great fame of *Faust* has partially obscured the reputation of Gounod's distinguished church music, which to many critics represents his greatest artistic achievement. As Saint-Saëns has said: "When, owing to the fatal march of time, in a distant future, the operas of Gounod will have entered forever the dusty sanctuary of libraries known only to students, the *Messe à Ste. Cécile, Rédemption, Mors et vita* will remain alive, and will teach future generations what a great musician France could boast of in the nineteenth century."

Principal works by Charles Gounod:

OPERA: *Sapho*; *Le Médecin malgré lui*; *Faust*; *Philémon et Baucis*; *Mireille*; *Roméo et Juliette*; *Polyeucte*.

CHORAL: *Rédemption*; *Mors et vita*; cantatas; masses; requiems; motets; *Choeurs orphéoniques*; *Dans une étable*; *Les Gaulois*, etc.

ORCHESTRA: Two symphonies; *Marche romaine*; *Le Calme* (for violin and orchestra); *La Reine des apôtres*.

Pieces for the piano, songs, etc.

About Charles Gounod:

Bellaigue, Camille. *Gounod;* Bouvet, M. A. de. *Gounod*; Dubois, Th. *Notice sur Charles Gounod*; Gounod, Charles. *Memoirs of an Artist*; Prodhomme, Jacques Gabriel (with A. Dandelot) *Gounod*.

Important recordings of music by Charles Gounod:

OPERA: *Faust*, complete (COLUMBIA-Beecham).

SELECTIONS FROM OPERA: *Mireille*, "Ouverture" (ODEON); "Chantez, chantez" (ODEON); "O légère hirondelle" (GRAMOPHONE); "La brise est douce" (COLUMBIA); "Anges du Paradis (COLUMBIA-Thill); *Roméo et Juliette*, "Je veux vivre dans ce rêve" (COLUMBIA); "Ange adorable" (ODEON); "L'Amour, l'amour" and "Ah, lève-toi soleil!" (COLUMBIA-*Thill*); "O nuit divine" (DEON).

Enrique Granados *1867-1916*

ENRIQUE GRANADOS Y CAMPINA, one of Spain's major composers, was born in Lérida on July 29, 1867. His family moved to Barcelona while he was still a child; here he was given piano instruction, first by Francesco S. Jurnet, then by Joan Baptista Pujol. His pianistic talent was marked, and a career as a virtuoso was planned for him. Before long, however, Granados came under the influence of Felippe Pedrell, often designated as the father of Spanish music, who, as his harmony teacher, not on'y directed him towards composition but also awakened his national consciousness.

In 1887, Granados went to Paris with the hope of entering the Conservatory. Typhoid fever prevented him from taking the entrance examinations with the result that he never became more than a mere auditor in some of the classes. During this period, he lived at Rue de Trevise, together with Ricardo Viñes, the famous pianist; theirs was a characteristic Parisian-Bohemian life in which music and painting were the major interests.

Granados returned to Barcelona in 1889. On the 20th of April of the following year he gave a piano recital that launched a successful virtuoso career. As a composer, he was introduced with two books of *Goyescas* and *Spanish dances*, both for piano, in which (following the banner of Felippe Pedre'l) he attempted to produce native Spanish music, far different from the meretricious music by which Spain was known to the rest of the world. As he wrote: "The musical interpretation of Spain is not to be found in tawdry boleros and habañeras, in *Carmen*, in anything accompanied by tambourines and castanets. The music of my nation is far more complex, more poetic and more subtle."

Between 1892 and 1898, Granados earned his living by giving concerts on the piano, and by teaching. At the same time, he was busily occupied in outlining new and greater plans for composition. One of his pupils at this time, Joaquin Nin, well-known Spanish composer, recorded the following impressions of Granados: "I was seduced by his exuberant imagination, his delicious blunders, his unexpected confusion, his nobility, his tragic-comic outbursts, his large eyes always ready to weep, to laugh, to admire or to show astonishment at everything, the fantastic recitals of his extraordinary adventures, his talks streaked with irony and candor, with refinement, with elegance, with contemplation and with activity, with humor and with gravity, with uneasiness and with serenity."

In 1898, Granados' first important opera, *María del Carmen,* was heard successfully in Madrid. The enthusiasm which this work elicited, convinced the composer that he had found the proper medium for his music. In 1903, he produced another operatic work, *Folleto.* His most important opera, however, did not come until 1914: *Goyescas,* re-developed from his famous piano pieces, on a libretto of Fernando Periquet's.

Goyescas was scheduled to make its début at the Paris Opéra, but the World War shattered this plan. It was accepted for its première by the Metropolitan Opera House of New York. Granados personally attended the first performance, which took place on January 25, 1916, and was, therefore, able to witness the rousing reception that was accorded his most ambitious work.

Invited by President Woodrow Wilson to play at the White House, Granados was forced to cancel his steamship reservation to Europe and to postpone his home sailing for one week. It was a fatal decision. He left America full of high hopes and ambitions, "nourished by a world of projects," as he wrote to a friend. At Folkstone, he boarded the *Sussex* for Dieppe which, one hour and ten minutes after sailing, was torpedoed by a German submarine. On March 24, 1916, Enrique Granados met death near the coast of France.

ENRIQUE GRANADOS

Granados was an inveterate collector, his particular preferences being books, paintings and firearms. "The home life of the composer is delightful," wrote a friend, Francesco Gandara. "In his home, Granados gives evidence of keen humor. . . . He is an ardent sportsman, an enthusiastic automobilist and motor-cyclist. [At one time] some of his pupils gave him on his saint-day a new motor-cycle."

Francesco Gandara recorded the picture he will always retain of Granados. "It was at the Academy of Art and Literature in Barcelona, whose members had gathered to honor the memory of a poet . . . who had just died. . . . Enrique Granados was present. He was asked to do something to express his grief at the poet's death. Without a word, he rose, walked to the piano, and struck three solemn, vibrant chords. Then, on the spur of the moment, he produced, amid the rapt silence of the listeners, a most tender and beautiful dirge."

Leigh Henry has discussed Granados' music in the following fashion: "He may be said to represent in modern Spanish music the dramatic element which finds fluid expression in the melodic flow and poetic themes of the Malaguenas, and in the rhythmic nuances and movements of the popular Spanish dances. In so treating Spanish characteristics, however, Granados was objective and concerned with tonal and rhythmic-dynamic effects, not subjective, as the folk-cult 'nationalists' are."

"What Granados introduced into the music of Northern Europe might be described as a gesture," wrote J. B. Trend. 'Stately Spanish grace' is the first thing that strikes one in such a piece as *Los Requiebros* in the first book of *Goyescas.* In his way of writing for the pianoforte he owed much to Liszt; the texture of his music is definitely nineteenth century—that is to say, German. Yet his sense of form—or, as some critics hastily conclude, the absence of it—was also new; he rambled on, making his points by repetition (like a Spanish poet) and saying the same things in a number of delightful and decorative ways."

Principal works by Enrique Granados:

OPERA: *María del Carmen*; *Folleto*; *Goyescas*.

ORCHESTRA: Incidental music to *Liliano*; *La Nit del mort*; *Dante*.

CHAMBER MUSIC: *Piano quartet*; *Piano trio*.

PIANO: *Goyescas*; *Spanish dances*. Songs.

About Enrique Granados:

Collet, Henri. *Albéniz et Granados*; Trend, J. B. *De Falla and Spanish Music*.

Musical Observer 13:78 February 1916; *Musical Times* 60:465 September 1, 1919.

Important recordings of music by Enrique Granados:

SELECTIONS FROM OPERA: *Goyescas*, "Intermezzo" (COLUMBIA-Arbós).

PIANO: Twelve Spanish dances (ODEON).

Karl Heinrich Graun   *1701-1759*

KARL HEINRICH GRAUN, son of an excise collector, was born in Wahrenbrück, Saxony, on May 7, 1701. As a child he was taken to Dresden where his beautiful voice gained him, in 1713, the appointment of treble singer to the town council. At the same time, he pursued the study of music at the Kreuzschule where his instructors were Christoph Schmidt, chapel-master of Dresden, and Grundig, cantor of the school. Composition began early with him; during his student days he composed a number of motets and sacred works which were performed by the chorus of the Kreuzschule.

In 1725, Graun left Dresden to become tenor in the Brunswick Opera. It was not long before his initiative and talent brought him rapid promotion. It is said that, shortly after his arrival in Brunswick, he was scheduled to sing in an opera composed by Schurmann, chapel-master of Brunswick. Some airs of the opera displeased Graun so violently that he substituted others of his own composition. Strange to say, not only was he not reprimanded for this affrontery, but he was given a promotion to assistant chapel-mastership, and commissioned to compose an opera. *Pollidoro* was, in consequence, composed in 1726, and on its performance was

successful. During the next few years Graun composed both operatic and church music with fertility.

His reputation grew sufficiently, by 1735, for Crown-Prince Frederick (later Frederick-the-great) to invite him to become court-composer at Rheinsberg. During this time, Graun composed many works of high merit, including concertos for flute for his eminent patron, and a series of distinguished choral works. In 1740, when Frederick became Emperor, he appointed Graun chapel master in Berlin and opera director. In his capacity of opera director, Graun toured Italy to gather a staff of singers for his company, returning to Berlin with a well-assembled staff of musicians.

Graun remained in Berlin for the remainder of his life, dividing his energies between the direction of opera and composition, in both of which he acquired a formidable reputation. He died in Berlin on August 8, 1759, and at the time of his death was considered one of the most celebrated composers of his period. When Frederick-the-Great heard the news of Graun's death, he wept and exclaimed: "Never shall I find such a man again!"

Certainly, he was one of the most prolific composers of his day. There was no field of musical composition in which Graun did not leave a copious heritage. Besides thirty-six operas, he composed passions and cantatas for the Church, oratorios (one of which, *Der Tod Jesu,* is even today frequently performed in Germany), concertos for the flute and piano, a library of chamber music, and even a singing method.

"Graun was, without a doubt, one of the most gifted classical composers of his generation," we learn from an anonymous monograph published in the *Allgemeine Musik-Gesellschaft.* "His composition, above all, was clean and neat, the harmony full, but at no time was the principal voice overburdened. His fugues and choruses are neither topheavy nor polished, neither affected nor frivolous. In all of his works there is apparent a genuine order of modulation. In this respect he was very sensitive to the slightest harshness. His melody is the most pleasant which one

KARL HEINRICH GRAUN

Principal works by Karl Heinrich Graun:

OPERAS: *Rodelinda*; *Artaserse*; *Catone in Utica*; *Adriano in Siria*; *Demofoonte*; *Mitridate*; *Semiramide*; *Ezio*; *Merope*.

CHORAL: Passions; oratorios; cantatas; motets; Te Deums, etc.

INSTRUMENTAL: Concertos for the flute; concertos for harpsichord; concertos for the violin; chamber works for trio, etc.

About Karl Heinrich Graun:

Mayer-Reinach, Albert. *Karl Heinrich Graun als Opernkomponist*; Mennicke, Karl Heinrich. *Hasse und die Brüder Graun.*

Allgemeine Musik-Gesellschaft in Zürich 48:1 (no. 38); *Monthly Musical Record* 33: 121, 141, 161 July-September 1903; *Musical Opinion* 54:594 April 1931.

Christoph Graupner *1683-1760*

CHRISTOPH GRAUPNER was born in Kirchberg, Saxony, on January 13, 1683. Here he attended public school where he learned the first principles of music under the organist Küster. When Küster was called to the organ-post of Reichenbach, Graupner accompanied him, continuing study under his guidance for two additional years.

From Reichenbach, Graupner came to Leipzig where for nine years he studied at the St. Thomas Schule, his instructors being Schell (at the harpsichord) and Kuhnau (in composition).

In 1706, the invasion of Saxony by Sweden compelled Graupner to escape to Hamburg, where he arrived with only two thalers in his pocket. Fortunately, he succeeded in procuring a position as accompanist at the Opera, and he remained in this position for three years. These were important years for Graupner's artistic development. The director of the Hamburg opera, at the time, was the eminent composer, Reinhard Keiser, who served as a model for the young musician in his first ventures as an operatic composer.

Amatory troubles compelled Graupner to leave Hamburg sooner than he wished. In 1710, he came to Darmstadt where he received an appointment as vice-chapel-master. Here his musicianship and artistry were important in improving the quality of court performances. His prestige as a musician grew rapidly,

might hear, and . . . . altho his adagios were long, it was necessary—as Hiller said—for Graun to develop them for them to seem not long at all."

Ebenezor Prout pointed out that "Graun seems to have had a fine feeling for tone color; there is more variety in his scoring than is to be found in much of the music of his contemporaries."

He was, wrote Marpurg, "the greatest ornament of the German muse, the master of pleasing melody . . . . tender, sweet, sympathetic, exalted, stately and terrible by turns. All the strokes of his pen were equally perfect. His genius was inexhaustible."

Two of Karl Heinrich Graun's brothers were eminent musicians. The oldest, August Friedrich Graun (1697-1765) was the cantor of Merseburg where he acquired considerable reputation. Johann Gottlieb Graun (1698-1771) was not only a famous violinist but also an esteemed composer of instrumental music. During the latter part of his life, Johann Gottlieb Graun was the conductor of a royal band in Berlin. His compositions, which have been praised for their variety of mood and elasticity of style, included sonatas for the violin, for flute, concertos for the harpsichord, for the violin, symphonies, cantatas and chamber works.

and he was finally elevated to the post of full chapel-master.

When, in 1723, the post of cantor at the Thomas Schule in Leipzig became vacant, Graupner was suggested as a candidate, together with Johann Sebastian Bach and Telemann. He was, however, comfortable in Darmstadt and, therefore, reluctant to consider a change.

During the remainder of his life Graupner remained in Darmstadt. The last ten years were marked by complete blindness, brought on by overwork. He died on May 10, 1760.

Christoph Graupner was a fertile composer in every musical form. He produced many operas between the years of 1707 and 1719 which made his name well-known in music circles. Between 1719 and 1745 he composed no less than 1300 works for the church services at Darmstadt. He also composed many works for chamber orchestra, for piano and for small chamber groups. His name is virtually forgotten today; but he was an important influence in the development of symphonic and piano music.

Principal works by Christoph Graupner:

OPERA: *Dido*; *Die lustige Hochzeit* (with Keiser); *Hercules und Theseus*; *Antiochus und Stratonice*; *Telemach*; *Berenice und Lucio*, etc.

ORCHESTRA: 115 symphonies; 80 overtures; 50 concertos, etc.

CHORAL: Chorales; pieces for one or more voices, etc.

Pieces for harpsichord.

About Christopher Graupner:

Roack, F. *Christoph Graupner's Kirchenmusik.*

André Ernest Grétry   *1741-1813*

ANDRÉ ERNEST MODESTE GRÉ-TRY, an important figure in French opera of the eighteenth century, was born in Liège on February 8, 1741. At an early age he showed unusual curiosity for music in every form. He loved to listen to his father perform on the violin or sing folk melodies. At four, he was attracted to a bubbling pot of water because it produced pleasant sounds while boiling; in attempting to discover what produced these sounds,

he overturned the pot, scalded himself badly, and permanently impaired his eyesight.

Possessing a beautiful voice (his biographer, José Bruyr, commented that "he sang like an angel") he was placed by his father in the choir of St. Denis, where his strict and methodical music master almost smothered his great love for the art. Fortunately, his next teachers—the organists Renekin and Moreau—were sympathetic and affectionate. Under them, Grétry acquired the elements of musical composition.

As a child, Grétry was, by temperament, a mystic, profoundly religious and God-fearing. In his *Memoirs* he has recorded the fact that at one time, on his way to the St. Denis, he begged God for death if he could not make him "an honest man and a good musician." The same day a rafter fell on his head and almost killed him. The first comment Grétry made upon recovering was: "I did not die. Then God has decided to make me an upright man and a good musician!"

While still a boy, he was introduced to the sparkling operas of Pergolesi, when an Italian company of singers came to Liège for a series of performances. He "nearly died with pleasure" on hearing *La Serva padrona* for the first time, and he attended every performance of this work which the company gave. These performances convinced Grétry of the direction in which he would travel in his own music: He would compose operas in the style of Pergolesi. Thus, Pergolesi's influence upon him, which persisted thruout Grétry's entire life, had its origins in early boyhood. As he later wrote: "Pergolesi was the creator. My music is but a continuation of his."

His boyhood was marked by fertile composition. Creation was not an easy task for him, not only because he was insufficiently equipped in technique, but also because he suffered intensely from poor health. At the age of sixteen, he had an internal hemorrhage. Frequently, his composition was interrupted by these painful attacks. However, his productivity did not seem to suffer; in 1758 alone he produced six symphonies.

ANDRÉ ERNEST GRÉTRY

These symphonies attracted the Chanoine du Harlez, who was prepared to help the young musician. At that time, Grétry's great ambition was to go to Rome; the Chanoine financed the journey. With a smuggler for a companion, Grétry made the trip from Liège to Rome, part of the way by foot, and was enrolled in the *Collège de Liège,* founded by a compatriot for the benefit of Liège citizens in Rome. Here, Grétry became a pupil of the contrapuntist Casali who, strange to say, found his student hopelessly dull.

His innate resource and tact enabled Grétry to earn a fair-sized annual income in Rome. He heard of a nobleman, an amateur flautist, who commissioned every musician that came to his door to compose a flute concerto for him; invariably, he dismissed the composer abruptly because the commissioned concerto displeased him. Grétry decided to visit the nobleman. Before accepting the commission, he begged to hear the nobleman perform. Then, in composing a work for his future patron, he meticulously inserted all the runs and technical tricks which he had noted the flutist had delighted in utilizing. The result was that the Concerto earned for Grétry a handsome annual salary.

In Rome, Grétry composed his first work for the theatre, *La Vendemmiatrice,* performed in 1765 at the Alberti Theatre with marked appreciation. Shortly after this, he stumbled across a score of Monsigny's *Rose et Colas,* a work which convinced him that his field should be that of the *opéra-comique.* From that moment on, Rome began to stifle him. He yearned for Paris.

In 1768 he was back in Paris, determined to make himself successful, naively wondering how he "could please everybody." Always an opportunist, Grétry now made valuable friendships—with Diderot, Count Creutz (the Swedish ambassador), the painter Vernet, and the Abbé Arnaud—all of whom exerted their influence on his behalf. At the close of 1768, a two-act opera of Grétry, *Le Huron,* received performance. The following year, two more operas—*Lucile* and *Le Tableau parlant*—brought him his first emphatic success.

During the next twenty years, Grétry composed so many operas (it has been recorded that more than fifty of his operas were performed in this period) that to attempt to list them would be a formidable task. Of these, the most famous were *Zémire et Azor* (1771), *La Fausse magie* (1775), *L'Épreuve villageoise* (1784) and *Richard Coeur de Lion* (1784). After the performance of *La Fausse magie,* Jean Jacques Rousseau—who until now had looked with little favor upon Grétry—sought out the composer, clasped his hand and told him that he was now fully convinced of his genius.

Always keeping his finger upon the pulse of the times, Grétry became an ardent revolutionist, during the French Revolution. For this reason, though the revolution deprived him of his great fortune, his distinguished reputation remained unimpaired. In 1785, the municipality of Paris named a street after him; soon afterwards a statue of him was erected at the Opéra Comique. When the Conservatory was founded, Grétry became an Inspector; with the inauguration of the Institut, he was chosen a member.

With the return of the monarchy, Grétry nimbly reversed his position and became a violent counter-revolutionary —publishing in 1801 a treatise against revolution entitled *Concerning Truth:*

What We Were, What We Are and What We Ought to Be. Because of his new stand, Grétry was rewarded by Napoleon III with the order of the Legion of Honor, and a yearly pension.

During the last ten years of his life, Grétry virtually abandoned composition to devote himself to philosophy and musical theory. Towards the close of his life, he derived considerable personal satisfaction and pleasure from living in the former home of Jean Jacques Rousseau, *L'Érémitage* near Montmorency, which he had bought from the philosopher.

He died at *L'Érémitage* on September 24, 1813. Three days later he was honored with a magnificent funeral, which attested to the great honor with which he was esteemed.

This short biography of Grétry has already disclosed certain of Grétry's more obvious personal traits: his shrewd opportunism, his infinite resource and tact, his lack of scruples. Fétis has further commented that Grétry was a formidable egoist whose conversation invariably consisted only of his own achievements, plans and creations. Certainly, he was not above advertising himself and his work. It was said that frequently he joined a group of strangers, and would suddenly say: "I see that they are playing Grétry's *Épreuve* to-night. I must surely see it!" Then, passing off to another group of strangers, he would repeat the remark. He was, however, a likable person, generous, affectionate, deeply religious. He was highly superstitious.

Thruout his life, Grétry suffered bad health. The early hemorrhage persisted with him until the end of his life. To this were frequently added fevers and chest-coughs. His delicate health necessitated a strict diet often consisting of nothing more than a glass of water and a pound of dry figs. Frequently, too, he suffered from musical obsessions. At one time, a theme from his opera, *Les Deux Avares,* tormented him until he thought he would go mad. "My brain was like a pivot," he later explained, "on which that piece of music everlastingly turned, and I could do nothing to stop it."

As a composer, Grétry possessed many faults which have been subject to severe censure by many critics. Certainly his technique was deplorably deficient. His form was monotonous, his ensemble writing poor, his instrumentation weak, and his harmonic construction often full of obvious errors. It was remarked that "a coach and four could pass between the bass and treble in some of his arias."

The truth was that Grétry looked upon the science of instrumentation with contempt; at least thirty of his operas were orchestrated by other musicians. Two other of his operas have undergone radical revision in instrumentation by other composers—*Richard,* by Adam, and *L'Épreuve,* by Auber. To Grétry, the most important consideration in composition was the production of beautiful melody. "The melody which lingers in one's mind like beautiful poetry," he once wrote, "bears the mark of genius."

And that, without a doubt, is the great strength of his music—its inexhaustible flow of beautiful melody. Even his declamations are freshly melodic. Wrote Karl Maria von Weber: "Grétry is perhaps the only one among French composers whose spirit is essentially lyric, at times even romantic. It would be impossible to equal the really exquisite purity of his melodies, which are always inspired to suit the exigencies of the moment and not according to stereotyped forms."

Except for their wealth of melodic content, his operas cannot be said to be of importance from present-day standards. "There was nothing like deeply thought-out, coherent artistic scheme of modern music drama," wrote Mary Hargreave. "The primitive style of instrumentation, the simplicity of the score, the well worn lines of conventional routine, all favored the quick throwing together of compositions of merely 'occasional' *raison d'être.*"

It is the opinion of Frederick Niecks that our generation would not find many appealing qualities in Grétry's operas, with the exception of some poignantly beautiful airs. "Our time would feel too much the absence of wealth of harmony, counterpoint, orchestration and elaborate form, to be content with the exquisite simplicities of Grétry. Our time would also feel Grétry's limited compass of emotional expression, which did not reach the grand intensities and puissances of tragedy and heroism, but which comprised all the shades of the pastoral, domestic and other temperate affections of the heart and mind that fell short of the violently passionate emotions."

Grétry himself knew his artistic limitations. In his *Memoirs* he wrote: "I received from Nature the gift of appropriate melody but she denied me that of strict and complicated harmony."

It is interesting to notice that, in his theoretical writings, Grétry dreamt of a theatre for opera which strangely foreshadows the Bayreuth of Wagner by almost a century. The theatre which Grétry envisioned was to have the symphony orchestra completely concealed, was to consist of one class of seats (no boxes) and was to have a curved stage which would be clearly visible from every part of the house.

Principal works by André Ernest Grétry:

OPERA: *Les Deux avares*; *Zémire et Azor*; *L'Amant jaloux*; *L'Épreuve villageoise*; *Céphale et Procris*; *La Rosière republicaine*; *Richard Coeur de Lion*; *La Fausse magie*, etc.

ORCHESTRA: Six short symphonies; incidental music to many plays.

CHORAL: Requiem; Psalm 130; motets; mass.

CHAMBER MUSIC: Six string quartets; Two piano quartets (with flute).

Piano sonatas.

About André Ernest Grétry:

Bruyr, José. *Grétry*; Closson, Ernest. *André Modeste Grétry*; Curzon, Henri. *Grétry*; Grétry, André Ernest Modest. *Memoirs*; Hargreave, Mary. *Earlier French Musicians*; Hulst, Felix. *Grétry*; Lasserre, Pierre. *The Spirit of French Music*; Rolland, Romain. *Some Musicians of Former Days*.

La Revue Musicale 12:417 May 1931.

Important recordings of music by André Ernest Grétry:

OPERA: *L'Amant jaloux*, "Sérénade" (PATHE). *Céphale et Procris*, "Aria" (COLUMBIA); "Ballet music," arranged by Felix Mottl (COLUMBIA-Defauw), *Richard Coeur-de-Lion*, "Je crains de lui parler la nuit" (COLUMBIA). *La Rosière républicaine*, "Ballet music," arranged by Meyrowitz (COLUMBIA).

Edvard Grieg *1843-1907*

EDVARD HAGERUP GRIEG, Norway's greatest composer, was born on June 15, 1843, in Bergen, where his father was a consul from England. His mother, a gifted pianist, brought him his first musical impressions by frequently playing for him Mozart and Weber, thereby arousing in him a curiosity for an instrument that could produce such magic sounds. In later life he recalled "the wonderful satisfaction with which my arms stretched out to the piano to discover—not a melody, that was yet far off—no, it must have been a harmony, first a third, then a chord of three notes, then a full chord of four; ending at last with both hands. Oh joy! A combination of five, the chord of the ninth! When I found that out my happiness knew no bounds. That was indeed a success! No later successes ever stirred me like that. I was about five years old."

At school, he was an inattentive and irresponsible student. The school was about half-an-hour's walk from his home. Frequently, to avoid attending classes on rainy days, he would stand under a dripping roof until he was soaked. His master would then send him home to change his clothing which, because of the distance, meant that he would not have to return that day. "I played this prank pretty often; but when at last I carried it so far as to come one day wet thru, tho it hardly rained at all, they became suspicious and kept a look-out. One day, I was caught, and made an intimate acquaintance with the birch."

During these school days, Grieg already tried his hand at composition, producing a series of piano variations. These variations he showed to his school master who, already sufficiently prejudiced against him, called it "stupid stuff." At his home, however, the great Norwegian violinist, Ole Bull, caught sight of this work, and was so impressed with it that he told Grieg: "You must go to Leipzig and study music." Leipzig immediately became Grieg's most coveted goal.

In his fifteenth year, Grieg was taken by his father on an extended trip thru Norway. The beautiful scenery made so deep an impression upon him that, for the moment, he yearned to become a painter in order to record his impressions on canvas. From this time dates his great national consciousness.

Late in 1858, Grieg's precious goal was finally reached. He was sent to Leipzig to complete his music study under E. F. Richter (counterpoint), Reinecke and Reitz (composition) and E. F. Wenzel and Moscheles (piano). Strange to note, Grieg was here, too, the shiftless pupil. For this there were several reasons. For one thing, he detested routine exercises, and instead of attempting to master his lessons he spent his free hours in day-dreaming. Moreover, the fact that the music of several of his most loved composers (particularly Chopin, Wagner and Schumann) was taboo to Conservatory students aroused his antagonism and prejudice against the school. Finally, he preferred composition to study, sacrificing for it all of his study-periods. The result of his negligence was repeated failure in his school-work. Finally, ashamed to find himself at the bottom in the school-ratings, he decided that he would once and for all master his lessons. For the next few weeks he worked day and night. Then his health broke. Pleurisy set in, resulting in the calamity of leaving Grieg with only one lung for the remainder of his life. Partially recovered, Grieg was sent home in 1860 for a prolonged rest. Then, returning to Leipzig for the final examinations, he passed with high grades.

After Leipzig, Grieg went to Copenhagen, in an attempt to make, here, his mark as a musician. He met and was encouraged by the Danish composer, Niels Gade. In Copenhagen, too, Grieg became a close friend of a young Norwegian musician, Rikard Nordraak (cousin of the dramatist, Björnson)—whose flaming patriotism aroused Grieg. Together, they hoped to bring about a Norwegian school of music. They founded the Copenhagen Euterpe Society, with the aim of giving performance to the music of young, unrecognized composers.

In 1864, Grieg returned to his home in Bergen. Here his national ardor was further inflamed in talks with Ole Bull.

EDVARD GRIEG

Bull had arranged several Norwegian folk-songs for the violin which drew Grieg's interest towards the folk music of his country.

In 1864, in Copenhagen, Grieg had been secretly engaged to Nina Hagerup, a talented singer, daughter of a well-known Danish actress. To her, Grieg composed what is probably one of his best-known songs, *Ich liebe dich*. Marriage was for the time out of question because of Grieg's financial insecurity. When it was finally consummated, in 1867, it was the beginning of a long and idyllic relationship. Her faith in his genius and her encouragement were important factors to him during those years when he was unknown and unrecognized, fighting virtually a lonely battle on behalf of Norwegian music.

The winter of 1865 was spent by Grieg in Rome, where he received the news of the death of his friend and fellow-artist, Nordraak. This was a terrible blow, and inspired him to carry on alone the work that they had planned together: to bring Norwegian music to the fore. For this purpose, Grieg went to Christiana, Sweden, where he established the Musical Union and became its conductor. With this organization, Grieg gave a successful all-Norwegian program. But his success was only temporary. Before long, the novelty of new Scandinavian music began to pall, and Grieg confronted severe opposition and antagonism in his indefatigable efforts to present it.

The first sweet taste of success came to Grieg in 1869 when he received a letter from the great Liszt, congratulating him for his *Violin sonata in F*, a work which the master found full of promise. This letter, from one of the great musicians of the time, brought Grieg a government pension of 1,600 kronen, enabling him to make the voyage to Rome to meet Liszt personally. It was during this meeting that Grieg showed Liszt his latest work, the *Piano concerto*. "Carry on, my friend," Liszt told Grieg. "You have real talent. Don't ever permit them to frighten you!"

This *Piano concerto* is generally recognized as one of Grieg's great works Frederick Niecks found in it "life itself, in its press and stress." And Henry T. Finck: "The first movement is replete with beautiful, haunting melody, and nothing could be more lovely than the orchestral introduction to the slow movement—one of the saddest preludes ever written—a prelude illustrating Grieg's gift of creating an emotional atmosphere with the simplest means."

Upon his return to Christiana, Grieg went to Denmark where he was instrumental in forming a Danish Opera company of first importance at the Royal Theatre. Finally, in 1874, he returned home to Bergen. It was at this time that—at the request of the great dramatist, Henrik Ibsen—he composed the music that first brought him fame thruout the world, the incidental music to *Peer Gynt*.

During the decade of 1864 to 1874, Grieg composed his most representative music—including two violin sonatas, the *Peer Gynt* music, the *Piano concerto,* the *Norwegian dances,* and some of his most famous songs. Discussing this imposing output of music, Daniel Gregory Mason wrote: "One may point out . . . its persistently lyrical character. . . . It is intimate, suggestive, intangible. It voices the gentlest feelings of the heart, or summons up the airiest visions of the imagination. It is whimsical, too, changes its hues like the chameleon, and often surprises us with a sudden flight to some unexpected shade of expression. Again,

its finesse is striking. The phrases are polished like gems, the melodies charm us with their perfect proportions, the cadences are as consummate as they are novel. Then, again, the rhythm is most delightfully frank and straightforward; there is no maundering or uncertainty, but always a vigorous dancing progress, as candid as childhood."

In 1874, Grieg's imperial position in Norwegian music was officially recognized by the government when he was given a yearly pension which enabled him to fulfil his life-long dream of buying a home in the country and devoting himself exclusively to composition. He selected a spot at the Hardanjer Fjord, one-half hour by rail from Bergen. Troldhaugen became, before long, a Mecca to which music-lovers of an entire world came to do homage to a great composer. They came in such abundance that Grieg soon placed a notice at the entrance: "Edvard Grieg does not desire to receive callers earlier than four in the afternoon."

During the last thirty years of his life, Grieg was the recipient of many honors commensurate with his position in the world of music. In 1872, he was appointed member of the Swedish Academy of Music; in 1883, he became a corresponding member of the Musical Academy of Leyden. In 1890, the French Academy of Fine Arts elected him a member of its body, and three years later the University of Cambridge gave him an honorary doctorate in music (simultaneously with Tschaikovsky, Saint-Saëns, Boito and Bruch). The honor which he esteemed most highly came in 1903, when his bust was placed in the hall of the Leipzig Gewandhaus.

Edvard Grieg died on September 4, 1907 in a hotel room in Bergen, while enroute to Christiania. The evening before his death he said to his nurse: "I am not able to sleep. I shall have another restless night." A few hours later he knew he was dying. He called his wife to his side and told her: "This is my end."

His body was laid in the great hall of the Museum of Art and Industry of Bergen where over 7,000 people came ʻto see him for the last time. He was buried with all the ceremony and honor befitting the greatest composer of his country.

Tschaikovsky, who met Grieg in 1888, described him in the following sentence: "He had an uncommon charm, and blue eyes, not very large, but irresistibly fascinating." To this, we may add a few descriptive words of Ernest Classon: "His gaze is serious, indescribably tender, with a peculiar expression, at once ailing, restless and childishly naïve. The entire effect is that of kindness, gentleness, sincerity and genuine modesty."

Grieg possessed a headstrong temperament, was frequently petulant because of his life-long ill-health, was often guilty of lack of tact or consideration. Fishing was his favorite diversion; also, playing the piano in solitude. He detested having anyone near him when he was making music. He was an omniverous drinker of tea—strong tea in the morning, weak at night.

When he worked, he demanded monastic seclusion. He had a one-room cabin, surrounded by natural beauty, near the Hardanjer Fjord, where intrusion was never permitted while he was busy at composition. He loved the wild country landscapes near this cabin passionately.

Analyzing Grieg's major works, Lawrence Gilman wrote: "He is sometimes truly imaginative, as in passages in the *Peer Gynt* music, in the last two sonatas for violin and piano (opus 13 and opus 45), in certain of the songs and piano pieces. He has, too, achieved ideas; ideas of exquisite distinction, of noble breadth. But they lack the stamp of supreme excellence. . . . But in a surpassing degree, Grieg has individuality— individuality that is seizing and indubitable. That, one feels, is his distinguishing possession. His accent is unmistakable. His speech may sway one, or it may not; but always the voice is the voice of Grieg. . . . Grieg is thrice-admirable in this: he wears no one's mantle; he borrows no man's speech."

Principal works by Edvard Grieg:

ORCHESTRA: *Norwegian dances*; *Symphonic dances*; Incidental music to *Peer Gynt*; Incidental music to *Sigurd Jorsalfar*; *Lyric pieces*; *Concerto for piano and orchestra*; *Holberg suite* (arranged from the piano).

CHORAL: *Vor dem Klosterpforte*; *Landerkennung*; *Olaf Trygvason*, etc.

CHAMBER MUSIC: *Quartet in G-minor*; Two sonatas for violin and piano; *Sonata for violoncello and piano*.

About Edvard Grieg:

Songs, pieces for the piano, etc.
Finck, Henry T. *Edvard Grieg and his Music*; Gilman, Lawrence. *Nature in Music*; Mason, Daniel Gregory. *From Grieg to Brahms*; Rokseth, Yvonne. *Grieg*.
Contemporary Review July 1905; *Monthly Musical Record* 35:161 September 1905.

Important recordings of music by Edvard Grieg:

ORCHESTRA: Incidental music to *Peer Gynt* (COLUMBIA-Kerby); Incidental music to *Sigurd Jorsalfar* (COLUMBIA-Schneevoigt); *Lyric pieces* (VICTOR-Goossens); *Concerto for piano and orchestra* (VICTOR-Bachaus); *Norwegian dances* (VICTOR-Blech); *Symphonic dances* (COLUMBIA-Dobrowen).

CHAMBER MUSIC: *Sonata in G-major*, for violin and piano (POLYDOR); *Sonata in C-minor*, for violin and piano (VICTOR-Kreisler); *Sonata in A-minor*, for violoncello and piano (COLUMBIA-Salmond).

SONGS: *The first meeting* (GRAMOPHONE-Noréna); *I love you* (COLUMBIA-Tauber); *Springtide* (GRAMOPHONE-Noréna).

Charles T. Griffes *1884-1920*

CHARLES TOMLINSON GRIFFES, one of the outstanding composers that America has produced, was born in Elmira, New York, on September 17, 1884. The study of music was begun at an early age. Griffes made such rapid progress at the piano that, while still a student at high-school, he decided to become a concert pianist. He went to Berlin to complete his pianistic studies. While there, he came under the influence of Humperdinck, his instructor in theory, who—sensing that Griffes' importance as a musician rested more in the creative than in the interpretative field—succeeded in diverting the young musician towards composition. Under Humperdinck's influence, Griffes entered upon his first phase as a composer, producing German songs and piano pieces which, truth to tell, failed to reveal any of his latent power. This music, we are informed by Norman Peterkin, "is Teutonic in style, rather sentimental in spirit, and the best that one can say of it is that it is the work of a good and sure craftsman."

In 1907, Griffes returned to America. Soon afterwards he became a music teacher in the Hackley School of Tarrytown, New York, holding this position until his death. During these years, his industry was given principally to composition. He was a slow worker, each of his compositions being the result of careful and fastidious labor. As a result, Griffes' works were few and far between. And altho he succeeded in producing several works of considerable distinction (particularly the *Poem* for flute and orchestra, dedicated to and introduced by, Georges Barrère, and *Two pieces* for string-quartet, given a first performance by the Flonzaley Quartet in 1918) he worked in obscurity and neglect.

In 1920, his last work, the *Pleasure dome of Kubla Khan,* for orchestra, was accepted by the Boston Symphony. Too poor to engage a copyist to write out the parts for the orchestra, he set himself this task. His days, of course, belonged to his many duties at the Hackley School. He was, therefore, compelled to work at night. Never very strong, Griffes now weakened his health thru anxiety and hard work to so great an extent that, when he finished his copying work, he succumbed to an attack of pneumonia.

CHARLES T. GRIFFES

The first performance of the *Pleasure dome of Kubla Khan* was so successful that, overnight, Griffes became a famous composer. On his sick-bed he received not only tidings of the magnificent reception accorded his new work but also commissions from various important musical organizations thruout the country to prepare an opera, a ballet, and several symphonic works.

Unfortunately, this recognition came too late. Charles Griffes died in New York on April 8, 1920, at the premature age of thirty-six. There can be little doubt but that his untimely death robbed America of a composer of first importance. The few works he had already produced not only disclosed great promise but considerable fulfillment as well. With each succeeding work, Griffes was showing a greater mastery of his forms, a stronger individuality and musical speech.

Discussing the style of Griffes' maturer works, John Tasker Howard has written: "Like Debussy, whom he admired almost as much as Ravel, Griffes was more interested in tints than in solid colors. . . . Griffes has occasionally given us harmonies that are exquisite in themselves, dependent on nothing that goes before or that follows. Modes and oriental scales seem to have held a fascination for him. . . . Of Griffes' many gifts, the powers of description seem preeminent."

Griffes' works are continually performed in our present-day concert-hall, particularly his orchestral masterpiece, the *Pleasure dome,* and his highly effective pieces for the piano, the most famous of which are *The White peacock, Clouds* and *Roman sketches.* Of the *Two pieces* for string quartet, Philip Hale has written that it is "music of a strange beauty, yet not remote, but warmly human."

Griffes was gifted in directions other than music. He could draw skillfully with pen and ink, could produce tasteful water-colors, and during the last years of his life, frequently made etchings in copper. He was a great lover of literature, his favorite authors being Lafcadio Hearn, Edgar Allan Poe and the Celtic school of William Butler Yeats and Fiona McLeod. He rarely read fiction.

Principal works by Charles Tomlinson Griffes:

ORCHESTRA: *The Pleasure dome of Kubla Khan*; *Poem* (for flute and orchestra).

CHORAL: *Scherzo bacchanale* (with orchestra); *These things shall be.*

BALLET: *The Kairn of Koridwen*; *Schojo.*

CHAMBER MUSIC: Two pieces (for string quartet).

Songs, pieces for the piano, etc.

About Charles Tomlinson Griffes:

Howard, John Tasker. *Our American Music.*

Chesterian N.S. 30:161 March 1923.

Important recordings of music by Charles Tomlinson Griffes:

ORCHESTRA: *The Pleasure dome of Kubla Kahn* (VICTOR-Ormandy).

PIANO: *The White peacock* (COLUMBIA-Hess); *The Fountain of Acqua Paola* (ROYCROFT).

SONGS: *By a lonely forest pathway* (COLUMBIA).

Jacques Halévy *1799-1862*

JACQUES FRANÇOIS FROMENTAL ÉLIE HALÉVY, the son of a distinguished Hebrew poet, was born in Paris on May 27, 1799. He revealed his love for music as a child when he spent tireless hours drawing melodies from the piano. In his tenth year, therefore, he was sent to the Paris Conservatory where he soon proved his talent by winning, one year later, first prize in solfeggio, and second prize in harmony. He finally came to the fugue and composition class of Cherubini, under whose instruction he reached maturity.

After two unsuccessful attempts to gain the Prix de Rome, Halévy was awarded this coveted music prize, in 1819, for a cantata, *Herminie*. The three years in Italy were spent in industrious study and composition, and it was here that he first turned to the opera.

Returning to France via Vienna, where he was met and warmly welcomed by Beethoven, Halévy strove industriously to gain a performance for his early operas. The authorities turned a deaf ear to him. Halévy had already given up the hope of seeing an opera of his reach performance when, unex-

pectedly, the Opéra Comique sent him a notice that it had accepted *Phidias* for early production. It was presented in 1827 and received such warm acclaim that the director of Opéra Comique commissioned Halévy to compose a work expressly for that institution. *L'Artisan* came in 1828, likewise appealing strongly. A few months after this, *Clari* was produced with Mme. Malibran in the principal rôle, and Halévy was definitely on the road to fame.

In 1827, Halévy was appointed professor of harmony at the Conservatory, holding his post for many years of valuable service. Two years after this, he was appointed to assist Hérold as director of singing at the Théâtre Italien. During this same year, Halévy was widely discussed in Parisian music circles because of his *Le Dilettante d'Avignon*, a lusty satire on Italian opera, which was so successful that it ran for two consecutive seasons.

Notwithstanding the appeal of his early works, Halévy was still not recognized as a composer of importance. A certain prestige came to him, in 1833 when he accomplished a distinguished task in bringing to completion *Ludovic*, the opera by Hérold, left unfinished because of death. But Halévy was still esteemed a composer of smaller stature, possessing a deft and ingratiating style but a limited artistic canvas.

On February 23, 1834, Halévy's masterpiece, *La Juive*, the one opera by which he is today remembered, was given its première at the Académie de Musique. With *La Juive*, Halévy definitely came into his own as an important operatic composer. With a score which, as R. A. Streatfeild pointed out, was full of "dignity and sobriety," Halévy proved that he owned a dramatic instinct, a rich feeling for melody, and an unusual ability to express emotion poignantly in tone.

La Juive took Paris by storm. It was soon afterwards introduced in the leading capitals of Europe with almost equal success.

For the next few years, Halévy's enormous fertility produced a long string of operas and operettas, but in none of these did he succeed in attaining the power and originality of his masterpiece. Only in the *Queen of Cyprus,* produced in 1841, did he suggest the talent and strength of *La Juive.* It is of interest to note that at this time, Richard Wagner—obscure and starving in Paris—was assigned to prepare the piano arrangement of *Queen of Cyprus.*

However, though Halévy failed to duplicate *La Juive* in any of the operas that followed it, his fame did not suffer. His was a formidable popularity. His *Valley of the Andorra,* for example, succeeded, in 1848, in extricating the Opéra Comique from financial difficulties. In 1850, Halévy visited London where he was greeted with a storm of approval. Four years later, he was appointed secretary of the Académie des Beaux-Arts.

Ill-health compelled Halévy, in 1861, to seek the warmer climate of Nice. Here he underwent rapid disintegration, mentally and physically. One morning, he violently demanded a copy of Pergolesi's *La Serva padrona,* and his daughter was forced to ransack every music-store in Nice to find a copy before he would be appeased. Several days later, seated upon a couch, he attempted to stretch out and could not do so. Calling to one of his daughters he said: "Lay me down like a gamut." Then, as she helped him stretch out, he accompanied each of his motions with "do-re-mi-fa," etc. Finally, his head sank into the pillow, his muscles grew tense, and then—with the final note of the scale on his lips—he passed away.

His death took place on March 17, 1862. Five days after his burial, in Paris, *La Juive* was revived at the Opéra.

While Halévy's greatest work is a serious opera, his style was best suited for lighter creation. Here, as Paul Bekker has written, "he shows the hand of a master, very happily inspired by his inner ear for vocal effects."

"Certainly the talent of Halévy lacks neither freshness nor grace," was the opinion of no less a musician than Richard Wagner. "His vigorous constitution, his concentrated energy that characterized his energy, assured him from the very first a leading position in our lyric theatre. He knew how to

JACQUES HALÉVY

succeed, in the *opéra comique,* in attaining a gait of gracious elegance."

Principal works by Jacques Halévy:

OPERA: *La Juive*; *L'Éclair*; *Les Mousquetaires de la reine*; *Le Juif errant*; *Le Nabab*; *La Magicienne*; *Queen of Cyprus,* etc.

About Jacques Halévy:

Halévy, Léon. *Jacques Halévy, Sa Vie et ses Oeuvres*; Wagner, Richard. *Gesammelte Schriften.*
Guide Musicale 49:863 December 6, 1903; *Musical Courier* 82:6 June 16, 1921.

Important recordings of music by Jacques Halévy:

SELECTIONS FROM OPERA: *La Juive,* "Introduction" (GRAMOPHONE-Blech); "Si la rigeur et la vengeance" (VICTOR-Pinza); "O Dieu, Dieu de nos pères" and "Si trahison" (GRAMOPHONE-Martinelli); "Dieu que ma voix tremblante" (VICTOR-Martinelli); "Vous qui du Dieu vivant" (VICTOR-Pinza); "Rachel! quand du Seigneur" (VICTOR-Martinelli).

Andreas Hammerschmidt *1612-1675*

ANDREAS HAMMERSCHMIDT was born in Brüx, Bohemia, either in 1611 or, more probably, in 1612. His father was driven from Brüx by the Thirty Years War to Freiberg in Saxony, where Andreas began his music study. In 1633, he was appointed organist by Count von Bünau at his castle in Weesenstein, and here Hammerschmidt published his first work, an eight-part chorus to commemo-

ANDREAS HAMMERSCHMIDT

rate the victory of the Saxon army at Liegnitz in 1634.

In 1636, Hammerschmidt became organist of the St. Pierre church in Freiberg. Three years later he received an even more important post at the church St. Johann in Zittau. He held the latter position until the end of his life. He died on October 29, 1675. Shortly after his death, the city of Zittau erected a monument in his honor.

Between 1638 and 1642, Hammerschmidt published his series of *Musikalische Andachten,* settings of German sacred words for one to six voices. His most famous work was published in Dresden in 1647, the *Dialogues Between God and the Believing Soul,* secular pieces for one to three voices with instrumental accompaniment. In these works, Hammerschmidt applied the *ars nuova* to polyphonic writing with considerable success.

Fétis has commented that Hammerschmidt possessed "an original genius, an exalted style and a manner of writing that was simpler and purer than most of the compositions of his time." C. Hubert Parry finds in Hammerschmidt a modern element. He wrote in the *Oxford History of Music*: "One of the most important features of modern musical art is the clear definition of the musical idea; but it took composers a long time to arrive at the conception,

and they often tried to express what touched them most in a rather indefinite way. But Hammerschmidt often shows a lively instinct for the path along which art was destined to travel. . . . His efforts in the direction of expression extend even to occasional harmonic subtleties."

Principal works by Andreas Hammerschmidt:

CHORAL: *Musikaliche andachten* (five parts); *Dialogues between God and the believing soul*; Odes; Madrigals; Motets; Missae Sacrae, etc.

INSTRUMENTAL: *Tafelmusik.*

About Andreas Hammerschmidt:

Denkmäler der Tonkunst in Österreich (vol. 16); Parry, C. Hubert. *Oxford History of Music* (vol. 3).

Important recordings of music by Andreas Hammerschmidt:

CHORAL: *Musikalische andachten,* "Sei nun wieder zufrieden" (LUMEN). *Machet die Tore weit,* motet (POLYDOR).

George Frederick Handel *1685-1759*

"He is the master of us all."—JOSEF HAYDN

"To him I bend the knee. For Handel is the greatest, ablest composer that ever lived."—BEETHOVEN

GEORGE FREDERICK HANDEL was born in Halle, Saxony, on February 23, 1685. His father, a village surgeon, was determined to have his son procure a social position by becoming a lawyer. He frowned therefore on every effort of the boy to acquire a musical education, severely forbidding him any instruction in the art. Thru the intervention of George Frederick's nurse and several friends of the family, a spinet was smuggled into the garret. Upon this—with the strings deadened by strips of cloth—the boy practised late each night while his father was asleep.

When George was seven years old, his father took a journey to the court of Saxe-Weissenfels to visit a son of a former marriage, a valet to a duke. Young George begged for permission to accompany his father, and when his request was refused, he followed the coach on foot until his father was forced to acquiesce. At the court of the duke,

George Frederick was permitted to play upon the organ and harpsichord, making so profound an impression on the duke that he filled the boy's pockets with gold and persuaded father Handel to permit the boy to follow the study of music.

On their return to Halle, father Handel permitted the son to begin the study of music, but only on condition that academic study, principally that of law, would not be abandoned. F. W. Zachau, the organist of the Liebfrauen-kirche was engaged as the boy's music teacher—an admirable pedagogue who gave Handel an intensive training in singing, on the organ, clavier, oboe, violin and in composition. For three years, this comprehensive course of study continued. Handel made such great progress that, finally, Zachau confessed that there was nothing more he could teach him.

In 1696, Handel was taken to Berlin to exhibit his musical talent. He created a sensation among musicians with his phenomenal exploits. The elector of Brandenburg wished to attach him permanently to his court, and offered to send him to Italy for additional study. Father Handel, however, still clinging obstinately to his ambition of making his son a lawyer, ordered the boy back to Halle. One year later, the father died, leaving his family in straightened circumstances. Compelled to help in the support of his family, Handel accepted a post as organist at the Dom und Schlosskirche, at the same time entering the University with the intention of bringing to realization his father's ambition for him.

After a year of study at the University (during this period Handel had composed hundreds of works for the church), he definitely decided that the legal profession was not for him. He now turned whole-heartedly to music. The music life of Halle was limited, and Handel soon began to cast anxious eyes beyond the horizon. He decided to settle in Hamburg, then a musical metropolis. Here he came in 1703, obtaining a post as second violin at the Opera House, which was under the distinguished direction of Reinhard Keiser. Intimacy with this operatic world, and friendship with Johann

Mattheson, a celebrated musician in Hamburg, were powerful influences in bringing maturity to Handel's artistry.

In 1703, Handel went to Lübeck with the hope of receiving the post of chapel-master held by Buxtehude. He, like Johann Sebastian Bach, was considered seriously as Buxtehude's successor, but was rejected when he refused to marry Buxtehude's daughter, as was prescribed by the ru'es.

It was not long before Handel made his mark as a musician in Hamburg. When Reinhard Keiser disappeared from Hamburg to escape the claws of creditors, Handel took his place at the harpsichord and directed the opera performances with such competence that, after Keiser's return, he was retained as one of the directors of the Opera. This position brought him into conflict with his friend Mattheson. Mattheson's opera *Cleopatra* was produced at the Opera under Handel's direction, with Mattheson himself singing the principal rôle of Antony. Because Antony dies early in the opera, Mattheson insisted that, at this point, Handel relinquish the direction of the opera to him. Handel stoutly refused. At the end of the opera, Mattheson struck Handel squarely on the cheek, challenging him to a duel. It was Mattheson's contention that Handel's life was saved only because the former's sword broke on a heavy metal button on Handel's coat.

On January 8, 1705, Handel's first opera, *Almira,* was given its first performance at the Hamburg opera. It succeeded in spite of its apparent deficiencies, and ran for twenty performances. *Almira* was succeeded in Hamburg by three more operas, *Nero, Daphne* and *Florinda.*

In 1706, Handel bade farewell to Hamburg. For the next thirteen years he was to wander across the face of Europe. His first destination was Italy. In Florence, he produced his first Italian opera, *Rodrigo,* the success of which was so great that it earned for Handel many gifts—and the love of the prima-donna. She followed Handel to Venice, where she appeared in a still more striking success, Handel's second Italian opera *Agrippina.* Early in 1708, Handel was in Rome, under the protection of

Cardinal Ottoboni, for whom he composed his oratorio *La Resurrezione,* and his cantata *Il Trionfo del tempo.* But his fame in Italy stemmed not only from his compositions; his performances on the harpsichord were the wonder and awe of Italy. It was Domenico Scarlatti who, hearing a performance on the harpsichord at a masquerade, exclaimed that the performer must perforce be either "the celebrated Saxon or else the devil himself."

After a short stay in Naples where Handel was greeted with festivity and honor, he returned to Venice, meeting there the Abbé Steffani, chapel-master of Hanover. Steffani induced Handel to come to Hanover and succeed him in his post. He was given the generous salary of ten thousand thalers, and was permitted as much leisure as he desired, as well as enough vacations to permit him to continue his musical education.

Hardly was he installed in this new position when, encouraged by his English friends, he decided to take his first leave-of-absence from Hanover for the purpose of visiting London. He came late in 1710, and upon a special commission composed *Rinaldo* in two weeks. *Rinaldo* took London by storm after its first performance on February 24, 1711. Handel was the man-of-the-hour, courted by society, honored by the music public.

In June, 1711, Handel was back in Hanover, attending diligently to his duties as chapel-master. But he could not forget his London triumphs. Before long—in the autumn of 1712—he took a second leave of absence for the purpose of revisiting England. With this visit, his fame and fortune were to take even deeper root in English soil. As a result, Handel remained in England far beyond the time granted him by his leave of absence, unable to desert the scenes of such triumphs and adulation.

Upon the death of Queen Anne, in 1714, the Elector of Hanover mounted the throne of England, placing the truant Handel in an embarrassing position. It is a familiar legend that the Elector of Hanover, bitter at Handel's desertion of the Hanover post, refused to have any contact with the composer in England. Two of Handel's friends, Lord Burlington and Baron Kielmansegge, arranged a tactful reconciliation. A royal water party on the Thames was to take place in honor of the new king. Handel's friends arranged that the royal barge be followed by a band of musicians, conducted by Handel, and performing special Handel music. The music made a deep impression upon the king, and he inquired who the composer was. When the king learned that the composer was none other than Handel, he readily forgave him for his former transgression, at the same time bestowing upon him a life pension of two hundred pounds a year. It is doubtful, however, whether this frequently repeated tale of the origin of the celebrated *Water music* has much basis of truth.

From this time on, Handel definitely established himself in England. He anglicized his name, and accepted England as his permanent home. It is, of course, impossible in space as limited as this to present his career in England comprehensively, nor is it necessary. It is sufficient to note that in England he reached his highest artistic triumphs and composed his greatest masterpieces. Petty rivalries frequently brought stress to his career—particularly during his short and ill-fated period as opera impresario—but from all of these he finally emerged triumphant. His crowning position in the English music of his time was recognized by his grateful contemporaries.

By 1740, Handel reached a definite landmark in his career. At this time, he had permanently abandoned opera (of which he had composed some forty works) and turned his genius to the oratorio. With this change, a new and greater composer made his appearance. For Handel, despite all the great moments he achieved periodically in his operatic writing (particularly in some sublime songs), was never a supremely great composer for the theatre, and his operas are dated. He was not, as C. F. Abdy Williams pointed out, "a reformer like Gluck and Wagner. He took the opera as he found it and simply embellished it by means of his great genius. He was content to work on the forms that he found established. . . . His operas have disappeared from the stage (and altho attempts have been made to revive some of the best of them, especially in Germany, it cannot be pretended that they are ever likely to attract the public again, however interesting they might be to connoisseurs). Handel, in his operas, was essentially a man of his time. . . . He simply took the forms he found ready-made and adorned them with all the beauty and solidity he was capable of producing, which far surpassed the operatic efforts of his contemporaries. . . . The orchestration of Handel's operas would probably seem monotonous to an audience accustomed to the brilliancy of modern instrumentation. . . . The subject-matter of the operas is perhaps another bar to their acceptance. . . . A third obstacle is that the vocal parts were written to suit the powers of special singers and were invariably altered when it was necessary that they should be sung by others. It is scarcely possible that singers could be found to execute the more difficult songs nowadays, to say nothing of the fact that artificial male sopranos are an extinct species."

With *Saul,* in 1738, and *Israel in Egypt,* in 1739, Handel composed two oratorios in which his creative genius expanded and flowered as it had rarely succeeded in doing in the operas. "Instead of the stereotyped harmonic structure of dominant-tonic, subdominant-tonic," wrote César Saerchinger, "which stamps so much of his work as tedious and antiquated, we have rich chromatic progressions and colorful modulations; the clear-cut note-for-note harmony is varied by a setting of a polyphonic web which eloquently betrays Handel's early fugal training, a polyphony as diverse almost as that of the a cappella masters of the past, but resting firmly on a pure harmonic foundation, euphonious, sonorous, guided by solid laws of progression, but unrestrained in its freedom of movement. The chorus *They loathed to drink,* adapted from one of his own organ fugues, is a fine example. It is in

GEORGE FREDERICK HANDEL

moments like these that Handel shows his kinship to his great countryman, Bach."

The greatest of these oratorios, *The Messiah,* composed in twenty-three days, came in 1741 and received its first performance on April 3 of the following year. "When I composed the *Hallelujah chorus,*" explained Handel, "I did think I did see all heaven before me, and the great God himself." The present-day custom among audiences everywhere of standing during the performance of the *Hallelujah chorus* dates from the opening performance of the work. At that time, explained Dr. Beattie in one of his letters, "the audience was exceedingly struck and affected by the music in general; but when the chorus struck up *For the Lord God Omnipotent* in the *Hallelujah,* they were so transported that they all together, with the King (who happened to be present) started up and remained standing till the chorus ended."

"The work is too well known to require extended comment," to quote César Saerchinger once again. "Let us only remind the reader of the exquisite beauty of such lyric passages as 'I know that my Redeemer liveth,' 'How beautiful are thy feet,' and 'Behold and see' which are among the rarest gems of aria form in our possession. Powerful and passionate expressions such as occur in 'The people that walked in darkness' are as rare in the literature of dramatic music, while the highly dramatic recitatives like 'Thy rebuke hath broken' are, without question, one of the completest realizations of the ideal of Peri and Monteverdi. The glorious choral effects in the *Hallelujah chorus,* the stirring polyphony, now simultaneous, now imitative, reflect a potency and spiritual elevation that will perhaps never be surpassed. Lastly, let us not forget the beautiful *Pastoral symphony* in which the exquisite Calabrian melody, the song of the *piferari* that Handel heard in the early days in Rome, is introduced."

The Messiah was followed by a magnificent series of oratorios which, as Arnold Schering was tempted to say in his *Geschichte der oratoriums,* is the greatest period in oratorio history. *Samson* was composed in 1741, *Joseph* in 1743, *Semele* in 1744, *Belshazaar* and *Hercules* in 1744, *Judas Maccabeus* and *Joshua* in 1747, *Solomon* in 1748, *Theodora* in 1749, *The choice of Hercules* in 1750, and *Jephtha* in 1751.

Early in 1751, Handel began to suffer from failing eyesight, which made composition painful. By 1753, his physicians despaired of his sight (he was suffering from *gutta serena*), and soon afterwards total blindness set in. Blindness, however, did not interrupt his magnificent activity. He continued his many duties as a musician—directing his own music, playing the organ, and composing.

On April 6, 1759, after directing a charity performance of *The Messiah,* he was seized with a fainting spell. He was taken home and put to bed, from which he was never again to rise. On April 14, Handel died; he had been conscious until the end. He was buried in the poet's corner of Westminster Abbey. His burial place is marked by a statue by Roubilliac, representing Handel leaning over a table covered with musical instruments, a pen in his hand, and before him the score of the *Messiah* open at the portion "I know that my Redeemer liveth."

Romain Rolland has given us an eloquent verbal portrait of Handel in *A Musical Tour Thru the Land of the Past.* "They used to call him 'The Great Bear.' He was gigantic, broad, corpulent, with big hands and enormous feet; his arms and thighs were stupendous. . . . He walked bow-legged, with a heavy, rolling gait, very erect, with his head thrown back under its huge white wig, whose curls rippled heavily over his shoulders. He had a long horse-like face, which with age became bovine and swamped with fat; with pendant cheeks and triple chin, the nose large, thick and straight, the ears red and long. His gaze was very direct; there was a quizzical gleam in his bold eye, a mocking twist at the corner of his large, finely cut mouth. His air was impressive and jovial. . . . He was full of humor. He had a 'sly pseudo-simplicity' which made the most solemn individuals laugh though he himself showed an unsmiling face. No one ever told a story better. . . . This huge mass of flesh was shaken by fits of fury. He swore almost with every phrase. . . . Spiteful, he was not. 'He was rough and peremptory,' says Burney, 'but entirely without malevolence.' There was, in his most violent fits of anger, a touch of originality which, together with his bad English, made them absolutely comical. Like Lully and Gluck, he had the gift of command; and like them, he combined an irascible violence that overcame all opposition with a witty goodnature which, though wounding to vanity, had the power of healing the wounds it had caused. . . . This masterful character, with its violence and its transports of anger and genius, was governed by a supreme self-control. In Handel . . . tranquility prevailed. . . . No one had any suspicion of the nervous tension or the superhuman determination which he must have needed in order to sustain this tranquility."

Handel composed easily, spontaneously, as naturally as man breathes. His Concerti grossi, for example, were composed each in a single day at a single sitting. He wrote straight off, and frequently needed no revision. As a matter of fact, he wrote so easily that the abundance of his ideas surpassed his ability to put them down on paper; he therefore adopted a system whereby he could jot down his ideas in an abbreviated form.

We have already commented upon Handel's operas and oratorios. There remains one more field in which he was preeminent—orchestral music. His orchestral works include twelve concerti grossi, six oboe concerti, symphonies from his operas and oratorios, his open-air music (the *Water music* and the *Fireworks music*) and concerti for horns. Here, as Romain Rolland has written, "he had . . . an exquisite sense of form. No German surpassed him in the art of writing beautiful melodic lines. Mozart and Hasse alone were his equals in this. . . . He did not work so much thru the brilliancy, variety and novelty of his tone-colors as by the beauty of his designs, and his effects of light and shade. With a voluntarily restrained palette, and by satisfying himself with the sober colors of the strings, he yet was able to produce surprising and thrilling effects. Volbach has shown that he had less recourse to the contrast and mixing of instruments than to the division of the same family of instruments into different groups. On the other hand, Handel, when he considered it advisable, reduced his instrumental forces by suppressing the violin and the second violin, whose places were taken by the harpsichord. All his orchestral art is in the true instinct of balance and economy which, with the most restricted means in managing a few co'ors, yet knows how to obtain as powerful impressions as our musicians today, with their crowded palette."

C. Hubert Parry has discerningly contrasted the music of Handel with that of his great contemporary, Johann Sebastian Bach: "Where Handel aimed at beauty of melodic form, Bach strove for characteristic expression. Where Handel used orderly progressions of simple harmony, Bach aimed at contriving elaborate interweavings of subtly disposed parts to give the effect of the subtlest shade of human feeling. Where Handel used the most realistic means to convey the hopping of frogs, or the rattling of hailstones. . . Bach attempted to express the inner feelings of human creatures under the impress of any exciting causes. . . Nowhere is the difference of their attitude better illustrated than in their use of the recitative. Handel, accepting the conventions of the Italian art without hesitation, ruined an enormous number of his works by the emptiest, baldest and most mechanical formulas; while Bach, dissatisfied with anything which had not significance, endeavored by the contours and intervals of his solo part, by the progressions and harmonies of his accompaniment, and by every means that was available to intensify from moment to moment the expression of the words.

"Bach's feeling for melody was not so happy as Handel's. . . . In instrumentation both of these giants among composers were equally backward, though their aims and methods, and the rest they achieved, were very different. . . . Handel did as little as it is possible for a great master to do in adding to the resources of the instrumental side of music. . . . Bach, on the other hand, looking always forward, gives proof of much more purpose in his use of instrumental resources. . . The oratorios of Handel were nearly all dramatic or epic, and the subjects were treated as nearly as possible histrionically. . . . But (with Bach) they are the direct outcome of personal devotion, and in them the mystic emotionalism of the Teutonic nature found its purest expression."

Principal works by George Frederick Handel:

OPERA: *Almira*; *Nero*; *Daphne*; *Rodrigo*; *Agrippina*; *Rinaldo*; *Silla*; *Radamisto*; *Rodelinda*; *Lotario*; *Arianna*; *Alcina*; *Atlanta*; *Arminio*; *Serse*; *Jupiter in Argos*; *Giulio Cesare*, etc.

CHORAL: Two passions; Nineteen oratorios (including *The Messiah, Esther, Saul, Israel in Egypt, Samson, Judas Maccabaeus, Joshua, Solomon, Susannah, Jephtha*, etc.); *Ode for St. Cecilia's day*; *L'Allegro*; *Il Pensoroso*, etc.

ORCHESTRA: Twelve concerti grossi; suites for full orchestra (including *Water music, Fireworks music*); concertos for solo instruments and orchestra; overtures.

Organ concertos; sonatas for the violin, for viola, for oboe; suites for the harpsichord; preludes and fugues for organ; trios, etc.

About George Frederick Handel:

Chrysander, Friedrich. *G. F. Handel*; Dent, Edward J. *Handel*; Flower, Newman. *George Frederick Handel*; Rockstro, W. S. *The Life of George Frederick Handel*; Rolland, Romain. *Handel*; Schering, Arnold.

Geschichte der Oratoriums; Schoelcher, Victor. *The Life of Handel*; Streatfeild, R. A. *Handel*; Williams, C. E. Abdy. *Handel.*

Important recordings of music by George Frederick Handel:

SELECTIONS FROM OPERA: *Alcina*, "Orchestral suite," arranged by Göhler (VICTOR-Mengelberg). *Atlanta*, "Cara selve" (GRAMOPHONE); "Comme alla tortorella langue" (COLUMBIA). *Rinaldo*, "Lascia ch' io pianga" (GRAMOPHONE-Olszewska). *Serse*, "Largo" (VICTOR-Schipa), etc.

CHORAL: *The Messiah*, complete (COLUMBIA-Beecham). *Judas Maccabaeus*, "Mourn ye afflicted children" (COLUMBIA); "Arm, arm ye brave" (GRAMOPHONE); "Sion now her hand shall raise" (PARLAPHONE); "Fall'n is the foe" (COLUMBIA); "Sound an alarm" (GRAMOPHONE). *Samson,* "Overture" (DECCA); "Awake, the trumpet's lofty sound" (GRAMOPHONE); "Honour and arms" (COLUMBIA); "Death march" (GRAMOPHONE); "Let the bright Seraphim" (COLUMBIA); "Let their Celestial concerts unite" (GRAMOPHONE). *Joshua*, "O Had I Jubal's lyre" (VICTOR-Schumann). *Solomon,* "What though I trace" (GRAMOPHONE); "Nightingale's chorus" (COLUMBIA); "Entrance of the Queen of Sheba" (COLUMBIA-Beecham).

ORCHESTRA: Twelve concerti grossi (DECCA-Ansermet); *Concerto for harp and orchestra* (DECCA); *Concerto in D-major,* for orchestra and organ (COLUMBIA-Harty); *Concerto in B-flat major*, for harpsichord and orchestra (VICTOR); *Fireworks music* (COLUMBIA-Harty); Water music (VICTOR-Stokowski); *Origin of design*, arrangement of Handel airs (COLUMBIA-Beecham); *Suite*, arrangement of Handel airs (COLUMBIA-Harty).

HARPSICHORD: Six suites (HIS MASTER'S VOICE-Landowska).

Many recordings of sonatas, etc.

Johann Adolph Hasse *1699-1783*

NOTWITHSTANDING his German birth, Johann Adolph Hasse is considered one of the important composers of the Neapolitan school of opera.

He was born in Bergedorf, near Hamburg, on March 25, 1699. His father, organist and schoolmaster at Bergedorf, gave him his first musical instruction, which he soon supplemented with self-study. In 1717, Hasse left for Hamburg where he became acquainted with Ulrich König, poet to the King of Poland. Attracted to Hasse because of his beautiful voice and musical sensitivity, König introduced the musician to Reinhard Keiser, one of the foremost operatic composers of the period and the director of the Opera House.

Keiser engaged Hasse as tenor for the opera. For the next four years, Hasse devoted himself both to the study of music and to his duties as an operatic singer. Then, in 1722, König procured for him a more important post as singer at the Brunswick Theatre. It was here that, in 1723, Hasse's first dramatic work, *Antigonus,* was given performance.

Altho *Antigonus* was praised, Hasse recognized his technical shortcomings sufficiently to embark for Naples, in 1724, and become a pupil of Porpora. It was Hasse's great ambition to study under Alessandro Scarlatti, master of the Neapolitan opera. This Hasse felt to be an impossible dream. At a social gathering, he met Scarlatti who soon became so impressed with his personality that he decided to accept him as a pupil. Scarlatti's influence over Hasse was powerful; it was because of this influence that Hasse was henceforth to compose operas in the distinct style of the Neapolitan school.

In 1725, Hasse was commissioned by a banker to compose a *Serenade,* for two voices. When performed before a brilliant gathering, the work made so deep an impression that, literally overnight, Hasse became famous in Naples. As a direct result of this success, he was commissioned to compose an opera for the Theatre Royal. *Il Sesostrato* was performed in 1726, becoming an immediate favorite with Neapolitans.

In 1727, Hasse went to Venice where he was appointed professor at the Conservatory. During this period, the charm of his personality, the beautiful quality of his singing voice, the fame of his compositions and his great talent as a performer on the harpsichord all combined to make him one of the most attractive musicians in Italy. Here, he met the charming singer, Faustina Bordoni, who several years later became his wife.

August II of Dresden invited Hasse to his court in 1731 to become chapelmaster. Here, his opera, *Alessandro nell' Indie* (which included in its cast some of the greatest singers of the time, including Hasse's own wife) was a triumph. During the next few years,

Hasse toured with his wife thru the principal cities of Italy, then went to London (where he did not enjoy great success principally because Handel was the composer of the hour) and, finally, returned to Dresden in 1739.

When, in 1745, Frederick the Great triumphed at the battle of Kesseldorf and made a triumphant entry into Dresden, he sent one of his generals to Hasse and begged him to arrange a private performance of his opera, *Arminio*. The performance delighted the Emperor so greatly that, during the remaining days of his stay in Dresden, he insisted that Hasse officiate over all the musical activities. Upon his departure, he awarded Hasse a diamond ring and a thousand thalers.

Beginning with 1755, Hasse knew less happy days. For one thing, his voice had not only lost its beautiful quality but was disappearing completely, with the result that towards the end of his life he became completely dumb. Then, in 1760, during the siege of Dresden, he lost most of his property, including many of the manuscripts which at that time he was preparing for publication. Finally, in 1763, the Seven Years War compelled the court of Dresden to adopt strict economy, necessitating the dismissal of both Hasse and his wife.

Disappointed that fate should have taken so unkind a turn, Hasse and his wife left for Vienna where, fortunately, he was engaged by the court. Between 1763 and 1766 he composed six operas whose appeal was great. In 1770, he was once again in Italy to attend a performance of his last opera, *Ruggiero*. *Ruggiero* was performed simultaneously with a short serenade, *Ascanio in Alba*, composed by thirteen-year-old Wolfgang Amadeus Mozart. It is recorded that when Hasse heard *Ascanio*, he exclaimed: "This child will cause all of us to be forgotten!"

During the last decade of his life, Hasse lived in retirement in Venice, composing music principally for the church. He died there on December 16, 1783.

Charles Burney has described Hasse: "He was tall and strongly built. His face must have been handsome and finely chiselled. . . . He was very . . . kindly in manner. He was very talkative and full of commonsense; equally devoid of pride and prejudice; he spoke ill of no one. On the contrary, he did justice to the talents of several of his rivals. He had an infinite respect for Philipp Emanuel Bach, and spoke of Handel only with reverence."

Johann Adolph Hasse was an enormously prolific composer. He created more than a hundred operas (he set all of Metastasio's librettos to music, some of them three or four times), and a rich output of oratorios, cantatas and instrumental music. He was a composer who produced his music easily, spontaneously and abundantly. His works were so numerous that, as he himself said, he might very well fail to recognize one of them. As a matter of fact, he frequently confessed that he derived far more pleasure from creation than from preserving what he had written.

Charles Burney has referred to Hasse as the most learned and the most elegant composer of his time. From present-day standards it would seem that Burney's statement is overenthusiastic, and that the critical evaluation of Fétis is much more discerning: "In expression of tender sentiments," wrote Fétis, "his music had an irresistible charm, but in general he lacked effectiveness in energetic feeling, and his forms did not pos-

JOHANN ADOLPH HASSE

sess sufficient variety. His harmonies were less strong, less rich in modulation than the works of other German composers of his time; they appeared feeble later when Mozart and Haydn threw into their music all the splendor of their art. As for his church music, his style had clarity but one perceived too much affinity with his dramatic writing, and his melodies lacked both grandeur and masculinity."

Principal works by Johann Adolph Hasse:

OPERA: *Sesostrato*; *Artaserse*; *Alessandro nell'Indie*; *Didone abbandonata*; *Antigono*; *Semiramide*; *Il Re pastore*; *Zenobia*; *Ruggiero*, etc.

CHORAL: Oratorios; cantatas; misereres; psalms; Te Deums, etc.

INSTRUMENTAL: Concertos; selected orchestral pieces, etc.

About Johann Adolph Hasse:

Fétis, F. J. *Biographie Universelle des Musiciens*; Kamienski, Lucian. *Die Oratorien von Johann Adolph Hasse*; Menicke, Karl Heinrich. *Hasse und die Brüder Graun*.

Hans Leo Hassler *1564-1612*

HANS LEO HASSLER, descended from a long line of eminent organists, was born in Nuremberg on October 25, 1564. His father is believed to have been his only teacher in Nuremberg, but he was a competent master, for Hans Leo Hassler soon distinguished himself as an organist.

In 1584, Hassler left for Venice (it is the opinion of many musicologists that the community of Nuremberg financed the trip) to complete his studies under the contrapuntal master, Andrea Gabrieli —being the first German composer to travel across the Alps for higher musical education. Here he was introduced intimately to the music of Palestrina, whose influence upon him became marked. One year later, Hassler was summoned back to Germany to become private organist to Octavian Fugger at Augsburg. He held this position for fifteen years, at the same time continuing his studies in composition and counterpoint.

In 1601, he was called to Vienna by Emperor Rudolph II as court composer and organist, and so pleased the

HANS LEO HASSLER

Emperor with his talent that he was soon knighted. In 1604, he became organist at Ulm where he married and settled for a short period. Four years later, he was called by Prince Christian II of Saxony to Dresden.

In 1612, Hassler journeyed to Frankfort-on-the-Main, in the suite of Prince George I, for the purpose of attending the coronation of Emperor Matthias. Here, attacked by phthisis, he died on June 8, 1612.

A composer of distinguished contrapuntal music for the church, Hassler's importance in musical history rests in the fact that he gave to the German school a style of harmonic writing which persisted for a long time among German composers.

Karl Nef esteems Hassler's church works as "pearls of Protestant church music." "How splendidly the polyphonic arrangement of *Ein Feste Burg* depicts the proud defiance of the opening words, how well it delineates the 'cruel enemy,' and in what a beautifully flowing line it calmly draws to its conclusion! Not less beautiful . . . are the simple four-voice arrangements of the church melodies which Hassler published in 1608. This is golden treasure which the church choirs should ever cherish. Even he who stands far removed from a genuine musical appreciation can surmise what depth of spirit lay in this master who wrote the melody *O haupt voll Blut und Wunden*. . . . His masses are highly esteemed for their melodic wealth, and he achieved delightful results as a composer of madrigals and secular songs."

Both brothers of Hans Leo Hassler distinguished themselves as musicians. The older, Kaspar Hassler (1562-1618) was an organist at the Lorenz Kirche in Nuremberg, and distinguished himself by editing several important collections of sacred motets by Italian composers. The younger, Jacob Hassler (1569-1618?) was likewise a prominent organist, editor of a collection of church works, and the composer of several pieces for organ.

Principal works by Hans Leo Hassler:
CHORAL: Masses; canzonets; magnificats; madrigals; songs; motets; psalms, etc.

About Hans Leo Hassler:
Fétis, F. J. *Biographie Universelle des Musiciens*; Leichentritt, Hugo. *Meisterwerke Deutscher Tonkunst*; Nef, Karl. *An Outline of the History of Music.*

Important recordings of music by Hans Leo Hassler:
CHORAL: *Christ ist erstanden* (GRAMOPHONE); *Mein lieb'will mit mir kriegen* (PARLAPHONE); *O haupt voll blut und wunden* (VICTOR); *Wenn ich einmall soll scheiden* (KANTOREI).

Joseph Haydn *1732-1809*

"A genius of this kind never before existed and probably never will be surpassed. He is . . . the father of us all."—GEORGE THOMSON

"He alone has the secret of making me smile, and touching me to the bottom of my soul."—MOZART

FRANZ JOSEPH HAYDN was born on March 31, 1732, in Rohrau, a village in Austria near the border of Hungary. He came from peasant folk. His father, Mathias Haydn, was a wagoner and parish sexton; his mother, Elizabeth, was a woman of simple tastes and humble origin.

Music was an instinct with these people. During the evening Mathias would play the harp, and Elizabeth would sing, as the children sat at their feet and listened. Of these younger Haydns, Franz Joseph was most keenly affected by the music he heard, and most clearly showed aptitude for the art. When his father discovered him one day, sitting outside the schoolhouse and simulating playing the violin by scraping two sticks of wood against each other, he determined to give the boy as competent a musical training as he could. For this purpose, he enlisted the cooperation of his kinsman, Johann Mathias Frankh, a choir-master, who was to teach the boy of six the violin and harpsichord. Haydn later commented that he received "more blows than victuals" from his teacher, but Frankh was a competent teacher, and in two years the boy was able to enter the choir school of St. Stephen's church in Vienna.

At St. Stephen, Haydn was under the tutelage of Reutter, the chapel-master, who failed to discern any particular talent in the boy. Reutter not only neglected Haydn but frequently maltreated him. Joseph Haydn, however, found musical guidance elsewhere. With a few gulden, which he had succeeded in saving, he bought several treatises on counterpoint and thorough bass, which he virtually learned by rote. Thus he acquired training in musical theory.

When Haydn was seventeen years old, his voice broke. Being of very little use to the church, he was summarily dismissed from the choir—a pretext being one of Haydn's practical jokes on a fellow pupil. There followed bitter days for young Haydn. He was without a home, friends or money. The first night away from the church he was forced to sleep in the streets. An acquaintance from St. Stephen pitied him and gave him temporary lodging. Before long, Haydn succeeded in finding a few pupils and a few engagements as violinist. Thus he was able to subsist. His free moments still belonged to music study: each evening was spent in the study of the sonatas of Philipp Emanuel Bach.

In a short while, Haydn's fortunes improved. He had composed a mass which attracted some notice, bringing the composer several commissions. There followed a lucrative post as music teacher in the home of an influential family in Vienna. Then, Haydn became acquainted with Michael Porpora—a singer of great reputation—who at the time was in the employ of the Venetian ambassador at Vienna. Porpora engaged Haydn as his accompanist, and thru this engagement Haydn was given an opportunity to meet some of the outstanding musicians in Vienna at the time, including Gluck and von Dittersdorf.

Haydn composed his first string-quartet in 1755 on the encouragement of a musical amateur, von Fürnberg, who conducted chamber music performances at his home. This form of composition, which he inherited from the hands of Boccherini, so intrigued Haydn that for the next few months he created one string-quartet after another, establishing this form of composition as one of the major vehicles for musical expression. These quartets delighted von Fürnberg with their spontaneity and charm; in partial gratitude, he enthusiastically recommended the composer to Count Morzin as worthy of filling the position of chapel master on the Count's private estate in Bohemia. Haydn eagerly accepted the position, which included salary and board. Here, Haydn found the peace, quiet and leisure necessary for composition. His pen became increasingly fertile; and it was here that he composed his first symphony.

At this time, Haydn married Maria Anna Keller, daughter of a wig-maker. This was an ill-fated marriage. Surly, supremely selfish, extravagant, Maria Anna was hardly the suitable wife for Haydn. She was little interested in her husband's art, frequently used his manuscripts as curling papers. There were endless squabbles. The couple lived together several unhappy years, and then separated permanently. Haydn supplied her with a generous income until the end of his life.

Haydn's position at the private home of Count Morzin was soon succeeded by an even more important post, that of second chapel master to Prince Esterhazy of Eisenstadt. Five years later, he rose to the rank of first chapelmaster. For twenty-five years he held this post. Here Haydn was in charge of the daily concerts. The magnificent festivals which regularly took place at

JOSEPH HAYDN

the palace proved to be colorful backgrounds for Haydn's music making. Dressed in a costume which consisted of bright blue coat decorated with silver braid and buttons, white collar and cuffs as well as his powdered wig and shining pumps, Haydn personally directed the concerts. His pen likewise contributed a mountain of instrumental music for orchestra and chamber groups for these festivities.

At this time, Haydn became acquainted with Mozart. Much to his credit, Haydn recognized Mozart's genius. Until the end of Mozart's life, Haydn fought vigorously to bring the genius recognition. In 1785, Mozart composed a series of six quartets which he affectionately dedicated to Haydn. When Haydn heard these quartets, he told Mozart's father: "I must tell you before God, and as an honest man, that I think your son the greatest composer I ever heard of."

The death of Prince Esterhazy in 1790 enabled Haydn to accept an offer which had been extended him by Johann Peter Salomon, concert-manager and violinist —namely, to come to London, direct a few concerts, and supply six new symphonies. In 1791, Haydn visited London for the first time. From March until May he directed orchestral concerts featuring his new works. His success was brilliant. Haydn's music became the conversation of the hour, and he himself was the recipient of much honor. Oxford bestowed upon him the degree of doctorate of music; the Prince of Wales invited him as a guest to his home.

Haydn remained in London a year and a half before returning to Vienna. En route homewards, he stopped off at Bonn where he became acquainted for the first time with Ludwig van Beethoven (then still in his adolescence) who showed him a cantata he had recently composed. This work Haydn "greatly praised, warmly encouraging the composer to proceed with his studies." Later on, in Vienna, Beethoven became a pupil of Haydn, but their relationship was never successful: Beethoven was far too much the iconoclast, Haydn too much the classicist, for these two temperaments to harmonize.[1]

In 1794, Haydn was once again a visitor to London, six new symphonies in his bag. Once again he was the recipient of great honor. At this time, he became a friend of Mrs. Schroeter, to whom he became closely attached. "She was a very handsome woman, though over sixty," Haydn commented, "and, had I been free, I should certainly have married her." Three piano trios were dedicated by the composer to Mrs. Schroeter.

Haydn was likewise greeted with honor in his own country. Upon his return to Vienna from London, he found himself recognized as the greatest Austrian composer of his time. Concerts of his music were planned in his honor in Vienna; a bust of him was erected in his native city. In 1797, on the occasion of the birthday of Emperor Franz II, Haydn's national anthem (which was originally the second movement of his famous *Kaiser Quartet*) was performed and sung in every principal theatre in Austria. One year later saw the first performance of one of Haydn's greatest works, *The Creation,* modeled after Milton's *Paradise Lost.* The success of *The Creation* was instantaneous. Choral societies were founded in Austria expressly to give it performance. *The Creation* was followed by Haydn's last great work, also for chorus, *The Seasons.*

Haydn's old age was quiet and dignified, although touched with a gentle melancholy brought on by illness. In 1805, on Haydn's birthday, Mozart's fourteen-year-old son came to the home of the master to bring him a cantata he had composed especially for his father's close friend. In March of 1808, Haydn heard a performance of his work for the last time, *The Creation,* directed by Salieri. From that time on he was confined to his home thru weakness and ill-health.

Joseph Haydn died in Vienna on May 31, 1809. In his will he forgot no one— old friends, acquaintances, people who had done him favors in his youth and those who had been kind to him in his old age. "I commend my soul to my all-merciful Creator," he concluded his will reverently. Haydn was buried in an obscure churchyard near his home in Vienna. Eleven years later, however— at the request of one of the Esterhazys— his body was brought to the parish church of Eisenstadt, where it rests today.

Haydn was of middle height, with very short legs. His complexion was dark, marked by smallpox, his nose aquiline, the expression of his eyes soft and generous. He always wore a wig, with side-curls and queue. He considered himself a very ugly man, and was consistently bewildered that so many striking women should have been attracted to him.

His generosity, warm heart and simplicity have frequently been subject for comment. "Anybody can see by the look of me," he once said of himself—an accurate stroke of self-appraisal, "that I am a good-natured sort of a fellow." He was fervently religious. Habitually, he began and ended his manuscripts with the words: "In nomine Domini" and "Laus Deo"; and when he was composing *The Creation* he fell on his knees each day and prayed to God to give him strength to bring the work to successful completion. By nature he was thrifty, hard-working, extremely methodical. He possessed a sunny sense of humor, and a lovable disposition. He was not a particularly educated man; he read very little, and was only superficially ac-

[1] See sketch on Beethoven.

quainted with any subject out of the realm of music.

When he composed, he preferred to wear his best clothing, his diamond ring and his most ornate pendants. He worked industriously and systematically. He sketched his works on the piano, then, a few hours afterwards, developed them on paper. He worked regularly each day, never waiting for inspiration or inclination. He was well aware of his importance and greatness. "I know," he once said, "that God has bestowed a talent upon me, and I thank him for it. I think I have done my duty and have been of use in my generation and by my works. Let others do the same."

Haydn's importance in the history of music has been so great that it is difficult to summarize his many achievements in a few paragraphs. He inherited the sonata form from Philipp Emanuel Bach and not only solidified it but infused into it such vital genius that it became one of the most pliant forms of musical expression. He definitely established the form of the symphony, preparing the way for Mozart and Beethoven. He was the father of the string quartet; Mozart frequently confessed that it was from Haydn that he learned how to compose for four stringed instruments. He enriched the harmonic language of his day, increased the resources of orchestration. He was one of the pioneers in the creation of program music. It is, therefore, with considerable justification that he is frequently termed the "father of instrumental music."

His most successful medium for artistic expression was in the symphony and the string quartet. "It is not often," wrote Otto Jahn, "that a composer hits so exactly upon the form suited to his conceptions; the quartet was Haydn's natural mode of expressing his feelings." And, in commenting upon Haydn's symphonies, C. Hubert Parry wrote: "His predecessors had always written rather carelessly and hastily for the band, and hardly ever tried to get refined and original effects from the use of their instruments, but he naturally applied his mind more earnestly to the matter in hand and found out new ways of contrasting and combining the tones of different members of his orchestra, and getting a fuller and richer effect out of the mass of them when they were playing. In the actual style of music, too, he made great advances; in his hands, symphonies became by degrees more vigorous and, at the same time, more really musical."

J. Cuthbert Hadden neatly summed up Haydn's style of composition when he wrote: "To say that a composition is 'Haydnish' is to express in one word what is well understood by all intelligent amateurs. Haydn's music is like his character—clear, straightforward, fresh and winning, without the slightest trace of affectation or morbidity. Its perfect transparency, its firmness of design, its fluency of instrumental language, the beauty and inexhaustible wealth of its melody, its studied moderation, its child-like cheerfulness—these are some of the qualities which mark the style of this most genial of all composers."

A distinguishing trait of Haydn's works was his frequent use of Croatian folk music for his melodic material. Wrote W. H. Hadow: "The Croatian melodies are bright, sensitive, piquant, but they seldom rise to any high level of dignity or earnestness. They belong to a temper which is marked rather by feeling and imagination than by any sustained breadth of thought, and hence, while they enrich their own field of art with great beauty, there are certain frontiers which they rarely cross, and from which, if crossed, they soon return." Even many of Haydn's original melodies are characterized by typical rhythmic and melodic qualities to be found in the Croatian folk songs. However, as Franz Bellinger has added, "Haydn's speech, like that of every genius, was not only that of his race, but of the world." To these Croatian characteristics, Haydn added his high inspiration and sensitivity, and produced a type of melody which, for the most part, is unmistakably his.

Principal works by Joseph Haydn:

ORCHESTRA: More than 125 symphonies; divertimenti; German dances; nocturnes; serenades; cassations; concertos for violoncello and orchestra; *Concerto for harpsichord and orchestra*; symphonies concertantes, etc.

OPERA: *Le Pescatrici*; *La Vera Costanza*; *La Fedeltà premiata*; *Orlando Paladino, etc.*

CHORAL: *Seven words of the Saviour on the cross*; *Stabat Mater*; cantatas; masses; *The Creation*; *The Seasons, etc.*

CHAMBER MUSIC: More than eighty string quartets; sextet; quintets; Thirty-eight piano trios; Thirty trios for strings; Fifteen trios for combinations of wind and strings; sonatas for violin and piano.

Sonatas for the piano, songs, etc.

About Joseph Haydn:

Brenet, Michel. *Haydn*; Hadden, J. Cuthbert. *Haydn*; Hadow, W. H. *Oxford History of Music* (vol. 5); Mason, Daniel Gregory. *Beethoven and his Forerunners*; Parry, C. Hubert. *Studies of Great Composers*; Pohl, Carl Ferdinand. *Haydn*; Townsend, Pauline D. *Joseph Haydn.*

Important recordings of music by Joseph Haydn:

CHORAL: *The Creation,* "Rolling of foaming billows" (VICTOR); "With verdure clad" (GRAMOPHONE); "Awake the harp" (GRAMOPHONE); "The heavens are telling" (COLUMBIA); "Achieved is the glorious work" (GRAMOPHONE). *The Seasons,* "Komm, holder Lenz" (GRAMOPHONE); "Schon eilt froh der Ackersmann" (GRAMOPHONE-Schorr).

ORCHESTRA: *German dances* (TELEFUNKEN-Kleiber); *Farewell symphony* (COLUMBIA-Wood); *Symphony in G-major,* no. 13 (VICTOR-Krauss); *Oxford symphony* (VICTOR); *Surprise symphony* (VICTOR-Koussevitzky); *Military symphony* (COLUMBIA); *Clock symphony* (VICTOR-Toscanini); *Drum roll symphony* (COLUMBIA); *London symphony* (VICTOR-Barbirolli), etc.; *Concerto for violoncello and orchestra,* in D-major (COLUMBIA-Feuermann).

CHAMBER MUSIC: Four volumes of the principal string quartets (HIS MASTERS VOICE-Pro Arte); *Trio in G-major* (VICTOR).

Stephen Heller *1813-1888*

STEPHEN HELLER was born as Jacob Heller in Pesth, Hungary, on May 15, 1813. In his twelfth year, his parents made him a Catholic to save him from the anti-Semitic persecutions that, at the time, were taking place in Hungary. At the same time, his birthname was changed to Stephen.

His father, a clerk in a cloth factory, had visions of a great career as virtuoso for Stephen. When Stephen was still a child, he studied the piano under Franz Brauer, and harmony under Cibulka. He made sufficient progress to make a public appearance in Pesth together with his teacher, Franz Brauer, in a two-piano concerto by Dussek.

His encouraging performance urged his parents to send him to Vienna to continue the study of the piano under the distinguished Karl Czerny. He came to Vienna in 1826. During this period he met Beethoven and Schubert, and gave a concert which promised much for his future. In 1828, his studies were prematurely interrupted, when his father —impatient to see his son embark upon a glorious career—called him back home for the purpose of beginning an extended concert tour. For three years, the Hellers toured Hungary (where Chopin heard him play) and Germany. Stephen's concerts were only moderately successful.

The strain of travel and concertizing, however, finally proved too great for the boy. He suffered a nervous breakdown. The Hellers were compelled to interrupt their tour at Augsburg, where they settled. Here, Stephen Heller continued his piano studies under Chelard. At the same time, he essayed composition—pieces for the piano—which he sent to Robert Schumann for criticism. Schumann found that the pieces contained so great a talent that he wrote Heller an enthusiastic letter and published a favorable criticism in the *Neue Zeitschrift für Musik*. This was the beginning of a friendship between the

STEPHEN HELLER

two musicians which grew and developed with the passing of years thru the medium of a prolific exchange of correspondence; the two musicians, however, never met.

In 1838, Heller went to Paris, which then remained his home for the rest of his life. For a while he undertook concert work, and was not only an excellent virtuoso but equally remarkable at improvisation. Charles Hallé, the conductor of the Manchester Symphony Orchestra, wrote as follows, after hearing Heller's improvisations: "The change that came over him and his execution at such moments was marvelous. . . . Difficulties seemed to vanish. . . . Whether he improvised quite freely or on subjects given to him, he was equally fascinating, dominating his listeners and pouring out a wealth of ideas of which his published works gave no idea."

Notwithstanding Heller's pianistic gifts, he was never successful on the concert stage. For one thing, he did not possess a personality sufficiently striking to arouse curiosity and interest in his audiences; then, he was painfully self-conscious, persistently fleeing from public attention. As a result, his public appearances became less and less frequent. During his life, he pursued a quiet and unobtrusive existence, earning his living by teaching the piano, and devoting his free hours to composition.

In 1873, Heller developed eye trouble which became so serious during the next ten years that he was forced to consult specialists. For eighteen months he underwent incessant treatment without showing any improvement. His eyesight, finally, became so bad that he could neither read nor write. Composition was now out of the question, teaching as well. His income, therefore, came to an abrupt end. For a while, intense poverty faced him. However, he had a true friend in Charles Hallé, who now came to his rescue. Hallé made an appeal to music lovers thruout Great Britain and collected enough money to buy Heller an annuity that promised the composer comfort until the end of his days.

Stephen Heller died in Paris on January 14, 1888, in virtual obscurity. His piano works were known and admired only by a handful of musicians.

Much of the neglect which Heller suffered was the direct result of his own making. Obscurity inevitably follows a composer who fights public attention and flees from recognition as Heller consistently did. As a result, many composers, far less gifted than he, enjoyed a greater prominence. Moreover, Heller was known to have been an idler, a procrastinator where work was concerned. He was altogether incapable of rigorous application to the task of the composition. His music suffered, consequently. He was hopelessly addicted to time consuming daydreaming, and he was well aware of this great fault. In 1844, he wrote to Robert Schumann: "What are my plans? I have none. . . . I am a consummate dreamer and I forget for months, nay for years, what I live for, nay whether I live at all. . . . I puff away my whole life in this cursed dreaming and forget reality in mere poetic day-dreams."

Frederick Niecks has etched a verbal portrait of Stephen Heller. "When I saw Heller, he was living at no. 7 Cité Malesherbes, on the third story. . . . The sitting room into which I was ushered was decidedly small and was also very modest as to furniture. . . . The quiet and unpretentious atmosphere of the room, I found afterwards to be in perfect harmony with the character of the man who had his home here. . . . Heller made his appearance in a loose red Garibaldi blouse. All his being and doing was suffused with calm. . . . Another of his fundamental characteristics was simplicity, a third, kindliness. . . . Heller was not a man of strong resolves and steel muscles, not of fierce deeds and tenacious pursuits. Soft is the only epithet that fits his constitution. For the struggle for existence he had an unconquerable aversion. He turned away with disgust from what he likened to the fighting of dogs for any bones that many turn up. . . . Passivity was his element."

Heller's piano works have been relegated to comparative obscurity, rarely making an appearance on a modern concert program. However, it is the opinion of Isidor Philipp that Heller does not deserve this frigid neglect. Discussing

Heller's works, Philipp wrote: "Stephen Heller derives from Schumann, Mendelssohn and Chopin in the sense that he has certain affinities with all three of these great masters. But he developed a style peculiar to himself. The *Promenades d'un solitaire,* the *Nuits blanches,* his preludes and études, mark an epoch in the history of piano music. These pieces are written in a form that was new, that was personal to Heller. His talent may have been comparatively small, but it was pure and bore a stamp of its own. His music was not of large proportions, it did not plumb great depths; but it was essentially the music of good breeding, and as such, indeed, it belongs to a period that is no longer ours. Still, the best of it has lost nothing of its pristine bloom. In some of his works, Heller is a classicist, in others he is a romanticist; but he never fails to be original. His music occupies a distinctive and important place in the literature for the piano. It is music replete with imagination, charm and sincerity."

Principal works by Stephen Heller:

An entire library of piano music, including études, sonatas, Nocturnes, serenades, album-leaves, etc.

About Stephen Heller:

Marliave, Joseph. *Études Musicales;* Schütz, Rudolf. *Stephen Heller.*
Etude 26:691 November 1908; *Monthly Musical Record* 48:25 February 1918; *Musical Quarterly* 21:432 October 1935.

Sir George Henschel *1850-1934*
(See *Composers Of Today*)

Victor Herbert *1859-1924*

VICTOR HERBERT, prince of American operetta composers, was born in Dublin, on February 1, 1859. His grandfather was Samuel Lover—he of the phenomenal versatility: Lover was the author of such popular Irish novels as *Handy Andy,* and also painter, singer, actor, composer, poet and librettist.

When Victor Herbert was three years old, his father, an attorney, died in Paris. The boy was taken under the wing of his eminent grandfather, who was the first to introduce him to music. Victor's mother, a pianist, then gave

him lessons on the piano, and he made such progress that grandfather Lover prophesied a great musical career for the boy.

While Victor Herbert was still a boy, his mother married a German physician, settling in Stuttgart. Here, Victor was entered in the Gymnasium, where the studies were so numerous and exacting that he could devote but little time to music. However, he succeeded in finding spare moments, particularly at night, in which to play the flute and take some lessons on the violoncello. Before long, he revealed such unmistakable talent for the violoncello that his mother definitely decided to place him under intensive musical training. For this purpose, a distinguished violoncellist, Professor Cossman in Baden-Baden, was engaged as Victor Herbert's teacher. "I had exceptional advantages," Herbert wrote in later years, "advantages, it seems to me, not offered to students nowadays. My lessons were no fifteen minute affairs, and then away at something else. I was under the constant eye of my master, and I could not help making rapid progress."

For one year and a quarter, Herbert studied in this fashion under Professor Cossman. He then emerged a professional musician. For a while, he played the violoncello in the court orchestra at Stuttgart. Then he went on a concert tour, giving solo performances, and playing in important orchestras in Leipzig, Munich and Berlin. This concert tour convinced Herbert that he had still much to learn in his art. He returned to Stuttgart to continue his studies. Chief chapel master Seyfrytz gave him instruction in composition. It was under Seyfrytz's influence that Herbert first turned to composition—producing first a suite and then the *Concerto for violoncello and orchestra,* which he himself introduced at the concerts of the Royal Orchestra in Stuttgart.

During the years that followed, Herbert earned his living by playing in leading European symphony orchestras. He performed under the batons of such world famous musical figures as Liszt, Brahms, Anton Rubinstein, Saint-Saëns, Delibes and Eduard Strauss, acquiring thereby rigorous musical training.

In 1886, Walter Damrosch—who had inherited the baton of the Metropolitan Opera House from his recently deceased father—went to Europe to find new voices for the next season's opera. He heard Theresa Foerster sing, and was so delighted with her performance that he made an effort to engage her. Theresa Foerster, however, explained that she could not consider the contract. She was engaged to be married to a young violoncellist, Victor Herbert by name, from whom she would not consider separation. Finally, Damrosch decided to engage him as a violoncellist in the Metropolitan Opera House orchestra. In this way, Victor Herbert was brought to America.

It was not long before he became a prominent figure in America's musical life. For a few years, he played in the orchestra of the Metropolitan Opera House, and in symphony concerts under the leadership of Theodore Thomas and Anton Seidl. In 1892, he composed his first operetta, *Prince Ananias,* which, though it was still an abortive effort, was not without charm. Two years later, Herbert became bandmaster of the Twenty-second Regiment Band. At the same time he introduced his second *Concerto for violoncello and orchestra* with the Philharmonic Symphony Orchestra. In 1895, he composed another operetta, *The Wizard of the mill.* Three years later found him principal conductor of the Pittsburgh Symphony Orchestra. His creative energy, simultaneously, was flowing thru two channels— that of serious music (a symphony and a symphonic-poem) and operetta (*The Fortune teller*).

In 1903, Victor Herbert recognized where his greatest power as a musician rested. He resigned from his post as conductor in Pittsburgh, came to New York and devoted himself entirely to composition. *Babes in Toyland* was composed in 1903, followed by such triumphs as *Naughty Marietta, Mlle. Modiste* and *Eileen.* At the same time he was equally industrious in creating serious music. In 1911, his opera *Natoma* was given a première in Philadelphia, and received with great enthusiasm; three years later,

VICTOR HERBERT

the Metropolitan Opera House presented a second opera by Herbert, *Madeleine.*

But it was his lighter music that brought him world prestige. Between the years of 1904 and 1917, Herbert produced no less than thirty operettas, selections from which were heard from one coast of America to another, succeeding in making him one of the best loved composers in the country. With the advent of radio, Herbert's music literally crowded the air; whenever an orchestra was performing, it inevitably included selections from the music of Victor Herbert. The arrival of the talking picture likewise found Victor Herbert a favorite composer. He was one of the first composers brought to Hollywood to prepare an original score for the screen (*The Fall of the Nation*). Subsequently, several of his operettas became successful cinemas, including *Babes in Toyland* and *Naughty Marietta.*

The style of light music suited Herbert gracefully. He could compose with a pen that had variety, tunefulness and charm. As Herbert F. Peyser summarized: "The light opera manner in its truest form is an integral part of Herbert's musical nature. His characteristic utterance is in its way as distinctive, as individual, as free as that of every great composer of comic opera from Strauss to Arthur Sullivan. His melodic flow is facile, superabundant and generally original. To be sure, his excessive productivity has not suffered him to maintain anything like an even level of excellence. He has occasionally lapsed into banality and has not infrequently stooped to conquer. . . . On the other hand, his ability to surpass all his previous efforts in point of sheer melodic wealth, delicacy and refinement of feeling and amazing fineness of workmanship . . . is little short of marvelous."

Victor Herbert died suddenly of heart failure in New York City on May 27, 1924. It was said that overindulgence in food and drink curtailed his life. He died while in the midst of preparing a new musical score for Florenz Ziegfeld. He was at the height of his popularity.

Victor Herbert was a victim of soft living and luxury. He was a connoisseur of foods, ate prodigiously, enjoyed his meals with the delight of a true gourmet. He was frequently found at the Luchow restaurant in New York, where his favorite dish was boiled beef with horse-radish sauce and wine kraut. He was likewise a great drinker. He frequently asserted that to drink water was the height of vulgarity. He drank only fine wines and an enormous quantity of beer. Whenever he played at one theatre for any length of time he always installed an icebox in his dressing room for drinks.

He always wore the best clothing purchasable, had a magnificent car, and lived ornately. He was sublimely careless about money.

He was a placid and good natured person, but when roused gave vent to a flow of the most lurid vocabulary. He delighted in Rabelaisian humor, and had an inexhaustible supply of favorite stories. He was a man of great vanity, eager to be the object of obsequious adulation; nothing delighted him more than to have musicians bow to him, when he passed, in reverent honor. His generosity was famous. His greatest interest, besides music, was the fight of his native country, Ireland, for its independence, which, when achieved, reacted upon him as a personal victory.

In his composition, he worked industriously with very little vacation. He could work with lightning speed. Frequently, he was occupied with two scores at one time. He was never at a loss for melodic ideas. His greatest problem was to curb his almost irrepressible spontaneity.

He was proudest of his serious works, particularly of his opera *Natoma*. But he knew too well that his true self was in his operettas, with which he had conquered two continents.

"His musical ancestor," wrote Deems Taylor shortly after Herbert's death, "was Mozart, and the family of which he was so brilliant a younger son numbered Offenbach, Delibes, Bizet, the Strausses and Arthur Sullivan among its elders. What he had was what they all had, the gift of song. His music bubbled and sparkled and charmed, and he brought the precious gift of gaiety to an art that often suffers from pretentiousness and self-consciousness of its practitioners.

"Herbert was a far more important figure in American music than he has ever had the credit for being. His chosen field was the operetta, and though his achievements in this field have made him world famous, the fact that his medium was primarily a form of entertainment caused self-styled serious musicians to regard him with a certain measure of condescension. He felt this keenly. He was a talented composer and a serious one and he knew it. . . . They compare him with Sullivan, but I think he was a far more gifted man than Sullivan. Do not forget that Sullivan had Gilbert. Herbert never had a librettist who was worthy of him. . . . His tunes were neither glorified rhythmic patterns nor harmonic paraphrases. They were pure song, capable of being sung without accompaniment if need be, as pure in outline as the melodies of Schubert or Mozart."

Principal works by Victor Herbert:

OPERA: *Natoma; Madeleine; Wizard of the mill; Babes in Toyland; Naughty Marietta; Mlle. Modiste; Eileen; Algeria*, etc.

CHORAL: *The Captive.*

ORCHESTRA: *Symphony;* Two concertos for violoncello and orchestra; *Serenade* (for strings); *Suite romantique; Hero and Leander*, etc.

About Victor Herbert:

Goldberg, Isaac. *Tin-Pan Alley*; Kaye, Joseph. *Victor Herbert*. *Metronome* 37:63 September 1921; *Musical America* October 11, 1913.

Important recordings of music by Victor Herbert:

SELECTIONS FROM OPERA: Two albums of favorite excerpts from Victor Herbert's most famous operas, arranged by Shilkret (VICTOR-Shilkret).

Ferdinand Hérold *1791-1833*

LOUIS JOSEPH FERDINAND HÉROLD was born in Paris on January 28, 1791. His father, François Joseph Hérold, was a well-known musician, a pupil in Hamburg of Philipp Emanuel Bach, and a composer of many works for piano and chamber groups. Young Ferdinand, therefore, came under the influence of music at an early age. His adaptability for music must have heartened his father; at the age of six he could not only play the piano well but he was also the composer of several small pieces.

When he was ten years old, he was entered as a pupil at the Institution Hix. "His progress was more rapid than that of other pupils," Fétis, his instructor at the Institution, has recorded. "Nature had made him a musician."

In 1802, Hérold's father died. His mother, who was in financial difficulties, vacillated a long time between permitting her son to continue his studies and procuring for him a position in a government office which would greatly improve her circumstances. Finally, she decided to yield to wiser judgment than her own. She took some of Hérold's original compositions to Grétry, and asked him for a verdict. Grétry studied the works, smiled at some of their youthful errors, but finally announced: "Rest assured, madam. Your son will be a distinguished musician!"

This definitely decided Hérold's mother that her son should receive intensive musical training. When Hérold completed his brilliant career at the Institution Hix, he was placed in the Paris Conservatory where he was once again a brilliant student. In 1812, he was awarded the Prix de Rome for his cantata *Mlle. de la Vallière*.

In Italy, Hérold definitely decided that his lifework would be devoted to the theatre. He therefore felt that it would be wisest to go to Naples and come into closer contact with Italian opera. In Naples, he was fortunate in gaining the interest of Queen Caroline who appointed him court pianist. As a result of royal favor, Hérold's first opera—*La Jeunesse de Henri V*—was given a successful performance in Naples.

On his return to Paris, Hérold turned wholeheartedly to the composition of opera. At this time, he gained the friendship of Boieldieu, composer of *opéra-comique*, who opened for Hérold many opportunities by asking him to collaborate with him on an *opéra-comique*, *Charles de France*. As a result of his increased prestige brought on by this collaboration, Hérold was enabled to produce several operas between 1817 and 1820—principally *La Clochette*, *Le Premier venu*, *L'Amour platonique* and *L'Auteur mort et vivant*—in which his fresh approach, his novel instrumentation and his dramatic instinct won for him a wide and responsive audience. With the performance of *Le Muletier*, in 1823, Hérold's reputation as a prominent operatic composer was established.

During the succeeding years, Hérold served as accompanist in the Théâtre des Italiens (1820-1827), and as choirmaster at the Académie de Musique. Temporarily, his fecundity in writing operas came to a halt. He devoted his creative talent, instead, towards the production of works for the piano and ballet.

In 1831, Hérold produced the first of two operas that have immortalized his name, *Zampa*. *Zampa* failed to make the appeal to its first audiences that previous operas had succeeded in doing. Many critics—including Berlioz—found much to criticize severely in the work. Posterity, however, has learned to regard this as one of the most mature operas that Hérold has produced. Here, as B. Jouvin wrote in his biography, "the brain, the heart and the hand of the artist are fraternally combined to produce a complete and perfectly unified work. The melody of the composer,

FERDINAND HÉROLD

overflowing in abundance, is at turns passionate and buoyant. . . . The harmony, endowed with force and with elegance, adopts, under a skilled hand, all the undulations of sonority. . . . But all has not been said when one has praised the melody and the harmony. There is the Song, beautifully attired; the musician takes it by the hand and places it in a setting of instrumentation which has languor, grace, buoyancy and color."

"*Zampa* has been called a French *Don Giovanni*," remarks R. A. Streatfeild, "but the music owes far more to Weber than to Mozart, while the fantastic and absurd incidents of the plot have little of the supernatural terror of Mozart's operas. . . . It would be in vain to look in Hérold's score for an echo of the passion and variety of Mozart, but much of the music of *Zampa* is picturesque and effective. Hérold's tunes sound very conventional after Weber, but there is a good deal of skill in the way they are presented. His orchestration is of course closely modeled on that of his German prototype, and if it is impossible to say much for his originality, we can at any rate admire his taste in choosing a model."

Zampa was followed, in 1832, by *Le Pré aux clercs* (built upon a heroic national poem), which Frenchmen have always esteemed on a much higher plane

than its predecessors, and which was acclaimed from the very first performance.

This was Hérold's swan song. A month later he became a victim to a chest disease. He died at his home in Les Ternes on January 19, 1833. His dying words were: "I go too soon! I have only just begun to learn how to write for the theatre." His last opera, *Ludovic,* was lying unfinished upon his desk; *Ludovic* was brought to completion by Jacques Halévy.

"Hérold was the most important musician in the first half of the nineteenth century," in the opinion of Arthur Pougin, "and his name marks an important epoch in the history of national art. . . . With him, dramatic music freed itself from the fetters which had formerly bound it; it soared fully and freely into the air, definitely and permanently repudiating former formulas."

Principal works by Ferdinand Hérold:

OPERA: *La Clochette*; *Le Premier venu*; *Les Troquers*; *L'Amour platonique*; *Le Lapin blanc*; *L'Illusion*; *Zampa*; *Le Pré aux clercs*; *Ludovic* (completed by Jacques Halévy).

BALLET: *Astolphe et Joconde*; *La Somnambule*; *Lydie*; *La Belle au bois dormant*; *La Fille mal gardée.*

ORCHESTRA: Two symphonies.

CHAMBER MUSIC: Three string quartets.

About Ferdinand Hérold:

Jouvin, B. *Hérold: Sa Vie et ses Oeuvres*; Pougin, Arthur. *Hérold.*

Principal recordings of music by Ferdinand Hérold:

SELECTIONS FROM OPERA: *Le Pré aux clercs,* "Air de Nicette" (POLYDOR); "Ce soir, j'arrive donc" (PATHE); "Jours de mon enfance" (COLUMBIA); "Oui, Marguerite" (GRAMOPHONE). *Zampa,* "Ouverture" (GRAMOPHONE-Krauss).

Johann Adam Hiller *1728-1804*

JOHANN ADAM HILLER (whose original name was Hüller)—father of the *German Singspiel*—was born at Wendisch-Ossig, near Görlitz, Prussia, on December 25, 1728. His father, a parish clerk, died when Johann was barely six years old.

His mother sent him to the Gymnasium at Görlitz for his education. He remained here until his twelfth year, acquiring the elements of violin and harpsichord playing. At the same time, he sang in the Görlitz choir.

His unusual musical intelligence attracted the attention of George Roth, a teacher at the Gymnasium, who temporarily adopted Hiller and gave him a thorough musical education. Hiller, however, had no intention of becoming a professional musician. In 1754, he became secretary to a nobleman in Silesia, resigning the post only because he would not tolerate the immorality of his employer. Shortly afterwards, he was employed in Wurzen.

The death of his employer decided Hiller to continue his music study more assiduously. He went to Dresden, earned his living by singing in the choir and playing the violoncello, and studied harmony and the harpsichord under Homilius, organist of the Notre Dame Church. At this time, Hiller had the opportunity to listen to the music at the court. He heard the operas of Hasse and Graun which influenced him profoundly. Hasse's operas, as a matter of fact, appealed so strongly to him that he copied by hand the full orchestral parts of his operas.

In 1751, Hiller went to the Leipzig University to pursue legal study. Music was not neglected, Hiller continuing its study under Gellert and Jöcher. At the same time, he began composition, but only because he realized that his late start with the violin and harpsichord would never permit him to undertake a virtuoso career. He composed some twelve symphonies, several cantatas and a few German airs.

In 1754, Hiller left the Leipzig University, and became a teacher of Count Brühl. During the years that Hiller held this post, he continued his composition, publishing a volume of melodies on religious poems by Gellert and a suite of German songs.

At this period, Hiller was afflicted by several sicknesses—some real, others imaginary—which m a d e consecutive work difficult. He resigned his teaching position with Count Brühl (receiving a pension of one hundred Saxon écus). From this time on he became an im-

JOHANN ADAM HILLER

portant musical force in Leipzig. In 1762, he published a volume of harpsichord sonatas. Five years later, he founded a school of singing, where he conducted oratorios by Handel, Graun, etc. In 1776, he established the Concert Spirituel, a series of orchestral concerts which he himself conducted, for which he composed special symphonies and songs with orchestral accompaniment. In 1781, these concerts moved to the new Gewandhaus hall in Leipzig. Thus one of the greatest symphony orchestras in musical history, the Leipzig Gewandhaus Orchestra, began its career under Hiller's direction.

Coincident with these activities, Hiller began the composition of his famous *Singspiel*. Always gifted at producing the song form—which he brought to new development—Hiller turned his talents to the French operetta. By subjecting it to German influences, he evolved the *Singspiel* which was to reach a magnificent culmination with Mozart, and from that point to evolve into the future German opera. Some of Hiller's *Singspiel* possessed so much charm and freshness (*Lottchen am Hofe, Die Jagd* and *Der Teufel ist los*, for example) that they were performed for many years after his death. Burney wrote about *Der Teufel:* "The music was so natural and so agreeable that the favorite airs . . . were sung by all classes of the people, and some of them in the streets."

In 1785, Hiller resigned from his conductorial position at the Gewandhaus, and four years later was appointed organist and musical director of the St. Thomas Schule. He held this position until his death.

Johann Adam Hiller died in Leipzig on June 16, 1804.

While Hiller's creative works no longer hold an important position in the world of music (with the exception of a few scattered vocal works) he was an important influence in the development of the song as an art form and in the early history of German opera. Hiller, wrote Robert Haven Schauffler, "was one of the useful band of pioneers who were groping towards the truth that music can never be definite and concrete like words or pictures. Dimly, he saw that its chief glory is its indefinite, abstract, universal quality, and that whatever tends to constrict that glory to the concrete function of illustrator, sins against the art."

Principal works by Johann Adam Hiller:

SINGSPIEL: *Der Teufel ist los*; *Lottchen am Hofe*; *Die Jagd*; *Der Dorfbarbier*; *Die Muse*; *Der Krieg*; *Der neue gutsherr*, etc.

CHORAL: Passions; cantata; psalm; odes; part-songs; *Choralbuch*.

ORCHESTRA: Symphonies; partitas; songs with orchestral accompaniment.

About Johann Adam Hiller:

Einstein, Alfred. *Lebensläufe Deutscher Musiker*; Fétis, F. J. *Biographie Universelle des Musiciens*.
Allgemeine Musikgesellschaft in Zürich No. 36.

E. T. A. Hoffmann *1776-1822*

THERE is probably no composer in music history with so picaresque a life-story as E. T. A. Hoffmann, who has been immortalized in Jacques Offenbach's famous opera, *Tales of Hoffmann*.

Ernst Theodor Amadeus (originally Wilhelm) Hoffmann—composer, painter, poet, romancer, singer, impresario, critic, teacher, conductor, scientist—was born in Königsberg on January 24, 1776. As a youth, he studied both the sciences and the arts. Possessing an amazing intellect, he learned everything taught him with facility. His first music master was the organist Pobielsky, from whom he acquired sound training in the playing of the piano. At the same time, he learned to draw, paint, write poetry, and converse in several languages. For all of these widely diversified studies he showed equal aptitude.

Completing some of these studies, he decided to specialize by entering the University of Königsberg and beginning the study of law. Then, suddenly and inexplicably, he brushed aside his life of study and intellectual training and mysteriously gave himself up completely to debauchery and dissipation. As he himself wrote, his parents had been so intent upon giving him a complete education in the sciences and the arts that they neglected his moral training, with the result that he was always deficient in the latter. During this period, he earned his living by giving music lessons; for diversion, he painted grandiose subjects on enormous canvases.

Poverty, finally, drove him back into the arms of his family when, in 1796, he resumed his legal study in Glogau. In 1799, he was given a position as referendary of the court of justice in Berlin; shortly after this, he became assessor of the Tribunal in Posen. He was headed for a brilliant legal career. But his strange opinions on a variety of subjects, his lack of tact in relationship with superiors, and especially his delight in drawing absurd caricatures of those in power, made his circle of enemies increasingly large. At one festive ball, he arranged to have one of his friends, in disguise, distribute his strange caricatures of the most famous guests. As a result, thru the influence of his antagonists, he was removed from Posen to Plozk. Ennui with the routined work demanded by this post compelled him to seek diversion in music study. In 1801, one of his works—music to Goethe's *Scherz, List und Rache*—was performed in Posen.

In 1804, by permission of the officials, Hoffmann's government post was transferred from Plozk to Warsaw. Here, he married a charming Polish lady, and for the first time attempted to live a disciplined and reasonable existence. He

E. T. A. HOFFMANN

was turning with greater interest towards musical activity, founded a singing academy which he himself directed, and composed an *opéra-comique, Chanoine de Milan* (after a text by Alexander Dumas). His little opera, *Die Lustigen musikanten,* the first work to bring him fame as a composer, was also created at this time and performed in Warsaw.

The entrance of the victorious French army into Poland, in 1806, compelled Hoffmann to flee from Warsaw. He came to Berlin, penniless and without resources. Musical conditions in Berlin were in a sad plight; it was not easy for Hoffmann to find connections which might insure him a respectable living. A few of his friends, however, succeeded in securing for him several pupils. For two years, Hoffmann lived in dire poverty, studying the technique of musical composition with great intensity.

In 1808, the count of Soden planned to open a theatre in Bamberg, and engaged Hoffmann to direct the music and to compose a special opera. His financial problems at an end, Hoffmann went to Posen to bring his wife to Bamberg. On arriving at Bamberg, however, he learned that the theatrical venture had collapsed. There followed another two years of great poverty. In 1810, Hoffmann was engaged as the director of the theatre in Bamberg, by the members

of the royal family who lived in that city. He held this position for two years, then lost it, suffering once again keen want. In an attempt to alleviate his poverty, he wrote criticisms for the *Allgemeine Musikalische Zeitung* in Leipzig. It was at this time that he wrote the series of fantasy-romances on chapel master Kreisler which brought him fame. He also was the author of many fairy tales (one of which inspired Tschaikovsky to compose the *Nutcracker suite*) and several brilliant critical articles on music. He wrote a distinguished analysis of the Beethoven *Symphony in C-minor* which, on March 20, 1820, elicited from Beethoven a letter of deep gratitude.

Meanwhile, Hoffman's friends had interceded for him, procuring for him a post in the theatre in Dresden. At that time, Napoleon's retreating army reached Germany. Hoffmann, on his way to Dresden, passed thru the very battlefields, actually sitting in a house that was bombarded (and in which three men were killed) without suffering a scratch. In 1814, he left his Dresden position and came to Leipzig, and during the journey his carriage overturned and his wife suffered serious injury.

In Leipzig he once again knew poverty, cold and neglect. "I found him," wrote Rochlitz, who was Hoffmann's friend at this time, "in a little room in a miserable hotel. He was seated in a battered bed—poor protection from the cold—his feet contracted by gout. His wife, sad and in despair, sat near him."

It was precisely this note (dispatched to Prince of Hardenburg, first minister to the King of Prussia) that brought Hoffmann a comfortable post as judicial advisor in Berlin, a post he held until his death.

His last years were marked by nervous disorders which resulted in partial paralysis. He died in Silesia on June 25, 1822.

His life had been marked by the most ruthless dissipation and waste of energy which—as Thomas Carlyle wrote—"might have seasoned the nectar of the gods." He was an inveterate drinker, moved in the most suspicious company, indulged in emotional and nervous excesses. He was small in stature and piteous looking; during the greater part of his life he commanded from those with whom he came into contact not admiration (as his great talents deserved) but compassion. He was enormously eccentric, consistently fluctuated from violent dissipation to the most austere abstinence, from gaiety and lightheartedness to black morbidity. His great tragedy was that he did all things well, but that in nothing was he pre-eminent. He was the dilettante *par excellence,* talented in more directions than one can enumerate, great in none.

As a composer, he was strongly influenced by Mozart (whom he adored, and in honor of whom he adopted the name of Amadeus). Fétis comments that Hoffmann's music "lacked imagination and never rose above mediocrity." But there are other critics—among them, principally, A. B. Marx—who find much of charm, grace and appeal in his works, even where they lack individuality. In his operas, Hoffmann maintained Wagnerian principles many years before Wagner. His romanticism exerted a great influence, particularly on such outstanding composers as Robert Schumann.

Carl Maria Weber, who heard Hoffmann's opera *Undine* in Berlin, in 1817, wrote as follows about this work: "The work, as a whole, is one of the most ingenious creations which the present epoch has given us. It is the felicitous result of a most perfect understanding and knowledge of the subject, completed by a series of ideas profoundly thought-out and by all the artistic effects. And the most important aspect of this work of art is its sincere and beautiful melodies."

Principal works by E. T. A. Hoffmann:

OPERA: *Scherz, list und rache; Der Renegat; Faustina; Die Ungeladen gäste; Undine; Das Gespenst; Aurora.*

ORCHESTRA: Two symphonies; overture; incidental music to many plays.

CHAMBER MUSIC: *Quintet for harp and strings,* etc.

About E. T. A. Hoffmann:

Bellaigue, Camille. *Impressions Musicales et Littéraires;* Curzon, Henri de. *Musiciens du Temps Passé;* Fétis, F. J. *Biographie Universelle des Musiciens;* Mistler, Jean. *La Vie d'Hoffmann.*

Gustav Holst *1874-1934*
(See *Composers Of Today*)

Francis Hopkinson *1737-1791*

FRANCIS HOPKINSON, who shares with William Billings the distinction of being the first American composer, was born at Philadelphia on September 21, 1737. His father was an Englishman who had married the niece of the Bishop of Worcester.

Francis Hopkinson's education took place at the College of Philadelphia (later known as the University of Pennsylvania), and he was a member of the first class to receive the degree of bachelor of arts from that institution (1757). Hopkinson continued his studies at the College, receiving the degree of Master of Arts and Doctor of Law. He was admitted to the bar in 1761.

His musical education began comparatively late. It was not until his seventeenth year that he began the study of the harpsichord; it is believed that his teachers were John Beals, Charles Love, John Palma, and later, Robert Bremner. In that same year, he also began composition, publishing an *Ode to music.* In 1759, he participated even more actively in music by teaching singing to the children at Christ Church in Philadelphia, where, in 1770, he assumed a temporary post as organist.

Hopkinson's name features as prominently in the early political life of America as in its early musical history. He was one of the most active revolutionists among the colonists; in 1776, he resigned every office that demanded allegiance to King George III, including his seat in the Provincial Council of New Jersey (to which he was appointed in 1774) and his post as collector of the Port of Newcastle, which he had held since 1772. Soon thereafter, he became a delegate to the Continental Congress, was one of the signers of the Declaration of Independence, and—in the opinion of his biographer, George E. Hastings—was even the designer of the American flag.

With the establishment of the American government, Hopkinson was appointed Secretary of Navy. After that, his political positions included that of the judge of the Admiralty from Pennsylvania (1779). In 1787, he was an active participant in the framing of the constitution of the United States.

Strange to say, a life so rich in political activity, was also marked by musical achievements. During the height of his political power, he was the central musical figure in Philadelphia, conducting regular concerts and giving performances on the harpsichord. In 1781, Hopkinson composed an oratorio-opera *The Temple of Minerva* (an allegory to commemorate the American alliance with France) which was performed with George Washington in the audience. In 1788, Hopkinson published his *Seven songs* which he dedicated to his friend, George Washington.

It is with his songs, primarily, that Hopkinson has earned an important position in the history of American music (one of which, *My days have been so wondrous free,* has the distinction of being the first piece of secular music produced in America after the independence). "I will not tell you how much they have pleased us," Thomas Jefferson wrote to Hopkinson, upon receiving a bundle of songs from the composer as a gift, "or how well the last of them (*The Traveler benighted*) merits praise for its pathos. But I will relate a fact only, which is that while my elder daughter was playing it on the harpsichord, I happened to look towards the fire and saw the younger one in tears. I asked her if she was sick. She said, 'No, but the tune is so mournful!' "

Discussing the songs of Francis Hopkinson, the editor of this volume wrote in the *Musical Courier* as follows: "Francis Hopkinson possessed the Romanticist's gift to bend and adapt his melodic gift to express the varied emotions of the lyrics he couched in music. . . . Not the least intriguing quality of these songs is their broad, symphonic accompaniments, in which variety and originality are always predominant. Never does the accompaniment assume the guise of harmony textbook exercises, which is so often the case of other American songs of this

period; in Hopkinson's songs the accompaniment is the spine of the song— as it should be—as important and integral a part to the conception of the whole as the melody.

"Like Schubert and Wolf, Hopkinson's best songs are vibrant with an unaffected beauty that stabs the heart. Listen to such exquisite morsels as *See down Maria's blushing cheek, My love is gone to sea* and the *Traveler benighted* and you will soon realize that Hopkinson could sing of beauty in soft and unforgettable accents."

Francis Hopkinson died of apoplexy in Philadelphia on May 9, 1791.

John Adams described Hopkinson in the following words: "He is one of your pretty, little, curious men. His head is not bigger than a large apple. I have not met with anything in natural history more amusing and entertaining than his personal appearance, yet he is genteel, well-bred and is very social."

Francis Hopkinson's gifts ran thru varied channels. He was not only a distinguished political figure and a gifted composer. As a satirist, he often wrote brilliant and stinging pieces. As a poet and a painter he had a deft and varied touch. And as an inventor, he improved the method of quilling the harpsichord, created a keyboard for Benjamin Franklin's harmonica, and evolved a primitive metronome.

FRANCIS HOPKINSON

Francis Hopkinson's son, Joseph Hopkinson — a judge — distinguished himself by being the author of the famous song, *Hail Columbia.*

Principal works by Francis Hopkinson:

An entire library of excellent songs including *My days have been so wondrous free, O'er the hills, Enraptured I gaze, Come fair Rosina, Beneath a weeping willow shade, My heart disdain, See down Maria's blushing cheek. My love is gone to sea, The Traveler benighted,* etc.

About Francis Hopkinson:

Hastings, George E. *Francis Hopkinson;* Howard, John Tasker. *Our American Music;* Sonneck, Oscar George. *Francis Hopkinson and James Lyon.*

Johann Hummel   *1778-1837*

JOHANN HUMMEL

JOHANN NEPOMUK HUMMEL was born in Pressburg on November 14, 1778. His father, Joseph Hummel, director of the Imperial School of Military Music, attempted to teach his son the violin when the latter was still a child. Showing little aptitude for the violin, Hummel was soon redirected towards the piano; with this instrument he revealed remarkable potentialities.

When the Imperial School closed, father Hummel went to Vienna to become conductor of a theatre orchestra. At this time, Johann, aged seven, was brought by his father to perform at a musical soirrée held at the home of Wolfgang Amadeus Mozart. Mozart was so delighted with Hummel's performance that he offered to adopt the boy for a few years and personally superintend his musical education. For two years, Hummel lived under Mozart's roof, acquiring both a marvelous pianistic technique and a profoundly mature insight into music.

In 1787, Hummel made his debut as pianist in Dresden with such success that his father decided to take him upon an extensive concert tour. Their voyage brought them to the court of Cassel, to Holland, to Edinburgh (where his success was particularly striking, and where Hummel's first published work made an appearance) and, finally, to London. In London, the Hummel's settled momentarily to permit Johann to study the piano under Clementi. Then, after revisiting Holland, they returned to Vienna—after an absence of six years.

Johann Hummel, now fifteen years old, was considered among the foremost virtuosi of the German school of piano performers. But father Hummel had greater ambitions for his son than a virtuoso career. He therefore placed him under rigorous educational discipline; Albrechtsberger was engaged to teach him harmony, and Salieri, counterpoint. Under their guidance, Hummel composed his first operas.

After a concert tour in Russia, Johann Hummel returned to Vienna in 1803 to devote himself to creative work more seriously than before. Under the patronage of Nicholas Esterhazy—whose chapel-master he became—Hummel began the composition of piano pieces, ballets and operas which were frequently performed thruout Vienna. These early works—which, as one critic pointed out, "rings in our ears with Mozart's music,"—enjoyed great popularity, attracting even the praise of Joseph Haydn. As a matter of fact, by 1806 Hummel had become so well-known as a composer that, in Paris, his *Fantasie* was selected by Cherubini as an examination piece for the students of the Conservatory.

In 1811, Hummel left his position with Esterhazy, becoming a teacher of the piano in Vienna. He was not to remain without a musical post for long. By the end of the year he became chapel-master to the King of Wurtemburg. Four years later, he assumed a similar post at the court of Stuttgart, and in 1820 was selected as chapel-master in Weimar to the Grand Duke of Saxony.

In 1823, Hummel traveled extensively as a virtuoso, principally in Holland, Belgium and France, achieving soaring fame both for his interpretative abilities and for his extraordinary improvisations.

In 1827, Hummel visited Beethoven at the latter's deathbed. These two musicians had been estranged since the early part of the century, when, as chapel-master of the Esterhazy court, Hummel performed Beethoven's *Mass in C*, and made some caustic comments about the work which reached Beethoven's ears. On this later meeting, however, the two musicians clasped hands of friendship. "You are a lucky man," Beethoven said to Hummel at this meeting. "You have a wife who takes care of you—who is in love with you—while I, I am a poor, lonely man!"

The next two years found Hummel revisiting Paris and London, where his pianistic talents failed to arouse the admiration and acclaim they once knew. It is believed that, about this time, Hummel gave up concert work and turned to conducting. In 1831, he conducted the German Opera Company at the King's Theatre in London.

The last years of his life were spent quietly in Weimar. Here he died, on October 17, 1837.

Johann Hummel was small in stature, somewhat corpulent. He was known to have been extremely careless about his manners and dress, presenting far from a courtly appearance. He was charitable and generous, possessed a charming sense of humor, and had the talent of making close friends with whomever he came into contact with.

It is the opinion of Fétis that "if Beethoven were born twenty-five years later, Hummel would have been recognized as the greatest instrumental composer of his era."

"Unquestionably, Hummel was one of the most gifted composers of his time," wrote his biographer, Karl Benyovszky, "whose only misfortune it was to have been a contemporary of Beethoven."

Time, no doubt, has dwarfed Hummel's stature in the history of music. That his name is remembered at all, is principally the result of his piano music. "He was," wrote F. Bonavia, "the most attractive of the minor pianoforte composers of his time," even though, "he has been rather drastically dismissed by modern taste." Of his piano works, Robert Schumann considered the *Piano sonata* (Opus 81) Hummel's masterpiece. "It is," wrote Schumann, "in truth a big, epical, Titanic work; the painting of a large, struggling spirit."

Principal works by Johann Hummel:

OPERA: *Le Vicende d'amore*; *Mathilde von Guise*.

BALLET: *Hélène et Paris*; *Das belebte gemälde*; *Sappho*.

CHORAL: *Mass in B-flat*; *Mass in E-flat*; *Mass in D*.

ORCHESTRA: *Overture in B-flat*; *Double concerto for violin and piano with orchestra*; *Six piano concertos*; *Variations* (for piano and orchestra); *Potpourri* (for viola and orchestra); *Variations* (for oboe and orchestra).

CHAMBER MUSIC: *Septet in D-minor*; *Septet in C-major*; *Piano quintet*; *Two quintet-serenades*; *Three string quartets*; *Seven piano-trios*; *Eight sonatas for violin and piano*.

An entire library of music for the piano.

About Johann Hummel:

Benyovszky, Karl. *Johann Hummel*; Meugy, A. *La Poésie de la Musique*.

Important recordings of music by Johann Hummel:

PIANO: *Rondo in A-flat major* (VICTOR-Moiseivitch); *Rondeau favori* (COLUMBIA).

Engelbert Humperdinck 1854-1921

ENGELBERT HUMPERDINCK was born in Siegburg, near Bonn, on September 1, 1854. He entered the high school at Paderborn for the purpose of preparing himself for architectural studies in Cologne. Here—his musical talent being well known—he was asked to compose some incidental music for a performance of Goethe's *Claudia von Willabella*. The joy of creation proved to be so great that Humperdinck, unhesitatingly, packed his bags and left for Cologne in order to have Ferdinand Hiller, the well-known musician, pass judgment on this first fruit. Hiller found it to be a youthful effort, but discovered sufficient merit there to encourage its composer to discard his architectural ambitions and to begin the study of music seriously. In 1872, therefore, Humperdinck entered the Cologne Conservatory, becoming a pupil of Hiller, Gernsheim and Jensen.

Four years of patient study brought him sufficient proficiency to enable him to win the Frankfurt Mozart Award, which made it possible for him to go to Munich to continue his studies under Lachner, and later, under Rheinberger at the Royal School of Music. In 1879, Humperdinck won the Mendelssohn Stiftung, which now made it possible for him to take a trip to Italy.

This trip proved to be the most important single influence in Humperdinck's artistic career. It was during this voyage that he met Richard Wagner, at the Villa D'Angri near Naples. Wagner soon became fond of the young musician (whom he called "Humpchen"), and urged him to come to Bayreuth to help him prepare *Parsifal* for production. Humperdinck, who worshipped Wagner, assented eagerly. In 1882, he came to Bayreuth, acting as rehearser and stage-manager; he even wrote out patiently the orchestral parts of *Parsifal*.

After the festival, Wagner left for Venice, where he wished to celebrate the birthday of Frau Wagner by a performance of his own *Symphony in C*. Wagner wrote to Anton Seidl, inviting him to Venice to conduct the *Symphony*. Seidl had other engagements, but reminded Wagner that Humperdinck might be an acceptable substitute. Humperdinck, therefore, conducted the *Symphony* at the Liceo Benedetto Marcello on Christmas Day of 1882. In gratitude, Wagner attempted to procure for Humperdinck the position of director of the Liceo, but failed because Italy at the time was strongly antagonistic to Germans.

At this time, Humperdinck won another musical award—the Meyerbeer Prize of $2000, which made it possible for him to take an extensive tour thru Italy, Spain and France. He arrived in Paris in 1883. Here he heard the tidings of the sudden death of Richard Wagner. Humperdinck was to remain a close friend of the Wagner family for the remainder of his life; the education of young Siegfried Wagner was, as a matter of fact, entrusted to him by Frau Cosima Wagner.

In 1885, Humperdinck went to Barcelona, where he was appointed professor of the Conservatory. It is said that he was the one to introduce the symphonies of Beethoven to Spanish audiences, in his short career there as orchestral conductor. Five years later, he was in the employ of the publisher Schött, in Mayence.

It was at this time that Humperdinck began to sketch the opera which made him world-famous. Originally, he planned *Hänsel und Gretel* as a little play with which to entertain his nephews and nieces. In developing the play, however, he sensed its operatic possibilities and began to outline his musical ideas.

In 1890, Humperdinck became professor at the Hoch Conservatory in Frankfurt, at the same time serving as music critic of the *Frankfürter Zeitung*. Such spare hours as he could find, he devoted to composition. On December 23, 1893, *Hänsel und Gretel* was given its first performance in Weimar, and was phenomenally successful. Overnight, Humperdinck (who previously had been known rather obscurely as the composer of a pleasant orchestral *Humoresk*, a popular choral piece, *Das Glück von Edenhall,* and a few smaller pieces) became one of the most famous composers in Germany.

The fame of *Hänsel und Gretel* spread like a conflagration thruout Europe. It was, finally, introduced to America by Anton Seidl at the Daly's Theatre in New York in 1895 where, strange to say, it was a failure. However, upon further acquaintance with this opera, America began to appreciate its subtle charm and appeal; it was presented by the Metropolitan Opera House in 1905 and was successful.

Hänsel und Gretel has maintained its popularity to this day. For, as R. A. Streatfeild has pointed out, "Hum-

ENGELBERT HUMPERDINCK

perdinck's music reproduced, with
infinite art, the tender and childlike
charm of the delightful old fairy tale.
His score is amazingly elaborate . . . yet
the whole thing flows on as naturally as
a ballad. The voice parts are always
suave and melodious, and the orchestral
score, however complicated, never loses
touch of consummate musical beauty."

H. E. Krehbiel has noted that, in
composing *Hänsel und Gretel*, Humperdinck was strongly under the influence
of his beloved master, Wagner. "Humperdinck built up his musical structure
in *Hänsel und Gretel* in the Wagnerian
manner, and he has done so with such
fluency and deftness that a musical layman might listen to it from beginning to
end without suspecting the fact, save
from the occasional employment of what
may be called Wagnerian idioms. The
little work is replete with melodies nearly all of which derive their physiognomy
from two little songs which the children
sing at the beginning of the first and
second acts, and which are frankly borrowed from the folk-song literature of
Germany. These ditties, however . . .
contribute characteristic themes out of
which the orchestral part is constructed;
and these themes are developed in accordance with an interrelated scheme
every bit as logical and consistent as
the scheme at the bottom of *Tristan und
Isolde*."

The great success of *Hänsel und
Gretel* enabled Humperdinck to resign
his positions as teacher and critic and,
retiring to Boppard on the Rhine, to
devote himself entirely to composition.
Two years later, he produced another
opera, the *Königskinder*, which (partially because Humperdinck employed an
unorthodox style in which the actors
spoke in rhythm to the music) was
received co:dly. *Königskinder* was
introduced to America at the Metropolitan Opera House in the winter of 1910
in the presence of the composer.

In 1900, Humperdinck returned to
pedagogy by becoming director of the
Akademische Schule in Berlin. During
the next five years, he produced two
more operas—*Dornröschen* and the *Die
Heirat wider willen*—both of which
were failures. Somewhat discouraged,
Humperdinck momentarily abandoned
operatic composition. For the next six
years, he composed considerable incidental music for stage productions by
Max Reinhardt—including such Reinhardt successes as *The Miracle, The
Merchant of Venice, Lysistrata, A
Winter's tale* and *The Blue bird*.

In the winter of 1911, Humperdinck
suffered an attack of apoplexy which
left his left arm paralyzed. He recovered, but required henceforth the services of an attendant. During the war, he
was a staunch chauvinist, and drew up a
manifesto—signed by ninety-five professors thruout the country—which
repudiated the German atrocities, firmly
maintaining that Germany was not the
aggressor in the war but the victim.

Engelbert Humperdinck died in Berlin
on September 27, 1921 after a fresh
attack of apoplexy.

Although, of his many operas, only
one enjoyed fame, Humperdinck's influence upon the German operatic composers of his time was great, particularly in
arousing interest in German folk music
forms. Paul Kekker relates: "The example set by Humperdinck's treatment
of the orchestra—combination of simple
song-melody with an appearance of artistic polyphony and harmonic logic—
proved handy for German composers of
household music, and was exploited in a
rich practical literature of genre-pieces,
idylls, comic or light operas in small

forms." Of German opera composers, the one who has probably been most strongly influenced by Humperdinck is the modern Hans Pfitzner, composer of *Palestrina*.

Principal works by Engelbert Humperdinck:

OPERA: *Hänsel und Gretel*; *Dornröschen*; *Die Königskinder*; *Die Marketenderin*; *Gaudeamus*; *Die Heirat wider willen*.

CHORAL: *Das Glück von Edenhall*; *Die Wallfahrt nach Kevlaar*, etc.

ORCHESTRA: *Symphony in C*; *Humoreske*; *Maurische rhapsodie*; incidental music to many plays.

About Engelbert Humperdinck:

Besch, Otto. *Engelbert Humperdinck*.
The Looker-On 1; 105 November 1895; *Musical America* 34:5 October 8, 1921.

Important recordings of music by Engelbert Humperdinck:

OPERA: *Hänsel und Gretel*, abridged (BRUNSWICK).

SELECTIONS FROM OPERA: *Die Königskinder*, "Vater, Mutter, hier will ich knien" (GRAMOPHONE); "Verdorben—gestorben" (TELEFUNKEN).

SONGS: *Am Rhein* (BRUNSWICK-Schlusnus); *Weihnachten* (VICTOR-Schumann-Heink).

Vincent D'Indy *1851-1931*
(See *Composers Of Today*)

Michael Ippolitov-Ivanov *1859-1935*
(See *Composers Of Today*)

Leoš Janáček *1854-1928*
(See *Composers Of Today*)

Adolph Jensen *1837-1879*
"Jensen must be pronounced the heir of Franz Schubert."—HUGO RIEMANN

ADOLPH JENSEN, eminent composer of the *Lied*, was born on January 12, 1837, in Königsberg, descended from a distinguished family of musicians. His grandfather, Wilhelm Gottlieb Jensen, was a talented composer of choral and organ music, a pupil of Graun and Hasse.

As a child, Adolph Jensen revealed musical talent, beginning the composition of songs in his sixth year. He was advised by the rector of his town to follow music study seriously, but for many years his knowledge of the art was acquired by self-instruction. He was finally permitted by his parents to complete his musical training under Louis Ehlert and Friedrich Marpurg.

In his nineteenth year he went to Brest, Russia, as a teacher of music to a nobleman's family. He returned to Germany one year later, and became conductor in several theatres in Posen and Glogau. In 1859, he received an important post as conductor of German opera in Copenhagen; here he became a close friend of Niels Gade.

Between 1860 and 1866, Jensen devoted himself to teaching; simultaneously, he was occupied with composition and with the direction of a musical academy in his native city. To this period belongs a great portion of his works, and as, at this time, Jensen was strongly under the influence of Robert Schumann, whom he adored, his music revealed perceptible traces of Schumann's style.

In 1866, Jensen was called to Berlin by Karl Tausig, who had founded a musical school. For the next two years, he taught the piano at this institution. Ill-health compelled him to give up these pedagogical tasks. He migrated to Switzerland with the hope that its climate might benefit him.

Hard work (Jensen would frequently compose during the entire night) finally exacted its heavy penalty, in 1867, when Jensen suffered a nervous breakdown. From this time on he suffered illness and intense pain. "Health, health!" he wrote bitterly in 1871. "It is that for which I would sell myself to the devil!" And in 1873: "I have become so nervous that on the most insignificant occasions I tremble like aspen leaves."

During the last seven years of his life, Jensen was driven by illness and restlessness from one place to another, persistently seeking rest and alleviation from pain in different climates and surroundings. His composition did not cease during these trying years. Having come under the influence of Richard Wagner, for whom he expressed his admiration in many letters, his music at this time disclosed obvious Wagnerian traces. "In all my recent composition,"

ADOLPH JENSEN

he himself wrote during the closing years of his life, "I have endeavored and I think with success, to transfer to smaller forms Wagner's idea of 'beauty and truth.'"

In 1875, Jensen settled in Baden-Baden. Here, he died on January 26, 1879, a man broken in spirit and body. The score of an unfinished opera was found after his death. It was brought to completion by Wilhelm Kienzl.

In an illuminating discussion of Jensen's music, Frederick Niecks has written: "No composer after Schubert, Schumann and Robert Franz has enriched the lyrical literature more than Jensen. . . . Jensen's individually distinctive art has its roots in Schumann; but also Chopin was an important factor in the formation of his character and style; and in later life Wagner's influence made itself powerfully felt. . . . Jensen, in describing his temperament as soft, describes also his music. However, the development of his character and style, the emotional deepening of the one and the expressional strengthening of the other, must not be overlooked. Nor is this all that should be noted. The naïvete, freshness, joyousness and serene tenderness which we find in the earlier works—notably in the *Wander-bilder* (Opus 17) and in the *Roman-tische studien* (Opus 8)—disappear

more and more in the later works, many of which are darkened with sadness."

Principal works by Adolph Jensen:

OPERA: *Turandot* (completed by Wilhelm Kienzl).

CHORAL: *Jephthas tochter*; *Der Gang der Jünger nach Emmaus*; *Adonisfeier*; *Donald Caird ist wieder da*; *Gesang der Nornen*; *Brautlied*.

ORCHESTRA: *Overture in E-minor*.

About 160 songs (including the cycles *Der Ungenannten, Liebeslieder, Spanisches lieder-buch, Dolorosa, Gaudeamus,* etc.) ; pieces for the piano.

About Adolph Jensen:

Niggli, Arnold. *Adolph Jensen*; Schweizer, Gottfried. *Das Liedschaffen von Adolph Jensens.*

Allgemeine Musikgesellschaft in Zürich 83:1 January 1895; *Monthly Musical Record* 12:49 March 1. 1882.

Important recordings of music by Adolph Jensen:

SONGS: *Murmelndes lüftchen* (PARLAPHONE-Lehmann) ; *O lass' dich halten* (PARLAPHONE-Lehmann).

Joseph Joachim *1831-1907*

JOSEPH JOACHIM, whose great eminence as a violinist has tended to obscure his distinction as a composer, was born in Kittsee, near Pressburg, on June 28, 1831. His father, a merchant, was fond of music, possessing enough perception to recognize that his son was born with unusual musical talent. At the age of five, therefore, Joseph Joachim received a violin as a gift. Soon afterwards, he became a pupil of Szervaczinski, leader of the opera band in Pesth. His progress was phenomenal. Two years later, Joseph Joachim made his first public appearance. "This genius-boy," wrote a prophetic critic in the *Spiegel*, "seems likely to become an epoch maker in the art of music. It would give us great pleasure should we be the first to have contributed to his fame."

In 1841, Joachim was sent to Vienna to continue his study under Hellmes-berger, who felt that the boy could never become a great violinist because of his weak bow arm. At this time, Joachim met Ernst, the famous violinist, who urged him to become a pupil of Joseph Böhm. "I lived in Böhm's house, and he took enormous pains with me night and day," Joachim wrote in later years. "The room in which I practised had a glass door, and Böhm used to peep in at all times unknown to me. . . . I breathed in a thoroughly musical atmosphere while I was under Böhm's roof."

Two years later found Joachim in Leipzig, where he became a close friend of Felix Mendelssohn, "the revered benefactor of my early days who unceasingly looked after me with fatherly care." Mendelssohn discouraged Joachim from entering the Conservatory, advising him to become a private pupil of Ferdinand David (in violin) and Hauptmann (in composition). On August 19, 1843, Joachim made his first appearance in Leipzig as violinist, playing de Bériot's *Rondo*, with Mendelssohn himself at the piano. Two months later, Joachim appeared as a soloist with the Leipzig Gewandhaus Orchestra, playing Ernst's *Othello fantasy*.

In the Spring of 1844, Joachim visited London, taking with him flattering letters of recommendation from Mendelssohn. On March 28, he appeared at the Drury Lane Theatre and scored an emphatic success. His great ambition, however, was to appear as soloist with the famous Royal Philharmonic Orchestra of London. He soon learned that one of the abiding rules of the Philharmonic forebade the appearance of prodigies with the orchestra. Fortunately, Mendelssohn arrived in London at this time and assured the managers of the Philharmonic that the artistic standards of the orchestra would by no means be lowered by the appearance of this extraordinary prodigy. Mendelssohn's influence carried weight. On May 27, 1844, Joachim's great ambition was realized.

It was a memorable concert, indeed! It introduced England to the complete *Midsummer night's dream* music of Mendelssohn (of which only the overture had previously been heard), and it inaugurated Joachim's great career officially, in his performance of the Beethoven *Concerto*. Wrote J. W. Davis in the *Musical World* in review: "Joachim's rendering of the *Concerto* was astonishing. Not only was it astonishing coming from a comparative

JOSEPH JOACHIM

child, but astonishing as a violin performance, no matter from whom proceeding."

It was at Mendelssohn's request that Joachim, during the next two years, reduced the number of his public appearances to a minimum, devoting himself, instead, to intensive study. Returning to Leipzig, Joachim taught for a short period at the Conservatory, and served temporarily as leader of the Gewandhaus Orchestra. In 1849, Liszt appointed him the leader of the Grand Duke's band at Weimar. In 1853, he was given a similar position with the court orchestra of the King of Hanover, retaining this assignment for twelve years. It was here that he met Johannes Brahms for the first time. Brahms, then in his youth, had come to Hanover to accompany the violinist, Reményi. Joachim was so impressed with Brahms' performance at the piano that he gave the young musician a letter of introduction to Robert Schumann. In this fashion the lifelong friendship between Brahms and Joachim began. It was for Joachim that Brahms, at the height of his career, composed his great *Violin concerto*.

In 1868, Joachim was appointed director of the *Hochschule für ausübende Tonkunst*, which under his guidance became one of the leading musical institutions in Germany. One year later, he founded the world-famous Joachim String Quartet, which during its long existence, held a preeminent position among chamber groups, terminating only with the death of its founder. One of the distinctions of the Joachim Quartet is that it was the first to bring prominence to the then neglected and much criticised last quartets of Beethoven.

Thus, during his long musical career, Joachim's influence was felt in many directions. He was accepted as one of the great violinists of his generation; there were many critics who felt that no other violinist could equal the depth and profundity of his performances of the Bach solo sonatas and the concertos of Beethoven, Mendelssohn and Brahms. He was a potent force in music pedagogy and in chamber music. His efforts were, therefore, rewarded by great honor. He was conferred the order of knighthood by Germany. In 1877, he received an honorary degree from the University of Cambridge. In 1889, he became the object for a world-wide celebration—the occasion of his fiftieth anniversary as a professional musician. In 1904, England became festive to commemorate the sixtieth anniversary of his first appearance in London.

Joseph Joachim died in Berlin on August 15, 1907. The entire world of music mourned his passing.

As a composer, Joachim may have left less of an impression than he did in other musical activities. But he was a composer of talent. Ernest Walker speaks of the "grave sweetness and stern purity" of his music. J. A. Fuller-Maitland refers to Joachim's music as "masterly, often intricate in design," full of "nobility of conception." "There is often a note of tender melancholy, as in the *Romance in B-flat.*"

Joachim's best works include the *Gozzi overture* (which Professor Tovey had referred to as "Haydn up-to-date"), two concertos for violin and orchestra, the *Variations in E-minor* and *Notturno,* both for violin and orchestra, the *Scena* for contralto and piano, the *Romance in B-flat,* and the *Kleist overture.* Joachim, however, is perhaps best known for the cadenzas which he wrote for the violin concertos of Beethoven and Brahms.

In June, 1931, the centenary of Joseph Joachim's birth was celebrated in London by a concert of the London Philharmonic Society (under the direction of Sir Henry J. Wood and Professor Francis J. Tovey) which featured works by Joachim, including the *Gozzi overture* and the *Hungarian violin concerto.*

Principal works by Joseph Joachim:

ORCHESTRA: *Concerto in G-minor* (for violin and orchestra); *Hungarian concerto for violin and orchestra; Gozzi overture; Kleist overture;* Overtures to *Hamlet* and *Henry IV; Notturno* (for violin and small orchestra); *Concerto in G-major* (for violin and orchestra).
Songs.

About Joseph Joachim:

Fuller-Maitland, J. A. *Joseph Joachim. Monthly Musical Record* 59:324 November 1, 1929; *Musical Times* 72:599 July 1, 1931; *Strad* 42:193 August 1931.

Niccolò Jommelli   *1714-1774*

NICCOLÒ JOMMELLI, a prominent figure in the Neapolitan school of opera, was born in Aversa, near Naples, on September 10, 1714. After preliminary musical instruction under a canon, he continued his studies at the Conservatory Poveri di Gesù Cristo, and concluded them at the Conservatory Pietà de'Turchini where his masters included Leo, in composition, and Prato and Mancini in cholar music.

As a composer, he made his bow with several ballets and a church cantata, the latter of which elicited the high praise of Leo who prophesied a great future for the young composer. In 1737 came Jommelli's first opera, *L'errore amoroso,* Jommelli being so uncertain about its merit that, upon its first performance at the Teatro Nuovo in Naples, he affixed to it a pen name. This precaution was unnecessary. The performance was successful, receiving considerable praise from musicians in Naples. Encouraged by this reception, Jommelli composed his second opera, *Odoardo*—presented under his own name—which was so popular that it brought the composer a commission from the Cardinal Duke of York, at Rome, to compose operas expressly for him.

In 1740, Jommelli went to Rome. Under the patronage of the Cardinal he produced two more operas—*Ricimero* and *Astianatte*—which increased his prestige. As a result of these successes, Jommelli received a commission from Bologna. While visiting this city to bring his opera to completion, he visited Padre Martini—probably the most famous musician of Italy at the time— begging to become his pupil. As was his custom, Martini gave Jommelli a subject for a fugue, asking the young musician to develop it. This Jommelli did with so much ease, imagination and skill that Martini said: "Did you come to mock me? It is I who should study under you!"

Jommelli's reputation as a composer soon spread thruout Italy. In 1747, he was appointed professor at the Conservatory degli Incurabili. His position in Italian music had become so important that when the post of chapel-master was vacated in Naples, he was sent the manuscripts of all the contestants and asked to select the successful candidate.

In 1748, Jommelli was invited to Vienna, where his opera *Didone* was given its first performance. This work brought Jommelli as much fame in Vienna as his previous works had brought him in Italy. As its librettist, Cesareo, wrote in a letter to the Princess of Belmont: "Its music fairly aston-

NICCOLÒ JOMMELLI

ished the court. It is so full of elegance of ideas, novelty of harmony, and above all deep expression." The Empress, Maria Theresa, showered him with gifts and favors; and even so great a personality as the poet Metastasio did him honor.

Jommelli, back in Rome towards the close of 1749, was appointed assistant chapel master at St. Peter, a post he held for four years. From there he went to Stuttgart, summoned by the Duke of Württemberg. For sixteen years he fulfilled his duties as chapelmaster at the exceptional salary of 4000 florins a year, exclusive of apartment and necessities.

The poor health of his wife brought Jommelli back to Italy, in 1769, when he received handsome offers from the King of Portugal to come to his country and compose operas for him. Jommelli was too old and tired to begin travel anew and declined the generous offer. The King of Portugal, however, was so eager to do honor to the great composer that he specified, should he receive a copy of each of Jommelli's operas, the composer need not come to Portugal to receive the handsome income.

This stipend enabled Jommelli to retire to Aversa and devote himself to composition. In 1770, his opera *Armida* —one of his most distinguished works— was performed in Naples; young Mozart, aged fourteen, heard the work on his trip to Italy and wrote to his sister praising it highly. In 1771, his opera *Ifigenia* was produced and became one of the few failures that Jommelli encountered during his life. This failure broke his heart and spirit. From that time on, he was unable to turn his hand to the composition of opera. During the last two years of his life, Jommelli devoted himself almost entirely to church music—producing a *Miserere* which many critics believe to be his masterpiece.

Niccolò Jommelli died of apoplexy in Naples on August 25, 1774. His friend, Saverio Mattei, has described the grandiose funeral: "Yesterday all the musicians of the city united in celebrating the funeral of the great Jommelli. The church was very finely ornamented; and a great number of wax tapers were placed about the pompous bier. Two orchestras of three rows . . . executed the music that was expressly composed on the occasion by the worthy Sabatini. . . . At the desire of Signor Manna, not only every musician attended the funeral and performed gratis, but contributed likewise towards the expenses of this solemnity."

In appearance, Jommelli was corpulent, clumsy in gestures, abrupt and awkward in speech. He was a man of culture, possessed a kind heart which was the object of admiration among the many musicians whom he had helped generously. He never catered to public taste, but success was a necessity for his happiness. He wrote with great facility, was able to compose an air while opening and reading a book of poetry—retaining it in memory, sometimes for several weeks, until he put it down on paper.

Charles Burney, in surveying Jommelli's output as a composer, finds three prevailing styles: "Before he went to Germany, the easy and graceful flow of . . . Pergolesi pervaded all his productions; but when he was in the service of the Duke of Wurtemberg, finding the Germans were fond of learning and complication, he changed his style in compliance with the taste and expectation of his audience. And on his return to Italy, he tried to think and simplify his dramatic music."

Principal works by Niccolò Jommelli:

OPERA: *Ezio*; *Merope*; *Achille in Sciro*; *La Clemenza di Tito*; *Armida*; *Ifigenia in Aulide*; *Demetrio*; *Il rè pastore,* etc.
CHORAL: *Isacco*; *Betulia Liberata*; *S. Elena*; *Passion*; masses; *Requiem*; *Miserere*; motets.

About Niccolò Jommelli:

Abert, H. *Niccolò Jommelli als Opernkomponist.*
Musical Standard N.S. 9:36 June 2, 1917.

Josquin des Prés *1445-1521*

"He is the master of the notes; they have to do as he wills; other composers have to do as the notes will."—MARTIN LUTHER

"He is the type of all musical excellence at the time at which he lived."—CHARLES BURNEY

THE greatest composer produced by the Netherland contrapuntal school,[1] recognized by his contempo-

[1] See sketch on Dufay.

raries as the foremost musical master of his age, was Josquin des Prés, who was born in Hainault about 1445. As a child, he sang in the choir of the collegiate college at St. Quentin, where he rose to the position of canon and choirmaster. He is said to have continued his studies under Okeghem, who, in turn, had been a pupil of Dufay. If so, it was from this master that Josquin inherited the traditions of the Netherlands school of music.

In his twenty-fifth year, Josquin went to Milan, where for five years he remained at the court of Galeazzo Maria Sforzai. For a short period, Josquin was in Florence, associated with the brilliant court of Lorenzo the Magnificent. In 1486, he entered the Papal choir, remaining there for eight years under the papacy of both Innocent VIII and Alexander VI. By 1490, Josquin had left Italy to join the chapel of Louis XII of France. Towards the close of his life, he returned to his homeland where he pursued the tasks of composition and pedagogy with considerable vigor. His last days were spent in the little town of Condé-sur-Escant, where, as Provost of the Chapter, he died on August 27, 1521.

As a composer, Josquin des Prés was known to have been very critical of himself, refusing to publish any work unless it had satisfied him for several years.

JOSQUIN DES PRÉS

He composed only when it suited him to do so; not even the most flattering commissions could tempt him to produce music when he was not in the mood. As a teacher, his influence was profound. One of his pupils, Adrian Petit Coclicus, wrote as follows about his master: "My teacher never gave a lecture on music, or wrote a theoretical work, and yet he was able in a short time to form complete musicians. He did not keep his pupils busy with long and useless instructions, but he taught them the rules in a few words during the singing."

Julien Tiersot points out that contrapuntal music was brought to its first stages of important development with Josquin des Prés. The interweaving of the counterpoint became more intricate; modulation was strongly suggested; accidentals were used more freely; imitation and canon acquired greater plasticity. As a matter of fact, Fétis mentions that Josquin was the first to write regulariy in more than two parts, thereby being virtually the inventor of canonic art.

But Josquin des Prés' works are important not merely as milestones in contrapuntal development. Ambros refers to Josquin as "the first musician who impresses us with genius. There speaks in the music of Josquin a warm sensitiveness, a capacity for urgent emotion, a mystic awe of worship. His *Masses* are noble with the nobility of the heart's depth. . . . In his other works, the abstract, elevated style of the earlier composers is broken up by the prism into a glowing play of many colors. Here is sadness, pain and bitter revolt; and here is intimate love, tender sympathy, and playful jest. It is an unprecedented stride forward which occurs with Josquin; in him there is 'lived thru' an art development such as is found in no artist previously."

Josquin's influence upon his contemporaries was marked. An entire school of disciples arose to compose in his idiom and to profit by his examples. Of these, the most important was Nicho'as Gombert, composer of many distinguished songs, psalms and motets. Of Gombert, Fétis wrote: "The art of writing in the style of the fugue with facility brought him distinction. He was no less remarkable for the elevation of his style in certain works, whose words possess a grace character—a type of merit very rare and practically unknown during the first half of the sixteenth century. In this, Gombert was the precursor of the style of Palestrina, who produced nothing more beautiful than the *Pater Noster* of this composer."

Principal works by Josquin des Prés:
Masses; motets; secular songs, etc.

About Josquin des Prés:
Ambros, August Wilhelm. *Geschichte der Musik*; Sollitt, E. R. *From Dufay to Sweelinck*; Wooldridge, H. E. *Oxford History of Music*, vol. 2.
Proceedings of the Musical Association 53:1 1926-1927; *Revue Internationale de Musique* 21:1322 February 1, 1899.

Important recordings of music by Josquin des Prés:
CHORAL: *Ave, verum corpus natum* (VICTOR); *Ave versa virgintas* (PATHE); *Et incarnatus est* (PARLAPHONE).

Vassily Kalinnikov *1866-1901*

VASSILY SERGEIVICH KALINNIKOV was born in Voima, near Orlow, on January 13, 1866. He was the son of an official in the Russian police service. As a boy, he was educated in the Orlowsky Seminary.

His miserable financial condition brought him to Moscow in his youth with the hope of improving his fortune. Here, in 1884, he entered the music school of the Philharmonic Society, becoming a pupil of Iljinsky and Blaramberg.

In 1893, he received his first important musical post when he was appointed second conductor of the Italian Opera in Moscow. Unfortunately, he was unable to hold this post for more than a year. In 1894, he discovered that he had a tubercular condition of the lungs. In an attempt to cure himself, he resigned his conductorial position and went to the south of Russia. Here he devoted himself principally to composition. It was during this period that he composed his most celebrated works.

Kalinnikov is best known to present-day concert audiences thru his *Fifth symphony* which has been recognized by critics as one of the more significant additions to the repertoire of the symphony in our time. This symphony, which was introduced in Vienna, in 1898, and was shortly thereafter performed in Berlin, enjoyed popular acclaim from its very first performance principally because of the dignity of its style, its majestic concept, the broad richness of its melody and the ingenuity of its development.

Vassily Kalinnikov died in Yalta on January 11, 1901, at the premature age of thirty-five. He left behind him only a handful of works, but these are of sufficient distinction and originality to convince us that his early death robbed us of an important composer.

Principal works by Vassily Kalinnikov:

ORCHESTRA: Two symphonies; *Suite*; Two intermezzi; *The Nymphs*; *Cedar and palm*; Music for *Tsar Boris* (Tolstoy); *1812 Prologue.*

CHORAL: *Russalka*; *John of Damascus*; *Beatitudes.*

CHAMBER MUSIC: *String quartet.*
Songs, pieces for the piano.

Reinhard Keiser *1674-1739*

THE· first outstanding composer of German opera, Reinhard Keiser, was born in Teuchern, near Weissenfels, Leipzig. The precise date of his birth is unknown, but in view of the fact that he was baptized on January 12, 1674, it is strongly believed that he was born in the early part of that month.

From his father, Gottfried Keiser, a respectable composer of church music, Reinhard Keiser acquired the elements of music. He then entered the St. Thomas Schule in Leipzig where, as a pupil of Johann Schelle, he attained maturity.

In 1692, he received an appointment as court musician in Brunswick. There, his first opera, *Basileus,* was performed. In 1694, he came to Hamburg as chief composer to the Opera. Five years after this, his opera *Ismene*—a revision of an earlier pastorale, *Die wiedergesundenen verliebten,* originally introduced at Brunswick—was performed with such extraordinary success that it made Keiser one of the most beloved operatic composers in Hamburg.

For the next forty years, Keiser devoted himself to prolific operatic composition for Hamburg, producing a series of one hundred and sixteen operas which assured him a magisterial position over the operatic composers of his day, and firmly established German opera. Fétis has noted that the outstanding characteristics of these operas were "the correctness and profundity of his expression, combined with originality of form. . . . He had a strong and penetrating harmony, and an instinct for instrumentation." He brought operatic form to crystallization, enriched the dramatic expressiveness of melody. He was, unquestionably, the highest esteemed operatic composer in his time, his operas the models for all other operatic composers in Germany. J. A. Hasse considered him the first composer in the world; Mattheson—a rival operatic composer in Hamburg—confessed that Keiser had no equal. Scheibe and Reichardt likewise expressed their admiration and respect in no uncertain vocabulary.

In 1700, Keiser inaugurated in Hamburg a series of brilliant winter concerts in which a specially selected orchestra, the foremost vocalists and instrumentalists, joined to perform outstanding music. Three years later, together with Druiske, he became director of the Hamburg Opera. Their extravagance in expending funds for production brought ruin to the opera-house. Druiske absconded, and for a period Keiser was forced to go into hiding to evade the clutches of creditors. In 1709, however, Keiser married the daughter of a rich Hamburg merchant, thereby returning to full respectability. Always extravagant and a lover of luxury, Keiser now led a life of greater self-indulgence than before.

Self-indulgence, however, did not interfere with his musical career. In 1716, he visited Copenhagen where he became an idol of its music public. Between 1719 and 1721 he officiated as court composer in Stuttgart. In 1723, he returned to Copenhagen as royal chapel master. Five years later, he accepted a position as cantor and canon of the Hamburg Cathedral. In 1729, he visited

St. Petersburg where he was immediately engaged to take charge of the opera. In this post, he was sent to Italy to search for new singers. However, while passing through Hamburg, he found it so difficult to separate himself from old associations that he decided to give up his St. Petersburg post peremptorily. He settled permanently in Hamburg at the home of his daughter where, for the remainder of his years, he led a quiet and retired existence. He died in Hamburg on January 12, 1674.

Karl Nef has referred to Keiser as "one of those fortunate creatures who always have an inspiration, with whom everything turns into song. He might be compared with Mozart or Schubert, if his nature had been somewhat more profound. Depth is a quality which is always lacking in Keiser. He delights, flatters, pleases, but scarcely ever is one really moved by his music. He understood his trade, and his forms are artistic."

Principal works by Reinhard Keiser:

CHORAL: Passions, motets, psalms, oratorios, cantatas, etc.

OPERA: *Basileus*; *Ismene*; *Almira*; *Oktavia*; *L'inganno felice*; *Der lächerliche Prinz Jodelet*; *Ulysses*; *Störtebecker*, etc.

About Reinhard Keiser:

Leichentritt, Hugo. *Reinhard Keiser als Opernkomponist*; Nef, Karl. *An Outline of the History of Music.*

Friedrich Kuhlau   *1786-1832*

FRIEDRICH DANIEL RODOLPHE KUHLAU was born in Ülzen, Hanover, on September 11, 1786. As a boy, he was sent to draw water out of a well and, losing his balance, he hit his head in such a manner as to injure his right eye; a few years later, he lost the eye completely.

Although his parents were poor, they succeeded in procuring adequate musical instruction for him. In his eighth year, Friedrich Kuhlau took lessons on the piano. A few years later, he was sent to Brunswick to begin singing lessons, and to undertake the study of the flute— earning his living, during this period, by singing songs on the streets. He went next to Hamburg where he pursued the

FRIEDRICH KUHLAU

study of harmony under Schwencke. It was at this time that he published his first compositions for flute and piano.

In 1810, Napoleon occupied Hamburg. In order to escape from army conscription, Kuhlau fled to Copenhagen. Here his ability was soon recognized, and he was appointed first flute of the court orchestra. By 1814, he became an important figure in Danish musical life, a vital force in the restoration of national opera (for which he composed *Roeverbergen,* a work that made him famous thruout Copenhagen).

Comfortably established, Kuhlau brought his parents from Germany and settled with them in Lyngbye, a small town near Copenhagen, earning a satisfactory living by teaching piano and theory. It was at this time that he composed the bulk of his works for flute— works which brought him great honor. In 1818, Kuhlau was appointed court composer.

In 1825, Kuhlau made a short visit to Vienna, where he met Beethoven. It cannot be said that Beethoven was impressed with Kuhlau's improvisations but, notwithstanding this fact, a friendship developed between the two musicians. Before his departure from Vienna, Kuhlau received from Beethoven a parting gift—a canon composed on a verse which punned upon the name of Kuhlau.

Returning to Lyngbye, Kuhlau devoted himself principally to compositions for the piano. In 1830, his property, and many valuable manuscripts, were destroyed by fire. His grief over the loss was so great that it undermined his health. He died in Lyngbye on March 12, 1832, and the splendid funeral he was given bespoke the high position he had maintained in Copenhagen's musical life.

Friedrich Kuhlau is perhaps best known for his numerous works for the flute which, as Philip Hale once wrote, "afford estimable models of construction and originality." His piano works, particularly his *Sonatinas,* are familiar to students of the pianoforte; in their clarity and succinctness they have proved to be valuable studies for beginners of the piano.

An anonymous critic, discussing in *The Etude* the qualities of Kuhlau's style commented upon the fact that, in all of his music, it is evident that the composer's instrument was the flute. "The influence of the flute is quite evident in his piano works which abound in charming passages in the higher octaves of the piano. It is also noticeable in the flowing style of his music—a style peculiar to composers who are accustomed to play on an instrument capable of sustaining long voice-like tones and at the same time capable of great flexibility."

Principal works by Friedrich Kuhlau:

OPERA: *Roeverbergen*; *Elisa*; *Lulu*; *Hugo and Adelaide*; *The Magic harp*; *Castle of brigands.*

ORCHESTRA: Music for Boyce's *Shakespeare*; Music for Heiberg's *Elverhöi*; Two concertos for piano and orchestra.

CHAMBER MUSIC: Three quintets for flute and string quartet; *Grand quartet in E for four flutes*; Seven grand trios for flute; Six sets of three duets for two flutes; Three piano quartets; Sonatas for flute and piano.

Pieces for the piano, for the flute, songs, etc.

About Friedrich Kuhlau:

Thrane, Karl. *Friedrich Kuhlau.*

Etude 32:712 October 1914; *Flutist* 8:186 October-November 1927; *Musician* 14:260 June 1909.

Johann Kuhnau *1660-1722*

JOHANN KUHNAU, frequently designated as the father of the piano sonata, was born in Geising, Bohemia, in April of 1660. In his ninth year, he was sent to the Kreuzschule of Dresden where he studied under Alexander Hering and Jacob Bental. He soon attracted the notice of chapel-master Vincenzo Albricci, who took a personal interest in his musical development and welcomed him as a household guest.

An epidemic, which ravaged Dresden in 1680, brought Kuhnau to Zittau where he continued his study of music. At the same time, he entered the University with the intention of entering upon law as a life career. Composition, however, was not neglected. On the occasion of a municipal election he composed a motet for two choirs which met with such extraordinary success that it brought its composer a position as cantor at a substantial salary.

In 1682, Kuhnau came to Leipzig to complete his legal studies at the University. Here, too, his musical talent was recognized. He was offered a post as organist of the St. Thomas Schule. In 1688, Kuhnau officially became a lawyer. The same year he also entered more actively into the music field by founding the Collegium Musicum, which gave series of concerts in Leipzig.

For the next thirteen years, Kuhnau assiduously followed the practise of both law and music. His intelligence, however, was too restless and keen to find satisfaction in these two pursuits alone. He also studied Greek, mathematics and Hebrew; he translated several books from the French and the Italian; and he wrote a satiric romance.

On May 6, 1701 Kuhnau was offered the post of cantor of the St. Thomas Schule on the condition that he would renounce his legal profession. He conceded to this demand eagerly. For the next twenty years, he directed the famous choristers of the St. Thomas Schule and devoted himself industriously to the composition of music.

Johann Kuhnau died in Leipzig on June 25, 1722. His last years were unhappy ones, embittered by the tragic loss of two sons and a daughter. His post at the St. Thomas Schule was assumed by Johann Sebastian Bach.

While Kuhnau composed many admirable works for chorus, works in which, as Camille Bellaigue pointed out, "one finds . . . young and truly fresh . . . these grandiose scholastic forms which Bach was soon to bring to maturity." He is most famous for his piano music. It was Kuhnau who was the inventor of the piano sonata. The first of these was published in 1695 with the following introductory comment: "I add a sonata which may please amateur musicians. Why should not one try to write for the piano in a form which has been utilized for other instruments?"

Kuhnau was so well satisfied with his initial experiment in this direction, that he composed thirteen additional sonatas. "While writing these . . . sonatas," Kuhnau himself wrote, "I experienced such eagerness, that without neglecting my other occupations, I wrote one every day, so that this work, which I began on a Monday, was completed by the Monday of the following week." Seven of these sonatas appeared under the title of "Fresh Piano Fruits"; the other six were grouped under the heading of "Musical Representations of Some Stories of the Bible. Perhaps the most famous of these sonatas is *The Combat between David and Goliath* which, even today, is occasionally featured in piano recitals.

"He did, indeed, possess a depth of feeling, and at the same time a beauty of form, a grace compounded of strength and lucidity which even today would make his name a household word," wrote Romain Rolland. "Kuhnau was one of the creators of the modern sonata; he wrote 'suites' for the clavier which are models of spirited grace, occasionally tinged with reverie. He composed some descriptive poems— 'program music'—under the title of *Biblical sonatas*; cantatas, sacred and profane, and a Passion which makes him, if we are to tell the truth, not only the immediate predecessor of Bach at the St. Thomas Schule in Leipzig, but

JOHANN KUHNAU

also, in a great many respects, his indisputable model."

Musicologists have repeatedly acknowledged Kuhnau's historical importance. Scheibe regarded him as one of the four greatest German composers of his time. Spitta points out frequently how Kuhnau's liturgical music influenced Bach. Shedlock reveals similarities between the music of Kuhnau and Handel.

Finally, Kuhnau was not only the father of piano music but also, as Romain Rolland mentioned briefly in the above quotation, a pioneer in the composition of program music. Camille Bellaigue wrote in this connection: "Program music existed before his time, it is true; but it was less felicitously expressed, and certainly less musical."

Principal works by Johann Kuhnau:

CHORAL: Motets; chorales; passion; cantatas, etc.

INSTRUMENTAL: Suites for the piano; sonatas for the piano.

About Johann Kuhnau:

Bellaigue, Camille. *Études Musicales* (2e série); Rolland, Romain. *A Musical Tour thru the Land of the Past.*
Le Guide Musicale 50:43 January 17, 1904.

Important recordings of music by Johann Kuhnau:

INSTRUMENTAL: *The Combat between David and Goliath* (ANTHOLOGIE-SONORE).

Édouard Lalo *1823-1892*

VICTOR ANTOINE ÉDOUARD LALO was born in Lille, France, on January 27, 1823. His father, an officer of the Grande Armée, was three times wounded in the battle of Lützen, in spite of which he continued to hold command until the very end of the battle, thereby earning a decoration from the Emperor himself on the field of battle. That decoration was Édouard Lalo's proudest possession thruout his life.

Édouard Lalo's strong gift for music brought him to it at an early age. He was entered in the Conservatory of Lille, and then was placed under the private tutelage of Pierre Bachmann, a sensitive musician who had played under Beethoven's baton in Vienna, who gave Lalo rigorous and thorough musical training. Lalo's aptitude for music was matched only by his love for the art; even as a boy, he was firmly determined to adopt music as a life profession. His father, however, had visions of making his son a soldier in the French army, and vigorously opposed his son's wishes. A bitter battle of words took place, one day, between father and son. Édouard Lalo, rather than submit to his father's will, left the paternal home, vowing never again to return. The breach between father and son was not healed until the former's death, when Edouard Lalo rushed back from Paris in time to hear his father's dying words of forgiveness.

Freed from his father's domination, Lalo—now in his sixteenth year—came to Paris, entering the Paris Conservatory. These were trying days for the young musician, but not even starvation could smother his high spirits. Lalo did not remain at the Conservatory long, for the rigid formalism irritated him. Instead, he turned to textbooks and the scores of musical masterpieces for his lessons, deriving from them a consummate technique. In 1845, he composed his first major work, a trio of great originality and talent. Two years later, he won the second Prix de Rome.

His professional musical career was begun in 1855 when he joined the Armingaud-Jacquard Quartet as violist.

To this group, was soon added a wind-section which, now known as the Société classique, gave brilliant concerts thruout France.

At this time, Lalo became a friend of the distinguished painter, Eugène Delacroix, who was also a lover of great music. Each Friday evening, Delacroix would be one of the visitors at Lalo's house in Rue Duphot, where there took place musical soirées. After the music there were discussions. Delacroix's penetrating aesthetic theories had a vital influence upon the young composer's artistic growth.

In 1865, Lalo was teaching harmony to private pupils, when he fell in love with his favorite student, Mlle. Julie Marie Maligny, an excellent singer. They were married in July of that year. Two years later, Lalo came to prominence for the first time. In that year, the Minister of the State in Paris announced a competition among French composers for a work suitable for performance in the lyric theatre. Lalo submitted his first opera, *Fiesque* (based upon Schiller's *Fiesco*) and was awarded third prize. Several prominent musicians, who saw the score of Lalo's opera, were so infuriated that a work of such extraordinary merit should be awarded third prize that one of them—Monsieur Perrin, director of the Paris Opera—decided to produce it. The opera never reached production, even though it attained rehearsal, but the incident brought considerable advertisement to the composer.

It was many years, however, before Lalo fully came into his own as a composer. On January 18, 1874, his personal friend, Pablo Sarasate, the great violinist, introduced Lalo's *Violin concerto* at the concerts of the London Philharmonic. The work enjoyed so great a success that Lalo decided to compose still another large work for Sarasate. The following year, therefore, Sarasate introduced at the Concert Populaire of Paris the *Symphonie espagnole*. With these two works, Lalo firmly established his reputation as a composer of importance.

On May 7, 1888 there took place at the Opéra Comique the first performance of Lalo's masterpiece, the opera *Le Roi d'Ys.* "When two years ago I destroyed the first score of *Le Roi d'Ys*," Lalo wrote in 1888, "I had the desire of making it a lyrical drama in the modern acceptance of the term; but, after some months of reflection, I drew back, frightened at this task which seemed much too heavy for my strength. Until now, the colossus Wagner, the inventor of the real lyrical drama, has alone been strong enough to carry such a weight; all those who have had the ambition to walk in his footsteps have failed, some piteously, others honorably. ... It will be necessary to surpass Wagner in order to fight on his own ground with advantage, and the fighter capable of doing so has not yet revealed himself. As for myself, I have realized in my time my impotence, and I have written a simple opera."

This "simple opera"—based upon a Breton legend—took Paris by storm. One critic of Lalo's day found it "noble, strong, puissant, not free from faults, but evidently the work of an artist of the first rank, and endowed in a superior degree." The audiences were thunderously enthusiastic, acclaiming Lalo the composer of the hour.

"*Le Roi d'Ys* is an excellent specimen of the kind of opera which French composers of the second rank used to write before the sun of Wagner dawned upon their horizon," wrote R. A. Streatfeild. "It is redolent of Meyerbeer and Gounod, and though some of the scenes are not without vigor, it is impossible to avoid feeling that in *Le Roi d'Ys* Lalo was forcing a graceful and delicate talent into an uncongenial groove. He is at his best in the lighter parts of the work, such as the pretty scene of Rozenn's wedding, which is perfectly charming."

The last years of Lalo's life were touched with tragedy. Although he was appointed a member of the Legion of Honor in 1880, and an officer ten years later, he sincerely felt that he had failed to receive the honor he deserved, principally because he had not been chosen for the Institut. Paralysis, moreover, crippled his body just as disappointment smothered his spirits.

He died in Paris on April 22, 1892, and was buried at Père Lachaise. "Lalo," said Jules Massenet in his eulogy over the fresh grave, "will be counted among the French composers of whom we must be proud because his music, sometimes exquisite or sparkling, sometimes dramatic or elegiac, is always the pure music of Lalo."

Discussing the qualities of Édouard Lalo as composer, Julien Tiersot wrote: "The music of Lalo is essentially an aristocratic art. It is a sculpture created with extreme delicacy, outlined without any visible effort, and brought to being—so it seems—with the utmost of naturalness. It possesses no romanticism, discloses little restlessness, and its intimate feeling is not very profound. But his forms are of a rare ingenuity. Its tonality is clear and endowed with a color not too excessive but always bathed in light; it is founded upon a diatonism that is almost constant and hardly ever depends upon the resources of chromaticism. His melodies, generally short, are elegant and fresh. His rhythms are well formed, so neat that they often give the feeling of energy."

Principal works by Édouard Lalo:

ORCHESTRA: *Concerto for violin and orchestra*; *Divertissement*; *Allegro symphonique*; *Concerto for violoncello and orchestra*; *Rhapsodie norvégienne*; *Concerto russe* (for violin and orchestra); *Symphony*; *Concerto for*

ÉDOUARD LALO

piano and orchestra; Symphonie espagnole (for violin and orchestra).

OPERA: *Fiesque; Le Roi d'Ys; La Jacquerie* (completed by Coquard).

CHAMBER MUSIC: Two quintets; Two quartets; Three trios.

BALLET: *Namouna; Néron.*

About Édouard Lalo:

Seré, Octave. *Musiciens Français d'aujourd'hui;* Tiersot, Julien. *Un Demi-siècle de Musique Française.*
La Revue Musicale 4:97 March 1923.

Important recordings of music by Édouard Lalo:

ORCHESTRA: *Concerto for violoncello and orchestra* (COLUMBIA-Maréchal); *Symphonie espagnole* (VICTOR-Menuhin); *Namouna,* suite from ballet (BRUNSWICK-Wolff); *Rhapsodie norvégienne* (ODEON-Pierné).

SELECTIONS FROM OPERA: *Le Roi d'Ys,* "Ouverture" (COLUMBIA-Gaubert); "En silence pourquoi souffrir" (COLUMBIA); "Prélude" and "De tous côtés j'aperçois" (PARLAPHONE); "Aubade" (GRAMOPHONE).

CHAMBER MUSIC: *String quartet in E-flat major* (GRAMOPHONE).

Orlando de Lasso   *1532-1594*

"One of the peaks in the history of music."—CHARLES VAN DEN BORREN

ORLANDO DE LASSO, the last of the masters produced by the Netherland school of counterpoint[1], was born as Roland de Lattre in Mons, Hainault, in February of 1532. His father appears to have been convicted as a counterfeit coiner, and as punishment was forced to walk three times round the public scaffold with a collar of counterfeit coins dangling from his neck. It is said that Orlando witnessed this disgraceful episode, which affected him so vitally that he ran away from home and called himself Orlando de Lasso.

At the age of seven, he became a choirboy in the church of St. Nicholas, beginning formal music study one year later. Being in possession of a beautiful voice, he was kidnapped three times by the agents of powerful nobles who were eager to include him in their choirs. The first two times, the rape was unsuccessful. The third attempt, however, brought Orlando de Lasso into the service of Ferdinand Gonzaga, viceroy of Sicily. For four years, he remained in the employ of Ferdinand, traveling with him as

far as Munich where Orlando became a member of the choir of the chapelmaster.

In 1548, Orlando de Lasso's voice broke, and—leaving the service of Ferdinand permanently—he went to Naples, and was engaged by the Marquis della Terza, an important patron of art. 1552 found de Lasso in Rome where, in all probability, he became personally acquainted with Palestrina, seven years his senior. In Rome, de Lasso became chapel master at the Basilica of St. John Lateran. From Rome he went for a brief visit to London. Here the news of the serious illness of his parents came to him, and he rushed back to his homeland. Towards the close of 1554, Orlando settled in Antwerp; it was here that his first book of madrigals, revealing the influence of Willaert, was published.

In 1556, Orlando de Lasso was invited to Munich where he was installed in the court of Duke Albert of Bavaria. Here, during the ensuing years, he grew in importance and power. After the first six years, the Duke entrusted him with the direction of all the musical activities of the court. In 1558, Orlando de Lasso was married to Regina Wäckinger.

It was not long before his fame as a composer grew until it reached the farthest boundaries of Europe. In 1562, he published his first book of wholly sacred music in Nuremberg, and a volume of cantiones in Venice; two years later there followed a French publication of his entire output up to the time. His fame grew so great in the years that followed that, in 1570, Maximilian II gave him a patent of nobility which was to remain valid for his descendants as well.

In 1571, Orlando de Lasso visited Paris. The regal pomp and honor with which he was received expressed the admiration of the French music public for this great composer. Three years later, Orlando was further honored in Rome by Pope Gregory II with the title of Chevalier de St. Pierre. By 1579, his reputation was so formidable—and offers for his services from foreign courts so plentiful—that he was asked to sign an agreement to remain in the

[1] See sketch on Dufay.

ORLANDO DE LASSO

Bavarian court for the remainder of his life in return for an admirable yearly salary. Thus—with the exception of a brief excursion into Italy, which took place in 1585—Orlando de Lasso remained attached to the Bavarian court until his death, generally recognized by his contemporaries as the greatest musician of the day.

The last years of de Lasso's life were marked by gloom and morbidity, brought on by fear of insanity. He talked constantly of death. Shortly before his death, he was seized by a fit of insanity during which time he did not even recognize his wife; the period of mental upheaval, however, was only temporary.

He died in Munich on June 14, 1594, leaving as a heritage more than two thousand compositions. He was buried in the cemetery of the Franciscans. The following year a monument was erected in Munich in his honor.

Discussing the qualities of Orlando de Lasso as a composer, Charles van den Borren wrote: "Profoundly human, and a profound believer—such was Orlando. With this was combined a propensity to interest himself in everything, to leave nothing in the shade, to explore to the further-most depths all the domains of his art. Universality and fecundity—these were the distinctive traits of his genius. . . . If one penetrates more deeply into the labyrinth of his immense production, one is struck by the multiplicity of his attention to detail, and the infinity of his means which is combined with this diversity. . . . The motet is. . . the form in which he gave expression to his highest and most personal inspiration, the one in which, more than in any other, he gives witness of his lofty genius."

H. E. Wooldridge points out in the *Oxford History of Music* that Orlando de Lasso's characteristic works are often "deficient in melodic beauty" that often "the voice parts seem not to spring complete from the imagination of the composer and to flow thence in parallel streams, but rather to have been put together with a view to create an harmonic effect." Notwithstanding such defections in his art, de Lasso's music remains an imposing artistic achievement because of its "grandeur and pathos."

Ernest Closson makes an interesting comparison between Orlando de Lasso, and his great contemporary of the Roman polyphonic school, Palestrina. "Lasso has less grace than the Italian, he is less luminous, less perfect, above all else less mystic. However, if he is inferior to him from the point of view of religious sentiment, he surpasses him in secular composition thru the originality of his harmony, his energy, his vigor and puissant vivacity, his strong conceptions, and more especially thru his vernal freshness."

It is the opinion of many critics that the most famous of Orlando de Lasso's works is the *Seven penitential psalms,* written before 1560. "These powerful, magnificent, serious pieces," wrote Hugo Leichentritt, "are eminent classical masterpieces of the first rank, and find their equal only in certain Palestrina and Bach compositions. They show, besides, the fullest mastery of contrapuntal technique, Lasso's individuality, with its dark pathos, its passionate outcries, differing considerably from Palestrina's more serene, more celestial pure manner."

Principal works by Orlando de Lasso:
Motets; masses; magnificats; passions; madrigals; villanelles; moresques; psalms; French and German songs, etc.

About Orlando de Lasso:

Borren, Charles van den. *Orlande de Lassus*; Closson, Ernest. *Orlande de Lassus*; Expert, Henri. *Orlande de Lassus*; Wooldridge, H. E. *Oxford History of Music* (vol. 1).

Jean Marie Leclair *1697-1764*

JEAN MARIE LECLAIR l'aîné, often called the "Corelli of France," was born in Lyons on May 10, 1697, the oldest son of eight children. In his youth, he followed in the footsteps of his father by becoming an apprenticed lacemaker.

In 1716, Leclair was married in Lyons to Rose Castignie, a singer, and shortly after this followed the study of music with great assiduity. In 1722, he became ballet-master in Turin, at the same time undertaking the study of the violin and beginning the composition of charming interludes and ballets. Six years later, he went to Paris where he made his mark as a violinist. His phenomenal technique attracted considerable notice within a limited circle of connoisseurs who regarded him as one of the great violinists of the time. At this time, too, he published his first book of violin sonatas.

From 1728 until 1736, Leclair enjoyed considerable success at the Concert Spirituel, and at the concerts of the court where he was leader of the royal band. From 1729 until 1735 he performed in the orchestra of the Paris Opéra. During this period he did not neglect music study, pursuing the science of composition under Chéron.

Meanwhile, Leclair had become a widower, and was married a second time—now to Louise Roussel, wealthy widow, who had formerly been the engraver of Leclair's music and with whom he had entered into business relationship for several years. Being a lady of considerable means, she brought to Leclair comfort and affluence.

After 1736, Leclair resigned from his many activities as a violinist, devoting himself to teaching and to composition. For the next sixteen years he published an entire library of music for the violin which placed him among the important pioneer composers of that instrument.

Critics have pointed out what remarkable strides violin music made thru Leclair's works: a new limpidity was brought to its harmonic writing; *tempo* acquired greater flexibility; dynamics became more subtly expressive; the variation-form assumed greater resourcefulness; and, finally, the binary-form began to assert itself as the basis for the opening movement of the sonata.

Except for a brief visit to Holland, at the invitation of the Princess of Orange (where he heard Locatelli, the famous violinist) and for a fleeting excursion into Spain in 1743, Leclair lived a comparatively secluded existence during the last thirty years of his life—momentarily interrupted, in 1746, when his opera *Scylla et Glaucus* was given a successful performance, and once again, two years later, when the Duke of Gramont appointed him leader of a private orchestra.

Towards the close of his life, Leclair was estranged from his second wife. He built for himself a home, remote from the city of Lyon, far removed from any other house. Here he lived a lonely and quiet existence. On October 22, 1764, Leclair was murdered in this house. His gardener found him sprawled upon the floor; upon closer examination it was discovered that the composer had been murdered by three strokes of a sharp tool. Although both the gardener and Leclair's nephew were in turn suspected of the crime, the murderer was never discovered.

Leclair's face has been described by a French contemporary as "full, with very large eyes that possessed a uniquely strange expression, heavy eyebrows and an enormous brow."

His acquaintances remarked that he was modest, sincere and generous, inclined towards melancholy, somewhat of a misanthrope. He detested applause and the *haut monde*, finding happiness only in complete and monastic solitude. He was a man of great simplicity, a lover of books. By temperament, he was pensive and introspective.

He left a prolific library of works, the most important of which are those which he composed for his own instrument. Wrote Lionel de Laurencie: "Here one confronts most often, together with a

JEAN MARIE LECLAIR

perfect clarity of design, an austere nobility which does not progress without a touch of coldness; also a poignant and anxious pathos which seems to lose itself in the scintillating and sparkling gaiety of his lively movements. . . . Leclair. . . . gave proof of a fecund resourcefulness which. . . . has opened up for the instrumental art the greater part of its future vistas."

Principal works by Jean Marie Leclair:

OPERA: *Glaucus et Scylla*; *Apollon et Climène*, etc.

CHAMBER MUSIC: Concerti grossi for three violins, viola, violoncello and organ; overtures and sonatas for trio; trios for two violins and bass; sonatas for two violins without bass; concerti for violin and chamber orchestra; forty-eight sonatas for violin.

About Jean Marie Leclair:

Laurencie, Lionel de. *L'école Française du Violon.*

La Revue Musicale 4:12 February 1923; *Sammelbände der Internationalen Musik-Gesellschaft* 6:250 1904-1905; *Strad* 40:676 April 1930.

Important recordings of music by Jean Marie Leclair:

VIOLIN AND PIANO: *Sonata in D-major* (POLYDOR).

Charles Lecocq *1832-1918*

ALEXANDRE CHARLES LE-COCQ, famous composer of French *opéra-comique,* was born in Paris on June 3, 1832. "I was a good little boy," he wrote in reminiscent mood in later years, "not turbulent, timid, even inclined to be shy on account of the weakness in my legs which, alas! prevented me from running and frisking about like my happier comrades. When recess came, not being able to join their gambols, I amused myself by drawing sounds from a primitive and absurd instrument, the flageolet. I played by instinct without knowing a word of music."

A music teacher, Monsieur Laffont, noticed him and, impressed with the boyish improvisations on the flageolet, decided to take the boy under his supervision. Thus, young Lecocq was taught *solfège,* and the elements of the violin and piano. He made such rapid progress that, in his fourteenth year, Lecocq was able to draw an income by teaching the piano.

At the age of eighteen, Lecocq entered the Conservatory, where he became the pupil of Bazin in harmony and Jacques Halévy in composition. He showed marked signs of his musical talent by winning several awards, including first prize in harmony and second prize in fugue. He remained at the Conservatory for four years. Upon leaving the institution, he attempted to earn a living by teaching the piano and publishing church songs.

For several years, his ambition had been to compose music for the theatre. Finally, an opportunity presented itself when Jacques Offenbach, director of the Bouffes Parisiens, announced a competition for a one-act operetta based upon a libretto of Ludovic Halévy and Léon Battu, *Le Docteur Miracle.* Lecocq worked assiduously on this operetta, and received the full fruits of his labor by winning the award and having his work performed at Offenbach's theatre on April 8, 1857. Even in this early work, Lecocq's style possessed charm and appeal; there were many critics who praised this piece as a work of great promise.

Success, however, had not yet arrived. Encouraged by the performance of his one-act operetta, he worked industriously upon his first major *opéra-*

CHARLES LECOCQ

comique, *Huis clos,* which, upon its performance in 1859, was a complete failure. There followed several further unsuccessful efforts to gain public attention. Then, when Lecocq despaired of every emerging from his obscurity, his *Fleur de thé*—presented in 1868—aroused considerable admiration and enthusiasm.

From that time on, his rise to fame and success was marked. On December 4, 1872, his masterpiece, *La Fille de Mme. Angot,* was presented in Brussels. It was so great a success that it ran for five hundred consecutive nights, establishing Lecocq as one of the outstanding composers of *opéra-comique* of his day. Two years later, he achieved another overwhelming triumph in Brussels, with *Giroflé-girofla.*

Success seemed to be the dynamo supplying Lecocq with indefatigable energy, and from this time on his pen was tirelessly producing a long series of light-operas, their melodic freshness, ingenious instrumentation, pungency of wit and grace finding enthusiastic audiences everywhere. Between 1874 and 1900, Lecocq produced more than thirty operettas, the majority of which were acclaimed. His musical importance was acknowledged in 1894 when he was appointed a member of the Legion of Honor.

Charles Lecocq died in Paris on October 24, 1918. For more than forty years he had occupied a reigning position over composers of French *opéra-comique,* and he was mourned thruout France.

Principal works by Charles Lecocq:

OPERA: *Le Docteur Miracle; Liline et Valentin; Les Ondines de champagne; L'Amour et son carquois; Fleur de thé; Le Beau Dunois; La Fille de Mme. Angot; Giroflé-Girofla; La Petite mariée; Le Petit duc; La Jolie Persane; Le Marquis de Windsor; Le Jour et la nuit; La Princesse des Canaries; La Vie mondaine; Plutus; Nos bons chasseurs; Ruse d'amour; La Belle au bois dormant; Yetta,* etc.

BALLET: *Barbe-bleu; Le Cygne; Les Fantoccini.*

Songs.

About Charles Lecocq:

Schneider, Louis. *Les Maîtres de L'opéretta Française.*

New Music Review 12:294 July 1913; *Revue Internationale de Musique* 14:851 October 15, 1898.

Guillaume Lekeu   *1870-1894*

"Next to Franck, Lekeu is one of the most remarkable representatives of the Belgian school."—DEBUSSY

IN musical history, the career of Guillaume Lekeu stands virtually unparalleled. Dead at the age of twenty-four, he succeeded in producing works of such power that critics unanimously proclaimed them the creation of true genius; works of such originality that they made his name prominent in the music of the past half century.

Guillaume Lekeu was born in Heusy, near Verviers, on January 20, 1870. In 1879, his parents moved to Poitiers, where Guillaume was entered in the Lycée. Here he revealed unusual talents, particularly for science, ancient and modern literature, and the plastic arts. Graduating from the Lycée in 1888, he entered the University of Paris. After taking his bachelor's degree in philosophy, he suddenly turned his entire energy to music.

In music, he was virtually illiterate until his fourteenth year when he began the study of the art. In 1885, however, he heard some work of Beethoven which stirred him so deeply that he decided to devote himself to music. He began the study of solfeggio and the piano, spending four industrious years poring over the scores of Beethoven, Bach and Wagner. When, on completing his bachelor's degree at the University, he decided to become a musician, he became a pupil of Gaston Vallin in harmony. Under Vallin he made such phenomenal progress that he was urgently advised to become a student of César Franck.

For a full year, between 1889 and 1890, Lekeu studied under Franck. There developed a close bond between teacher and pupil. In the summer of 1889, Lekeu made a pilgrimage to Bayreuth to hear Wagner's music dramas, and was profoundly impressed. Now more than ever he knew that music would be his lifework.

The death of César Franck in 1890 affected him intimately, but, fortunately, another great musician was at hand to take him under his wing—Franck's disciple, Vincent d'Indy. D'Indy, convinced of Lekeu's genius, urged him to enter the Belgian competition for the Prix de Rome. Lekeu succeeded in gaining only the second prize, in 1891, a source of great disappointment to him.

For the next three years of his life, Lekeu worked industriously upon his composition, and enjoyed a measure of recognition. On March 27, 1892, his choral work, *Andromède,* was performed at the Conservatory of Verviers under Louis Keter, finding an appreciative audience. In the Fall of 1893, his *Fantasie symphonique,* for orchestra, was performed under his own direction at Anjou, which succeeded in attracting further attention to the young, brilliant composer.

His life's span, however, was drawing to a rapid close. He contracted typhoid fever and died in Angers on January 21, 1894. A few hours before his death, he was gay, exuberant, full of hope for the future, little aware that his life was at an end. Then delirium set in, and Lekeu knew he was dying. His last words were: "So many works unfinished—my quartet!"

Four months after his death, his friends arranged a concert in his memory at the Salle d'Harcourt in Paris; it was directed by Vincent d'Indy and

GUILLAUME LEKEU

Eugène Ysaye performed. Lekeu's *Violin sonata,* selections from *Andromède* and the *Fantasie symphonique* were featured.

On February 1, 1896, Lekeu's *String quartet,* to which he had referred in his dying words and which had been brought to completion by Vincent d'Indy, was introduced by Claude Debussy under the auspices of the Société nationale. On November 16, 1904, the Hoffmann Quartet performed the work in Boston. "Lekeu's voice was his own," wrote Philip Hale after hearing the work. "His music is not like that of other men; he thought in his own way and his emotional eloquence in this quartet is genuine and convincing. . . . Such music does not suffer when played after a noble work by Beethoven, but it makes a work like that of Dvořák, which followed, unendurable."

Although Lekeu did not compose many works, what he created is sufficient, in the opinion of Romuald Vandelle "to place this young artist at the head of all composers of his generation. None of his rivals. . . . manifested a genius more original, or an inspiration more exalted. From his music there comes a breath of grandeur and an intensity of life which are not deceiving. . . . When faith took possession of him, when for a moment he attained the peaks towards which he threw his gaze, his song became unique and large, powerfully harmonized with an intuitive feeling for timbres which astonishes and ravishes. . . . These moments mark the peak of his inspiration."

Principal works by Guillaume Lekeu:

OPERA: *Barberine* (sketches); *Les Burgraves* (sketches).

CHORAL: *Chant lyrique*; *Andromède*.

ORCHESTRA: *Two études symphoniques*; *Adagio* (for quartet and orchestra); *Poème* (for violin and orchestra); *Introduction and Adagio*; *Fantasie symphonique*.

CHAMBER MUSIC: *Adagio* (for two violins and piano); *Sonata for violin and piano*; *Trio*; *Sonata for violoncello and piano* (unfinished); *Quartet* (brought to completion by Vincent d'Indy).

Songs, pieces for the piano.

About Guillaume Lekeu:

Seré, Octave. *Musiciens Français d'aujourd'hui*; Sonneck, Oscar George. *Miscellaneous Studies in the History of Music.*
Musical Quarterly 5:109 January 1919; *La Revue Musicale* 2:122 January 1921.

Important recordings of music by Guillaume Lekeu:

CHAMBER MUSIC: *Quartet* (POLYDOR); *Sonata for violin and piano* (POLYDOR).

Ruggiero Leoncavallo *1858-1919*

RUGGIERO LEONCAVALLO, composer of *Pagliacci*, was born in Naples on March 8, 1858. He was a student at the Naples Conservatory where, as a boy of sixteen, he composed a talented cantata. After receiving his diploma from the Conservatory, he went to Bologna to attend the University, taking a course of literary training under Carducci. Music, however, was not neglected. At this time, he composed an opera, *Chatterton,* arranging with a local impresario for a production of the work by placing with him a large sum of money necessary for the expense. The impresario, however, escaped from Bologna with the money, leaving Leoncavallo penniless.

Restlessness and self-dissatisfaction brought on wanderlust. In his twentieth year, he traveled thruout Europe—to England, France, Germany and Holland —attempting to find some permanent musical connection, but succeeding only in earning the most meagre living thru teaching the piano and singing. It was a miserable existence, fraught with disappointment, futility and despair. Leoncavallo's spirit was succored, during this time, only by a gargantuan plan which he conceived for composing a grandiose operatic trilogy, along Wagnerian lines, with the Italian Renaissance as a setting.

His voyages, finally, brought him to Egypt, where he received an appointment as pianist to the viceroy's brother. Shortly after his arrival, an Arabian insurrection broke out against England. In danger of his life, as all Europeans in Egypt were, he escaped from Cairo in the middle of the night, arrived at Port Saïd and, after organizing a special concert to raise funds, sailed for Paris.

In Paris, Leoncavallo knew the life of a true Bohemian. Reduced to beggary and hack-work in order to keep from starving, he went from one *café-chantant* to the next in search of random employment as pianist. He also earned some twenty francs a day by composing popular chansonettes for the proprietor of the Eldorado Music Hall, one of which became an emphatic success.

This sordid existence was brought to termination when Leoncavallo met and became a friend of Victor Maurel, celebrated French baritone. Maurel was on his way to Milan, and he urged Leoncavallo to accompany him. There, Mau-

RUGGIERO LEONCAVALLO

rel introduced the young composer to Ricordi, the influential publisher, who listened to Leoncavallo's plans for an operatic trilogy on the Renaissance with interest. Ricordi gave Leoncavallo a substantial sum of money to begin work on the first of the trilogy, promising it production. When, however, *I Medici* was finished, procrastinations and delays greeted it until, finally, it was permanently discarded.

Meanwhile, Mascagni's great success with the one-act *Cavalleria rusticana* induced Leoncavallo to put aside, momentarily, the composition of a Renaissance trilogy and to create a work similar to *Cavalleria* which might attract public attention. This work—it was *Pagliacci*—came to the notice of Lison Frandin, celebrated primadonna, who, touched by Leoncavallo's inability to get a hearing, urged the powerful editor, Sonzogno, to use influence on his behalf. "Really," Sonzongo told the singer, "the house is full; there are too many competitors in the field." Frandin, however, was insistent, and finally succeeded in arranging an interview. During this meeting, Leoncavallo played *Pagliacci* for the editor. During the first act, Sonzogna appeared apathetic; but in the second, he could restrain himself no longer. He embraced the composer and promised to help him.

It was Sonzogno's influence that procured a performance for *Pagliacci* at the Dal Verme theatre on May 7, 1892. The conductor was Arturo Toscanini.

"Well do I remember that eventful evening when it first saw the light," Claude Trevor has recorded. "No one knew anything much about it except that it was a novelty, and of sufficient importance to have attracted the attention of Maurel, who created the baritone part. The crowded Dal Verme theatre was literally in a frenzy on the above occasion, and at the fall of the curtain a scene of such wild enthusiasm took place as is only to be seen rarely."

F. Bonavia has explained the reason for the phenomenal success of *Pagliacci*. "The text has the rare merit of a poignant story and rapid action, and the music has all the lyrical flow of the Italian school; but the texture is in-finitely more substantial than is the case with Mascagni. . . . The orchestration is also carefully balanced, and is free from vulgarities."

The success of *Pagliacci* brought performance to Leoncavallo's earlier opera, *I Medici*, in 1893. *I Medici*—possessing none of the lyrical freshness or spontaneity of *Pagliacci*—was a failure. "The music is the work of an extremely clever man," wrote R. A. Streatfeild. "It is seldom original, it is true; indeed, it teems with the most audacious plagiarisms, but it is cleverly strung together, and the orchestration is full of fancy and even imagination. Nevertheless, as a serious work of art its value is absolutely *nil*. It is the work of a cultivated student of contemporary music, a man who has read and digested the best scores of the best musicians of Europe during the past fifty years. It is a brilliant exercise, a triumph of eclecticism."

The failure of *I Medici* influenced Leoncavallo to abandon his plan for a Renaissance trilogy. Instead, he turned to the composition of operas similar in spirit and style to *Pagliacci*. He composed many operas in this vein, none of them able to recapture his early fire and freshness. He remained, notwithstanding his prolific production, essentially a one-opera man—a fact which greatly embittered him in the closing years of his life.

Ruggiero Leoncavallo died of nephritis at his villa in Montecatini on August 9, 1919.

Principal works by Ruggiero Leoncavallo:

OPERA: *Pagliacci*; *I Medici*; *La Bohème* (composed before Puccini's opera); *Zaza*; *Der Roland*; *La Jeunesse de Figaro*; *Maia*; *Malbruk*; *La Reginalla delle rose*; *Gli Zingari*; *Ave Maria*; *Goffredo Mameli*.

ORCHESTRA: *Serafita*.

BALLET: *La Vita d'una Marionetta*. Songs.

About Ruggiero Leoncavallo:

Streatfeild, R. A. *Masters of Italian Music*. *Monthly Musical Record* 49:193 September 1919; *Musical America* 30:26 September 6, 1919; *Musical Times* 60:476 September 1, 1919.

Important recordings of music by Ruggiero Leoncavallo:

OPERA: *Pagliacci*, complete (VICTOR-La Scala).

SELECTIONS FROM OPERAS: *Zaza,* "Buona Zaza" and "Zaza, piccola zingara (COLUMBIA).

SONGS: *Mattinata* (VICTOR-Martini); *Sérénade napolitaine* and *Sérénade française* (POLYDOR).

Jean François Lesueur   *1760-1837*

JEAN FRANÇOIS LESUEUR was born in a small French hamlet, Plessiel, near Abbéville, on February 15, 1760, the son of poor peasant folk. As a child, the only music he heard was the hymns in church. It was reported that, at one time, when he was seven years old, a military band passed thru his town. The magic concord of sound so entranced him that he followed the music for miles until he fell exhausted on the road. This incident must have made an impression upon his parents for, soon afterwards, he was placed in a monastery school, the only school near Plessiel where he could procure instruction in music. Here he remained until his sixteenth year, when he was transferred to another monastery. Then, completing his studies under Abbé Roze and serving as a choirmaster in Dijon, he turned to Paris, in 1784, where he was appointed chapel master at the school of the Innocents. At this time, his first works to reach performance were featured at the Concert Spirituel— a group of motets.

In 1786, Lesueur was given the post of chapel-master at Notre Dame. Feeling convinced that church music was in sad need of reform, he began to inaugurate large-scale church performances in which, during festival days, he would perform grandiose religious music-dramas of his own composition, to the accompaniment of elaborate orchestras. These performances attracted the poor folk from distant corners of Paris, and became so celebrated that before long Marie Antoinette herself attended them.

Notwithstanding the popularity of these performances, Lesueur confronted considerable opposition. There were many devout souls who felt that, thru these spectacles, cathedral service was being degraded into a "beggar's opera." To the churchmen of Notre Dame these services were likewise undesirable because of their exorbitant expense. Be-

fore long, the church officials began to seek an excuse for dismissing their ambitious chapel-master. When, therefore, Lesueur asked, at one time, for a brief leave of absence to visit England, the churchmen found here the pretext they had been seeking, and Lesueur was cursorily dismissed.

In an attempt to justify his reforms of church music, Lesueur now published his *Essai de musique sacrée,* in which he clearly expounded his theories. He attempted to apply to church music the imitative principles utilized so successfully in opera by Gluck. He felt strongly that the character of music should vary with different festivals of the year, that it should attempt to express the context of the words as closely and as dramatically as possible. Music, he felt strongly, should be essentially imitative, it should be endowed with a descriptive program and, hence, full of expression. It is interesting to point out that in more instances than one did Lesueur prove to be one of the first theorists to champion the cause of program-music, and also one of the first to formulate definitely a theory for *leit-motif.*

Upon his dismissal from Notre Dame, many prominent people rose to champion his cause. André Chenier, the poet, wrote a poem defending him; and the Canon of Notre Dame offered him the hospitality of his summerhouse, of which Lesueur availed himself for several years.

It was at this time that, momentarily, Lesueur turned from the composition of church to dramatic music. In 1793, his first opera, *La Caverne* (taken from *Gil Blas*) was given a successful performance. This was followed by *Paul et Virginie* which brought Lesueur additional prestige. As a result of the success of these operas, Lesueur was appointed, in 1793, professor at the École de la garde nationale, and, two years later, Inspector at the Conservatory.

His fame continued to grow until 1801 when, once again, Lesueur suddenly found himself stranded without a post. In that year, he began to object strenuously to the course of study given at the Conservatory. Finding that his complaint reached deaf ears, he published a

JEAN FRANÇOIS LESUEUR

monograph *Projet d'un plan général de l'instruction musicale en France*. This monograph incurred the enmity of his superiors, who utilized the first pretext to dismiss Lesueur. For a period, he knew poverty. Then, in 1804, he was appointed director of music to Napoleon, a post vacated by Paisiello. With this appointment, his fortune took a radical turn. On July 10, 1804, his new opera, *Ossian, ou les Bardes*, was performed at the Opéra, with Napoleon in the audience. Napoleon was so pleased with the work that he sent the composer a gift of a snuffbox filled with gold pieces.

From that time on, Lesueur was the favorite composer of Napoleon, consequently enjoying great prosperity and fame. Upon Napoleon's coronation in 1804, he composed a *Te Deum* which pleased the new Emperor considerably. Two years later, Lesueur was married to the charming Mlle Adeline Jamart de Courchamp; Napoleon and Josephine signed the marriage contract. In 1813, Lesueur succeeded Grétry as a member of the Institut.

The downfall of Napoleon was a severe personal blow to Lesueur, but it did not materially change his fortunes. He continued in his many positions, adding to them the significant post of superintendent of the Chapel of Louis

XVIII. In 1818, Lesueur became professor at the Conservatory, holding this assignment until the end of his life. He was a brilliant teacher, and he exerted an influence over a large group of famous French composers, including Gounod, Thomas and Berlioz.

Jean François Lesueur died in Paris on October 6, 1837. Fifteen years after his death a monument was erected in his honor in Abbéville. For this occasion, his pupil, Ambroise Thomas, composed a special *Song of triumph*.

Lesueur was described by one of his contemporaries as follows: "His features were hard, noble, lit with a superior intelligence which, so to speak, embellished his face. His brow was high and polished like a marble-top table, destined to receive and efface the thousand impressions which confronted it. His mouth was finely shaped, his lips were sensitive. . . . His cheeks were pale, made thin by constant study and by the many battles of his life." With his shock of gray hair, with his eyes of piercing intensity, underneath arches of heavy brows, and with his fine ascetic face, he made a majestic impression. "He had the air of an old patriarch," Gounod once said.

He was unworldly and impractical, his head perpetually in the clouds. But his character was not untouched by pride and vanity. It was said that his life was guided by three ideals: Homer, the Bible and Napoleon.

Lesueur is, today, better remembered as a personality and teacher than as composer. "His music is a mixture of simplicity and complexity," wrote Mary Hargreave. "He was a poet, philosopher and a writer, as well as a musician, and was full of ideas which were too difficult of execution, especially with his primitive notion of harmony."

Lesueur's most important accomplishment rests with his theories on music. In this field, he was a precursor of Berlioz (whom he influenced profoundly), and left a permanent impression upon musical development.

It was Octave Fouqué who commented facetiously that "Lesueur's best work was—Berlioz."

Principal works by Jean François Lesueur:

OPERA: *La Caverne*; *Paul et Virginie*; *Ossian, ou les Bardes*; *La Mort d'Adam*; *Alexandre à Babylone*, etc.

CHORAL: *Débora*; *Rachel*; *Ruth et Noémi*; *Ruth et Booz*; *L'Ombre de Sacchini*; Thirty masses; Three Te Deums; psalms; motets; odes; choruses, etc.

ORCHESTRA: *Coronation march*; *Fête music*; *March séraphique*.

About Jean François Lesueur:

Fouqué, Octave. *Les Révolutionnaires de la Musique*; Hargreave, Mary. *The Early French Musicians*; Lamy, F. *Jean François Lesueur*; Servières, Georges. *Épisodes d'Histoire Musicale*.

Anatol Liadov   *1855-1914*

ANATOL CONSTANTINOVICH LIADOV, well-known Russian nationalist composer, was born in St. Petersburg on May 11, 1855. In his autobiography, Rimsky-Korsakoff has given us a vivid description of Liadov's early background: "Anatol Constantinovitch was the son of Constantin Nikolaievich Liadov, conductor of the Russian opera. . . . The brilliant musical gifts of Anatol's father were stifled in continuous revelling and carousing. He frittered away his activity as a composer on mere nothings, composing dance music and pieces to order. . . . Of Anatol's mother, I know nothing; she had long departed the world, when I first came to know him. Anatol and his sister had been left to grow up as best they might. Their father, deep in his carousing and his liaison with the singer L., was never at home and never laid eyes on his children for weeks at a stretch. Though he drew a very good salary, he frequently left his children without a copper so that they had to borrow money occasionally from the servants to escape starvation. Of formal education and instruction there could be no question at all. On the other hand, however, Anatol had unrestricted access behind the scenes of the Maryinsky Theatre, where, one and a'l, from the leading singer to the last lamplighter, spoiled him as the conductor's son. At rehearsals, he lurked in the wings and clambered all over the boxes. . . . He could observe to his heart's content. . . . The pet of the opera-troupe, the pet who frequently had nothing to eat at home, was irresistibly drawn by the operatic stage. Glinka he loved, and knew by heart. . . . Of singers, chorus and orchestra he had heard enough and more than enough. Amid such surroundings, his boyhood passed, without supervision and without system."

He was entered in the St. Petersburg Conservatory where, despite his love for music, he at first proved to be a listless and lazy pupil. Frequently he did not come to class; on those days that he did attend, his mind was far removed from the classroom. As a result, he was soon suspended. His pleas and promises of repentance brought reinstatement. From this time on, Liadov suddenly became the brilliant student. He completed his course in counterpoint, fugue, instrumentation and musical form under Johansen and Rimsky-Korsakoff. Upon graduation, he composed so remarkable a work for orchestra, *The Bride of Messina*, that he was recommended for the teaching staff at the Conservatory. In 1878, he was appointed professor of harmony and theory at this institution.

From this time on, he was active as pedagogue, associating himself likewise with the Imperial Chapel. In 1894, he became conductor of the Musical Society, and was instrumental in bringing to the fore many prominent works of younger Russian composers. Shortly after this, he was appointed by the Geographic Society a member of an important committee to investigate Russian folk music. In this capacity, he did valuable work in unearthing important folk songs and in giving them significant modern adaptations.

Anatol Liadov died in St. Petersburg on August 28, 1914.

In a letter to Stassov, Moussorgsky described Liadov as "fair-haired, thick-lipped, the forehead not very high but full of character, especially in conjunction with the high cheek-bones. Irregular wrinkles run around his nose and mouth. He is extraordinarily nervous and highly strung, and even more extraordinarily taciturn."

He was known to have been a man of singular attractiveness and charm, whose simplicity and retiring disposition (he detested making public appearances, even at concerts where his works were performed) were frequently subject of comment. Perhaps his most distinguishing trait was an incorrigible laziness. He detested hard work, or activity of any kind. His entire life was dominated by this lethargy and inertia. He detested movement of any kind: he lived in one city for more than thirty years, retaining in all that time the same summer house. He was happiest when idle in a chair indulging in vacant dreams. It was said, likewise, that the weather had an effect on his creative energy. He was unab'e to work at all in fair or warm weather.

Notwithstanding his inertia, Liadov composed many works of distinction. These works, wrote Ellen von Tidebohl, reveal him to be a "true Slav. . . . His fertile imagination gave to his compositions a distinctly fertile Russian character. . . . Liadov's music is entirely national. He continued the work begun by Glinka, the father of Russian music, and his followers, Dargomijsky, Borodin, Moussorgsky and Rimsky-Korsakoff. Compared with the latter, his forms are much smaller."

It is the opinion of many critics that Liadov is most important in his adaptations of Russian folk music. Here, as Alfred J. Swan commented, "Liadov's soul . . . . blossoms forth, radiates brilliant light. He has set in all about one hundred and fifty songs. . . . Liadov's harmonies are distinguished by certain peculiar traits that fit the songs to an almost incredible degree. . . . Coupled with elegance, taste and economy, which is yet exuberant, they make Liadov's settings unique from a purely musical point of view. But, of course, the main charm of them lies in the peculiar spiritual affinity between Liadov's genius and the Russian folk song."

Principal works by Anatol Liadov:

ORCHESTRA: *The Bride of Messina; Two polonaises; Eight Russian songs; Baba-jaga; The Fairy lake; Kikimora; Dance of Amazons; From the Apocalypse; Two scherzos.*

CHORAL: Choruses to *The Bride of Messina*; Choruses for *Soeur Béatrice*; Choruses for women's voices.
A library of piano pieces including mazurkas, variations, preludes, sketches, etc. A library of songs, including adaptations of Russian folk music.

About Anatol Liadov:

Calvocoressi, M. D. and Abraham, Gerald. *Masters of Russian Music*; Rimsky-Korsakoff, Nicholas. *My Musical Life.*
Chesterian N.S. 18:45 October 1921; *Monthly Musical Record* 45:9 January 1915; *Musical Record and Review* 498:4 July 1, 1903.

Important recordings of music by Anatol Liadov:

ORCHESTRA: *Baba-jaga* (BRUNSWICK-Wolff); *Kikimora* (ODEON); *Eight Russian songs* (VICTOR-Stokowski).

ANATOL LIADOV

Serge Liapunov *1859-1924*

SERGE MICHAELOVITCH LIAPUNOV was born in Yaroslav on November 30, 1859. His first systematic musical education he received at the Imperial Music School in Nijny-Novgorod. In 1878, he entered the Moscow Conservatory remaining there for five years. His teachers included Klindworth and Pabst at the piano, and Tschaikovsky, Taneyev and Balakirev in composition. It was Balakirev who had the strongest influence over the young musician; in all of his future composition, Liapunov imitated many of Balakirev's musical mannerisms.

His studies ended, Liapunov was appointed subdirector of the Imperial Choir in Petrograd, in 1884. For

SERGE LIAPUNOV

eighteen years he held this position, earning the respect and admiration of the foremost musicians in Russia. His reputation assumed such imposing stature that, in 1893, he was appointed member of a folk-song commission of the Geographical Society which, in 1897, succeeded in publishing almost three hundred unfamiliar Russian folk songs.

In 1902, Liapunov resigned his post at the Imperial Choir to become inspector of music at the St. Helene Institute. Five years later, he embarked on an extensive concert tour thru Germany and Austria as conductor and concert-pianist, bringing many Russian works to the attention of these music audiences. After 1910, Liapunov served as professor at the Petrograd Conservatory.

One year before his death, Liapunov came to Paris, spreading there valuable propaganda on behalf of Russian music. On November 11, 1924, he died in Paris of paralysis of the brain.

It is Rosa Newmarch's opinion that, in his composition, Liapunov is at his best in writing for the piano. "Here, Liszt was his ideal. His influence shows clearly in the twelve *études d'exe-cution transcendente*. . . . Liapunov's piano music demands a high degree of digital skill but is . . . redeemed from empty virtuosity by the poetic lyricism

which suffuses it and penetrates the hard surface of the technical polish."

Liapunov's importance, however, is greater historically than creatively. "In the evolution of Russian music," wrote Boris de Schloezer, "Liapunov played an important rôle which the historian will never forget even when his music is completely abandoned. . . . [His works] imposed upon Russian musical genius a strict discipline, they inculcated into it a taste for perfection of form, enriching it with all the acquisitions of Western musical culture, making it possible for the emergence of the art of Scriabin, as well as that of Stravinsky or Prokofieff."

Principal works by Serge Liapunov:

ORCHESTRA: *Symphony*; *Yelasova Vola*; *Haschisch*; *Ouverture solennelle*; Two concertos for piano and orchestra; *Rapsodie* (for piano and orchestra); *Ballade*; *Polonaise*, etc.

PIANO: Preludes, études, dances, etc. Songs.

About Serge Liapunov:

Calvocoressi, M. D. and Abraham, Gerald. *Masters of Russian Music*; Montagu-Nathan, Montagu. *A Short History of Russian Music*. *Chesterian* 6:116 January 1925; *Musical America* 41:47 November 29, 1924; *La Revue Musicale* 6:142 December 1924.

Franz Liszt *1811-1886*

"Liszt, Liszt, qui changerait sans changer de délire,
Les notes pour les vers, le clavier pour la lyre."—ÉMILE DESCHAMPS

ROMANTIC biographers have found the life of Franz Liszt singularly rich in glamor and episode. He was born in Raiding, Hungary, on October 22, 1811. From his father, Adam Liszt —an impoverished officer in the imperial service, who was a devoted amateur of music—Franz Liszt inherited his love for music. From his mother, Liszt acquired a devotion for religion. His entire life was governed by these two influences.

Franz Liszt disclosed his talent for music at an early age. He was taught the elements of music by his father, making such progress, even under this inadequate instruction, that he was able to make an impressive debut at Ödenburg at the age of nine. Encouraged by the praise his son received, Adam Liszt took the boy to the Esterhazy palace in Eisenstadt, where his talent once again made a vivid impression, and urged a group of noblemen to raise a fund to provide for his musical education.

The Liszts now established themselves in Vienna, where Franz became a piano student of Karl Czerny, and the aged Salieri's pupil in composition. For two years, Franz continued his studies, making appearances on the concert stage at the same time. At one of his concerts, in 1823, it is said that Beethoven was in the audience, and was so moved by what he heard that he came upon the stage and kissed the young virtuoso. 1823 likewise marked Liszt's official debut as a composer, when his variations on a Diabelli waltz were published in a collection entitled *Vaterländische Künstler-Verein.*

Towards the close of 1823, the Liszts went from Vienna to Paris (stopping en route for Franz to give two successful concerts) to enroll the young musician in the Paris Conservatory. Cherubini, however, would not be moved by the boy's soaring reputation, not by his indisputable gifts, nor even by the letter of introduction from Prince Metternich which Franz had brought with him, to alter the rules of the Conservatory which forbade admittance to foreign-born musicians. Franz, therefore, was placed under Reicha and Paër, under whose instruction this young genius was matured.

During this period, Franz Liszt became the darling of the French salon. On March 8, 1824, he made a public appearance at the Opéra, assisted by a symphony orchestra; it has been recorded that, in the Hummel *Concerto,* his beautiful playing so enchanted the musicians in the orchestra that, in one passage, they forgot to play their parts. Two months later, Franz was in London, where he delighted not only the great music public, including the highest society, but even George IV, for whom he gave a command performance. On October 25, 1825, this genius emerged with new powers: His opera, *Don Sancho,* was produced enthusiastically at the Opéra. Unfortunately, this early

FRANZ LISZT

example of Liszt's creative talent is no longer in existence; it was destroyed in the fire that consumed the library of the Opéra about fifty years later.

For the next two years, Liszt concertized with great success. In August of 1827, Adam Liszt died in Boulogne-sur-mer, with the warning on his lips that his son be careful not to permit women to ruin his great career. With these words still ringing in his ears, Franz experienced the first genuine love affair of his life. He had settled in Paris with his mother, earning a livelihood by teaching the piano. One of his pupils was the beautiful Caroline de Saint-Cricq. It was not long before they contemplated marriage. The Count de Saint-Cricq would not hear of such an alliance, and crushed whatever hope the lovers entertained.

The loss of his beloved was a severe blow to Liszt, who sought consolation in solitude and religion. For the first time he thought seriously of abandoning music and entering the church. At the same time, he turned avidly to literature and philosophy, devouring the works of Montaigne, Chateaubriand, Voltaire, St. Beuve, Lamartine, Rousseau, etc. Once aroused, his appetite for literature became insatiable. At one time, he turned impetuously to the Avocat Crimieux and cried: "Monsieur Crimieux, please teach me *all* of French literature!" These interests so absorbed Liszt that he neglected himself, ate and slept irregularly, and suffered a nervous breakdown. At one time, he was so sick that a rumor spread thruout Paris that he was dead.

The July revolution of 1830 deflected Liszt's ardor from religion and philosophic study to the proletarian cause. It was only with difficulty that his mother restrained him from fighting in the barricades.

Two years later, Liszt returned to music—inspired by Paganini's phenomenal performances on the violin, and by Liszt's friendship with such musicians as Berlioz and Chopin. He now hurled his enormous energy into developing his pianistic technique. "Here is a whole fortnight that my mind and fingers have been working like two lost spirits—Homer, the Bible, Plato, Locke, Byron, Hugo, Lamartine, Chateaubriand, Beethoven, Bach, Hummel, Mozart, Weber are all around me," he wrote to a friend at this time. "I study them, meditate on them, devour them with fury; besides this, I practise four to five hours of exercises (thirds, sixths, eighths, tremolos, repetitions of the notes, candenzas, etc.). Ah! provided I don't go mad, you will find an artist in me! Yes, an artist such as you desire, such as is required nowadays."

In 1833, Franz Liszt fell in love with the Countess d'Agoult, who deserted her husband and children to come to the composer. "Strong affinities of race and temperament brought them together, but the extreme differences in their education and station in life of necessity raised up innumerable difficulties around them. A thousand obstacles arose between them and endowed the passion that drove them towards each other with a dolorous intensity which, in more balanced days than these, love will never know again." This quotation appears in a book of *Memoirs* written by "Daniel Stern," a pseudonym for the Countess d'Agoult herself, who, in later years, adopted a literary career.

The lovers fled to Geneva, where their first child was born. Liszt and the Countess remained attached to one another for six years. After this, differences of temperament brought a rupture.

Three children had been born to them, one of whom was the celebrated Cosima —wife of Hans von Bülow and later of Richard Wagner.

Upon returning to Paris after his love escapade in Geneva, Liszt discovered that in his absence a new pianist had risen to fame—Sigismund Thalberg. Liszt's vanity piqued, he determined to prove to all Paris that he was still the greatest pianist of his time. There followed a bitter musical duel between these two great pianists, each of whom had his own devoted band of followers. Finally, the two pianists appeared at an exclusive salon, playing their own works, and what was surely one of the monumental concerts in musical history became a personal victory for Liszt.

Betwen 1840 and 1848, Franz Liszt travelled thruout the music world, proving beyond contradiction that he was one of the foremost virtuosos of his generation. Triumph, acclaim, fawning adulation met him everywhere. Men were enchanted by the vast scope of his interpretative art as well as by the magic and magnetism of his personality; women, everywhere, succumbed to his unique fascination. In 1847, he performed in Kiev, where he made so striking an impression upon Princess Caroline von Sayn-Wittgsenstein, that she urged the musician to live with her at one of her estates. This was the prelude to a lifelong relationship between Liszt and the Princess.

In 1848, he was appointed chapelmaster to the Grand Duke of Weimar and, settling with the Princess in that city where he remained for thirteen years, he exchanged the piano for a baton. These years as chapel-master were marked by a valiant battle to bring important works of unknown composers to recognition. Among the new works which Liszt introduced were *Benvenuto Cellini* of Berlioz, *Alfonso und Estrella* of Schubert, *Lohengrin* of Wagner, *King Alfred* of Raff, and the *Barber of Bagdad* of Cornelius.

In 1849, Richard Wagner, a political fugitive from Dresden, visited Franz Liszt at Weimar. Wagner and Liszt had met several times previously, but during Wagner's stay at Liszt's home in Weimar, the bond between these two great musicians became a close one. From that time on, Liszt devoted his life towards bringing the great music dramas of his friend to the notice of the music world. As a matter of fact, Liszt was one of the forces to bring Wagner's dream of Bayreuth to realization. In later years, when Richard Wagner encouraged Liszt's daughter, Cosima, to desert her husband, Hans von Bülow, and to live with him, Liszt was so bitterly infuriated that for many years he became a personal enemy of Wagner. It speaks nobly for Liszt's artistic integrity that, even during these years of enmity towards Wagner, his zeal and industry in publicizing Wagner's music dramas remained undiminished.

In 1861, as a result of intrigue and antagonism—brought on principally by opposition to Liszt's efforts on behalf of new music—Franz Liszt resigned his post at Weimar, after a stormy reception accorded his performance of Cornelius' *Barber of Bagdad*. "I had dreamed of a new art period for Weimar," he wrote, "like that of Karl August, in which Wagner and I should have been leaders, as formerly Goethe and Schiller were; but unfavorable circumstances brought these dreams to naught." From this time on, Liszt was drawn more and more closely to the church, spending much of his time in Rome in close contact with the Pope. In 1865, he was given the honorary title of Abbé. In 1879, he submitted to the tonsure, and then took the vows of four minor orders.

In 1870, Liszt was appointed president of an academy of music in Budapest. Formerly distinguishing himself as pianist, conductor and composer, he was now to carve a new great career for himself as teacher. The same high ideals and integrity that governed his artistic activity in other fields of endeavor now characterized his work as a teacher. He brought to his pupils that fine insight, that enormous knowledge of piano technique and that scholarship and high artistry that succeeded in making him one of the foremost piano teachers of all time. The greatest pianists of the past and present generation were at one time pupils of Franz Liszt including Hans von Bülow,

Karl Klindworth, Tausig, Sgambati, Moritz Rosenthal, Emil Sauer, Frederic Lamond, etc.

Reconciliation between Wagner and Liszt took place in 1872. With the inauguration of the Bayreuth Festival in 1876, Liszt was a familiar figure at the small Bavarian town which had become the shrine for the Wagnerian music drama.

When Richard Wagner died, on February 13, 1883, Liszt was in Budapest, and the news struck him as a hammer-blow. Cosima Wagner, who could not forget that her father did not sanction her union with Wagner, would not permit him to come to the funeral.

After a short tour in 1886—which took him to France, England, Belgium and Germany—Liszt returned to Bayreuth. Compelled to remain on the train all night, he caught cold. Negligence—notwithstanding his illness he insisted upon hearing *Tristan*—brought on pneumonia.

Franz Liszt died in Bayreuth on July 31, 1886. The last word he had been heard to utter was—"Tristan."

Amy Fay, whose charming volume, *Music Study in Germany,* contains many illuminating paragraphs about musical celebrities, describes Liszt as follows: "Tall and slight, with deep-set eyes, shaggy eyebrows, and long iron-gray hair which he wears parted in the middle. His mouth turns up in the corners, which gives him a most crafty and Mephistophelian expression when he smiles, and his whole appearance and manner have a sort of Jesuitical elegance and ease. His hands are very narrow, with long and slender fingers that look as if they had twice as many joints as other people's! They are so flexible and supple that it make you nervous to look at them. Anything like the polish of his manner I never saw. When he got up to leave the box, for instance, after his adieu to the ladies, he laid his hand on his heart and made his final bow—not with affectation, or in mere gallantry, but with quiet courtliness which made you feel that no other way of bowing to a lady was right or proper. It was most characteristic. But the most extraordinary thing about Liszt is his wonderful variety of expression and play of feature. One moment his face will look dreamy, shadowy, tragic. The next he will be insinuating, amiable, ironic, sardonic; but always the same captivating grace of manner."

Franz Liszt's personality has been the subject for endless paragraphs. He has described himself as "half gypsy and half Franciscan." Certainly, he was a strange mixture of wordliness and godliness. Religion was always an important element in his life; thruout his life he was a devout and pious soul. Yet this never kept him from indulgence of the flesh. One writer has recorded that Liszt had no less than twenty-six love-affairs; both of his principal relationships (with the Countess, and with the Princess) were without benefit of clergy. Moreover, soft living, comfort, aristocratic pomp and ceremony were necessities with him. It is only the sentimental biographer who can speak of Liszt as a man of "simplicity."

He was a man of strange contradictions. His generosity and warm heart were well known: his great influence, his purse, his advice and encouragement were always at the service of deserving musicians. And yet, Ernest Newman points out in *The Man Liszt,* he was likewise guilty of snobbery, and periodic streaks of insincerity. Liszt was, at turns, humble and self-advertizing, self-effacing and egotistic, a recluse who loved solitude and a man of the world who demanded attention and adulation. He could be a staunch friend and a venomous enemy. He could be the high artist whose integrity could never be questioned, and, at other times, he could compose obvious potboilers.

Liszt's career as a composer is divided into two distinct periods. In the first, he composed principally brilliant fantasias and transcriptions for the piano, as well as songs. In the second period, beginning with 1848—under the influence of Princess Wittgenstein—he turned to more ambitious ventures, producing those imposing symphonic and choral works that have brought him immortality.

Liszt is, first and foremost, a composer and transcriber for the piano. Wrote Camille Saint-Saëns: "The influence of Liszt on the destiny of the piano was immense. . . . We owe to him the invention of picturesque musical notation, thanks to which, by an ingenious disposition of the notes, and an extraordinary variety in presenting them to the eye, the author contrived to indicate the character of the passage, and the exact way in which it should be executed. Today, these refined methods are in general use. But above all, we owe to Liszt the introduction on the piano of orchestral effects and sonority."

In his symphonic music, Liszt's method—as Daniel Gregory Mason pointed out—consisted in "combining the musical organization of the classicists with the dramatic organization of Berlioz." Continuing, Prof. Mason wrote: "By the use of program and leading motives, he secured the advantages of the realistic school: freedom from the shackles of the strict traditional sonata form and a 'poetic' principle of coherence. By retaining thematic development, he reenforced this poetic coherence by musical logic, and avoided to some extent the fragmentary effects into which unmodified realism generally falls. To the thirteen orchestral pieces in which he most strikingly embodied this plan of interlinked dramatic and musical structure he gave the name of *Poèmes symphoniques,* generally translated as "symphonic-poem." He owes his chief historical importance to his creation of this form, which he exemplified also on a larger scale in his *Faust* and *Dante* symphonies."

While no critic denies the powerful influence that Liszt exerted on musical development in his composition (his harmonic writing greatly influenced Wagner, his symphonic-poem gave birth to an entire new school of which Richard Strauss is today dean, his piano music brought writing for the piano to new stages of development, etc.), the modern musical authority is inclined to exclude Liszt from the first rank of great composers. Frederick Niecks wrote in explanation: "The eloquence of his tone-speech does not make up for the less happy lyricism, the richness of the chordal harmony for the poverty of the polyphony; the virtuosity of his diction and orchestration for the inequality of his thought and its presentation. As to the last point, the thought in Liszt's larger compositions is apt to be without the continuity, the evolution, the logic which distinguish that of the supreme masters. He too readily contents himself with fragments of ideas joined together by transitions of inferior stuff. Both his style of mind and his early practise incline him to the improvisational fantasia-like and cumulative form. Sketching was more natural to him than elaboration; indeed, revision did not amount with him to a deepening and interpenetrating. . . . His music is full of exclamatory interjections, dashes, impressive sequences, and the natural accents of the emotions."

Principal works by Franz Liszt:

ORCHESTRA: *Dante symphony; Faust symphony*; Thirteen symphonic poems (including *Tasso, Les Préludes* and *Mazeppa*); Two concertos for piano and orchestra; *Danse macabre* (for piano and orchestra); *Hungarian fantasy* (for piano and orchestra); *Mephisto waltz.*

CHORAL: *Fest-messe in D*; *Ungarische Krönungs-messe*; *Requiem*; psalms; motets; *Die Legende von der heiligen Elisabeth*; *Christus*; *Die heilige Cäcilia*; *Die Glocken des Strassburgen Münsters*; *Missa Choralis,* etc.

PIANO: *Sonata in B-minor*; Hungarian rhapsodies; études; legends; *Années de pèlerinage,* etc.
Songs.

About Franz Liszt:

Bekker, Paul. *Franz Liszt*; Corder, Frederick. *Franz Liszt*; Hervey, Arthur. *Franz Liszt and his Music*; Huneker, James Gibbons. *Franz Liszt*; Kapp, Julius. *Franz Liszt: Eine Biographie*; Newman, Ernest. *The Man Liszt*; Nohl, Ludwig. *Life of Liszt*; Pourtalès, Guy de. *Life of Franz Liszt*; Sitwell, Sacheverell. *Franz Liszt*; Siloti, Alexander. *My Memories of Liszt.*

Important recordings of music by Franz Liszt:

ORCHESTRA: *Faust symphony* (PATHE); *Mazeppa* (BRUNSWICK-Fried); *Les Préludes* (COLUMBIA-Mengelberg); *Concerto in E-flat major* (COLUMBIA-Gieseking); *Concerto in A-major* (VICTOR-De Greef); *Hungarian fantasy* (VICTOR-De Greef); *Second Hungarian rhapsody* (VICTOR-Stokowski); *Mephisto waltz* (COLUMBIA-Defauw).

CHORAL: *Missa choralis* (POLYDOR).

PIANO: Thirteen Hungarian rhapsodies (GRAMOPHONE-Hambourg); *Sonata in B-minor* (VICTOR-Horowitz); *Liebestraum* (COLUMBIA-Grainger). Innumerable other recordings of smaller piano pieces.

Pietro Locatelli *1693-1764*

PIETRO ANTONIO LOCATELLI was born in Bergamo in or about 1693. In his early youth, he was sent to Rome, where he became a pupil of the violin under the great Corelli. When his study under Corelli was completed, he entered professional ranks.

In 1725, Locatelli entered the service of the Landgrave of Hesse-Darmstadt at Mantua. In 1732, he went to Amsterdam, which he then made his permanent home. There, he conducted concerts, gave performances on the violin which were sensational, and published his first important works. He achieved considerable renown for his violin playing which, in technical skill, was said to have been without parallel. He had a phenomenal command of his instrument; his virtuoso feats were the wonder and awe of his contemporaries.

Pietro Locatelli died in Amsterdam on April 1, 1764.

Despite the fact that Charles Burney esteemed Locatelli "a voluminous composer of music that excites more surprise than pleasure," Locatelli was a composer of genuine merit. His work, as Edmund van der Straeten pointed out, contains much "that is excellent, and his share in the development of the sonata form is by no means inconsiderable. Paganini owes a great deal of his art

PIETRO LOCATELLI

to the close study of Locatelli's twenty-four caprices, which are really transcendental technique."

Locatelli was, in truth, the father of modern violin virtuosity. He was the first composer to use high positions of the violin, and in his caprices went to the very end of the fingerboard, using the highest A of which the violin is capable.

It should likewise be mentioned—as Arnold Schering has said—that Locatelli was likewise an innovator in the concerto-grosso form. Inheriting the form from his master, Corelli, he brought it greater solidity, expressiveness and variety of emotion.

Principal works by Pietro Locatelli:

ORCHESTRA: Twelve concerti grossi; Thirty concerti for violin and chamber orchestra.

CHAMBER MUSIC: Trio sonatas for two violins and bass; quartet-concertos; sonatas for flute and bass; sonatas for violin and bass.

VIOLIN: Caprices; sonatas, etc.

About Pietro Locatelli:

Phipson, Thomas Lambe. *Biographical Sketches of Celebrated Violinists*; Reuchsel, Maurice. *L'École Classique du Violon*; Straeten, Edmund van der. *The History of the Violin*.

Important recordings of music by Pietro Locatelli:

VIOLIN: Caprice, *Le labyrinthe* (POLYDOR); *Sonata da camera* (COLUMBIA).

Matthew Locke *1630-1677*

MATTHEW LOCKE, the foremost English dramatic composer before the time of Henry Purcell, was born in Exeter in or about 1630. He began his musical career as a chorister in the Exeter Cathedral, where he was trained by Edward Gibbons (the brother of the celebrated Orlando) and William Wake.

In 1644, when Cathedral services in England were suppressed, Locke was turned adrift. He went to London. A few years after this, he was on the continent on some secret mission—possibly carrying with him letters and propaganda of the Royalists. During this period he did not neglect music study, developing himself in the rules of composition.

In 1651, he was back in England, where he produced his first major work,

MATTHEW LOCKE

the *Little consort of three parts.* Two years later, he turned to the creation of dramatic music, when he collaborated with Christopher Gibbons in the composition of a masque, *Cupid and Death.* Thus began his endeavors in the dramatic field. Between 1653 and 1660, he produced many works for the theatre, including the *Siege of Rhodes,* which Roger North has called "semi-operas" and which have tempted more than one musicologist to refer to their composer as the originator of English opera.

Matthew Locke soon achieved so prominent a position in English music that the coronation of Charles II was accompanied by music which he composed for the event. In acknowledgment, Charles II appointed Locke "composer in the private musick" and "composer in Ordinary" on June 16, 1660.

Towards the end of his life, Locke officiated as organist of the chapel Somerset House, where his performances were considered too heavy-handed and distasteful.

Matthew Locke died in London in August of 1677, and was buried in the chapel of Savoy Palace. Henry Purcell wrote an ode in commemoration of Locke's death.

Locke's music was, as Frederick Bridge pointed out, "exceedingly dramatic and melodious," containing a harmony which—in the words of W. H.

Cummings—"evinces a freshness and variety far in advance of the period in which it was composed." It had a strong-muscled robustness, a strength and vigor which placed it quite apart from the music of other English composers of the period. "All his work," remarked Jeffrey Pulver, "is marked by an obvious desire to do his best—often in a style that did not suit him. Thus his sacred music, though good, lacks that spontaneity which his dramatic work exhibits."

Principal works by Matthew Locke:

OPERA: *Siege of Rhodes*; *The Stepmother*; *Macbeth*; *Psyche*; *The Tempest*.

CHORAL: Anthems; hymns; ayres; songs, etc.

INSTRUMENTAL: *Little consort of three parts*; *Courtly masquing ayres*; *Musick's delight on the cithern*; *Apollo's banquet*; *Musick's handmaid,* etc.

About Matthew Locke:

Bridge, Frederick. *Twelve Good Musicians*; Pulver, Jeffrey. *A Biographical Dictionary of Old English Music*; Walker, Ernest. *A Short History of English Music*. *International Music Society Congress* 4:100 May-June 1911.

Important recordings of music by Matthew Locke:

INSTRUMENTAL: *String quartet,* arranged by Warlock-Mangeot (NATIONAL GRAMOPHONIC SOCIETY).

Charles Martin Loeffler *1861-1935*

(See *Composers Of Today*)

Karl Loewe *1796-1869*

JOHANN KARL GOTTFRIED LOEWE, genius of the ballad, was born in Löbejün, near Halle, on November 30, 1796. His father, Andreas Loewe, was the village schoolmaster and choirleader, who knew enough music to initiate his son into the art. Karl Loewe took to music instinctively. From earliest childhood, his play hours were spent in singing and drawing melodies from the piano.

At the age of ten, he was sent to the school of Cöthen where, as he later wrote in his autobiography with charming frankness, "the people admired and made much of me." Three years were

spent here, after which Loewe became a pupil at the Gymnasium in Halle.

During this time, Andreas Loewe was eager to ascertain if his son was particularly gifted in music. To convince himself, he took the boy to Professor Türk, a theorist in Halle. Professor Türk gave the boy a severe examination, from which Karl emerged triumphant. He had given such convincing signs of talent that Professor Türk took him under his wing and taught him musical theory and the art of singing. Under Professor Türk's guidance he developed into an excellent singer. Before long he gave performances in Halle which brought him many words of praise. At one of these performances, the celebrated Mme. de Staël was so moved by his singing that she showered upon him effusive praise, pressing into his hand an eight-groschen piece. At another performance, King Jerome, brother of Napoleon I, was present and so pleased with Loewe's singing that he endowed the young musician with three hundred thalers a year to permit him to complete his music study.

The downfall of Jerome's kingship in 1813 deprived Loewe of his annuity, rudely curtailing his intensive music-study. He re-entered the Gymnasium, completed his studies there, and in 1817 entered the University. At this time, a vocal quartet was formed in Halle under the leadership of Adolf B. Marx, in which Loewe interested himself keenly because the first soprano was the beautiful Julie von Jacob, upon whom he had directed admiring glances long before this. The success of the vocal quartet permitted expansion. Before long, this society was capable of performing the oratorios of Handel and Haydn and the operas of Gluck and Spontini. In this way, Loewe was brought into contact with some great masterpieces of music, which aroused in him such enthusiasm that he determined to pursue the career of a composer. Shortly after this—in 1818—he composed two of his most admirable ballads, *Edward* and the *Erlkönig* (not to be confused with the famous *Lied* of Schubert). These two ballads impressed Adolf B. Marx who published them at his own expense.

KARL LOEWE

In 1819, Loewe visited Dresden where he met and became a friend of Karl Maria von Weber, the operatic composer. Returning to Halle, Loewe alternated between musical and military activity—giving song recitals and, at the same time, fulfilling his military service in the Halle rifle battalion where he was a champion marksman. He served in military service only one year, relieved from all further military duty by Crown Prince William IV of Prussia.

In 1820, Loewe came to Jena where he visited Goethe, the printed copy of his ballad, the *Erlkönig*, bulging from his pocket. "Goethe was exceedingly kind," Loewe wrote later, "and while walking up and down with me, conversed pleasingly about the nature of the ballad. . . . I told him that I liked the ballad above all other forms of poetry, and how the popular legend of the *Erlkönig* in the grand romantic garb of his poem had quite captivated me; so much so, indeed, that I could not help setting it to music."

It is interesting to comment parenthetically that eighteen years later the oldest grandson of the great poet, Walter von Goethe, was Loewe's pupil in theory and composition.

From Jena, and his interview with Goethe, Loewe went to Berlin where he took a musical examination under Zelter, director of the Singakademie. The re-

sults were brilliant and he was instantly appointed choirmaster of St. Jacob's Church in Stettin, where he became at the same time a student of theology, preaching sermons at periodic intervals. At this time, too, he received an appointment as teacher in the Gymnasium of Stettin.

Financially secure, he was now able to marry his first love, Julie von Jacob, in September of 1821.

He retained both positions, as choirmaster of St. Jacob and as teacher in the Gymnasium, for almost forty-six years. During this period he composed the bulk of his ballads and oratorios that brought him world-wide fame.

In 1823, one year and a half after his marriage, his wife, Julie, died. The catastrophe immersed him in great melancholy. For the next year he lived in lonely sorrow—refusing to come into contact with society—giving expression to his great grief by composing his poignant songs to Byron's *Hebrew melodies.* Fortunately, before the end of the second year of this voluntary seclusion, one of his pupils, Augusta Lange, attracted his interest. Before long, he emerged from his solitude, and married a second time.

By 1830—when he composed his oratorio, *Die Zerstörung Jerusalems*—Karl Loewe had reached fame as a composer. In 1832, the University of Greifswald gave him an honorary degree of doctor of philosophy, and shortly afterwards he was elected Fellow of the Royal Society of Fine Arts in Berlin. Between 1844 and 1848, he toured extensively as concert artist, giving song recitals in Berlin, Dresden, Frankfurt, Prague, Vienna, and finally before Queen Victoria in England.

His active career came to a sudden halt in 1866 when he was stricken with paralysis. Ordered by the municipality of Stettin to resign from all his official positions, Loewe retired to Kiel where he spent the last three years of his life. He died there on April 20, 1869. He was buried near the organ of St. Jacob's church in Stettin.

As a composer of both ballads and oratorios, Karl Loewe enjoyed considerable distinction before and after his death. The foremost musicians of his time—including Spontini, Weber, Schumann, Mendelssohn and Wagner—recognized his genius and esteemed him highly. Posterity has paid homage to him as well. "Loewe is the most important of all minor song writers," commented Francis Toye and Dyneley Hussey, "owing to the fact that he may be said definitely to have created the German dramatic ballad. Even now his setting of the *Erlkönig* has not been entirely swamped by Schubert's, and in the opinion of some competent judges his interpretation of the text is more conscientious if not more effective."

Wrote Hugo Riemann: "The musical form of the ballad was first created thru Loewe, so far as he understood it by clinging to the development of a plastic principal motive of epical breadth without losing any of the sharp characteristic details."

Principal works by Karl Loewe:

OPERA: *Rudolph der deutsche herr*; *Malek Adhel*; *Die drei wünsche*.

CHORAL: *Die Zerstörung Jerusalems*; *Die sieben schläfer*; *Die Apostel von Philippi*; *Die Festzeiten*; *Die Auferweckung des Lazarus*; *Palestrina*; *Die erste Walpurgisnacht*, etc.

ORCHESTRA: Symphonies; overtures; concertos for piano and orchestra.

CHAMBER MUSIC: Four string quartets; *Piano trio*.

About 250 songs. An entire library of celebrated ballads. Pieces for the piano, etc.

About Karl Loewe:

Bach, Albert B. *The Art Ballad*; *Loewe and Schubert*; Bulthaupt, H. *Karl Lowe, Deutschlands Balladenkomponist*; Loewe, Karl. *Autobiography*; Wellmer, August. *Karl Loewe*.

Important recordings of music by Karl Loewe:

BALLADS: *Archibald Douglas* (GRAMOPHONE-Bender); *Edward* and the *Erlkönig* (GRAMOPHONE-Bender); *Fridericus Rex* and *Prinz Eugen* (POLYDOR); *Hochzeitlied* and *Tom der reimer* (GRAMOPHONE-Bender); *Die Uhr* (COLUMBIA-Tauber), etc.

Albert Lortzing *1801-1851*

GUSTAV ALBERT LORTZING, composer of comic operas, was born in Berlin on October 23, 1801. He was a descendant of a family of actors; his father had given up the leather trade to join the stage.

Following in the traditions of the family, Albert Lortzing took to acting in his fourth year, combining his histrionic efforts with music study at the Singakademie. Unfortunately—because his parents were itinerant actors—it was impossible for him to complete his studies. His childhood was spent in travelling from one town to another, in continual poverty; for a short period, he attempted to alleviate his family's financial difficulties by copying opera parts.

In 1819, Albert Lortzing definitely turned to composition, producing several airs. Some of these early creative ventures attracted the notice of Karl Herlssohn, novelist, who thought he recognized in them the germs of a definite musical talent. He encouraged Lortzing, who now turned industriously to the composition of operettas. In his twenty-first year, Lortzing composed the first of his operettas, *Ali Pascha von Janina*, which was performed in Münster four years later.

In his twentieth year, Lortzing married a young actress, Rosina Regina Ahles. For a while, the young pair knew great poverty. This was, to a degree, alleviated in 1826, when Lortzing and his wife received employment in a theatre in Detmold. The salary was poor but it promised some leisure in which Lortzing could turn to composition. In 1833, Lortzing went to Leipzig, employed as a tenor at the Leipzig Opera. After his successful debut in the cast of *Die Schlachtmaschine*, he enjoyed a great vogue. However, his success as a singer did not disturb his fertility as a composer.

On February 30, 1837, Lortzing witnessed the first decided success of his creative career when he appeared in a performance of his own operetta, *Die beiden schützen*, which caught the fancy of the audiences. *Die beiden schützen* was performed successfully in Dresden, Prague, Berlin, Munich, and, finally, Vienna. This operetta was followed, in December of that year, by a still more successful venture, the *Zar und Zimmermann*, the work by which Lortzing is best known. Given at the Stadt Theatre in Leipzig on December 22, 1838, it was so successful that it was immediately introduced in leading cities in Germany and Austria.

In 1844, Lortzing was appointed a conductor of the Leipzig Opera. "This," he wrote enthusiastically at the time, "is first the beginning of my good luck." But, as Lortzing soon discovered, it was merely the prelude to his misfortunes. After several months, he lost his conductorial position because of intrigues in the institution. There followed for Lortzing two years of great want when the composer earned nothing from his music because it was being widely sold in pirated editions. In 1846, Lortzing had respite from his troubles when, invited to Vienna to conduct his own *Waffenschmied* he made so great an impression upon the Viennese music public that he was engaged as conductor of the Theatre-an-der-Wien. The Revolution of 1848 brought this assignment to an end. Brokenhearted, Lortzing returned to Leipzig to seek some post commensurate with his talent.

Broken in health and spirits, his hearing markedly impaired, Lortzing—who could find no musical post—was compelled to return to acting in small German towns, where his earning was so meagre that he frequently could not afford to buy coal. This trying period was finally brought to a close when Lortzing was appointed conductor of ballet and vaudeville at the Friedrich-Wilhelmstädter Theatre in Berlin, a post not particularly satisfying but which, in contrast to his previous engagements as itinerant actor, seemed affluence, indeed. But once again misfortune was Lortzing's companion, and after a few months he lost this post as well.

This was the last straw. This dismissal broke Lortzing's spirit and health, and in a short time he became a human wreck. He died in Berlin on January 21, 1851. "At half past six. . . . I heard him moan painfully," described his wife. "I turned around and touched him. A cold perspiration was on his forehead. I called him—shook him—no answer. I immediately called the girl and told her to bring vinegar and fetch the doctor. He came with a surgeon. They bled him in both arms—blood came—he

ALBERT LORTZING

made a few sounds, opened his eyes, but only a short time, to close them forever. By half past seven he was no more."

No critic will attempt to assign outstanding importance to Lortzing as a composer (he does not even occupy an all-important position in light music). But he will confess that, in Lortzing's best works—such as the *Zar und Zimmermann* and *Der Wildschütz*—the composer possessed a pleasing style full of humor and charm. "His is a kindly, sunny humor," wrote Eric Blom, "for he never ruffled his placid audiences by any too cruel thrusts of satire. It has, in fact, a great deal of the sentimentality of the old German *Singspiel,* a quality which often characterizes and frequently disfigures his music. The comic portions of his operas always have a lively aptness, enhanced by a happy knack of neat orchestration; but where it is a question of displaying tender or melancholy feelings, he lapses sadly into an almost unendurable triviality."

Richard Wagner looked upon Lortzing as a "skilful composer" and Liszt found sufficient merit in the *Zar und Zimmermann* to perform it in Weimar in 1851. Other musicians, however—Robert Schumann, of example, or Hans von Bülow—found very little to admire in Lortzing's works.

After Lortzing's death, Giacomo Meyerbeer, the famous operatic composer, helped raise a fund of sixteen thousand dollars to provide for the composer's family.

Principal works by Albert Lortzing:

OPERA: *Die beiden schützen*; *Zar und Zimmermann*; *Hans Sachs*; *Der Wildschütz*; *Undine*; *Der Waffenschmied*; *Die Rolandsknappen*; *Regina*.

CHORAL: Choruses; *Die Himmelfahrt Christi*.

ORCHESTRA: Overtures; music to *Drei Edelsteine*.

About Albert Lortzing:

Blom, Erich. *Stepchildren in Music*; Dueringer, Philip Johann. *Albert Lortzing: Leben und Wirken*; Webster, Clarinda Augusta. *Albert Lortzing*; Wittman, Hermann. *Lortzing*.
Musical America 44:5 October 9, 1926; *Musical Opinion* 46:355 January 1923; *Proceedings of the Musical Association*, 58th Session, 1931-1932.

Important recordings of music by Albert Lortzing:

OPERA: *Zar und Zimmermann,* abridged (POLYDOR).

SELECTIONS FROM OPERA: *Undine*, "Overture" (PARLAPHONE-Knappertsbusch); "Vater, mutter, schwestern, brüder" (POLYDOR-Tauber); "Ballet music" (GRAMOPHONE). *Der Waffenschmied,* "Overture" (POLYDOR); "Auch ich war ein Jüngling" (PARLAPHONE-List); "Lied an die flasche" (ODEON-Hoffmann); "Nun ist's vollbracht" (POLYDOR-Schlusnus). *Der Wildschütz*, "Overture" (GRAMOPHONE); "Heiterkeit und fröhlichkeit" (POLYDOR); "Kann es im erdenleben" (GRAMOPHONE).

Jean Baptiste Lully *1632-1687*

"I do not believe that there exists any other sweeter music under heaven than Lully's."—MME. DE SÉVIGNÉ

JEAN BAPTISTE LULLY, the father of French opera, was born in Florence, Italy, on November 29, 1632, the son of a peasant. As a child, he learned to play the guitar and acquired the elements of music from a Franciscan monk. He revealed such musical aptitude, that he interested Chevalier de Guise who had come from Paris to Florence to find an Italian boy who might serve as a page in the household of Mademoiselle de Montpensier. Chevalier de Guise took Lully back with him to Paris. Unfortunately, Lully's awkward mannerisms and ugly face repelled De Montpensier and, instead of engaging

him as a page, she placed him in the kitchen as a scullion.

His leisure hours he devoted to music —playing the violin and guitar and composing. A nobleman accidentally heard him play the violin and was sufficiently pleased to entreat Mademoiselle de Montpensier to place the boy in the orchestra. Here, Lully revealed his talent for music. He would no doubt have risen to high rank but for a malicious and pointed verse which he wrote one morning about his employer which resulted in his dismissal.

It was shortly after this dismissal from Mademoiselle de Montpensier's household that he found employment in the orchestra of Louis XIV. From that time on, his star rose and soared until he became one of the most famous musicians in the court. It was said that Louis XIV adored Lully's music, expressly establishing a new orchestra, called "Les Petits violons" so that Lully might direct it and compose for it original works. During this period, Lully composed some thirty ballets, to which Louis XIV himself danced.

Lully was, therefore, accorded great honor. Louis XIV conferred upon him the patent of nobility and appointed him "secretaire du roi." In 1862, Lully rose to the rank of "Maître de musique" to the royal family, a post bringing with it handsome remuneration. At this time, Lully's fame as a composer was so great that poets and essayists expressed their admiration for him in their writings.

In 1669, Abbé Perrin was given the patent to create an *Académie de Musique*. Lully, severely jealous of any competitor, indulged in petty court intrigues until the patent was transferred from the Abbé Perrin to himself. Thus, Lully became the director of an opera house. From that time on stemmed his great importance in musical history. With the aid of a sensitive poet, Quinault, Lully composed a long list of operas which definitely established French opera, bringing to that art form new phases of development. Modeling his operas after those of Caccini, Lully enriched instrumentation, substituted accompanied recitatives for the *secco recitativo,* (modeling it more closely after speech), and developed harmonic language.

Lully, as we learn from the writings of Lecerf de la Vieville, "produced one opera a year, and he took three months to write it. He applied the whole of his energies to it, and worked with extreme assiduity. The rest of the year he did little to it, except for an occasional hour or so at night when he could not sleep, and on mornings, which he could not spend in pleasure. He kept his mind always fixed, however, on the opera that he was evolving, or had just evolved, and if anyone happened to learn what he was singing at any time, it always proved to be an extract from an opera on hand."

Discussing Lully's achievements in opera, C. Hubert Parry wrote: "Lully developed a scheme of opera which was more mature and complete than any other of his time. The texture of his work on the whole is crude and bald, but the definition of the various items which go to make up his operatic scheme is complete as far as it goes. . . . In the first place, the plan of his overture is thoroughly distinct, and very happily conceived as an introduction to what it follows. . . . Lully shows excellent sense of relief and proportion, and in regulating the relation of the respective acts and scenes to one another; and he is

JEAN BAPTISTE LULLY

conspicuously successful for his time in shaking himself free from the ecclesiastical associations of the modes, and adopting a thoroughly secular manner. . . . His instinct for orderliness and system in laying out the musical material was in advance of the age. . . . He was among the first to make a notable use of what is called the aria form. . . . Lully's type of opera was an immense advance over the first experiments in plan, in definiteness of expression and rhythm, and in variety of subdivision into component ballet movements, choruses, instrumental interludes, arias, recitatives and so forth."

In January of 1687, Lully directed the performance of a *Te Deum* which he had composed in honor of the King's recovery from a serious illness. Two months later, on March 22, Lully died in Paris. There are some historians who maintain that Lully's death was the result of negligence. In rehearsing, Lully would beat time by pounding his heavy walking stick upon the ground. He accidentally hit his foot so often, while beating time, that he developed a fatal gangrene. Placing himself in the hands of incompetent physicians, Lully soon found that the gangrene had spread, poisoning his entire body.

There is an amusing anecdote told in connection with this illness. Realizing that his life was in danger, Lully called upon his father confessor. His father confessor told Lully that he was being punished because he had composed music for a theatre, advising Lully—if he was penitent—to destroy his last opera. This the composer did, and received absolution. Shortly afterwards, Lully confided this fact to a friend, who was horrified that Lully should have destroyed an opera. "That's nothing to worry about," Lully told his friend calmly. "You see, I had another copy in my desk."

George Hogarth described Lully as follows: "In person, Lully was rather thick and short. His complexion was dark, and his features very far from handsome; but his face had the expression of spirit and talent. He had not the politeness which might have been expected from so long a residence at the

French court; but he was gay, good-humored and his deportment was not without dignity. He was too much addicted to the pleasures of the table. . . . He was fond of money, and left behind him a sum equal to a hundred thousand dollars. He was called a miser by the extravagant courtiers. He had much vivacity and wit, and told a story with admirable humor."

Hogarth might have added that Lully was very ambitious, often unscrupulous in his methods to gain his ends; he loved drink and food excessively; he was untidy in his dress; he did not possess a capacity for hard work, and in composing his music he frequently dictated his melodies to a secretary who would fill in the harmonies.

It is the opinion of Henri Prunières, that *Acis et Galatée* is Lully's most important work.

Principal works by Jean Baptiste Lully:

OPERA: *Alceste*; *Atys*; *Isis*; *Psyché*; *Amadis*; *Roland*; *Armide*; *Acis et Galatée*; *L'Amour médecin*; *Le Bourgeois gentilhomme*; *Persée*, etc.

CHORAL: *Te Deum*; *Miserere*; *Libera*; motets.

ORCHESTRA: Concertos; overtures; suites. Ballets.

About Jean Baptiste Lully:

Hargreave, Mary. *Some Earlier French Musicians*; Hogarth, George. *Musical History, Biography and Criticism*; La Laurencie, Lionel de. *Lully*; Noirville, Duruy de. *Histoire du Théâtre et de l'opéra en France*; Parry, C. Hubert. *Evolution of the Art of Music*; Prunières, Henri. *Lully*.

Important recordings of music by Jean Baptiste Lully:

SELECTIONS FROM OPERA: *Alceste*, "Ouverture" (VICTOR-Stokowski); "Scène funèbre" (ULTRAPHONE); *Atys*, "Air pour la suite de flore" (PATHE); "Les Songes agréables (GRAMOPHONE-Landowska); *Persée*, "O Mort!" (PATHE); "Que n'aymez vous" (COLUMBIA). *Thesée*, "Ouverture et Marche" (PATHE); "Revenez, amours, revenez" (COLUMBIA).

SONGS: *Au clair de la lune* (GRAMOPHONE-Printemps); *Air tendre et courante* (VICTOR).

Edward Macdowell *1861-1908*

EDWARD ALEXANDER MAC-DOWELL, considered by many critics the foremost of American composers, was born in New York City, at 220 Clinton Street, on December 18, 1861. His ancestry was Scotch-Irish.

In his eighth year, Macdowell was given his first piano lessons by Juan Buitrago, friend of the family. Macdowell was no prodigy, but he proved to be alert in learning his piano lessons and in acquiring the rules of composition. After a few years of study under Buitrago, he became a pupil of Paul Desverine and Teresa Carreño. By this time, he had developed sufficiently to promise a successful future as pianist.

When he was fifteen years old, his mother took him to Paris where she entered him in the Conservatory as a pupil of Marmontel in piano, Savard in theory and composition. It is interesting to mention the fact that a fellow pupil of his at this time was Claude Debussy.

There now occurred an incident which almost changed the entire direction of his life. He was taking private lessons in French and, to relieve the monotony of grammatical drill, he sketched a portrait of his tutor. He was caught at this task. The tutor was so intrigued by the drawing that he confiscated the work and showed it to a friend, a teacher at the École des Beaux-Arts. The painter, in turn, found the sketch a talented one, and offered to teach Macdowell free of charge for three years. Macdowell's mother faced a pressing problem: Should Edward be permitted to continue his study of music or should he be redirected towards art? She questioned Marmontel at the Conservatory and consulted Edward's own wishes. It was, decided, finally, that he should continue his career as a musician.

Considerably dissatisfied with the instruction he received at the Paris Conservatory, Edward Macdowell, finally left Paris and went to Stuttgart. Here, he was even less happy; the method of teaching at the Stuttgart Conservatory was so different from that in Paris that he would have to begin his studies almost from the starting point. The stay in Stuttgart was, therefore, brief. The Macdowells next went to Wiesbaden, where Edward became a pupil of Louis Ehlert in composition and theory. That autumn, he was entered in the Frankfurt Conservatory, becoming a pupil of Raff and Carl Heymann.

Completing his studies at the Frankfurt Conservatory, Macdowell entered the ranks of professional musicians by accepting private pupils. One of these was Marian Nevins, who was later to become the charming and devoted Mrs. Edward Macdowell.

In 1881, Macdowell became head piano teacher at the Conservatory in Darmstadt. The work was arduous and the pay small, but it insured financial independence. It was at this time that he devoted himself industriously to composing (writing his *Modern suite* for piano) and to the reading of great English and German poetry.

The hard work at Darmstadt began to affect his health. He decided to resign his position and return to Frankfurt. Here, he divided his time between composition and pedagogy. One of the works on which he was engaged at this time was the *First piano concerto*. Raff saw the manuscript and was so impressed by the high quality of the music that he decided to send the young composer to Liszt. In 1882, Macdowell visited Liszt with the manuscript of his concerto under his arm. A fellow visitor at this time was Eugène D'Albert, the great pianist. With D'Albert playing the orchestral part of the work on the second piano, Macdowell performed his composition for the master. Liszt praised the work highly, finding it a ripe achievement.

On July 12, 1882, Macdowell played his *First piano suite* at the Allgemeiner Deutscher Musikverein. One year later, on Liszt's warm recommendation, the *Second modern suite* was published by Breitkopf and Härtel.

In June of 1884, Macdowell returned to America for a brief visit to marry Marian Nevins. For their honeymoon, they returned to Europe, visiting London and Paris, and finally settling in Frankfurt. Macdowell now applied himself more conscientiously to composition, producing at this time the orchestral *Hamlet and Ophelia*.

In the spring of 1887, the Macdowells bought a cottage in Grubweg, near Wiesbaden. In these idyllic surroundings, the composer was especially productive. He was now to see the fruits of his labor; his fame began to spread in several directions. *Hamlet and Ophelia* was performed successfully in Darmstadt, Wiesbaden, Baden-Baden, Frankfurt, and finally in New York under Franz van der Stucken. Teresa Carreño played the *Second modern suite* in a recital in New York. And, in 1888, the *First piano concerto* was introduced in New York. Wrote W. F. Apthorp at the time: "We can hardly recall a composition so full of astonishing and unprecedented effects. The work was evidently written at white heat; its brilliancy and vigor are astounding."

These successes inspired Macdowell to return to America. In 1888, he regretfully sold his cottage, crossed the ocean and settled in Boston. He now immersed himself in varied activities as teacher, pianist and composer. During the next few years, America heard several important performances of his works. In 1893, *Hamlet and Ophelia* was performed by Arthur Nikisch; one year later Anton Seidl introduced the *Second piano concerto* at the concerts of the New York Philharmonic. And, in 1896, the Boston Symphony Orchestra, on a visit to New York, performed both the *Indian suite* and the *First piano concerto* at the Metropolitan Opera House.

In 1896, a department of music was founded in New York at Columbia University. The professorship was accorded to Macdowell, the "greatest musical genius America ever produced." The work was prodigious—particularly for the first two years when he did not have an assistant. Always thorough and conscientious, Macdowell hurled all of his energy and industry into his duties, taxing his health considerably. His years at Columbia University affected his strength vitally. When he retired in 1904—partially because of his illness but principally because a severe misunderstanding had arisen between the composer and the University authorities—he was a sick and broken man.

Instead of retiring to quiet and rest, Macdowell continued his hard work as

EDWARD MACDOWELL

teacher, pianist and composer, until he was able to work no more. In 1905, the first signs of nervous disorder made an appearance. Before long, it developed into complete disintegration of the brain tissues. Finally, Macdowell's mind became like that of a child. He would sit near a window, perpetually smiling, completely oblivious of his surroundings or his fate, thumbing the pages of a fairy tale book which seemed to bring him singular pleasure.

He died on January 24, 1908, at Westminster Hotel in New York. His body was taken to his farm at Peterboro, New Hampshire, where he was buried on an open hilltop commanding a view he loved well. Several years after his death, Mrs. Macdowell established her home in Peterboro, in memory of her great husband, as a colony for artists, writers and poets, where for a negligible sum they might come to work in felicitous surroundings.

T. P. Currier has given us the following description of Macdowell: "His finely shaped head, carried a little to one side, was well set on slightly drooping shoulders. His very dark hair was close-cut. . . . There was about him no trace of the 'professional artist.' . . . His skin was light and clear, showing a slight color in his rather delicately rounded cheeks. Light blue eyes, with light bordering of eyebrows and lashes,

a well-cut aquiline nose, and an agreeable mouth and firm chin, completed what anyone would call a handsome face.

"It was equally expressive. Even casual acquaintances could read in it a kindly disposition, strong sense of humor, energy and determination. In conversation, he regarded one frankly and intently; and his face mirrored with extreme quickness his instinctive response. Anything pleasant or humorous would bring a lively twinkle into the eyes, rapid winking of eyelids, and a contagious smile, or deep hearty laugh, as the case may be. Profuse compliments would be received with a mingled look of boyish bashfulness and sly suspicion."

Edward Macdowell had a singularly well-rounded intellect. He was thoroughly versed in literature, was a student of philosophy, and a radical in politics. He was known for his fine sense of humor which was spiced with a keen irony; "witticisms seemed constantly to sparkle with him," commented H. F. Gilbert. His generosity towards young students of the arts made him well-loved among all those with whom he came into contact.

Discussing Macdowell's style of composition, Lawrence Gilman wrote that it was "as pungent and unmistakable as Grieg's, and far less limited in its variety. Hearing certain melodic turns, certain harmonic formations, you recognize them at once as belonging to Macdowell and to no other. . . . He suggested, at his best, no one save himself. He was one of the most individual writers who made music. . . . His manner of speech was utterly untrammeled, and wholly his own. Vitality—an abounding freshness, a perpetual youthfulness—was one of his traits; nobility—nobility of style, another." The outstanding characteristics of Macdowell's music, continued Mr. Gilman, were "great buoyancy and freshness," an "abounding vitality," "a constant juxtaposed tenderness and strength," a "pervading nobility of tone and feeling." His music "is charged with emotion. Yet it is not brooding or hectic, and it is seldom intricate or recondite in psychology. It is music curiously free from fevers of sex."

Macdowell is probably best known for his piano works—his two concertos for piano and orchestra and his celebrated sonatas (*Tragica, Eroica, Norse* and *Keltic*). In writing about the sonatas, James Gibbons Huneker has spoken of their "broad, colored narrative tone, their heroic and chivalric accents, poetic passion and feminine. . . . It is noble, noble as the soul of the man who conceived it. Elastic in form, orchestral in idea, these sonatas—which are looser spun in the web than Liszt's—will keep alive the name of Macdowell."

The *Second piano concerto* is, in the opinion of John F. Porte, "a work full of feeling, brilliantly cohesive and logical, with good material that is handled with confident skill. . . . Its character. . . . is strong and virile, containing many passages of pure tonal beauty and eloquent expressiveness."

Principal works by Edward Macdowell:

ORCHESTRA: *Hamlet and Ophelia*; *Lancelot and Elaine*; *Lamia*; *First suite*; *Indian suite*; Two concertos for piano and orchestra; *Romance* (for violoncello and orchestra); *The Saracens, Lovely Alda* (fragments of a symphony).
An entire library of piano music including sonatas, two suites, woodland sketches, fantasiestücke, études, etc.
Songs, choruses.

About Edward Macdowell:

Brown, Abbie Farwell. *The Boyhood of Edward Macdowell*; Gilman, Lawrence. *Edward Macdowell*; Huneker, James Gibbons. *Unicorns*; Porte, John F. *Edward Macdowell*; *A Great American Tone-Poet, His Life and Music.*
American Mercury 7:50 January 1926; *Musical Quarterly* 1:17 January 1925; *Musician* 13:160 April 1908; *New Music Review* 11:494 November 1912.

Important recordings of music by Edward Macdowell:

ORCHESTRA: *Second piano concerto* (VICTOR).
PIANO: *A.D. 1620* (COLUMBIA-Hess); *In Autumn* (GRAMOPHONE); *Nautilus* (VICTOR-Barth); *To a water lily* (VICTOR); *To a wild rose* (VICTOR); *To the sea* (VICTOR-Barth); *Witches dance* (BRUNSWICK-Godowsky).

Sir Alexander Mackenzie *1847-1935*

SIR ALEXANDER CAMPBELL MACKENZIE was born in Edinburgh on August 22, 1847. He was de-scended from a family of musicians: his great grandfather was an army bandsman; his grandfather was a violinist in Edinburgh; and his father was both a violinist and a conductor.

Alexander Mackenzie was a precocious child, revealing a sensitive ear for music and a retentive memory. At the age of eight, he was already in professional ranks, earning a salary as violinist in his father's orchestra. Two years later, he was sent to Sonderhausen, Germany, to receive a comprehensive musical training. Here, as he himself later wrote, "I played second fiddle in the Ducal orchestra, and thus drank deeply from the well-springs of 'advanced music.' For instance, we were the second town in Germany to perform *Lohengrin,* and we played the *Tristan* prelude before the opera was brought out."

He was back in London in 1862. "When I first arrived. . . from Germany, my hair was very long, and as I wore a turban hat, my somewhat feminine appearance aroused the curiosity of the boys in the street, who followed me with an attention more obtrusive than pleasant. In sheer despair, I made for the first barber's shop I could find in the Blackfairs Road, and had my hair cut."

In London, Mackenzie became a student at the Royal Academy of Music, at the same time earning his living by accepting odd jobs in theatre orchestras. He was a brilliant student; in a few months' time, he was awarded the King's scholarship.

His academy career came to an end, in 1865, when he returned to Edinburgh, making his mark as a violinst. He organized chamber concerts, introducing to Edinburgh many chamber music classics (such as the Schumann *Quintet*). He also devoted himself to teaching and conducting. He found time for composition as well: during this period he produced a piano trio and two piano quartets.

Under this strenuous activity, his health gave way. His doctor ordered a year of quiet and rest, which he spent in Florence. There he achieved such splendid results in developing his health and in producing successful music that he decided to make Florence his permanent home. There he produced some of his best music, including the cantatas *The Bride* and *Jason* (produced in Worcester in 1881 and Bristol in 1882, respectively) ; the opera *Colomba*; an orchestral ballad, *La Belle dame sans merci, The Rose of Sharon* (Norwich, 1884) and the *Concerto for violin and orchestra* (Birmingham, 1885).

These compositions brought him a formidable reputation. The demand for his presence in England became so pressing that, in 1885, Mackenzie returned to his native country. Once again, he undertook an active musical life. He became conductor of the Novello concerts in 1885, assumed the post of principal of the Royal Academy (which he retained for thirty-six years with great distinction), and took over the baton of the Royal Philharmonic in 1892. In recognition of these services, he was honored with knighthood in 1895.

For the remainder of his life, Sir Alexander Mackenzie maintained a distinguished position in the musical life of his country—as composer, conductor and teacher. On the occasion of his eighty-sixth birthday, more than forty of the most eminent musicians of England presented him with a silver tray inscribed with the facsimile autographs of Elgar, Delius, Sir Henry J. Wood, Sir Edward German, Sir Landon Ronald, etc.

Sir Alexander Mackenzie died in London on April 28, 1935. The obituary paragraphs spoke of his geniality, personal charm and warm generosity which attracted to him all those with whom he came into contact. He was essentially a cosmopolitan, at home with foreign languages and in foreign literature, a man of rich cultural background. A quiet wit spiced his conversation. He approached his many musical tasks with prodigious zest, high idealism and inexhaustible enthusiasm. In his art, he was essentially a conservative and as he himself wrote "a thorough-going eclectic, appreciating all that is good in its own period."

"In his music," wrote Charles Willeby, "he steered a middle course. At times it is eclectic to a fault. If for the nonce—to use his own words—he puts on the Wagner greatcoat, we probably discover that he wears the vest of Berlioz under-

SIR ALEXANDER MACKENZIE

neath. There is music from his pen which could own Massenet for a master. . . . He has avoided flippancy in his art, even if in doing so he has at times bored us, and of his force when occasion demands it, there can be no doubt, though it is descriptive rather than emotional. But it is never the force of accident; he is ever conscious of his purpose, clear in his method and design. Of all his works those which represent him most happily are *La Belle dame* and *Twelfth night*. . . . I have found little of pathos in his music, little that goes very deep, yet I am inclined to think that his greatest strength lies in the sphere of realism rather than in that of idealism. But the sweep of his imagination is sometimes tremendous. The orchestra, in his hands, is a thing of might, and some of his works give one the impression that, their conception being so broad, the intricacy of detail in treatment is not always to their advantage. His highest point in the realm of idealism has been reached in his *Dream of Jubal*; his greatest directness of expression, in the *Story of Sayid.*"

Principal works by Sir Alexander Mackenzie :

OPERA : *Colomba*; *The Troubadour*; *Phoebe*; *His Majesty*; *The Cricket on the hearth*; *St. John's Eve*; *The Knights of the road.*

CHORAL : *The Rose of Sharon*; *Bethlehem*; *The Bride of Jason*; *The Story of Sayid*;

The Cottar's Saturday night; *The Dream of Jubal*; *Witch's daughter*; *The Sun-God's return*, etc.

ORCHESTRA: Three rhapsodies; *Scherzo*; *La Belle dame sans merci*; *London, day by day*; *Coronation march*; *Invocation*; Four overtures; *Concerto for violin and orchestra*; *Scottish concerto* (for piano and orchestra); *Highland ballad* (for violin and orchestra).

CHAMBER MUSIC: *Piano quartet in E-flat*; *Piano trio*, etc.

Songs, pieces for the piano, etc.

About Sir Alexander Mackenzie:

Mackenzie, Sir Alexander. *A Musician's Narrative*; O'Connor, T. P. *In the Days of My Youth*; Willeby, Charles. *Masters of English Music*.

Monthly Musical Record 63:152 September 1933; *Musical Opinion* 45:781 June 1922; *Musical Times* 68:785 September 1927.

Gustav Mahler *1860-1911*

"We know today that he was one who was destined to be lord and leader; one whom we must follow. It was a duty to combat for him. It is a joy to be certain of his victory."—PAUL STEFAN

"No one will gainsay me when I say, 'Truly he was a great man!' "—ARNOLD SCHÖNBERG

GUSTAV MAHLER—of whose symphonies Adolf Weissman has written that they are "the last supremely great works of this class given to the world"—was born in Kalischt, a small town in Bohemia, on July 7, 1860. His parents were Jewish shopkeepers. From his earliest years, Gustav lived in a world of his own. In grammar school, he was known to stare vacantly into space, whistling a note or two to himself, unconscious of what was happening about him. At home, he was equally oblivious of everything except his books and the piano, which he found in his grandfather's home in his sixth year. There is an anecdote told of his boyhood which gives us a particularly illuminating insight into his strangely self-centered personality. One afternoon he was taken by his father into the forest. His father suddenly recollected that he had forgotten something at home. Placing the boy on a stump, he warned him to remain there until he returned. On arriving home, the father discovered that some unexpected guests had arrived; in the confusion, Gustav was completely forgotten. Several hours passed before

his father remembered him. Rushing back to the woods, he discovered that the boy was still sitting on the tree-stump, lost in the fog of his meditation and reveries, completely unaware of the fact that he had been left alone during all these hours.

His father noticed his unusual love for music, and, although he had hoped to make his son a shopkeeper, decided he would permit Gustav to study music if he had the necessary talent. To decide the issue, he took the boy to Professor Epstein of the Vienna Conservatory. Gustav played a few of his own compositions, and Professor Epstein announced: "That boy is a born musician."

Thus, Gustav Mahler, at the age of fifteen, became a pupil at the Conservatory of Vienna. Here he remained for three years, winning awards for piano playing and composition.

His flaming idealism and profound love for great music made the first years of his professional life difficult. His first position was at a music hall where he conducted light operetta for $12.50 a month. Finding the position unbearable, he sought escape by accepting a post as conductor at Olmütz—an abominable music-house where masterpieces were performed together with cheap musical farces and subjected to shabby treatment. Once again he could tolerate this post for only a short period, passing on to Cassel where he became "royal director of music." Here, he was compelled to direct a vulgar parody of Wagner's *Tannhäuser* which so infuriated him that he handed in his resignation peremptorily.

In 1885, Mahler was selected to conduct Mendelssohn's *St. Paul* at a music festival in Leipzig. This was the first performance in which he gave a strong indication of his talent as a conductor. It resulted in his appointment, the same year, by Angelo Neumann as conductor of his opera house in Prague. After a trial performance of Cherubini's *Water carrier*, Mahler was entrusted with the performances of Wagner's *Ring* and Mozart's *Don Giovanni*, giving performances of such eloquence and power that he was engaged for the Opera House in Pesth.

GUSTAV MAHLER

fortissimo; his climaxes, obtained by the simplest means; his whispering *pianissimo*; his instinct for the needful alternation of tranquility and agitation; his sense of sharpness of the melodic line; all these were elements which equally went to make up his power."

Notwithstanding his active career with the baton, Mahler found the time and energy to compose those works which brought him fame. Unfortunately, from the very first, his music aroused antagonism and hostility. When his *First symphony* was introduced in Budapest in 1889, it was received with disconcerting indifference. This indifference grew to antagonism when, the following year, Richard Strauss conducted the *Second symphony*. When Felix Weingartner performed the *Third symphony*, in 1897, there were hissing and catcalls.

It was here that Mahler's importance as a conductor soared. Each of his performances enjoyed increasingly mounting success. Brahms said of his Mozart: "Such a *Don Giovanni* performance as has been heard in Pesth is not to be heard even in Vienna." Critics proclaimed that "everything that took shape under Mahler's fingers was as born again."

From Pesth, Mahler went to the Hamburg Opera, and from the Hamburg Opera to Vienna where—as conductor of the Vienna State Opera and the Vienna Philharmonic, he was recognized as one of the great conductors of the period. From 1908 until 1911, Mahler visited the United States annually to direct, both at the concerts of the Philharmonic Society and at the Metropolitan Opera House.

In discussing Mahler's many extraordinary qualities as a conductor, Paul Stefan informs us that "he had an aim which only Wagner before him had sought with such tenacity to attain: Distinctness. The experience of many years had given him unerring knowledge of the capabilities of every instrument, of the possibilities of every score. Distinctness, for him, was an exact ratio of light and shade. His *crescendi*, his storms, growing from bar to bar, now taking breath for a moment, now crashing into

In 1902, Gustav Mahler was married to Alma Maria Schindler. One year later a daughter was born to them. During this period, he was working on the *Kindertotenlieder,* a set of elegies written by Rückert. When, in 1906, his little daughter died of scarlet fever, Mahler was obsessed with the thought that he had tempted fate by composing the *Kindertotenlieder,* that he was in a great measure responsible for his daughter's death. This morbid feeling lingered with him until the end of his life.

In 1908, Mahler was invited to America by the Metropolitan Opera House. His friends urged him to decline the offer, knowing well that he was not physically fit to undertake such an exacting assignment. He turned a deaf ear to all advice. After a strenuous season in New York, he returned home broken in health. A physician-friend told him that, unless he gave up all activity, his heart would no longer withstand the strain. Mahler, however, was stubborn. He refused to reduce his work, continuing his many assignments as conductor and composer on two continents.

On September 12, 1910, after harrowing rehearsals, he conducted in Munich the first performance of his grandiose *Eighth symphony,* the "symphony of a thousand voices." This performance brought Mahler probably the only sincere triumph of his creative career. In the winter of 1910, he was back in New York, undertaking a rigorous schedule with the New York Philharmonic. The hard work, coupled with the biting criticisms he received resulting from his freedom in interpreting the classics, soon exacted a heavy toll: He collapsed on February 21, 1911. Taken back to Paris for serum treatments, he was told by physicians that they could do nothing. He asked, therefore, to be carried to his beloved Vienna. There, on May 18, 1911, he died, a broken and unhappy man.

He was buried in the cemetery at Grinzing in silent reverence; he had left instructions that not a word was to be spoken nor a note of music sung at his burial. One day after the services, Emperor Francis Joseph decreed that a special performance of the *Eighth symphony* take place in honor of the dead composer.

Altho Mahler was frequently referred to as "the ugly Mahler," those who knew him explain that his face had a particular appeal and attractiveness. "He was a little below average height," wrote Gabriel Engel, in his monograph on the composer, "but a wiry, slender figure of perfect proportions obviated any impression of shortness. He had flowing black hair and dark brown eyes which under the stress of great emotion would take on an almost fanatical gleam." His appeal, however, rested in his scorching eyes, the tense muscles of his face, his square jaw, all of which suggested strength and power.

He was a man of great irritability and nervousness, a man of inexhaustible energy which made hard work essential for peace of mind, a man of unswerving stubbornness. Perhaps the outstanding quality of his personality was his high idealism. He looked upon music as a ritual in which he was high priest. Thruout his life, therefore, he could never accept any compromises with the unalterably high standards he had set for himself in his art. Consequently, as a conductor in Prague, he resigned from his post (preferring unemployment and poverty) because his commands were not followed to the letter; and several

years later, he resigned once again from a highly lucrative post in Vienna because Francis Joseph insisted that a favorite tenor of his—whom Mahler had given a pension, because he was too old to fulfil his position satisfactorily—be reinstated. And the same uncompromising idealism he brought to his composition, preferring the abuse of his contemporaries to the lowering of his own creative standards.

Few composers have been subject to such extreme opinion as Gustav Mahler. Even today, the musical world is definitely divided into two camps—those who are with him heart and soul, and those who are against him. There are those who feel that Mahler was a prophetic voice in music; that his major works—the nine symphonies, the *Lied von der Erde,* the *Kindertotenlieder*—represent the apotheosis of musical expression. These disciples of Mahler include such eminent musicologists as Adolf Weissman, Paul Bekker, and Paul Stefan, such famous composers as Arnold Schönberg, and Richard Strauss, such eminent conductors as Mengelberg, Klemperer and Bruno Walter. On the other hand, there are many who feel that, altho in his best pages Mahler reached sublimity, he is often too discouragingly prolix, too hysterical, too bombastic, too effusive to deserve the mark of greatness. Permitting Philip Hale to represent this group of critics: "One has found thru his symphonies restlessness that at times becomes hysterical; reminders of Wagner, Berlioz, Strauss; melodies in folk song vein, often naïve, at times beautiful, but introduced as at random and quickly thrown aside; an overemployment of woodwinds, used too often as solo instruments; passages for the bass which recall the fact that as a child Mahler delighted in military bands. Sudden changes from screaming outbursts to thin and inconsequential instrumentation; trivial moments when the hearer anticipates the movement of a country dance; diffuseness, prolixity that becomes boresome; an unwillingness to bring speech to an end; seldom genuine power or eloquence; yet here and there measures that linger in the memory."

However, when all the necessary subtractions are made, there is much left of genuine importance. As H. T. Parker explained: "In orchestration and in form particularly, Mahler made tremendous forward strides. His orchestra does not indulge in the riot of color characterizing the German school at the end of the last century. Melodic contours matter more to him than orchestral colors. For him the orchestra is a single, sounding unit, a cosmos alive with a host of embryonic or evolutional possibilities; always a far more closely welded unity than a mere sum of the various coloristic parts. But in this cosmos the various sonorous elements often assume huge proportions. . . . Mahler, who can write a symphony for a thousand performers, is never afraid of an economy of instruments. . . . Nor does he shrink from sparse groups in widely separated spacings. He never miscalculates. No matter how great his economies, no matter how distant his spacings, his scores always 'sound.' For Mahler knows his instruments."

Gustav Mahler's widow is today the wife of Franz Werfel, the world-famous writer.

Principal works by Gustav Mahler:

ORCHESTRA: Nine symphonies; *Das Klagende lied* (for soprano, alto, tenor soli, mixed chorus and orchestra); *Das Lied von der Erde* (for tenor and alto soli, and orchestra).

SONG-CYCLES: *Des Knaben wunderhorn* (with orchestra); *Kindertotenlieder*; *Rückert lieder*, etc.

An entire library of songs with piano or orchestral accompaniment.

About Gustav Mahler:

Engel, Gabriel. *Gustav Mahler: Song Symphonist*; Specht, Richard. *Gustav Mahler*; Stefan, Paul. *Gustav Mahler: A Study of his Personality and Work.*

Important recordings of music by Gustav Mahler:

ORCHESTRA: *Second symphony* (VICTOR-Ormandy); *Fifth symphony*, "Adagietto" (COLUMBIA-Mengelberg).

SONGS: *Kindertotenlieder* (POLYDOR-Rehkemper); *Um Mitternacht* (COLUMBIA); *Des Knaben Wunderhorn*, "Rheinlegendschen" and "Der Tambourgesell" (POLYDOR-Schlusnus).

Benedetto Marcello   *1686-1739*

BENEDETTO MARCELLO was born in Venice on July 24, 1686, the descendant of an ancient and illustrious family that had included senators, ambassadors, prelates and a doge. His father, a competent violinist, frequently gathered the leading musicians at his home (the Marcello palace which still stands on the Grand Canal). In this way, Benedetto was brought into contact with music from earliest childhood. His father hoped to make him a great violinist, and sent him to study under Tartini. But from his early student days, the boy showed greater aptitude for and interest in musical theory than in violin exercises. His principal instructors in theory were Francesco Gasparini and Lotti.

Between the ages of seventeen and twenty, Marcello was so deeply immersed in music that he hardly ever stepped out of his study. He memorized the theoretical writings of Zarlino, and pored over the music of Monteverdi, Palestrina and Stradella. He worked so hard that his health was vitally affected. His father was compelled to send him to the country, forbidding the introduction of any music-paper into the house. This could hardly discourage Marcello's industry. At night, when he was supposed to sleep, he ruled lines on blank paper and worked on his music.

In his twenty-first year, he entered the legal profession, soon achieving considerable renown in this field. At twenty-five he became a member of the Great Council. In 1711, he was appointed to the Council of Forty. His music, however, was not abandoned. He composed industriously. In December of 1711, he was elected a member of the Accademia Filarmonici of Bologna.

Marcello's biographer, Leonida Busi, relates two interesting anecdotes in connection with the life of the composer. One occurred in 1728, when he went to the Church Saint Apostoli to take part in musical services. Going up to the altar, he stepped upon a sepulchral slab which gave way, causing him to fall into the grave. Marcello was not hurt, but the incident had a far-reaching effect on his life. He seemed to see in this a

BENEDETTO MARCELLO

warning of coming death. From that time on, he abandoned his formerly gay life—devoted entirely to parties, theatres and the company of pleasure-mongers—and, going into almost monastic retirement, devoted himself to piety and religion. From this time on, too, he became melancholy, serious and brooding. One of the important works that he created during this sombre period was his famous *Psalms*. "In your sublime and imperishable psalms," wrote the German chapel master, Telemann, to him, "there reigns a majesty which all masters before you have failed to enthrone."

The other incident occurred shortly after this. He was standing upon his balcony in Venice when a gondola passed under him. In it was a young girl, singing so beautifully that Marcello ordered his servant to stop the gondola. He found that the singer was a beautiful young girl of humble origin. He was so moved by the quality of her voice that he offered to become her teacher. On March 28, 1729—despite the fact that it was scandalous for a man of noble descent to marry a humble woman—Marcello married his pupil, Rosana Scalfi.

In 1730, Marcello was appointed purveyor at Pola in Istria. About this time, his health gave way. He returned to Venice after a few years, and accepted

the post of treasurer in Brescia. Despite these official positions, he did not interrupt his prolific composition.

Benedetto Marcello died in Brescia on July 24, 1739, and was buried in the church of S. Giuseppe. His epitaph referred to him as a "nobleman, magistrate, philologist, poet and musician."

Benedetto Marcello is known principally as a composer of a considerable library of choral music, including psalms, madrigals, oratorios and cantatas. Musicologists have been divided as to the importance of this musical output. On the one hand, Burney, who studied the eight volumes of Marcello's music, found that "there is no considerable merit in the work," and that "the author has been overpraised." Fétis, on the other hand, saw in Marcello's music "a rare merit of poetic expression, much originality and boldness in ideas, and lastly a singular variety of means."

"The music of Marcello was essentially lyric," wrote Camille Bellaigue. "But, to me, Marcello's power is more to be admired than his sweetness—now, in the assurance of his faith and the impetuosity of his prayer, now in the tragic emotion of his repentance. [His] musical individuality was noble, proud and vigorous; in every particular, it stemmed from the force and beauty which the Renaissance created thruout all art. To be convinced of this, one has but to read a certain *Sonata in F-major*, written for violoncello and piano; we cannot but feel that it is full of strength, pride and nobility. . . . The glowing and triumphant Psalms are the most characteristic of Marcello's genius. Veritable odes of music, how clear and high they rise in their beauty, and, above all, with what sudden bursts of emotion do they spring forth!"

Benedetto Marcello was likewise the author of *Il Teatro alla moda*, a stinging satire in prose on the pretenses and affectations of the Neapolitan opera.

Principal works by Benedetto Marcello:

CHORAL: Psalms, madrigals, oratorios, cantatas, etc.

CHAMBER MUSIC: Concerti for 5 instruments; sonatas for cembalo and flute, for cembalo and violoncello, etc.

About Benedetto Marcello:

Bellaigue, Camille. *Portraits and Silhouettes*; Busi, Leonida. *Notizie sulla Vita e le Opere di Marcello.*
Monthly Musical Record 20:49 March 1890.

Important recordings of music by Benedetto Marcello:

CHAMBER MUSIC: *Sonata in G-minor,* for viola de gamba and harpsichord (VICTOR); *Toccata* (COLUMBIA); *Adagio in D-minor* (VICTOR); *Sonata in F-major,* for violoncello and harpsichord (PARLAPHONE).

"Padre" Martini *1706-1784*

GIOVANNI BATTISTA MARTINI —better known as "Padre" Martini—was born in Bologna on April 24, 1706. His father, a violinist, taught him the elements of music. Martini made such progress that before long his father could teach him no more. Other instructors were, therefore, summoned to train him—including Predieri, at the harpsichord, and Antoni Riccieri, in counterpoint.

However, the church appealed to Martini even more strongly than music. As a young man, he followed theological studies with the monks of San Filippo Neri. He soon passed his novitiate at the Franciscan convent at Lago and on September 11, 1722 he was ordained a priest.

In 1725, he returned to his native city, giving himself up to the study of many varied subjects. He absorbed philosophy, undertook the study of mathematics under Zanotti, learned medicine. The same thoroughness he brought to music, plunging into an intensive study of its theory and practice. As a result, he acquired an extraordinary knowledge of music and science, amassing a culture which was the wonder of his contemporaries. His library consisted of some 17,000 volumes, considered by many one of the foremost private libraries in Europe.

In 1725, Martini received an appointment as chapel-master at Saint Francesco. Shortly after this, he opened his own music school in Bologna. His reputation as a scholar being world-famous, he attracted to his school musicians from all parts of the world. In this way, his influence was felt far and wide. There were few musicians of the eighteenth century who did not—directly or indirectly—profit by his great wisdom and experience.

The last years of Martini's life were marked by pain: he suffered from asthma and a disease of the bladder. His spirit—always resigned and gentle— was not darkened by his suffering. In spite of declining strength and increased suffering, his enormous energy knew no respite.

Giovanni Battista Martini died in Bologna on October 3, 1784.

Charles Burney, who met Martini when the latter was an old man, wrote in the following vein: "He is advanced in age, and in bad health. He has a distressing cough; his legs are swollen; and his whole appearance is that of a sick man. . . . His character is such that it inspires not only respect but affection. With the purity of his life and the simplicity of his manners he combines gaiety, kindness and philanthropy. I have never liked anyone so well after so slight an acquaintance. I was no more reserved with him at the end of a few hours than I should have been with an old friend or a beloved brother."

Martini's principal compositions were for the church. He was not a preeminently gifted composer, altho there is much in his music to disclose careful construction and good taste. Romain

"PADRE" MARTINI

Rolland pointed out that Martini's work "exhibited a certain rococo grace" which was its distinguishing characteristic. He followed in the traditions of the old Italian school, being neither an experimentalist nor an innovator. His works have charm and poise, but lack real individuality and artistic importance.

Martini was likewise an important musical theorist, his most significant works in this direction being a three-volume history of music (the first extensive, scientific history of music in existence) and a two-volume thesis on counterpoint.

Two very popular morsels are frequently erroneously ascribed to Martini. The world-famous song, *Plaisir d'amour*, was not the composition of Giovanni Battista Martini but of Martini Il Tedesco (1741-1816). An *Andantino*, frequently featured by Fritz Kreisler, has recently been discovered to be, not an arrangement of a Martini melody by Kreisler, but an original work by Kreisler himself.

Principal works by Giovanni Battista Martini:

CHORAL: Requiems; motets; hymns; canticles; Three oratorios; Twenty cantatas; litanies; antiphons; canons; intermezzi; madrigals, etc.
Organ pieces; pieces for harpsichord, etc.

About Giovanni Battista Martini:

Busi, Leonida. *Il Padre G. B. Martini*; Fétis, François Joseph. *Biographie Universelle des Musiciens*; Parisini, Federico. *Della Vita e delle Opere del Padre Martini*.

Important recordings of music by Giovanni Battista Martini:

CHAMBER MUSIC: *Balleto*, arranged for string quartet (COLUMBIA).

Giuseppe Martucci *1856-1909*

GIUSEPPE MARTUCCI was born in Capua on January 6, 1856. His father, a trumpet player and leader of a military band, taught him the piano. Giuseppe made such rapid progress that he was able to make a successful début in his eleventh year.

At sixteen, Martucci made an extensive tour as concert pianist thru Italy and England, his performances evoking the high admiration of many musicians.

Returning to Italy, late in 1872, he entered the Naples Conservatory. Here, he remained for two years, acquiring maturity under the instruction of Costa, Serrao and Rossi.

When he completed his studies, he devoted two years to teaching and concert work. Finally, he received an appointment as professor of piano at the Conservatory of Naples. At this same time, his fine musicianship was recognized when he was assigned the direction of the Neapolitan Quartet Society (in which he first revealed his great interest in chamber music), and was given the conductorial post with an orchestra founded by Prince d'Ardore. The latter was Martucci's debut as a conductor. He adapted himself so well to the baton that, within a short period, he attained considerable fame. In 1888, he gave the first Italian performance of Wagner's *Tristan und Isolde* in Bologna. After this—being one of the strongest disciples of Wagner in Italy—he gave such stirring performances of the Wagnerian music dramas in Bologna that the city soon became something of a Wagnerian shrine in Italy.

In 1902, he was appointed director of the Naples Conservatory which post he held until his death.

Giuseppe Martucci died in Naples on June 1, 1909.

GIUSEPPE MARTUCCI

In his compositions—the most famous of which are the *Concerto for piano and orchestra* and the *Second symphony*— Martucci strikingly reveals the influence of Wagner and Liszt on his musical thought. His orchestration is drenched with Wagnerian color, while in its dramatic intensity his music follows in the tradition of the Liszt tone poem. His style was, therefore, an eclectic one, but as a critic in the *Musical Courier* noted, its foundations were "broad and deep," couched in scholarly erudition and musicianly good taste. He belonged, as Hugo Riemann pointed out, to that school of Italian composers—including Sgambati and Bossi—which attempted to divert Italian composers from opera towards the creation of symphonic and chamber music according to German formulas.

Principal works by Giuseppe Martucci:

ORCHESTRA: Two symphonies; Two concertos for piano and orchestra; Four piccoli pezzi; *La Canzone dei ricordi* (for voice and orchestra); nocturnes; novelettes, etc.

CHAMBER MUSIC: *Piano quintet*; Two piano trios; *Sonata for violoncello and piano*.

CHORAL: *Samuel*.

Pieces for the violin; pieces for the piano; songs.

About Giuseppe Martucci:

Musical Courier 40:26 March 14, 1900; *Musician* 14:367 August 1909; *Symphonia* 1:3 June 1910.

Important recordings of music by Giuseppe Martucci:

ORCHESTRA: *Notturno in G-flat minor* (PARLAPHONE); *Novelletta* (GRAMOPHONE).

Jules Massenet *1842-1912*

JULES ÉMILE FRÉDÉRIC MASSENET, youngest son of a family of twenty-one children, was born in Montaud, a suburb of Saint-Étienne, on May 12, 1842.

"My father was a superior officer under the First Empire," he later recorded, "but when the Bourbons were restored, my father resigned. He was a graduate of the Polytechnic School, and later devoted himself to manufacturing and to starting the famous iron-works near Saint-Étienne. My mother gave me my first piano lessons. How well I remember the day! It was February 24,

1848. The lesson was strangely interrupted by the noise of street-firing. The revolution had begun."

The Revolution not only interrupted that first piano lesson but all the manufacturing activities of father Massenet, ruining him completely. In 1851, therefore, the Massenet family transferred its home from Montaud to Paris in an attempt to begin life anew. Here, because Jules had already shown unmistakable musical talent, he was entered at the Paris Conservatory. Curious to say, in Bazin's class, he was considered a poor student. At one time, Bazin was so infuriated at his ungifted pupil that he insisted Massenet leave the class. Massenet's next teacher in composition was Ambroise Thomas, who instinctively understood the sensitive boy and adapted the studies to suit his temperament. Under Thomas, Massenet made prodigious progress. Between 1859 and 1863, Massenet won awards in piano playing and fugue, and finally the Prix de Rome for composition.

"It was in Rome that I began to live," Massenet wrote. "There it was that, during my happy walks with my comrades, painters or sculptors, and in our talks under the oaks of the Villa Borghese, or under the pines of Villa Pamphili, I felt my first stirrings and admiration for nature." In Italy, Massenet met Sgambati, the great pianist, and then Franz Liszt. Curiously enough, it was thru Liszt that Massenet met his future wife. Liszt, having decided to give up his piano pupils and turn completely to the church, recommended Massenet as a teacher for one of the pupils, Mlle. de Saint-Marie. There followed an affectionate relationship between Massenet and his pupil which culminated on October 6, 1866 in marriage.

Upon returning to Paris, Massenet began work on his first opera which, thru the intervention of Ambroise Thomas, was accepted for performance by the Opéra Comique in 1867. *La Grand'tante* ran for fourteen performances only, but it attracted notice among the critics by virtue of its clever instrumentation, its dramatic appeal and its original melodic line. In 1872, another Massenet opera, *Don César de Bazan*,

JULES MASSENET

was hardly more successful. But one year later, Massenet suddenly soared to fame. An oratorio, and incidental music to Leconte de Lisle's *Les Erynnies*—the latter work containing the world-famous *Élégie,* originally entitled *Invocation*—were performed at the Odéon with so great a success that their composer achieved instantaneous fame. Three years later, Massenet became a member of the Legion of Honor. In 1878, he was elected to the Académie des Beaux-Arts and appointed professor of composition at the Paris Conservatory.

Between 1880 and 1900, Massenet was at the peak of his fame as a composer, and was recognized as one of the foremost operatic composers in France at the time. He produced one extraordinary success after another, beginning with *Hérodiade* in 1881—including *Manon* (1884), *Le Cid* (1885), *Werther* (1892), *Thaïs* (1894).

There can be little doubt but that it was in his operas that Massenet proved his greatest gifts as a composer. As G. Jean-Aubry wrote: "Massenet had the theatrical sense developed to a degree the more rare insomuch as he makes no use of blatant means. He is always able to retain a degree of distinction that is indisputable even when it is only relative. He has yielded no more to noisy realism than he has attempted to attain

to lofty grandeur." And, continued Edouard Schuré, Massenet's operas were particularly distinguished for "the elegant . . . thrust with which he drove to the very source of a melody of which he availed himself with so much grace. . . . Massenet had two personal and original notes: on the one hand, an intriguing tenderness which rises at times to passion; on the other hand, a penetrating melancholy, singularly incisive."

It is Louis Schneider's opinion that Massenet, in his operas, "is the musician of Woman and Love. Love, he sang of it in every possible form—mystic or carnal, idealistic or romantic; he even submitted it to the caprices of fashion."

After 1900, Massenet—who had become the foremost French composer of his time—suddenly degenerated artistically. Truth to tell, he had been ruined by success. More eager to retain his enormous popularity than to compose music of growing power and originality, he began to repeat himself endlessly until he could produce nothing more than ineffectual and unimpressive works, following definite formulas. Altho he remained a singularly prolific composer until the end of his life, he could produce only two operas which are worthy to stand near his best achievements—*Le Jongleur de Notre Dame* (1902) and *Don Quichotte* (1910). As Claude Debussy remarked so aptly: "Massenet fell a victim to the butterfly-play of fascinating lady admirers."

Massenet had come in from Egreville to consult his physicians, when he was suddenly stricken. He died in Paris on August 13, 1912. His body was taken back to Egreville, and there the funeral services, following his express wishes, were simple and dignified.

Describing Massenet as he knew him, Georges Servières wrote: "His eyes are very quick in their movements; the expression is very gentle. His profile is finely cut. His shoulders are slightly stooping, and he seems short, altho. . . . of medium height. His movements are full of an ever-present, nervous vivacity."

Massenet always considered *Le Jongleur,* and not *Thaïs,* as his greatest score.

"The chief idiosyncracy of Massenet as man and artist," in the opinion of

M. D. Calvocoressi, "is an overwhelming desire to court success. His object was to seduce; and from the time when he found that his music proved effective and became popular, he carefully avoided changing his manner. The characteristic melody *à la Massenet,* graceful and elegant enough, but almost stereotyped, runs thru all of his scores. . . . His early scores are, for the greater part, his best. . . . Later, and for the plain reason that he never attempted to renovate his style, he sank into sheer mannerism. Indeed, one can but marvel that so gifted a musician, who lacked neither individuality nor skill, should have so utterly succeeded in throwing away his gifts."

It should not be forgotten that Massenet enjoyed a great career as a teacher of compositions. His pupils included such distinguished composers as Alfred Bruneau, Gustav Charpentier and Gabriel Pierné.

Principal works by Jules Massenet:

OPERA: *Hérodiade; Manon; Le Cid; Werther; Thaïs; La Navarraise; Sapho; Grisélidis; Le Jongleur de Notre Dame; Don Quichotte,* etc.

ORCHESTRA: Seven suites; incidental music to *Les Erynnies* (including the world-famous *Élégie*); *Concerto for piano and orchestra; Fantasie* (for violoncello and orchestra); *Visions; Devant la Madone; Marche solennelle;* incidental music to *Théodora,* to *Phèdre,* to *Le Manteau de roi,* etc.

CHORAL: *Marie Magdeleine; Eve; Narcisse; La Vierge; La Terre promise.*

BALLET: *Le Carillon; Cigale; Espada.*

Songs, etc.

About Jules Massenet:

Bouvet, Charles. *Massenet;* Brancour, René. *Massenet;* Chantavoine, Jean. *De Couperin à Massenet;* Delmas, Marc. *Massenet and His Works;* Finck, Henry T. *Massenet and His Operas;* Hervey, Arthur. *Masters of French Music;* Jullien, Adolphe. *Musiciens d'hier et d'aujourd'hui;* Schuré, Edouard. *Profils des Musiciens.*

Important recordings of music by Jules Massenet:

OPERA: *Manon,* complete (COLUMBIA); *Werther,* complete (COLUMBIA).

ORCHESTRA: Incidental music to *Les Erynnies* (PARLAPHONE); "Ballet music" from *Le Cid* (VICTOR-Hertz); "Ballet music" from *Hérodiade* (ODEON); "Meditation" from *Thaïs* (VICTOR-Fiedler); *Scènes alsaciennes* (COLUMBIA); *Scènes pittoresques* (BRUNSWICK).

SONGS: *Élégie* and *Enchantment* (PATHE-Vallin); *Noël païen* and *Ouvre tes yeux bleus* (COLUMBIA).

Innumerable recordings of excerpts from the operas.

Étienne Henri Méhul 1763-1817

"Méhul is a very great master, one who has brought the greatest honor to the French school."—SAINT SAËNS

"He was a product of the true French school."—WAGNER

ETIENNE NICOLAS (HENRI) MÉHUL was born in Givet, in Ardennes, on June 22, 1763. His father, the owner of a wineshop in Givet, recognized his son's talent for music and placed him in care of the organist, Abbot Wilhelm Hauser. Méhul remained a pupil of Hauser for some five years, finally becoming his assistant at the organ.

One day, a wealthy amateur heard him play the organ and, recognizing signs of genius, offered to finance Méhul in a trip to Paris. In this way, Méhul went to Paris in his fifteenth year, taking with him a letter of introduction to the eminent Gluck. When he arrived at Gluck's home, the master was in a state of almost complete undress, playing at the harpsichord; but to the idolatrous Méhul "all the magnificence of Louis XIV *toilette* could not fascinate me as much as Gluck's négligée!"

Gluck seemed to have been impressed with Méhul, for he undertook not only to guide him in his musical career but also to teach him philosophy and poetry. He advised Méhul to continue his studies under Edelmann, the harpsichordist, and to turn his creative efforts from the composition of sonatas to opera. At this time, Méhul composed two operas which have completely disappeared.

As a composer for the theatre, Méhul groped and stumbled until he met François Hoffmann, a poet, who offered to write librettos for him. Their first collaborative effort was *Euphrosine et Coradin* which, on its first performance in 1790, was an acknowledged success. Overnight, Méhul found himself a famous composer whose music was favorably compared with that of Grétry and

Gluck. During the next four years, he firmly established his position with two more operatic successes, *Stratonice* and *Horatius Coclès*.

During the French Revolution, Méhul composed patriotic songs for the revolutionists which brought him still greater prestige in the eyes of the masses. One of these songs, *Le Chant du départ* soon rivalled the *Marseillaise* in popularity. Principally because of *Le Chant du départ*, Méhul won official recognition. "In the front rank of Republican composers," ran a proclamation, "the nation places and proclaims Citizen Méhul." In 1795, Méhul was further honored by being appointed a director of the Conservatory.

For the next few years, Méhul composed several operas which failed to make an appeal particularly because of their bad librettos. One of these, *Le Jeune Henri*, presented in 1797, was hissed because the book suggested propaganda for royalty. But the music's merit was recognized, and the overture—known today as *La Chasse du jeune Henri*, one of Méhul's most distinguished pieces—was encored.

Méhul's reigning position in the French music of the period was not endangered by these successive failures. In July, 1800, he was called upon to compose a special work to commemorate the storming of the Bastille and to celebrate the victorious return of the French army, under Napoleon. At the same time, his native city held a remarkable fête in his honor. With Napoleon's rise to power, Méhul acquired even greater importance by becoming one of the Emperor's favorite composers, and a guest at Malmaison.

The composition of his masterpiece, *Joseph*, was the direct result of a challenge. During a dinner at one of the fashionable salons in Paris, the conversation turned to a discussion of Baour-Lormian's *Joseph in Egypt*, which was then being performed at the Comédie Française. The theme was being attacked, but Méhul insisted that the subject was an excellent one, even highly serviceable as an opera. One of the guests at the dinner, the poet Alexandre Duval, offered to write the libretto if

ÉTIENNE HENRI MÉHUL

Méhul would compose the music.

Joseph was first performed on February 17, 1807. Though it ran for only thirteen performances it was widely praised as an artistic work of outstanding merit. Poems were written in its honor:

> *"In this seductive work,*
> *Brilliant with the fire of your genius,*
> *Everywhere your original harmony can be found,*
> *Capturing and ravishing our hearts."*

wrote the distinguished Guizot. Napoleon gave it the five thousand franc prize for the best operatic work in ten years—a prize which, incidentally, Méhul never collected.

"The music is nearly always simple, touching, rich in successful if not very bold modulations," was Berlioz's estimate of the score, "in broad, full harmonies, in graceful accompaniments; the expression is always truthful."

Joseph was Méhul's last outstanding work for the theatre, even though his industry in this field persisted. Between 1808 and 1810, he concentrated on composition of symphonies, inspired by the examples of Haydn, and produced a series of charming works for orchestra.

The fall of Napoleon was a severe blow to Méhul's fortunes. He found himself demoted from Inspector at the Conservatory to professor with a sharp decrease in salary. His spirit, crushed by the disgrace brought to his idol, Napoleon, was further smothered with envy by the rise of Spontini as a composer of importance.

In 1817, Méhul was a sick man. He was rushed to the island of Hyères, with the hope that the climate might restore his health. "I have broken up all my habits," he wrote at this time. "I am deprived of all my old friends; I am alone at the end of the world, surrounded by people whose language I scarcely understand; and all this sacrifice to obtain a little more sun."

Méhul recovered slightly, sufficiently to be present at a grandiose demonstration held in his honor in Marseilles. But, on returning to Paris, he relapsed. He was reduced to sitting by the fire, all day, stifling his coughs. He died in Paris on October 18, 1817, and was buried at Père Lachaise.

Méhul was of medium height with regular features, attractive eyes and a beautiful speaking voice. He was a man of great ambition; "I love glory with madness," he once confessed. It is for this reason that, despite his imposing position in French music almost from the dawn of his career, he was also the victim of frequent depression, feeling that none of his operas enjoyed the success they deserved. Towards the close of his life, he suffered intensely from a haunting persecution-complex; he felt that he was the victim of innumerable jealousies and intrigues. He was bitterly envious of the success of every other composer, particularly that of Spontini.

Notwithstanding these objectionable qualities, he was well-loved and greatly admired. "Whilst other people have generous traits," wrote one of his librettists, Arnault, "Méhul's whole life was generosity." Méhul was a particularly fluent conversationalist, a born storyteller. His greatest diversion was with flowers, for which he bore an extraordinary affection.

The outstanding qualities of Méhul as a composer, according to Karl Maria von Weber, were "dramatic truth, animated advance free from injudicious repetitions, the great effects, frequently by the simplest means, and economy in instrumentation, giving, in fact, only that which is absolutely essential."

Méhul's importance in musical history rests principally in the fact that he placed light opera on a firmer and more substantial basis.

Principal works by Étienne Henri Méhul:

OPERA: *Euphrosine et Coradin*; *Stratonice*; *Horatius Coclès*; *La Caverne*; *Le Jeune Henri*; *Épicure* (with Cherubini); *L'Irato*; *Une Folie*; *Le Trésor supposé*; *Joanna*; *L'Heureux malgré lui*; *Héléna*; *Joseph*; *La Journée aux aventures*; *Trancrède et Clorinde*; *Uthal*; *Les Amazones*; *Ariodant*.

CHORAL: *Le Chant du départ*; *Chant national*; cantata; mass, etc.

ORCHESTRA: Four symphonies; Fourteen overtures.

Sonatas for piano.

About Étienne Henri Méhul:

Brancour, René. *Méhul*; Curzon, Henri de. *Musiciens du Temps Passé*; Hargreave, Mary. *Earlier French Musicians*; Pougin, Arthur. *Méhul: Sa vie, son Génie, son Caractère*; Vieillard, P. A. *Méhul: Sa Vie et ses Oeuvres*.

Important recordings of music by Étienne Henri Méhul:

SELECTIONS FROM OPERA: *Ariodant*, "Romance du barde" (PATHE). *Le Jeune Henri*, "Ouverture" (BRUNSWICK-Lamoureux). *Joseph*, "Vainement Pharon" (COLUMBIA-Thill).

VOCAL: *Le Chant du départ* (COLUMBIA-Thill).

Felix Mendelssohn *1809-1847*

"I am Saul and thou art David. Come to me when I am sad and discouraged and quiet my soul with thy sweet harmonies."
—GOETHE

JAKOB LUDWIG FELIX MENDELSSOHN, one of the glories of the Romantic period in music, was born in Hamburg, on February 3, 1809. His ancestry was distinguished: His grandfather, Moses Mendelssohn, often referred to as "the modern Plato," was a celebrated metaphysician who, it is believed, was the prototype for Lessing's *Nathan der weise*. Moses Mendelssohn's son, Abraham, became a prosperous banker, who married Leah Salomon, a woman of singular attainments about whom H. F. Chorley wrote: "There have lived few women more honorably distinguished than she by acquirement." It was at the instigation of Leah Salomon's brother that Abraham Mendelssohn yielded to expediency and had his family converted to the Lutheran religion, adopting the new name of Bartholdy.

Under the guidance and inspiration of understanding parents, Felix knew a happy childhood. When he was three years old, the French occupation of Hamburg compelled the Mendelssohn family to flee to Berlin. When the French army reached Berlin, the Mendelssohn family crossed the frontier and went to Paris. In Paris, Felix received his first systematic instruction at the piano, from Mme. Bigot.

On returning to Berlin, Felix was given an intensive musical education—piano with Ludwig Berger, and musical theory with Zelter. He made marked progress. At the age of nine, he made his first appearance in public as pianist; at eleven, he turned to composition for the first time. His early fruits as a composer were disclosed at weekly concerts which took place at the Mendelssohn home. It was apparent that Felix was handsomely endowed with musical talent, and his name was much spoken of in musical circles.

Sir Jules Benedict, who first met Mendelssohn in 1821, has recorded his first impressions of the genius. "Walking in the streets of Berlin with my master and friend, Karl Maria von Weber, he directed my attention to a boy, apparently about eleven or twelve years old, who, on perceiving the author of the *Freischütz*, ran towards him, giving him a most hearty and friendly greeting. 'This is Felix Mendelssohn,' said Weber, introducing me at once to the prodigious child, of whose marvelous talent and execution I had heard so much at Dresden. I shall never forget the impression of that day on beholding that beautiful youth, with his auburn hair clustering in ringlets round his shoulders, the ingenuous expression of his clear eyes, and the smile of innocence and candor on his lips. He would have it that we should go with him at once to his father's house; but as Weber had to attend a

rehearsal, he took me by the hand and made me run a race till we reached his home. Up he went briskly to the drawing-room where, finding his mother, he exclaimed: 'Here is a pupil of Weber's, who knows a great deal of his music and of the new opera. Pray, mama, ask him to play it for us.' And so, with an irresistible impetuosity, he pushed me to the pianoforte, and made me remain there until I had exhausted the store of my recollections. When I then begged of him to let me hear some of his own compositions, he refused, but played from memory such of Bach's fugues or Cramer's exercises as I could name."

One of the most important influences in Felix's early life was his intimacy with Goethe, whom he met in his thirteenth year, spending a fortnight at his home and enchanting the great poet with his musical gifts. At one of these meetings, at Goethe's request, young Felix played a Bach fugue, in the middle of which the young musician's mind went blank. Rather than interrupt the flow of music, Felix spontaneously constructed the remainder of the work. "You will be a very great composer, Felix," Goethe told him.

It was while he was still a child that Felix Mendelssohn became enthusiastic about the music of Johann Sebastian Bach. His teacher, Zelter, possessed a copy of the *Passion according to St. Matthew* which had not been performed since Bach's death and was virtually forgotten. One day, in thumbing the pages of this dusty score, Felix was struck by the high nobility and moving power of Bach's music. He went home and begged his mother for a copy of this great music. On Christmas day of 1823, Felix found a copy of the *Passion* under his Christmas tree. From that time on, he became an enthusiast of Bach's music.

Notwithstanding his youth, Felix Mendelssohn composed industriously in many forms of musical composition—sonatas, songs, cantatas, organ-works and even a symphony were given performance at the weekly musicales at the Mendelssohn home. In 1824, his comic-opera, *The Two nephews,* was given a hearing with orchestral accompaniment. "My dear boy," his master, Zelter, told

FELIX MENDELSSOHN

him after the performance, "you are no longer an apprentice but an independent member of the brotherhood of musicians. I proclaim you an independent in the name of Mozart, Haydn and the older Bach."

In 1825, the Mendelssohns bought a new, spacious home on Leipzig Road in Berlin. Here, the Sunday musicales were greatly enlarged, and the foremost musicians of Germany were frequent visitors. One of these who attended these concerts was Moscheles, the great pianist, who found so much merit in Felix's works that he decided to teach him the piano. "Today," recorded the great teacher in his diary, "I gave Felix his first lesson. . . . He is a mature artist, altho only fifteen."

During this period, Mendelssohn composed two important works. The first of these came in 1826, the overture to *A Midsummer night's dream* which he originally composed for two pianos, but later orchestrated. This—a creation of a boy of seventeen—is in some respects Mendelssohn's most felicitous work. "The bloom of youth lies suffused over it," as no one less than Robert Schumann wrote, "as over scarcely any other work of the composer. The finished master took in his happiest minute, his first and highest flight." The other of the two works was an opera, *Die Hóch-zeit des Camacho,* which after many ob-stacles—raised by such envious musicians as Spontini—reached performance in 1827 when it was sharply criticized by the newspapers. It is more than probable that it was because of this adverse criticism that Mendelssohn never again composed an opera.

In 1829, there took place one of the important events in Mendelssohn's career. From boyhood, when he had first come into contact with Bach's *Passion according to St. Matthew,* it had been his ambition to introduce this masterpiece to the world. In 1829, Mendelssohn organized a special chorus for this purpose and, after many painstaking rehearsals, performed the work on March 11. The performance was so successful that, ten days later, it was repeated. "It was an actor and a Jew," Mendelssohn told Devrient, who also participated in the performance, "who restored this great Christian work to the people."

Musicologists have frequently asserted that if Mendelssohn had not been a great composer, his name would have loomed large in musical history by virtue of the fact that he rescued this Bach masterpiece from neglect and obscurity.

For the next few years, Mendelssohn traveled extensively. In May of 1829 he went to England where he was elected honorary member of the Philharmonic Society. This was the beginning of a long association between England and Mendelssohn. With the exception of Handel, no foreign composer was ever esteemed so highly in England as Mendelssohn. From London, Mendelssohn went to Scotland, where he composed his *Fingal's Cave overture* and planned his *Scotch symphony.* Arriving in Berlin, Mendelssohn was offered the chair of music, recently founded at the University, which he declined. By 1830, he was in Italy, recording his impressions of Italian art and music in vivid letters. After a short visit to Switzerland, he went to Paris where he became acquainted with Chopin and Liszt. Finally, he returned to Berlin, once again doing a great service to music by performing Beethoven's *Fourth concerto* which, for some mysterious reason, had been neglected until now.

In 1833, Mendelssohn was appointed music director at Düsseldorf. After a short and not altogether pleasant association with this city, Mendelssohn was offered, in 1835, the conductorial post of the Leipzig Gewandhaus Orchestra.

A new facet of Mendelssohn's genius was now revealed more forcefully than ever before—his talent with the baton. Under his guidance, the concerts of the Leipzig Gewandhaus Orchestra achieved new artistic peaks. In his fastidious attention to details in his conducting, Mendelssohn virtually heralded the modern era of orchestral direction. However, during this active period with the baton, his creative pen was not idle. In 1836, he completed his oratorio *St. Paul,* which was given its first performance at the Lower Rhine Festival in Düsseldorf, by a chorus of more than three hundred singers and a double orchestra.

After Düsseldorf, Mendelssohn arrived for a short visit in Frankfurt. Here he met the charming Cécile Jeanrenaud who, in March of 1837, became his wife. Their marriage was a romantic episode until the very end. As Mendelssohn once wrote: "The best part of every pleasure is gone if Cécile is not there!"

In 1840, Mendelssohn was appointed chapel-master by Wilhelm IV, King of Prussia—with full charge of the music department of the Academy of Arts. He was not happy here, for musical standards were not of the highest and he persistently encountered petty intrigues among the high officials and members of the orchestra. Finally, Mendelssohn succeeded in procuring the King's permission to abandon his post and to return to Leipzig. In his position as chapel-master, Mendelssohn composed for the King, music for *Antigone, Athalia* and, most important of all, the *Midsummer night's dream suite,* the overture to which he had composed as a boy.

In April of 1843—after many years of effort—Mendelssohn finally brought a life-long dream to realization in Leipzig. Financed by a legacy, he was able to establish—with the cooperation of Robert Schumann and Ferdinand David— the Leipzig Conservatory of Music.

For the next few years, Mendelssohn worked at a feverish pace. His pedagogical duties at the Conservatory were many, absorbing his time and energy. At the same time, he was busy conducting the concerts of the Gewandhaus Orchestra and giving guest performances in England and principal German cities. Finally, he was working upon his most ambitious composition, the oratorio *Elijah,* which was first performed by the Birmingham Festival in 1846 amid phenomenal ovations.

Hard work overtaxed his energy and weakened his body. He began to feel pains in the head. Despite his growing illness, he went to London, in April of 1847, to conduct *Elijah.* When he returned to Frankfurt in September of that year, he appeared a tired, old, sick man—even though he had not as yet seen his fortieth birthday. The news of the death of his beloved sister, Fanny, struck him when he had neither the physical strength nor the spirit to withstand the shock. There followed fits of depression, recurrent pains in the head, chills and fevers.

Finally, in Leipzig, he collapsed completely. On the fourth of November (1847) he suddenly sat up in his bed and emitted a cry of pain. He sank back unconscious. A few hours later he was dead.

Eduard Philipp Devrient described the magnificent funeral that was Germany's expression of love for its great musician. "In the afternoon the immense throng of the funeral procession began to gather in front of the house. . . . The coffin was covered with a rich funeral pall of velvet embroidered in silver. . . . Streets and open places were filled with people; all the windows were crowded on the long and circuitous road that the procession was to pass, thru the town and by the Gewandhaus, the scene of Mendelssohn's labors. The musicians led the way, playing a hastily instrumented *Song without words* by Mendelssohn (the one in E-minor, book 5). Six clergymen in full robes followed the bier. . . ." Memorials were likewise held in London, Manchester, Birmingham, Paris and principal cities of Germany.

After the funeral services in Leipzig, the body of Felix Mendelssohn was transferred to Berlin where it was buried in the family vault of the Mendelssohn family.

Both the attractiveness of his appearance and the charm of his personality have been the subject for many pages. As the music, so was the man. Refinement, sensitivity and softness were his integral qualities as an individual. Generally in good spirits and a lover of quips, Mendelssohn was a favorite of the salon. He was a great lover of children and Nature. His favorite composers were Bach and Beethoven.

He often carried the germ of an idea for a composition in his mind for many weeks or months before he put it down on paper. He was highly self critical, and often subjected a work to minute revision even after it received public hearing. He was not easily satisfied with his creations, even after they achieved resounding acclaim.

In his music Mendelssohn approached his greatest individuality when he attempted to paint landscapes of Nature in tone. "The *Scotch* and *Italian* symphonies are entirely occupied in giving thru music the local color of the landscapes and life of the two countries indicated, or, more properly, the impression which they produced in the composer's imagination," wrote H. H. Statham. "The same is true of the *Hebrides* (*Fingal's Cave*) *overture, The Meerstille overture,* etc. In the *Midsummer night's dream overture* it is so in effect, though not nominally, where the sentiment of the quiet moonlight is so exquisitely conveyed by the few slow chords for the wind instruments, bringing us at once into the scene for seeing fairy revels."

What are the distinguishing qualities of Mendelssohn's music? Together with a form of clear and polished symmetry, Mendelssohn's music is characterized, as Frederic H. Cowen has written, by "extreme grace and refinement and musicianly scholarship, at times full of sparkling vivacity, at others tinged with melancholy. If he had comparatively few really great moments, so are there few traces of absolute weakness, as may often be found in the lesser works of Mozart and other composers. . . . He was an inspired melodist, though his themes, beautiful as they were, were not infrequently moulded after the same pattern. He also possessed a strongly marked style and individuality (one of the surest attributes of genius). . . . He possessed . . . in addition a gaiety and animation, a *joie de vivre* which were the outcome of his happy and light-hearted nature."

Though few would deny that Mendelssohn at his greatest exerts a peculiar fascination, evoking a world of magic uniquely his own, critics are generally agreed that he is not of the stature of Beethoven, Mozart, Bach or Handel. If we were to compare Mendelssohn with the giants of the musical art, we would discover, as Daniel Gregory Mason did, that "we cannot escape the impression of a certain thinness of blood, straitness of sympathy and inelasticity of mind. His personality is tenuous, overrarefied; he seems more like a faun than a man. And hence it comes about that when, leaving his world of fairies, elves, visionary landscapes, and ethereal joys and sorrows, he tries to sound a fuller note of human pain and passion, he is felt to be out of his element. His style is too fluent, too suave, too insinuating and inoffensive, to embody tragic emotion. It lacks the rugged force, the virile energy, the occasional harshness and discordance even of the natural human voice; its reading of life, in which there is ugliness, crudity and violence as well as beauty, is too fastidiously expurgated."

However, as Frederic H. Cowen summed up: "If Mendelssohn did not rise to the greatest heights, he came within measurable distance of them. His music bears the stamp of his cultured mind, and his high level of excellence is undeniable."

Principal works by Felix Mendelssohn:

ORCHESTRA: *Italian symphony; Scotch symphony; Reformation symphony; A Midsummer night's dream suite; Fingal's Cave overture; Ruy Blas overture; Trauer-marsch; Concerto for violin and orchestra;* Two concertos for piano and orchestra; music for *Antigone, Athalie, Oedipus in Colonos; Meerestille overture.*

CHAMBER MUSIC: *Piano octet; Piano sextet;* Two string quintets; Seven string quartets; Three piano quartets; Two piano trios;

Violin and piano sonata in F-minor; Two sonatas for violoncello and piano.

CHORAL: *St. Paul*; *Elijah*; Psalms; *Die Erste Walpürgisnacht*; *Te Deum*; *Magnificat*; hymns, etc.

OPERA: *Die Hochzeit des Camacho*.

Songs.

About Felix Mendelssohn:

Benedict, Jules. *Sketch of the Life and Works of Felix Mendelssohn*; Dahms, Walter. *Mendelssohn*; Devrient, Eduard Philipp. *Recollections of Felix Mendelssohn-Bartholdy*; Dorn, Heinrich. *Recollections of Felix Mendelssohn and His Friends*; Gotsch, Rosamund Brunel (editor). *Mendelssohn and His Friends in Kensington*; Hensel, S. *The Mendelssohn Family*; Lampidius, W. A. *Life of Felix Mendelssohn-Bartholdy*; Reissmann, August. *Felix Mendelssohn-Bartholdy*; Rockstro, W. S. *Mendelssohn*; Stratton, Stephen Samuel. *Mendelssohn*.

Important recordings of music by Felix Mendelssohn:

ORCHESTRA: *Italian symphony* (VICTOR-Koussevitzky); *Scotch symphony* (COLUMBIA-Weingartner); *A Midsummer night's dream suite* (VICTOR-Hertz); *Fingal's Cave overture* (VICTOR-Boult); *Ruy Blas overture* (VICTOR-Boult); *Concerto for violin and orchestra* (COLUMBIA-Szigeti); *Meerestille overture* (VICTOR-Blech).

CHAMBER MUSIC: *Piano octet* (GRAMOPHONE); *Quartet in E-minor* (VICTOR-Budapest); *Trio in C-minor* (COLUMBIA); *Trio in D-minor* (VICTOR-Casals, Thibaud, Cortot).

CHORAL: *Elijah,* complete (COLUMBIA).

PIANO: *Songs without words,* selected (VICTOR-K. U. Schnabel).

André Messager *1853-1929*

ANDRÉ CHARLES PROSPER MESSAGER was born in Montluçon on December 30, 1853. As a child, he would drink in greedily the popular music he heard at his home, and he told his parents that some day he would compose similar music. His parents objected to a musical career, hoping that he would become a government official. Financial ruin changed their outlook on life, and they permitted André to obtain a musical education. His studies were first pursued intensively at the École Niedermeyer. They were concluded under Saint-Saëns who recognized his talent and persistently exerted his influence to bring him recognition.

In 1874, Messager was appointed assistant organist at the church St. Sulpice in Paris. Six years later, he became director at the Théâtre Éden in Brussels. He held the latter post only a short period, returning to Paris to officiate as organist at the Church St.-Paul-et-St. Louis, and as choirmaster of the church Ste. Marie des Batignolles.

His creative career was officially launched when his *Symphony,* composed in 1875, was crowned by the Société des compositeurs and performed at the Colonne concerts with acclaim. This success brought the Folies Bergères management to introduce his ballet *Fleur d'oranger.* The ballet was so great a success that it ran for two hundred nights. After this, Messager turned his talent towards comic opera. After two ungratifying attempts, he produced his first decided success, *La Béarnaise,* at the Bouffes Parisiens, in 1885. One year later, *La Béarnaise* duplicated its Parisian success in London. There followed, in the footsteps of this first triumph, several other prominent *opéra-comiques,* including *La Basoche, Les Petites Michus* and *Mirette.*

At the same time that he was successfully following his creative career, Messager was achieving great prominence with the baton. From 1898 to 1903 he was conductor at the Opéra Comique, from 1901 to 1907 he served as artistic director of Covent Garden, London, and from 1907 until 1919 he was director at the Paris Opéra. From 1908, he con-

ANDRÉ MESSAGER

ducted symphonic music with the Concerts du Conservatoire, visiting America with this orchestra in 1918.

His distinguished musical career brought him many honors. In 1907, he became an officer of the Legion of Honor, and in 1926 he was elected a member of the Académie des Beaux-Arts.

André Messager died in Paris on February 24, 1929. He had been married to an English song composer, Miss Hope Temple.

Altho Messager composed a talented symphony and several cantatas and songs, he is best known for his *opéra-comique*. Here, as Adolphe Boschot wrote, "Messager has the force of talent and charm, knowing how to assume a style that is simple, natural and facile; and his obvious facility is the distinguishing trait of mastery. He could escape from pedantry and gravity because. . . Fate, or some gentle guardian angel, gave him the wings of a Parisian wren or sparrow. She likewise gave him a nimble song which fluttered heavenwards, and was harmonized. . . with elegant lines."

Roland-Manuel discovered in Messager's style "elegance, dryness and sensibility. The harmonic language of Messager is extraordinarily original. . . . André Messager, gentleman of music, did not at all imagine that his art could do anything more than delight us."

Principal works by André Messager:

OPERA: *La Béarnaise*; *Le Bourgeois de Calais*; *Isoline*; *Le Mari de la reine*; *La Basoche*; *Mirette*; *Les Petites Michus*; *Véronique*; *Fortunio*; *Béatrice*; *Monsieur Beaucaire*.

BALLET: *Mignons et vilains*; *Les Deux pigeons*; *Scaramouche*; *Amants eternels*; *Le Procès des roses*; *Une Aventure de la Guimart*.

ORCHESTRA: Symphony; incidental music for *Hélène*, *La Montagne enchantée*, etc.

CHORAL: *Don Juan et Haydée*; *Prométhée enchaînée*.

Songs, pieces for the piano, etc.

About André Messager:

Boschot, Adolphe. *Le Mystère Musical*; Seré, Octave. *Musiciens Français d'aujourd'hui.*
Musical Opinion 42:489 May 1919; *Musical Times* 70:367 April 1929; *Musique* 2:837 April 15, 1929.

Important recordings of music by André Messager:

SELECTIONS FROM OPERA: *La Basoche*, "Ouverture et Passepied" (ODEON); "À ton tour simple et sincère" (POLYDOR); "Elle m'aime" (COLUMBIA). *Les Deux pigeons*, "Ballet suite" (GRAMOPHONE). *Véronique*, "Fantasia" (POLYDOR); "Ouverture" (ODEON); "Adieu, je pars" (COLUMBIA).

Giacomo Meyerbeer *1791-1864*

"Meyerbeer's operas inaugurated a new epoch in operatic writing."—FRANZ LISZT

JAKOB MEYER BEER (it was not until much later in life that he contracted and Italianized his name to Giacomo Meyerbeer) was born in Berlin on September 5, 1791, to wealthy Jewish parents. He showed early signs of musical talent. He proved to be in possession of a keen ear and a retentive memory. As a child, he frequently startled his parents by the accuracy with which he reproduced melodies he had heard but once. They, therefore, soon decided to place him under capable musical instruction. At five, Meyerbeer became a pupil of Franz Ignaz Lauska, who taught him the piano. Four years later he made his first public appearance, performing the Mozart *D-minor concerto*. He acquired great fame as a prodigy of the piano, some critics esteeming him one of the most gifted pianists in Berlin at the time.

In 1802, Muzio Clementi—who had, by this time, gone into retirement as a teacher of the piano—visited Berlin where he heard Meyerbeer play. Clementi was so carried away by the performance that he decided to become Meyerbeer's teacher. Meyerbeer's other musical studies were pursued under Zelter, the eminent theorist (teacher of Mendelssohn), and, shortly afterwards, Anselm Weber.

At this time there occurred a much-quoted anecdote of Meyerbeer's student days. Meyerbeer composed a fugue which pleased his master, Anselm Weber, who decided to send it to Abbé Vogler, master of counterpoint. The reply received from Abbé Vogler was keenly discouraging—in the form of a tremendous and voluminous thesis written by the Abbé on the method and manner of composing fugues, in which was included a vivisection of Meyerbeer's fugue with all of its many errors clearly noted. Meyerbeer, however, was not disheartened. He composed another fugue, according to the instruction set forth in the thesis, which he also despatched to Abbé Volger. This time a far different reply came to his door: "Art opens to you a glorious future. Come to me at Darmstadt, where you will be to me as a son."

In this way, Meyerbeer went to Darmstadt in 1810, becoming not only a pupil but also the household guest of Vogler. He remained here for two years, composing his first large works: a cantata, *God and Nature,* the four-part *Sacred songs of Klopstock,* and his first opera, *Jephtha's vow.* It should be pointed out that Meyerbeer's fellow-pupil, at this time, was Karl Maria von Weber, between whom and himself there arose an intimate friendship.

After these two years, Vogler told Meyerbeer that his studies were at an end, since there was nothing more he could teach him. Meyerbeer, therefore, went on to Munich to attend a performance of his *Jephtha's vow,* which was highly unsuccessful. From Munich he went to Vienna with the intention of pursuing a career as piano virtuoso. But on the night of his arrival there, he heard a recital of Hummel and was so appalled by his own shortcomings in contrast to this great pianist that he decided to go into complete retirement and redevelop his piano style. In 1813, he emerged from this seclusion and gave a concert in Vienna, and was acclaimed an outstanding artist. During this time, too, his second operatic venture—a comic opera, *Alimelek*—was performed in Vienna, meeting with a cold reception.

Discouraged by his two creative failures, Meyerbeer decided to give up all intentions of composing for the theatre. Salieri, however, urged him to reconsider his decision and to go to Italy to study operatic style more closely. Meyerbeer followed Salieri's advice and arrived in Venice in 1816. "All my feelings became Italian," he later wrote, "all my thoughts became Italian. After I had lived a year there it seemed to me that I was an Italian." It was to be expected, therefore, that in his composition his style should become Italian as well, particularly because he was closely attracted to Rossini's operas which he heard so extensively at this time.

In 1818, he composed his first Italian opera, *Romilda e Costanza,* which received acclaim upon its performance in Turin. There followed several commissions from important opera houses. For the next few years, Meyerbeer produced a string of Italian operas which, though they enjoyed great vogue in their day, have failed to survive. Meyerbeer was penetratingly self-understanding when he referred to these early Italian operas as his "wild oats."

In 1823, Meyerbeer returned to Berlin where he completed another opera, *Il Crociato in Egitto,* which was a sensation in Venice the following year. A performance of this work in Paris brought Meyerbeer to the French capital, which appealed so strongly to him that he decided to settle there permanently. He became a close friend of leading musicians in Paris, including Adam, Auber, Boieldieu and Halévy. Association with these composers brought him a stifling dissatisfaction with all of his previous operatic achievements. For several years, therefore, he abandoned the composition of operas completely. When he emerged from this retirement, it was no longer as a composer of Italian opera that he made his appearance but as a composer of French opera.

The first of his French operas, *Robert le diable*—on a libretto by Scribe—was presented on November 22, 1831. Its striking effects and colorful scenes brought it so magnificent and permanent a success that it firmly established the Opéra on a financial basis. It brought in more than four million francs within the next twenty years, receiving some three hundred and thirty performances.

While Meyerbeer's second opera, *Les Huguenots,* performed in 1836, did not equal the success of *Robert,* it showed his increasing powers as a composer. *Les Huguenots* remains one of the famous Meyerbeer operas, the one in which he reached his highest development and enrichment. "Had he written

GIACOMO MEYERBEER

During a leave of absence from Berlin, Meyerbeer visited Paris where he received from his librettist the book for a new opera. Meyerbeer worked enthusiastically on his new task. In April of 1849, *Le Prophète* was introduced at the Opéra in Paris. It was a tremendous success from the very first. And it has maintained its success to this day.

For the next ten years, Meyerbeer devoted himself principally to comic opera. In 1854, the Opéra Comique performed *L'Étoile du nord* whose success was so great that, within the year, it ran to more than one hundred performances. Five years later came *Dinorah,* and once again Meyerbeer's creation found an enthusiastic response.

The last years of Meyerbeer's life were devoted to the composition of his *magnum opus,* the opera, *L'Africaine*—a task made doubly difficult by his poor health and failing eyesight. He was never destined to hear his last creation. On April 23, 1864, he took to his bed, a hopeless invalid. And on the morning of May 2, he died.

His body was taken to Berlin. Everywhere, en route, the body was greeted with reverent ceremony. He was buried in the family tomb in Berlin.

One year after his death, his last opera, *L'Africaine,* was performed for the first time in Paris amid thunderous acclaim.

Meyerbeer, who was a man of great culture, made a striking personal impression. He had charm and poise; he was a fluent and absorbing conversationalist. He was, by inheritance, a man of great wealth. Yet he lived in Paris in such simplicity that he was frequently accused of being miserly. That he was liberal with his money was, however, repeatedly proved thruout his life by his open-handed generosity in assisting musicians, his endless contributions to charities and his handsome trust-fund which he raised for musicians' families. He was addicted to neither drinking nor smoking.

His greatest fault, both as a man and as an artist, was his love of glory and his indefatigable effort to attract it. Just as in his operas he always catered to public taste—and, therefore, concerned

nothing else but the fourth act," wrote Arthur Hervey, "he would be entitled to rank as one of the greatest dramatic composers of all time." Berlioz was tremendously enthusiastic about this opera. "The effervescence of the emotions excited by this masterpiece makes one desire to be a great man in order to place one's glory and one's genius at the feet of Meyerbeer." And Richard Wagner—before his anti-Semitic prejudices brought a reversal of his judgment—considered the fourth act one of the greatest acts in all operatic music.

Meyerbeer was now one of the most famous operatic composers of his time. Honors came to him from many directions. From the Netherlands, the Order of the Oak Crown was bestowed upon him; from London arrived an appointment to the Royal Academy; from Germany, an offer to become chapel-master to King Friedrich Wilhelm IV.

For the next few years, Meyerbeer lived in Berlin, devoting his creative energy to the composition of music for the king in his post as chapel-master. He produced many choral works for the chapel, several marches, and one opera (*Das Feldlager in Schlesien*), the last of which was successful principally because it boasted of Jenny Lind in its cast. At the same time he was busy with the baton, performing operas of Spohr, Weber and Wagner.

maturity under the instruction of Costa,

fect his operas produced than with their content—so, by word of mouth and by every action, he attempted to draw endless attention and admiration towards himself and his work. It was Heinrich Heine who criticized Meyerbeer for this shortcoming in a devastating quip: "When Meyerbeer is dead," Heine once asked, "who will look after his glory?"

Discussing Meyerbeer's operatic output, C. Hubert Parry wrote: "Musically it is a huge pile of commonplaces, infinitely ingenious and barren. There is but little cohesion between the scenes, and no attempt at consistency to the situations in style and expression. No doubt Meyerbeer had a great sense of general effect. The music glitters and roars and warbles in well-disposed contrasts, but the inner life is wanting. It is the same with his treatment of characters. They metaphorically strut and pose and gesticulate, but express next to nothing; they get into frenzies but are for the most part incapable of human passion. The element of wholesome musical sincerity is wanting in him, but the power of astonishing and bewildering is almost unlimited. His cleverness is equal to any emergency."

Notwithstanding these lamentable faults, Meyerbeer was an operatic composer of importance. "Meyerbeer was an innovator," wrote Arthur Hervey, "his operas contain great beauties; he showed extraordinary dramatic perception and marked originality; he devised new instrumental effects; he helped to prepare the way for the modern music-drama. . . . With more strength of character, Meyerbeer would have done yet greater things. He had at his command the genius and the opportunities."

Hugo Riemann thus summed up Meyerbeer's historic importance: "History will point to Meyerbeer's music as one of the most important steps to Wagner's art."

Principal works by Giacomo Meyerbeer:

OPERA: *Il Crociato in Egitto*; *Robert le diable*; *Les Huguenots*; *Das Feldlager in Schlesien*; *Le Prophète*; *L'Étoile du nord*; *Dinorah*; *L'Africaine*.
CHORAL: *Gott und die Natur*; *Gutenberg*; *Maria und ihr genius*; *Festhymnus*; *Das*

Genius der musik am grabe Beethovens; *Stabat Mater*; Psalms; *Miserere*.
ORCHESTRA: *Fackeltänze*; march; overture. Songs.

About Giacomo Meyerbeer:

Blaze de Bury, Angé Henri. *Meyerbeer: Sa Vie, ses Oeuvres et son Temps*; Curzon, Henri. *Meyerbeer*; Duariac, Lionel Alexander. *Meyerbeer*; Kapp, Julius. *Meyerbeer*; Kohut, Adolphe. *Meyerbeer*.

Important recordings of music by Giacomo Meyerbeer:

SELECTIONS FROM OPERA: *L'Africaine*, "Overture" (GRAMOPHONE-Blech); "Adieu, mon doux rivage (COLUMBIA-Rethberg); "Fille des rois" (ODEON); "Adamastor, roi des vagues" (VICTOR-Ruffo); "Prélude; Marche indienne" (GRAMOPHONE-Blech); "O Paradis" (VICTOR-Gigli). *Dinorah*, "Ombre légère" (PATHE); "En chasse" (COLUMBIA). *Les Huguenots*, "Nobles seigneurs, salut!" and "Une dame noble et sage" (VICTOR-Onegin); "O beau pays de la Touraine" (COLUMBIA-Noréna); "Ballet music" (GRAMOPHONE-Blech); "Gloire au grand Dieu vangeur" (GRAMOPHONE); "O Ciel! où courrez-vous" (GRAMOPHONE). *Le Prophète*, "Ah, mon fils!" (VICTOR-Onegin); "Prélude" (GRAMOPHONE-Blech); "Coronation march" (VICTOR-Mengelberg); "Roi du ciel". (PATHE); "O prêtres de Baal" (VICTOR-Onegin). *Robert le diable*, "Ouverture" (GRAMOPHONE-Blech); "Voici donc le débris" (COLUMBIA).

Stanislaus Moniuszko   *1819-1872*

"The composer of *Halka* must be considered a musician of very original powers."—HANS VON BÜLOW

STANISLAUS MONIUSKO was born in Ubiel, near Minsk, on May 5, 1819, the son of a former officer in the army of Napoleon. From his mother, he received his first instruction in music. After acquiring the elements, he was placed under Augustus Freyer in Warsaw. In 1837, he went to Berlin where for two years he was a student under C. F. Rundenhagen. One year later, he emerged as a composer, with *Three songs*, which G. W. Fink described in the *Allgemeine Musikalische Zeitung* as "national in word and tune. . . distinguished by surety and decisiveness." In 1842, he published the first part of his *Home song book*, and was instantly recognized as a song composer of great distinction.

"Not for a moment do I hesitate to put the songs of Moniuszko in the

STANISLAUS MONIUSZKO

highest class of lyric composition," wrote the Russian composer, Serov, in 1869, "as represented by the great names of Schubert and Schumann in Western Europe, and in our country by Glinka and Dargomijsky."

From Berlin, Moniuszko went to Vilna where for many years he earned his living by playing the organ at St. John's Church, and teaching the piano. He did not neglect composition. In 1846, there was produced in Warsaw his opera-bouffe, *The Lottery,* which enjoyed great popularity. During the next year, Moniuszko was engaged in the task of composing his monumental folk-opera, *Halka*—often designated as the first national Polish opera. *Halka* was given its first performance at the Vilna concert-hall on January 1, 1848.

Discussing *Halka,* Zdzislaw Jachimecki wrote: "The listener is carried upon the stream of the music, and always feels the personality of the composer, and the sincerity of his inspiration. The songs of the opera are very melodious, characteristic and dramatic. There are, however, also other remarkable factors which raise it to the rank of a masterpiece. No Polish dramatic composer had previously expressed by dance scenes the Polish national temperament so perfectly as Moniuszko did."

Ten years after its first performance at the Vilna concert-hall, *Halka* was introduced with great success to the Warsaw opera house. Since that time it has been performed by the foremost opera houses thruout the world, coming to Prague in 1868, St. Petersburg, Kiev and Moscow in 1892, and, finally, to New York in 1905. *Halka* has also made its appearance in a Polish talking film, in which version it was released thruout Europe and America.

Moniuszko followed the success of *Halka* with another popular opera, *The Terrible castle,* performed in Warsaw on September 28, 1865.

In 1858, Moniuszko changed his permanent home from Vilna to Warsaw, where for many years he was busily engaged in conducting at the opera house, in teaching theory at the Conservatory, and in composing. During the last years of his life, he produced two operas which were decided failures, *The Pariah* in 1869 and *Beata* in 1872. These failures broke his heart and spirit, bringing on his fatal illness. He died in Warsaw on June 4, 1872.

In April of 1926, the Vienna Volksoper revived *Halka* with overwhelming success.

Principal works by Stanislaus Moniuszko:

OPERA: *The Lottery*; *Halka*; *Flis*; *The Countess*; *The Terrible ~castle*; *The Pariah*; *Beata.*

CHORAL: *Sonnets from the Crimea*; *Spectres*; Seven masses; Two requiems; *Four Ostrobramer litanies*; hymns, etc.

ORCHESTRA: *Bajka overture*; incidental music to *Hamlet, Merry wives of Windsor,* etc.

About 400 songs; piano pieces, etc.

About Stanislaus Moniuszko:

Jachimecki, Zdislaw. *Stanislaus Moniuszko. Musical Quarterly* 14:53 January 1928; *Poland-America* 5:93 August 1924.

Important recordings of music by Stanislaus Moniuszko:

ORCHESTRA: *Bajka* (SYRENA).

SELECTIONS FROM OPERA: *Halka,* "Gydyby rannem slenkiem" (GRAMOPHONE), "I ty mu wierzysz" (ODEON); "Overture," "Mazurka," "Mountaineer's dance," "Polonaise," etc. (SYRENA).

Pierre Monsigny *1729-1817*

ONE of the creators of the French *opéra-comique*, Pierre Alexander de Monsigny, was born in Franquembergues, near St. Omer. He was given an intensive education at the Jesuit College of St. Omer, where one of the Jesuits taught him the violin. In his eighteenth year, the death of his father placed the burden of the support of his family upon his shoulders. Realizing that the opportunities in his native city were few and far between, he left for Paris, with thirty francs in his pocket. Soon after his arrival in the French capital, he secured a position as clerk in the Bureaux des Comptes du Clergé.

In 1752, an itinerant operatic company from Italy presented in Paris Pergolesi's sparkling *La Serva padrona*. This sparkling opéra-bouffe stirred Monsigny who felt that he had, at last, found the medium in which he wished to express himself musically. He decided to return to music study with greater intensity as preparation for creative work. He took lessons in harmony from Gianotti, a disciple of Rameau, making such progress in five months that he was able to submit to his teacher the manuscript of a comic-opera, *Les Aveux indiscrets*.

This comic-opera was performed at the Théâtre de la Foire on February 7, 1759. The following year, another Monsigny opera, *Le Maître en droit* received presentation. With *Le Cadi dupé,* produced in 1761, Monsigny became one of the most popular composers of his time. *Le Cadi dupé* attracted the attention of Sedaine, eminent librettist, who presented himself to Monsigny and offered to write the books for his operas. Together, they produced such overwhelming successes as *On ne s'avise jamais de tout, Le Roi et le fermier* and *Rose et Colas.*

In 1768, Monsigny was given the position of *maître d'hotel* in the household of the Duke of Orleans. This was, for the most part, a sinecure enabling Monsigny to live in great luxury, amass considerable wealth and, at the same time, to devote himself uninterruptedly to composition. During the next few years, Monsigny produced some of his most resounding successes, including *Le Déserteur* (1769)—concerning which Berlioz was later to write some rapturous paragraphs of praise—*Le Faucon* (1772), *Le Rendezvous bien employé* (1774) and *Félix* (1777).

Curiously enough, altho *Félix* was an overwhelming success and despite the fact that it revealed Monsigny at the height of his creative power, Monsigny was never again to compose another work. Monsigny, himself, in later years explained his silence to Fétis by confessing that not another idea came to his head after *Félix*, that *Félix* "was like death for me."

In 1785, the Duke of Orleans died, and his son—greatly appreciative of Monsigny's music—appointed him administrator of his affairs and inspector of the canals of Orleans. The French Revolution not only brought these positions to an end, but also wiped out Monsigny's sizable fortune. There followed poverty and suffering. In 1798, the Opéra Comique gave Monsigny an annuity of $500 a year. When Napoleon heard about this grant—surprised to learn that the great composer Monsigny was still alive—he increased it to $1500. In 1800, upon the death of Piccinni, Monsigny was appointed Inspector at the Conservatory. He was, however, unfitted for the post, due to his inadequate musical technique, and was forced to

PIERRE MONSIGNY

give it up two years later. In 1813, Monsigny succeeded Grétry at the Institut, and in 1816 he was awarded the Legion of Honor.

Pierre Alexander de Monsigny died in Paris on January 14, 1817. An impressive funeral ceremony at St. Laurent attested to the high respect and admiration which his work still commanded in Paris.

A contemporary of Monsigny described him as follows: "He was of medium height; his appearance was noble and benevolent, and his manners were at the same time both simple and elegant. He preserved until his extreme old age all that distinguished a man who has lived in the best society. His character, full of sweetness and kindness, without a trace of pettiness or envy, brought him the affection and high esteem of all those who knew him. The most salient trait of his make-up was a most exquisite sensibility."

While it is quite true that none of Monsigny's comic-operas have survived, they were all-important in serving as models for all future French composers of the *opéra-comique*. Monsigny had an inadequate musical technique which, more than once, revealed appalling gaps in his musical construction. But what he lacked in science he more than compensated for in charm, grace and melodic beauty. Adolphe Adam, famous composer of *opéra-comique,* has spoken of the "exquisite sensibility," the "comic verve," the "dramatic movement and expressive force" of Monsigny's music. Berlioz has expressed the opinion that Monsigny was as genuine and as important in his own field, as Gluck was in his.

Principal works by Pierre Alexander de Monsigny:

OPERA: *Les Aveux indiscrets; Le Maître en droit; Le Cadi dupe; On ne s'avise jamais de tout; Le Roi et le fermier; Rose et Colas; Le Déserteur; Le Faucon; Le Rendezvous bien employé; Félix.*

About Pierre Alexander de Monsigny:

Adam, Adolphe. *Derniers Souvenirs d'un Musicien;* Boschot, Adolphe. *Chez les Musiciens;* Pougin, Arthur. *Monsigny et son Temps.*

Philippe de Monte *1521-1603*

PHILIPPE DE MONTE, the last of the great representatives of the Flemish school of contrapuntal music, was born in Malines in 1521. Material about his early life is meagre, but it is known that as a boy he was a chorister at the St. Rumold's Cathedral, which was under the patronage of Queen Margaret of Austria. In early manhood he came to Naples where for fifteen years he followed the trade of tutor. Here he came into intimate friendship with Orlando de Lasso.

II, consort of Queen Mary. One year accompanied de Monte on a tour thru Italy in 1554. At any rate, in that year de Monte came to Rome, met Palestrina, and succeeded in publishing his first book of five-part madrigals. From Rome he went to Antwerp, then to London where he joined the choir of Philip II, consort of Queen Mary. One year later, he returned to his native country.

For the next ten years, Philippe de Monte toured Italy extensively as composer, singer and performer, acquiring a great reputation for his contrapuntal music. One of his contemporaries, Chancellor Selt (in 1555), referred to him as "the best composer in the whole century." In 1572, he was awarded the honorary and non-resident position of treasurer at the Cathedral of Cambrai, and three years after this was elevated to canonicate.

In 1586, De Monte went to Vienna where he was given his most important musical post—choirmaster to Emperor Maximilian II. He retained his position until the end of his life.

Philippe de Monte died in Vienna on July 4, 1603. After his death, his prolific output passed into complete obscurity. It was not until our time that a group of distinguished musicologists—principally G. van Doorslaer and Charles van den Borren—unearthed his work and revealed its outstanding artistic importance. There has recently been sponsored and launched the publication of the complete works of Philippe de Monte under the editorship of Charles van den Borren and Canon van Nuffel.

PHILIPPE DE MONTE

Philippe de Monte composed a library of masses, madrigals, motets, etc. These works, G. van Doorslaer informs us, are characterized by "a simple, pure and elegant style, and at the same time by a profound technique of harmony and counterpoint."

"With Monte," wrote Charles van den Borren in analyzing de Monte's style, "the edifice is slowly and patiently put together by means of little pieces fitted one upon another with the most marvelous suppleness and most impeccable sureness. He has, like Lasso, a vigorous *sens-plastique* of which the delicate materiality is in opposition with the more ethereal substance of Palestrina's work."

Principal works by Philippe de Monte:

CHORAL: Thirty-five masses; about 1,000 madrigals; motets, etc.

About Philippe de Monte:

Doorslaer, G. van. *La Vie et les Oeuvres de Philippe de Monte.*
Chesterian 11:70 December 1929; *Musical Times* 72:1036 November 1, 1931; *Proceedings of the Musical Association* 57:99, 1930-1931.

Claudio Monteverdi   *1567-1643*

CLAUDIO MONTEVERDI, the first of the great Italian opera composers, was born in Cremona on May 15, 1567. The existing facts of his early life are not very informative. It is known that, while still young, he was a pupil of Ingegneri, one of the most important musical theoreticians of the time. Monteverdi acquired such a thoro musical education from him that he was able, in 1583, to publish his first book of madrigals which disclosed a contrapuntal skill of great mastery.

In 1589, Monteverdi became a violist in the court orchestra of the Duke of Mantua. From this time on, biographical material about him becomes more plentiful. His salary was twelve and a half Mantuan crowns a month (a decent income), but in view of the fact that he was expected to live in style he was always in financial difficulties. However, this was an important post for Monteverdi, for here he found recognition for his unmistakable musical gifts. He enjoyed such great esteem in the eyes of the Duke that when, in 1595, the Duke traveled to Hungary, and, in 1599, to Flanders and Spa, he insisted upon taking his gifted musician with him.

The latter trip was of far-reaching importance to Monteverdi's artistic development, bringing him into contact with the French school of composers, their technique and style of composition which he was to utilize extensively. We are informed by Monteverdi's brother that Claudio Monteverdi was the first composer in Italy to "practise the French manner of vocal writing in the new style which has been much admired during the last three or four years, whether as the accompaniment of words of motets or madrigals, or songs and arias."

In 1601, Monteverdi was appointed chapel master to the house of Gonzaga in Mantua, and as an additional mark of honor was accorded full citizenship. His salary was small; it was said that he was frequently compelled to fight the treasurer to receive that little which was due him. The work was exacting, particularly to a composer of Monteverdi's temperament, who could work only slowly and painfully. Frequently the compulsion to complete assignments on a few days' notice depressed him and made him violently ill. "I do most heartily pray your most Serene Highness," he was compelled to write to the

Duke at one time, "for the love of God, no longer to put so much work on me; and to give me more time, for my great desire to serve you, and the excess of my fatigue will not fail to shorten my life."

In 1605, Monteverdi published his fifth book of madrigals. With this publication, one phase of his artistic career came to an end. From this time on, he was to go in an altogether new direction, a direction which was to bring him a permanent position of importance in musical history.

The marriage of the Duke's son to Margherita, the Infanta of Savoy, in 1607, inspired Monteverdi to compose a work for the occasion in the then new art form of the opera. During his trip to Flanders, in 1599, he had heard reports about that group in Florence who, under Giovanni Bardi's wing, had evolved a new type of musical art.[1] The report interested him excessively. On his return to Italy, he attended a performance of Peri's *Euridice,* when his enthusiasm for the opera form grew. When, therefore, he wished to commemorate the wedding of his employer's son, he decided to try his hand at the new form. The opera was *Arianna,* and it was so triumphant during its performance at the wedding ceremony, that Monteverdi decided to continue in this new sphere of composition.

One year later, Monteverdi published his masterpiece, the opera *Orfeo,* which is frequently credited as being the first great opera.

Discussing the score of *Orfeo,* Henri Prunières wrote: "The whole score shows considerable attention to variety of effect. . . . Contrast abounds. . . . The powerful Venetian colorist is at work. The first act is a luminous tone picture in clear-tints. It is almost entirely given up to joyous shepherd choruses with dancing. . . . The atmosphere of the second act is sombre thruout. . . . In Act III, by the substitution of brass for strings, Monteverdi produces a dark and truly malevolent effect. The Fourth Act is all in half-tints, suited to the pale light which reigns in the infernal regions, and in Act V there is a progression from the dark despair of Orpheus

to the golden glow of musical apotheosis. . . . He shows an astonishing sensitiveness to the expressive value of each instrument, and to what we call instrumental color."

"One of the most remarkable features of this work," in the opinion of Frank Howes, "is the great flexibility and power of the recitative, which is very light, and carries the drama forwards more rapidly than does a good deal of the recitative in later works."

In 1613, Monteverdi left Mantua to compete for the post of chapel-master of St. Mark's Cathedral in Venice. His performance on the organ so impressed the Procurators that, then and there, they offered him a salary of three hundred ducats a year, instead of the usual two hundred. In this position, Monteverdi remained until the end of his life, living simply and in seclusion in a monk's cell and devoting his time to the composition of church music and operas and to the training of his choir.

Meanwhile, his name grew more and more famous thruout the entire world of music. In 1637, the first opera house in Venice opened its doors. Its frequent performances of Monteverdi's operas brought him enormous prestige. There was hardly a musician thruout Europe who was not acquainted with some of his music and who did not revere his name.

In 1643, Monteverdi decided to take one last glimpse of the city of his birth. Unfortunately, his wish never reached realization. Falling seriously ill on the voyage, he was brought back to Venice, where he died on November 29, 1643. He was buried with pomp and ceremony, accorded a funeral usually given only to princes.

Monteverdi was known to have been a man of austere simplicity, very serious and grave in his behaviour, proud and self-assured in his conduct. He was intimately acquainted with the classics and philosophy. He worked hard thruout his life. He knew only one diversion, the practice of alchemy.

Casting a glance over the formidable output of Monteverdi's genius—his church and secular music—Henri Prunières commented as follows: "This immense work is inexhaustible. It astonishes by its richness as by its in-

[1] See sketch on Caccini.

CLAUDIO MONTEVERDI

credible variety. Yet the personality of Monteverdi gives to this work, written in styles not only different but incongruous, a surprising unity. Everything bears the mark of his genius; the contrapuntal motets, the madrigals with their barbaric dissonances, the graceful canzonette, the dramatic narrations. The slightest arietta by Monteverdi has so peculiar a quality that the composer can be recognized in the very first bars. . . . The music of Monteverdi, like that of Bach, is never empty of thought and feeling; it does not find its end in itself but in the emotions it expresses. His vehement soul is revealed entire, with its passionate sadness, its powerful sensuality, its love of life; for this great Latin artist, who suffered so greatly, preserved to the end that love and feeling for life."

Monteverdi's importance in musical history rests not with his church music—which, though often labored, possessed great imagination and power—but in his operas. As Paul Bekker pointed out, his outstanding contribution lay in "shaping their [Florentines] achievements, which though bold and of genuine worth were still rather tentative, into a vigorous form of art." While the pioneer efforts of Caccini and Peri should not be minimized in importance, it was Monteverdi who first definitely pointed the direction towards which Italian opera was to travel.

Monteverdi is frequently referred to, by the musical historian, as the "father of modern orchestration." Truth to tell, the orchestration of his operas was many years ahead of its time. He introduced such new effects as pizzicato and tremolo, which were electrically new for their days; his dissonances enriched harmonic language immeasurably; he first evolved a dramatic style of composition for the orchestra. But, most important of all, he made a sharp distinction between an "instrumental" style of composition and "vocal." "He produced music," wrote Adam Carse, "which is only possible on string instruments; music, in which the interest is that of harmony, texture and tone-color, and is completely independent of imitative movement of parts."

Recently, the eminent Italian composer, Francesco Malipiero, edited for publication the complete works of Monteverdi. Another recent composer, Vincent d'Indy, restored the L'Incoronazione di Poppea, which was presented by the Juilliard School of Music in New York in 1932-1933.

Principal works by Claudio Monteverdi:

OPERA: *Arianna*; *Ballo delle ingrate*; *Maddalena*; *Didone*; *Armida*; *Adone*; *L'Incoronazione di Poppea*; *Orfeo*, etc.

CHORAL: Eight books of madrigals; scherzi musicali; motets; masses; requiems, etc.

About Claudio Monteverdi:

Mackie, M. D. *Monteverdi, His Life and Works*; Prunières, Henri. *Claudio Monteverdi.*
Musical Times 65 :509 June 1924.

Important recordings of music by Claudio Monteverdi:

SELECTIONS FROM OPERA: *Arianna*, "Lasciatemi morire" (PARLAPHONE). *L'Incoronazione di Poppea*, "Lullaby" (COLUMBIA). *Orfeo*, "Ecco purch'a voi ritorno" (VICTOR).

CHORAL: *Lagrime d'amante al sepolcro dell' amata*, madrigal-sestina, (COLUMBIA).

Cristobal Morales *1500-1553*

CRISTOBAL MORALES, one of the earliest of great Spanish church composers, was born in Seville about 1500. As a boy, he sang for six

CRISTOBAL MORALES

years in the choir of the Seville Cathedral under Fernandez de Castilleja, the chapel master. His beautiful voice brought him to Rome, in 1535, where he joined the choir of the Pope. Three years after this, his first known work—a cantata for six voices—was given performance. There followed a fertile outpouring of choral compositions, including several magnificats, three volumes of motets, and two volumes of masses.

In 1540, Morales was given leave from the papal choir to return to his native country. Between 1545 and 1553, he held the post of chapel-master first in Toledo and then in Malaga. It seems that, in the latter year, he took a leave of absence from his Malaga position expressly to apply once again for his former chapel-master assignment in Toledo. At any rate, all trace is lost of him from this time on, and it is believed that he died somewhere in Spain, sometime between September 4 and October 7 in 1553.

The singular importance of Morales as a composer rests in the fact that he was one of the first great Spanish composers to disclose to the rest of Europe the peculiar individuality of the Spanish mind. His prolific óutput of church music is characterized by an amazing technique. No less a theoretician than Padre Martini greatly admired, and frequently commented upon, Morales'

choral structure. However, as J. B. Trend pointed out, "Morales is saved from dullness by his imagination; he had such a complete command of the methods of his time that he could afford to break the strictest rules. . . when the occasion demanded it."

"The art of Morales," wrote Cecil Gray, "is perhaps less directly moving than that of most of his compatriots, and it has in it something of the ceremonious stiffness and solemn, courtly demeanor of a Spanish grandee; nevertheless, this somewhat forbidding aspect conceals a vein of sombre and passionate intensity which is often exceedingly compelling and impressive."

Cristobal Morales' works have been published in the first volume of the *Hispaniae scholae música sacra*, edited by Felipe Pedrell.

Principal works by Cristobal Morales:
CHORAL: Cantatas; magnificats; motets; masses.

About Cristobal Morales:
Gray, Cecil. *A History of Music*; Mitjana y Gordon, Rafael. *Estudios sobre Algunos Músicos Españoles del Siglo XVI*; Trend, J. B. *The Music of Spanish History*; Van Vechten, Carl. *The Music of Spain*.

Thomas Morley   *1557-1606*

THE first of the great English madrigalists, Thomas Morley, was born in England in 1557. As a boy, he was a chorister in St. Paul's Cathedral. In 1573, his voice broke and, leaving the St. Paul choir, he became a pupil of William Byrd.

In 1589, Morley was appointed organist at St. Paul's Cathedral, a position he held for almost four years. During this time, he was strongly implicated as a political agent in Flanders—becoming reconciled to the Catholic Church so that he might better allay suspicion—and was discovered by Paget, a Roman Catholic, who intercepted some letters of Morley's. With imprisonment, perhaps death, facing him, Morley came (in the words of Paget himself) "asking on his knees forgiveness. I was content to let him go."

Scorched by this contact with politics, Morley contented himself with devoting the remainder of his life to music. In 1592, he became a gentleman of the Chapel Royal. One year later, he published his first volume of Canzonets. 1594 saw the publication of his first book of madrigals which, with the exception of the solitary examples produced by William Byrd, were the first important specimens of madrigal form in England.[1]

Discussing English madrigal composers from Thomas Morley on, Ernest Walker wrote: "So far as greatness in handling of material there can be no doubt that the concerted vocal music of the chief men of the time represents the supreme flower of English art. . . . Limited by necessary historical conditions as their technical resources are, they can between them cover a wide range of emotional expression, and portray it from end to end, with a subtle directness that places their work very high among the things worthy of permanent remembrance by musicians of all nationalities. . . . They can look in the face any composer who has ever lived; if they are not among the supreme divinities they are at any rate Titans among the earth-born."

All of Thomas Morley's published work falls within the span of a few years. Following the publication of his madrigals, he produced a set of ballets in 1595 (including such gems as *Now is the month of Maying* and *About the Maypole new*), in 1598, a second volume of madrigals, in 1599, a book of Consort Lessons and, in 1600, a book of airs.

On September 28, 1598, Thomas Morley was granted the patent for printing songbooks and music paper. A competitor, John Day, claimed priority to the patent. After considerable altercation, the matter was brought before the House of Commons which decreed that the patent was to remain exclusively with Morley until his death, after which it would become public property.

Ill-health compelled Morley to abandon composition and retire from the Chapel Royal in 1602. In 1603, he edited the charming book of madrigals, *The Triumphes of Oriana*, written in honor of Queen Elizabeth, to which the foremost madrigal composers in England contributed numbers.

Thomas Morley died in London sometime between 1603 and 1606. Historians have for a long time give 1603 as the definite date, but modern musicology tends to 1606 as more accurate. Besides his compositions, Morley wrote a sparkling dialogue entitled *A plaine and easie introduction to practicall musicke,* published in 1597.

What Edmund Horace Fellowes wrote about Morley's canzonets might well apply to all of his secular works, his ballets and madrigals as well. They reflect, wrote Fellowes, "the light-hearted spirit of the composer, who excelled all the English madrigalists in this particular vein. . . . They are written with consummate skill and with extraordinarily full harmonic effect, while their phrasing and melodic beauty go near perfection."

Principal works by Thomas Morley:

CHORAL: Canzonets; ballets, madrigals; airs.

INSTRUMENTAL: Fantasias.

About Thomas Morley:

Anderton, H. Orsmond. *Early English Music*; Becker, Oscar. *Die Englischen Madrigalisten*; Fellowes, Edmund Horace. *English Madrigal Composers*; Heseltine, Philip. *The English Ayre*; Walker, Ernest. *A Short History of English Music.*

Important recordings of music by Thomas Morley:

CHORAL: *Fire, fire my heart* (COLUMBIA); *Hard by a crystal fountain* (ROYCROFT-English Singers); *It was a lover and his lass* (COLUMBIA); *Now is the month of Maying* (ROYCROFT-English Singers); *O mistresse mine* (GRAMOPHONE); *Sing we and chant it* (ROYCROFT-English Singers).

INSTRUMENTAL: *Fantasias for two viols* (COLUMBIA-Dolmetsch).

Moritz Moszkowski *1854-1925*

MORITZ MOSZKOWSKI was born in Breslau on August 23, 1854. He began the study of the piano in Dresden, continuing it at the Stern Conservatory in Berlin. His studies were completed at the Kullak Conservatory.

In 1873, Moszkowski made an impressive debut as concert pianist in Berlin. Shortly after this, he was engaged as teacher of the piano at the Kullak Con-

Moszkowski: Mŏsh-kof'ski

[1] For a discussion of the madrigal, see sketch of William Byrd.

servatory, holding this position with distinction for many years.

After a successful concert tour as pianist, which took him thruout Europe, Moszkowski settled in Paris in 1897. He had, by this time, acquired a soaring fame as a composer. He had already composed many small pieces for the piano (including his frequently performed *Spanish dances*) which made his name known thruout the length and breadth of Europe. His opera, *Boabdil*, was given an impressive first performance in Berlin in 1892. His *Concerto for piano and orchestra* was acclaimed in Germany and England.

In recognition of his importance as a composer, Germany selected him as a member of the Berlin Academy in 1899.

Moszkowski's last years were in striking contrast to his fame and success of early manhood. He had disposed of all his copyrights for a handsome figure, enough to insure him financial stability for the remainder of his life. Unfortunately, he invested all this money in Russian, Polish and German securities. The World War, therefore, brought him financial ruin. The closing years of his life were spent in dire penury and ill-health. An effort was made by the music world to raise funds for him sufficient to bring him material comforts. But when this plan reached realization, Moszkowski was a dying man. He passed away in Paris on March 4, 1925.

Fannie Edgar Thomas, a pupil of Moszkowski, has recorded the following description of the composer: "Moszkowski is one of those 'ever-will-be-youthful' types of men, tall, slender, of a certain easy grace in carriage, a gentle air. . . . Hair and mustache are somewhat auburn and not over plenteous, face rather long, with high brow, kindly eyes, the hands long and slender, with a few freckles on them, the speaking tones clear, gentle, good-humored and haunting."

As a composer, Moszkowski is best known for his pieces for the piano which, as Paderewski once commented, embraced the whole gamut of piano technique.

"The music of Moszkowski," wrote George Lowe, "follows in legitimate line

MORITZ MOSZKOWSKI

that of Schumann and Chopin. It is romantically conceived and built up out of well sustained melodies and bold harmonies not too remotely related. The wealth of melody and the generally attractive quality of the rhythms are marked features in the work of this composer. There is no hesitancy in the sequence of his musical themes. They flow from a source that is clear and undisturbed. . . . It is by his delightful dance music that Moszkowski will probably always be best known. . . . Moszkowski like Chopin has shown how dance music may be both scholarly and artistic, and if he fails to stimulate our intellect or stir any depths of emotions, he sets our pulses tingling, and makes us feel the glamour of the world, wayward doings of youth beneath sunny Spanish skies, and the various characteristics that dominate the people of his country—Poland. It may be the life of action only that he has the power to picture vividly, but he does it with a subtle and compelling fascination. That is the essence of his genius."

Principal works by Moritz Moszkowski:

OPERA: *Boabdil*.

BALLET: *Laurin*.

ORCHESTRA: *Jeanne d'Arc*; *Phantastischer zug*; *Aus aller Herren Länder*; (orchestrated) Two suites; *Prelude and fugue for strings*;

Concerto for violin and orchestra; Concerto for piano and orchestra, etc.

An entire library of piano music (including two books of Spanish dances, Skizzen, Tarentella, Études, etc.) ; songs.

About Moritz Moszkowski:

Collins, W. F. *Laurel Winners.*
Gramophone Magazine 3:58 July 1925; *Monthly Musical Record* 45:128 May 1915, 57:72 March 1927; *Musical Opinion* 50:1088 August 1927.

Important recordings of music by Moritz Moszkowski:

SELECTIONS FROM OPERA: *Boabdil,* "Malagueña" (VICTOR).

ORCHESTRA: *Aus aller Herren Länder,* arranged (GRAMOPHONE) ; *Spanish dances,* Book 1, arranged (COLUMBIA-Kerby) ; *Suite no. 1* (VICTOR-Damrosch).

PIANO: Serenata (COLUMBIA-Friedmann) ; *The Juggleress* (VICTOR-Levitzki) ; *Étude in G-flat major* (GRAMOPHONE-De Greef).

VIOLIN AND PIANO: *Guitarre* (VICTOR-Heifetz).

Modest Moussorgsky   *1839-1881*

MODEST PETROVICH MOUSSORGSKY, one of the component parts of that important nationalistic school known as the "Russian five" was born in Karevo, in the government of Pskov, on March 21, 1839. His father, a prosperous landowner, had married a serf.

We learn from his autobiography (which, curiously enough, Moussorgsky wrote in the third person) that his was a happy childhood, in which music played an important rôle from the first. "Under the influence of his nurse," Moussorgsky wrote, "he became familiar with the old Russian tales. It was mainly his familiarity with the very spirit of the life of the people that impelled him to extemporize music before knowing even the most elementary rules of piano playing. His mother gave him his first piano lessons."

It was not for music, but for the army, that Moussorgsky was at first intended. After completing his preliminary studies in St. Petersburg, he entered, and finally graduated from, the Military School for Ensigns, becoming an officer of the Preobrajensky Regiment. Military routine was hateful to him from the first, and thruout his three years in the army he constantly sought escape.

[1] See sketch on Balakirev.

An officer in the regiment, recognizing Moussorgsky's great love for music, introduced him to that distinguished composer, Dargomijsky. Dargomijsky, in turn, introduced Moussorgsky to Balakirev and Borodin. "He was a true little fop," wrote Borodin about his first meeting with young Moussorgsky, "all spick and span in a well-fitting uniform, well groomed, his hair carefully brushed, his hands perfectly manicured. He spoke mincingly, interlarding his sentences with French words. He was very popular with the ladies."

The enormous enthusiasm of Balakirev and Borodin for music, and their high ideals for a new nationalistic art, infected Moussorgsky. He decided to join them in their heroic battle to create a new school of Russian music.[1] Realizing now that his life was destined to go in an entirely new direction, he resigned from the army, in 1858, and devoted himself exclusively to music. Balakirev and Borodin gave him advice, and under their guidance he composed his first large works.

For a short period, he was absorbed with composition. Then, family reverses necessitated his return to work. In 1863, he accepted a government post. He was a careless and irresponsible worker and was dismissed from one position after another. He remained a government employee, however, until 1879—two years before his death.

For several years, Moussorgsky lived partly in the country, partly at his mother's home, and partly with his brother and sister-in-law. During these years, he came into close contact with Russian peasants and their folk music. He was so intrigued by the homely and simple beauty and unpretentiousness of the Russian spirit that, more than ever before, he decided to devote his art to giving it expression. "The goal of the artist," as he wrote, "should be to study the most subtle features of human-beings and of humanity in mass."

At this time, he witnessed a little episode which was said to have had a far-reaching influence upon him. Passing thru a Russian village, one day, he saw the town simpleton make love to the belle. Moussorgsky was enchanted

MODEST MOUSSORGSKY

by the weird, vibrant haunting sentences of the simpleton—sentences which seemed to the composer to possess more musical poignancy than any concocted melody. It was from that time on, it is believed, that Moussorgsky definitely decided to make his music a literal translation of speech. "What I want to do is to make my characters speak on the stage as they would in real life, and yet write music which will be thoroughly artistic."

The first compositions, in which he disclosed his individuality and power, came in 1867—a choral number, *The Rout of Sennacherib,* several poignant songs, and the first draught of his only orchestral composition, *A Night on a bald mountain.* But all this was merely the apprenticeship for the great task which yet stretched before him: the composition of a Russian opera which would give expression to the soul of the Russian people.

His first effort in this direction was a one-act opera based on Gogol's comedy, *The Marriage,* composed in 1868. It was here that he first experimented with melodies that resembled human speech. "If you forget all operatic conventions," Moussorgsky wrote to Rimsky-Korsakoff, "and admit the principles of musical discourse carried out in all simplicity, then *The Marriage* is an opera. If I have managed to render the straight-

forward expression of thoughts and feelings as it takes place in human speech, and if my rendering is artistic and musicianly, then the deed is done." It cannot be said that the other members of the Russian five appreciated the direction which Moussorgsky's art took in *The Marriage.* When this opera was given a private performance at the home of César Cui, it was regarded more as an interesting experiment than as an artistic achievement.

But Moussorgsky saw his direction clearly before him. He would permit neither advice nor criticism to swerve him from his goal. He had crossed the Rubicon with *The Marriage,* as he himself had picturesquely described it, and was prepared to explore a new world which he had discovered. Late in 1868, he began work upon Pushkin's drama, *Boris Godounoff.* The composition of this new opera intoxicated him, inflamed his imagination, and, as he termed it, "it went on boiling and bubbling" under his pen. "While I was writing *Boris,* I was *Boris,*" he remarked. It was a colossal labor of love, composed in white heat of inspiration.

In *Boris Godounoff,* Moussorgsky struck new paths even more boldly than he had done in *The Marriage.* In utilizing a prose, instead of a poetical libretto, he once again made an effort at producing his new type of song-form which would be more recitative than melodic, more speech than song. "I foresee a new kind of melody," wrote Moussorgsky in defence of *Boris,* "which will be the melody of life. With great pains I have achieved a new type of melody evolved from that of speech. Some day, all of a sudden, the ineffable song will arise, intelligible to one and all. If I succeed, I shall stand as a conqueror in art—and succeed I must."

But *Boris* was unorthodox in directions other than melodic form. It was built upon an entirely unconventional operatic pattern. There were no major love scenes, no efflorescent melodies, no ballets, no exhibitionistic tenor rôles.

The directors of the Imperial Opera, to whom Moussorgsky submitted *Boris,* were frankly puzzled by this strange work, which, to them, was neither fish, flesh nor fowl. They, finally, refused it. In an attempt to please the directors, Moussorgsky began to revise the opera—injecting a few love situations and several more singable passages for the principal characters. But even in this form the opera was too unconventional, and the committee of the Imperial Opera returned it to its composer.

Three scenes from *Boris* were performed at a benefit at the Imperial Opera on February 3, 1873, creating so striking an impression that it was finally decided to give the entire work performance. As a result, *Boris Godounoff* was introduced to the world on January 27, 1874. It received a chill reception. The critics were unusually vitrolic; Hermann Laroche, perhaps the foremost of them, referred to the opera as a "patchwork version" of Pushkin, full of "coarseness and cacophony," with accompaniments that sounded like "a perpetual strumming on the piano, with the loud pedal down most of the time." Even Moussorgsky's astute confederates were blind to the originality and greatness of the work. Rimsky-Korsakoff saw hardly more than its "clumsiness and illiteracy" and at first completely failed to perceive behind them a work of first magnitude. · César Cui wrote a denunciatory review. After twenty performances, *Boris* passed into obscurity.

Moussorgsky attempted to smother his disappointment with hard work: he was planning another folk-opera, *Khovanstchina,* and working intensively upon *The Fair at Sorotchintsi.* In 1879, his work was interrupted by a tour of Southern Russia which he took with Daria Leonova, a singer. The trip had an exhilarating effect upon him. He returned home with renewed spirits, determined to work harder than ever before.

Unfortunately, a lifetime of excessive drinking and dissipation were exacting its price. Moussorgsky was stricken with epilepsy. Paralysis followed. On March 28, he drew his last breath, without a friend or a relative at his bedside. He died as he had lived—alone.

"I went into the private room at the Nikolai Hospital," wrote M. M. Ivanov, shortly after Moussorgsky's death. "My heart failed me. The environment in which Moussorgsky was doomed to die, the setting in which this genius was extinguished, made one shudder. . . . You could see at once that a true Bohemian had died there. . . . Close to the door stood a cupboard, a desk, two chairs, and two small tables with newspapers and five or six books, among them Berlioz's *Traité de l'instrumentation.* He had died like a soldier, sword in hand. . . . A feeling of bitterness rose up in me—strange is the fate of our countrymen! That a genius like Moussorgsky . . . possessed of all the qualities that fitted him to scale the highest heights of life, should die in a hospital, among strangers, without one friendly hand to close his eyes."

After Moussorgsky's death, Rimsky-Korsakoff and Stassov took upon themselves the task of editing and revising Moussorgsky's compositions for publication. Truth to tell, his compositions were in sad need of editing. His musical education had been inadequate, so inadequate that frequently he had difficulty in putting down his ideas correctly on paper. Coarseness, clumsiness, awkwardness abounded in Moussorgsky's writings. "He did not want to increase his means of expression," wrote Pierre d'Alheim in justification of Moussorgsky's mistakes, "he simply tried to translate into sound the soul's cries which struck upon his ears from without or rose from within himself. In very truth, he trampled on the rules and crushed the life out of them by the sheer weight of his thought."

In this colossal task of editing, the most important work was done by Rimsky-Korsakoff, who not only completed and polished *Khovanstchina,* revamped *A Night on a bald mountain,* but reorchestrated and drastically revised *Boris Godounoff.* It was in Rimsky-Korsakoff's new version that *Boris Godounoff* emerged from obscurity, in 1904, with Chaliapin in the title rôle. Its triumph was unmistakable. In 1908, Rimsky-Korsakoff prepared a second version of *Boris Godounoff,* in which he restored many of the portions he had previously deleted. In this final form, *Boris* conquered the entire world of music. Recently, Moussorgsky's original form of *Boris* was published, and performed in Philadelphia and Boston in concert form under the batons of Stokowski and Koussevitzky respectively. At that time, it became apparent that *Boris* had lost something of its elemental power and colossal strength in Rimsky-Korsakoff's refined and manicured edition.

"With *Boris Godounoff*," wrote Kurt Schindler, "a new type of 'historical opera' has been founded. . . . This is the work of the simple and compelling logic of a master playwright, in which the great emotional forces, the revolutionizing sentiments of a period are depicted thru the medium of music.

"Moussorgsky was not only a wonderful composer individually, but behind him lay the unexplored musical wealth of the great Slav nation—a mine of rhythmically and melodically unusual folk songs; of Byzantine church chants flavoring of the mysterious early Christian periods; of old bard tunes, rhapsodical and full of grandeur; of new and violent vocal inflections rooted in the dialects of a rich and varied language. . . .

"In *Boris Godounoff*, the people are actually in the foreground of the happenings, the great masses are really the principal actor; at first dumb, oppressed, easily guided, then stirred up, threatening, finally in open revolt and jubilant war spirit. The strong veracity of these folk scenes can be likened without blasphemy to such eternal master-pieces as Shakespeare's *Coriolanus* and *Julius Caesar*. And in all dramatic music there is nothing so near to *Macbeth* as the specter scene of *Boris*.

"Since Wagner's death there is no work that has so stirred the musical world thru its freedom from convention, its direct truth, and its compelling sincerity."

Discussing Moussorgsky's individual type of melody, Paul Bekker commented: "Moussorgsky proceeds from the sentence structure and not, like Wagner, from the individual word. From the sentence structure he builds a sort of recitative-like arioso. For this construction, to be sure, the simple and natural singable quality of the Russian language was a prerequisite. There is,

in fact, no language except Italian that lends itself so readily to singing as Russian, and none that disposes of such rich material as Russian, particularly among men's voices. Moussorgsky found formal support for his style in Russian folk song, and for his treatment of speech-melody and of harmony in Russian church music."

"Of the 'Five,'" wrote Montagu-Nathan, "he alone appears to have possessed the true seer's vision. His art is to be described as an expression of socialism in simultaneous relation to people and to music. In opera, as in song, he was close follower of his master (Dargomijsky). His dramatic, as well as his vocal works, are informed by that steadfast desire for naturalness which Dargomijsky seems to have been the first to awaken in him. For more than either Balakirev, Cui or Borodin, Moussorgsky reflects the spirit of the sixties in Russia; his works are in much closer touch with the literature and painting of that period. They show us that, altho he was regarded with some alarm by his friends as a revolutionary, his ideals were of a kind that could not fail, when realized, to promote the evolution of the musical art."

The fame of *Boris Godounoff* has, to a large degree, obscured the fact that Moussorgsky was likewise a great composer of song.

Principal works by Modest Moussorgsky:

OPERA: *The Marriage*; *Boris Godounoff*; *Khovanstchina*; *The Fair at Sorotchintsi* (completed by N. Tcherepnine).

ORCHESTRA: *A Night on a bald mountain*; *Pictures at an exhibition* (orchestrated by Maurice Ravel).

CHORAL: *Joshua*; *The Rout of Sennacherib*. Songs; pieces for the piano.

About Modest Moussorgsky:

Calvocoressi, M. D. *Moussorgsky*; Riesemann, Oskar von. *Moussorgsky*.

Important recordings of music by Modest Moussorgsky:

SELECTIONS FROM OPERA: *Boris Godounoff*, "Opening chorus" (COLUMBIA); "Coronation scene" (VICTOR-Chaliapin); "Varlaam's song" (VICTOR-Chaliapin); "I have attained the highest power" (GRAMOPHONE-Chaliapin); "Clock scene" (GRAMOPHONE-Chaliapin); "Polonaise" (COLUMBIA); "Come, let us vote" (GRAMOPHONE-Chaliapin); "Farewell, my son,

I am dying," and "Death of Boris" (Victor-Chaliapin). *The Fair at Sorotchintsi,* "Introduction" (Parlaphone); "Why, my sad heart" (Gramophone-Rosing); "Hopak" (Brunswick-Wolff). *Khovanstchina* "Prelude" (Columbia-Harty); "Dances of the Persian slaves" (Victor-Coates); "Entr'acte" (Victor-Stokowski).

Orchestra: *A Night on a bald mountain* (Columbia-Paray); *Pictures at an exhibition,* orchestrated by Ravel (Victor-Koussevitzky).

Songs: Moussorgsky Song Society, collected songs (Parlaphone-Rosing).

Wolfgang Amadeus Mozart
1756-1791

"I declare to you on my honor that I consider him the greatest composer I have ever heard."—Joseph Haydn
"A most prodigious genius has raised him above all the masters of all time and in all the arts."—Richard Wagner

WOLFGANG AMADEUS MOZART—christened Johannes Chrysostomus Wolfgangus Theophilus Mozart—was born in Salzburg on January 27, 1756. His father, Leopold Mozart, was a famous musician in his own right. In his twenty-fourth year, Leopold received an appointment as violinist in the orchestra of the Archbishop of Salzburg, finally rising to the position of chapel master. He composed with fertility, and produced a famous violin method. But, as Leopold himself realized, his greatest work was not his own music, but—his son, Wolfgang.

Much has been written about Wolfgang Amadeus Mozart's phenomenal precociousness. At the age of three, he already sat in front of the harpsichord attempting to find harmonic successions of thirds; whenever he succeeded, his shrill voice rang out joyfully. When Wolfgang was four, his father began to teach him the elements of the harpsichord and, playfully, the rules of composition. Wolfgang learned these lessons with such ease that, by his sixth year, he had produced an imposing quantity of minuets, sonatas and even a concerto. His sensitive ear could recognize that the violin of his father's friend (which Wolfgang jestingly called a "butter-box") was tuned an eighth of a note lower than he himself tuned his own instrument; and it could

rebel so violently against a raucous sound that at the blast of a trumpet, he swooned with pain. Music, obviously, came as naturally to him as breathing.

Leopold Mozart, recognizing the extraordinary gifts of his two children (for Marianne, five years Wolfgang's senior, was also strongly talented) decided to exhibit his children before all Europe. When Wolfgang was six years old, therefore, an extensive concert tour brought him to the foremost concert halls and royal courts of Europe. Wherever he performed, the sweet charm of his personality and his incredible genius conquered the hearts of music lovers. Francis I of Vienna lovingly referred to him as *"ein kleine hexenmeister"* ("a little master-wizard"). In Frankfurt, Mozart gave something of a one-man circus show: "He will play," ran the announcement in the Frankfurt newspaper, "a concerto for the violin, and will accompany symphonies on the clavier, the manuel or keyboard being covered with a cloth, with as much facility as if he could see the keys; he will instantly name all the notes played at a distance, whether singly or in chords as on the clavier or any other instrument, bell, glass or clock. He will, finally, both on the harpsichord and the organ, improvise as long as may be desired and in any key."

"I was only fourteen years old," wrote Goethe many years later to Eckermann about this Frankfurt performance, "but I see, as if I were still there, the little man with his child's sword and his curly hair. . . . A phenomenon like that of Mozart remains an inexplicable thing."

In Paris, Wolfgang became the darling of Versailles. He was, as Grimm wrote "so extraordinary a phenomenon that one finds it difficult to believe it unless one has seen him with one's own eyes and heard him with one's own ears." The Paris visit was marked by the appearance of Mozart's first published work, four sonatas for the harpsichord.

From Paris, the Mozarts came to London, where Wolfgang won the heart of Johann Christian Bach, chapel master. In London, Wolfgang gave several sensational performances at the Vauxhall

Gardens which were the subject of great wonder.

The Mozarts were back in Salzburg in 1766, after an absence of four years. The tour had been a greater success artistically than materially. True, Mozart was given many gifts by royalty, but the principal goal towards which Leopold aspired had been unachieved—the acquisition of a permanent, lucrative post by Wolfgang in one of the principal European courts.

One year later, the Mozarts were once again on tour. They had come to Vienna where Wolfgang was commissioned to compose his first opera. Intrigues, created by envious composers, prevented this first opera achieving a performance. In Vienna, however, another charming theatrical work of Mozart, *Bastien and Bastienne*, an opéra-bouffe, was performed at the home of a friend, Dr. Messner.

Towards the close of 1769, the Mozarts made their first journey to Italy, a journey crowned with glory. In Mantua, they attended a concert of the Philharmonic orchestra which performed a few of Wolfgang's compositions in his honor. In Milan, they received a commission for Wolfgang to compose an opera seria for the following year. Bologna brought Mozart into contact with the great Martini, who welcomed the young genius with open arms of admiration and respect. In Rome, there took place that phenomenal proof of Mozart's genius which has frequently been quoted. Young Mozart attended a performance of the celebrated *Miserere* of Allegri which could be heard only in Rome during Holy Week performed by the papal choir. By papal decree it was forbidden to sing the work elsewhere, and its only existing copy was guarded slavishly by the papal choir. Any attempt to copy the song or to reproduce it in any form was punishable by excommunication. Mozart, however, had heard the work only once when, returning home, he reproduced it in its entirety upon paper. This incomparable feat soon became the subject for awed whispers in Rome; it was not long before the Pope himself heard of this amazing achievement. The Pope summoned Mozart, but instead of punishing the young genius with excommunication he showered praise upon him and gave him handsome gifts. A few months later, the Pope bestowed upon Mozart the Cross of the Order of the Golden Spur.

The following autumn, the Mozarts were back in Italy for Wolfgang to fulfill his commission for Milan and bring to completion his opera seria, *Mitridate, King of Ponte*. "Before the first rehearsal," Herr Leopold Mozart wrote to his wife, "there was no lack of people to run down the music and pronounce it beforehand in satirical language to be something poor and childish, alleging that so young a boy, and a German to the bargain, could not possibly write an Italian opera and that, altho they acknowledged him to be a great executant, he could not understand or feel the *chiaroscuro* required in the theatre. All these people have been reduced to silence since the evening of the first rehearsal with small orchestra, and say not a word."

At the first performance of *Mitridate* on Christmas day of 1770, the work was a phenomenal success. One of the soprano airs, contrary to all precedent, was encored. Cheers greeted the diminutive composer as he reached the stage. The newspapers commented upon that "rarest musical grace" and that "studied beauty" which seemed to be Wolfgang's intuitive idiom.

The next few years of Mozart's life were drab. Except for two brief intermissions, he remained in Salzburg whose limited intellectual world chafed him considerably. Moreover, his musical labor at the Court of the Archbishop was an endless humiliation. He was the principal composer and virtuoso at the Court, but his salary was so meagre and his work so unappreciated that each day was for him crowded with trials. His fellow musicians at the Court were dissolute scoundrels, whose musical tastes were vulgar and whose interests centered upon gambling and drink. "Tell me," Wolfgang wrote at this time, "how could a decent fellow possibly live in such company?"

It was, therefore, with a yearning heart that Wolfgang dreamt of escaping

WOLFGANG AMADEUS MOZART

from Salzburg. A new extensive tour was, therefore, planned for Mozart in 1777, and since Herr Leopold was refused by the Archbishop a leave-of-absence, Wolfgang Mozart left in the company of his mother to conquer the music world anew.

But the music world was this time not so easily conquered by Mozart. He was now twenty-one years old—a child prodigy no longer. The music world had in the past lavished its adoration upon a little pug-nosed child who could achieve miraculous musical feats. Now that the child had entered man's estate, he had lost his great appeal. Munich and Mannheim turned a deaf ear to his pleas for a permanent post at the court; even random commissions were not forthcoming.

These disappointments, however, did not smother Mozart's high spirits. Now a man, he found consolation from his disappointments in frequent love affairs. In Augsburg there was his cousin, Basle, his first genuine love. "Basle," he wrote to his father, "seems to have been made for me, and I for her—for both of us have that little bit of badness in us." In Mannheim, where he was a household guest of a musical family called Cannabich, he in turn courted Rosa Cannabich and then Aloysia Weber, a singer, daughter of a copyist. He thought seriously of marrying Aloysia; only the heated and embittered letters of his

father convinced him that it was wiser to delay marriage until he had procured his desired post. The road, therefore, next brought him to Paris, where in the summer of 1778 Mozart's mother passed away.

In Paris, too, Mozart met disappointment. There were those who were acutely jealous of his phenomenal genius; the others thought of him only as a one-time child prodigy who had outgrown his talent. Because of these people, it was impossible for him to receive the appreciation he deserved. Small commissions fell to him, but they were so slight and of such negligible importance that they failed to support him adequately. Even Grimm, once so idolatrous, now lost interest in Wolfgang, complaining in a long letter to Herr Leopold Mozart, that Wolfgang was "too confident, too little a man of action, too much ready to succumb to his own illusions, too little *au courant* with the ways that lead to success."

It was not long before Mozart, convinced that no important post was open for him, decided to return to Mannheim and marry Aloysia Weber. To his bewilderment and humiliation, he learned upon his arrival that Aloysia had forgotten him so completely during his absence that she did not even recognize him when he entered

Disappointment and disillusionment now completely overwhelmed him. He returned to Salzburg (a town he detested with increasing strength each time he returned to it) for a brief and sombre period. In 1780, a commission from Munich for an *opera seria* brought him escape. This commission resulted in the first of Mozart's great opera, *Idomeneo*. *Idomeneo*, upon its first performance on January 29, 1781 was a rousing success. Ramm, the oboe-player, and Lange, the horn-player "were half-crazy with delight," and the latter exclaimed: "I must own that I have never yet heard any music which made such a deep impression upon me!" The audience expressed its enthusiasm in no uncertain responses.

This success inspired Mozart to sever all connections with Salzburg and his employer, the Archbishop, and to settle permanently in Vienna. Shortly after he made Vienna his permanent home, he was commissioned by Joseph II to compose a *Singspiel*. *The Abduction from the Seraglio* duplicated in Vienna the success that *Idomeneo* enjoyed in Munich. Gluck, the foremost composer of operas at the time, had the work especially performed for him, his praise being lavish. Joseph II honored Mozart with rewards. And Prince Kaunitz, after hearing the opera, openly expressed the opinion that a genius like Wolfgang Mozart could appear only once in a century.

On August 4, 1782 Mozart was married to Constance Weber, youngest sister of his one-time beloved Aloysia. The ceremony was a simple one, the only ones present being the bride's mother and youngest sister, two witnesses, and a friend of the family. "The moment we were made one," Mozart wrote to his father, "my wife and I began to weep, which touched everyone, even the priest. . . . We are married now; we are man and wife! And we love each other enormously. We feel that we are made for one another."

It was shortly after his marriage that Mozart met and became a close friend of Joseph Haydn. Haydn recognized Mozart's genius, and until the end of his life exerted his every effort to bring recognition and fame to the younger composer who, he sincerely felt, was without an equal in all music.

On May 1, 1786, Mozart's *The Marriage of Figaro* was introduced in Vienna. "I can still see Mozart," wrote Michael Kelly, a singer, in his *Reminiscences* "dressed in his red fur hat trimmed with gold, standing on the stage with the orchestra, at the first rehearsal, beating time for the music. . . . The players on the stage and in the orchestra were electrified. Intoxicated with pleasure, they cried again and again, and each time louder than the preceding one: 'Bravo, maestro! Long live the great Mozart!' . . . It seemed as if the storm of applause would never cease. . . . Had Mozart written nothing but this piece of music it alone would, in my humble opinion, have stamped him as the greatest master of his art. Never before was there a greater triumph than Mozart and his *Figaro*!"

Despite this emphatic success, Mozart knew at this time a period of great trial and depression. His child, Raimund, had died three months after birth, inspiring in the composer a fit of melancholy which was not easily dissipated. Moreover, at this time, Mozart knew appalling poverty. Repeatedly, he wrote pitiful letters to his publishers, to friends, to distant acquaintances for small loans to relieve his trying circumstances. Finally, his wife Constance was ill, her sickness brought on by undernourishment.

Yet, in spite of these trying years, Mozart's pen knew no recess from the production of imperishable masterpieces. In October of 1787 he produced for Prague *Don Giovanni,* which more than one critic has designated as Mozart's greatest opera. *Don Giovanni* was greeted with thunderous cheers; but to the impoverished composer it meant only one hundred meagre florins. One year after *Don Giovanni*, Mozart composed his three greatest symphonies—the *G-minor*, the *E-flat major* and the *Jupiter* —all in the incredible span of two months. In 1790, came *Così fan tutte,* followed closely by the *Magic flute*. And between the composition of these monumental works, Mozart was composing a prolific library of concertos for solo instruments and his masterpieces for string quartet.

Mozart's last work was composed under mysterious circumstances. In 1791 a stranger, masked and dressed in gray, accosted Mozart and commissioned him to compose a requiem. The stranger was representing a wealthy nobleman who frequently asked great composers to produce works for him which he later presented under his own name. But to Mozart, ill and morbid as he was at this time, it appeared that this stranger was a messenger from the other world sent to warn the composer that the time had come for him to compose his own requiem. Through sleepless, delirious nights, the messenger from the other world haunted Mozart's thoughts. Feverishly he worked upon his requiem, refusing both rest and food so that he might finish his work before it was too late. "Willingly would I follow your advice," he wrote to a friend who tried to persuade him to take a holiday, "but how can I do it? . . . I know by my feelings that my hour has come. It is striking even now! I am in the region of death."

He was found at his desk unconscious. He was taken to bed, and the physician who had been summoned soon announced that Mozart was seeing his last days. Mozart knew he was dying. To his pupil, Süssmayer, he explained precisely how the *Requiem* was to be brought to completion. Shortly before his last breath left him, he attempted to sing parts of his last great work. On December 5, 1791, he said farewell to his family and turned his face to the wall; shortly afterwards he was dead.

Mozart's remains were thrown into a pauper's grave in the churchyard of St. Mark. One week later, when Constance returned with flowers to Mozart's body, she could not find the grave. Because Mozart had died like a pauper, his grave had been left unmarked, his body unidentified.

Mozart was short and slim, and though his head was slightly too large for the body its well-proportioned features gave him an attractive appearance. His face had a softness that was almost effeminate, his cheeks always being sickly pallid. His eyes, piercing in their intensity, were eloquently expressive. His hair, of which he was considerably proud, was a rich shock.

Well-poised, meticulously well dressed (he frequently sported laces and jewelry) and possessed of charming manners he made a deep impression upon those with whom he came into contact. Though moody by temperament and introspective, he was considerably fond of the society of pleasant people. He adored dancing, and it was with great difficulty that Constance could keep him from frequenting places of questionable reputation. His recreation consisted of bowling and playing billiards. "He was generally cheerful and in good humor," Constance Mozart has recorded, "rarely melancholy, though sometimes pensive. His speaking voice was gentle, except while directing music when he became loud and energetic—would even stamp with his feet, and might be heard at a considerable distance."

Commenting upon Mozart's method of composition, Robert Pitrou wrote: "With him, both stages—the birth of ideas and their elaboration—were probably unconscious. His mind was constantly creating, without ever a break. When he came to the third stage—to committing to paper—he used to give his ideas at one stroke the very form he was aiming at. . . . When at his desk, he always seems . . . to have been copying out music already fully written down in his mind. We even know, from his letters, that his mind could turn to other music the while. Sending a prelude and fugue to his sister on April 20, 1792, he wrote: 'Forgive the untidy arrangement. I had composed the fugue first, and while writing it out, I was thinking out the prelude.'"

Mozart himself has written: "When I am in the right mood, ideas teem within me. Those I like I retain. Then there are scraps which might go to the making of many a good dish. When I start composing I draw upon the accumulation in my brain."

Commenting succinctly on Mozart's principal operas, Eric Blom has written: "With *Idomeneo* mastery may well be said to have been reached. . . . Fine work Mozart certainly did put into *Idomeneo,* and in spite of the influence of Piccinni and of certain conventions (mainly choral) of French grand opera, he was becoming an independent musical personality. His treatment of accompanied recitative shows a very sensitive readiness to apply expressive touches. . . . In *The Abduction from the Seraglio* Mozart was at last wholly in his element, not because of any especial liking for the German *Singspiel* . . . but chiefly because by 1782 he was a fully matured master of his craft and had learnt a good deal about life. . . . Indeed one would not have a note different even where it falls a little short of greatness, for it never ceases to be delicious as it is apt to its type and subject. . . . It is a structure and a collection of tunes of such fascinating grace that one would like to call back every phrase of it to hug it over and over again. . . . And then came *The Marriage of Figaro* . . . the perfect *opéra-bouffe.* . . . Beaumarchais' exposure of a refined but pernicious civilization is here made the pretext for music as sunnily civilized as the world ought to have if the dreamers of Mozart's age had been right. . . . These qualities *Figaro* has to a degree never again attained in music, and it has moreover a profound humanity, a sympathetic penetration into the hearts of men and women—especially women. . . . *Figaro* is Italian comic opera in its final stages of perfection. . . . With all its overwhelming perfection, *Figaro* still shows an almost disconcerting readiness to use the current idiom of the time. . . . But the next opera, the greatest of all . . . *Don Giovanni,* makes a tremendous advance in achieving originality already, so to speak, at the fountainhead of inspiration. . . . It is impossible to conceive that any notion as here set down by Mozart could have come from the pen of any other composer, then or later. What is more, not a single number in *Don Giovanni* can be imagined to occur in any other opera by Mozart himself. Everything is in character, everything colored by the particular mood into which this great tragi-comic subject cast him. . . . After *Don Giovanni* we are magically transported into yet another world: that of *Così fan tutte.* Well, scarcely a world at all; only a show of marionettes. . . . Once again Mozart achieved the miraculous feat of writing a score which, consistent in style from start to finish, could not by any conceivable chance lend a single one of its numbers to any other work of his. The whole perfume and flavor of the music is new and unique. Artifice is the keynote of it. . . .

"What Mozart wanted was not declamation but spontaneous emotional expression, not grandly ordered drama but the variety of life. . . . That is why he was not in the least disturbed by the hair-raising inconsistencies, the pantomime absurdities of *The Magic flute.* . . . Here was a great deal of nonsense, but it was good theatre, it was alive, and there was a multiformity of setting, of situation, of character such as he had never before had occasion to handle. . . . The variety of *The Magic flute* score ought to be bewildering; somehow it is

only astonishing in a favorable sense. . . . The music itself is much more diversified than that of any opera of Mozart's. . . . The flashy Italian arias of the Queen of the Night next to Sarastro's solemn utterances in Mozart's 'masonic' manner, the popular ditties of Papageno side by side with the profound humanity of Pamina's tear-compelling G-minor lament and the wonderful dramatic truth of her brief mad scene . . . all this and more is by some marvel of genius fashioned into a single gem of many facts— and of inestimable value."

Edvard Grieg, the famous composer, has written an illuminating essay on Mozart which is not widely known. In it, he has discussed Mozart's greatest symphonies in the following manner: "We note at once the great step from Haydn's to Mozart's treatment of this the highest of instrumental forms, and our thoughts are involuntarily transferred to the young Beethoven who, without any specially noteworthy break, rises from where Mozart left off to those proud summits which none but he was destined to reach. In the introduction of the E-flat major symphony, just before the first allegro, we come upon harmonic combinations of unprecedented boldness. They are introduced in so surprising a way that they will always preserve the impression of novelty. . . . In the G-minor symphony, Mozart shows himself to us in all his grace and sincerity of feeling. It is worth noting what astonishing effects he gets here by the use of chromatic progressions. In the *Jupiter symphony* we are astounded, above all, by the playful ease with which the greatest problems of art are treated. No one who is not initiated suspects in the finale, amid the humorous tone gambols, what an amazing contrapuntal knowledge and superiority Mozart manifests. And then this ocean of euphony! Mozart's sense of euphony was, indeed, so absolute that it is impossible, in all his works, to find a single bar wherein it is sacrificed to other considerations."

Mozart's importance in the development of the musical art has been so great that it is not easy to summarize his contribution in a few paragraphs. C. Hubert Parry has admirably suggested

·the stride the musical art made under Mozart in his discerning paragraphs on the contribution of both Haydn and Mozart: "Before their time, the only two branches in which first-rate and mature work of the harmonic kind had been done were the violin sonatas written chiefly by the great Italian violinists and their pupils in other countries and the clavier sonatas. The scope of the movements was small and without much development, and the ideas even in the best examples were rather indefinite. By the end of their time instrumental art had branched out into a very large number of distinct and complete forms, such as symphonies, concertos, quartets, trios and sonatas for violin and clavier. The style appropriate to each had been more or less ascertained, and the schemes of design had been perfectly organized for all self-dependent instrumental music. Both Haydn and Mozart immensely improved upon their predecessors in the power of finding characteristic subjects, and in deciding the type of subject which is best fitted for instrumental music. . . . They improved the range of the symphonic cycle of movements by adding the minuet and trio to the old group of three movements; thereby introducing definite and undisguised dance movements to follow and contrast with the central cantabile slow movement. Between them they had completely transformed the treatment of the orchestra. . . . Even in detail the character of music is altered in their hands; all phraseology is made articulate and definite; and the minutiae which tend themselves to refined and artistic performance are carefully considered, without in any way diminishing the breadth and freedom of the general effect. There is hardly any branch or department of art which does not seem to have been brought to high technical perfection by them; and if the world could be satisfied with the ideal of perfectly organized simplicity, without any great force of expression, instrumental art might well have stopped at the point to which they brought it."

Principal works by Wolfgang Amadeus Mozart:

OPERA: *Idomeneo*; *Abduction from the Seraglio*; *The Marriage of Figaro*; *Don Giovanni*; *Così fan tutte*; *The Magic flute*; *La Clemenza di Tito*; also operettas, dramatic cantatas, etc.

CHORAL: Fifteen masses; *Requiem*; Two masonic cantatas; Four litanies; Two vespers; Te Deum; Nine offertoriums; Four kyries, etc.

ORCHESTRA: More than forty symphonies; divertimenti; serenades; cassations; Twenty-five concertos for piano and orchestra; Eight concertos for violin and orchestra; Concertos for two pianos, for three pianos, for flute, for flute and harp, for horn, for clarinet; *Concertante sinfonie* (for violin, viola and orchestra); *German dances*; marches, etc.

CHAMBER MUSIC: Nine string quintets; Twenty-six string quartets; Seven piano trios; Forty-two sonatas for violin and piano.

PIANO: Seventeen sonatas; Three fantasies; Fifteen variations; shorter pieces.

Pieces for organ; arias, etc.

About Wolfgang Amadeus Mozart:

Blom, Eric. *Mozart*; Curzon, Henri de. *Mozart*; Dent, Edward J. *Mozart's Operas: A Critical Study*; Dunhill, Thomas. *Mozart's String Quartets*; Jahn, Otto. *The Life of Mozart*; Kelly, Michael. *Reminiscences*; Mozart, Wolfgang Amadeus. *Letters*; Paumgartner, Bernhard. *Mozart*; Ponte, Lorenzo da. *Memoirs*; Prod'homme, J. G. *Mozart, Raconté par Ceux qui l'ont Vu*; Sitwell, Sacheverell. *Mozart*.

Important recordings of music by Wolfgang Amadeus Mozart:

OPERA: *The Marriage of Figaro*, complete (HIS MASTERS VOICE-Glyndebourne Festival); *Così fan tutte*, complete (HIS MASTERS VOICE-Glyndebourne Festival).

SELECTIONS FROM OPERA: *Don Giovanni*, "Overture" (GRAMOPHONE-Blech); "Madamina, il catalogo" (GRAMOPHONE-Chaliapin); "Là ci darem la mano" (GRAMOPHONE); "Della sua pace" (POLYDOR); "Batti, batti" (VICTOR-Schumann); "Minuet" (VICTOR-Landowska); "Serenata" (VICTOR-Pinza); "Vedrai, carino" (VICTOR-Schumann). *The Abduction from the Seraglio*, "Overture" (BRUNSWICK-Furtwängler); "Wer ein Liebchen hat gefunden" (VICTOR-Kipnis); "Kostanze, Kostanze" (POLYDOR); "Durch Zärtlichkeit" (PARLAPHONE-Pons); "Marten aller Arten" (BRUNSWICK). *Idomeneo*, "Overture" (BRUNSWICK); Choruses (GRAMOPHONE). *The Magic Flute*, "Overture" (VICTOR-Mengelberg); "Der Vogelfänger bin ich" (PARLAPHONE); "Hm, hm, hm!" (BRUNSWICK); "Bei männern" (BRUNSWICK); "March of the priests" (GRAMOPHONE-Blech); "In diesen heil'gen hallen" (VICTOR-Kipnis); "Ach, ich fühl's (PARLAPHONE-Lehmann); "O Isis und Osiris" (VICTOR).

ORCHESTRA: *Symphony in C-major*, K. 338 (COLUMBIA-Beecham); *Haffner Symphony* (VICTOR-Toscanini); *Symphony in C-major*, K.425 (VICTOR-Busch); *Prague symphony* (GRAMOPHONE-Kleiber); *Symphony in E-flat major*, K. 543 (VICTOR-Walter); *Symphony in G-minor*, K. 550 (VICTOR-Koussevitzky); *Jupiter symphony* (COLUMBIA-Beecham); *Divertimento in D-major, and F-major* (DECCA); *Divertimento in C-major* (GRAMOPHONE); *Divertimento in B-major* (BRUNSWICK); *Divertimento in D-major* (COLUMBIA); *Eine kleine nachtmusik* (VICTOR-Ormandy); *Concerto in A-major*, for piano and orchestra (COLUMBIA); *Concerto in D-minor*, for piano and orchestra (VICTOR-Fischer); *Concerto in B-flat major*, for piano and orchestra (VICTOR-Schnabel); *Coronation concerto*, for piano and orchestra (DECCA); *Concerto in G-major*, for piano and orchestra (COLUMBIA-Dohnanyi); *Concerto in G-major*, for violin and orchestra (GRAMOPHONE-Menuhin); *Concerto in D-major*, for violin and orchestra (COLUMBIA-Szigeti); *Concerto in A-major*, for violin and orchestra (VICTOR-Heifetz); *Concerto in E-flat major*, for violin and orchestra (COLUMBIA); *Concerto in D-major*, K. 271a (VICTOR-Menuhin); *Adelaide concerto*, for violin and orchestra (VICTOR-Menuhin); *Concertante sinfonie* (COLUMBIA); *Concerto for flute, harp and orchestra* (VICTOR); *German dances*, no. 1 to 6 (COLUMBIA).

CHAMBER MUSIC: *Quartet in G-major*, K. 387 (COLUMBIA); *Quartet in D-minor*, K. 421 (VICTOR-Flonzaley); *Hunting Quartet* (VICTOR-Budapest); *Quartet in A-major*, K. 464 (VICTOR-Roth); *Quartet in C-major*, K. 465 (VICTOR-Budapest); *Quartet in D-major*, K. 575 (GRAMOPHONE-Flonzaley); *Quartet in F-major*, K. 590 (GRAMOPHONE-Budapest); *Quartet for flute and strings*, K. 285 (NATIONAL GRAMOPHONIC SOCIETY); *Quartet for oboe and strings*, K.370 (COLUMBIA); *Quartet for piano and strings*, K.478 (VICTOR-Pro-Arte, Schnabel); *Quintet in C-major* for strings, K. 515 (VICTOR-Pro-Arte); *Quintet in G-minor*, for strings, K. 516 (VICTOR-Pro-Arte); *Quintet for clarinet and strings in A-major*, K.581 (COLUMBIA); *Trio in B-flat major*, K. 502 (POLYDOR); *Trio in E-major*, K. 542 (COLUMBIA); *Trio in G-major*, K. 564 (COLUMBIA); *Sonata in A-major*, for violin and piano (VICTOR-Menuhin); *Sonata in B-flat major*, for violin and piano (GRAMOPHONE).

Eduard Nápravnik *1839-1915*

EDUARD FRANTSOVITCH NÁPRAVNIK was born in Beischt, near Königgratz, Bohemia, on August 24, 1839. At the age of five he displayed an aptitude for music. His father, a music teacher, placed him under the instruction of a local tutor, Pugonny.

By his thirteenth year, Nápravnik could play the organ well enough to officiate at church services. In 1850, he was sent to the Modern School at Prague to continue his musical education. There his studies were soon interrupted by the sudden death of his father. For a short period, Nápravnik knew great want and suffering. Then, thru the generosity of a patron, he was enabled to enter the Organ School in Prague. When his studies were completed he received an appointment as piano teacher in Maidel's Piano Academy. At the same time, he continued advanced music study under Kittel, director of the Prague Conservatory.

Nápravnik began composition at an early age. During his trying period of self-adjustment, he produced a symphony, a mass, an overture on Czech themes and many smaller works. None of these succeeded in bringing him any measure of recognition.

In August of 1861, Nápravnik received an invitation from Prince Youssipof to come to Russia to conduct his household orchestra. This was the turning point in Nápravnik's career. He now settled in Petrograd, which became for him his second home. Here he became acquainted with Constantin Liadov, father of the Russian composer, whose influence brought Nápravnik a position

EDUARD NÁPRAVNIK

as assistant conductor and organist at the Imperial Opera in Petrograd.

In 1869, Nápravnik was appointed principal conductor of the Petrograd Opera. Thus began a celebrated career as conductor which spanned forty years and in which Nápravnik assumed a regal position among the batonists of Russia. Thru Nápravnik's influence, the Opera was completely reformed, new methods introduced, new singers engaged and a new repertory installed. During his long tenure of the directorial post, Nápravnik conducted more than three thousand works and gave sixty-two first performances, half of which were devoted to new Russian operas.

In 1868, Nápravnik's opera, *The Citizens of Nijni,* was given its première in Petrograd. Rimsky-Korsakoff found the work unimpressive, too derivative in style and filled with plebian ideas. The work, therefore, made very little impression. Tschaikovsky, however, wrote to Nápravnik in 1885 telling him that he esteemed *The Citizens* highly.

Whatever fame Nápravnik enjoyed as a composer was the result of his operas. *Harold,* given in 1886, *Doubrovsky,* in 1895, and *Francesca da Rimini,* in 1903, still left much to be desired, but the music public derived great pleasure from their warm melodic content and their skillful workmanship.

In his music, wrote Leonid Sabaneyev, Nápravnik "recalls the music of Rubinstein and, in some respects, that of Tschaikovsky, though his later period suggests the more contemporary influences of the Russian national school. Nevertheless, his compositions are by no means lacking in musical quality, and show him to have been a fine master and fully equipped in the technique of musical writing."

Eduard Nápravnik died in Petrograd on November 10, 1915.

Principal works by Eduard Nápravnik:

OPERA: *The Citizens of Nijni; Harold; Doubrovsky; Francesca da Rimini.*
ORCHESTRA: Four symphonies; *The Demon; The East; National dances; Solemn overture;* Marches; *Concerto for piano and orchestra; Fantasia on Russian themes* (for piano and orchestra); *Fantasia* (for violin and orchestra); *The Song of the nightingale.*

CHAMBER MUSIC: *String quintet;* Three string quartets; *Piano quartet;* Two piano trios; *Sonata for violin and piano;* Two suites for violoncello and piano.
CHORAL: *Don Juan;* Three male choruses; Five a cappella choruses, etc.

About Eduard Nápravnik:

Montagu-Nathan, Montagu. *A Short History of Russian Music;* Rimsky-Korsakoff, Nicholas. *My Musical Life.*
Musical Opinion 40:305 February 1917; *Musikliterarische* Blätter 1:1 January 1904.

Important recordings of music by Eduard Nápravnik:

SELECTIONS FROM OPERA: *Duobrovsky,* "Give me oblivion" (VICTOR).
ORCHESTRA: *The Song of the nightingale* (VICTOR-Panizza).

Pietro Nardini   *1722-1793*

PIETRO NARDINI was born in Fibiana in 1722. As a child he was brought to Leghorn where he began the study of music. After taking lessons from Tartini, in Padua, in his twenty-fourth year, Nardini returned to Leghorn, playing in church concerts.

In 1753, he became attached to the chapel of the Duke of Wurtemberg at Stuttgart. Here he made his reputation as a violinist. "I have heard a violin player named Nardini," wrote Leopold Mozart (father of the great composer), in 1753, "who in beauty, equality and purity of tone is not to be surpassed." When Emperor Joseph II heard Nardini perform he was so pleased that he presented him with a richly enammeled gold snuffbox.

In 1767, Nardini left Stuttgart, returning to Leghorn, where he composed most of his music. Two years later, he came to Padua, the home of Tartini, renewing his friendship with his former master. During Tartini's fatal illness, Nardini tenderly and solicitously nursed him, remaining at his master's side until Tartini died.

In 1770, Nardini became first violinist and court chapel-master in Florence. After this, he entered the service of the Grand Duke of Tuscany. His last years were spent in comparative seclusion in Florence, where he died in 1793.

Nardini's music, commented Thomas Lambe Phipson, "like his character was

PIETRO NARDINI

of serious cast. . . . His style is large, his ideas and his expression natural."

Principal works by Pietro Nardini:

ORCHESTRA: Six concertos for violin and orchestra.

CHAMBER MUSIC: Six string quartets; Six trios for flute and bass; Six sonatas for two violins; Six sonatas for violin and bass.
Many compositions for solo violin, etc.

About Pietro Nardini:

Phipson, Thomas Lambe. *Biographical Sketches of Celebrated Violinists*; Reuchsel, Maurice. *L'École Classique du Violin*; Straeten, Edmund van der. *The History of the Violin.*

Important recordings of music by Pietro Nardini:

INSTRUMENTAL PIECES: *Andante cantabile,* from a violin concerto (COLUMBIA-D'Aranyi); *Aria* (COLUMBIA); *Adagio cantabile,* arranged for violoncello from a violin concerto (TELE-FUNKEN).

Ethelbert Nevin *1862-1901*

ETHELBERT NEVIN, celebrated American song composer, was born at Vineacre, the homestead of his father, in Sewickley, Pennsylvania, on November 25, 1862. His father, of Scotch-Irish descent, whose immediate ancestors had for several generations been farmers in Pennsylvania, was a business man of moderate means.

Ethelbert Nevin showed obvious musical talent at an early age. At ten, he played the piano with such fluency that his teachers pronounced him a genius. One year later, he turned to composition, producing a polka. In his thirteenth year, he composed a song, *Good night, good night beloved,* which knew considerable popularity.

His father had visions of a successful business career for Ethelbert, and entered him in Western University for a thoro academic training. Nevin's scholastic career, however, was short. He was too strongly devoted to music. In the autumn of 1881, he continued the study of music under Benjamin J. Long and Stephen Emery. Then, in 1884, he embarked for Berlin to complete his piano studies and prepare for a virtuoso career under Karl Klindworth. Klindworth recognized that Nevin's greatest talent in music rested not in his piano playing but in his compositions. He, therefore, urged him to devote all of his time and energy towards completing his theoretical education. After a short period of further study under Hans von Bülow, Nevin returned to America. On December 10, 1886 he made his first appearance as concert-pianist, featuring at his concert several pieces of his own.

In 1888, Nevin married Anne Paul, a boyhood sweetheart, settling shortly after this in Boston where, for the first time, he turned away from a career as virtuoso to that of a composer. In 1891, Nevin published his suite for piano, *Water scenes.* It was one of these pieces that first brought him a brilliant success—the world-famous *Narcissus.*

Nevin, himself, has explained the origin of this celebrated piano piece. "I remembered vaguely that there was once a Grecian lad who had something to do with the water and who was called Narcissus. I rummaged about my old mythology and read the story over again. The theme, or rather both themes, came as I read. I went directly to my desk and wrote out the whole composition. Afterwards, I rewrote and revised it a little. The next morning, I sent it to my publishers. Until the proofs came back to me I never tried it on the piano. I left almost immediately for Europe and was surprised when a publisher wrote to me of the astonishing sale of the piece."

Narcissus was a best-seller, bringing great fame and prosperity to its composer. During Nevin's lifetime, more than 125,000 copies were sold. It was performed from one coast of America to another. The striking success of *Narcissus* not only surprised its composer but frequently disgusted him. He regarded it as one of his slightest efforts, and it brought him continual annoyance that, of all his works, this should have aroused the admiration of the music public. He frequently referred to this piece as his "nasty *Narcissus.*"

Restlessness took Nevin to Europe in 1892 and again in 1895, and for extended periods he enjoyed travel in France, Germany, Italy and Algiers. When he returned to America in 1897, after his second voyage, he settled in New York City. It was here that, early in 1898, he composed a song whose success surpassed that of *Narcissus* and established Nevin as the most famous composer of serious songs in America of his day.

Francis Rogers has recorded the incident attending the first performances of this song, in the *Musical Quarterly.* "After dinner, Nevin sat down at the piano, as was his custom, and began to play. After a little while, he handed me a slip of music-paper with the voice part and the words of a song scribbled on it in pencil, saying as he did so, 'Here is a song I want you to sing at our concert next week.' I deciphered my part as best I could, while Nevin played the accompaniment from memory. . . . The song was *The Rosary.* . . Our little audience approved of our efforts, but Mr. Skelding professed to doubt our ability to get the song ready for public performance in so short a time, and after some good-natured discussion offered to bet Nevin a champagne supper for all present that the song would not be sung at the New York concert. Nevin accepted the wager and won it, for the following week, February 15, 1898, in Madison Square Garden Concert Hall, we gave *The Rosary* its first public performance."

The Rosary remains one of the best selling serious songs of any American composer. From 1898 to 1928, more than two and a half million copies were sold.

"It is in his songs that Nevin's peculiar charm asserts itself most potentially," wrote Louis Campbell-Tipton, "for here his ultra-lyric moods are reflected without challenging invidious comparison. Here is his vantage ground; and it is remarkable the number of songs he has written with a similar harmonic basis, all of which are beautiful. . . . Altho he has never followed the modern tendency to atmospheric word-painting in music. . . . The most steadfast advocate of word-painting must recognize the aesthetic beauty of the best examples of the lyric school of which Nevin in his songs is a representative."

In 1900, Nevin settled in New Haven. During the last period of his life he was severely addicted to morbidity, and to resorting to alchoholic stimulants in solitude. Excessive drinking undermined his strength and weakened his heart. He died of an apopleptic stroke in New Haven on February 17, 1901. After his death, malicious rumors were spread that he had committed suicide, but these rumors have long ago been proved to be false.

In estimating Nevin's position as a composer, John Tasker Howard wrote:

ETHELBERT NEVIN

"It is unfair either to overrate or under-rate Ethelbert Nevin. A great master he never was and never could be. He lacked completely the power to paint with a large brush on a broad canvas. He had no ability to develop his materials to works of large dimensions, to sustain a prolonged melodic line or to reach soul-stirring climaxes. As a miniaturist he wrought exquisite cameos, music that reflected the kind of man he was and the sort of life he led."

Francis Rogers described Ethelbert Nevin as follows: "He was of medium height and very slender. Without being emaciated, his frame appeared to carry neither flesh nor muscle. He had no liking for sports of any kind and seldom walked if a cab was available. Indeed, in his distaste for physical exercise he was somewhat Oriental. Oriental, too, was his habit of squatting on one heel while he read and smoked contentedly. . . . His senses were abnormally keen, especially his sense of smell and his hearing. He could recognize his friends. . . . not only by their footfall but also by their odor."

For many years, it was the custom in the Nevin family to conduct musicales every evening when, with the family about him, Ethelbert Nevin sang and played his new works.

Principal works by Ethelbert Nevin:

CHORAL: *The Quest.*

PANTOMIME: *Lady Floriane's dream.*

SONGS: An entire library of famous songs including *The Rosary, Mighty lak' a rose, Captive memories* (song-cycle), etc.

PIANO: *In Tuscany*; *Water scenes*; *Sketchbook*; *In Arcady*, etc.

Pieces for the organ, for violin and piano, etc.

About Ethelbert Nevin:

Howard, John Tasker. *Ethelbert Nevin;* Vance, Thompson. *The Life Of Ethelbert Nevin.*
Music 19:573 April 1901; *Musical Quarterly* 3:358 July 1917; *Musician* 6:67 March 1901.

Important recordings of music by Ethelbert Nevin:

SONGS: *Music by Ethelbert Nevin*, principal works of Nevin arranged for orchestra by Shilkret, including *Narcissus, Day in Venice*, selections from *In Arcady, Mighty lak' a rose, Little boy blue, At twilight, In winter I get up at night, It was a lover and his lass, The Rosary*, etc. (VICTOR-Shilkret).

Otto Nicolai *1810-1849*

KARL OTTO EHRENFRIED NICOLAI was born in Königsberg on June 9, 1810. He had a miserable childhood, principally because of an autocratic father who beat him frequently. In his twelfth year, therefore, Otto ran away from home, for five years subsequent to which he knew appalling starvation and cold.

In 1827, he came to Berlin where he was introduced to two eminent musicians, Berger and Zelter, who decided to help him in his music study. Nicolai made rapid progress. In 1830, he published a vocal duet, which was followed by a vocal quartet, and a book of *Lieder* dedicated to Mendelssohn. Between 1832 and 1834, he composed a *Christmas overture*, a symphony and a Te Deum which were performed in Berlin and in Leipzig, attracting to the composer some attention.

In 1834, Nicolai arrived at Rome where, thru the influence of Karl von Bunsen, Prussian ambassador at the Papal Court, he was given the position of organist at the Prussian Embassy. Here, he was given the opportunity to study sacred music under Giuseppe Baini. During these studies he copied and collected rare manuscripts which became the nucleus of his magnificent library, with which Royal Library in Berlin was later endowed.

It was in Rome that Nicolai first interested himself in opera. After producing two unsuccessful works, he composed *Il Templario* which, upon its presentation in Turin in 1840, was a striking success. *Il Templario* spread Nicolai's reputation thru half the music world, being produced in Vienna, Berlin, St. Petersburg, Constantinople and New York.

In 1840, Nicolai received an appointment as conductor of the Hofoper at Vienna where, soon after his arrival, he presented his own *Il Templario*. He proved to be a uniquely gifted conductor; under his direction the Hofoper enjoyed great artistic success. In 1842, he founded the Vienna Philharmonic Orchestra which, under his baton, began its distinguished career as one of

OTTO NICOLAI

the great symphony orchestras of the world.

In 1844, Nicolai began work upon his masterpiece—his opera based upon Shakespeare's *Merry wives of Windsor,* and after a libretto of H. S. Mosenthal. It was from the first bar a labor of love. "My new opera," he wrote at that time, "has, in its composition, made me very happy. The happiest hours of an artist are those which he spends in creation."

It was several years before the *Merry wives of Windsor* reached performance. In the meanwhile, in 1847, Nicolai was appointed chapel-master and director of the *Domchor* in Berlin. Two years after this appointment, the *Merry wives of Windsor,* upon royal request, was introduced in Berlin. It was a tremendous success. Altho Nicolai was ill at the time, he conducted the first four performances.

Apoplexy brought Nicolai's life to a premature close. He died in Berlin on May 11, 1849, on the very day on which he was elected a member of the Berlin Academy of Arts.

In his earlier operas, Nicolai followed Italian models closely, but in his crowning achievement he reverted to the type of German comic opera which had been brought to popularity by such composers as Lortzing. "But," as Paul Bekker pointed out, "Nicolai works with more

plentiful musical capital, both as to invention and craftsmanship. He brings with him from Italy, above all, the urge to sing, which his work shows much more markedly than that of Lortzing. . . . All the characters sing in German, but their creator knows Italian articulation. He gives them a melodic line of such freedom, a *parlando* of such lightness, that the listener notices with astonishment how well the German language is learning to sing. But Nicolai is not satisfied with solo voice. He is again writing ensemble-opera; the first German ensemble-opera since *Figaro.*"

Principal works by Otto Nicolai:

OPERA: *Rosmonda d'Inghilterra*; *Il Templario*; *Odoardo e Gildippe*; *Il Proscritto*; *The Merry wives of Windsor.*

CHORAL: Motets; *Requiem*; *Te Deum.*

ORCHESTRA: Two symphonies; *Overture on Ein' Feste Burg*; *Concerto for piano and orchestra.*

CHAMBER MUSIC: *String quartet*; *Sonata for violoncello and piano.*

Songs, pieces for the piano.

About Otto Nicolai:

Bekker, Paul. *The Changing Opera*; Kruse, Georg Richard. *Otto Nicolai: Ein Kunstlerleben*; Mendel, Hermann. *Otto Nicolai.*

Important recordings of music by Otto Nicolai:

SELECTIONS FROM OPERA: *The Merry wives of Windsor,* abridged recording (POLYDOR-Berlin State Opera).

Jakob Obrecht 1430?-1505
(See sketch on Guillerme Dufay)

Jacques Offenbach 1819-1880
". . . the Mozart of Champs-Élysées."—
ROSSINI

JACQUES OFFENBACH was born in Cologne, Germany, on June 21, 1819, the son of a synagogue chorister whose original name was Judah Ebersct. Delicate in constitution, Jacques was forbidden to indulge in the study of music for which he manifested unusual enthusiasm. He was, therefore, compelled to study the violoncello surreptitiously. One day, in his tenth year, he startled his relatives and friends by offering to substitute for the absent violoncellist in a performance of a Haydn quartet, playing his part with

JACQUES OFFENBACH

sureness and skill. Three years after this, he made a public appearance, playing several of his original compositions. He created such a stir with this performance that for many weeks he was the talk of Cologne.

In his fourteenth year, young Offenbach set out for Paris, in his pocket a letter of introduction to Cherubini. Cherubini was so impressed with Offenbach's talent that he entered him as a student in the Conservatory in spite of its rules which forbad admission to foreigners. At the same time, Offenbach earned his livelihood by playing in the orchestra of the Opéra Comique, where his love for prank and mischief (one of his favorite pranks was to play only the alternate notes of a work!) cost him so many fines that he frequently drew no salary.

In 1848, Offenbach made a trip to Germany to visit his relatives. On his return, the following year, he accepted the post of conductor at the Comédie Française. At this time, he harbored dreams of owning his own theatre where he might produce musical plays according to his own fancy. His dream did not reach realization until 1855 when he took the lease of Bouffes Parisiens and introduced his own *Deux aveugles*. The success of his performances of comic-opera at the Bouffes-Parisiens was so great that, before long, Offenbach was compelled to take larger and more prominent quarters. At the Bouffes Parisiens, Offenbach presented a succession of operettas that brought great popularity to his name.

It was at the Bouffes Parisiens that, in 1858, Offenbach presented one of his outstanding works, *Orphée aux enfers*. (*Orpheus in der Unterwelt*). At first, *Orphée* was a dismal failure. Jules Janin of the *Figaro* viciously attacked it with withering denunciations; and the audience was confused by its satiric theme. It was not until fifteen years later that it came into prominence.

"The score is full of sparkling wit and melodious charm," wrote Gabriel Grovelz concerning *Orphée*. "It is impossible to analyze adequately a piece wherein the sublimest idiocy and the most astonishing fancy clash at every turn. The overture is gay and lively, the recitative of the Shepherd Aristée is almost on the level with one of Iopas in *Les Troyens* of Berlioz. The songs of Cupid and Venus are accompanied by the snores of the sleeping Gods, and those of John Styx are masterpieces of fatuity and naivete. . . . Offenbach never produced a more complete work."

For the ensuing few years, Offenbach produced operettas with varying degrees of success, ranging from *Barkouf* (1861) which was a dismal failure to *La Belle Hélène* (1864) which was sensational. Of the many operettas, Offenbach produced in this period, the most important was, of course, *La Belle Hélène,* a worthy successor of *Orphée*. "One is astonished at the extraordinary tunefulness," writes Arthur Hervey, "the wonderful *entrain* which never flags, the peculiar sense of humor, the real originality displayed in its pages."

In 1866, Offenbach relinquished his ownership to the Bouffes Parisiens. But the theatre was too much in his blood for him to surrender production permanently. He returned, in 1872, to manage the Gaîeté which, though it attracted large audiences, involved him in such expense that it collapsed. "My children," he said to his musicians, the night before the Gaîeté was forced to close, "you will be paid to the last centime. If I have been incautious, I shall at least be honor itself."

To help defray the enormous expense of paying the many debts that he had accumulated as manager of the Gaîeté, Offenbach left for a tour of America which brought him a 100,000 franc profit. He has recorded his impressions of this trip in *Notes d'un musicien en voyage.*

The last years of Offenbach's life were sombre. He suffered from a painful gout and a harrowing cough. He had only one wish left, and that was to live long enough to hear a performance of his last opera, *The Tales of Hoffmann,* upon which he had been working many years. He was not fated to see the realization of his great wish. He died in Paris on October 4, 1880. Four months after his death, *The Tales of Hoffmann* was given a successful première.

As a personality, Offenbach possessed a naive vanity which made him as proud of his attractive appearance as of his musical talent. Essentially he was a *boulevardier,* fond of fine living and display. Applause and appreciation were indispensable to him; he acquired his greatest happiness from public acclaim.

Principal works by Jacques Offenbach:

OPERA: *Orphée aux enfers; La Belle Hélène; Barbe bleue; La Vie parisienne; La Grande duchesse; Madame Favart; Les Contes d'Hoffmann.*

About Jacques Offenbach:

Bekker, Paul. *Jacques Offenbach*; Hensler, Anton. *Jacques Offenbach*; Martinet, André. *Jacques Offenbach: Sa vie et son Oeuvre*; Northcott, R. *Jacques Offenbach: A Sketch of His Life.*

Important recordings of music by Jacques Offenbach:

OPERA: *The Tales of Hoffmann,* abridged recording (POLYDOR-Berlin State Opera); *Orphée aux enfers,* abridged recording (ODEON-Berlin State Opera); *La Vie parisienne,* abridged recording (ODEON).

Jean De Okeghem *1430?-1495*

(See sketch on Guillerme Dufay)

Niccolò Paganini *1782-1840*

NICCOLÒ PAGANINI, one of the foremost violinists of all time, was born in Genoa on October 27, 1782. His father, Antonio Paganini, was engaged in shipping. He was known to have been a man of hardness and unscrupulous severity, who raised his son with a hand of iron.

As a child, Niccolò Paganini was attacked so severely by measles that it was thought that he was dead. His body was wrapped in a shroud, and it was only by accident that it was not prematurely buried. This early illness left Paganini sickly for the remainder of his life.

He began the study of the violin at a very early age. His father, dreaming of wealth which a prodigy might bring him, applied cruelty in keeping Niccolò at his musical tasks, punishing each mistake severely, and permitting the child no relaxation or play. Under his early teachers—Giovanni Servetto and Giacomo Costa—Paganini made startling progress. At the age of eight he composed a violin sonata of surprising merit; a half year later, he played the *Concerto* of Pleyel in church so successfully that he was frequently engaged for church functions. Antonio Paganini was rapidly realizing his dreams, but far from relenting his despotic rule over his son, increased it with the hope of bringing his vision sooner to fruition.

In 1795, Paganini—then thirteen years old—gave a performance at a theatre in Genoa that was so phenomenal that he was henceforth known as the "wonderchild." His father decided to take him to greater teachers. He therefore began the study of composition under Ferdinando Paër in Leghorn. In 1797, Paganini undertook an extended concert tour to Milan, Bologna, Florence, Pisa, Leghorn, startling the audiences with his phenomenal technique.

By this time, Antonio Paganini's tyranny over his son was proving unbearable to Niccolò, who became determined to free himself once and for all from his father's rule. In November of 1798, he went with his older brother to the St. Martin Festival at Lucca, where he gave a successful performance.

NICCOLÒ PAGANINI

From Lucca, he visited nearby cities giving outstanding performances. He earned enough money to support himself more adequately, and he firmly decided never again to return to his father's home.

This newly-won freedom, however, turned his head. He was only sixteen years old, but he began to plunge into dissipation with women, and gambling. Of these two vices, the latter proved to exert so strong a hold upon him that he would frequently lose more at one sitting than he earned in several weeks. More than once he was forced to pawn his violin to pay off a debt of honor. At one time, he was scheduled to give a performance, but his violin was in pawn. A friend, Monsieur Livron, offered to lend him his own valuable Guarnerius, and at the concert was so enchanted with Paganini's playing that he urged the violinist to retain the precious instrument as a gift. Shortly after this, Paganini almost lost this famous violin in gambling. When, the following morning, the realization came to him that he had almost gambled away his most precious possession, he swore never again to approach a gaming table; and he kept his promise.

Between 1801 and 1805, Paganini disappeared from public sight. It is believed that he lived during these years in complete retirement in the chateau of a Tuscan lady, a guitarist, devoting his time to mastering the playing of the guitar and to composing music for that instrument.

In 1805, Paganini returned to the concert stage. Once again, he knew triumph. Towards the close of the year, he was employed by the Princess of Lucca as court violinist. Here he experimented indefatigably with violin technique and continually attempted to perform on less than four strings by the use of harmonics. He actually composed at this time a sonata for the G-string alone.

Paganini remained in the employ of the Princess of Lucca until 1813. For the next few years he concertized extensively in Italy. He left no question as to his supremacy over all violinists of his day.

Ill-health made it impossible for Paganini to give concerts outside of Italy for many years. Finally, in 1828—after a rest cure in Sicily had brought him renewed strength—Paganini went to Vienna where he was a sensation. Clothes, food, delicacies were named after him; his picture was featured on walking sticks and snuffboxes. In 1831, Paganini surpassed even this Viennese triumph in Paris. Franz Liszt expressed the wonder of the French music public when he exclaimed: "What a man! What a violin! What an artist! Heavens! What sufferings, what misery, what torture in those four strings!"

By this time, Paganini had become something of a legend. It was not only his incredible technique—his digital feats on the fingerboard seemed miraculous to his audiences—but his cadaverous appearance that aroused the superstitious terror and awe of his audiences. "Five feet five inches in height, built on long, sinuous lines, a long pale face with strong lineaments, a protruding nose, an eagle eye, curly hair flowing to his shoulders and hiding an extremely thin neck," was Castil-Blaze's description of Paganini in 1831. "Two lines, one might say, were engraved on his cheeks by his profession, for they resembled the f f of the violin."

His pale, long-drawn face with its hollow cheeks, his thin lips that seemed to curl into a sardonic smile, piercing expression of his eyes which were like flaming charcoals, gave him a diabolic appearance which tempted many of his admirers to circulate the rumor that he was the son of a devil. People frequently crossed themselves if they were accidentally touched by him. At one time, Paganini was forced to publish letters of his mother to prove that he had human parents. At any rate, he aroused awe and terror wherever he played. In Paris he was called Cagliostro; in Prague he was deemed to be the original wandering Jew; the Irish circulated the rumor that he had reached their land on the Flying Dutchman.

Notwithstanding his delicate health, Paganini continued concertizing extensively, and succeeded in amassing a considerable fortune. In 1836, however, he entered a speculative venture—the establishment of a "Casino Paganini" in Paris, a fashionable gambling resort where concerts were given—which was a failure and in which he lost a fortune. His unhappiness at the loss of his wealth aggravated his illness. He left for Marseilles and Nice for rest and recovery. But he was doomed. His illness grew worse, he coughed incessantly, and finally he lost his voice completely. He died in Nice on May 27, 1840.

A few days before his death, the Bishop of Nice was called to his bedside, but Paganini refused to see him, insisting that he was not dying. He died, therefore, without the final sacraments, and the church refused to grant him a burial on holy ground. For a long period his coffin remained in the hospital in Nice, then was removed to Villafranca. It was not until five years after Paganini's death that his son, by appealing directly to the Pope, received permission to bury the body of the great violinist in the village church near Villa Gaiona.

Thruout his life, Paganini suffered from a nervous disease which compelled him to assume a nomadic existence. This disease resulted frequently in violent fevers which compelled him to follow long periods of inactivity. Because of his ill-health, he observed a rigorous diet: frequently, for an entire day he ate no more than some soup, a cup of chocolate and a cup of camomile tea. He required an excessive amount of sleep.

He possessed an unusually sensitive ear, even for a great musician, that could detect even the faintest whisper from a great distance; loud talk caused him extreme physical pain. Thruout his life he was capricious and unmanageable, disorderly in his personal appearance and in the state of his home. His friends have frequently commented on the fact that he was tight-lipped and reticent. Where money was concerned, he was a man of greed.

Robert Schumann held Paganini the composer in as high esteem as Paganini the virtuoso. "His compositions," wrote Schumann, "contain many pure and precious qualities." Berlioz was equally enthusiastic about Paganini's works: "A volume might be written in telling all that Paganini has created. . . of novel effect, of ingenious contrivances, noble and grandiose forms, and orchestral combinations unknown before his time. His melodies are broad Italian melodies, but full of passionate ardor seldom found in the best pages of dramatic composers of his country. His harmonies are always clear, simple and of extraordinary sonorousness. His orchestration is brilliant and energetic without being noisy."

Certainly, Paganini's greatest importance as a composer rests with his brilliant pieces for the violin, in which he developed the resources of his instrument prodigiously and profoundly affected all violin-writing that was to follow. Of his works for the violin, perhaps the most famous are the twenty-four caprices which, in the opinion of Florizel von Reuter, are "Paganini's most important work. . . and reveal such a wealth of pedagogic lore, coupled with such inexhaustible fantasy and poetical romance that they may be considered as convincing proof of Paganini's worth as a musician and composer."

Both Franz Liszt and Robert Schumann have transcribed the twenty-four caprices for piano. Johannes Brahms composed a series of piano variations on the twenty-fourth caprice, as did the modern Russian composer Serge Rachmaninoff.

Principal works by Niccolò Paganini:

VIOLIN AND ORCHESTRA: Two concertos; *Variations on a theme by Süssmayer; Variations on God save the King; Allegro de concert; Moto perpetuo,* etc.

CHAMBER MUSIC: Three quartets for strings and guitar; Two sonatas for violin and guitar, etc.

VIOLIN: *Twenty-four caprices; Witch's dance; Le Carnaval de Venise; Sixty variations upon Baracubà,* etc.

About Niccolò Paganini:

Day, Lillian. *Paganini of Genoa;* Istel, Edgar. *Niccolò Paganini;* Kapp, Julius. *Paganini: Eine Biographie;* Prodhomme, J. G. *Niccolò Paganini;* Stevens, Peter John. *The Paganini;* Stratton, Stephen S. *Paganini: His Life and Works.*

Important recordings of music by Niccolò Paganini:

ORCHESTRA: *Concerto in D-major,* for violin and orchestra (VICTOR-Menuhin); *Moto perpetuo,* arranged for orchestra (VICTOR-Ormandy).

VIOLIN AND PIANO: Caprices no. 2 and 9 (COLUMBIA-Szigeti); Caprice no. 20 (VICTOR-Heifetz); Caprice no. 24 (VICTOR-Heifetz); *La Campanella* (VICTOR-Menuhin).

John Knowles Paine *1839-1906*

JOHN KNOWLES PAINE was born in Portland, Maine on January 9, 1839. His earliest musical education was received in Portland from Hermann Kretschmar. For a short period, in 1837, he officiated as organist. Then, a few months later, he left for Berlin where for three years he followed the study of the organ, composition, singing and instrumentation under Haupt, Wieprecht and Teschner.

After giving a few successful organ recitals in Berlin, Paine returned to America in 1861 to engage actively in musical activity. One year later, he was appointed instructor of music at Harvard University where he worked so devotedly and conscientiously in the building of the department of music that, in 1875, he received his professorship in music—the first occupant of such a chair in any American university. He was known to have been an inspiring teacher and a potent influence on his students, many of whom—including Arthur Foote, Louis A. Coerne, Frederick Shepherd

Converse, Henry T. Finck, Richard Aldrich and William Foster Apthorp—later became prominent in various fields of musical endeavor.

Pedagogical activity, however, did not absorb all of his energy for, during his long career as a teacher, Paine was likewise a fertile composer. In 1867, he directed his own Mass at the Singakademie in Berlin in the presence of Crown Princess Victoria, achieving his first distinct success as a composer. Six years after this, his oratorio, *St. Peter*—first performed in Portland, Maine, and then repeated by the Handel and Haydn Society in Boston—brought him increased prestige. With the performance of his *First symphony* (a work which Paine regarded as "the turning point in my career") by Theodore Thomas' orchestra in Boston, in 1876, Paine's important position among American composers became firmly established.

Within the next few years he produced outstanding music in various fields. The most important of these were the *Spring symphony* and the symphonic-poem *An Island fantasy,* both performed by Theodore Thomas, and such choral works as *A Song of promise,* (composed for the Cincinnati Festival of 1888), and *Oedipus Tyrannus,* performed widely in Boston and New York and receiving a gold medal in Ber-

JOHN KNOWLES PAINE

lin, in 1909, on the occasion of the un-
veiling of a monument to Wagner. In
1901, Paine produced his most ambitious
work, his opera *Azra*, which was published by Breitkopf and Härtel. The
Moorish dances, from this opera, was
featured prominently in symphony concerts.

In 1905, Paine resigned his position
as professor of music at Harvard to
turn more extensively to composition.
Unfortunately, his liberation from pedagogical activity was short-lived. Ill-
health made intensive creative work impossible. On April 25, 1906, Paine
died of pneumonia at his home in Cambridge, Massachusetts. On his piano
rested the unfinished score of his last
work, a symphonic poem, *Lincoln,* upon
which he had been working intensively
for several months.

"He certainly can be classed as a
musician and composer in whom the
elements of old and the new are happily
blended," wrote Louis C. Elson. "He
has written in the classical forms, and
he has also shown a romantic spirit in
his more recent works; he has attained
the dignity of the old Hellenic tragedy
in his *Oedipus Tyrannus,* and he has
given most modern touches in some parts
of his opera, *Azra,* notably in the *Moorish dances* and in the beautiful forest
scenes."

"As a master of orchestration," commented Henry T. Finck, "he has few
. . . equals."

Principal works by John Knowles
Paine:

ORCHESTRA: *Symphony in C-minor*; *Spring
symphony*; *The Tempest*; *An Island fantasy*;
As you like it overture; *Duo concertante* (for
violin, violoncello and orchestra).

OPERA: *Azra.*

CHORAL: *St. Peter*; *The Realm of fancy*;
Phoebus, arise!; *The Nativity*; *A Song of
promise*; *Oedipus Tyrannus*; *Choral hymns,*
etc.

CHAMBER MUSIC: *String quartet*; *Piano
trio*; *Larghetto and scherzo* (for trio); *Sonata for violin and piano,* etc.

Pieces for the organ, for piano; part songs;
songs, etc.

About John Knowles Paine:

Howard, John Tasker. *Our American
Music.*
Aeolian Quarterly 3:13 September 1899;
Etude 24:104 March 1906.

Giovanni Paisiello *1741-1816*

GIOVANNI PAISIELLO, composer
of Italian operas, was born in Taranto on May 9, 1741. His father, a
veterinary surgeon who acquired such
fame in this practice that he was employed by the King of Naples, entered
his son in the Jesuit School where Giovanni remained for eight years. There,
his beautiful voice attracted notice.
One time Chevalier D. Girolanio Carducci asked him to sing from memory,
which Paisiello did with such self-
assurance that Carducci urged the boy's
parents to send him to Naples to continue music study under masters. The
parents, at first, refused adamantly to
part from their only son. But Carducci's
entreaties finally won out. When, therefore, Giovanni Paisiello had completed
his preliminary music study under a
priest, Don Carlo Presta, he went with
his father to Naples in 1754, entering the
Conservatory of St. Onofrio as a pupil
of Durante.

For nine years, Paisiello remained a
student at the Conservatory, devoting
special effort to the study of church music, and composing psalms, motets and
oratorios. Towards the close of his
student days, however, he composed a
comic interlude which was performed
at the Conservatory. This piece attracted so much attention that it procured for its composer a commission
from Bologna to compose an opera. In
this way, Paisiello was brought to that
field of music in which he won world
renown.

Paisiello composed two comic operas
for Bologna—*La Pupilla* and *Il mondo
a Rovescio*—which achieved such great
fame that the composer received commissions to compose operas for leading
opera houses in Italy. His pen was productive; during the next few years he
composed a long string of operas which
spread his fame from one end of Italy
to the other. When he settled in Naples,
his fame rivalled that of Piccinni and
Cimarosa, two of the most popular
operatic composers of the time.

But his reputation was not confined to
Italy alone. In 1776, he received an invitation from Catherine II, to serve as
her music-master, at a yearly salary of

4,000 rubles, excluding expenses. For nine years, Paisiello remained in the employ of Catherine. This period was especially distinguished by the fact that it produced *Il Barbiere di Siviglia*, probably the best of Paisiello's operas and the first to utilize a subject which Rossini was later to make world famous.

On his way back to Italy, after his extended sojourn in Russia, Paisiello stopped at Vienna, where he composed twelve symphonies upon an order from Joseph II, and an opera, *Il Rè Teodoro*. Proceeding to Naples, he was appointed chapel master to Ferdinand IV, in 1784. In this post he produced some of his most famous operas, including *Nina* and *La Molinara*.

In 1799, the revolution in Naples established a republican government, and the court withdrew to Sicily. Paisiello, however, did not lose his prominent musical post, immediately being appointed composer to the Nation. With the Restoration, his former patrons refused to reinstate him. For two years, therefore, Paisiello held no official post. Then, called to Paris by First Consul Napoleon to direct the music of his chapel, at a salary of 12,000 francs a year excluding expenses, Paisiello came to the French capital, remaining two and a half years in Napoleon's employ. During this period, he composed considerable church music and an opera, *Proserpine*. His music was esteemed highly by Napoleon, who considered Paisiello one of his favorite composers.

The ill-health of Paisiello's wife, brought on by the climate of Paris, compelled the composer to resign from his attractive position and to designate the-then-unknown Leseuer as his successor. Returning to Naples, Paisiello found honor and fame awaiting him. He was accorded a handsome pension by Joseph Buonaparte and reinstated in his one-time position as chapel-master. The return of the Bourbon family into power in Naples however ended this good fortune. Deprived of his pension, Paisiello was faced by comparative penury.

The loss of his high position affected Paisiello vitally, undermining his health. The death of his beloved wife, in 1815,

GIOVANNI PAISIELLO

was the last blow. Giovanni Paisiello died in Naples on June 5, 1816.

The critics of his day assigned a crowning position to Paisiello in the world of opera. We read, for example, in the *Quarterly Musical Magazine and Review* of 1818 that Paisiello's qualities as a composer were "fertility of invention, an extraordinary and happy facility of finding subjects full both of nature and originality, a talent unique in developing them by the resources of melody, and embellishing them by interesting details, an arrangement always full of fancy and learning, a taste, grace and freshness of melody. . . . His composition is always very simple, and divested of all affectation of learning. . . exceedingly elegant; his accompaniments are always very clear and at the same time full of brilliant effect. . . . He knows perfectly how to introduce variety. . , to pass from the comic, from the simple and unaffected, to the pathetic, to the majestic, and even to the terrible without losing. . . grace and elegance."

Time, however, has not confirmed the enthusiasm of Paisiello's contemporaries. R. A. Streatfeild remarked tersely in *The Opera*: "Paisiello, a composer whose works though immensely popular in their day, did not possess individuality enough to defy the ravages of time. Paisiello deserves to be remembered as the first man to write an opera on the tale of the 'Barber of Seville.' "

Principal works by Giovanni Paisiello:

OPERA: *L'Idolo cinese*; *L'Olimpiade*; *La Serva Padrona*; *Il Barbiere di Siviglia*; *Nitteti*; *La Molinara*; *Nina*; *Zenobia*, etc.

CHORAL: More than thirty masses; *Requiem*; *Passion*; *Te Deum*; cantatas; motets.

ORCHESTRA: Twelve symphonies; *Funeral march*; Six concertos for piano and orchestra.

CHAMBER MUSIC: Six string quartets; Twelve piano quartets, etc.

About Giovanni Paisiello:

Abert, Hermann. *Paisiellos Verhältniss zu Mozart*; Parker, John R. *A Musical Biography*; Streatfeild, R. A. *The Opera*.
Quarterly Musical Magazine and Review 1:308 (1818).

Giovanni Pierluigi da Palestrina
1525-1594

"He was the ocean towards which all streams flow."—GIOVANNI MATTEO ASOLA (1591)

"In a general history of ancient poetry Homer would doubtless occupy the most ample and honorable place; and Palestrina, the Homer of the most ancient music that has been preserved, merits all the reverence which it is in a musical historian's power to bestow."—CHARLES BURNEY

THE age of vocal polyphony was brought to a magnificent culmination by Palestrina, the foremost musical genius of the sixteenth century. This composer, whose name was derived from the town of his birth, was born as Giovanni Pierluigi Sante in Palestrina, Italy. The date of his birth has been subject to much controversy, but it has been placed somewhere towards the close of 1525. It has been recorded by Zoë Kendrick Pyne that the long-existing enigma of Palestrina's birth was about to reach solution in 1912 when a musicologist discovered in an Augustian monastery, a Palestrina manuscript which seemed to contain the composer's exact date of birth, but which was difficult to decipher. The musicologist asked the monastery for permission to photograph the manuscript, but when he returned to do so discovered that someone had, in the meanwhile, stolen the manuscript; it has never been heard of since.

A legend informs us that, shortly after his arrival in Rome in 1540, Palestrina walked past the Basilica S. Maria Maggiore Janetto, singing to himself as he walked. The choirmaster, overhearing him, was so struck by the quality of his voice that he urged the boy to enter his choir. It is doubtful if this story has even the germ of truth. It has also been recorded that Palestrina became a pupil of the Flemish contrapuntist, Goudimel, another statement that is subject to controversy.

However, it is known definitely that, on October 28, 1544, Palestrina was appointed organist and choirmaster at the cathedral San Agapito, in Palestrina, and that in this position Palestrina enjoyed the happiest period of his life. He was busily engaged in musical activity without interference of jealous antagonists, and enjoyed marked appreciation and a satisfactory salary. Three years after this appointment, Palestrina married Lucretia de Goris. Palestrina's biographer, Giuseppe Baini, has described the intense poverty that Palestrina suffered during the early years of this marriage, but modern research has disproved Baini. As a matter of fact, Lucretia de Goris was the daughter of a prosperous landowner, and soon after her marriage, received an inheritance of a house, vineyards, fields and meadows. There is more reason to believe, therefore, that during the early years of his marriage, Palestrina was in comfortable circumstances, able to devote his entire attention and industry to music study and composition.

In 1551, Palestrina returned to Rome to receive the appointment of Master of the Boys in the Julian choir in St. Peter's. Three years later, he published his first volume of music—containing four masses for four voices, and one mass for five voices—which he dedicated to Pope Julius III. Flattered by this dedication, Pope Julius III appointed Palestrina the following year to the collegiate of singers in his private chapel. This year was also marked by the publication of Palestrina's first book of madrigals for four voices.

On the death of Pope Julius III the papacy went to Marcellus II, who died almost as soon as he assumed his pontifical position. The new Pope was Paul IV, who decided to reorganize the Papal choir. Palestrina was summarily dismissed—primarily because he was married, and married singers were not permitted in the papal choir. It is said that the dismissal affected the composer so acutely that for several weeks he was ill in bed with nervous disorders. However, Palestrina did not remain without employment for a long time. Soon after his recovery, he was given the post of chapel master at the Basilica St. John Lateran, when he composed his book of thirty-five magnificats and his lamentations for four and eight voices.

In 1561, Palestrina became the chapel-master of S. Maria Maggiore, and with this appointment is inaugurated one of the richest creative periods in Palestrina's life. 1562 was the date of the Council of Trent which decreed that Italian Church music must be radically reformed. The following year, Pope Pius IV created a commission of eight cardinals to bring this decree to realization. One of the first moves of this commission was to engage Palestrina to compose a mass which would serve as a model for all church composers. Palestrina composed three masses (including his world-famous *Missa Papae Marcelli*) which were first performed at the home of Cardinal Vitellozzi. This mu-

sic was accorded lavish enthusiasm and praise and was immediately accepted as the prototype for all future ecclesiastical music. This episode established Palestrina as the foremost church composer of the period.

In 1565, Palestrina assembled five of his masses, including the *Papae Marcelli,* and sent them with an appropriate dedication to Philip II, monarch of Spain, who rewarded the composer with nothing more than effusive gratitude. Three years later, these masses were published. A third volume of masses was published in 1570, and likewise dedicated to Philip II.

In 1569, Palestrina entered the service of Cardinal d'Este, a prominent figure of the Renaissance who encouraged Palestrina to compose some of his greatest choral works, including the first book of motets. The second book of motets appeared in 1572, followed three years later by the third volume.

It was not until March of 1571 that Palestrina returned to the Papal choir, this time as chapel-master. He was now the foremost composer in Italy and was accorded great honor and reverence. In 1575, he received what was probably the greatest triumph of his career. It was the year of the Jubilee, and to celebrate the event, fifteen hundred singers from the town of Palestrina, subdivided into three mammoth choruses, entered Rome on foot, singing the music of Palestrina as they marched.

The death of his wife, in 1580, caused Palestrina great grief. One year later, however, he remarried. The last years of Palestrina's life were sombre. Of the four children of his first wife, three died, after revealing considerable musical talent; the fourth proved to be dissolute and irresponsible. But sorrow could not dam the flow of his inspiration, which continued to pour in magnificent abundance.

The early part of 1594, Palestrina published his last work, a collection of thirty madrigals. While preparing this publication, he was stricken with pleurisy which completely undermined him. He took to bed on January 26 of 1594 and one week later—on February 2—he passed away. His last words to his son

GIOVANNI PIERLUIGI DA PALESTRINA

expressed gratitude in knowing that the remainder of his works, which were as yet unpublished, would soon be issued.

"The boy genius from the Sabine hills had done his work," to quote Zoë Kendrick Pyne. "Step by step, emerging from obscurity to fame, he bore music aloft and taught it to express all that the tongue dare not utter, because such emotion, such ecstasy, is too great for words defiled by common use."

Palestrina was buried on the day he died. His body was encased with a plate of lead, on which his name was enscribed in Latin together with the designation "Musicae Princeps." On February 14, a Requiem Mass was performed in his memory in the chapel of S. Maria del Soccorso.

Giuseppe Baini has, somewhat pedantically, subdivided Palestrina's music into ten different periods or styles. However, Cecil Gray is probably more accurate in finding three, rather than ten, distinct styles in Palestrina's lifework. "In his first book of masses, and in several other compositions published later, but probably written about the same time, he appears rather in the light of a disciple and follower of the Netherland school. . . . They are highly complex and artificial, and as full of ingenious contrapuntal contrivances as the most elaborate productions of the Flemish school. His second period is characterized by a constantly increasing tendency in the direction of melodic suavity and harmonic clarity, culminating in the *Missa Papae Marcelli*—the most famous as it is likewise one of the best of all his Masses—in which the utmost sensuous beauty is united to a great wealth and subtlety of technical resource, without, however, detracting from the profoundly devotional character of the music. Finally, in the work of his third period, the formal structure becomes more concentrated and precise, the polyphonic texture still more refined and simplified, and the harmonic and melodic idiom undergo a further process of clarification, resulting in the formation of a style from which every vestige of the old Flemish style has been eliminated."

Palestrina was not, essentially, a revolutionist in music; he did not create any new vocabulary or forms. He was, as Richard R. Terry pointed out, "content to work in the modes as his forefathers had done, and we see no signs of his attempting to break away from this mediaeval system of tonality. . . . Unlike his English contemporaries, he tried no bold experiments in the direction of a newer tonality, and this contented habit of mind gives his music very frequently an uneventful character. But the note of mysticism was always present. Serene, aloof, and detached from mundane affairs, there is no note of materialism to be found in it. When he rises to his highest flights, they are flights of spiritual ecstasy, not those of declamation or pictorialism."

A complete edition of Palestrina's works—numbering thirty-three volumes and including some nine hundred and fifty compositions—was published by Breitkopf und Härtel under the editorship of Witt, Espagne, Commer and Haberl.

Principal works by Giovanni Pierluigi da Palestrina:

CHORAL: Thirteen books of masses; Four of madrigals; Seven books of motets; lamentations; hymns; offertories; magnificats; litanies, etc.

About Giovanni Pierluigi da Palestrina:

Brenet, Michel. *Palestrina*; Cametti, Alberto. *Palestrina*; Fellerer, Karl Gustatav. *Palestrina*; Pyne, Zoë Kendrick. *Palestrina*; *His Life and Times*; Raugel, Félix. *Palestrina*; Schmitz, Eugen. *Palestrina*.

Important recordings of music by Giovanni Pierluigi da Palestrina:

CHORAL: *Missa Papae Marcelli*, complete (VICTOR-Westminster Choir); *Missa assumpta est Maria*, complete (VICTOR-Dijon Choir); *Stabat Mater*, complete (SYRENA); *Sicut cervus* (VICTOR-Sistine Chapel).

Horatio W. Parker *1863-1919*

HORATIO WILLIAM PARKER, one of the most gifted of American composers, was born in Auburndale, near Boston, Massachusetts, on September 15, 1863. His father was a distinguished Boston architect; his mother, a woman of rare literary talent who distinguished herself by her translations in

English from Latin, Greek and European languages.

As a child, Horatio Parker disclosed a remarkable memory, as well as an unusual love for natural history. Music, however, seemed to make no impression upon him. Time and again, his mother attempted to arouse a love for music in him, but failed.

His interest in music was suddenly and mysteriously aroused sometime in 1877. Once stirred, his appetite became insatiable. His mother informed us that he used "to spend literally whole days at the piano, beginning at daylight and stopping only when his father sent him to bed, perhaps at 11 P.M. From that time onwards he had one object. Sports and recreation were left out of his life, and the necessary education was with great difficulty imparted in the intervals of music study."

His mother gave him his first instruction at the piano. He made gargantuan strides. He soon turned to composition, and at the age of fifteen set to music fifty poems of Kate Greenaway's *Under the window* in a period of two days. He also studied the organ. In his sixteenth year he was appointed organist and director of music at St. Paul's Church in Dedham.

Apparently destined for a musical career, Parker soon followed an intensive training. Stephen Emery was engaged to teach him harmony; John Orth, the piano; George W. Chadwick, composition. George W. Chadwick has recorded his impressions of Parker as a student: "As my pupil, he was far from docile. In fact, he was impatient of the restrictions of musical form and rather rebellious of the discipline of counterpoint and fugues. But he was very industrious and did his work faithfully and well. His lessons usually ended with his swallowing his medicine, but with many a wry grimace. It was quite natural that before long our relation should develop from that of teacher and pupil into a warm and sincere friendship."

In his eighteenth year, Parker went to Munich where he studied the organ under Josef Rheinberger. Parker became so much of a favorite pupil of this organ master that when Rheinberger completed his *Organ concerto in F* he selected Parker to introduce it in Munich. In Munich, too, a few of Parker's early works reached performance at the concerts of the Royal Music School.

In 1885, Parker returned to America, becoming director of musical instruction at St. Paul's and St. Mary's School in Garden City, Long Island. There followed several positions as organist, first at St. Andrew's Church in New York, then at the Holy Trinity Church, also in New York. At the same time, Parker taught counterpoint at Thurber's National Conservatory.

In 1893, Parker transferred his home from New York to Boston, becoming organist and director of the choir of Trinity Church. For eight years, he held this position with great distinction. In 1894, he was appointed professor of music at Yale University, thereby coupling pedagogy with the playing of the organ and the conducting of choral music.

And at the same time, his creative pen was not idle. On May 3, 1893—while still in New York—Parker directed the first performance of his most famous choral work, *Hora novissima* at the Holy Trinity Church—composed during a period of illness and depression. This performance was so successful that the following year the Handel and Haydn Society in Boston performed it. The Springfield Festival likewise featured it prominently. In 1899, Parker was invited to England to conduct this work, receiving a heart-warming reception.

"The solid musical worth of *Hora novissima*," commented George W. Chadwick, "its skilful and impressive choral writing, the poetic beauty of the solos, and the varied and colored instrumentation, endear it to musicians, while its lofty spiritual atmosphere, its fervent religious expression, altho tinged with romantic mysticism, make a strong appeal."

Horatio Parker's prestige as a composer rose gradually after the performances of *Hora novissima*. In 1897, Walter Damrosch introduced his oratorio, *St. Christopher*, with the Oratorio

HORATIO W. PARKER

Society of New York. The musical merits of this work were proved when it was featured prominently at the Norwich and Bristol music festivals in England. In 1901, Parker was awarded the Paderewski prize for a cantata, *A Star song*. Ten years later, he won the prize of $10,000 offered by the Metropolitan Opera House for the best opera written in English by an American composer, with *Mona* (on a libretto by Brian Hooker), performed on March 14, 1912. Another opera, *Fairyland,* won the first prize offered by the National Federation of Women's Clubs for an American opera.

Walter Henry Hall pointed out that Parker's outstanding importance as a composer does not rest with his two operas which won him great fame. "His ventures into opera, while they proved his complete mastery of musical material, and enhanced his reputation, also showed that his greatest gift was in the direction of pure choral music."

Horatio William Parker died of pneumonia at his home in Cedarhurst, Long Island, on December 18, 1919. His last published work, the choral *Dream of Mary*, reveals a modification of his former complex style with the result, as Walter Hall commented, that Parker produced "music direct, beautiful and impressive."

Thruout his life, Parker suffered severely from rheumatism. Notwithstanding this ailment, he was a passionate lover of sports. He played golf frequently, and enjoyed nothing more than cycling and mountain climbing. His summers were frequently spent in the Bavarian, Tyrolean or Swiss Alps, either on foot or on bicycle.

Principal works by Horatio W. Parker:

OPERA: *Mona*; *Fairyland*.

CHORAL: *Hora novissima*; *St. Christopher*; *A Wanderer's psalm*; *A Star song*; *Spirit of beauty*; *A Song of the times*; *The Dream of Mary*, etc.

ORCHESTRA: *Symphony in C-minor*; *Symphonic poem*; *Venetian overture*; *Collegiate overture*; *Scherzo in G*; *A Northern ballad*; *Concerto for organ and orchestra*; *Crépuscule* (for mezzo-soprano and orchestra); *Union and liberty* (for solo and orchestra, composed for the inauguration of Theodore Roosevelt as president).

Pieces for the organ, for the piano, etc.

About Horatio W. Parker:

Chadwick, George W. *Horatio Parker*; Howard, John Tasker. *Our American Music*. *Musical Quarterly* 16:153 April 1930; *Musical Times* 43:586 September 1902; *New Music Review* 19:58 January 1920.

C. Hubert Parry *1848-1918*

SIR CHARLES HUBERT HASTINGS PARRY—called by some English critics the "greatest English composer since Purcell"—was born in Bournemouth, on February 27, 1848. He was the second son of Thomas Gambier Parry, a Gloucestershire squire, talented amateur painter, and a well-known collector of Italian art-works.

Parry disclosed musical sensitiveness at an early age. At eight, he composed chants and hymn tunes. At preparatory school he came under the influence of Samuel Sebastian Wesley who brought him more intimately into contact with music. From there, he went to Eton where his musical talent became recognized.

In 1868, Parry's *Intermezzo religioso* for strings was introduced at the Gloucester Festival. The exhilaration of hearing his own work convinced him that he wished to become a composer. He decided, therefore, to continue his music study under such well-known professors as Sterndale Bennett, G. A. Macfarren and H. H. Pierson.

On graduation from Oxford, Parry engaged for three years in business. The lure of music, however, was too great. He finally discarded all thought of a permanent business career and entered the profession of music. He was fortunate, at this time, in becoming a close friend of Edward Dannreuther, the musicologist, whose advice and encouragement were of immeasurable importance in the growth of Parry's artistic career. It was for the musical gatherings which Dannreuther held at Orme Square (the very same studio where, one afternoon in 1877, Wagner read to a group of friends his libretto of *Parsifal*) that Parry's early chamber works reached performance. And it was Dannreuther who introduced Parry's *Concerto for piano and orchestra* at the concerts of the Crystal Palace in 1880.

It was probably this performance that procured for Parry a commission from the Gloucester Festival to compose a special choral work. Late in 1880, scenes from *Prometheus unbound* were performed at the Festival. The performance was a disheartening failure. Parry, however, did not wait long for recognition. In 1883, his eloquent setting of Shirley's Ode, *The Glories of our blood and state* was performed at the Gloucester Festival with considerable enthusiasm. Four years later, the Bach Choir sang his *Blest pair of sirens,* convincing the critics of the originality and imagination of the composer. From this time on, Parry's music found appreciative ears. With the performance of the third and fourth symphonies, in 1889, there were already many critics to hail him as the greatest English composer of his time.

In 1894, Parry succeeded Sir George Grove as the director of the Royal College of Music—a position he held until the end of his life. Altho he was henceforth burdened by innumerable administrative duties, he did not neglect composition. He was enormously prolific, producing music in every possible form, with the exception of the opera.

C. HUBERT PARRY

Parry's eminent position in English music was recognized; he was the recipient of many honors and distinctions. In 1898, he received the honor of knighthood. Five years later—at the coronation of King Edward VII, for which he composed a special anthem—he was created a Baronet. In 1900, Parry succeeded Sir John Stainer as professor of music at Oxford University, holding this position until 1908 when ill-health compelled him to resign.

Sir Charles Hubert Parry died at Knight's Croft in Rustington on October 7, 1918. His body was cremated and placed in an urn in St. Paul's Cathedral in London.

Parry's musical style is not, wrote R. O. Morris, "superficially an attractive one. He scarcely ever wrote a good tune in the sense in which, for instance, Purcell, Schubert and Brahms wrote good tunes. . . . Even in his finest musical declamations there is hardly a trace of the true lyrical rapture. His rhythm is often too square and too heavy-footed. . . . His harmony, again, is staid and unadventurous. . . . All these things hit you right in the face at the outset."

Intimacy with Parry's music, however, discloses many of its fine qualities. "His instrumental work," to quote W. H. Haddow, "is firm and dignified; it contains no cheap and no unworthy phrase, but it has not the sense of color and contrast on which orchestral writing so much depends, and it holds so far aloof from sensationalism that it even discountenances adventure. His chief strength, and here his has no rival thruout our history, is his gift of entering into the very heart of a noble poetry, not by the reflected light of illustration or comment but by a glow of inspiration which has been kindled at the same fire."

Sir Charles Hubert Parry has also distinguished himself as an eminent musicologist, producing many works of unquestionable musicological significance— including the *Evolution of the art of music,* the third volume of the Oxford History of Music (*The Seventeenth Century*), and a biographical and critical study of Johann Sebastian Bach. He also contributed many penetrating articles to George Grove's *Dictionary of Music and Musicians.*

Principal works by C. Hubert Parry:

ORCHESTRA: Five symphonies; *To an unwritten tragedy; Suite moderne; Variations in E-minor; Suite in F; Concerto for piano and orchestra;* Incidental music to Aristophanes' *The Birds, The Clouds* and *The Frogs,* to Hobbes' *Repentance,* Aeschylus' *Agamemnon.*

CHAMBER MUSIC: *Wind nonet; String quintet in E-flat; String quartet in G; Piano quartet in F-minor;* Three piano trios; *Violin sonata in D; Violoncello sonata in A.*

CHORAL: *Judith; Job; King Saul; The Glories of our blood and state; Ode to a solemn music; Ode on St. Cecilia's day; L'Allegro; Il Pensoroso; Invocation to music; Song of darkness and light; The Pied piper of Hamelin; A Vision of life; Hymn to the Nativity,* etc.

About C. Hubert Parry:

Fuller-Maitland, J. A. *The Music of Parry and Stanford;* Graves, Charles L. *Hubert Parry;* Hadow, W. H. *Collected Essays;* Willeby, Charles. *Masters of English Music.*

Monthly Musical Record 46:3 January 1916; *Musical Quarterly* 5:299 July 1919; *Musical Times* 59:489 November 1918

Important recordings of music by C. Hubert Parry:

CHORAL: *Coronation anthem* (COLUMBIA); *Jerusalem* (GRAMOPHONE).

SONGS: *Three aspects* (GRAMOPHONE-McCormack).

Felipe Pedrell   *1841-1922*

"For my part, I affirm that it is to the lessons of Pedrell and to the powerful stimulation exercised on me by his works that I owe my artistic life."—MANUEL DE FALLA

THE father of modern Spanish music, Felipe Pedrell, was born in Tortosa, on February 19, 1841. As a boy, he sang in the choir of the Tortosa Cathedral, which brought him into intimate contact with Spanish church music. Feeling drawn to music, he began its study autodidactically, succeeding in acquiring a competent education. Then, as a student of Juan Antonio Nin y Serra, he reached maturity. It was Serra who first introduced him to native Spanish music and who urged him to compose works based on folk melodies.

In 1871, Pedrell's first published work appeared, and three years later was succeeded by his first opera, *El Ultimo abencerraje.* His music attracted very little attention. To earn his living, Pedrell turned to pedagogy, becoming professor of musical history and aesthetics at the Madrid Conservatory.

Ill-health compelled Pedrell to resign from his professorial post. Going to Barcelona, which he then made his home, Pedrell published his famous opera *Los Pirineos,* which was not performed until 1892. It was at this time that he first began his monumental work on behalf of Spanish music, publishing a pamphlet, *Por nuestra música,* in which he maintained that national music art must rest upon the foundation of the folk song. From this time on, he devoted inexhaustible energy towards historical and archaeological research. In 1887 came his *Estudios de Bibliografia músical,* which was followed by a biographical and bibliographical dictionary of Spanish, Portugese and Spanish-American writers and composers. From 1892, he began the publication of a series of articles, entitled *Los Músicos anonimos,* filled with important documentary information about Spanish folk lore.

In 1894, Pedrell began to edit his famous *Hispaniae scholae música sacra,* an eight-volume anthology of great Spanish church music. This monumental endeavor was succeeded by a still

FELIPE PEDRELL

more gargantuan venture, the editing and publication of the complete works of Vittoria, the great Spanish church composer of the sixteenth century. Between 1905 and 1908, Pedrell edited an anthology of classical organ works by Spanish composers, and the last years of his life were devoted to the selection, editing and publication of *Cancionero músical popular español,* the first comprehensive anthology of Andalusian, Moorish, Catalonian and Basque folk-music.

Despite these enormous archaeological and historical labors, Pedrell did not neglect composition. In a long series of works, including operas, choral and symphonic compositions, he attempted to put into practice his theories on Spanish music. He was, however, never accorded that recognition for his compositions that he received for his historical and critical labors. When, in 1911, his seventieth birthday was the object of considerable festivity and congratulations, it was not because he was a composer but rather because he had accomplished monumental research in Spanish folk and church music.

The realization that his music never achieved recognition embittered him considerably. As he once told Manuel de Falla, towards the close of his life: "They have never done me justice either

in Catalonia or in the rest of Spain. They have constantly tried to belittle me, saying that I was a great critic, or a great historian, but not a good composer. It is not true. I *am* a good composer! I do not want respect for my years, but for my work. Let them hear it and study it; they will then be able to judge!"

However, as Anthony Clyne wrote, Pedrell's importance does not rest in his creative work. "He was himself incapable of entirely discarding the meretricious sentimentality, acquired thru the influence of foreigners, especially the Germans, of an age when true romance was in all the arts so often counterfeited. So anxious to make his music expressive, he did not see that it was not sufficient to use the material of folk music with the technique of European music, but that its own technique must be involved. Its rhythmic and modal characteristics were the essence of its beauty and value. Intensely patriotic, he nevertheless overlaid the racial and traditional qualities with a structure un-Spanish, producing a mixture of irreconcilable styles."

Pedrell's great importance in musical history rests almost exclusively with his research work, and with his influence upon the succeeding generation of Spanish composers. Almost single-handed he caused a renaissance of Spanish music, and pointed out a new direction for Spanish music towards which his contemporaries traveled eagerly. Thus he achieved a new epoch in Spanish art music. His influence was felt strongly not only by his immediate successors, Isaac Albéniz and Granados, but also by the entire school of modern Spanish composers. "He has made of Spanish music a living and vibrant art," wrote André Coeuroy. "The Joaquin Turinas and the Manuel de Fallas of our day would not have become what they are if this predecessor—he of the white beard—had not guided them. Thus Pedrell has known the purest joy that can be experienced by pioneers—that of having assisted, while living, to the triumph and culmination of his life's ideal."

Felipe Pedrell died in Barcelona on August 19, 1922. During the last years of his life he knew not only illness but poverty as well, a poverty which was only partially alleviated by the support of his pupils.

J. B. Trend has discovered three striking qualities in Pedrell's music: "There are individual peculiarities in his style, serenity as well as strength in his emotions, and an unusual sense of mystery, or of poetry."

Principal works by Felipe Pedrell:

OPERA: *El Ultimo abencerraje*; *Quasimodo*; *Mazeppa*; *Cléopâtre*; *La Celestina*; *Los Pirineos*.

CHORAL: *Cançon*; *Messe di gloria*; *Hymne à Ste. Thérèse*; *Requiem*; motets; antiphons.

ORCHESTRA: *Excelsior*; *El Comte Arnau*; *Glose* (with chorus); *I Trionfi; Cant de la montanya; Marche à Mistral*.

Songs.

About Felipe Pedrell:

Coeuroy, André. *Le Panorama de la Musique Contemporaine*; Curzon, Henri. *Felipe Pedrell et Les Pyrénées*; Salazar, Adolfo. *La Música Contemporánea en España*; Trend, J. B. *Manuel de Falla and Spanish Music*.

Monthly Musical Record 52:277 November 1922; *Music and Letters* 7:265 July 1926; *Musical Quarterly* 11:164 April 1928; *La Revue Musicale* 4:1 February 1922.

Important recordings of music by Felipe Pedrell:

SONGS: *C'était en avril* (VICTOR); *Sur l'eau* (VICTOR).

Giovanni Pergolesi *1710-1736*

THE history of opera bouffe virtually begins with Giovanni Pergolesi's *La Serva padrona*, the first great opera bouffe in musical history.

Giovanni Battista Pergolesi was born in Jesi, near Ancona, on January 3, 1710. His first musical instruction was on the violin under Francesco Santini and Francesco Mondini.

In his sixteenth year, his musical talent attracted the attention of an intelligent patron of the arts, Count Cardolo Maria Mannelli, whose influence made it possible for Pergolesi to enter the Naples Conservatory, Poveri di Gesú Cristo, where his teachers were Gaetano Greco, Francesco Durante and Francesco Feo.

In 1731, Pergolesi emerged officially as a composer when his sacred drama *La Conversione di San Guglielmo d'Aquitania* (which contained a comic intermezzo) was performed at the monastery S. Angello Maggiore. The success of this performance procured its composer a commission to compose an opera for the court theatre. *La Sallustia* was produced in the winter of 1731 and was warmly acclaimed, altho there were many who did not like the comic intermezzo which Pergolesi had inserted into this opera, too. In 1732, another Pergolesi opera made its appearance, *Ricimero*, but it was a complete failure.

All of Pergolesi's works were created winthin the short span of five years (1731-1736). But his industry in this period was phenomenal and he produced a rich succession of works for the theatre, for chorus, chamber-groups and solo voice. It was often difficult for him to compose because his creative labors would frequently be interrupted by violent hemorrhages. Yet, despite his illness, he worked at a breath-taking pace. In these five years, he composed twelve operas, thirty oratorios, four masses, four Salve Reginas, psalms, airs, cantatas, sonatas, trios, a Stabat Mater as well as four volumes of vocal exercises. It was almost as though he knew that he had not long to live.

Pergolesi's masterpiece, that jewel of comic opera—*La Serva padrona*—was first presented in Naples, in 1733, to vigorous and triumphant applause. Built about a theme of almost threadbare simplicity and utilizing only three characters, of which one is entirely silent, this little play, as Karl Nef commented pithily "is so lively in its music, so telling in its characterization, so full of jests and humor, that it has continued as a masterpiece of the first rank until the present day."

Twenty years after its first performance in Naples, *La Serva padrona* was introduced thruout Europe by a group of itinerant Italian singers, and was everywhere received with tumultuous acclaim. It was performed in Paris in 1752 and made so profound an impression that it brought into being an entire cult of musicians, including Jean Jacques Rousseau, Diderot and Grimm, who proclaimed this as the only true musical art, condemning such French composers as Rameau for enmeshing music with intricate technique and elusive emotions.[1]

La Serva padrona, commented Paul Bekker, "is among the most astonishing things the theatre has to show in any age. Two speaking characters, no decorations —nothing could be more primitive. . . . The astonishing thing is the variety exhibited within that narrow circle. Nothing more can be said about the interplay of man and woman than bass and soprano tell each other and enact in their raving, dancing and singing. It may be this element of eternal validity that gives Pergolesi's work its incomparable effect. . . . It remains. . . alive and inimitable. While it contained, as the first work, the essence of the entire species, it left to later times the possibility of formal expansion and productive elaboration. But everything essential it had itself established beyond excelling."

Early in 1734, Pergolesi was engaged by the Duke of Maddaloni as court musician. One year later, another of his distinguished works, the opera *L'Olimpiade,* was introduced under his own direction at the Tordinona Theatre in Rome. The performance was a dismal failure. Grétry reported that someone in the balcony threw an orange at the composer's head! This failure affected not only Pergolesi's spirits but his health as well, aggravating his illness and

GIOVANNI PERGOLESI

bringing on a period of great despondency. Momentarily, he deserted the composition of operatic music, but fortunately this desertion was only temporary. In the autumn of 1735, he presented another comic opera in Naples, *Il Flaminio,* which aroused some enthusiasm and praise.

Biographers of Pergolesi relate that at this time, the composer fell in love with a girl of high rank, Maria Spinelli. Her brothers swore that they would kill Pergolesi if she did not promise to forget him completely. Three days later, the brothers returned for the girl's final answer only to find that the girl had left to enter a convent.

This loss of his beloved was a fatal blow to Pergolesi. His health disintegrated rapidly. Early in 1736 he went to Pozzuoli for a rest cure. It is believed that he composed his remarkable *Stabat Mater* here, on a commission from the Confraternity of S. Luigi di Palazo at Naples. He composed the *Stabat Mater* in illness and pain, and when his friends begged him to take a short respite he answered: "Alas, I have no time to lose!"

It is a penetrating commentary upon Pergolesi's personality that at this time— with illness as his companion and death facing him—he should compose a lusty and vulgar musical jest, a satiric scherzo about the Capuchin monks.

Giovanni Pergolesi died at Pozzuoli, Italy, on March 17, 1736. He was buried in the town cathedral. *"Giovane e moribondo"* ("Young and dying") was the inscription on his grave.

Many critics, including Paul Marie Masson, have found a close affinity between the style of Pergolesi and that of Wolfgang Amadeus Mozart. Wrote Masson: "There exists between Pergolesi and the author of *Don Giovanni* a close parental tie. One finds with each of them the same quality of soul, the same nimble gaiety or, in the sadness, the same elegiac sweetness. And it is not only in sentiment that they resemble each other but in style as well, by the general form of their art. There are entire pages of Pergolesi which one would say had been written by Mozart; there are the same melodic outlines, the same method of harmonization and accompaniment."

The world-famous modern composer, Igor Stravinsky, has arranged several famous Pergolesi melodies for chamber-orchestra and adapted them into two suites, *Pulcinella* and *Suite italienne.*

Principal works by Giovanni Pergolesi:

OPERA: *La Sallustia; Ricimero; La Serva padrona; L'Olimpiade; Il Flamino*, etc.

CHORAL: Thirty oratorios; Four masses; Four Salve Reginas; psalms; cantatas; *Stabat Mater; Orfeo; Giasone*, etc.

ORCHESTRA: *Concerto for violin and strings; Symphony in G; Concerto for flute and orchestra.*

CHAMBER MUSIC: *Sonata for violoncello and continuo*; Twenty-six sonatas for two violins and bass, etc.

Airs.

About Giovanni Pergolesi:

Bekker, Paul. *The Changing Opera;* Bellaigue, Camille. *Portraits and Silhouettes;* Colini, Francesco. *Pergolesi e Spontini.*
Le Guide du Concert 1:149 January 14, 1911.

Important recordings of music by Giovanni Pergolesi:

SELECTIONS FROM OPERA: *La Serva padrona,* "Donne vaghe" (GRAMOPHONE); *Vocal selections* (DECCA).

CHORAL: *Stabat Mater,* "First Chorus" (PARLAPHONE); "Vidit suum" (PARLAPHONE).

ARIAS: *Se tu m'ami* (COLUMBIA).

ORCHESTRA: *Pulcinella* and *Suite italienne,* Pergolesi melodies adapted by Stravinsky (COLUMBIA).

Jacopo Peri

(See sketch on Caccini)

Niccolò Piccinni *1728-1800*

NICCOLÒ PICCINNI, well-known composer of Italian opera who was the principal character in the famous Gluck-Piccinni feud of musical history,[1] was born in Bari, Naples, on January 16, 1728. His father hoped to make of him a priest, and it was only surreptitiously that Niccolò was able to study the harpsichord. One evening, while visiting the home of the Bishop of Bari with his father, Niccolò found a harpsichord in an empty room. Thinking he would be undetected, he began to play quietly.

[1] See sketch on Gluck.

His music, however, attracted the Bishop's notice who, recognizing the talent of the performer, urged father Piccinni to permit the boy to study music.

In this manner, Piccinni became a pupil at the Conservatory St. Onofrio in 1742. He was at first displeased with the instruction at the school, seeking diversion by composing oratorios, psalms and operatic arias secretly. The director of the Conservatory, Leo, soon heard that one of the younger pupils was composing in pretentious forms, contrary to the rules. Leo, therefore, summoned Piccinni to his office. He discovered so much talent and merit in the works that Piccinni brought with him that Leo— whose original intention it had been to reprimand the student severely— caressed the boy and placed him under the personal care of Francesco Durante.

Piccinni remained at the Conservatory for twelve years. On leaving that institution he found a patron in the influential Prince of Ventimiglia, who utilized his power to procure a production of Piccinni's first opera, *Le Donne dispettose,* in Naples in 1755. The success of this opera was extraordinary. Despite the fact that many intrigues were working against the young composer, instigated by the followers of Logroscino, celebrated composer of comic opera at the time, Piccinni produced several rousing successes shortly after his initial product.

In 1758, Piccinni was summoned to Rome on a commission to compose *Alessandro nelle Indie.* Here, two years later, he composed the comic opera, *La Cecchina,* one of the most famous opera bouffes in musical history. *La Cecchina* was first performed in leading theatres in Rome, then introduced to the important cities of Italy. Its fame and popularity grew so great that it was even known in China, where the Emperor had a special performance of the work prepared for him.

This opera, as Eric Blom wrote, "is replete with a fluency and vivacity that are quite in the best vein of the comic opera of the period. . . . It is mellifluous, pretty music, written without any great care to fit it to the stage situation, yet with more of that care than the public of the time, who simply wanted to hear agreeable music, ever suspected. There is some delightful harmony and surprising modulation in this little opera, besides occasional attempts to create dramatic effect by means of tremolos, and other conventional tricks."

Piccinni's fame was now at its height. In 1761, he composed six operas which were performed simultaneously in six different leading opera houses, each enjoying great popularity. For several years, Piccinni was without a rival.

This dominant position, however, was soon menaced. In 1773, a pupil of Piccinni—Anfossi, by name—produced a comic opera, *Incognita perseguitata,* whose charm brought momentary popularity to its composer. Anfossi's newly won fame reacted unfavorably to Piccinni's reputation. At one performance of a Piccinni opera, there were some to hiss the work. To Piccinni, this was a severe blow. His health became affected, and for an extended period he was seriously ill. When he recovered, he swore never again to compose an opera for Roman production. He transferred his home to Naples, devoting his energy to the preparation of operas for the Neapolitan stage. In Naples he had lost none of his stature. One of the first comic operas he composed upon his return, *I Viaggiatori,* ran for four consecutive seasons.

In 1776, as a result of repeated invitations, Piccinni went to Paris where, for a salary of six thousand francs a year, he agreed to compose operas expressly for the French stage. He enjoyed high favor at the Court; twice each week he went to Versailles to give singing lessons to the Queen.

His first French opera was *Roland,* a subject which had likewise been given to Gluck. This was the beginning of an artistic war between Piccinni and Gluck which split musical Paris into two battling camps: The Gluckists were on the side of dramatic expressiveness and complex orchestrations and harmonizations; the Piccinnists were for simplicity, agreeable melody and unpretentious forms.

The director of the Opéra, recognizing the valuable publicity of this rivalry,

NICCOLÒ PICCINNI

decided to settle once and for all the comparative greatness of these two composers by commissioning both of them to compose an opera on the same subject—*Iphigénie en Tauride.* Piccinni had been promised that his opera would be performed first, but, at the last moment, the manager went back on his word and gave precedence to Gluck. Gluck's *Iphigénie* was a masterpiece, and it captured its audience by storm. After a success as great as this, Piccinni suffered inevitably. To add to Piccinni's misfortune, the principal singer of his opera appeared on the stage obviously intoxicated. The performance was, therefore, a fiasco. There was no longer a question in the minds of the Parisian music public that in the Gluck-Piccinni feud it was the former who was the victor.

In the meanwhile, Piccinni produced two more operas in Paris—*Atys* and *Adèle de Ponthieu*—which were only moderately successful. When Gluck left Paris, in 1780, Piccinni was momentarily the centre of interest again. But, three years later, a new rival appeared—Sacchini—whose great popularity brought failure to many of Piccinni's operas. It is worthy of mention, and singularly indicative of Piccinni's personality, that his rivalry with Gluck and Sacchini did not embitter him against his antagonists. When they died Piccinni extended gestures of admiration and respect, going so far as to say of Gluck that "the lyrical theatre is as much indebted to him as is the French stage to the great Corneille."

The French Revolution sent Piccinni back to Naples, where the King gave him a flattering reception and a handsome pension. Several of Piccinni's operas were revived successfully. Once again he knew adulation. Unfortunately, Piccinni brought back with him the germs of revolutionary ardor. He began to express loudly sentiments on behalf of proletarian revolution, even permitting his daughter to marry a French revolutionary. Immediately, he lost caste in the eyes of the royalty. For four years, he was viciously persecuted, virtually kept a prisoner in his own home. In 1798, however, he received a commission from Venice to compose two operas. Safely out of Naples, he decided to return once again to France. Here, he tasted glory for the last time. He was created an Inspector of the Conservatory, and given a small pension.

His many misfortunes, however, had wrecked his health. Paralysis set in, and his health was persistently undermined by continual bleedings by surgeons. Finally, he left for Passy with the hope that rest and quiet might restore his health. There he died on May 7, 1800.

Piccinni has been described by one of his contemporaries as "under middle size, but well-made, his carriage bespeaking dignity. His figure had been very agreeable, his forehead was large and open, his eyes blue and. . . . with an expression both sweet and spirited and sometimes animated and sparkling. . . . The form of his nose, and the union of this feature with the forehead, reminded one of the Greeks. . . . His mind was quick, extended and cultivated. . . . His principles in art were severe."

In musical history, Piccinni is remembered principally because of the feud with Gluck, in which German opera triumphed over Italian. Piccinni's operas have been relegated to obscurity. However, there exist a number of outstanding critics in our day who believe that Piccinni's obscurity is undeserved, and that he is worthy of a much higher

artistic position than the musical historian has accorded him. Cecil Gray, for example, has written: "That such a noble and highly gifted artist as Piccinni . . . should be held up in musical histories to derision and contempt, and regarded as a typical representative of all the most pernicious tendencies in operatic art, is probably the cruelest injustice and the most glaring example of shallow prejudice and ignorance in the whole history of musical criticism. Gluck is incontestably a great musical dramatist, but as a musician pure and simple he is incontestably the inferior of his rival."

Bernard van Dieren is equally enthusiastic about Piccinni's art: "He was a strong personality and a considerable intellect, and technically well equipped. His music has an elegant stateliness, an easy flexibility, and a balanced clarity such as are rarely found combined with so much strength and purpose. He has dramatic muscle, together with exquisite nervous sensibility. His melody emotionally pulsated with a subtlety that has been rarely equalled before the advent of Verdi."

Niccolò Piccinni's grandson, Louis Alexandre Piccinni (1779-1850), was likewise a composer of operatic music. Born in Paris, he was engaged in that city as pedagogue, violinist, accompanist, and chorus master at the Opéra. He composed more than two hundred works for the stage, some of which were very popular in their day.

Principal works by Niccolò Piccinni:

OPERA: *Le Donne dispettose*; *Alessandro nelle Indie*; *Siroe*; *L'Olimpiade*; *Demetrio*; *La Cecchina*; *Demofoonte*; *Berenice*; *Catone in Utica*; *Antigono*; *Roland*; *Atys*; *Iphigénie en Tauride*; *Didon*, etc.

CHORAL: Three oratorios; mass, etc.

About Niccolò Piccinni:

Blom, Eric. *Stepchildren of Music*; Curzon, Henri. *Les Dernières Années de Piccinni à Paris*; Della Corte, Andrea. *Piccinni*; Dieren, Bernard van. *Down Among the Dead Men*; Gray, Cecil. *A History of Music*.

Important recordings of music by Niccolò Piccinni:

SELECTIONS FROM OPERA: *Didon*, "Air de Didon" (GRAMOPHONE).

Amilcare Ponchielli *1834-1886*

AMILCARE PONCHIELLI was born in Cremona on September 1, 1834. At the age of nine he was entered at the Milan Conservatory, where he remained for eleven years. While still a student, he made abortive attempts at operatic composition which elicited the praise of his teachers.

Upon leaving the Conservatory, he began the composition of a major operatic work based upon Manzoni's *I Promessi sposi.* This work was given a first performance in Cremona, in 1856, with moderate success. For several years following this operatic debut, Ponchielli earned his living as a bandmaster in Piacenza. At this same time, he composed several operas, none of which revealed sufficient individuality to attract notice.

The opening of a new opera house in Milan—the Teatro dal Verme—brought Ponchielli a commission for an opera for the opening performance. In 1872, Ponchielli revised his early *I Promessi sposi* radically, and—with his wife singing a principal rôle—the work achieved a tremendous success. There followed a commission from La Scala in Milan for a ballet. When *I Lituani,* the commissioned work, was performed in Milan in 1874, it was riotously acclaimed.

AMILCARE PONCHIELLI

Ponchielli was now a famous composer. With the self-assurance which fame brings with it, he now set upon the task of composing a new opera. On April 8, 1876, he produced *La Gioconda* on a libretto by Tobia Gorria (who was none other than Arrigo Boito, famous composer and librettist). The opera did not completely satisfy the composer and, after having put the final touches upon it, he changed it radically. In this new form, *La Gioconda* was again performed at Genoa, in December of 1876. There followed a La Scala performance the following February. The triumph which this opera achieved definitely placed Ponchielli among the leading composers of Italian opera in his day.

"Ponchielli's score," wrote a critic in review shortly after the first performances of *La Gioconda,* "shows that he has fully grasped the poet's intentions. True to the school of which Boito made himself the champion, and after many years of hard struggle, Ponchielli had endeavored to write dramatic music which being descriptive of the action abounds in coloring and instrumental effects. . . . *La Gioconda* is an energetic and laudable effort to infuse fresh vigor into Italian opera."

Probably the most famous portions of *La Gioconda* are the ballet sections, principally the famous *Dance of the hours,* which have been favorites with opera audiences everywhere. "The ballet music is unusually good," wrote R. A. Streatfeild, "and shows many favorable examples of Ponchielli's fondness for fanciful melodic designs, a mannerism which has been freely imitated by his pupils and followers."

Altho Ponchielli produced three operas after *La Gioconda,* he failed to duplicate his brilliant success. He remained the composer of one extraordinary opera, but that one opera was sufficient to bring him immortal fame in operatic history.

During the last years of his life, Ponchielli served as chapel-master at the Cathedral of Bergamo. He died in Milan on January 16, 1886.

"His creative power," summed up William Foster Apthorp, "was considerable. He was decidedly a man of genius, if of second rank. If he lacked Verdi's vigor of temperament, he had a fine dramatic gift, and his technical musicianship was rather in advance of his day."

Principal works by Amilcare Ponchielli:

OPERA: *I Promessi sposi*; *La Savojarda*; *Roderico*; *Bertrando del Bornio*; *La Stella del monte*; *Il Parlatore eterno*; *La Gioconda*; *I Mori di Venezia* (completed by A. Cadora).

BALLET: *Le Due gemelle*; *I Lituani*, etc.

CHORAL: *Cantata in honor of Donizetti*; *Hymn in memory of Garibaldi.*

About Amilcare Ponchielli:

Apthorp, William Foster. *The Opera: Past and Present*; Streatfeild, R. A. *The Opera.*

Musical Times 24:338 June 1, 1883; *Musician* 10:95 March 1905; *Neue Musik Zeitung* 42:216 September 1916.

Important recordings of music by Amilcare Ponchielli:

OPERAS *La Giaconda*, complete (COLUMBIA-La Scala).

SELECTIONS FROM OPERA: *I Promessi sposi*, "Overture" (GRAMOPHONE).

Giacomo Puccini *1858-1924*

"Within his period, Puccini stands as the perfecter of lyric opera."—PAUL BEKKER

GIACOMO ANTONIO DOMENICO MICHELE SECONDO MARIA PUCCINI—successor to Giuseppe Verdi as the foremost composer of Italian opera—was born in Lucca on June 22, 1858. He was descended from a long line of musicians. For two centuries the family of Puccini had been prominent musicians in Lucca. Giacomo Puccini was, therefore, trained musically from earliest childhood.

Altho he disclosed unusual musical precociousness, Giacomo was as a child unruly and undisciplined. He was hot-tempered, obstinate and irresponsible. At school—the seminary of San Michele —he was the leader of his companions in all mischief. In singing class, he displayed a supreme indifference, and at home was frequently kicked by his uncle because of the frequency with which wrong notes appeared in his practising. In San Pietro at Somaldi, where he studied the organ, he often scandalized the priests by introducing operatic arias in his improvisations. It was

probably only his indifference which made him fail in a competition for a hymn, which he entered in 1877.

He loved music passionately, however; at one time he went on foot to Pisa, thirteen miles distant, to hear Verdi's *Aïda.* The performance enchanted him. From that moment on, he was determined to go to Milan and study music intensely, perhaps even to meet the great master personally. Fortunately, his mother understood him sympathetically, and did everything in her power to bring his dream to realization. She applied to Queen Margherita, convinced her of Giacomo's gifts, and procured three hundred lira, enough to support Giacomo for one year. In October of 1880, Puccini entered the Reale Conservatorio, after passing the entrance examinations.

"I like Milan," he wrote to his mother, after he had become acclimated. "I am not hungry. I eat a great deal, and I fill up on substantial soup. My appetite is satisfied. In the evenings I go to the Gallery for a stroll, then come home footsore: reaching my room, I do a little counterpoint, I do not play the piano, because it is not allowed at night. After that I go to bed where I read seven or eight pages of a novel. This is my life."

While still a student at the Conservatory, Puccini composed a *Capriccio sinfonico* which, upon its performance at the Conservatory concert, was successfully received. Franco Faccio promised to perform it at the concerts of the La Scala, and it was published by a well-known house in Milan. Thus, upon leaving the Conservatory, Puccini had his first taste of success, which encouraged him to undertake the laborious work of composing his first opera.

To earn a livelihood, Puccini taught the piano in Milan, working between lessons upon his first opera, *Le Villi.* When the opera was completed, he submitted it for the Sonzogno competition, but it was not even read because it was too illegible. Shortly afterwards, however, Puccini played the score for Arrigo Boito, well known critic, librettist and composer, who was so impressed with the work that he started a special subscription to have the work performed. It was presented at the Theatre dal Verme in May of 1884, and was so phenomenally successful that it brought Puccini a reward of 2,000 lira. Ricordi accepted the work for publication, giving the composer one thousand lira in advance.

Puccini was now in comparatively affluent circumstances. He has recorded how, shortly after the success of *Le Villi,* he went into his favorite restaurant in Milan, called *The Aïda*—where during his long period of penury he had accumulated a bill of several hundred lira—ordered a sumptuous meal and then, to the bewilderment of the restaurant keeper, took out a thousand lira note and paid off his long-standing debt. "That was for me the greatest, the most memorable satisfaction."

Puccini's second opera, *Edgar,* was presented at the La Scala on April 21, 1889. It was a failure, even though there were many critics who praised the mastery of its construction. But Puccini did not wait long for permanent success. In February of 1893, his third opera—*Manon Lescaut*—was introduced at the Teatro Regio in Turin. *Manon Lescaut* made Puccini world-famous, being introduced with enormous success in London and Paris as well as in Italy.

With *Manon Lescaut,* Puccini's career, as the greatest Italian operatic composer since Verdi, was definitely launched. "Puccini's work," wrote D. C. Parker in discussing *Manon,* "contains some of the most vigorous and spontaneous melody which he has given us. . . . The Puccini 'manner'. . . is not absent. Indeed, considering the chronological position of the opera, it is surprising that there is so much of the mature Puccini in it."

While in Paris for the French première of *Manon,* Puccini worked industriously on his new opera, *La Bohème,* on a libretto by Giuseppe Giocosa and Luigi Illiaca based on the famous novel by Henri Murger, *Scènes de la vie de Bohème.* The opera was completed in his villa at Torre del Lago, and given its first performance at the Teatro Regio in Turin in February of 1886, under the direction of Arturo Toscanini.

GIACOMO PUCCINI

The opera was a sensation. With one stroke, Puccini had surpassed all of his previous operatic efforts, producing a work which placed him unquestionably at the head of all Italian operatic composers of the time. "Puccini has caught the fanciful grace of Murger's style," in the critical estimate of R. A. Streatfeild, "with the dexterity of genius. His music is thoroughly Italian in style, but he never strikes a false note. He dashes off the irresponsible gaiety of the earlier scenes with a touch which though light is always sure, and when the action deepens to tenderness, and even to pathos, he can be serious without falling into sentimentality and impressive without encroaching upon the boundaries of melodrama. *La Bohème* is one of the few operas of recent years which can be described as a masterpiece."

The success of *La Bohème* brought Puccini financial security. He built a beautiful Florentine villa at Torre del Lago. Here, during the next three years, he planned and worked on his new opera, *Tosca,* after the tragedy of Sardou. It seemed as if success had now become a habit, for *Tosca,* on its performance at the Teatro Costanzi in Rome on January 14, 1900, equalled the phenomenal success of *La Bohème.*

In February of 1903—while driving his car at high speed late one night, near his home—Puccini missed a curve and went. over an embankment of some thirty feet. Both his wife and son escaped injury, but Puccini broke his leg and suffered intense pain while he was rushed back to his villa at Torre del Lago. Three days later, a specialist from Florence arrived to set the broken leg, but the recovery was long and painful. For several months, Puccini suffered excessively, but during this period he did not interrupt his composition. He was working on *Madame Butterfly,* and was frequently forced to interrupt his labors in the middle of a line because the pain in his leg was too poignant. He was confined to an invalid's chair, and whenever he wished to try out a new harmony or melody he would be carried to his piano.

When *Madame Butterfly* was given its first performance at La Scala, on February 17, 1904, it met a chill reception. Its exotic theme failed to create a favorable impression, and, *mirabile dictu!* Puccini—idol of Milan—was hissed and booed at the end of the opera. This failure prompted Puccini to withdraw the score from the La Scala after one performance. After revising the music slightly, Puccini permitted another performance of the work in Brescia, on May 28, 1904. At this time, the audience was more appreciative. In October of 1905, *Madame Butterfly* was presented to America in English by the Henry W. Savage Opera Company.

Late in 1906, the Metropolitan Opera House of New York decided to introduce *Madame Butterfly* into its repertoire. For this event, it invited Puccini to America. Puccini arrived in New York early in January of 1907, and received a regal welcome. At the first performance of *Madame Butterfly* he was given a thunderous ovation.

While in America, Puccini attended a presentation of David Belasco's *Girl of the golden West.* When, shortly before his return to Italy, he was commissioned by the Metropolitan Opera House to compose an opera expressly for that institution, he decided to convert the David Belasco play into an opera. The libretto was prepared by Carlo Zangarini and Carlo Civinini. In 1910, upon the completion of the opera, Puc-

cini returned to America to help assist at the rehearsals; David Belasco officiated as the stage director. On December 10, 1910, the opera was given its première with a cast that included Caruso, Emmy Destinn and Scotti. It was a gala event which the élite of musical New York attended. But—perhaps because of an unappealing libretto—the opera was a failure.

For the next seven years, Puccini's pen was idle; and not until 1917 did he emerge from his retirement with a new opera—*La Rondine,* a work written in a lighter vein. *La Rondine* was followed by three one-act operas. Puccini's last opera was *Turandot,* based upon an eighteenth century play of Count Carlo Gossi.

Late in 1924, while working on *Turandot,* Puccini was troubled by persistent sore throat and hoarseness. He went to a specialist in Florence who was vague about the nature of Puccini's ailment. To Puccini's son, however, the specialist confessed that the master was suffering from a cancer of the throat. It was decided that only an operation might spare his life. On November 4, Puccini and his son set off for Brussels where he was to undergo an operation under the hand of one of the foremost surgeons in Europe. It was a difficult operation, but Puccini emerged from it miraculously. However, a heart attack set in the following day, and on November 29, Giacomo Puccini died. The news spread thruout the music world, and was met everywhere with grief. In Rome, a performance of *La Bohème* was interrupted to permit the orchestra to play Chopin's *Funeral march* as the audience stood in respect.

The Italian government defrayed the expenses for Puccini's funeral. After impressive ceremonies in Brussels, his body was brought back to Lucca for burial.

Two years after Puccini's death—on April 25, 1926, his last opera, *Turandot,* was presented in its unfinished form at the La Scala in Milan under the direction of Arturo Toscanini. In the middle of a phrase, the work came to an abrupt stand-still. Toscanini, turning around to the audience, tears streaming down his face, announced: "Here—here—the maestro died!" *Turandot* was completed by Franco Alfano, and in this form has been presented in leading opera houses in Europe and America.

In appearance, Puccini hardly suggested a composer. Always carefully attired, he seemed more the successful business man than the creative artist. There were, however, sensitive lines to his face, delicacy to his lips and alert intelligence in the expression of his eyes.

His passionate hobbies were motoring and hunting. He was sensitive to beautiful women ("I am always in love," he once confessed laughingly), an epicure (his favorite food was beans!), a lover of soft living. Solitude was essential to him; most of his life, he lived in privacy far removed from adulation and praise. He was not a prolific composer. He frequently required a long period of rest after completing an opera before he could begin work upon another. When he worked, however, he worked intensely, unable to tolerate the slightest disturbance. "When I am working, do not trouble me. I am capable of levelling a gun at you," he frequently warned his guests. He was a man of great culture, his favorite relaxation being reading. One of his favorite authors was Maxim Gorky. In his own opinion, his two best operas were *Manon* and *Madame Butterfly*.

In his operas, Puccini's canvas is not a very great one, even in his most successful creations. Ildebrando Pizzetti has referred to Puccini's works as *"opera di arte non grande."* Puccini himself has said of his own works: "I love small things, and the only music I can or will make is that of small things. . . so long as they are true and full of passion and humanity, and touch the heart."

However, though Puccini's canvas is small, there can be no question but that he always reveals himself a master of his equipment, an artist in the finest sense of the word. "There is never anything coarse, vulgar or effusively banal in his approach," wrote Richard Specht, "but always a noble and fastidious delicacy, the quintessence, so to speak, of exquisite music. . . . His ideas are full of an inimitable elegance, a quivering grace, and a sure feeling for artistic tact and grace which colors even the smallest phrase with personality . . . he has his own peculiar, unforgettable note, and further, a bitter-sweet, gently irritating aroma that is all his own, not only in his orchestration, but also in pure tone and harmony."

Principal works by Giacomo Puccini:

OPERA: *Manon Lescaut*; *La Bohème*; *Tosca*; *Madame Butterfly*; *The Girl of the golden West*; *La Rondine*; *Il Tabarro*; *Suor Angelica*; *Gianni Schicchi*; *Turandot* (completed by Franco Alfano).

CHORAL: *Solemn mass*; *Juno*.

About Giacomo Puccini:

Dry, Wakeling. *Giacomo Puccini*; Specht, Richard. *Giacomo Puccini: His Life and Work*; Weissman, Adolf. *Giacomo Puccini*.

Important recordings of music by Giacomo Puccini:

OPERA: *Manon Lescaut*, complete (COLUMBIA-La Scala); *La Bohème*, complete (Columbia-La Scala); *Tosca*, complete (COLUMBIA-La Scala); *Madame Butterfly*, complete (COLUMBIA-La Scala).

Gaetano Pugnani   *1731-1798*

GAETANO PUGNANI was born in Turin on November 27, 1731. His first important instruction on the violin was pursued under Somis, and brought to completion under Tartini. In 1752, Pugnani was appointed first violinist at the Royal Chapel in Turin. He then began an extensive concert tour which established his fame as a violinist. In 1754, he received an extraordinary reception at the Concert Spirituel in Paris, and, in 1768, surpassed this success in London.

He was a violinist of unusual brilliance, but his performances were distinguished particularly by the depth and profundity of his artistic insight. When Pugnani played on the concert stage, he was so absorbed in his music that he would forget his surroundings and frequently walk up and down the platform, while playing, imagining himself to be entirely alone.

In 1770, Pugnani returned to Turin to become general director of the Royal Chapel, where he established his fame

GAETANO PUGNANI

both as a composer and as a teacher of the violin. One of his most famous pupils was Viotti.

Gaetano Pugnani ,died in Turin on July 15, 1798. He has been described by his contemporaries as of middle height, deep-set eyes of brilliant intensity, emaciated cheeks that gave his face an unusual spiritual quality. His nose, of enormous length, was frequently the subject of much ridicule. One artist of his day caricatured him as leading an orchestra, all the orchestra players sheltered under the roof of his nose!

R. Sodenheimer pointed out that Pugnani, in his compositions, was something of a link between Sammartini and Boccherini. "Pugnani was also the particular Italian composer to assimilate the Italian with the German sonata form. His significance is, for us, however, hardly more than a go-between. . . . Altho his works, as Funker so aptly puts it, are 'suffused with a tint of melancholy,' and altho our ear is captured by the sorrow-laden, even cloying tones which Italian music was to hand on to the classical composers thru Sammartini, Pugnani and Boccherini, his creative power did not suffice to divest the strongly marked outlines of their mechanical effect. . . . In detail, he was undoubtedly successful in formulating many new idioms. . . . but to create a great and convincing new form out of

the new formulas. . . . was denied him."

Ironically enough, the two compositions by which Pugnani is today remembered—the celebrated *Praeludium and Allegro* and the *Tempo di minuetto,* both supposedly arranged for the violin by Fritz Kreisler—have recently been discovered to be not pieces by Pugnani but original compositions by Kreisler.

Principal works by Gaetano Pugnani:

ORCHESTRA: Nine concertos for violin and orchestra; sinfonias.

CHAMBER MUSIC: Thirteen octet-sinfonias (strings and woodwind); Six quintets (for strings and flute); Six string quartets; triosonata; violin duets; Fourteen sonatas for violin and piano.

Operas, cantatas, ballets, etc.

About Gaetano Pugnani:

Cobbett, Walter Willson. *Cyclopedic Survey of Chamber Music*; Pamparato, S. Cordero di. *Gaetano Pugnani: Violinista Torinese*; Straeten, Edmund van der. *The History of the Violin.*

Important recordings of music by Gaetano Pugnani:

VIOLIN AND PIANO: *Largo espressivo* (COLUMBIA-Enesco).

Henry Purcell   *1658-1695*

"Sometimes a hero in an age appears,
But scarce a Purcell in a thousand years."
—JOHN DRYDEN

"THE Father of English Music," as Henry Purcell has been called, was born, it is believed, in Westminster in or about 1658. His father, who was an esteemed musician in his own right, a gentleman of the Chapel Royal, died when Henry Purcell was six years old. The boy was adopted by his uncle, Thomas Purcell. Shortly after this, Purcell was admitted as a chorister of the Chapel Royal, and it has been said that while still a chorister he composed several anthems.

In 1670, Purcell set to music a loyal address from the children on the occasion of His Majesty's birthday. This work attracted wide attention, bringing the boy into favor with the English royalty. In consequence, when his voice broke in 1673, necessitating his dismissal from the Chapel Royal, he was immediately engaged as "keeper, maker, mender, repairer and tuner" of the king's in-

Purcell· pĕr'cĕl

struments at a salary of thirty pounds a year and an additional sum for his wardrobe. It is strongly believed that at this same time, Purcell was a pupil of the celebrated organist and composer, John Blow.

Thru the influence of John Blow, Purcell was appointed to the post of copyist at the Westminster Abbey, in 1675. Four years later, when Blow resigned from his post as organist at the Abbey, Henry Purcell, aged twenty-one, was named successor. In 1680, Purcell first revealed creative genius with his famous *Fantasias* for strings, in various parts, one of the most strikingly original instrumental works of the period. This year was also marked by his marriage.

In 1682, Purcell was appointed organist of the Chapel Royal, the same year in which his first son was born. One year later, he published a set of sonatas for two violins and a bass in the Italian style. In 1685, he returned to his one-time post as copyist at Westminster.

It was on a commission from a boarding school for girls in Chelsea that, at this period, Purcell composed the work that proved to be his masterpiece, the opera *Dido and Aeneas*. This composition is one of the landmarks of English opera; it has frequently been said that if Purcell had composed nothing else he would have remained one of the great English composers of all time.

"It is one of the most original expressions of genius in all opera," wrote the composer, Gustav Holst. And Hubert J. Foss commented: "In the variety of its style, in its power of crystallizing instantly a situation, a new scene, a character, it is dramatic music of the first order. In this last particular the special greatness of Purcell's achievement lies most. He has the power to vivify each of the characters, puppet-like though they appear to be in the libretto; he enlivens each scene, so that it seems as if paper flowers and property trees had blossomed into real fragrance and were oozing the real sap of spring. His gaiety is as lively as his sorrow is poignant; his crowds are as sharply characterized as his principals."

Dido and Aeneas was completed in 1689 and performed shortly afterward

HENRY PURCELL

at the Josias Priest School for Girls in Chelsea. On the celebration of the bicentenary of the composer's death in 1895, *Dido* was revived by Sir Charles Stanford at the Royal College of Music in London.

The success of *Dido and Aeneas* encouraged Purcell to continue his composition for the theatre. During the next few years he produced the music for *The Tempest*, *The Massacre of Paris*, for Beaumont and Fletcher's *The Prophetess* and for Dryden's *Amphitryon*. The music for *Amphitryon* attracted the attention of John Dryden who was so impressed that he sought out the composer; a close friendship followed. Purcell and Dryden collaborated several times on dramatic works, and in 1691 produced their most ambitious effort, *King Arthur*. It is the opinion of many critics that the music to *King Arthur* represents one of Purcell's maturest achievements. Wrote Ernest Walker: "Purcell never wrote anything more finely organized than the spacious *Passacaglia* in the fourth act, the structure of which is remarkable."

During the remaining years of his life, Purcell produced one more major work, *The Fairy queen*, after Shakespeare's *A Midsummer night's dream*, as well as a large quantity of sacred choral music.

It is believed that hard work undermined his ever-delicate constitution and that his death—which took place on November 21, 1695—was the result of his low physical resistance. Another theory, based on apocryphal evidence, has it that Purcell's death was caused by a cold, contracted while waiting outside the doorstep for his wife to let him enter. According to this legend, Purcell's wife—infuriated at his disposition to keep late hours and indulge in drink—ordered the servants, one night, not to admit their master if he returned after midnight. Having drunk profusely at the tavern, Purcell arrived home past midnight, considerably heated from the drinks, and was forced to wait several hours in the cold before he was admitted. A cold set in which developed, the following day, into his final fatal illness.

Henry Purcell was the first musician to be honored with burial in Westminster Abbey. On the tablet, near his grave, was inscribed: "Here lyes Henry Purcell, Esq. who left this life, and is gone to that Blessed Place where only his harmony can be exceeded."

John Dryden wrote a celebrated ode in honor of Henry Purcell.

Purcell was known to have been a lovable, amiable, bright spirit. A witty tongue and a pleasant disposition endeared him to many friends. He was a great lover of drink. He frequently confessed that his happiest hours were spent in the tavern in the company of friends, consuming great quantities of wine.

Henry Purcell was an eminent theorist as well as a composer. His most important theoretical writing appears in the 1694 edition of Playford's *An Introduction to the skill of music.*

Historians have always accorded a position of pre-eminent importance to Henry Purcell, who, had he lived a full life's span, might have changed the entire course of English music. He was one of music's geniuses. "Purcell's genius. . . was equal to that of the greatest masters," wrote Burney with unfaltering insight a century and a half ago, "and though his dramatic style and recitative were formed in a great measure on French models, there is a latent power and force in his expression of English words, whatever be the subject, that will make an unprejudiced native of this island *feel,* more than all the elegance, grace and refinement of modern music, less happily applied, can do."

The most predominating quality of Purcell's genius was his ability to produce melodies of unforgettable beauty. "Few musicians have possessed the melodic sense to such a degree as Purcell," wrote Henri Dupré. "Not the slightest trace of effort can be felt in the melodies of the English master, they spring spontaneously to life. Purcell sings as naturally as a bird."

However, it would be a mistake to believe that all is gold in Purcell's prolific output of music. Frequently, Purcell fluctuated from sheer genius to the commonplace. W. H. Hadow has pointed out the three outstanding faults in Purcell's works. "The first is that his melody is not always. . . of the supremely highest rank. It is pure, it is lucid, it is imbued with national feeling, but it does not worship in the inner courts. . . . The second is that no artist of his eminence has ever been so completely under the control of one tiresome mannerism. On almost every occasion when the music speaks with a cheerful voice . . . we have the same lilting figure of dotted notes constantly appearing until we come to expect it as a matter of course. . . . The third is one which he shares with other composers of the seventeenth and eighteenth centuries. . . . the construction of a song on a simple quatrain, or an even more slender foundation, the words of which were constantly repeated in order to eke out the music."

But, notwithstanding his faults, Purcell remains "the ornament not only of his age, but also of his country," as Henri Dupré wrote. "Purcell, whose work with its marvelous variety is one of the rarest jewels in the poetic treasury of Great Britain; Purcell, in short, whose name has been handed down thru the ages, and will always be so handed down, because he knew how to express human feelings in a language all divine."

Principal works by Henry Purcell:

OPERA AND THEATRE MUSIC: *Dido and Aeneas; King Arthur; The Fairy queen; The Tempest; Amphitryon; The Prophetess; The Massacre of Paris,* etc.

CHORAL: Anthems; services; hymns; odes; songs; trios; catches, etc.

INSTRUMENTAL: Fantasias in 3, 4, 5, 6, 7 and 8 parts for strings; Twelve sonatas in three parts; Ten sonatas in four parts; overtures; pieces for the harpsichord; pieces for the organ, etc.

About Henry Purcell:

Arundell, Dennis Drew. *Henry Purcell*; Dupre, Henri. *Purcell*; Holland, A. K. *Henry Purcell: The English Tradition.*

Important recordings of music by Henry Purcell:

OPERA: *Dido and Aeneas,* complete (DECCA).

INSTRUMENTAL: *Nine four part fantasias, The Golden sonata* (COLUMBIA); *Ayres for the theatre,* arranged by Bernard (DECCA); *Suite in G-major,* for harpsichord (COLUMBIA-Dolmetsch).

CHORAL: *Catches,* "I gave her cakes" and "To thee and to a maid" (COLUMBIA); *Airs,* "If music be the food of love" and "How long, great God" (COLUMBIA).

JOACHIM RAFF

Joachim Raff *1822-1882*

JOSEPH JOACHIM RAFF was born at Lachen, on the lake of Zürich, on May 27, 1822. As a child he disclosed remarkable capacity for learning languages. It is said that at the age of seven he could translate Homer. His parents, therefore, decided to give him an intensive classical education. After completing preliminary studies at the Würtemburg Institute, Joachim Raff became a student at the Jesuit Lyceum of Schwyz where he won first awards in Latin and mathematics. During this period, music was merely a hobby; it was only for diversion that he learned to play the violin and piano.

Indigence compelled Raff to discontinue his academic studies, and in his twentieth year he became a schoolmaster. Music now began to hold a stronger attraction for him and from this time on he devoted more conscientious effort towards composition. Upon the whim of a moment, Raff sent some of his compositions to Felix Mendelssohn, in 1843, who found therein so much talent that he immediately wrote to his publisher, Breitkopf and Härtel, urging publication. "The composition is elegant and faultless thruout," Mendelssohn wrote, "and in the most modern style. If my hearty

recommendation will have any weight, I most willingly add it to the request of my young friend."

Breitkopf and Härtel published Raff's early pieces. This publication, together with Mendelssohn's enthusiastic praise, tempted him to give up school teaching completely and to become a musician. There followed several years of privation, during which time Raff continued his creative work indefatigably.

At this time, Raff met Franz Liszt. Liszt, who always had a keen scent for true talent, was strongly impressed by Raff's gifts—so much so that he urged Raff to accompany him on a tour thru Switzerland. In 1846, Raff met Mendelssohn personally for the first time. Mendelssohn urged Raff to become his pupil, but, unfortunately, the sudden death of the great composer ended this plan. Instead, Raff went to Stuttgart, where he turned even more seriously to music study than before, principally under Hans von Bülow. In 1848, von Bülow introduced Raff's first major work, a *Concertstück,* for piano and orchestra.

In 1850, Raff went to Weimar where, for six years, he served as secretary, assistant—as well as pupil—of Franz Liszt. During this period, Liszt exerted every effort to bring recognition to the young composer, going so far as to present Raff's early opera, *König Alfred,* at the Court Theatre.

Dr. William Mason, fellow-pupil of Raff under Franz Liszt, gave us the following word-portrait of the young composer. "He was hard to become acquainted with, and not disposed to meet one half-way. He was fond of argument, and if one side was taken, he was apt to take the other. . . . Upon better acquaintance. . . one found a kind heart and a faithful friend. . . . He was very poor and there were times when he seemed hardly able to keep body and soul together. Once he was arrested for debt. . . . He was a hard worker and composed incessantly."

In Weimar, Raff met and fell in love with Doris Genast, the beautiful daughter of an actor. When Doris left for Wiesbaden in 1856, Raff followed her. They were married in that city in 1859.

Meanwhile, Raff's star as a composer was rising. In 1858, he composed incidental music to a drama by Wilhelm Genast, *Bernhard von Weimar,* the overture to which proved to be so popular that it was performed thruout Germany. In 1863, Raff's first symphony won the prize offered by the Gesellschaft der Musikfreunde of Vienna, focussing more attention upon him. In 1870, a comic opera, *Dame Kobold,* finally established his reputation as a composer. Seven years later, Raff was appointed the director of the Hoch Conservatory in Frankfurt, a position he held until the end of his life.

Joachim Raff died in Frankfurt on June 24, 1882. At the time of his death he was held in high repute as a composer. Since his death, however, his music has suffered neglect, and performances of his works have been few and far between.

Perhaps the outstanding characteristic of Raff's music is its graceful fusion of classical forms with the romantic spirit. "The wonderful ease with which he was able to employ scholastic devises revealed itself in all his larger compositions," wrote Arthur Hervey, "and if he was occasionally prolix in his utterances

and not invariably inspired, he was always comprehensible and rarely dull. . . . His romanticism was grafted on a classical stem, and the broadness of his outlook resulted in his endeavoring to conciliate opposing tendencies."

Raff is best known as a symphonist. Ebenezer Prout has analyzed the predominating qualities of Raff's best symphonies. "The first point that strikes the student of these symphonies is their individuality. They possess, it is true, that family likeness which shows them to be productions of the same brain. . . . His ideas are by no means of equal merit, but at all events the well never runs dry, and inexhaustible fluency seems to be one of the composer's striking characteristics. . . . I have no hesitation in saying that since Beethoven nobody has equalled Raff in the absolute mastery of thematic treatment. By his skill in this respect, he frequently succeeds in constructing an interesting movement out of the most unpromising material; and when, in addition, he has been happy in the choice of themes, he produces music worthy to rank with the masterpieces of our art. No less remarkable. . . is his complete command of counterpoint."

Principal works by Joachim Raff:

ORCHESTRA: *An das Vaterland; Im walde; Symphony in G-minor; Lenore; Symphony in D-minor; In the Alps; Frühlingsklänge; Im sommer; Zur herbstzeit; Suite; Jubilee overture; Festival overture; Ein' feste burg overture; Concerto for violoncello and orchestra;* Two concertos for violin and orchestra; *Concerto for piano and orchestra; Suite for piano and orchestra; Ode au printemps* (for piano and orchestra); *Suite* (for violin and orchestra).

OPERA: *König Alfred; Dame Kobold.*

CHORAL: *Wachet auf!; Psalm 130; De profundis; Die Tageszeiten,* etc.

CHAMBER MUSIC: *String octet; String sextet; Piano quintet;* Two piano quartets; Four piano trios; *Sinfonietta* (for wind instruments); Sonatas for violin and piano.

About Joachim Raff:

Raff, Helene. *Joachim Raff: Ein Lebensbild.*

Monthly Musical Record 12:175 August 1, 1882; *Neue Musik-Zeitung* (Stuttgart-Leipzig) 43:254 March 1922.

Jean Philippe Rameau *1683-1764*

"Rameau has made of music a new art."—
VOLTAIRE

JEAN PHILIPPE RAMEAU was born in Dijon on September 25, 1683. His father was an organist who, though poor, was determined to give his son a thorough education. While still a mere child, Rameau was taught music; at the age of seven, he could play the harpsichord competently. However, to an exacting father it seemed that the musical progress Jean made was much too slow to warrant further study in the art. As a result, the boy was sent to a Jesuit college for an academic training. He was, however, an inattentive and indifferent pupil to any study unrelated to music. When he left the college, he had hardly succeeded in carrying away with him any perceptible degree of education.

His great love for music ineluctably drew him to Italy, the home of the opera. Depending upon his knowledge of music for a livelihood, Rameau wandered, in his eighteenth year, thru the northern Italian cities, now playing in town bands, now performing the organ for church services, coming at all times into intimacy with the Italian music of the day. It cannot be said that this music pleased him. Before long, he returned to his native France, to assume the post of

JEAN PHILIPPE RAMEAU

organist, first at Avignon, and then in Clermont. At the same time, he began his first intensive efforts at composition.

The musical life of a small town in France was inadequate for Rameau. After six years of organ playing at Clermont, he migrated to Paris. Here he settled in the home of a wig-maker in the Rue du Temple, not far from the church where Louis Marchand, world-famous organist, performed regularly. For a while, Rameau was Marchand's pupil, earning at the same time a meagre existence by playing the organ. For several years he knew intense poverty in Paris, but during this period he was absorbed in music study.

In 1723, Rameau first came into prominence, not as a composer, but as a theoretician, by publishing the first of his remarkable studies on harmony, *Nouveau système de musique théorique*. In later years, Rameau was to supplement this volume with several other studies on harmony. These were to form the basis for the science of modern harmony.

It was Rameau's eminence as a theorist that brought him, in 1727, to the notice of the foremost art patron in France—Monsieur Riche de la Pouplinière. Convinced that Rameau was a musician of genius, La Pouplinière was determined to give him every opportunity to grow and develop. He placed an organ at his disposal, permitted him to conduct his private orchestra, and introduced him to the foremost artists of the day in his salon. It was here that Rameau met, for the first time, appreciation and recognition as a composer. The instrumental music that he composed for La Pouplinière's orchestra found attentive ears.

In 1733, Rameau composed his opera, *Hippolyte et Aricie,* based upon Racine's *Phèdre,* which, after several rehearsals at the home of La Pouplinière, was presented at the Opéra. Four years later came the famous *Castor et Pollux,* which enjoyed a great success. In 1745, Rameau's *La Princesse de Navarre,* on a libretto by Voltaire, definitely placed him in preeminent position among the French composers of the time, earning for him a yearly pension of two thousand francs and the honorary title of "Compositeur de la musique de chambre."

Despite this recognition and honor, Rameau did not attain ultimate success without a fierce struggle. There were those who found his music too intricate for their tastes, and too unmelodious, who preferred the less taxing music of Lully. These adherents of the Italian tradition in opera were vicious critics of Rameau's music and abused him considerably. As a matter of fact, one of the most circulated verses of the time had, for its butt, Rameau:

> "If the difficult is pretty,
> What a great man is Rameau!
> If, by chance, whate'er is witty
> Must be simple, then I know
> He is but a little man!"

With the passing of several years, this hostility to Rameau grew rather than decreased. In 1752, an Italian company presented Pergolesi's *La Serva padrona*. The charming simplicity and ingenuousness of this music inspired many to proclaim this as the only true musical art and to condemn viciously composers like Rameau and even Lully who enmeshed the musical art in the labyrinth of a complex technique. At the head of this group were such outstanding men as Jean Jacques Rousseau, Diderot and Grimm. "The French airs are not airs at all," wrote Rousseau in his *Lettres sur la Musique Française,* "and the French recitative is not recitative. I conclude, therefore, that the French have not and cannot have a music of their own; or if they have one, it will be so much the worse for them!"

Musical Paris was split by a veritable war, known as the *"guerre des bouffons."* Those who sided with Rousseau upheld the Italian tradition in opera; those who were with Rameau, fought on behalf of "French art." Rousseau, as a matter of fact, composed a delightfull comic opera, *Le Devin du village,* in 1752, following the style of Pergolesi. It is interesting to note parenthetically that, several years later, when a similar battle split musical Paris—the fight of Gluck against the Italian Piccinni, Rousseau was once again in the heat of the battle, but this time his fight was against the Italian tradition and for Gluck.

During the last ten years of his life, Rameau lived a quiet and secluded existence, producing his several important treatises on harmony, and composing ballets, operas, instrumental music with an industrious pen. The last years of his life found him generally accepted as the greatest composer of his period; and he saw his "French art" winning a decisive victory.

Jean Philippe Rameau died at his home in the Rue des Bons Enfants on September 12, 1764. It is said that on his death-bed he reproved the priest for intoning his prayers out of tune. He was buried with ceremonious reverence.

Rameau, who was tall and thin, was frequently compared by his contemporaries to an organ-pipe. His voice was loud and harsh, his actions awkward, his mannerisms obstreperous. He was known to have been avaricious, capable of driving a hard bargain. Altho he earned well, he lived with a simplicity that bordered upon the threadbare. He much preferred saving his money to spending it. His was not a pleasant personality, often acid in his conversation and unscrupulous in his actions. Long solitary walks in the country were his favorite diversion.

In composing, he frequently created his works while holding violin in hand, and not—as so many other composers did—at the harpsichord. He possessed an extraordinary self-assurance. He frequently said that he could, if he wished, set the *Gazette de Hollandie* to music. He looked upon music more with the eyes of a theoretician than of a creator, considering it an imitative art, and maintaining that it was entirely based upon a routined system of harmony.

Rameau is of significance in musical history as a forerunner of Gluck in the development of the music drama. Generally recognized as being the first modern colorist, Rameau—because of the striking originality of his harmonies and his startling orchestral effects—definitely drew opera away from the stereotyped traditions of the Italian school and introduced it to an expressiveness entirely unknown in his day.

"Rameau embodies the most astonishing balance of science, will-power and inspiration," wrote G. Jean-Aubry. "Nothing extravagant characterizes him. It may be that he is crabbed and savage, because the obsession of the problems on which he aspires to throw light compels him to solitude; but how much the more thoroughly does the most vivid feeling pierce thru in a thousand places! . . . . Plasticity of rhythm, a sense of orderly life, delicacy, and care to maintain the balance of expression, these are the features of Rameau."

Karl Nef, in considering Rameau's operas, believes that he "belongs to the most original discoverers of all times. He treated the recitative, like Lully, in strictly French manner, and, like him, but with greater skill, he drew upon the chorus for dramatic purposes. In his own manner, Rameau created a well-rounded work of art which combines in unified manner poetry, action, solo, chorus and orchestra, an accomplishment that is to be reckoned among the greatest achievements in the field of musicodramatic art."

Between 1895 and 1924, Durand in Paris published a complete edition of Rameau's works in eighteen volumes under the editorship of Camille Saint-Saëns and several other prominent French musicians.

Principal works by Jean Philippe Rameau:

OPERA: *Castor et Pollux*; *Dardanus*; *Les Fêtes d'Hébé*; *La Princesse de Navarre*, etc.

Ballets; an entire library of music for the harpsichord; instrumental pieces for various combinations of instruments, etc.

About Jean Philippe Rameau:

Hargreave, Mary. *Some Earlier French Musicians*; Masson, P. M. *L'Opéra de Rameau*; Nef, Karl. *An Outline of the History of Music.*

Important recordings of music by Jean Philippe Rameau:

SELECTIONS FROM OPERA: *Castor et Pollux*, "Ballet suite" (BRUNSWICK-Wolff); "Air de Thélaïre" (COLUMBIA). *Dardanus*, "Rigaudon" (POLYDOR). *Les Fêtes d'Hébé*, "Tambourin," arranged for harpsichord (VICTOR-Landowska).

INSTRUMENTAL: *La Poule*, for harpsichord (GRAMOPHONE-Landowska); *Les Sauvages* for harpsichord (GRAMOPHONE-Landowska); *Theme and variations*, for harpsichord (NA-TIONAL GRAMOPHONIC SOCIETY); *Les Tricotets*, for harpsichord (GRAMOPHONE-Landowska).

Max Reger *1873-1916*

MAX REGER, for a long time a controversial figure in recent German symphonic music, was born in Brand, Bavaria, on March 19, 1873, the son of the village school master. He was born with an amazingly sensitive ear: As a child he frequently aroused wonder and admiration by his ability to name correctly, when blindfolded, any note played on the piano or organ. At one time, a military band passed his home. When it was gone, Max Reger sat at the piano and without hesitation played the march from beginning to end.

His first instruction in music was received from both his father and his mother. Progressing rapidly, he was placed under Adalbert Lindner, who perfected his piano technique and mellowed his musical understanding. It was not long before Reger made appearances at school concerts, exciting considerable enthusiasm for his performances of Beethoven and Chopin. Between 1886 and 1889, he served as organist of the Weiden Catholic Church.

One time, Lindner urged Reger to undertake composition, and Reger—already manifesting his life-long disposition towards profusion—composed a long and complicated overture for a small orchestra. Lindner was so impressed with the result that he sent it to Hugo Riemann, the eminent musicologist. Riemann damned the work with faint praise, found some talent in it but many faults as well, prescribing a rigorous course in Bach and Beethoven for the young student. This criticism dampened Reger's enthusiasms but not his productivity. In the year that followed he produced several songs, a string quartet and a movement of a quintet. These were sent to Hugo Riemann who now showed greater enthusiasm.

By 1890, Riemann decided that Reger was sufficiently talented to warrant acceptance as a pupil. Reger, therefore, went to Sondershausen and lived at Rie-

MAX REGER

mann's home where he underwent a rigorous course in harmony and counterpoint. The works of Bach and Beethoven were studied with painstaking minuteness. This intensive musical training brought Reger a marked artistic development. As a musician, he acquired a mature and profound insight; as a pianist, he attained not only a remarkable technical equipment but a great interpretative capacity as well. Finally, as a composer, he developed his own personal style and idiom. Hugo Riemann found much to commend in Reger's compositions at this time, going so far as to recommend the composer enthusiastically to an English publisher, Augener, Ltd. Augener signed a contract with Reger accepting for publication all works produced during the next seven years. The relationship between Augener and Reger, however, soon became strained. Reger's ponderous style found little favor in England and his music sold badly. Upon the request of Augener to simplify his music, Reger demanded the termination of his contract. It was later reassumed by the German publisher, Schott.

In 1896, musical activity was rudely interrupted when Reger was called to military duty. Sensitive in spirit and body, the privations of military service played havoc with his health. He became seriously ill, and for a while

puzzled the physicians at the hospital as to the nature of his ailment. He was, finally, returned to his father's home. There, for three years, he lived under the scrupulous eye of the house physician. During these years of quiet and rest, Reger was voluminously productive, adding a considerable quantity of songs, organ pieces and chamber works to his already imposing list of works.

In 1901, Reger went to Munich and began to earn his livelihood by conducting and by playing the piano. He achieved considerable success as a concert pianist because of the sensitivity of his piano style and his profound interpretative talent. His engagements were so numerous that he soon overstrained himself, suffering from a stroke of paralysis in 1906. A long rest at Lake Chiem—where he wrote his famous *Introdution, passacaglia and fugue* for two pianos—brought his health back sufficiently to enable him to visit St. Petersburg where, as a conductor and pianist, he was given a royal reception.

In 1907, Reger was appointed music director of the University of Leipzig, and from 1907 until his death he was on the faculty staff of the Leipzig Conservatory. Professorial duties did not interfere with his composition. Violin sonatas, chamber works, symphonic music (including the imposing *Variations and fugue on a theme of J. A. Hiller*), choral works, sonatas, concertos were produced with amazing fertility.

Reger was not a popular composer. The complexity of his technique and the pedantry of his style aroused considerable antagonism and criticism among music critics, and the general public found little appeal in his ponderous works. However, his work did not pass entirely without honorable recognition. In November of 1907, Reger was honored with the title of professor by the King of Saxony. In 1908, the degree of Doctor of Philosophy was conferred on him by the University of Jena. Two years later, the Medical Faculty of Berlin University gave him an honorary doctor's degree.

When the World War began in 1914, Max Reger made an effort to volunteer, but was found physically unfit for military service. He therefore settled in Jena to devote himself to further composition. He died, suddenly, of heart-attack in Leipzig on May 11, 1916.

As a composer, Reger was more note-worthy as an artisan than as an inspired creator. He is, perhaps, one of the most skillful technicians that music has produced. He was, as André Coeuroy pointed out, essentially the skillful work-man, the musical craftsman *par excellence*. He could imitate the style of any composer with astounding cunning. The most complicated forms in music were mere child's play to him. His music, more often than not, is an amazing study in technical acrobatics. "Seated at his work-bench of a musical mechanic, in a shop whose windows were rarely opened to the outside world," wrote André Coeuroy, "he manufactured, like a shoemaker his shoes, fugues and more fugues. He did not wish either to dazzle or impress; he created problems, and found their solutions. He personi-fied abstract music; he was the man of Bach's polyphony, and of old forms brought back to life—toccatas and passacaglias."

Alexander Brent-Smith emphasized the fact that Reger's pedantry was his great fault as a composer. "He says everything that can be said, and he exhausts his hearers long before he has exhausted his subject. Furthermore, he not only says all that is to be said about his subject, but he says all that is to be said about each successive harmony, thus leaving nothing to the imagination. . . . His melodies are choked with notes, and have little chance to live. . . . Whenever he saw a crack in the counterpoint, he stuffed it up with two or three demi-semi-quavers; had a chord only four notes, he added two more; did a melody move in a single line, he instantly doubled it. . . . Thus he stifled his ideas with too many notes, just as some ostentatious jewelers crowd their windows."

Principal works by Max Reger:

ORCHESTRA: *Variations and fugue on a theme of J. A. Hiller*; *Symphonic prelude to a tragedy*; *Lustspiel overture*; *Konzert in alten stil*; *Romantic suite*; *Ballet suite*; *Variations and fugue on a theme of Mozart*; *Eine vaterländische overture*; *Concerto for violin and orchestra*; *Concerto for piano and orchestra*, etc.

CHORAL: *Der evangelische kirchenchor*; Four choral cantatas; Thirty-eight motets; psalms; *Requiem*; *Gesang der Verklärten*; *Die Nonne*, etc.

CHAMBER MUSIC: *String sextet*; *Piano quintet*; *Quintet for clarinet and strings*; Five string quartets; Two piano quartets; *String trio in A-minor*; Two piano trios; serenades for string trio; sonatas for violin and piano; suites for violin and piano; sonatas for violoncello and piano; sonatas for clarinet and piano, etc..

A voluminous library of music for the organ, for the piano (including the *Variations and fugue on a theme of Beethoven*), for two pianos (including the *Introduction, passacaglia and fugue*).

Songs.

About Max Reger:

Bagier, Guido. *Max Reger*; Kallenberg, Siegfried Garibaldi. *Max Reger*; Lindner, Adalbert. *Max Reger: Ein Bild seines Jugendlebens und Kunstlerischen Werdens*; Reger, Elsa. *Mein Leben mit und für Max Reger*; Ungar, Hermann. *Max Reger*.

Monthly Musical Record 46:161 June 1916; *Musical Times* 66:497 June 1925; *Strad* 37:167 June 1926.

Important recordings of music by Max Reger:

ORCHESTRA: Ballet music (GRAMOPHONE); *Konzert in alten stil* (BRUNSWICK); *Variations on a theme of Mozart* (POLYDOR-Busch).

CHAMBER MUSIC: *String trio in A-minor* (GRAMOPHONE); *String quartet in E-flat major*, "Scherzo" (GRAMOPHONE).

CHORAL: *Gloria in Excelsis Deo* (POLYDOR); *Und unser lieben frauen* (MUSICA SACRA).

Karl Reinecke *1824-1910*

KARL HEINRICH CARSTEN REI-NECKE was born in Altona, Denmark, on June 23, 1824. The son of a professional musician, he was brought into contact with music at an early age. At five he began the study of the piano, at eight he made his first essays at composition, and at eleven he made his first public appearance as piano virtuoso. After his debut, he continued the study of music with greater intensity, concentrating especially on the playing of the violin. In early youth, he served a valuable apprenticeship as violinist in orchestras.

At the age of eighteen, he toured Scandinavia as pianist, being especially successful in Copenhagen. By 1843, his music journey had brought him to Leipzig, where once again he turned to the study of music. In Leipzig he performed several of Mendelssohn's works and the piano part of Robert Schumann's *Quintet* in the presence of the respective composers, and it was not long before he became their close friend. In 1844, he continued his tour as virtuoso pianist, settling for two years in Copenhagen in a position as court pianist.

In 1851, he was appointed professor of piano and counterpoint at the Cologne Conservatory. Something of the esteem with which he was held in the eyes of Franz Liszt might be judged by the fact that Reinecke, in this year, was entrusted with the piano instruction of Franz Liszt's daughters.

His first efforts with the baton began in 1854, when he was appointed conductor of the Konzertgesellschaft in Barmen. His concerts enjoyed great popularity, and Reinecke soon acquired a formidable reputation as a conductor. After a short appointment as music director in Breslau in 1859, Reinecke received the musical post which brought him world-wide fame—the conductorship of the Leipzig Gewandhaus Orchestra. At the same time, he became a member of the faculty, in piano and

composition, of the Leipzig Conservatory.

Both as a conductor and teacher, Reinecke became one of the most influential musicians in Leipzig, the very center of its musical activity. People in the streets took off their hats to him when they passed him; there were not many in Leipzig who were unaware of his prominent position in the musical life of the city. When, therefore, the new Leipzig Gewandhaus auditorium was opened, in 1884, Reinecke was honored with a degree from the University. One year later—on the occasion of his twenty-fifth year of musical activity in Leipzig—the city became festive in his honor: his opera, *König Manfred*, was performed at the Opera, and at the Gewandhaus auditorium there took place a concert devoted to his works.

Reinecke's fame in musical history rests more with his work as teacher and conductor than with his creative efforts, although he produced more than two hundred works in every field of musical endeavor. Of his imposing output, only a handful of piano pieces (principally the sonatas) and choral works have survived him. J. A. Fuller-Maitland has written: "It is pretty certain that Reinecke will be remembered. . . not by his operas *König Manfred* or *Der Gouverneur von Tours*, his symphonies, his chamber compositions or even by his *Piano concerto in F-sharp minor*. . . but by certain works he has written for children, such as the pretty cantatas *Schneewittchen* and *Aschenbrödel* . . . and the like, and the many children's songs by which his name is endeared to thousands of small Germans. His works in the larger forms are reproached, and no doubt fairly enough, with poverty of invention and cold classicality, altho he is a master of the ordinary resources of the instruments for which he writes. . . . As an arranger of other men's works he is especially successful."

Karl Reinecke died in Leipzig on March 10, 1910.

Principal works by Karl Reinecke:

OPERA: *König Manfred*; *Auf hohen befehl*; *Der Gouverneur von Tours*; *Ein Abenteuer Händels*.

KARL REINECKE

CHORAL: *Schneewittchen*; *Dornröschen*; *Aschenbrödel*; *Traumfriedel*; *Sommertagsbilder*; *Schlachtlied*; *Festgesang*; *Der Deutsche sang*, etc.

ORCHESTRA: Three symphonies; *Kindersymphonie*; Overtures, *Dame Kobold, Fest, Zur Jubelfeier, Zenobia,* etc.; *Trauermarsch*; *Triumphsmarsch*; *Serenade for strings*; *Reformationsfeier*; Four concertos for piano and orchestra; *Concerto for violin and orchestra*; *Concerto for flute and orchestra*; *Concerto for violoncello and orchestra.*

CHAMBER MUSIC: *Octet* (for wind); *Sextet* (for wind); *Quintet*; Five string quartets; Two piano quartets; *String trio*; Four piano trios; *Trio for piano, oboe and horn*; *Trio for piano, clarinet and horn*; Sonatas for violin and piano; Sonatas for violoncello and piano, etc.

Songs, compositions for the piano, etc.

About Karl Reinecke:

Fuller-Maitland, J. A. *Masters of German Music;* Wasielowski, Wilhelm Joseph von. *Karl Reinecke: Sein Leben, Wirken und Schaffen.*
Musical Observer 26:11 February 1927.

Ottorino Respighi *1879-1936*
(See *Composers Of Today*)

Ernest Reyer *1823-1909*

ERNEST REYER (whose original name was Louis Ernest Étienne Rey) was born in Marseilles on December 1, 1823. His earliest musical education was pursued at the Free School of Music in his native city. In his early years, he showed greater affection than aptitude for his art, and his parents finally decided that it would be wisest to discourage him from adopting music as his life's profession. They therefore sent him in his sixteenth year to Algiers to stay with his uncle, who held a government post in the province of Constantine. Here, however, Reyer continued industriously with his musical occupations, teaching himself from textbooks he had brought with him. He also began composition; one of his works, during this period, was a mass, performed at the cathedral in Algiers. His prolonged stay in Algiers had a profound influence on his artistic development. It was, no doubt, chiefly responsible for his predilection, in later life, for Oriental subjects in his musical composition.

The revolution of 1848 brought Reyer back to Paris. His parents had by this time decided to permit him to follow his musical inclinations, and Reyer plunged deeply into study, principally with his aunt, Louise Farrenc, a composer. His studies completed, he approached composition with a new vitality, producing a work based on an Oriental subject—a symphonic ode, *Le Sélam*, to words by Théophile Gautier. *Le Sélam* was introduced in 1850 at the Théâtre Ventadour but, because it was modeled so closely after Félicien David's *Le Désert,* it failed to make an impression.

It was not until he produced his one-act opera, *Maître Wolfram*, which was produced at the Théâtre Lyrique in 1854 that Reyer began to attract attention. Critics noticed the freshness of his melodic material and the originality of his instrumentation. Berlioz, upon hearing this early work, exclaimed: "God be praised! We have gone out of the kitchen and into the garden. Let us breathe deeply!"

His next important work, a ballet-pantomime, *Sacountala*—which was presented at the Opéra in 1858—increased his prestige. With the first performance of his opera, *La Statue,* at the Théâtre Lyrique in 1861, Reyer's important position in French music was accepted. No less a musician than Georges Bizet considered *La Statue* the most remarkable

ERNEST REYER

opera given in France in twenty years, amazing praise when it is recalled that Gounod's *Faust* had been introduced to Paris two years before this. *La Statue* won for Reyer the decoration of the Legion of Honor.

In 1862, Baden-Baden presented the next of Reyer's operas, *Érostate,* which, because of its German première, Reyer dedicated to the Queen of Prussia. Ten years later, the opera was given a French performance, when it encountered such antagonism because it had been dedicated to the Queen of an enemy country, that it was closed after two presentations.

Between 1865 and 1875, Ernest Reyer devoted himself principally to music criticism, becoming editor of music of the Paris *Journal des Débats.* For this paper, he went to Cairo to attend the première of Verdi's *Aïda,* in 1871. On his return to Paris he became one of the most vigorous and fearless protagonists for such unappreciated or misjudged composers as Berlioz, Wagner, Lalo and Bizet. Many of his more important newspaper articles have been assembled into two books, *Notes de Musique,* published in 1875, and *Quarante Ans de Musique,* published posthumously in 1909.

In 1876, Reyer's important position in French music was confirmed by his appointment to the Institut. Meanwhile, he had been working for ten years on a new opera, *Sigurd,* based on a Nibelungen legend. It was not until 1884 that *Sigurd* received a performance— and not in Paris, but at the Théâtre de la Monnaie in Brussels. The following July, *Sigurd* was produced at Covent Garden, in January of 1885 in Lyons and, finally, in June of 1885 in Paris. The Paris version of *Sigurd* was so sadly handled that in the middle of the performance the composer ran out of the opera house and refused to listen to it.

Sigurd, in the opinion of Julien Tiersot, is full of "color, of movement and—in certain spots—of poetry. The melodic vein here is abundant. . . . It is 'full of ideas'. . . . His songs have a spontaneous force, a grace which is neither effeminate nor affected. And if his orchestra does not have that trans-

parency which one admired in the past, it is colorful, striking and expressive."

The Théâtre de la Monnaie of Brussels likewise presented the first performance of Reyer's last important work, *Salammbô. Salammbô* was a favorite from its first performance, and, when it was introduced to Paris in 1892, found enthusiastic admirers.

During the last years of his life, Reyer led a quiet and retired existence. Serving as a librarian for the Opéra, he lived on the fifth floor of the Opéra house in comparative seclusion. He died in Levandou, Hyères, on January 15, 1909.

"His style," commented Arthur Hervey, "has been described as proceeding from Gluck and Weber, while his admiration for Berlioz and Wagner reveals itself in the richness and variety of his instrumentation. . . . It may be said with truth that Reyer's individuality is not of the most marked, that his melodies sometimes lack distinction, and that his inventive faculty is scarcely equal to his skill in making the most of his materials; but none will contest the true artistic feeling that presides over all his compositions, nor deny him the possession of strongly pronounced convictions."

Principal works by Ernest Reyer:

OPERA: *Maître Wolfram; Sacountala* (ballet); *La Madeleine au désert* (scena); *La Statue; Erostate; Sigurd; Salammbô.*

CHORAL: *Victoire; Le Sélam* (with orchestra); *L'Union des arts; Le Hymne du Rhin; Le Chant du paysan; Choeur des buveurs; Choeur des assiégés.*

Songs.

About Ernest Reyer:

Hervey, Arthur. *Masters in French Music;* Imbert, Hughes. *Nouveaux Profils de Musiciens;* Jullien, Adolphe. *Ernest Reyer;* Tiersot, Julien. *Un Demi-siècle de Musique Française.*

Revue musicale de Lyon 6:436 January 24, 1909.

Important recordings of music by Ernest Reyer:

SELECTIONS FROM OPERA: *Salammbô,* "Airs des Colombes" (POLYDOR). *Sigurd,* "Ouverture" (GRAMOPHONE-Coppola); "Je savais tout" (POLYDOR); "J'ai gardé mon âme ingénue" and "Esprits gardiens" (GRAMOPHONE); "Salut, splendeur du jour" and "O Palais radieux" (GRAMOPHONE).

Josef Rheinberger *1839-1901*

JOSEF GABRIEL RHEINBERGER was born in Vaduz, in the upper Rhine valley, on March 17, 1839, the son of Peter Rheinberger, treasurer to Prince Lichtenstein. While still a child, Rheinberger would listen while his sisters took lessons upon the guitar and in singing; and it soon became apparent that he learned with far greater rapidity than they. His parents decided to include him in this musical instruction. He was first taught the piano. Then, making swift progress, he was sent to Sebastian Pöhly for lessons in theory. Pöhly, who recognized Rheinberger's talent, soon began to teach him the organ—actually inventing a special apparatus with which the organ pedals might be brought within easy reach of the feet of the little boy. Once again, Rheinberger was a receptive pupil, so much so that in his seventh year he was considered sufficiently proficient to be engaged as organist of the parish church.

The Bishop of Chur, hearing of Rheinberger's talent, decided to test the boy himself. He placed the music of a Salve Regina on the organ and asked the boy to play the work by sight, while the Bishop sang the vocal part. Young Rheinberger not only played fluently, but even corrected the Bishop whenever he sang out of tune.

In 1847, Rheinberger composed his first mass, which was performed in the parish church to enthusiastic comment. In the same year, Rheinberger disclosed his extreme intolerance of bad music by burning, on his own initiative, several volumes of organ masses which he found in the organ-loft and which did not meet with his approval.

For two years, Rheinberger studied theory with Philipp Schmutzer in Feldkirch—making the ten mile journey to Feldkirch by foot every week-end. In 1850, his studies with Schmutzer came to an end. He now worked intensively by himself to prepare for entrance examinations to the Munich Conservatory. Between 1851 and 1854, he was a pupil at this famous institution, studying the piano under Emile Leonhard, the organ under Professor Herzog and counterpoint under J. J. Maier.

JOSEF RHEINBERGER

On leaving the Conservatory, Rheinberger became a private pupil of Franz Lachner, at the same time earning his living by giving private lessons. In 1859, Professor Franz Lachner resigned from the faculty of the Munich Conservatory, selecting Rheinberger as his successor. One year later, Rheinberger rose to the position of professor of counterpoint. That year also marked his first publication—a set of four piano pieces.

In 1860, Rheinberger received an appointment as organist of the Court Church St. Michel in Munich. During the next few years, he was also employed as conductor of the Munich Oratorio Society (for which he composed many works for chorus and orchestra) and as solo-repetitor of the Hof-Theatre, where he created something of a furor by playing and transposing at sight a score of Wagner's *Flying Dutchman*. In 1867, when Hans von Bülow founded the Royal School of Music, Rheinberger was chosen professor of counterpoint and organ. In that same year, he was married to Fraülein Franziska Jägerhuber, a talented writer, who was influential in directing him towards great literature, thereby broadening his intellectual background.

. In 1877, Rheinberger was honored with an appointment as Royal chapelmaster. In this office, he composed many ecclesiastical works, including eleven masses, an oratorio and a Stabat Mater. The last years of Rheinberger's life were marked by ill-health, due to incurable lung-trouble which he had contracted in a mountain tour of the Tyrol. He died in Munich on November 25, 1901.

Josef Rheinberger was held in high esteem as a musician and was the recipient of many honors, including a degree from the University of Munich, knighthood of Gregory the Great from Pope Leo XIII, and election to the Academy of Berlin.

He was a sociable person, who frequently maintained that he derived his greatest pleasure from the society of agreeable people. His dinner-table was invariably filled with guests. Rheinberger himself superintended the cooking of every meal served at his home; he was an excellent cook, and frequently prided himself on the fact that his principal instructor in the culinary art had been a chef in the service of Napoleon III.

Before his marriage, he had been a great lover of hunting. His wife, however, being an intense humanitarian, put an end to this pastime. After marriage, Rheinberger frequently indulged in the hobby of histrionics. At one time, it was said, he appeared under an assumed name as Bottom in a production of *A Midsummer night's dream,* at the Royal Theatre in Munich. He was fond of reciting poetry to friends, while accompanying himself on the piano.

He was excessively generous and charitable. Each Christmas he distributed gifts widely to the poor, and he was always responsive to any charitable cause. He was a strict Roman Catholic.

His marriage was an ideally happy one. On the death of his wife, he lived in virtual seclusion, rarely visiting his friends or welcoming them to his home. He would visit his favorite restaurants and would enviously eye any happy couple until they would become embarrassed by his fixed gaze. His last years were unhappy.

Josef Rheinberger was a prolific composer. The list of his works occupies almost a full four-column closely-printed page in Grove's *Dictionary.* Discussing the qualities of this music, Frederick Niecks wrote: "Thoroughness of work-

manship is a feature which distinguished Rheinberger's productions. . . . And this quality of thoroughness is combined with another, not less characteristic of the artist and his work—namely, unpretentiousness. . . . Rheinberger is a master of his craft and yet never makes a bravado of his skill. The matter, the intellectual and emotional substance of his compositions, is of the nature of his workmanship—unpretentious. We may describe it as simple, and even as homely. . . . For him, the classic temperament predominates over the romantic. . . . Moreover, his romanticism differs . . . . in its being neither violent, extravagant, voluptuous, fantastic, nor transcendentally sentimental. . . . His art is deeply-rooted in folk-music; even in his grandest and most scholastic compositions the soil from which it sprang is easily discernible. Health, simplicity and clearness pervade everything he has written."

J. A. Fuller-Maitland pointed out that "the department of his work in which the highest level has been maintained thruout his career is beyond question that of organ composition. The whole series of organ sonatas, covering as they do a period of over twenty years, has a richness of coloring, a mastery of effect, and a constant flow of beautiful ideas that are by no means found in his other works."

As a teacher, Rheinberger was known to have been a very strict disciplinarian and pedant who subjected his students to a comprehensive and thoro technical training. He was frequently laughingly nicknamed by his pupils, "Herr Fugen-Seppel."

Principal works by Josef Rheinberger:
OPERA: *Die sieben raben; Die arme Heinrich; Das Zauberwort; Türmers töchterlein,* etc.

ORCHESTRA: *Wallenstein symphony; Florentiner symphony; Academic overture; Demetrius overture: Concerto for piano and orchestra;* Concertos for organ and orchestra.

CHORAL: *Toggenburg; Die todte braut; Johannisnacht; Die Rosen von Hildesheim; Montfort; Jairus' tochter; Christophorus; Der Stern von Bethlehem;* requiems; masses; passions; motets; hymns, etc.

CHAMBER MUSIC: *Nonet* (for wind and strings); *Sextet* (for wind); *String quintet; Piano quintet;* Two string quartets; *Piano* quartet; *Variations for string quartet*; Sonatas for violin and piano, etc.

Works for the organ, for the piano, etc.

About Josef Rheinberger:

Fuller-Maitland, J. A. *Masters of German Music*; Grace, Harvey. *The Organ Works of Rheinberger*; Kroyer, Theodor. *Josef Rheinberger*.

Monthly Musical Record 12:193 September 1882; *Musical Times* 67:812 September 1926.

Henry Joseph Rigel *1741-1799*

HENRY JOSEPH RIGEL (original-ly Riegel) was born at Wertheim on February 9, in 1741. After conclud-ing preliminary studies in music in his native city, he came to Mannheim to become a pupil of Franz Xaver Richter in harmony and counterpoint. His studies were brought to a conclusion in Stuttgart under Niccolò Jommelli.

Equipped with a letter of introduction from his former master, Richter, Rigel went to Paris in 1768. In a short while, he acquired a considerable reputation as a performer on the clavecin and as a teacher. He was held in high esteem by the foremost musicians in Paris of the time; no one less than Grétry, in the third volume of his *Essais sur la Musique,* referred to Rigel as an "expert master," commenting also upon the "excellence of his method."

Rigel likewise made his mark as a composer. On May 25, 1775, his oratorio, *La Sortie d'Egypte* was intro-duced at the Concert Spirituel, and was so highly esteemed by musicians thruout Paris that Rigel's fame as a composer was assured. "When one has composed a work like the oratorio *La Sortie d'Égypte,*" said Gluck, "one has composed a formidable work!" Three years later, two comic operas—*Le Savetier et le financier* and *Le Départ des matelots*—were presented at the Opéra Comique and the Comédie Italienne respectively. While certain critics—more in sympathy with the Italian standards of opera—found the music "pretentious," there was a chorus of praise for the originality and fresh-ness of the composer's style. Be-tween 1782 and 1786, Rigel directed a series of his own symphonies at the Concert Spirituel, and these works be-came so popular that the secure position of their composer in the French music of the time was assured. As a matter of fact, when Gluck left Paris, he said: "I am going—but I leave you Rigel."

In 1783, Rigel was appointed teacher in the Royal School of Singing in Paris. For more than ten years he taught there three times a week, receiving a liberal salary, commensurate with his high posi-tion as a musician. In 1795, when the Paris Conservatory was opened, he was named an Inspecteur together with Gossec and Cherubini. He maintained his position with the Conservatory until his death.

Henry Joseph Rigel died in Paris in May of 1799. He had composed in a variety of forms, including comic operas, oratorios, chamber-works and sym-phonies. It is generally conceded that he was artistically more successful in oratorios and instrumental music than in the opera.

In the *Lexikon der tonkünstler* of Gerber, published in 1790, we read that Rigel's works were generally character-ized by a spontaneity of ideas and purity of harmonic writing.

"Rigel is a man who tasted each style and did not devote himself exclusively to any one," wrote Georges de Saint-Fox. "His music is facile, pure, very exquisite and very pretty; with a sure art for modulation. What Rigel lacked from the point of view of melodic inven-tion he replaced with other qualities."

Rigel was one of the first composers to utilize the piano in instrumental ensemble music.

Principal works by Henry Joseph Rigel:

OPERA: *Le Savetier et le financier; Le Départ des matelots; Rosanie; Le Bon fer-mier; Blanche et Vermeille; Lucas; Les Amours du Gros-Caillou; L'Entrée du seig-neur; Aline et Dupré; Alix de Beaucaire; Pauline et Henri.*

CHORAL: *La Sortie l'Égypte; Jepthé; La Prise de Jericho; motets; Regina Coeli,* etc.

CHAMBER MUSIC: Six symphonies for cham-ber orchestra; *String quintet; Piano quartet;* sonatas for violin and piano.

About Henry Joseph Rigel:

La Revue Musicale 5:192 June 1924.

Nicholas Rimsky-Korsakoff
1844-1908

NICHOLAS ANDREIEVICH RIM-SKY-KORSAKOFF, acknowledged dean of the school of Russian composers known as the "Russian-five," was born in Tikhvin, in the government of Novgorod, on March 18, 1844.

He showed early signs of talent. "I was not fully two years old," he wrote in his autobiography, "when I clearly distinguished all the tunes that my mother sang to me. Later, when three or four years of age, I beat a toy drum in perfect time, while my father played the piano. Often my father would suddenly change the tempo and rhythm on purpose, and I at once followed suit. Soon afterwards, I began to sing quite correctly whatever my father played, and often I sang along with him. Later on, I myself began to pick out on the piano the pieces and accompaniments I had heard him perform and, having learned the names of the notes, I could, from an adjoining room, recognize and name any note of the piano." When he was six years old, he was given his first piano lessons, making rapid progress. At eight, he showed an unusual love for the music of Glinka's *A Life for the tsar*. One year after this, though entirely innocent of theoretical knowledge, he began composition.

Until his twelfth year, Rimsky-Korsakoff lived in his native city. There he had an opportunity to hear the folk-songs of peasants and to listen to the folklore of the Slavonic people, both of which made a deep impression upon his plastic mind. At the same time, he was vitally influenced by the music of a band of Jewish musicians, employed on his father's estate, who frequently played Russian folk-songs. His love for native Russian music, therefore, was deeply embedded in him from earliest childhood.

His aristocratic family, while realizing that he was uniquely talented in the direction of music, refused to permit him to enter the musical profession. Instead, they directed him towards a naval career. In 1856, therefore, Rimsky-Korsakoff was entered in the Naval College in St. Petersburg where he remained for six years.

His studies at the Naval College did not completely obliterate his musical interests; in his spare hours, he took lessons on the piano and on the violoncello. In 1861, Rimsky-Korsakoff became a friend of Balakirev, the Russian composer, and in their conversations on music, Rimsky-Korsakoff's one-time passion for it was again aroused. Balakirev introduced Rimsky-Korsakoff to César Cui, Borodin and Moussorgsky. These young musicians succeeded in transferring their ideals and enthusiasms for an indigenous Russian music to Rimsky-Korsakoff, who now knew that he must henceforth devote a great part of his life to serious musical activity.[1]

Rimsky-Korsakoff was sent abroad by his parents to complete his naval studies; he carried away with him his newly-awakened ambition to become a serious musician. During three years of cruising, Rimsky-Korsakoff composed his first symphony. In 1865, Balakirev introduced this symphony at the concerts of the Free School of Music in St. Petersburg where it aroused great praise.

The success of his symphony encouraged Rimsky-Korsakoff to continue his musical study and to devote more conscientious effort to his composition. A symphonic poem, *Sadko* (not to be confused with his opera of the same name which was produced at a later date), and an opera, *The Maid of Pskov*, emphasized his growing powers as a composer. In 1871, Rimsky-Korsakoff was appointed professor of composition and instrumentation at the St. Petersburg Conservatory; two years later, he definitely accepted music as his life profession by retiring from the Navy.

During the next three decades, Rimsky-Korsakoff's influence was felt in many directions. As a professor at the Conservatory, he directly influenced an entire generation of Russian composers in St. Petersburg. Between 1873 and 1884, he served—upon appointment by the Grand Duke Constantin Nicholaevitch—as the inspector of the naval bands; from 1874 to 1881, he was conductor of the Free School concerts, and from 1886 to 1900 he directed the Russian Symphony Concerts in St. Peters-

---

[1] For a discussion of the "Russian Five" see sketch of Balakirev.

NICHOLAS RIMSKY-KORSAKOFF

burg. While he was never acknowl-edged a great interpreter with the baton, his importance as a conductor rested in the fact that he was a vigorous pro-ponent for the younger Russian com-posers, a forceful instrument in bringing the most important Russian music of this period to the attention of the mu-sic public.

Notwithstanding his activity as a teacher and conductor, he did not neglect creative work. Beginning with *A Night in May*, on a text by Gogol—presented in St. Petersburg in 1878—he produced a long series of distinguished operas. *The Snow maiden*, his first truly per-sonal expression as an operatic com-poser, came in 1882. *The Snow maiden* was followed by *Sadko* (1895), *Mozart and Salieri* (1898) and the *Tale of Tsar Saltana* (1899). At this same time, Rimsky-Korsakoff was likewise indus-trious in producing symphonic music, creating the *Capriccio on Spanish themes* in 1887, the *Russian Easter overture* in 1888 and, most famous of all, the *Scheherezade* towards the close of 1888.

In 1905, Rimsky-Korsakoff published a letter in *Russ* in which he complained vigorously about the supervision by the police to which the St. Petersburg Con-servatory was subjected. As punish-ment for his rebellion, Rimsky-Korsa-koff was dismissed from the faculty. There followed a wave of indignation and resentment against this perfunctory dismissal of one who was unquestionably among the leading musicians in Russia. Such professors as Alexander Glazunov and Liadov peremptorily resigned from their posts. By the autumn of that same year, it was officially decided to reor-ganize the Conservatory completely. With the selection of Glazunov as direc-tor of the institution, Rimsky-Korsakoff was reappointed as professor of com-position and instrumentation.

He held this position until his death, which took place at St. Petersburg on June 21, 1908. He died after a third attack of angina pectoris. Glazunov, who was at his death-bed, said that Rimsky-Korsakoff's last regret was that he was unable to finish his course at the Conservatory.

Among Rimsky-Korsakoff's pupils were numbered such eminent Russian composers as Glazunov, Arensky, Liadov, Ippolitov-Ivanov and Gretchan-inoff.

Rimsky-Korsakoff was tall in stature, with narrow stooping shoulders, a chest that was flat, and a physical frame that suggested delicacy. His eyes, small and expressive, possessed an irrepressible ap-peal. "His long, brown beard," wrote Rosa Newmarch, "his spectacles and the natural gravity of his demeanor, gave him a slightly severe and pedagogic air. Where, I wondered, did he keep hidden away the rich stores of exquisite fancy and dainty humor that brightened every page of the *Snow maiden*?. . . . He was one of the delightful exceptions to those cosmopolitan, expansive and emotional and sometimes frothy Russians who give such false impressions of the national character. . . . Each time I saw Rimsky-Korsakoff, I was more and more struck by his simplicity and dignified reserve."

His foremost qualities as a man were his sympathy and good-humor; it was these qualities that made him the ideal teacher. He was a profound lover of Nature, and a man of profound intellect. His favorite composers were Bach, Mozart, Chopin and Schumann, but his tastes were sufficiently versatile to in-clude the waltzes of Johann Strauss.

Platon Brounoff has discovered four qualities in the music of Rimsky-Korsakoff: "His melodies are of the old

Russian style, entirely original in rhythm and character; his harmony is brilliant and daring, in which he uses the old Greek scales; he has an extraordinary talent for instrumentation—dazzling combinations of colors, strong, radiant and brilliant, and at the same time, transparent and clear; finally, qualities which you meet so seldom in the works of other Russian composers—namely, sunshine and warmth."

Commenting upon Rimsky-Korsakoff's operas, H. C. Colles wrote (Oxford History of Music) that they represent the "turning away from the naturalism of the historic drama [Moussorgsky's Boris] to the symbolism of the pictorial stage, of which the ballet is the ideal representation. Vocal melody was not Rimsky-Korsakoff's strong point as it was Tschaikovsky's. Rather the keen-edged instrumental phrase in appropriate coloring of violin, trumpet or oboe, the counterpart of gesture, the incisive rhythm, and the languorous arabesque were the groundwork of his inspiration. . . . In the main. . . if we say that it was Rimsky-Korsakoff who gave form and consistency to the Russian opera, we must also say that it was the Russian preoccupation with the ballet which imbued Rimsky-Korsakoff with a distinctive sense of those qualities."

"By his resolve to make a thorough study of the theoretical aspect of music, with which his comrades' acquaintance was far from exhaustive," wrote Montagu-Nathan, "he was eventually able to supplement and even to eclipse the efforts of César Cui in upholding the banner of nationalism against the onslaughts of a very determined opposition. . . . He proved that nationalism was not, as alleged, a mere cloak for technical ignorance, and in the course of time he gave the world a treasury of nationalistic musical art, and an army of pupils each of whom was able to reflect no little glory upon the master."

Rimsky-Korsakoff was the author of a remarkable book on instrumentation, and a charming autobiography. He also orchestrated important works of his compatriots, including Dargomijsky's The Stone-guest, a part of Borodin's Prince Igor, and Moussorgsky's Boris Godounoff and Khovanstchina.

Principal works by Nicholas Rimsky-Korsakoff:

OPERA: The Maid of Pskov; A Night in May; The Snow maiden; Mlada; Christmas Eve; Sadko; Mozart and Salieri; The Tsar's bride; The Tale of Tsar Saltana; Servilia; Kotscheï the immortal; Kitezh; The Golden cockerel.

ORCHESTRA: First symphony; Antar symphony; Symphony in C-minor; Sinfonietta on Russian themes; Overture on Russian themes; Russian Easter overture; Serbian fantasy; A Tale; Capriccio on Spanish themes; Scheherezade; Concerto for piano and orchestra; Fantasia on Russian themes (for violin and orchestra).

CHORAL: Slava; Two cantatas; Fragment from Homer; Four variations and fughetta (for female quartet); Two mixed choruses; 15 Russian folk songs; trios, etc.

CHAMBER MUSIC: String sextet; Quintet (for piano, flute, clarinet, horn and bassoon); String quartet.
Songs, works for the piano, etc.

About Nicholas Rimsky-Korsakoff:

Markevitch, Igor. Rimsky-Korsakoff; Montagu-Nathan, Montagu. Rimsky-Korsakoff; Rimsky-Korsakoff, Nicholas. My Musical Life; Pals, N. van Gilse van der. Rimsky-Korsakoff Opernschaffen nebst skisse über Leben und Wirken.

Important recordings of music by Nicholas Rimsky-Korsakoff:

SELECTIONS FROM OPERA: The Golden cockerel, orchestral suite arranged by Rimsky-Korsakoff (VICTOR-Coates). The Maid of Pskov, "Hunt and storm music" (VICTOR-Coates). A Night in May, "Overture" (VICTOR-Coates); "Sleep, my beauty" (GRAMOPHONE). Mlada, "Cortege des nobles" (VICTOR-Coates). Sadko, "Song of the Viking guest" (VICTOR-Chaliapin); "Song of India" (COLUMBIA-Tauber); "Berceuse" (VICTOR-Koshetz). The Snow maiden, "Full of wonders" (VICTOR); "Dance of the tumblers" (VICTOR-Coates). Tale of Tsar Saltana, "The Flight of the bumblebee" (COLUMBIA-Harty), etc.

ORCHESTRA: Antar symphony (VICTOR-Coppola); Scheherezade (VICTOR-Stokowski); Capriccio on Spanish themes (VICTOR-Fielder); Russian Easter overture (VICTOR-Stokowski).

Joseph Rode   1774-1830

JACQUES PIERRE JOSEPH RODE was born in Bordeaux on February 16, 1774. At the age of four he began the study of the violin under local teachers. He came to Paris in 1778 where a horn player heard him perform and was so impressed that he gave the boy a letter of introduction to the great violinist,

Viotti. Viotti gave Rode an audition, after which he immediately accepted him as a pupil. After two years of intensive study, Rode made his formal debut at the Théâtre de Monsieur, playing the Viotti thirteenth concerto.

Shortly after his debut, Rode was appointed leader of the second violins in the band of Théâtre Feydeau. He retained this position for four years, appearing occasionally as soloist. Then, in 1794, he made a tour of Holland and Germany, achieving great personal success. Embarking at Hamburg for Bordeaux, Rode was brought in a violent storm to England, where he made one appearance. Finally, the journey came to a close, and returning to Paris he was appointed principal professor of violin at the newly-founded Conservatory. At the same time, he held the position of solo violin at the Opéra. Rode, however, was too restless by temperament to remain imprisoned in any permanent post; one day, he resigned peremptorily and left for a Spanish tour.

In 1800, he was back in Paris, where he was honored by an appointment as solo violinist to Napoleon. He was now at the height of his fame, and at each of his public appearances he was cheered. "The more I heard of him," wrote Ludwig Spohr, "the more I admired his playing. Indeed, I do not hesitate for a moment to place his style. . . above that of my own master, Eck, and I did my utmost to master his style by a most careful study of same."

In 1803, in the company of the popular French composer Boieldieu, Rode toured the North German towns, finally extending his journey until he reached St. Petersburg, Russia. Here he settled, filling the post of solo violinist to Tsar Alexander, at a salary of more than $3,500 a year. For five years, Rode remained in Russia, working at a feverish pace. Then his health deteriorated. He returned to France with the hope of recovering his lost vitality and strength. This he succeeded in doing to a great extent, sufficient to enable him to undertake extensive tours in Switzerland, Germany and Austria. In Vienna, Rode met Beethoven, and the master was so moved by Rode's violin playing that he composed the Sonata in G (Opus

JOSEPH RODE

96) for him. In 1814, Rode settled in Berlin, where he was married. There he became acquainted with Felix Mendelssohn, then a child-prodigy.

After 1814, Rode's public appearances became few and far between, primarily because his technique had degenerated noticeably. He retired to Bordeaux where he bought a country home, and enjoyed the peace and serenity of solitude.

Unfortunately, in 1828, a few ill-advised friends urged him to emerge from his retirement and give a concert in Paris. The concert was such a fiasco that it brought laughter and ridicule upon Rode. Rode was severely affected by his appalling failure and brooded over the disgrace until his health gave way. For the next two years, he was a sick and broken man. He died at his chateau in Bordeaux on November 25, 1830.

Rode's principal works are for the violin, including ten concertos and twenty-four caprices. His fame, however, rests principally with his *Concerto in A-minor*, which appears in the repertoire of the concert violinist, and his twenty-four caprices, a valuable study book for the violinist.

Of the *Concerto in A-minor*, Alexander Brent-Smith has written: "It is remarkable in many ways. Written in an age which we, at this distance, regard dominated by Mozart, the Concerto, despite its many styles, shows no traces of Mozart's influence. . . . That the concerto is ill-knit, that it is a conglomeration of styles, that it has no intellectual development, is obvious criticism. But that it has endured and that it has very real beauties and freshness entitle it to our occasional release from the strings of students."

"Seen thru the late eighteenth century glasses," wrote I. M. Somerville of this concerto, "this is an attractive work, the first movement being noble and pathetic in feeling. . . . The slow movement, it must be confessed, is rather dull and gives the impression that not much trouble was taken with it. . . . The Rondo . . . is racy, compact and tuneful."

Arthur Pougin has commented upon Rode's caprices as follows: "[They] are truly model works in this form, and remain one of the best excercises for our young violinists. . . . [Most of them] are true pieces of style, with an inspiration that is sometimes melancholy and elegiac, sometimes ardent and fiery, sometimes warm and passionate."

Principal works by Joseph Rode:

ORCHESTRA: Ten concertos for violin and orchestra.

CHAMBER MUSIC: Five sets of string quartets; Three books of duos for two violins, etc.

VIOLIN: Twenty-four caprices; Seven sets of variations, etc.

About Joseph Rode:

Pougin, Arthur. *Notice sur Rode.* *Strad* 38:241 September 1927.

Gioacchino Rossini *1792-1868*

"He gave me the impression of being. . . . the most truly great and admirable man whom I ever met in the world of art."
—RICHARD WAGNER

GIOACCHINO ANTONIO ROSSINI, who was born in Pesaro, Italy, on February 29, 1792 was the son of the town trumpeter. Father Rossini, inspired with republican ideals by Napoleon's invasion of Pesaro, lost his municipal position while Gioacchino was still a child and—after a short period of incarceration—earned his living by traveling near the vicinity of Bologna as an itinerant musician. During this period of movement, he entrusted his son to the care of Gioacchino's aunt and grandmother.

In 1804, the Rossinis settled in Bologna. They were now able to concentrate upon Gioacchino's education. He had already disclosed unmistakable signs of genius. As a child, he possessed a beautiful soprano voice, and at the age of seven he made his debut in Bologna in an opera by Paër. By his twelfth birthday, he had not only undertaken composition (producing a great number of songs, duets and operatic arias) but had also learned to play the cembalo, horn and the viola with considerable competence.

As a result, Gioacchino was placed in the Liceo Musicale in Bologna, where his master, Mattei, gave him a comprehensive technical training. The rigorous schooling was not much to Rossini's taste, who found considerable more satisfaction in studying the scores of Haydn and Mozart by himself. However, he was an excellent pupil. In 1808, he was commissioned by the school authorities to compose a cantata on the occasion of the annual award of prizes.

In 1810, Rossini left the Liceo. After a few months of work as accompanist and teacher, he received a commission from Venice to compose a one-act opera. *La Cambiale di matrimonio* was successful, bringing its composer several more commissions to prepare other one-act operas.

Success came to Rossini almost at the dawn of his career. In 1813, his opera, *Tancredi,* was given its first performance in Venice—the first of Rossini's serious operas, or *opera seria.* The popularity of *Tancredi* spread like a contagious disease. All of Venice sang its arias; it is said that at a law court the public was ordered by the judge to stop humming them. Within four years, the opera encircled virtually half the world, greeted everywhere with the pleasure and enthusiasm which the Venetians first accorded it.

Only two and a half months after the emergence of *Tancredi,* Rossini produced a second great success, this time a comic opera, *L'Italiana in Algeri.* That Rossini had been able, within the space of less than three months, to produce two remarkable operas, and in contrary styles, so aroused the admiration of Venetians that Rossini immediately became the composer of the hour. The audiences, weary of pompous and stereotyped operas to which they had until now been subjected, reacted spontaneously to the exuberance and youth of Rossini's melodies, to the charm of his vocal ornamentations, and to his supple dexterity in composing nimble music.

In 1815, Rossini met the celebrated operatic impresario, Barbaja. Barbaja, realizing Rossini's enormous talent, urged the composer to come to Naples and assume the directorship of two operatic theatres there, and to compose one opera a year for each house. The first opera which Rossini composed for Naples, *Elisabetta,* blazed new operatic trails: It was the first opera which dispensed with accompaniments of recitatives by the cembalo, utilizing, instead, the full orchestra; it was also the first opera in which the singers were not permitted to indulge in their customary improvisations but were compelled to sing only those notes which Rossini had put down in the score.

Permitted by a flexible contract to take periodic vacations, Rossini went to Rome in November of 1815. In thirteen days' time, he composed for the Argentina Theatre in Rome the opera which made him immortal—the world-famous *Il Barbier di Siviglia.* Its first performance on February 5, 1816—under the title of *Almaviva*—was a failure, due principally to the fact that an opera on a subject similar to one formerly used by Rome's idol, Paisiello, could never hope to succeed. The failure, however, was only temporary. On its second performance the opera was cheered. It has ever since remained one of the most famous operas in the repertoire.

Rossini's popularity in Italy was now at a peak. Though the demand for his operas was enormous, his fertility was such that he was easily able to supply this prodigious demand. In a little more than five years, he composed sixteen operas, performed in Naples, Milan, Rome and Venice. The most famous of these included *La Cenerentola* (1817),

La Gazza ladra (1817), *Mosè* (1818) and *Zelmira* (1822).

In 1822, Barbaja, who had taken over the direction of Kärthnerthor Theater in Vienna, invited Rossini to the Austrian capital to help present *Zelmira.* For the first time in his life, Rossini crossed the border of Italy. In Vienna, he immediately became an idol. Altho there were some eminent musicians, like Karl Maria von Weber, who felt that Rossini, with his superficial art and lightness of touch was debasing the musical art, the music public was at his feet. In Vienna, Rossini visited Beethoven, and much to his credit, Rossini recognized the irony of fate that caused the composer of the *Eroica symphony* to live in penury and loneliness while he, Rossini, was a pampered pet of the music world, enjoying wealth and adulation. Rossini, as a matter of fact, attempted to raise a subscription for Beethoven, but it fell thru, due to the apathy of the Viennese music public to such a venture.

After returning to Italy where his latest opera, *Semiramide,* was presented in Venice (1823), Rossini once again took to travel. This time, he went to London, once again to be the object of adulation. From London, Rossini went to Paris, where—receiving an appointment as director of the Théâtre Italien at a munificent salary—he settled permanently. In 1826, Rossini retired from his directorial post and was given the honorary position of Composer to His Majesty, and Inspector General of Singing at an annual salary of twenty thousand francs.

On August 3, 1829, Rossini's last opera, *William Tell,* was first performed at the Opéra in Paris. Like its celebrated predecessor, *Il Barbier di Siviglia,* *William Tell* was not successful at first, though it achieved the respectable total of five hundred performances. The victim of a poor libretto, *William Tell* failed to exert that powerful appeal over its audiences that Rossini's previous operas had attained. It was many years before the work was acclaimed a characteristic Rossini masterpiece.

Rossini was now thirty-seven years old, probably the most famous operatic com-

GIOACCHINO ROSSINI

poser of his time, the creator of several masterpieces. His operatic style was continually disclosing new richness and depth; *William Tell* showed the growing powers of a great composer. It is, therefore, one of the inexplicable mysteries in musical history that, altho Rossini was to live for almost forty years after the composition of *William Tell,* he never again composed a work for the operatic stage. As a matter of fact, except for the *Stabat Mater* which came ten years after *William Tell,* and the *Petite messe solennelle,* which he composed towards the end of his life (together with several smaller pieces) Rossini's pen remained virtually idle.

For this amazing phenomenon many explanations have been offered. There are some to say that the failure of *William Tell*—as well as the rise of a rival, Meyerbeer, to great popularity— embittered Rossini so greatly that he swore never again to compose an opera. There are others to explain that his earlier productivity had sapped his energies, that—ill and tired—he was unable to devote himself to the hard work of composition. Still others say that, indolent by temperament, Rossini—now wealthy and comfortable—had no further incentive for composition. Rossini's own explanation (one cannot accept it too seriously!) was: "One more success would have added nothing to my glory, whilst a failure might tarnish it." In any case, musical history can offer no parallel of a composer who achieved greatness by his thirty-seventh birthday, and then, for the next forty years, went into almost complete retirement.

The last forty years of his life, Rossini spent partly in Paris and partly in Italy. Ill-health began to trouble him in 1836, but, at first, did not interfere with his capacity to enjoy life. By 1848, his health had degenerated so markedly that, in Florence, he suffered continual neurasthenia, unable to eat, sleep or enjoy tranquility. Returning to Paris for medical treatment, Rossini recovered partially. However, his ailment was chronic. After a short illness, he passed away in his villa in Passy, on November 13, 1868. It is curious to note that Rossini, who thruout his entire life had been superstitious, should have died on Friday the thirteenth.

Rossini was buried in Père Lachaise in Paris. Nineteen years after his burial, the Italian government removed his remains to Sante Croce church in Florence.

Rossini's personality is familiar to music lovers—his scintillating wit, his colossal laziness, his love of life and luxury. He was an epicure who took delight in preparing his own dishes. "I would rather be a sausage maker than a composer," he once commented. Luxury, comfort, adulation he found necessary to happiness; and he knew how to live fully and completely.

His bon mots are familiar, but only one or two need be mentioned as characteristic examples. When *William Tell* was given in a truncated form at the Opéra, the manager, meeting Rossini one day, told the composer that the second act would be performed that evening. "What, all of it?" Rossini asked with mock surprise. At another occasion, a young composer came to Rossini to play for him two original pieces. Rossini interrupted the first piece in the middle, and said acidly: "Indeed, I like the other one better."

Rossini loved long walks in the Bois de Boulogne. When he returned from these walks he would take off his wig, wrap a towel around his head and select the wig most appropriate for the activities of the evening. He was a very orderly man both in his dress and in his habits. His intellect was not wide. He was completely ignorant of politics, science or the other arts. He was excessively superstitious.

Rossini knew only too well his own strength and limitations as a composer. He knew, for example, that his musical facility made it possible for him to produce an abundance of music with spontaneous outpouring. "Give me a laundry list," he once said, "and I will set it to music." "He could, and did, compose music under any conditions," we are informed by Francis Toye, "amidst the chatter of friends . . . out fishing, or in bed." His abundance of ideas was such that a long-familiar anecdote speaks of the time when Rossini was composing in bed; a page of his manuscript fell to the floor; rather than go to the trouble of getting out of bed he composed the page over again.

Rossini, however, recognized the fact that he was altogether incapable of profundity or depth. "The German critics wish that I compose like Haydn or Mozart," he said after his visit to Vienna. "But if I took all the pains in the world, I should still be a wretched Haydn or Mozart. So I prefer to remain a Rossini. Whatever that may be, it is something, and at least I am not a bad Rossini."

Rossini's favorite composer was Mozart, whose works he adored.

As a composer Rossini's greatest talent lies in his deft touch, in his ability to produce volumes of sparkling, effervescent music that bubbles like champagne, and is often as intoxicating. There have been many critics, in his time and since, who have vigorously criticized Rossini's music as being so much surface veneer. Ingres, the painter, referred to Rossini's operas as "the works of a dishonest musician." Karl Maria von Weber held the opinion that with Rossini "the decay of music began." Many critics, too, have found fault with Rossini's simplicity in harmonizations and technical construction. To such accusations, however, one might well say what Grétry once levelled at similar onslaughts against his own music: "You know

that in the land of the sun one prefers to go nude."

Francis Toye is more than jusified in maintaining that Rossini's music "will never appeal greatly to those who attach supreme value to profundity of feeling or intellect. . . . Rossini was clear-headed, shrewd, urbane, but in no way intellectual." However, Francis Toye goes to considerable pains to explain that the world of music has room not only for Beethoven's profundity but for Rossini's gaiety and charm as well. In his own field—the production of music that chuckles and sparkles with each bar —Rossini was truly incomparable.

R. A. Streatfeild has clearly explained Rossini's historic importance: "The invention of the cabaletta, or quick movement, following the cavantina, or slow movement, must be ascribed to him, an innovation which affected the form of opera, German and French, as well as Italian, thruout the century. Even more important was the change which he introduced in the manner of singing . . . florid music. Before his day, singers had been accustomed to introduce cadenzas of their own, to a great extent when they liked. Rossini insisted upon their singing nothing but what was set down for them." Mr. Streatfeild might have added, what was mentioned earlier in the sketch, that Rossini was also the first to substitute the orchestra for the cembalo in accompanying the *secco recitativo*. Rossini also amplified the orchestra of his day, persistently introducing new instruments for the expression of new colors and effects.

Principal works by Gioacchino Rossini:

OPERA: *Tancredi*; *L'Italiana in Algeri*; *Elisabetta*; *Il Barbier di Siviglia*; *Otello*; *La Cenerentola*; *La Gazza ladra*; *Mosè*; *Zelmira*; *Semiramide*; *William Tell*, etc.

CHORAL: *Stabat Mater*; *Petite messe solennelle*; *Partenope*; *La Riconoscenza*; *Il Vero omaggio*; *L'Augurio felice*; *La Sacra alleanza*; *Il Bardo*; *Il Ritorno*; *I Pastori*; *Il Serto votivo*, etc.

Songs, canzonets, piano pieces, etc.

About Gioacchino Rossini:

Azavedo, A. *Gioacchino Rossini: Sa Vie et ses Oeuvres*; Beyle, Marie Henri (Stendhal). *Memoir of Rossini*; Curzon, Henri de. *Rossini*; Derwent, Lord. *Rossini—and Some Forgotten Nightingales*; Edwards, H. S. *Rossini's*

Life; Pougin, Arthur. *Rossini: Notes, impressions, Souvenirs, Commenaries*; Toye, Francis. *Rossini: A Study in tragi-Comedy.*

Important recordings of music by Gioacchino Rossini:

OPERA: *The Barber of Seville,* complete (COLUMBIA-La Scala).

SELECTIONS FROM OPERA: *La Cenerentola,* "Overture" (COLUMBIA); "Cavantina" (PARLAPHONE); "Aria and Rondo finale" (PARLAPHONE-Supervia). *La Gazza ladra,* "Overture" (BRUNSWICK-Furtwängler). *William Tell,* "Overture" (COLUMBIA-Beecham); "Coro dell'Imeneo" and "Tirolese" (COLUMBIA); "Cavantina" (COLUMBIA); "Ah, Mathilde," and "Troncar suoi di quell'empio" (GRAMOPHONE). *L'Italiana in Algeri,* "Overture" (PARLAPHONE); "Oh, che muso" (PARLAPHONE); "Per lui che adoro" (PARLAPHONE); "Amici in ogni evento" (PARLAPHONE-Supervia). *Semiramide,* "Overture" (COLUMBIA); "Bel raggio" (ODEON). *Tancredi,* "Overture" (VICTOR).

CHORAL: *Stabat Mater,* "Cuius animam" (GRAMOPHONE-Gigli); "Pro peccatis" (VICTOR-Journet); "Stabat Mater, Istud Agas" (GRAMOPHONE); "Inflammatus" (GRAMOPHONE).

ORCHESTRA: *Rossiniana,* arrangement for orchestra of famous Rossini piano pieces by Ottorino Respighi (COLUMBIA-Beecham).

Anton Rubinstein *1829-1894*

ANTON GREGOROVICH RUBINSTEIN, one of the great pianists of all time and a composer of distinction, was born in Volhynia, Russia, on November 28, 1829. His father, a manufacturer, left the village shortly after the birth of his son, establishing his family in Moscow. There, Anton Rubinstein's mother began to teach the boy the piano. He learned his exercises so rapidly that it was not long before the child outdistanced his teacher. He was then placed under the guidance of Villoing, a celebrated piano teacher in Moscow.

On July 11, 1839, Anton Rubinstein made his debut in Moscow, playing a movement from a Hummel concerto. "He certainly has the soul of an artist and the feeling for the beautiful," commented the Moscow *Galatea* the following morning, "and there lies with him so much musical talent that in time, after the complete perfecting and developing of it, the young artist will undoubtedly be able to procure himself

an honorable rank among European celebrities."

The success of that initial concert tempted Villoing to take his prodigy on a concert tour which extended as far as London and Paris. "In Paris, I remained a whole year," wrote Rubinstein in his autobiography, "but had no lessons except in music with Villoing, who jealously guarded me from all approach; not a being could gain access to me! At one of my concerts, Liszt, Chopin, Leopold Meyer, and other musical celebrities were present. In London, I was graciously received by the young and then-handsome Queen Victoria, and subsequently in all the aristocratic circles. Altho but a boy of twelve, I felt no shyness or timidity in the presence of these formal lords and ladies."

In 1846, Rubinstein came to Vienna, principally to seek the assistance of Franz Liszt. Liszt, however, gave Rubinstein a cold welcome, denying him any help. For a period, therefore, Rubinstein lived in want. "I lived in an attic of a large house, and often for two or three days in succession I had not money enough to pay for a dinner at the nearest restaurant, and so I went without food. The room was fairly bare, and soon I had crowded every corner and literally carpeted the floor with my writings. And what did I not write in those days of hunger! Every sort of composition, not only in the department of music—operas, oratorios, symphonies and songs—but articles, philosophical, literary and critical as well. . . . My prolonged absence at last reminded Liszt of my existence. He took it into his head to pay me a visit. . . . The first sight of my quarters seemed to shock . . . Liszt. He showed, however, much tact and delicacy, and in a most friendly manner invited me to dine with him on the same day—a most welcome invitation since the pangs of hunger had been gnawing me for several days. After this I was always on good terms with Liszt."

After a short stay in Berlin, where Rubinstein was active as pianist, teacher and composer, he returned to his native country. He settled in St. Petersburg, and for eight full years devoted himself

ANTON RUBINSTEIN

to study. At the same time, he worked industriously on his compositions. In 1852, an opera, *Dimitri Donskoi,* was produced with such great success in St. Petersburg that it procured for Rubinstein the patronage of the Grand Duchess Helen, who appointed him chamber-virtuoso. The Grand Duchess invited Rubinstein to spend his summers at her place at Kamennoi-Ostrow. It was there that Rubinstein composed three one-act operas, and also that famous piece which appears in the *Portraits,* for piano, *Kamennoi-Ostrow.*

In 1857, supplied with funds by the Duchess Helen and Count Vielhorsky, Rubinstein undertook an extensive concert tour as pianist, which established his reputation as one of the foremost virtuosos of his generation. "In power and execution he is inferior to no one," wrote Ignaz Moscheles. "This Russian boy has fingers as light as feathers, and with them the strength of a man."

Returning to Russia, Rubinstein gave a series of sensational concerts in St. Petersburg. He played an important rôle in Russia's musical life beginning with this period. He was appointed imperial concert-director, and in 1862, together with Karl Schuberth, he founded the St. Petersburg Conservatory, serving as its director for five years.

Another magnificent concert tour kept Rubinstein in the principal cities of Europe until the early part of 1870. Exhausted by the enervating strain of persistent travel, he expressed the hope of retiring permanently from all musical activity. However, his personality was too dynamic for inactivity. From 1870 until 1872, he directed the Philharmonic concerts and the Choral Society of Vienna. One year later he was in America, touring as concert pianist in the company of Henri Wieniawski, famous violinist. For the next fifteen years, Rubinstein's activities as concert pianist and composer knew few intermissions. Between 1885 and 1887, he gave a series of triumphant farewell concerts thruout all of Europe, returning to St. Petersburg in 1887 to resume the direction of the Conservatory. In 1889, he published his autobiography, to commemorate the fiftieth anniversary of his career as pianist.

Anton Rubinstein died suddenly in his villa at Peterhof, Russia, on November 20, 1894. Strange to say, he died a bitter and disappointed man—notwithstanding his magnificent career—because the music world refused to accord him recognition as a composer. "I confess to you frankly and honestly," he wrote to his Berlin publishers in 1889, "that complete disappointment is the sum total of all my artistic activity! That to which I have attached especial importance all my life, and to which I have devoted all my knowledge and built all my hopes upon—my work as a composer—has met with failure."

"He had the body of a Hercules, with a solid frame, huge developed chest, and broad, powerful shoulders," Arthur Pougin described Rubinstein. "His head was square, without either beard or moustache. The forehead was high and prominent, the hair was thick and black; the nose was strong, the mouth sensual, and the eyes which were sunk in their orbits had a look which, though piercing, seemed a little vague and undecided."

Rubinstein was fastidious about his food, preferring Italian cooking; he was fond of cucumbers. When he was on tour, he always arranged to have cucumbers sent to him, because no meal was complete without them. His favorite diversion was billiards, but he did not play well. Whenever he made a bad shot, he would always make the same apologetic remark: "I play billiards only for exercise." He was a passionate smoker of cigarettes.

Rubinstein was a prolific composer who produced an abundant number of works in every field of composition. Discussing Rubinstein's style, Leonid Sabaneyev wrote: "In most cases, Rubinstein shows himself to be a successor of Beethoven and Mendelssohn, but his defective sense of style leads him to blend these influences with those of Glinka, the Italian school, Meyerbeer and even Liszt. In his symphonic and chamber works, he is Mendelssohn without the stereotyped form and feeling for style of the original, but on the other hand, he often approaches Beethoven in the intensity and dramatic quality of his emotions (the *Fourth concerto for piano and orchestra*). In opera and music for the stage, he is more like Meyerbeer and Glinka. His work is inundated with an abundance of what are called commonplaces. Nevertheless, it cannot be denied that we find in it oases of inspiration which compel us to bear in mind his rank as a musician. . . . The oases of great thoughts and even of grandiose conceptions are evidence that if he had not written at journalistic speed, there was no reason why he should not have been the proclaimer of a great musical idea."

"Rubinstein may justly be accused of having produced with too much feverish haste, and of not having left himself time to give his works as much pruning and polishing as he should have done," commented Arthur Pougin. "Every now and again, too, he lapses into writing which is clumsy and is not characterized by purity of style; and he sometimes was rather too ready to be content with the first idea that came into his head. But these defects were more than counterbalanced by some splendid qualities. He had ample inspiration and wide, expansive temperament which made it possible for him to take up all branches of composition, if not exactly with success, at least with uncommon vigor. His music is undoubtedly alive, picturesque, and full of warmth and movement, and in moments of inspiration it carries the listener along in its train and rouses him to a high pitch of enthusiasm."

Principal works by Anton Rubinstein:

OPERA: *Dimitri Donskoi*; *Die Kinder der Heide*; *The Demon*; *Nero*; *Unter Räubern*; *Der Papagei*; *Gorjushka*; *Das verlorene paradies*; *Die Makkabäer*; *Moses*; *Christus*, etc.

ORCHESTRA: *Symphony in F*; *Ocean symphony*; *Symphony in D-minor*; *Dramatic symphony*; *Symphony in A-minor*; *Symphony in G-minor*; Overtures, *La Russie*, *Triomphale*, *Antony and Cleopatra*; *Suite in E-flat*; *Faust*; *Ivan IV*; *Don Quixote*; Five concertos for piano and orchestra; Two concertos for violoncello and orchestra; Two fantasias for piano and orchestra; *Caprice russe* (for piano and orchestra); *Romance* (for violin and orchestra); *Caprice* (for violin and orchestra).

CHAMBER MUSIC: *Octet in D*; *String sextet in F* (for piano and wind); *Quintet in G-minor* (for piano and strings); *Piano quartet in C*; Five piano-trios; Sonatas for violin and piano; Sonatas for violoncello and piano, etc.

Songs; pieces for the piano.

About Anton Rubinstein:

Bernstein, Nikolai Davidovitch. *Anton Rubinstein*; Lipsius, Ida Marie. *Anton Rubinstein*; Pougin, Arthur. *A Short History of Russian Music*; Rubinstein, Anton. *Autobiography*; Zabel, Eugen. *Anton Rubinstein: Ein Künstlerleben*.
Musical Quarterly 5:10 January 1919; *Musical Times* 70:977 November 1929.

Important recordings of music by Anton Rubenstein:

SELECTIONS FROM OPERA: *The Demon*, "Do not weep my child," and "I am he" (GRAMOPHONE); "Invocation to the night" (VICTOR). *Nero*, "O mein geschick" (GRAMOPHONE-Caruso); "Vindex's air" (ULTRAPHONE).

PIANO: *Étude*, no. 1 Opus 23 (GRAMOPHONE-Hambourg); *Melody in F* (BRUNSWICK-Godowsky); *Romance in E-flat* (COLUMBIA-Friedmann); *Staccato étude* (VICTOR-Levitzki); *Valse allemagne* (GRAMOPHONE-Hambourg); *Valse caprice* (VICTOR-Paderewski).

ORCHESTRA: *Kamennoi-Ostrow*, arranged for orchestra (VICTOR).

Many recordings of songs.

Camille Saint-Saëns 1835-1921

CHARLES CAMILLE SAINT-SAËNS was born in Paris on October 9, 1835. He was of humble origin: The ancestors of his father were peasant folk, while those of his mother were humble bourgeois.

His phenomenal precociousness has tempted more than one biographer to refer to him as another Mozart. As a baby of less than two years, he was sensitive to musical sounds, particularly those produced by bells. At two and a half, he was given his first lessons on the piano. A half year later, he began to learn musical notation, and at the age of five he made his first attempts at composition, the same year in which he made a public appearance with a violinist in a performance of a Beethoven sonata. Serious and intensive music study began in his seventh year, under Stamaty, at the piano, and Maleden, in theory. Saint-Saëns' progress was so lightning that, when he was ten and a half, he gave a piano recital at the Pleyel Hall, in a program devoted to Handel, Bach, Mozart and Beethoven.

In 1848, he was admitted to the Paris Conservatory, where he joined the organ class of Benoist, and the composition class of Halévy. Three years later, the first prize in organ playing rested in his hand.

He competed for the Prix de Rome in 1852, but failed to win the award. It is interesting to point out that Berlioz was one of those who voted against him. "I did not vote for Saint-Saëns," explained Berlioz. "He knows everything, but lacks melody." The disappointment of this failure, however, was alleviated a few months later when Saint-Saëns won first prize for his *Ode à Ste. Cécile*, in a composition conducted by the Société Sainte-Cécile in Paris; this work was performed in December of 1852.

On leaving the Conservatory, in 1853, Saint-Saëns was appointed organist of the Church Saint-Merry. In this year, his *First symphony* received performance at the hands of the Société Sainte-Cécile, and received a handsome measure of praise. A second symphony, following the first by three years, was likewise performed by the Société Sainte-Cécile. In 1857, Saint-Saëns received the important appointment of organist of the Madeleine; four years later, he joined the faculty of the Niedermeyer School of Music, as teacher of piano.

Nature had endowed him with inexhaustible energy; he was able to follow his many musical activities with equal industry. He not only performed his tasks at the Niedermeyer School and at the Madeleine Church with unique efficiency, but he was also following a career as piano virtuoso (distinguishing himself by the dignity of his style) and as composer, with equal success. And his activities did not end here. In 1871, he was one of the founders of the Société Nationale de Musique, whose mission it was to give performances of new works of French composers. Saint-Saëns, therefore, was a thoro musician who distinguished himself in numerous directions. It was no wonder, then, that when, early in the seventies Saint-Saëns visited Wagner's home and played the piano score of *Siegfried,* Hans von Bülow remarked that in his opinion Saint-Saëns had the finest musical equipment of any musician of that time.

Meanwhile, Saint-Saëns was achieving a formidable reputation as a composer. His two early symphonies, and his first symphonic poems (*Le Rouet d'Omphale, Phaëton* and *Danse macabre*) found enthusiastic audiences. Between 1865 and 1875, four of his piano concertos were performed in Leipzig and Paris, with the composer at the piano. In 1873, Pablo Sarasate introduced his *Violin concerto* in Paris. The competent workmanship of these works, the fluidity of the style and the freshness of the material aroused much enthusiasm, and finally succeeded in placing their composer at the head of all French composers of the day. By 1868, the importance of Saint-Saëns as a composer was recognized when he became a member of the Legion of Honor. In 1881, he was elected to the Institut.

His operas, however, failed to duplicate the success of his symphonic and chamber music. His early operas—including the famous *Samson and Delilah*—were persistently refused performance at the Paris Opéra. *Samson and Delilah*, as a matter of fact, was not performed until it was accepted by Weimar in 1877. When one act of *Samson* was performed in Paris at the Châtelet, it was bitterly attacked by the critics—one of whom wrote in the *Chronique Musicale*: "Never has a more complete absence of melody made itself felt as in this drama. And when to the lack of melodic motives there is added at times a harmony extremely daring, and an instrumentation which never rises above the level of the ordinary, you will have some idea of what *Samson* is like!"

It was not until Saint-Saëns became a member of the Institut that the Parisian opera houses opened their doors to his works. In 1883, the Opéra presented *Henry VIII,* beginning a series of consecutive performances of Saint-Saëns' operas, culminating in 1892 with a successful presentation of *Samson and Delilah.* However, it cannot be said that the operas of Saint-Saëns—with the exception of his masterpiece, *Samson and Delilah*—ever achieved the fame of his symphonic music.

Commenting upon the symphonic works, Louis Vuillemin wrote: "The Saint-Saëns symphonies, notably the one in C-minor with organ, are stylistic models. True to classical form, they extend it without doing much of the renovation until the *finale* makes its appearance. His symphonic-poems, on the other hand, better affirm the musician's personality. They instantly establish a genius: the 'poem for orchestra' has a legendary cast. As to the concertos for piano and orchestra, it seems to me that even more than anything already mentioned, they characterized the composer's 'manner.' Radiantly wrought, ingenious in their instrumental disposition, often rich in the picturesque, they dominate the ensemble of the composer's work and, I believe, constitute their most original feature."

Saint-Saëns was a uniquely productive composer; every field of musical composition has copious specimens of his talent. M. D. Calvocoressi, analyzing the general qualities of Saint-Saëns' style in all of his music, speaks of the "surpassing excellence of his technique . . . . his lucidity, his versatility, his sense of proportion, and the perfection of what he achieved within the limits of his outlook—limits carefully thought out, deliberately adopted, which he never fell short of nor overstepped. . . . His qualities of emotion and imagination

were inferior to his capacity for building and working out, but what his works lack in glow and profundity they almost make up for in technical interest and beautiful finish, in fineness of proportion and perfection of texture."

"He may not have the rugged power of a Berlioz, the emotional feeling of a Gounod, the mystic fervor of a César Franck, the insinuating charm of a Massenet," summed up Arthur Hervey, "but he possesses an extraordinary faculty for assimilation, and certain characteristics peculiarly his own. He has been taxed with dryness, with lacking that warmth of feeling which vivifies a work and establishes a communication between the composer and his audience. The fact is that, of all composers, Saint-Saëns is most difficult to describe. He eludes you at every moment—the elements constituting his musical personality are so varied in their nature, yet they seem to blend in so remarkable a fashion. . . . Saint-Saëns is a typical Frenchman. . . . He is pre-eminently witty. . . . It is this quality which has enabled him to attack the driest forms of art and render them bearable. There is nothing ponderous about him."

Camille Saint-Saëns died in Algiers on December 16, 1921. His body was brought back to Paris, where the funeral services were conducted with pomp and ceremony. Alfred Bruneau and Charles M. Widor delivered eloquent eulogies.

In his volume on modern French music, Georges Servières has given us this description of Saint-Saëns: "Saint-Saëns is of short stature. His head extremely original, the features characteristic: a great brow, wide and open where, between the eyebrows, the tenacity of the man reveals itself; hair habitually cut short, and brownish beard turning gray; a nose like an eagle's beak, underlined by two deeply marked wrinkles starting from the nostrils; eyes a little prominent, very mobile, very expressive."

Perhaps the most characteristic quality of Saint-Saëns as a man was his keen and penetrating intellect. He was not only a thoro musician, but a scholar as well. He was a brilliant amateur scientist, well versed in astronomy,

CAMILLE SAINT-SAËNS

physics and natural history. He was a student of philosophy. His knowledge of literature—classic and modern—was comprehensive. He was a good linguist, and could write a trenchant and striking prose.

Altho his social evenings at his home in Paris were frequent and famous—his weekly musical Mondays were known thruout Paris—he was essentially a lover of solitude. Frequently, he would slip away from his friends and would not be found for weeks at a time. At such time, he would take lonely holidays in foreign countries. He was a great traveler, and visited many countries of the world.

He was a brilliant conversationalist; his speech was always colored with a spicy irony that could wound an enemy as poignantly as a lance. He had a great love for mimicry. At some of his Monday evenings, he would startle his guests by impersonating Marguerite, of Gounod's *Faust,* in an indescribable costume, or else he would parody early Italian operas with a keen sense for their absurdity. He was likewise known for his obstinacy; there was no one who could change his mind, once he was determined to follow a certain course of action.

His greatest fault, both as artist and as man, was his intense love for speed. On vacations, he always chose the fastest trains and motor-cars. In his speech and actions, he was always electrically quick. And in his work, as well. He could not compose, or correct proofs with studied care—but did everything with a haste that frequently brought with it superficiality.

Camille Saint-Saëns was the editor of a comprehensive edition of Rameau's works published by Durand, and the author of two books of musical essays, *Harmonie et mélodie* and *Malade imaginaire*. It is also interesting to mention that Saint-Saëns was one of the first musicians in France to recognize the genius of Richard Wagner and to fight Wagner's battle heroically. During the World War, prompted no doubt by chauvinistic ardor, Saint-Saëns committed a *volte face* and became a bitter enemy of Wagner's music.

Principal works of Camille Saint-Saëns:

OPERA: *Samson and Delilah*; *Étienne Marcel*; *Henry VIII*; *Proserpine*; *Ascanio*; *Phryné*; *Les Barbares*; *Hélène*; *L'Ancêtre*; *Déjanire*.

CHORAL: *Le Déluge*; *The Promised land*; *Oratorio de Noël*; *Les Noces de Prométhée*; *La Lyre et la harpe*; *La Nuit*; *Ode à Ste. Cécile*; psalms; motets; *Messe solennelle*; *Messe de requiem*; choruses, etc.

ORCHESTRA: Five symphonies; Four symphonic poems (*Le Rouet d'Omphale, Phaëton, Danse macabre, La Jeunesse d'Hercule*); Two suites (*Algérienne, Ouverture de fête*); *Spartacus overture*; Five concertos for piano and orchestra; Two concertos for violin and orchestra; *Introduction et Rondo capriccioso* (for violin and orchestra); *Havanaise* (for violin and orchestra); Two concertos for violoncello and orchestra; *Rapsodie d'Auvergne* (for piano and orchestra); *Jota aragonesa*; *Sarabande et Rigaudon*; *Honneur à l'Amérique*; *Le Carnaval des animaux* (for two pianos and orchestra).

CHAMBER MUSIC: *Septet* (for piano, trumpet and strings); *Piano quintet*; *String quartet in E-minor*; *Piano quartet*; *Serenade* (for violin, viola, piano and organ); Two piano-trios; Sonata for violin and piano; Sonatas for violoncello and piano, etc.

An entire library of music for the piano, for the organ, etc.

About Camille Saint-Saëns:

Bonnerot, Jean Camille. *Saint-Saëns: Sa Vie et son Oeuvre*; Dandelot, Arthur. *La Vie et l'oeuvre de Saint-Saëns*; Hervey, Arthur. *Saint-Saëns*; Lyle, Watson. *Camille Saint-Saëns: His Life and Art*; Mason, Daniel Gregory. *From Grieg to Brahms*; Rolland, Romain. *Musicians of Today*; Servières, Georges. *Saint-Saëns*.

Chesterian 20:97 January 1922; *Etude* 25: 368 June 1907; *Monthly Musical Record* 52: 25 February 1922; *Musical Quarterly* 8:469 October 1922; *Musical Times* 63:90 February 1, 1922.

Important recordings of music by Camille Saint-Saëns:

SELECTIONS FROM OPERA: *Samson and Delilah,* "Orchestral selections," (COLUMBIA); "Air of the High Priest" (POLYDOR); "Trio" (GRAMOPHONE); "Printemps qui commence" (PARLAPHONE-Supervia); "Amour, viens aider ma faiblesse" (GRAMOPHONE); "Mon coeur s'ouvre à ta voix" (VICTOR-Onegin); "Vois ma misère," (GRAMOPHONE); "Bacchanale" (VICTOR-Stokowski). *Henry VIII,* "Ballet music" (VICTOR).

ORCHESTRA: Symphony no. 3 (VICTOR-Coppola); *Le Rouet d'Omphale* (VICTOR-Mengelberg); *Phaëton* (VICTOR-Coppola); *Danse macabre* (VICTOR-Stokowski); Suite Algérienne (ODEON); *Concerto in G-minor,* for piano and orchestra (VICTOR-de Greef); *Concerto in C-minor,* for piano and orchestra (GRAMOPHONE-Cortot); *Concerto in B-minor,* for violin and orchestra (COLUMBIA); *Concerto in A-minor,* for violoncello and orchestra (COLUMBIA); *Le Carnaval des animaux* (VICTOR-Stokowski).

CHAMBER MUSIC: *Trio in F-major* (COLUMBIA).

Pablo Sarasate *1844-1908*

PABLO MARTÍN MELITÓN SARASATE Y NAVASCUES, one of the great violinists of all time and a famous composer for his instrument, was born in Pamplona, in the province of Navarre, Spain, on March 10, 1844. He was a child prodigy who began study at an early age, making his first public appearance in Corunna at the age of six. Shortly after his debut, he set out upon his first successful concert tour thru Spain. In his twelfth year, he arrived in Paris, where he was enrolled in the Paris Conservatory in the classes of Jean Delphin Alard and Henri Reber. He was a brilliant pupil, succeeding in winning not only the first prize in violin playing but also the honorary *premier accessit* in harmony. It was not long, however, before he gave up his studies in harmony and composition to devote himself completely to his instrument. In his fifteenth year he was pronounced by his master fully prepared to begin a virtuoso career.

It is not necessary to trace the many tours that Sarasate took as concert violinist. He performed in every principal music center in the world—not only in Europe but in the Scandinavian countries, Portugal, Russia, North and South America as well. Everywhere he was greeted with the honor commensurate with his genius. "When one saw this little well-set man—with elegant figure, black eyes and abundant, flowing hair, holding in one hand both his fiddle and bow—advance to the platform, greet his public with great simplicity and without timidity, then place his instrument under his chin and prepare to launch upon his solo in his irreproachably correct position . . . one instantly felt that one was in the presence of a veritable artist," wrote Arthur Pougin. And an eminent critic of Sarasate's day wrote as follows about the great violinist's art: "Sarasate's distinguishing characteristics are not so much fire, force and passion, though of these he has an ample store, as purity of style, charm, flexibility, and extraordinary facility."

His career was a magnificent one, crowned with glory and adulation. Until his death he maintained an unquestioned supremacy over all other violinists of his day. Something of his importance may be judged by the fact that such composers as Lalo, Bruch and Sir Alexander Mackenzie wrote important works expressly for him.

PABLO SARASATE

A friend of Sarasate, Luisa Sobrino, has left us some vivid paragraphs about the personality of this great artist. "He was a model of courtliness and courtesy, particular to a degree as to the neatness and good-taste of his dress—exactness personified. At his Biarritz home, he breakfasted in his room, then walked for a little time in his garden, attended by his favorite dog. . . . Then he would drive to his favorite café—the same café, invariably—walk to the same table, and sit down in the same chair, Sarasate's chair. . . . He lunched to the minute at the appointed hour, and then there would be a short walk on the beach. At ten minutes to nine, precisely, he would take a cab and be driven to the Casino which he would always enter by the same door, sharp at the stroke of nine. . . . Then the homecoming—dominos—and a glass of beer.

"Sarasate, the man, was devoid of ostentation. . . . The possessor of a treasury of royal jewels, chiefly the gifts of admiring monarchs, he wore no jewelry but a simple chain. To money he gave no thought. . . . In his early days he was careless as to money. . . . Yet he had an eccentric fancy for carrying money about him. He liked to see it. I have often seen the special place in his violin case in which it was his habit to put his money and thus carry it about with him thru an entire season."

It is not without interest to note that Sarasate practised the violin only during the summer, and never during periods of engagements. His command of his instrument was so consummate that practice was not necessary for him. He was very near-sighted, but he possessed a remarkable photographic memory which made it unnecessary for him to refer frequently to the printed page.

Pablo Sarasate died in Biarritz—at his villa Navarra—on September 21, 1908, of acute bronchitis. In his will he bequeathed two Stradivari violins and five thousand dollars to the Pamplona Academy of Music, one Stradivarius violin and four thousand dollars to the Pamplona Conservatory and $20,000 to the Madrid Conservatory.

As a composer, Sarasate is best known for the repertoire of pieces which he composed for his instrument, in which he succeeded in exploiting and increasing the technical resources of the violin. Many of these pieces—including the famous *Zigeunerweisen, Jota Aragonesa* and *Spanish dances*—are favorites on programs of violin recitals.

Principal works by Pablo Sarasate:

An entire library of works for violin and orchestra or violin and piano including *Zigeunerweisen*; *Navarra*; *Airs ecossais*; Jota de San Fermin; Nocturne-Serenade; Chansons russes; sets of *Spanish dances*; Fantasias on *Carmen, Faust,* etc.; *Jota Aragonesa,* etc.

About Pablo Sarasate:

Altadill, Julio. *Memorias de Sarasate*; Bachmann, Alberto. *Les Grands Violinistes du Passé*; Villalba, Muñoz Luis. *Ultimos Músicos Españoles del Siglo XIX.*
Ménestral 74:306 September 26, 1908; *Monthly Musical Record* 38:222 October 1, 1908; *Musical Times* 49:693 November 1908.

Important recordings of music by Pablo Sarasate:

VIOLIN AND PIANO: *Carmen fantasy* (COLUMBIA-Zimbalist); *Habañera* (COLUMBIA); *Malagueña* (GRAMOPHONE-Heifetz); *Romanza Andalusa* (VICTOR-Menuhin); *Zapateado* (VICTOR-Heifetz); *Zigeunerweisen* (VICTOR-Elman).

Erik Satie   *1866-1925*

(See *Composers Of Today*)

Alessandro Scarlatti   *1659-1725*

ALESSANDRO SCARLATTI, the founder of the Neapolitan school of opera, which was the successor of the Venetian school of Caccini, Cavalli and Monteverdi, was born in Palermo in 1659.

The existing material on the early years of Scarlatti's life is meagre. It is believed that, when Alessandro was fourteen years old, his family migrated out of Palermo and, after two of its members had settled in Naples, went on to Rome. In Rome, Scarlatti began his first important studies in music, possibly under Carissimi, master of the Oratorio. There, too, his first opera was given performance in 1679.

For a short period, Scarlatti enjoyed the patronage of the Queen of Sweden, who admired his first opera sufficiently to endow him. Then, in 1682, Scarlatti decided to join the other members of his family in Naples, where, for the next twenty years, he made his home. In 1684, he succeeded Pietro Andrea Ziani as chapel master. The same year saw successful performances in Naples not only of his first opera, but of his second opera as well.

During the years that followed, Scarlatti composed prolifically for the stage. These works were performed regularly both at the royal palace and at the San Bartolomeo theatre, bringing him a powerful reputation and influence.

In 1702, political disturbances in Naples encouraged Scarlatti to visit northern Italy. His goal was Florence, where the son of the Grand Duke of Tuscany, Ferdinand III, was a famous patron and music lover. Unfortunately, Scarlatti's musical style did not appeal to Ferdinand III who, altho he was willing to commission the composer to produce several operas for his theatre, refused to give him a permanent appointment. Thus, Scarlatti passed on from Florence to Rome, somewhat regretfully, for he realized that opera in Rome at the time was at a very low ebb, due to the fact that the Pope did not countenance any productions for the stage.

While in Rome, Scarlatti met and became a friend of Cardinal Ottoboni, the same Cardinal Ottoboni who was a patron of Corelli. It was thru Otto-

boni's influence that Scarlatti was able to procure even so undesirable a post as assistant director of the S. Maria Maggiore. However, Scarlatti's lack of success did not smother his industry; in 1705, we find him confessing that he had just completed his eighty-eighth opera!

For several years, Scarlatti remained in Rome. Finally, Cardinal Grimani, Austrian Viceroy at Naples, made persistent gestures to him to return to Southern Italy. In 1713, enticed by his former post of chapel master at a greatly increased salary, Scarlatti returned to Naples. Here, except for intermittent trips to Rome to attend performances of his operas, he stayed for the remainder of his life.

His operas, which he continued to compose with an indefatigable pen, were enjoying an unprecedented popularity on the Neapolitan stage, exerting such a powerful influence on other operatic composers in Naples that they soon began to imitate his style. As Charles Burney wrote, Scarlatti's influence was so great not only upon his contemporaries but upon his immediate successors as well that "I find part of his property among the stolen goods of all the best composers of the first forty or fifty years of the eighteenth century." Morever, the fame of Scarlatti's operas soon drew the limelight of attention from Venice to Naples. Before long, a new school of operatic composition was functioning, known as the Neapolitan school.

Alessandro Scarlatti died in Naples on October 24, 1725. He was buried in the church of Montesanto. At the time of his death, he was recognized as the foremost operatic composer in Italy of his day. Commenting on his death, the *Gazzetta di Napoli* of October 30, 1725 wrote: "In the course of last week there died the celebrated Cavaliere Alessandro Scarlatti, to whom music owes much for the numerous works with which he enriched it."

Alessandro Scarlatti earned an all-important place in musical history for a variety of reasons. He is said, by some musicologists, to have been the first composer to write a string quartet. Moreover, in developing the "Italian" overture, as distinct from the "French" overture (the "Italian" overture consisted of

ALESSANDRO SCARLATTI

three movements—an "allegro", an "andante" and an "allegro"; while the "French" overture usually comprised a slow introduction followed by a fugue) he actually paved the way for the future symphony form. Finally, in the field of the opera, he inaugurated ensemble singing, chromatic harmony and brought the aria form to a high degree of perfection.

Discussing Scarlatti's operas, Edward J. Dent has written: "Scarlatti was not by temperament a reformer or an iconoclast. He took things as he found them, and did the best that could be done on the lines of his predecessors. The libretti of his day offered him hardly any guaranty of heroic sentiments which he could set to a dignified recitative, as well as straightforward obvious emotions, which he could express in a neat aria at the end of the scene. . . . Writing every air (and each opera would contain some fifty or sixty) in the same form, Scarlatti attained a wonderful mastery over his material, and besides displaying an infinite variety of style within the given limits, he gradually developed the form to a very high degree of emotional and structural organization."

As for Scarlatti's importance in musical history, Mr. Dent commented as follows: "He has gathered up all that was best of the tangled materials produced by that age of transition and experiment, the seventeenth century, to form out of them a musical language, vigorous and flexible as Italian itself, which has been the foundation of all music of the classical period."

Principal works by Alessandro Scarlatti:

OPERA: About 150 operas including *Mitridate Eupatore, Teodora, Tigrane, Il Trionfo del l'onore, La Rosaura, Telemaco, Turno Aricino, Griselda,* etc.

CHAMBER MUSIC: Symphonies for chamberorchestra); sonatas (for various combinations of instruments).

CHORAL: Two hundred masses; more than 600 cantatas and oratorios, etc.

About Alessandro Scarlatti:

Borren, Charles van der. *Alessandro Scarlatti, et L'ésthetique de L'opéra Napolitain;* Dent, Edward J. *Alessandro Scarlatti, His Life and Work;* Lee, Vernon. *Studies in 17th Century Italy.*
Musical Times 67:982 November 1926; *New Music Review* 17:312 September 1918.

Important recordings of music by Alessandro Scarlatti:

VOCAL: *Io vi miro ancor vestite di fior* (VICTOR-Galli-Curci); *O Cessate di piagarmi* (VICTOR); *Se Florindo fedele* (GRAMOPHONE); *Sento nel core certo dolore* (GRAMOPHONE); *Le Violette* (COLUMBIA).

INSTRUMENTAL: *Sonata for flute and strings* (VICTOR).

Domenico Scarlatti   *1685-1757*

"In the entire history of music there is perhaps no composer who is more remarkable than Domenico Scarlatti."—EDWARD J. DENT

DOMENICO SCARLATTI, son of Alessandro Scarlatti, was born in Naples on October 26, 1685, the same year that saw the birth of Bach and Handel. As in the case of his father, biographical facts about his life are not plentiful. He is known to have received his early musical education from his father, and to have gone to Rome when Alessandro left Naples in 1702. Three years later, he was engaged upon his first major musical task, remodelling Polaroli's opera *Irene* for its Naples production.

He disclosed an original talent both in his compositions and in the playing of the harpsichord, so much so that we find his father complaining to Ferdinand III of Florence, in 1705, that neither Florence nor Rome were environments

DOMENICO SCARLATTI

suitable for a talent so great as that of his son. "This son of mine is an eagle whose wings are grown; he ought not to stay idle in the nest, and I ought not to hinder his flight." As a result, Alessandro permitted Domenico to travel to Venice with Nicolini, a great singer of the day, for the purpose of studying under Gasparini.

Domenico Scarlatti acquired an unusual technical equipment at the harpsichord, becoming one of the most significant harpsichord virtuosos of his day. Shortly after his stay in Venice, he went to Rome, where Cardinal Ottoboni arranged a musical competition at the harpsichord between him and Handel. There were some who maintained that it was Scarlatti who emerged victorious from this duel. At any rate, from this time on dates a close bond of friendship between Handel and Domenico Scarlatti.

An appointment to the musical staff of Queen Marie Casimire of Poland, in 1709, turned Domenico Scarlatti seriously towards the theatre. During the next few years, he composed a series of operas which were performed at the Queen's theatre in Rome. In 1715, Scarlatti became chapel-master of St. Peter's in Rome, now turning his creative industry towards the Church.

In 1717, Domenico Scarlatti entered into legal proceedings in order to gain complete independence from the jurisdiction of his father. Victorious, he set out for London, where his opera *Narciso* was given a successful performance. From London, he went to Lisbon, where he became the darling of the court.

During the last twenty-five years of his life, Domenico Scarlatti lived in Spain, in the position of music master to the royal family. In this period, his fame as a composer and as a virtuoso on the harpsichord made his name known thruout the entire world of music. It was in Spain that Domenico Scarlatti composed his *Esercizi*, or exercises, for the harpsichord which have immortalized his name. These *Esercizi* (or "sonatinas" as they are known today)—composed expressly for the Infanta Barbara—not only foreshadowed the future sonata-form, but also inaugurated the modern age of pianoforte

playing. J. B. Trend, as a matter of fact, likewise considers these *Esercizi* as the origin of Spanish piano style.

In 1754, Domenico Scarlatti returned from Spain to the city of his birth. There he died three years later. An inveterate gambler, he had squandered all of his income in games of chance, leaving his family sadly in want.

While Domenico Scarlatti composed operas and church music with a fertile pen, his importance in musical history rests almost exclusively with the short morsels which he composed for harpsichord. These little pieces pointed towards new directions for many reasons. They introduced a new type of virtuosity—runs, arpeggios, and the crossing of hands—which definitely marked a new era in piano technique. In their form (they were usually divided into two parts, in which each part was repeated) they paved the way for the sonata form, to reach final crystallization with Haydn. Hans von Bülow has even suggested that some of the wittier pieces clearly foreshadowed the Beethoven "scherzo."

"His instinct for the requirements of his instrument," wrote C. Hubert Parry, "was so marvelous and his development of technique so wide and rich, that he seems to spring full armed into the view of history. That he had models and types to work upon is certain, but his style is so unlike that of familiar old suites and fugues and fantasias and ricercare, and other harpsichord music of the early times, that it seems likely that the work of his prototypes has been lost. . . . He knows well the things that will tell, and how to awaken interest in a new mood when the effects of any particular line are exhausted. Considering how little attention had been given to technique before his time, his feats of agility are really marvelous. The variety and incisiveness of his rhythms, the peculiarities of his harmony, his wild whirling rapid passages, his rattling shakes, his leaps from end to end of the keyboard, all indicate a preternaturally vivacious temperament; and unlike many later virtuosos, he is thoroughly alive to the meaning of music as an art, and does not make his feats of dexterity his principal object.

They serve as the means to convey his singularly characteristic ideas in forms as abstract as the modern sonatas. The definiteness of his musical ideas is one of the most surprising things about him. . . . He left behind him a most copious legacy to mankind, but his successors were very slow to avail themselves of it. . . . His influence did not bear full fruit till the development of genuine pianoforte playing began."

Two important modern composers have arranged Scarlatti's sonatinas for orchestral suites: Vincenzo Tommasini in *The Good humored ladies*, a ballet brought to prominence by Diaghilev, and Alfredo Casella in *Scarlattina*, for piano and orchestra.

Principal works by Domenico Scarlatti:

OPERA: *Sylvia*; *Orlando*; *Fatide in Sciro*; *Ifigenia in Aulide*; *Narciso*; *Amleto*.

CHORAL: *Stabat Mater*; *Salve Regina*, etc. Sonatinas for harpsichord.

About Domenico Scarlatti:

Parry, C. Hubert. *Evolution of the Art of Music*; Sitwell, Sacheverell. *A Background for Domenico Scarlatti*.
Monthly Musical Record 36:194 September 1906.

Important recordings of music by Domenico Scarlatti:

HARPSICHORD: Twenty sonatas (HIS MASTERS VOICE-Landowska).
ORCHESTRA: *The Good humored ladies*, a group of Scarlatti sonatinas arranged in an orchestral suite by Tommasini (DECCA).

Franz Schreker *1878-1934*
(See *Composers Of Today*)

Franz Schubert *1797-1828*
"He was a very little man, but he was a giant."—ANTON HOLZAPFEL

FRANZ PETER SCHUBERT, youngest son of a parish schoolmaster and a cook, was born in the Lichtenthal district of Vienna on January 31, 1797. The Schubert family was musical. Father Schubert played the violoncello, and Franz's older brothers, Ignaz and Ferdinand, were violinists. Their music-making gave Franz Schubert his earliest musical impressions. Before long, Franz, too, was given instruction in the art, under the guidance of his father,

his brother Ignaz, and Michael Holzer, choirmaster of the parish. "He seems to know the lessons perfectly before I begin to explain them to him," Holzer once told Schubert's father in amazement.

In his eleventh year, Schubert passed the entrance examinations for the Convict School, which trained choristers for the Imperial Court Chapel. Life at the Convict was not without hardship; the young music-students frequently suffered cold and hunger. "Hunger has become so pressing," Schubert wrote to his brother, Ferdinand, "that willy-nilly I must make a change. The two groschen that father gave me went in the first few days. If, then, I rely upon your aid, I hope I may do so without being ashamed (see Matt. ii, 4—So also thought I!) How about advancing me a couple of kreutzer monthly?"

When Schubert became acclimated to his new surroundings at the Convict he was far from unhappy. He was completely absorbed in music-study, finding therein endless fascination and adventure. He also made some intimate friendships, particularly one with Josef Spaun, seven years his senior, who remained his intimate friend for the remainder of his life.

In the Convict school, Franz Schubert began his first compositions. Supplied with note-paper by Spaun, Schubert composed his first song, *Hagar's Klage*, which came to the notice of Salieri, director of the Convict. Salieri was so impressed with this achievement that he placed Schubert under the personal guidance of Ruczizka, professor of harmony. Then, when Ruczizka confided to Salieri that Schubert "seems to have been taught by God himself, the lad knows everything," Salieri decided to take the boy under his own wing. One of the first exercises which Schubert composed for Salieri was—an opera! "Franz'l, you can do everything," Salieri told him. "You are a genius!"

In 1813, Schubert's voice broke; he was now compelled to leave the Convict school and return to his father's home. He was eager to devote himself entirely to composition (he had already produced a symphony, some church music, piano works, overtures and quartets!) but the necessity of earning a living compelled him to adopt the profession of teaching. A year of preparation at the Normal School of St. Anna enabled Schubert to assume a pedagogical post at his father's school. He was a miserable teacher. While in classroom, he was far removed from his pupils, troubling himself little with their attendance, work or behaviour, while his mind was busily conceiving melodies and development of themes. School-teaching was detestable to him, the four walls of a classroom a prison. When the school-day ended, however, Schubert found release; he could belong to music, and music alone. Nights were spent in the production of an incredible amount of music. In 1815 alone, Schubert composed two symphonies, two masses, five operas, four sonatas, several smaller choral works and one hundred and forty-six songs.

It was in 1815 that Schubert created the first of his indisputed masterpieces. His friend, Spaun, burst in upon him one day to find him in a fever of composition. Schubert had just stumbled across a ballad of Goethe, the *Erlkönig*, which inflamed his imagination. He reached for music-paper and, during the next few hours, set the great poem to music. When the song was completed, Spaun and Schubert hurried to the Convict school to perform it before several friends. But—as was to be expected of a song so far ahead of its time—it was greeted coldly.

The *Erlkönig* was one of Schubert's highest flights of genius, an amazingly one-piece and mature production for a boy of eighteen. Goethe, who first ignored it, heard it sung to him two years before his death when, with tears in his eyes, he acknowledged it to be a masterpiece. Jean Paul, the poet, begged a few moments before his death for a last hearing of this melody.

At this time, too, Schubert made several friendships which persisted until the end of his life. Together with Spaun, there were Mayrhofer, a poet, Vogl, a singer, Schober and Hüttenbrenner, two fervent admirers of Schubert's music. These, calling themselves "Schubertians," formed an intimate circle which,

FRANZ SCHUBERT

thruout the life of the composer, brought him encouragement, advice and material assistance. They held frequent social evenings devoted to music and entertainment—called "Schubertiaden"—which furnished Schubert the few moments of contentment and happiness he knew in his life.

In 1818, Schubert received a position as music teacher to the family of Count Johann Esterhazy in his estate at Zélesz, Hungary. The work was pleasant, the pupils agreeable, and the leisure abundant. However, Schubert did not remain at this post longer than one summer. The following winter, Schubert roomed with Mayrhofer, leading something of a Bohemian existence. The mornings belonged to intense composition. "He would sit down at the table clad only in his shirt and pants and compose the most beautiful things," recorded Spaun. In the afternoon, the two friends—often supplemented by Spaun, Vogel and Schober—would go to the café-house for relaxation.

Until this time, though Schubert had composed prolifically, his works had been completely ignored by the music world. In 1820, however, two important performances of Schubert's works took place in Vienna. Thru the efforts of Vogl, Schubert had received a commission from the Kärthnerthor Theatre to compose an opera, *Zwillingsbrüder.* At the same time, the Theatre-an-der-Wien engaged Schubert to prepare still another opera, *Zauberharfe.* It seemed that, at last, Schubert's star as a composer was rising. However, both productions were failures, leaving Schubert as comfortably obscure as he had been before. *Zwillingsbrüder,* after being bitterly reviewed, ran for only six nights. The *Zauberharfe* was not better received. One critic found there "a want of technical arrangement" and that the "harmonic progressions were too harsh; the instrumentation overladen; the choruses vapid and weak." Another critic felt that "the work was deficient in real melody."

An effort was made by Schubert's friends at this time to procure a publisher for some of his greatest songs. One publisher after another, however, found either that the accompaniments were too difficult or the composer too obscure. Finally, in 1821, Schubert's friends decided to publish some of these songs themselves. A hundred subscribers were found, and Schubert's first published work appeared. Following this publication, several other of Schubert's songs reached the presses. None of these publications, however, succeeded in alleviating Schubert's distressing poverty, his royalties from them amounting to only a few cents.

These failures were followed by still other misfortunes. In 1822, Schubert composed an opera, *Alfonso und Estrella,* the score of which he showed to Karl Maria von Weber. Weber,—embittered by the fact that Schubert had at one time severely criticized Weber's *Euryanthe*—said that "first operas and first puppies should always be drowned." After many futile and heartbreaking attempts to procure a production for the opera, Schubert finally was forced to discard his opera into his bulging trunk. In 1823, Schubert composed incidental music to a drama by Wilhelmina von Chezy, *Rosamunde,* which was performed in Vienna that same year. "Herr Schubert," wrote one critic, "shows originality in his compositions, but, unfortunately, *bizarrerie* also. The young man is passing through a

phase of development; we hope that he will emerge from it successfully. At present he is too much applauded [*sic* !]; in the future may he never complain of being too little recognized !"

These repeated failures plunged Schubert into an abysmal despondency. "Picture to yourself," he wrote brokenheartedly to a friend at this time, "a man whose health can never be reestablished, who from sheer despair makes matters worse instead of better; picture to yourself, I say, a man whose most brilliant hopes have come to nothing, to whom proffered love and friendship are but anguish, whose enthusiasm for the beautiful—an inspired feeling, at least—threatens to vanish entirely; and then ask yourself if such a condition does not represent a miserable and unhappy man. . . . Each night when I go to sleep, I hope never again to waken, and every morning reopens the wounds of yesterday."

In 1823, the Musikverein of Graz elected Franz Schubert an honorary member. This was no great honor, nor did it carry with it any remuneration. But, to Schubert—starved as he was for recognition—it brought considerable happiness. Overflowing with gratitude, Schubert decided to compose a symphony in honor of the Musikverein.

The work that Schubert composed was the world-famous *Unfinished Symphony,* so called because it comprises only two, instead of four, movements. Why Schubert never completed the work (the third movement, as a matter of fact, is abruptly halted after a few measures) has been a subject for much speculation. It is believed that, after the first two movements, Schubert was completely unable to maintain the high plane of ineffable beauty upon which the symphony was poised. Rather than permit the symphony to own two inferior movements, he preferred to keep it an unfinished masterpiece.

The remaining years of Schubert's life were not particularly eventful. There was continued and uninterrupted creation, which neither despair nor futility could smother. There were occasional excursions into the country; one particularly delightful holiday took place in

1825 when Schubert tramped the Tyrols with Vogl. Most important, however, was Schubert's visit to Beethoven's death-bed in 1827. Schubert worshipped Beethoven with an almost blind adoration. When, therefore, he heard that the master had seen a few of his songs and had praised them, he summoned courage and visited the sick-bed of the great composer, standing there in silent veneration for several hours.

At Beethoven's funeral, Schubert was one of the pall-bearers. When the ceremonies were over, Schubert and his friends stepped into a nearby tavern to drink to the memory of a departed hero. At that time, Schubert raised a toast to the one who would be the first among them to follow Beethoven to the grave. Then—as though in prophetic vision— Schubert begged his friends to promise him that, should he die soon, they would bury him next to Beethoven.

During these last years of Schubert's life, he composed some of his greatest works—the *Symphony in C-major,* the *Mass in E-flat,* some of his most poignant songs included the *Winterreise* cycle. Until the end of his life, however, he remained a comparatively obscure and unknown composer. Only one great honor came his way. On March 26, 1828 the Musikverein of Vienna gave a public concert devoted entirely to Schubert's music. The concert was overwhelmingly successful—the first and only taste of fame which Schubert had in his lifetime.

In the Fall of 1828, Schubert revealed more and more startling symptoms of illness. The physician recommended the country. Fortunately, his brother Ferdinand at that time had rented a house in the Neue-Wieden suburb of Vienna, and offered to take care of the composer. With the passing of a few weeks, Schubert's illness developed acutely. His body was a broken shell; before long, his physicians despaired completely of his recovery.

Schubert did not know that he was dying. He divided his time between correcting the proofs of his *Winterreise* and making important plans for the future. He sensed that, as a composer, he had technical deficiencies; he was

making arrangements, therefore, to study fugue and counterpoint under Sechter, court organist, when he recovered fully. He was making elaborate plans for future compositions, and for the first time he evinced a hope that his works would gain recognition.

On the night of November 16th, delirium set in. For three days after that, Franz Schubert lingered on half-insane with pain. Finally, the evening before his death, Schubert—still unconscious—called his brother Ferdinand to his side. "Ferdinand, I entreat you to put me into my own room. Don't leave me in this corner under the earth. Don't leave me here! Do I not deserve a place in the sunlight?" Ferdinand attempted to calm Schubert. "You are in your own room, Franz'l," he said. "But no!" Schubert answered hotly, "that cannot be true . . . . for Beethoven is not here!"

Late the next morning, Schubert once again called to his brother. "Ferdinand, am I lying next to Beethoven?" he asked. Ferdinand assured him that he was. "Then, Ferdinand, I am so happy."

Late that afternoon at three o'clock— the nineteenth of November of 1828— Franz Schubert passed away.

Two days later, Schubert was buried in the Während cemetery, near Beethoven, as he had requested. Franz Schober, Schubert's friend, read a poetical farewell:

"May Peace at last be with you! Angel-pure soul!
In the full bloom of Youth,
The stroke of Death has seized you
And extinguished the pure light within you!"

Shortly after Schubert's death a concert was held in his honor. With the proceeds from this concert, a monument was erected in Schubert's honor. This monument—with an inscription from a poem of Franz Grillparzer reading, "Here lies buried a rich treasure, and yet more glorious hopes"—still stands over Schubert's grave.

Anselm Hüttenbrenner, an intimate friend of Franz Schubert, has left us vivid word pictures of the great composer. "Schubert was not of a very striking appearance. He was very short, somewhat corpulent, with a full, round face. His brow had a very agreeable curve. Because of his near-sightedness, he always wore eyeglasses which he never removed, not even while sleeping. He never concerned himself with his dress, and he detested going into higher society because it necessitated careful dressing. In general, he found it impossible to discard his soiled frockcoat for a black suit. . . .

"His voice was weak, but very agreeable. . . . When Schubert would sing his own *Lieder,* in the company of musicians, he generally accompanied himself. When others sang them, he would generally sit in a remote corner of the room, or even in another room, and listen quietly. . . .

"Schubert never composed in the afternoon. After dinner, he would go down to the café, drink a cup of dark coffee, would smoke for several hours while reading papers. In the evening he would go to the theatre. Good plays interested him as much as good opera.

"Ordinarily, Schubert drank beer at the *Chat noir,* on Annastrasse, or at the *Escargot* at Peter—and smoked considerably. But when we were more affluent we would drink wine. . . . Before a glass of wine, Schubert was most loquacious; his opinions on music were pointed, brief and penetrating; he denounced with a strong feeling for justice. About his own works, Schubert spoke rarely. His favorite conversation concerned itself with Haydn, Mozart and Beethoven. He held the highest esteem of all for Beethoven. Schubert was enchanted by the operas of Mozart; but he could not find enthusiasm for Cherubini. The favorite works of Schubert were: the *Messiah* of Handel, the *Don Juan* and *Requiem* of Mozart, the *Mass in C-major* and *Symphony in C-minor* of Beethoven."

There remains but to add that Schubert was something of a practical jokester, frequently delighting his friends by whistling his own songs thru the teeth of a comb or by absurdly burlesquing operatic mannerisms at the piano; that he was fond of smoking his assortment of pipes, and fonder still of dancing; that, though he was fond of women, his natural shyness and self-consciousness made it impossible for him to associate

with them freely; that his few love-affairs were essentially of a schoolboyish nature; that his intellectual horizon was considerably limited—he knew little of painting, literature, philosophy or politics.

Schubert's greatness as a composer rests principally upon his amazing lyrical gift. Whether he composed a symphony, a string quartet or a song, he filled his mould with an endless wealth of beautiful ideas. He created beauty as freely as men breathe. Each of his thoughts possessed the wings of lyricism. His melodic output seemed inexhaustible both in its endless variety of mood and in its copiousness.

Since lyricism was his greatest gift, Schubert's genius found its aptest expression in the *Lied,* which he brought to an amazing development. "Simple in style and design, wonderfully direct and sincere, conceived as idealizations of the beautiful old German *Volkslieder,* and carried out with all the artistic perfection and appropriateness of detail that good craftsmanship could give, they are among the few things in music that are absolutely achieved," wrote Daniel Gregory Mason. "Especially remarkable is the art-concealing art by which Schubert, through some perfectly simple and unobtrusive feature of rhythm, melody or harmony, knows how to suggest exactly the spirit and atmosphere of his text. . . . In short, Schubert strikes at once . . . the exact tone and style needed to transfigure the particular feeling with all the magic of music, and throughout the song maintains the mood perfectly, with no mixture or clouding. And this, too, with the greatest actual diversity of mood in the different songs, to which his art flexibly responds. . . . Schubert is often sublimely simple . . . ; but sometimes he is merely flat and obvious. Indeed, writing as he did over six hundred songs in a score of years, not the most inspired of men could have always avoided platitude. Thus we must set aside many melodramatic and many trite compositions before we can get an unimpeded view of his real masterpieces. But after that has been done, we have left about twenty or thirty songs of such incomparable loveliness as to give him a secure place among the great masters of the musical lyric."

In considering Schubert's instrumental music—his remarkable chamberworks, his symphonies, his piano sonatas, etc.—it should be pointed out, as Philip Hale has done, that in them can be found the same "striking characteristics of Schubert's songs, spontaneity, haunting melody, a birthright mastery over modulation, a singular good fortune in finding the one inevitable phrase for the prevailing sentiment of the poem and in finding the fitting descriptive figure for salient detail."

"There is the spontaneous melody," wrote Philip Hale, "the simplicity praised by Walt Whitman. . . . To speak with the perfect rectitude and insouciance of the movements of animals and the unimpeachableness of the sentiment of trees in the woods and grass by the roadside is the flawless triumph of art. . . . Then there is the ineffable melancholy that is the dominating note. There is a gayety such as was piped naively by William Blake in his *Songs of Innocence*; there is the innocence that even Mozart hardly reached in his frank gayety; yet in the gayety and innocence is a melancholy—despairing, as in certain songs of the *Winterreise*, when Schubert smelled the mould and knew the earth was impatiently looking for him—a melancholy that is not the titanic despair of Beethoven, not the whining or shrieking pessimism of certain German and Russian composers; it is the melancholy of an autumnal sunset, of the ironical depression due to a burgeoning noon in the spring, the melancholy that comes between the lips of lovers."

Schubert's music, however, is not without marked defects. "The nicety of adjustment of details of form, after the manner of . . . masters, is defective, and self-restraint, concentration, conciseness and judgment are too often absent," pointed out C. Hubert Parry. One accepts these faults and recognizes them. Yet, when subtractions are made, there is a complete world of magic left, a world of Schubertian magic, a world flushed with a beauty that stabs the heart more poignantly than pain.

It is interesting to mention that many of Schubert's masterpieces were, for many years, lying neglected on dusty shelves and in obscure attics. The *Symphony in C-major,* for example, was found in a hidden corner by Robert Schumann who prevailed upon Ferdinand Schubert to send the manuscript to Felix Mendelssohn in Leipzig for its first performance. And *Rosamunde,* as well as forty songs, was discovered by Sir Arthur Sullivan and Sir George Grove in an attic of a physician in Vienna.

Principal works by Franz Schubert:

OPERA: *Alfonso und Estrella*; *Fierrabras*; *Die Zwillingsbrüder*; *Die Zauberharfe*; *Die Verschworenen*; Music for *Rosamunde*.

CHORAL: Six masses; Three kyries; Two Stabat Maters; *Magnificat*; Four Salve Reginas; Five offertoriums; *Deutsche messe*; Psalms; *Mirjams siegesgesang*; *Gott in der natur*; *Gebet vor der schlacht*; *Chor der engel*; *Gesang der geister*; Fifty other choruses and part-songs.

ORCHESTRA: Nine symphonies; Six overtures; *Konzertstück* (for violin and orchestra).

CHAMBER MUSIC: *Octet in F*; *String quintet in C*; *Piano quintet in A*; Sixteen string quartets; *String trio in B-flat*; Two piano trios; *Notturno* (for piano trio); *Trauermusik* (for nine wind instruments); Four sonatas for violin and piano; *Arpeggione* (or violoncello) *sonata*.

PIANO: More than fifteen sonatas; Eight impromptus; Eight moments musicaux; Two scherzos; Two sets of variations; *Wandererphantasie*; waltzes; ländler; other dances, etc.

More than 600 songs including the songcycles *Die Schöne Müllerin*; *Die Winterreise*; *Schwanengesang*.

About Franz Schubert:

Antcliffe, Herbert. *Schubert*; Audley, Agathe. *Franz Schubert, sa Vie et ses Oeuvres*; Bie, Oscar. *Franz Schubert: his Life and Works*; Dahms, Walter. *Schubert*; Deutsch, Otto Erich (editor) *Franz Schubert's Letters and other Writings*; Flower, Newman. *Franz Schubert: the Man and his Circle*; Kobald, Karl. *Franz Schubert and his Times*; Kreissle von Hellborn, Heinrich. *Franz Schubert*; Landormy, Paul. *La Vie de Schubert*; Mason, Daniel Gregory. *The Romantic Composers*; Pitron, Robert. *Franz Schubert: Vie Intime*.

Important recordings of music by Franz Schubert:

SELECTIONS FROM OPERA: *Alfonso und Estrella,* "Overture" (COLUMBIA-Harty); *Rosamunde,* selections (COLUMBIA-Harty).

CHORAL: *Mass in G-major* (GRAMOPHONE); *Deutsche messe* (CHRISTSCHALL) *Psalm 23* (PARLAPHONE); *Mirjams siegesgesang* (GRAMOPHONE).

ORCHESTRA: *Symphony no. 5 in B-flat major* (VICTOR-Blech); *Unfinished symphony* (VICTOR-Stokowski); *Symphony in C-major* (VICTOR-Boult); *Arpeggione sonata,* arranged for violoncello and orchestra by Cassado (COLUMBIA-Cassado).

CHAMBER MUSIC: *Octet in F* (COLUMBIA); *String quintet in C* (VICTOR-Pro Arte); *Piano quintet in A, "Forellen"* (VICTOR-Pro Arte, Schnabel); *Quartet in C-major* (POLYDOR); *Quartet in E-flat major* (COLUMBIA-Musical Art); *Quartettsatz* (VICTOR-Budapest); *Quartet in A-minor* (VICTOR-Budapest); *Quartet in D-minor, "Tod und das mädchen* (VICTOR-Budapest); *Quartet in G-major* (COLUMBIA-Kolisch); *Trio in B-flat major* (VICTOR-Thibaud, Casals, Cortot); *Trio in E-flat major* (GRAMOPHONE-Busch, Busch, Serkin); *Sonata in D-major,* for violin and piano (COLUMBIA); *Sonata in G-minor,* for violin and piano (GRAMOPHONE); *Sonata in C-major,* for violin and piano (VICTOR-Busch, Serkin); *Sonata in A-major,* for violin and piano (VICTOR-Kreisler).

PIANO: *Sonata in A-major* (COLUMBIA-Hess); *Sonata in G-major* (COLUMBIA); *Four impromptus* (COLUMBIA-Leginska); *Six moments musicaux* (COLUMBIA-Leginska).

SONGS: *Die Schöne müllerin,* complete (SCHÖNE MÜLLERIN SOCIETY); *Schwanengesang,* complete (GRAMOPHONE); *Die Winterreise,* complete (DIE WINTERREISE SOCIETY); *Seventeen songs* (GRAMOPHONE-Gerhardt); *Selected songs,* including the most famous of Schubert's *Lieder* such as *Ave Maria, Du bist die Ruh', Erlkönig, Die Forelle, Am Meer, Der wanderer, Der Tod und das Mädchen,* etc. (COLUMBIA).

Heinrich Schütz *1585-1672*

HEINRICH SCHÜTZ, who is frequently referred to by the musicologist as the "father of German music," was born in Köstritz, Saxony, on October 8, 1585. The son of a prosperous family, he was given a very thoro musical education from early childhood. He possessed a beautiful soprano voice which made so striking an impression upon the Landgraf Maurice of Hesse-Cassel, that the Landgraf, after many talks, finally prevailed upon Heinrich's parents to permit him to guide the musical and academic education of the boy.

In this way, Heinrich Schütz became a chorister of the Landgraf's chapel in 1599, and at the same time was enrolled as a student in the exclusive "Gymnasio"

to which only children of nobility were admitted. Schütz was an apt pupil in Latin, Greek and French, and the Landgraf decided to permit him to continue his academic study at the University of Marburg. It was during his early period at the University (where Schütz was enrolled to study law) that he manifested an extraordinary talent for music. Consequently, in 1609, his patron permitted him to leave the University for Italy to study music under Giovanni Gabrieli, master of counterpoint. There, in 1611, Schütz published his first musical work, a book of songs, which caused considerable stir among musicians.

On the death of Gabrieli, in 1612, Schütz returned to his native country to officiate as organist to the Landgraf Maurice. At this time, he was still undecided whether to adopt music or law as his career. In 1614, however, the Elector of Saxony, Johann Georg I, heard him conduct a musical performance, and was so impressed that he expressed his eagerness to procure this gifted musician as his chapel-master. The Landgraf was reluctant to part with his protegé, but persistent persuasion on the part of the Elector of Saxony finally won the day for him. Installed in Dresden as the chapel-master to the Elector, Schütz now definitely devoted himself entirely to music. He completely reorganized the music of the chapel on Italian lines, importing special instruments and players from Italy.

Heinrich Schütz remained in this post for fifty-seven years, retaining it until his death. He did not, however, hold this position without intermission. In 1628, he took a leave of absence to revisit Italy in order to study the advance made by the musical art during his absence. The Thirteen Year's War temporarily dissolved the Dresden chapel, and in 1633 Schütz served as a chapel-master in Copenhagen; when the chapel of Dresden was restored in 1645, Schütz returned to his former position, holding it uninterruptedly until the end of his life.

His position in Dresden gave him sufficient leisure to devote himself to composition. From the beginning of his tenure, he was amazingly fecund. His first important works came in 1619, a series of Psalms and Motets for eight or more voices. In 1627, to commemorate the marriage of the daughter of the Elector to the Landgraf of Hesse-Darmstadt, Schütz composed his only opera, *Dafne*, whose importance rests in the fact that it is probably the first opera in German music. However, it is not for his solitary production for the theatre that Schütz's name is prominent in musical history, but rather for his remarkable works for the Protestant Church—the oratorios, psalms, passions, etc.—works which have made him, together with Johann Sebastian Bach and Handel, one of the three greatest composers for the Protestant Church.

The complete works of Heinrich Schütz have been published, under the editorship of Philipp Spitta, by Breitkopf and Härtel. E. W. Naylor analyzed the distinguishing qualities of Schütz's works: First there is his care "to accent his words with intelligence and accuracy," coupled with "the tendency to let the course of the musical notes take the natural shape of ordinary speech"; second, there is an unusual dramatic expressiveness to his musical writing; and third, his harmonies are of unusual color and depth, with special emphasis upon the use of chromaticism.

"The most striking characteristic of Schütz's mature art lies in its expressive depth," wrote Cecil Gray. "In the art of Schütz every means of securing musical interest is ruthlessly sacrificed to his expressive purpose, with the result that he attains to a stark, elemental simplicity and a mystical grandeur and solemnity that are quite unlike anything else, and are among the most affecting things in all music. . . . It is incidentally interesting to note that Schütz became deaf in his old age, and that it is, therefore, probably no mere coincidence that we should encounter in his later work the same mysterious inner radiance, the same abstract and disembodied quality of thought, the same notes of wistful and tender resignation that we find in the later work of Beethoven."

Discussing Schütz's historical importance, Fr. Erckmann wrote: "When he was born, the purely polyphonic style had undergone a change. While studying under Gabrieli he became acquainted with the 'nuove musiche'—solo songs with figured bass, development of instrumental music, and union of vocal and instrumental music. With this new style he became thoroughly acquainted during a second stay in Italy, and he was the first German who introduced Italian methods and musical manners into Germany."

Heinrich Schütz died in Dresden on November 6, 1672. Martin Geier, who was at his death-bed, left us the following description of Schütz's last hours: "On the sixth of November . . . he arose . . . and dressed; and after nine o'clock, while he was searching for something in his room, he was seized by a sudden weakness and he was stricken by apoplexy. . . . The doctor, whom one had called without delay, applied all his care to succor him with excellent remedies . . . but there was nothing that could help him. At the same time, the spiritual father was called to his side. . . . He blessed him, and almost immediately, he [Schütz] rested very tranquil. . . . And when the fourth hour struck, he died quietly and peacefully, without the least convulsion, while we, at his side, were praying and singing."

Heinrich Schütz was buried in the church of Notre Dame in Dresden.

Principal works by Heinrich Schütz:
OPERA: *Dafne.*

HEINRICH SCHÜTZ

CHORAL: The Passions according to St. John and St. Matthew; *The Seven last words*; *The Christmas oratorio*; *Three Biblical scenes*; psalms; requiems; motets; Symphoniae sacrae; Geistliche concerte; madrigals, etc.

About Heinrich Schütz:
Einstein, Alfred. *Heinrich Schütz*; Müller, Erich Hermann. *Heinrich Schütz*; Pirro, Andre. *Schütz.*

Monthly Musical Record 52:309 December 1922; *Proceedings of the Musical Association* 32:23 (1905-1906).

Important recordings of music by Heinrich Schütz:
CHORAL: Geistliche concerte, "Also hat Gott die welt geliebt" and "Bringt her dem herren" (KANTOREI); "Eile, mich, Gott, zu erreten" and "Ich liege und schlafe" (KANTOREI); "Schaffe in mir, Gott" and "O süsser, o freundlicher, o gütiger Herr" (KANTOREI). *Symphoniae sacrae*, "Ich werde nicht sterben" (KANTOREI); "Saul was verfolgst du mich?" (GRAMOPHONE).

Robert Schumann *1810-1856*

"It matters little whether his monument be large or small, in either case it is imperishable."—W. H. HADOW

ROBERT ALEXANDER SCHUMANN was born in Zwickau, Saxony, on June 8, 1810. His childhood was tranquil. He moved in an environment that was distinctively cultured and in which he found sympathy and understanding. His father, a lover of great literature, was a successful publisher and a well-known author; his mother had a well-cultivated mind.

As a child, it was literature rather than music that attracted Robert Schumann. He read feverishly, devoting his play hours to the writing of dramatic sketches which he recited while accompanying improvisations on the piano. In his ninth year, he temporarily swerved his allegiance from literature to music. He heard Moscheles perform on the piano, and was so stirred that for a while he devoted himself to musical activity. He assembled many of his little friends into an orchestra which he directed; he also composed choral pieces. By his fourteenth year, he was once again in the arms of Muse. Poetry his major interest, he read voraciously the works of the Greeks, Goethe, Byron and —the poet who was probably the greatest

single influence in his life—Jean Paul. When he was fifteen, he founded a literary society among his friends for the purpose of reading and discussing great German literature.

While still in his adolescence, he was introduced by a friend of the family to the songs of Schubert. Once again, Schumann strongly felt the lure of music. For a period, therefore, he wavered between literature and music. "I possess imagination," he wrote at this time, taking stock of himself, "but I am not a profound thinker. Whether I *am* a poet—for I cannot *become* one—posterity must decide. The strange thing is that where my feelings make themselves felt most strongly, I am forced to cease being a poet: at such times I can never arrive at adequate ideas."

When Robert Schumann graduated from the Gymnasium, he was sent by his mother to Leipzig for the study of law. There he was attacked by a violent fit of melancholia (could it have been brought on by his aversion to adopting law as a profession?) which was only partially dispelled, and at infrequent intervals, by his preoccupation with music. He attended the concerts of the Gewandhaus, adopted musical friends and resumed a serious study of the piano under the guidance of a personal friend, Friedrich Wieck.

Schumann's mother, objecting violently to her son's neglect of law for music, decided to transfer him from Leipzig to Heidelberg. He remained in Heidelberg for a year, growing increasingly impatient with legal study and immersing himself more deeply in music. Finally, after a trip to Italy where he bathed himself in Italian music, he wrote to his mother on November 11, 1829, announcing his decision to become a musician. "If ever I were to have achieved anything in the world," he wrote, "it would have been in music. From the first I have had within me a powerful inclination towards music, and, not to overrate myself, the creative spirit as well." On July 30, 1830, he wrote once again: "I have . . . arrived at the conviction that with work, patience and a good master, I shall be able within six years to rival any pianist. . . . Besides this, I also possess imagination and perhaps talent for individual creative work." The letters, joined by others written by Friedrich Wieck, finally convinced the mother to give her consent. Late in 1830, therefore, Robert Schumann returned to Leipzig to begin a new life. He brought back with him the first draught of his first creative fruits for the piano, including the *Papillons,* the *Variations on Abegg* and the *Toccata.*

He hurled himself into his music study with assiduity, evolved his own method whereby he could, by indefatigable practise, acquire a prodigious technique at the piano. Unfortunately, he overstrained his fourth finger, completely paralyzing his hand. A virtuoso career, therefore, was now closed to him; he turned to composition. For two years, he studied theory under the guidance of Heinrich Dorn.

In 1833, Robert Schumann helped to found the Davidsbündler, a society of iconoclastic and idealistic music lovers who, just as King David conquered the Philistines, hoped to attack Philistinism, false musical standards, and false ideals, hoped to erect new and deserving altars and to shatter undeserving ones. Schumann himself has explained the origin of this society: "At the end of 1833, a certain number, for the most part of young musicians, would meet every evening in Leipzig, as though casually, in the first place for sociable purposes, but just as much in order to exchange ideas on the art which was their meat and drink, namely music. . . . Then, one fine day, an idea flashed across the minds of the young hotheads: 'Let us not be mere idle lookers on; let us set to work to make things better, so that the poetry of art shall be restored to its place of honor."

The voice of the Davidsbündler was the *Neue Zeitschrift für Musik,* edited by Robert Schumann, the first issue of which appeared on April 3, 1834. The Davidsbündler society did not enjoy a long life, but the magazine continued on for many years and, under the vigorous, fearless, and penetrating editorship of Schumann, was one of the most forceful weapons in Germany on behalf of great music.

The strain of work and study brought on neurasthenia. In 1833, Schumann began to suffer fainting fits, and violent rushes of blood to the head. During the night of October 17, 1833 he was attacked by a particularly violent fit in which he attempted to throw himself out of the window. For a short period, Schumann was certain that he was on the verge of insanity.

Recovery came slowly, and was followed by deep and brooding depression. Only in music did Schumann find some escape from his intense morbidity. In 1834, with the publication of his magazine, the *Neue Zeitschrift* and with the composition of his piano masterpieces the *Études symphoniques* and *Carnaval* something of his old zest for life returned to him.

At this time, Robert Schumann fell in love seriously for the first time in his life. She was Ernestine von Fricken, daughter of a rich baron and a passionate music lover, who frequented the home of Friedrich Wieck. Schumann spoke rhapsodically about his beloved, spoke of her "Madonna-like head" and described her as "gentle and bright as the eye of heaven shining blue thru the clouds." Though they were officially engaged, their relationship never developed into marriage. It is believed that either Ernestine's illegitimate birth or else the fear that marriage might hinder his artistic career caused a change of heart in Schumann.

By 1835, the affair with Ernestine became a forgotten incident. It was replaced by another love, this time for the young daughter of Friedrich Wieck —Clara, a brilliant pianist. On November 25, of 1835, Clara wrote to Schumann: "When you kissed me for the first time, I thought that I should faint. Everything went black before my eyes." The love affair grew in intensity, until Friedrich Wieck—not relishing the match—sent his daughter away to Dresden and forebade all correspondence between her and the young composer.

Schumann, however, was not discouraged from sending Clara poignant letters of devoted passion. When Wieck heard of this correspondence he flew into a rage, wrote to Schumann a letter full of

ROBERT SCHUMANN

poisonous vituperation, and threatened Schumann that he would not hesitate to kill him if he did not cease the correspondence. For some fifteen months, it was impossible for Schumann to exchange word with his sweetheart. However, he spoke to her thru his music: his *Sonata in F-sharp minor* was dedicated to her, his "unique cry of passion."

Thru the intervention of Clara Schumann's maid, the lovers, finally, resumed contact. On September 9, 1837 they met surreptitiously—for the first time in almost two years. The meeting was a disappointment to both; the prolonged absence had made both embarrassed and stiff. However, with renewed contact, the flame of their passion burst anew. In vain did Schumann plead with Friedrich Wieck for permission to marry Clara. At last, Schumann took the only step left him. Bringing the matter to court, he received legal sanction to marry. On September 12, 1840 Robert Schumann and Clara Wieck were married. Despite the many obstacles which perpetually arose during their married life, their union was a blissfully happy one.

It is more than likely that the influence of his happy marriage caused Schumann's creative genius to flower fully after 1840, to penetrate into new realms. In 1840, he turned from the piano to vocal composition, and as he himself realized, he "produced something quite new in that line." In 1841, he turned to the orchestra, producing the first two of his famous symphonies, as well as the *Overture, Scherzo and Finale.* One year later, he composed the greatest of his chamber works, three string quartets, the piano quintet and the piano quartet.

In 1844, ill-health compelled Robert Schumann to desert the strenuous musical life of Leipzig. Resigning his pedagogical and editorial activities, he settled in the more placid city of Dresden. There, for several years, he lived in virtual seclusion, which was only partially interrupted, at periodic intervals, by important concert tours.

In 1850, upon the recommendation of his friend Ferdinand Hiller, Schumann received the position of conductor in Düsseldorf. He could not, however, fulfill the exacting obligations of his new assignment adequately because of ill-health. His nervousness and irritability were growing rapidly; he soon lost the ability of intensive concentration. His efforts, therefore, received cold and antagonistic criticism. By 1853, his conducting had become so erratic and inept that a special committee discreetly suggested to him that, because of his ill-health, he give up his baton duties to devote himself entirely to composition.

It was during this trying period that Schumann met Johannes Brahms for the first time, welcomed him at his home as a household guest, and prophesied for the younger composer a magnificent future.

Early in 1854, Schumann arranged with a Leipzig publisher for the appearance of his more important essays on music in four volumes. These volumes proved Schumann's great discernment and penetration as a critic. Though many of these essays had been written fifteen to twenty years before this final publication, they had lost none of their intrinsic validity.

Schumann's nervous disorders were growing more apparent in 1854. His mind was tormented by a bedlam of musical sounds which seemed to haunt him incessantly. He frequently said that the great composers of the past—Bach, Mendelssohn and Schubert particularly

—held communion with him at his bedside, dictating melodies to him. In February of 1854, he left his home secretly and threw himself into the Rhine. Only the fortuitous circumstance of boatmen passing the scene at the moment saved him from drowning. After that, he was confined to a private insane asylum at Endenick, near Bonn. Occasionally, lucid moments returned to him when he would meet friends and devote himself to correspondence. But more frequently his spirits were smothered by crushing morbidity.

Robert Schumann died in the insane asylum in Endenick—in the arms of his wife—on July 29, 1856. Brahms, Joachim and Ferdinand Hiller accompanied his body to his grave in Bonn. In 1880, a monument was erected in his honor at the cemetery.

Schumann was moderately tall, built lithely, presenting a dignified appearance. His face, round and full and effeminately soft, invariably wore an expression of ineffable pain. His eyes were frequently clouded by revery. He was intensely self-centered, wrapping himself within a meditative cloak thru which few could penetrate. His spirits were rarely bright. It has been recorded that often, when he was in the company of boisterous friends, he would sit alone, apart from the crowd, and protected from the merrymakers by his reveries, would be little conscious of what was happening about him.

Robert Schumann had a well cultivated intellect. He was enormously well read in classical literature, the English poets, Dante, Petrarch and the foremost German writers. He not only studied Goethe, but interpreted him. His favorite author was Jean Paul, the poet. "I learned more counterpoint from Jean Paul than from my music-master," he once said.

He has confessed that three musical influences have shaped his development: "the simple Gluck, the more intricate Handel, and the most intricate of all—Bach. Only study the last named thoroughly and the most complicated of my works will be clear." He had a violent dislike for musical theory, considered a close study of the masters more important than an intensive study of harmony, counterpoint and composition.

Robert Schumann, who inherited the mantle of Romanticism from Franz Schubert, has produced masterpieces in many fields of musical composition. His piano works and his songs are, perhaps, the most integrated of his music; in smaller canvases, his touch was infallibly perfect.

"As a writer for the pianoforte, he may be said to rank beside Schubert," wrote W. H. Hadow. "He has less melodic gift, less sweetness, perhaps less originality, but he appreciates far more fully the capacities of the instrument and possesses more power of rich and recondite harmonization. His polyphony was a new departure in the history of pianoforte music, based upon that of Bach, but exhibiting a distinctive color and character of its own. The beauty of his single phrases, the vigor and variety of his accompaniments, the audacity of his 'bitter-sweet discords' are all so many claims on immortality. . . . His spirit, too, is essentially human. No composer is more companionable, more ready to respond to any word and sympathize with any emotion."

Of Schumann's songs, C. Hubert Parry has written that they "showed powers with which no one till then would have credited him. There was no laborious process of developing his style in this particular branch of art; he no sooner faced it than his mastery seemed complete. In this respect he resembled Schubert, who had written many of his finest songs in the earliest years of his mature productive period. Schumann adopted much the same method of dealing with his poems that Schubert did. He did not aim at making tunes with accompaniment and fitting the words to them, but he looked to the poet's conception to guide his own inspiration. Everything available was made to minister to the purpose of intensifying the design, thought, and meter of the poet by the music. The pianoforte part and the voice part had well-balanced functions. The voice did all that was possible in the way of melodious declamation, and the accompaniment supplied color, character, rhythm and all that must necessarily fall to its share, in the most perfect manner possible. Moreover, Schumann, by nature a poet himself, seized the purpose and spirit of the poems he set with an astonishing powerful grip, and conveyed infinite shades and varieties of meaning in forms which are almost always perfect works of art in detail and in entirety. He expressed with equal success pathos, passion, bitterness, humor, joy, exultation and even gaiety and sarcasm."

Schumann's symphonic works have been subject to great criticism by the musicologists, particularly for the feeble instrumentation and the meagre development of his ideas. Philip Hale has admirably summed up the strength and weakness of Schumann's symphonies. "It has been urged against Schumann that his symphonies were thought for pianoforte and then orchestrated crudely, as by an amateur. This, however, is not the fatal objection. . . . A more serious objection is this: the genius of Schumann was purely lyrical, altho occasionally there is the impressive expression of a wild and melancholy mood, as in the chords of unearthly beauty soon after the beginning of the overture to *Manfred*. Whether the music be symphonic, chamber, a pianoforte piece, or a song, the beauty, the expressive force lies in the lyric passages. When Schumann endeavored to build a musical monument, to quote Vincent D'Indy's phrase, he failed; for he had not architectonic imagination or skill.

"His themes in symphonies, charming as they often are, give one the impression of fragments, of music heard in sleep-chasings. Never a master of contrapuntal technique, he repeated these phrases over and over again instead of broadly developing them, and his filling in is generally amateurish and perfunctory.

"The best of Schumann's music is an expression of states and conditions of soul. This music is never spectacular; it is never objective. . . . In his own field, Schumann is lonely, incomparable. No composer has whispered such secrets of subtle and ravishing beauty to a receptive listener. The hearer of Schumann's music must in turn be imaginative and a dreamer. He must often anticipate the composer's thought. The music is not for a garish concert hall; it shrinks from boisterous applause."

Principal works by Robert Schumann:

ORCHESTRA: Four symphonies (including the *Spring symphony* and the *Rhenish symphony*); Overture, Scherzo and Finale; Overtures to *The Bride of Messina*; *Fest, Julius Caesar, Hermann und Dorothea*; *Concerto for piano and orchestra*; *Concerto for violoncello and orchestra*.

OPERA: *Genoveva*; Music for Byron's *Manfred*; Scenes for Goethe's *Faust*.

CHAMBER MUSIC: *Piano quintet*; Three string quartets; *Piano quartet*; Three piano trios; Two sonatas for violin and piano; Four fantasie-stücke for violin and violoncello, etc.

CHORAL: *Das Paradies und die peri*; *Adventlied*; *Der Rose pilgerfahrt*; *Der Königssohn*; *Des Sängers fluch*; *Vom Pagen und der königstöchter*; *Das Gluck von Edenhall*; *Abschiedlied*; *Requiem für Mignon*; *Nachtlied*; *Neujarslied*; *Missa sacra*; *Requiem*; *Spanisches liederspiel*; Part-songs for men's voices and for women's voices, etc.

PIANO: Three sonatas; *Papillons*; *Davidsbündlertanze*; *Carnaval*; *Fantasie-stücke*; *Kreisleriana*; Eight noveletten; Four nachtstücke; Nine waldscenen; Twenty albumblätter; *Etudes symphoniques*; *Variations on Abegg*; Twelve studies after Paganini's caprices; *Toccata*; *Fantasia in C*; *Arabeske; Humoreske*; Six intermezzi; Thirteen kinderscenen, etc.

An entire library of great songs.

About Robert Schumann:

Basch, Victor. *Schumann: A Life of Suffering*; Fuller-Maitland. *Schumann*; Hadow, W. H. *Studies in Music*; Jansen, F. G. *The Life of Robert Schumann told in his Letters*; Niecks, Frederick. *Robert Schumann*; Parry, C. Hubert. *Studies of Great Composers*.

Important recordings of music by Robert Schumann:

ORCHESTRA: *Symphony no. 1, "Spring"* (VICTOR-Stock); *Symphony no. 2* (BRUNSWICK); *Symphony no. 3, "Rhenish"* (VICTOR-Coppola); *Symphony no. 4* (COLUMBIA-Walter); *Concerto for piano and orchestra* (COLUMBIA); *Concerto for violoncello and orchestra* (VICTOR-Piatigorsky).

CHAMBER MUSIC: *Piano quintet* (VICTOR-Schnabel, Pro-Arte); *Quartet in A-minor* (VICTOR-Flonzaley); *Quartet in A-major* (VICTOR); *Piano quartet* (POLYDOR); *Trio in D-minor* (VICTOR-Casals, Thibaud, Cortot); *Trio in G-minor* (COLUMBIA); *Sonata in D-minor*, for violin and piano (VICTOR-Menuhin).

PIANO: *Sonata in G-minor* (VICTOR-Levitzki); *Carnaval* (COLUMBIA-Godowsky);

Davidsbündlertänze (COLUMBIA); *Études symphoniques* (VICTOR-Cortot); *Fantasia in C-major* (POLYDOR); *Kinderscenen* (VICTOR-Moiseivitch); Papillons (GRAMOPHONE-Cortot).

SONGS: *Dichterliebe,* complete (GRAMOPHONE); *Frauenliebe und Leben* (COLUMBIA-Lehmann), etc.

Alexander Scriabin   *1871-1915*
(See *Composers Of Today*)

Bernhard Sekles   *1872-1934*
(See *Composers Of Today*)

Alexander Serov   *1820-1871*

ALEXANDER NIKOLAEVICH SEROV, the son of a government official, was born in St. Petersburg on January 23, 1820. His intelligence as a child was extraordinary: he learned foreign languages with such facility that as a mere boy he was acquainted with Latin, Russian, English, French and German. Morever, he manifested a keen interest in natural history, the theatre, design and music. It was decided, therefore, to give him a thoro education as preparation for a government post. In 1834, he was enrolled in the School of Jurisprudence. Here he made only one friend—curiously enough, Vladimir Stassov, later a famous music-critic and one of Serov's most bitter adversaries.

In 1840, Serov left the School of Jurisprudence and became a clerk in a government office. His leisure hours were spent in studying the violoncello and composition; up to that time, his only formal training in music had been as a child under a spinster-aunt. Study in music convinced him that he was more interested in art than in law. When, in 1842, he met and became a friend of Glinka—and was deeply moved by the score of *A Life for the Tsar*—he definitely decided to turn to composition and began searching for an appropriate libretto for an opera.

The projected opera was interrupted, at the very beginning, when Serov was transferred from his government office in St. Petersburg to Simferopol, where his growing passion for music made him neglect his governmental duties. "I

used to write little fugues during the proceedings in court—nice little fugues," he later confessed. Finally, he made the inevitable step: he suddenly gave up his legal career, returned to St. Petersburg and decided to devote himself entirely to musical endeavors. To earn his living, he accepted a post as newspaper censor.

At this period of his life, he became a devoted disciple of Beethoven's last quartets. Feeling that the essential technical characteristic of these last quartets was the predominating use of old Greek modes, Serov decided to utilize such modes extensively in his own composition. For a while, he refused to compose any music in modern scales.

Serov first made his mark in the music world, not as a composer but as a critic. Eager to spread his ideas on Beethoven, the opera, and Russian music, he published a series of polemical letters in the *Pantheon* which attracted great attention because of the clarity of his writing and his profound scholarship. It was not long before he received recognition as the "first great Russian music critic."

In 1857, Serov traveled to Germany where he was virtually hypnotized by Wagner. "I am now Wagner mad," he wrote from Germany. "I play him, study him, read of him, talk of him, write about him and preach his doctrines. I would suffer at the stake to be his apostle." Returning to Russia, Serov brought his Wagner fever with him. By word of mouth and pen he attempted to spread propaganda thruout Russia for the great music-dramas. Unfortunately, Serov was so completely hypnotized by Wagner that he became blind to every other musical idiom. In a series of vitriolic essays, he viciously attacked the new national school of Russian music, headed by Balakirev, because he felt that it was traveling in a wrong direction. The national school found its champion in the critic Stassov. There ensued an acrimonious battle of printed words between Stassov and Serov which, for many years, rocked musical Russia to its very foundations.

It was primarily because he wished to give a concrete proof that the national school of Russians were adopting a false idiom that Serov decided, in his fortieth year, to turn to composition. In 1860, a famous Italian tragedienne, Signora Adelaïde Ristori, came to St. Petersburg with *La Giuditta.* Serov saw in this drama an excellent theme for an opera. He wrote his own libretto, and in May of 1863, his first important work— under the title of *Judith*—was given its first performance at the Russian Opera House.

"If the score of *Judith* is frequently open to adverse criticism," wrote César Cui, "one can at least point to a certain number of passages which deserve praise. In the first act . . . . there is a striking prayer; in the second, there is a long monologue for Judith which is really beautiful. . . . Then in the third act there is the exceedingly powerful and effective symphonic episode of the triumphal march . . . . as well as the delightful chorus of female slaves with its curiously broken rhythms."

Judith was something of a sensation, and for a long while proved to be the most vigorous argument that Serov had posed on behalf of his artistic position. In 1863, when Wagner visited St. Petersburg, he saw the score of *Judith* and was considerably pleased with the orchestration.

Spurred on by his first success, Serov turned with great enthusiasm to the composition of a second opera. In 1865, he completed *Rogneda,* which was produced the same year. *Rogneda* surpassed even the success of *Judith.* Tschaikovsky wrote as follows about this work: "The continued success of *Rogneda,* and the firm place it holds in the Russian repertory, is due not so much to its intrinsic beauty as to the subtle calculation of effects which guided its composer. . . . Serov knew how to catch the crowd; and if his opera suffers from poverty of melodic inspiration, from want of organic sequence, from weak recitative and declamation, and from harmony and instrumentation which are crude and merely decorative in effect—yet what sensational effects the composer succeeds in piling up!" Another critic, Gustave Bertrand, commented that *Rogneda* "bears the mark of undoubted inspiration but still more of deliberate endeavor."

ALEXANDER SEROV

As a result of his second success, Serov's popularity as a composer could not be questioned. The Tsar recognized his fame by compensating him with an annual pension of twelve hundred rubles.

Though Serov's first two operas were influenced by Wagner, they were not built strictly along the lines of the Wagnerian music-drama. His success now tempted Serov to attempt the composition of a major operatic work, which —by embodying Wagnerian theories in a music-drama on a Russian subject, written in Russian—would be the final argument to prove emphatically that the nationalist Russians were on the wrong trail. With this end in view, Serov composed *The Power of evil* in 1867. Fortunately, Serov did not live to realize how dismally he had failed. In its first performance in 1871, *The Power of evil,* with its overdressed instrumentation and cumbersome structure, appealed very slightly to Russian tastes.

Alexander Serov died suddenly of heart failure on February 1, 1871. Wagner wrote the following tribute: "For me Serov is not dead; for me, he still lives, actually and palpably. Such as he was to me, such he remains and ever will, the noblest and highest minded of men. His gentleness of soul, his purity of feeling, his serenity, his mind which reflected all these qualities made the friendship which he cherished for me one of the gladdest gifts of my life."

Vladimir Stassov has written as follows concerning the artistic importance of Serov: "A fanatical admirer of Meyerbeer, he nevertheless caught up all the superficial characteristics of Wagner, from whom he derived his taste for marches, processions, festivals, every sort of pomp and circumstance, every kind of external decoration. But the inner world, the spiritual world, he ignored and never entered; it interested him too little."

Principal works by Alexander Serov:

OPERA: *Judith*; *Rogneda*; *The Power of evil*.

ORCHESTRA: *Christmas Eve suite*; Incidental music to *Nero*; *Danse Cosaque*.

CHORAL: *Stabat Mater*; *Lied von der glocke*; *Ave Maria* (for soprano and orchestra).

About Alexander Serov:

Pougin, Arthur. *A Short History of Russian Music*; Riesemann, Oskar von. *Monagraphien zur Russischen musik*.
Zeitschrift der Internationalen Musik Gesellschaft 4:173 (1903).

Important recordings of music by Alexander Serov:

SELECTIONS FROM OPERA: *The Power of evil*, "Merry Butterweek" (GRAMOPHONE-Chaliapin).

Giovanni Sgambati *1843-1914*

GIOVANNI SGAMBATI was born in Rome on May 28, 1843. His father was a lawyer; his mother, an Englishwoman, was the daughter of an eminent sculptor.

It was originally intended by his parents that he be directed towards law, but his musical precociousness was so pronounced that they did not hesitate to assign music as his life's career. His first teacher was Amerigo Barberi, under whose instruction Sgambati disclosed marked genius.

When he was six years old, his father died, and his mother took him to Trevi, Umbria, where she married again. There, Giovanni Sgambati studied under the distinguished Natalucci, under whom he made such swift progress that he was able to make public appearances as a pianist, and as a conductor of small orchestras.

In 1860, Sgambati returned to Rome where he made his mark as concert pianist He became an ardent protagonist for great piano music, introducing at all of his concerts great German piano music which at the time was completely unknown in Italy—particularly the works of Robert Schumann. Despite the fact that Sgambati cluttered his programs with so many unfamiliar (and, to many Italians, unpalatable) piano works, he achieved considerable fame as a virtuoso. Bettina Walker in her charming volume, *My Musical Experiences*, has spoken of "his lovely, elastic touch, the weight and yet the softness of his wrist staccato, the swing and go of his rhythmic beat, the coloring rich and warm, and yet most exquisitely delicate, and over all, the atmosphere of grace, the charm, and the repose which perfect mastery alone can give." And Franz Liszt, who was in Italy during this period and became a close friend of Sgambati: "In Sgambati there is something of both Bonsart and Tausig."

At this same time, Sgambati proved his importance as a conductor. When, in 1866, the Dante Gallery was inaugurated in Rome, Liszt selected Sgambati to conduct his *Dante symphony*. After this, Sgambati was an important factor in introducing many great German symphonic works to Italian audiences—including the *Eroica symphony* and the *Emperor concerto* of Beethoven.

In 1869, Sgambati toured with Liszt thruout Germany, meeting many of the great personalities of the time, including Wagner, Rubinstein and Saint-Saëns. Wagner became so interested in Sgambati that he interested the publisher Schott in his early works, which included two quintets.

Upon his return to Rome, Sgambati founded a free piano class at the Academy of St. Cecilia. In 1878, he became professor of piano at the Academy, and later its director. His high position in Italy's musical life was recognized by royalty; he was the recipient of many honors from King Victor Emmanuel III. A familiar anecdote about Sgambati relates of the time when, with his customary absent-mindedness, he came to a court function without having put on his tie; Queen Margherita saved the situation by cutting a ribbon from her gown and adjusting it about the collar of the musician.

Recognition for his composition was likewise accorded him. His *Quartet in B-flat* was familiar on the programs of the Kneisel and the Joachim Quartets in their concerts thruout the music-world. In 1887, his *Second Symphony* and his *Piano quintet* received performances in Paris and Cologne respectively, and were well received. His *Epitalamio sinfonico* brought him high praise not only in Italy but in England as well. Finally, his *Requiem,* composed in memory of King Humbert I, was accorded a rousing reception upon its performances in Italy and Germany.

In 1903, Sgambati retired from all musical activity. For many years he lived a quiet existence in Rome, devoting himself only occasionally to teaching assignments. He died in Rome on December 15, 1914.

"Much of his work in the larger forms," wrote Edward Burlingame Hill, "has neither the spontaneity and melodic invention which characterize Italian music nor the depth which his German models possess. . . . In spite of the dryness of much of his chamber music, the somewhat futile classicism of the symphony, and the pretentiousness of the piano concerto, we must recognize Sgambati as a composer for the piano of real distinction. His piano pieces are original in technical style, and also in musical conception; they are elevated in artistic standards."

Alfredo Casella has taken considerable pains to point out that Sgambati's works are of considerable historical importance in the development of Italian instrumental music. "He marks the beginning of the renaissance in that country of instrumental music which had been in abeyance for a whole century. . . . The work of Sgambati, the first advocate and supporter of this return, is of real importance in musical history; if he said nothing that was absolutely new, it was he, at all events, who pointed the way which Italian composers are now treading in ever greater numbers, with grow-

GIOVANNI SGAMBATI

ing confidence and with increasing success."

Principal works by Giovanni Sgambati:

ORCHESTRA: Two symphonies; *Ouverture solennelle; Epitalamio sinfonico; Piano concerto in G-minor; Te Deum laudamus.*

CHAMBER MUSIC: Two piano quintets; *String quartet.*

CHORAL: Requiem.

Pieces for the piano, including études, nocturnes, pièces lyriques, transcriptions, etc.

About Giovanni Sgambati:

Etude 25:714 November 1907; *Monthly Musical Record* 40:125 June 1910; *Music and Letters* 6:304 October 1925; *Musical America* 21:2 December 19, 1914.

Bedřich Smetana *1824-1884*

BEDŘICH SMETANA, the founder of the modern school of Bohemian music, was born in Leitomischl, Bohemia, on March 2, 1824. His father, a wealthy brewer, was a lover of good music and introduced Bedřich to music study at an early age. Bedřich Smetana disclosed unusual talent as a child. At the age of five he was a member of a string quartet; a year and a half later, he made his debut as a pianist in an entertainment given in honor of Emperor Francis I. Soon after this, he turned his hand to composition. His talents found many admirers; for a period, he was the pampered pet of the aristocratic circles in Bohemia.

Between 1831 and 1839, he pursued his academic education in German schools at Neuhaus, Iglau and Deutsch-brod. After this, he was entered as a student in the Gymnasium in Prague where his preoccupation with music was so great that he neglected his other studies. In 1840, he was sent to Pilsen to complete academic study under the vigilant eye of a relative, Josef Franz Smetana, eminent scholar and historian. Josef Franz Smetana was keen enough to realize that his ward was squandering precious talent in devoting himself to any study but that of music. He therefore tried to use his influence in acquiring the consent of Bedřich's father for a musical career for the boy.

Father Smetana refused to permit his son to follow a musical career as a profession. When Bedřich insisted, his father abruptly terminated his support. Without resources, Smetana went to Prague in 1843, where he earned a meagre living by giving piano lessons and serving as a resident music teacher to Count Leopold Thun. At the same time, he turned with greater industry to music study, fortunate in procuring the instruction of Josef Proksch, a distinguished musical scholar.

In 1847, Smetana set out on an extended concert tour, the proceeds of which were to be expended in establishing a music school in Prague. The tour was a financial failure, but Smetana succeeded in gaining possession of some additional funds. In 1848, he established a musical institution in Prague. On August 27 of that same year, he was married to Katharina Ottilie Kolář, whom he had met in Pilsen.

In 1850, thru the intervention of his teacher, Proksch, Smetana received an appointment as concertmaster to the former Emperor of Austria, Ferdinand I. The security of this position enabled him to compose with greater fertility than before. Three years later, he composed his first significant work, the *Triumphsymphonie*, to commemorate the marriage of Emperor Franz Joseph of Austria, a work utilizing the Austrian National Anthem as a principal theme.

In 1855, Smetana's elder daughter, Frederike died at the age of four. As an escape from his sorrow, Smetana composed his poignant *Trio in G-minor*. He continued to brood over the death of his child until he was urgently recommended to seek a change of scene. In 1856, he went to Gothenburg, Sweden, where he immediately became an influential force in its musical life. He was appointed conductor of the Harmoniska Sällskapet, and from 1856 until 1861 served as director of the Philharmonic Society of Gothenburg.

The ill-health of his wife compelled him to return to Bohemia. On April 19, 1859 occurred the second great tragedy of Smetana's life—the death of his beloved wife. One year later, he returned to Gothenburg, where he remarried and resumed his activities as conductor.

He was back in Bohemia in 1861. After an extended concert tour thru Germany and Holland which was successful, he settled permanently in his native country and was henceforth to play an all-significant rôle in the musical development of his country. When, in 1863, an art society was founded in Prague, Smetana was appointed head of the music section. In this capacity, Smetana began his first significant efforts on behalf of native Czech music. Between 1863 and 1865, he conducted

BEDŘICH SMETANA

the Hlahol Singing Society, which he himself had founded, and in 1863, together with Ferdinand Hiller, he opened a new music school in Prague.

Despite his many efforts as conductor, teacher and virtuoso, he was not idle as creator. "I want to give my nation that which I owe to it and which I carry in my heart—a work of grand volume," he expressed at this time. The first significant effort in this direction came in 1863, his opera *The Brandenburgers in Bohemia*. The importance of this opera rests principally on the fact that it is the first opera of a truly national spirit by a Bohemian composer. At its first performance at the National Theatre in Prague on January 5, 1866 it was unsuccessful, principally because of an effete libretto. But there were many musicians in the audience who realized strongly that, with this work, Bohemian music was turning in a pioneer direction.

On May 30, 1866, Bohemian national music achieved its first milestone with the first performance of Smetana's most famous opera, *The Bartered bride*. Here, the success of his national style could not be questioned. Its appeal on Bohemian audiences was extraordinary.

"*The Bartered bride* is a simple *opéra-comique*, full of vivacity, movement and color," remarked Julien Tiersot. "The action, which takes place entirely in a public square, in an inn of a village of Bohemia, during a festival day, has for a subject a typical vaudeville situation. . . . This is a work full of verve and gaiety; its author had certainly conceived with pleasure." As for the score of the opera, Tiersot commented: "All the music which expresses all the states of soul (however simple) of the characters, is enframed here and there by purely picturesque episodes: choruses of peasants, drinking songs and, above all else, by popular elements which contribute greatly in giving life to this musical work and to justify its reputation as a representation of the art of a people."

The Bartered bride in its original form consisted of two acts, with musical episodes interspersed with spoken dialogue. It was later revised by Smetana, extended into three acts, with

spoken dialogue supplanted by recitatives. In this new form, it received its first great success outside of Bohemia in June of 1892, in Vienna, where it was a sensation. Thus began the great success of *The Bartered bride* thruout the entire world of music. It was introduced to America on February 19, 1909 at the Metropolitan Opera House, under the baton of Gustav Mahler.

The great success of *The Bartered bride* brought Smetana an appointment as conductor of the National Theatre in Prague. One of the members of this orchestra was a young musician, Antonín Dvořák; there soon developed an intimate friendship between the older and younger musician. Smetana exerted a great influence upon the artistic development of Dvořák, and was instrumental in arousing in the younger composer a national consciousness.[1]

In 1869, Smetana founded a dramatic school for the Bohemian Theatre in Prague, becoming its director four years later. At the same time, his industry as a composer knew no recess. He produced two additional operas at this period, including *Libuša* (which won a prize of one thousand gulden), a work, concerning which Herbert F. Peyser wrote in the *New York Times*, after a recent revival in Prague: "It is not necessary to be a Czech to realize that *Libuša* is one of the larger experiences of a musical lifetime. . . . For this is music . . . . now lyrical in the grand manner (and revealing some singular and beautiful relationships to Chopin), now heroic or epic and cast, as it were, in bronze—music that has the tread of armies in it."

By 1874, Smetana began to suffer deafness, as a result of which he was finally forced to resign his position as conductor at the Opera. Deafness, however, could not smother his creative ardor. During this period of storm and stress, he composed his most pretentious symphonic work, a symphonic cycle of six poems entitled *Má Vlast* (My Fatherland), and which includes the world-famous *Vltava* (On the Moldau), performed frequently at symphony concerts thruout the world. He also composed two new operas—*The Kiss*, given a very successful performance in 1876,

[1] See sketch on Dvořák, which also contains a comparison of the music of Dvořák and Smetana.

and *The Secret.* In 1880, he gave the world his greatest chamber work, the string quartet *Aus meinem leben.*

The last years of his life were bitter. His last opera, *The Devil's wall,* produced in 1882, was a miserable failure. It had been decided that the proceeds of the third performance go entirely to the composer, but when the sum was computed it was found to be a beggar's stipend. This failure deeply wounded the composer. "I shall write nothing more," he wailed, "no one wants to hear from me. . . . I am too old!" Late in 1882, he suffered a nervous breakdown, and—forgetting his former vow never again to compose—insisted upon violating the physician's orders by completing his last string quartet. His health went from bad to worse, and he became more and more subject to depression.

By the time his sixtieth birthday was celebrated in Bohemia, he was no longer able to realize what was happening about him. He had lost his mind completely, and on April 20, 1884 was interned in an asylum near Prague. There he died on May 12, 1884—a sombre end to a tragic life that had produced one of the gayest operas of all time.

It is impossible to overestimate Smetana's importance in the history of Bohemian music. "It was Smetana," summarized Jan Löwenbach, "who was priveleged not only to hear and imitate the spirit of the rich melodies and varied rhythms of his nation, but also to invent, to *feel,* and to *express* it in a *new way,* and to adapt it to the spirit of modern times. He created the new song and the first symphony and great symphonic poems filled with new poetical and national ideas, he invented a modern national style of piano music . . . . and he was the first to introduce a discreetly intimate note to chamber music. For national opera, he found, thru his ingenious intuition, his own lyrical and dramatic purity of style which has its personal cadence and retains its value as something intermediate between Mozart and Wagner. All this makes him the great founder of the modern music of the nineteenth century, and one of the most important factors in the culture of his nation."

Principal works by Bedřich Smetana:

OPERA: *The Brandenburgers in Bohemia; The Bartered bride; Dalibor; Libuša; Two widows; The Kiss; The Secret; The Devil's wall; Viola* (unfinished).

ORCHESTRA: *Hakon Jarl; Triumphsymphonie; Má Vlast* (1. *Vyšehrad;* 2. *Vltava;* 3. *Šarka;* 4. *From the fields and groves of Bohemia;* 5. *Tábor;* 6. *Blaník); The Prague carnival.*

CHAMBER MUSIC: *Aus meinem leben* (string quartet); *String quartet in C-minor; Piano trio in G-minor.*
Works for the piano, for chorus, etc.

About Bedřich Smetana:

Nejedlý, Zdeněk. *Frederick Smetana;* Ritter, William. *Smetana;* Rychnovsky, Ernst. *Smetana;* Tiersot, Julien. *Smetana;* Wellek, Bronislav. *Smetana's Leben und Wirken.*
Chesterian N. S. 37:137 February 1924; *Musical America* 39:5 March 1, 1924; *Musical Courier* 88:6 February 28, 1924; *La Revue Musicale* 5:193 October 1924.

Important recordings of music by Bedřich Smetana:

OPERA: *The Bartered bride,* complete (VICTOR-Prague National Opera).

ORCHESTRA: *Má Vlast,* complete (GRAMOPHONE).

CHAMBER MUSIC: *Aus meinem leben,* string quartet (VICTOR-Flonzaley); *Trio in G-minor* (COLUMBIA-Malkin).

Louis Spohr *1784-1859*

LOUIS SPOHR was born in Brunswick on April 5, 1784, the son of musical parents. His father, a physician, played the flute with virtuoso skill; his mother, was both a pianist and a singer. In such setting, Louis Spohr awakened to musical consciousness at an early age. At four, he sang duets with his mother. "Soon after," he informs us in his autobiography, "I had lessons [on the violin] from Herr Riemenschneider. I still remember that first lesson in which I had learned to play the G-major chord on all four strings. In ecstasies over the harmony, I hastened to the kitchen to my mother, and arpeggioed the chord to her so incessantly that she was obliged to drive me away."

Spohr's first important lessons on the violin came in his seventh year from Dufour, in Sessen, whither his family had transferred its home. His progress was such that, when he reached his twelfth birthday, his master felt that there was nothing more he could teach him. Spohr, therefore, was sent back to Brunswick for more advanced study of the violin under Kunisch, and for training in harmony and counterpoint under Hartung. It should be mentioned that upon Hartung's death (which occurred soon after Spohr began his lessons), Spohr's theoretical study came to a complete end; from that time on, the only instruction Spohr received in theory he drew from a personal study of the musical masterpieces of great composers.

In his fourteenth year, he was already a fully equipped virtuoso. His father felt that the time had come for the boy to earn his own living. For this purpose, Louis was sent to Hamburg, where for a period fortune refused to recognize him. After many discouraging months in which he failed completely to attract notice to his talent, he returned to Brunswick where he petitioned the Duke for help. He was engaged in the Court orchestra where his life was far from happy. Concerts at the court were not taken too seriously, invariably interrupted by noise of conversation and card-games; more than once was Spohr rebuked by the court for playing the violin with too much spirit, thereby disturbing the card-players!

This position, however, was not without importance for Spohr, for it enabled him to continue his violin study under Ferdinand Eck, one of the celebrated violin masters of the time. Late in 1802, master and pupil set out for an extensive concert tour. For the first time, Spohr's playing, which had now achieved maturity, aroused comment. A second concert tour came in 1804, when Spohr made an even more vivid impression in the principal cities of Germany. On December 10, his recital in Leipzig was a triumph; he was hailed both as a supreme violinist and as an outstanding composer. Rochlitz, the critic of the *Leipzig Music Journal*, wrote as follows about the two Spohr violin concertos which the violinist introduced at this concert: "His concertos rank with the finest existing, and in particular we know no concertos superior to the D-minor, whether as regards conception, soul and charm, or also in respect to precision and firmness. His peculiar

LOUIS SPOHR

style inclines most to the grand, and then to a soft and dreamy melancholy."

In the Spring of 1805, Spohr returned from his concert travels, and was appointed director of the ducal orchestra at Gotha. This launched Spohr's distinguished career as a conductor; from this time on his name loomed as large in the field of conducting as in those of violin-playing and composition. In 1812, he went to Vienna to direct the orchestra at the Theatre-an-der-Wien, when he met Beethoven whom he described in his autobiography as "blunt," "rough" and "even repulsive in manner." In 1815, Spohr became director of the Frankfurt Theatre where his prestige as a conductor became so great that, in 1820, he was invited to London to direct the symphony concerts of the Royal Philharmonic Society.

His first appearance with the Royal Philharmonic made conducting history, for it was the first time that a conductor attempted to direct a symphony concert with a baton. "I took my stand . . . in front of the orchestra," wrote Spohr in his autobiography, "drew my baton from my coat-pocket and gave the signal to begin. Quite alarmed at such a novel proceeding some of the directors protested against it, but when I besought them to grant me at least one trial they became pacified. The symphonies and overtures that were to be rehearsed were well known to me, and in Germany I had already directed their performances. I, therefore, could not only give the *tempi* in a very decisive manner, but indicated also to the wind instruments and horns all the entries, which ensured to them a confidence such as hitherto they had not known. . . . Surprised and inspired by this result, the orchestra immediately after the first part of the symphony expressed aloud its united assent to the new mode of conducting and thereby overruled all further opposition on the part of the directors. . . . The triumph of the baton as a time-giver was decisive."

Notwithstanding his activity as violinist and conductor, Spohr found sufficient energy for composition. Besides his violin concertos, commented upon above, he had produced many works for orchestra and for voices which received high praise. His opera, *Faust,* was introduced in Prague by Karl Maria von Weber in 1816; another opera, *Zemire und Azor,* was performed under his own direction in Frankfurt in 1819; and in 1820, he conducted his own *Symphony in D-flat* with the London Royal Philharmonic.

In 1822, Spohr received an appointment as director of the Court Theatre orchestra in Cassel, a period in which he produced several works of importance. In 1823, his operatic masterpiece, *Jessonda,* was given a brilliant reception at the Cassel Court Theatre. In 1826, his oratorio, *Die letzten Dinge* —performed at the Cassel Lutheran Church—spread Spohr's reputation as composer thruout Europe. In addition he composed several symphonies, including the famous programmatic *Die Weihe der Töne*—which, for half a century, was esteemed on a level with Beethoven's symphonies—many works for chamber groups, several additional operas, and a violin method which to this day is utilized by students of the instrument.

For thirty-five years, Spohr remained court-director in Cassel, maintaining his great reputation as violinist, conductor and composer. His activities knew no recess; he frequently traveled thruout Europe as violinist and composer, and

his industry as a composer succeeded in producing a prolific library of music in every form.

In 1857, because of his republican sympathies, he was asked to withdraw from his position with a pension. When, one year later, a broken arm brought to a close his virtuoso career, he went into complete retirement, whence he emerged only for a brief appearance, in the Spring of 1859, when he came to Meiningen to make a last appearance as a conductor. A bust of him was in a prominent position on the stage, flowers surrounded his music stand; when he came upon the platform he was greeted with thunderous ovation. This was his last public appearance. On October 22, 1859 he died in Cassel, after several months of illness and sleeplessness.

Very little of Spohr's music has survived him; but he was an important creative force in music. "Undoubtedly," wrote C. à Becket Williams, "the greatness of Spohr consists in his originality. He was decidedly an innovator, and stands out as such in an age of conventionalists. . . . Spohr freely introduced the romantic element into the oratorio. . . . Again, it must be remembered that 'program-music,' so-called, though not invented by him, received a considerable contribution to its waning health by the production of his symphony, *Die Weihe der Töne.* Also, his opera *Jessonda* shares with Weber's *Euryanthe* the honor of introducing for the first time accompanied recitative thruout, in place of spoken dialogue. He also invented various forms of composition, *e.g.* the double string-quartet, the quartet-concerto, the symphony for two orchestras, etc."

Without question, Spohr's most important works are his concertos for violin. Discussing them, Arthur M. Abell wrote: "Spohr gave to the violin concerto a depth, breadth and nobility such as had been quite unknown before him. He took a big step in advance of Viotti; he made the violin concerto an organic whole, giving it greater unity of construction, and greater wealth of ideas. . . . Spohr, like his predecessors, recognized the fundamental nature of the violin and treated it first as a 'singing' instrument; thus his slow movements are among the most beautiful cantabile writing in existence for the violin. Unlike Paganini, he avoided showy writing for effect. There is no froth or foam in Spohr's works. . . . He had an abundance of ideas, and in melodic outlines his concertos are lyric, elegiac and oftimes of a certain melancholic sentimentality."

Spohr venerated one composer, and only one composer—Mozart, whom he always used as a model for his own composition.

Principal works by Louis Spohr:

OPERA: *Alruna*; *Faust*; *Zemire und Azor*; *Jessonda*; *Der Berggeist*, etc.

CHORAL: *Das Jüngste gericht*; *Die letzten Dinge*; *Des Heilands letzte stunden*; *Das befreite Deutschland*; mass; hymns; psalms, etc.

ORCHESTRA: Nine symphonies; Fifteen concertos for violin and orchestra; *Concerto for quartet and orchestra*; *Concertante* (for two violines and orchestra); Two concertos for clarinet and orchestra; overtures, etc.

CHAMBER MUSIC: *Nonet*; *Octet*; *Septet*; *String sextet*; Seven string quintets; *Piano quintet*; *Quintet for piano and wind*; Four double string quartets; Thirty-four string quartets; Three quartet variations; Five piano trios; Twenty duos for two violins; Duos for violin and viola; Sonatas for violin and piano; Sonatas for harp and violin, etc.

Pieces for the harp, for clarinet, for the piano, for the violin; Nine books of songs, duets, part-songs, etc.

About Louis Spohr:

Crowest, Frederick. *The Great Tone Poets*; Malibran, Alexandre. *Louis Spohr: Sein Leben und Wirken*; Schletterer, Hans Michel. *Louis Sphor's Werke*; Spohr, Louis. *Autobiography*.
Monthly Musical Record 60:228 August 1930; *Musical Courier* 51:5 July 26, 1905; *Musician* 8:245 July 1903.

Important recordings of music by Louis Spohr:

ORCHESTRA: *Concerto in A-minor*, for violin and orchestra (TELEFUNKEN).

Gasparo Spontini   *1774-1851*

"Spontini was the last member of a series of composers whose first member was Gluck."—RICHARD WAGNER

GASPARO LUIGI PACIFICO SPONTINI was born in Majolati, Jesi, on November 14, 1774. His parents had hoped to train him for the church, and for this purpose they sent him to an uncle, a priest, for private instruction. The Church, however, held but small appeal for young Spontini. When, at one time, he was subjected to physical maltreatment by his uncle because he neglected religious studies for music, he ran away to Monte San Vito where another uncle, of kindlier disposition, permitted him to follow his musical bent unmolested.

By 1791, it was definitely decided that Spontini would be trained as a musician and not for priesthood. In that year, he was enrolled at the Conservatorio de' Turchini in Naples. There, under the careful guidance of Sala and Tritto, he made rapid progress, revealing such creative gifts that the well known impresario of the Argentina Theatre in Rome, Sigismondo, commissioned him to compose an opera. It was forbidden for students at the Conservatory to accept any commissions. Spontini, therefore, left the Conservatory and set to work upon his first opera. It was *I puntigli delle donne*, performed successfully in Rome.

The success of Spontini's first opera convinced the director of the Conservatory in Naples that so great a talent must be forgiven transgressions. Spontini was permitted to return to his studies. Meanwhile, he did not neglect the composition of operas, producing fifteen of them in a light vein, one of which (*L'Eroismo*) was performed in leading Italian theatres with great success.

In 1803, Spontini decided to seek new victories. He left Italy for Paris. There, by coming into contact with such composers as Méhul and Cherubini and by studying the scores of Mozart and Gluck, he was influenced into seeking an entirely new path in his operatic composition—to abandon his former light Italian style and to adopt the more elaborate manner of the French composers. In 1804, he introduced his first two operas in the new vein—*Julie* and *La Petite maison*—but neither possessed sufficient distinction to attract attention. *Milton*, which came in 1805, was also a failure.

It was while he was working on his masterpiece, *La Vestale*, that Spontini procured the patronage of the Empress Josephine. This patronage proved providential. *La Vestale* confronted innumerable obstacles before it saw first performance. The artists were prejudiced against the work, and rehearsals were usually interrupted by ridicule. Many enemies, envious that an Italian composer should be performed so frequently in Paris, attempted to use their influence to keep the opera from the stage. The patronage of Empress Josephine, however, insured its presentation. On December 6, 1807, therefore, Spontini's masterpiece was introduced.

It was a triumph. The applause of the first-night audience was thunderous. The opera was immediately accepted by public and critic as one of the great ones of the time. It succeeded in winning the decennial prize founded by Napoleon, unanimously accepted by a distinguished committee that included Méhul, Gossec and Grétry. "This opera," ran Méhul's report, "has had a brilliant and lasting success. The composer has had the advantage of applying his talents to an interesting and really tragic subject. His music has verve, brilliancy, and often grace. . . . The incontestable merit and superiority of the success of *La Vestale* do not allow the jury to hesitate in commending this opera as worthy of the prize."

While *La Vestale* is only infrequently performed today (it was last revived in America at the Metropolitan Opera House in 1926), its niche in musical history is established. It is an important transition-opera which bridges the gap between the eighteenth century classicism of Gluck and the French grand-opera period of Meyerbeer.

Discussing the merits of this opera, Ebenezer Prout wrote: "The melodies are all of an Italian cast; the recitatives, always remarkable for the truth of their expression, are modelled on those of Gluck, though without servile imitation; the great ensemble movements were in their day a novelty. Berlioz speaks of him as the inventor of the 'colossal crescendo'. . . . There is little doubt but that his great finales were the patterns which, consciously or not, were imitated by many of the opera composer who have followed him."

The success of *La Vestale* was not an overnight phenomenon. It became a permanent attraction at the Paris Opéra, enjoying more than two hundred performances by 1830. *La Vestale* was first introduced to America in Philadelphia and New York by a company from New Orleans as early as 1828.

Spontini's second great operatic success followed *La Vestale* by two years. *Fernand Cortez,* given its first performance on November 28, 1809, proved to be almost as popular as its eminent predecessor. The only other opera by which Spontini is today remembered—*Olympie* —came on December 22, 1819, and was a complete failure.

His bitterness at the failure of *Olympie* led him, in 1820, to resign his assignments as conductor of Italian Opera in Paris and to brush the dust of Paris from his boots. He visited Germany—coming to Dresden where he became acquainted with Weber, whom he treated with condescension. From Dresden, he went to Berlin where he was installed by Wilhelm III of Prussia as chief conductor and general music director.

In this position, he composed many operas, none of which was successful. His failure to recapture his one-time glory embittered him considerably. He composed less and less and began to assume a pose of arrogance and tactlessness which brought him many enemies. His increasing blatant arrogance, at one time, caused him to insult his patron, Wilhelm III of Prussia, with the result that he was tried in law-court and convicted. In 1842, therefore, Spontini was compelled to retire from his musical posts in Berlin.

In 1844, he was invited by Richard Wagner to come to Dresden and conduct a performance of *La Vestale.* Wagner, too, was treated by Spontini with haughty condescension. A famous anecdote, in this connection, is worth quoting. When Wagner confided to Spontini that, he, too, was a composer of opera, Spontini answered with arrogance: "In *La Vestale,* I treated a Roman subject, in *Agnes von Hohenstaufen,* a German subject, in *Fernand Cortez,* a Spanish-Mexican subject and in *Olympie* a Greek-Macedonian subject—all the rest is worth nothing. How do you imagine that you can invent anything new when

GASPARO SPONTINI

brilliantly when at the climaxes of his subjects his soul is stirred. It is in these qualities that Spontini's greatness lies. . . . Among the shortcomings, Spontini's poverty of harmony and awkwardness and inexpertness of part-writing strike one first."

Principal works by Gasparo Spontini:

OPERA: *Berenice*; *La Petite maison*; *Milton*; *Julie*; *La Vestale*; *Fernand Cortez*; *Pélage*; *Les Deux rivaux*; *Olympie*; *Alcidor*; *Agnes von Hohenstaufen*, etc.
Cantatas, hymns, songs, etc.

About Gasparo Spontini:

Bouvet, Charles. *Spontini*; Bury, Henri Blaze de. *Musiciens Contemporains*; Colini, Francesco. *Pergolesi e Spontini*; Wagner, Richard. *Collected Writings*.
Ménestral 93:1 January 2, 1931; *Monthly Musical Record* 42:494 December 1912; *Musical Times* 51:779 December 1910; *La Revue Musicale* 6:403 September 1906.

Important recordings of music by Gasparo Spontini:

SELECTIONS FROM OPERA: *La Vestale*, "Overture" (COLUMBIA); "Tu che invoco" and "O nume tutelar" (VICTOR-Ponselle).

Sir John Stainer *1840-1901*

SIR JOHN STAINER, composer of English church music, was born in London on June 6, 1840. From his father, a schoolmaster of the parish school of St. Thomas in Southwark, he inherited a great love for music. His father was so passionate an amateur of the musical art that he possessed in his house no less than six pianos, as well as a pipe-organ.

When John Stainer was tall enough to reach the keyboard of the organ while standing, his father began to give him instruction. At the age of seven, John could already play Bach. One year later, he became a probationer in the choir of St. Paul's Cathedral, rising to rank of full chorister in the Dean's vestry at the termination of twelve months.

In 1856, Frederick Ouseley, professor of music at Oxford, came to St. Paul's for the purpose of finding a suitable organist for a vacant position in St. Michael's College in Tenbury. After hearing Stainer perform, he felt convinced that he had found the candidate.

I, Spontini, declare myself unable to surpass my own works?"

Towards the close of his life, Spontini returned to his native city. His closing years were marked by miserable health: he was growing deaf, and his memory was failing him rapidly. He died on January 14, 1851 in the city of his birth. His entire belongings were left to the poor of Jesi and Majolati.

In view of the neglect into which the operas of Spontini have fallen, it is interesting to note with what high esteem and reverence they have been held by his contemporaries and immediate successors. Berlioz frequently spoke of his great admiration both for Gluck and Spontini. Robert Schumann wrote in his diary, after hearing *Fernand Cortez*: "Heard it for the first time with rapture." Richard Wagner wrote: "Let us bow profoundly and reverently before the grave of the creator of *La Vestale, Cortez* and *Olympie*."

Frederick Niecks has admirably summed up the present-day opinion of Spontini. "Spontini's earnestness, nobleness of aim and breadth of conception raise his operas to a high level. In their form there is an imposing largeness and a striving after unity that made him impatient of the littleness produced by the stringing together of self-contained pieces. His dramatic power and skill, which never foresake him, shine

The years Stainer spent in Tenbury were devoted to hard work. As the warden of St. Michael later recorded: "Stainer worked hard at the organ and pianoforte and did a good deal of composition. Besides playing at the two early services, he gave pianoforte lessons to the boys for two hours each day. He was fond of out-of-door sports and joined in the cricket games with the boys and pastors. And so his days passed, each like the other." At the same time, Stainer did not neglect his own study, receiving his bachelor degree in music from Oxford in 1859.

In 1860, Stainer was appointed organist and chorusmaster of Magdalen College in Oxford. One year later, he became organist at the University of Oxford, a rare honor for a youth who had only recently seen his twentieth birthday. 1864 marked his official debut as a composer, when a collection of eight madrigals was published by private subscription. In 1865, Stainer received his doctorate in music from Oxford, his exercise being the oratorio, *Gideon.*

After many years of successful activity as organist, Stainer was honored in 1872 with an appointment as organist of St. Paul's Cathedral. "In a very short time his influence and genius made the services at St. Paul's a model for cathedrals and churches thruout the land," commented an editorial writer in the *Musical Times.* "His masterly accompaniments—always devotional and in perfect taste—no less than his remarkable extemporizations, were listened to by organists from all parts of the world."

But his activity was not confined to the playing of the organ alone. For many years, he was professor of harmony and composition at Crystal Palace School, finally becoming professor of organ at the National School of Music in 1876. At the same time, he was industriously producing an entire library of distinguished choral music. In 1878, his oratorio, *The Daughter of Jairus,* was featured at the Worcester Festival, revealing him to be a strongly endowed musical creator. This was followed by important performances of *St. Mary Magdalen* at the Gloucester Festival of

SIR JOHN STAINER

1887, and of *The Crucifixion* at the St. Marylebone Church in the same year.

In 1888, failing eyesight compelled Stainer to resign his post as organist at St. Paul. One year later, he accepted a professorial position at Oxford University. He held this distinguished assignment for ten years, resigning finally in order to retire from all musical activity. On July 10, 1888 he was knighted by Queen Victoria in recognition of his eminent musical services to his country.

He was on a holiday trip to Italy when death took him suddenly. On Palm Sunday (March 31) of 1901 he reached Verona and spent the morning visiting the amphitheatre. After lunch at the Hôtel de Londres, he decided to take a nap, while his wife visited the Church. Upon her return to the hotel she found Sir John shivering, attacked by pains in the chest. Remedies, which were hurriedly applied, proved futile. A few hours later Sir John was dead.

Sir John Stainer has been described by his friends as a lovable, charitable, pious man of most simple character, to whom jealousy and malice were completely alien. Until the end of his life, his personality was marked by an innocent boyishness which was one of his most engaging qualities. His favorite hobby was his library of some 3,000 volumes to which he always referred with affectionate pride. He was likewise deeply interested in campanology. His favorite pleasure was an evening of conversation with intelligent friends, in which he indulged with considerable gusto between vigorous puffs at a cigar.

As a composer, he is best known for his Church music which is frequently performed. This, at its best, is characterized by melodic inventiveness, a passionate sincerity, simplicity of architectonic construction; at its worst, its sentimentality becomes maudlin. Critics are generally agreed that though Stainer is not a composer of first importance, he has at least succeeded in producing several works—headed by his world-famous *Crucifixion*—which have emotional appeal.

"It is not difficult to estimate his worth as a composer," wrote William Alexander Barrett. "His whole output, practically devoted to the Church, is characterized by sound workmanship, effectiveness and a ready appeal. Of the oratorios and cantatas, *The Crucifixion* and the *Daughter of Jairus* have achieved immense popularity; indeed, the former may be said to be the serious rival of *The Messiah* in the affection of the masses."

Sir John Stainer is likewise known for his critical pen, having produced several important volumes on Dufay, early Bodleian music, and many text-books on harmony and organ playing.

Important works by Sir John Stainer:

CHORAL: *Daughter of Jairus*; *St. Mary Magdalen*; *The Crucifixion*; services; anthems; madrigals; part-songs; Italian songs, etc.

Pieces for the organ.

About Sir John Stainer:

Barrett, William Alexander. *English Church Composers.*

Musical Times 42:293 May 1901; *Musician* 15:210 April 6, 1901.

Important recordings of music by Sir John Stainer:

CHORAL: *The Crucifixion*, complete (VICTOR). Hymns, "Gracious Spirit, Holy Ghost" (DECCA); "Hail, gladdening light" (COLUMBIA); "I am Alpha and Omega" (COLUMBIA).

Johann Wenzel Stamitz 1717-1757

"Haydn and Mozart rest absolutely on the shoulders of Stamitz's symphonies."
—HUGO RIEMANN

JOHANN WENZEL ANTON STAMITZ—the dean of the Mannheim school of instrumental music—was born in Deutschbrod on June 19, 1717, the son of a schoolmaster. He began the study of music at an early age, showing particular talent for the violin. In 1742, he performed as solo violinist at the festivities held in Frankfurt in honor of the coronation of Emperor Karl VII, and created so much enthusiasm for his performance that he attracted the notice of the Elector Palatine Karl Theodore who took him, one year yater, to Mannheim as chamber musician.

In 1745, Stamitz rose to the rank of concertmaster and conductor of the Mannheim orchestra. It was in this position that he made conductorial history, not only by establishing the "Mannheim school of conducting" (which laid considerable emphasis upon careful preparation of each composition performed, and rigid disciplining of the orchestra-men) but also by developing his orchestra as one of the most technically perfect of the time. Charles Burney referred to this Mannheim orchestra under Stamitz as a "band of generals." "No orchestra of the world has ever surpassed the Mannheim orchestra in execution," he wrote. "Its forte is thunder, its crescendo is cataract, its diminuendo is a crystal stream babbling along in the distance, its piano a breath of spring." Stamitz toured thruout Germany with the Mannheim Orchestra, creating a sensation everywhere with the performances.

But Stamitz's importance in musical history rests even more with his compositions, in which he proved to be one of the fathers of the symphony, one of the distinguished forerunners of Haydn. Stamitz's symphonies enjoyed great popularity in their day, and as early as 1751 they received performance in Paris. In these symphonies, Stamitz brings new development to the then embryonic sonata form. Analyzing Stamitz's symphonies, Karl Nef wrote: "His first movements already approached classical structure of the sonata-form: first and second theme, development and reprise. His slow movements are charming in their expression of tender sentiment, and frequently they are already scored in that flexible mobile manner, which is a characteristic of the newer orchestral music. . . . Stamitz also regularly inserted the minuet into the symphony. In this, he anticipated Haydn."

Hugo Riemann, who was one of the first to recognize that Johann Wenzel Stamitz was one of the important composers in musical history, asserted in his *Handbuch der Musikgeschichte* that Stamitz is historically the most significant composer of the middle eighteenth century because of the change from the classic to the romantic point of view in his instrumental music. Riemann pointed out these distinguishing features in the style of Stamitz: General avoidance of the conventional, pedantic, contrapuntal and fugal style; the discarding of the figured bass; frequent use of dynamic expression. It is these qualities which have made more than one recent critic refer to Stamitz as one of the first of the great instrumental composers in music history.

In 1755, Johann Wenzel Stamitz went to Paris to visit his sons, and he sojourned in the French capital for a brief period. He died in Mannheim on March 30, 1757.

Discussing the music of Johann Wenzel Stamitz, Romain Rolland wrote: "The roots of Beethoven exist already . . . in the Mannheim symphonies, in the work of that astonishing Johann Stamitz. . . . Thru him, instrumental music becomes the supple garment of the living soul, always in movement, perpetually changing, with its unexpected fluctuations and changes. . . . I have no hesitation in saying that the symphonies of a Stamitz, though less rich, less beautiful, less exuberant, are much more spontaneous than those of a Haydn or a Mozart. It is made to its own measure; it creates its forms; it does not submit to them."

Two sons of Johann Wenzel Stamitz distinguished themselves as composers, helping their father to bring the symphony form to integration and technical development. Karl Stamitz was born in Mannheim on May 7, 1746, and after studying the violin under his father, he joined the Mannheim orchestra as second violin. He went to Paris, in 1770, where he distinguished himself as a performer on the viol. In 1778, he went to England. Between 1785 and his death he traveled extensively thru Europe, as far as Russia. He died in Jena in 1801. He composed more than seventy symphonies, seven violin concertos, concertos for the viola and for the piano, some chamber music and several operas, including *Dardanus* and *Der verliebte Vormund*.

Johann Anton Stamitz, another son of Johann Wenzel, was born in Mannheim in November of 1754. Like his brother, he studied the violin with his father. With Karl, he visited Paris, where he held the office of "ordinaire de la musique du roi." Johann Anton Stamitz died in Paris in or about 1820, and was the composer of thirteen symphonies, three piano concertos, several violin concertos, fifty quartets and many trios and duets.

Principal works by Johann Wenzel Stamitz:

ORCHESTRA: About fifty symphonies; Ten orchestra trios; Twelve concertos for violin and orchestra; concertos for harpsichord and orchestra, etc.

CHAMBER MUSIC: Sonatas for the violin; sonatas for harpsichord, etc.

About Johann Wenzel Stamitz:

Denkmäler Deutscher Tonkunst (2nd series), vol. 3; Eitner, Robert. *Biographisch-Bibliographisches Quellen-Lexikon*, vol. 9; Nef, Karl. *An Outline of the History of Music.*

Sir Charles Villiers Stanford
1852-1924

"His music is in the best sense of the word Victorian, that is to say it is the musical counterpart of the art of Tennyson, Watts and Matthew Arnold."
—VAUGHAN WILLIAMS

SIR CHARLES VILLIERS STANFORD, the son of an examiner in the Irish Court of the Chancery, was born in Dublin on September 30, 1852. From his parents and his grandmother (the latter had been a pupil of Moscheles) he received his earliest lessons in music. At the age of six, he began to turn his hand to composition. Two years later, one of his compositions was featured during a pantomime performance at the Theatre Royal in Dublin.

He began serious study of music under Levey and Stewart. In his tenth year he visited London where he continued study under O'Leary and Ernest Pauer. He made swift progress; in 1870, he had so complete a musical training that he was able to win the organ scholarship at Queen's College in Cambridge. One year later, when he won the classical scholarship as well, he proved that his talents were not for music alone.

In 1873, he received appointments as organist of Trinity College, and as conductor of the Cambridge University Musical Society. After receiving his Bachelor of Arts degree at Cambridge in 1874, he left for Germany to complete his study of music under Reinecke in Leipzig and Kiel in Berlin. On his return to England he made his official bow as a composer when his incidental music to Tennyson's *Queen Mary* was performed, in 1876, at the Lyceum Theatre. This was followed by a performance of his *Festival overture* at the Gloucester Festival of 1877.

These early performances of his music encouraged a prodigious fertility. During the next few years he produced an abundance of works in every form of music, including his first opera *The*

SIR CHARLES VILLIERS STANFORD

Veiled prophet of Khorassan (1881) and his first two symphonies (1876 and 1882).

In 1883, Stanford was appointed by Sir George Grove as professor of composition and conductor of the orchestra and operatic class at the Royal College of Music. Two years later, Stanford supplemented this activity with conductorial duties with the Bach Choir. From this time on, his life was rich in achievement, and his energy poured thru many channels. In 1887, he was appointed professor of music at Cambridge, a position he held with prestige until the end of his life. In 1901, he succeeded Sir Arthur Sullivan as conductor of the Leeds Festival. He also made periodic appearances as conductor in principal cities of Europe and America. Thus, for many years, he exerted his influence in many fields.

To honor his crowning position in the world of English music, Stanford was knighted by King Edward VII in 1901. Three years later, he was elected a member of the Royal Academy of Arts in Berlin.

Sir Charles Villiers Stanford died in London on March 29, 1924. He has left an indelible mark as teacher, writer and composer. As a teacher, his influence can best be judged by the long list of distinguished pupils who studied under him, including Eugene Goossens, George Dyson, Vaughan-Williams, Frank Bridge, John Ireland and Gustav Holst. As a writer he is best known for his *History of Music,* his book of critical essays entitled *Interludes,* and several volumes of memories.

As a composer, the distinguishing quality of his music, as an anonymous critic wrote in the *Musical Times,* was his "versatility. There is no branch in which he did not do work varying from the merely sound to the first-rate—oratorio, opera, orchestral and chamber music, choral works, etc. . . . As is inevitable in so vast an output, there is much that is unoriginal, but impeccable workmanship is always evident. The matter may be perfunctory, the manner never. . . . His scores of all kinds are models of economy, though perhaps, this quality is best shown in his songs." W. H. Hadow added: "In all his works he is a craftsman of almost uncanny skill: with these and their like he rises above craftsmanship into the pure serene of poetry." It might be added that another distinguishing characteristic of Stanford's music is its undiluted classicism.

It is the opinion of Thomas F. Dunhill that Stanford will best be remembered for those songs which he composed in his later years. "In the familiar *Songs of the sea* and the *Songs of the fleet,* Stanford touched a note of romantic patriotism in strains which quicken the ardor of our spirit, and are stirring, manly and dignified. . . . But even better, because of sheer lovableness, were his Irish songs. It is safe to say that no one has approached Stanford in Irish music, either in the new settings he has provided for the old folk tunes of his race, or in those songs in which the melodies are entirely his own."

Harry Plunket Greene, in his charming book on Stanford, has given us vivid personal glimpses at the composer. He has shown Stanford to be Irish in his wit, gentleness, speech and temperament. He had a sharp tongue and a combustible temper and was, therefore, not always easy to get along with. As a teacher he was brusque, sometimes merciless. To one pupil, he exclaimed: "Your music comes from hell. From hell, my boy, H-E double L!" To Harold Samuel, the famous Bach performer, he once said: "You are playing Bach like a blacksmith." However, at other moments, he could be soft and solicitous; and, as a matter of fact, he always regretted his sharp remarks a moment after he made them, making great effort to placate his victim.

He was a methodical worker. For this reason, no doubt, he was able to accomplish as much as he did. He was smothered by the mass of routine which enmeshed him as teacher and conductor, but he never neglected his composition, which he always felt was the most important part of himself. Until the end of his life, he kept the fresh morning hours for his creative work, permitting no one and nothing to interfere with this custom.

He was a vicious opponent of modernism in music. "Anybody can write in the extreme modern style," he once

told a friend. "It is largely a matter of having enough spare time to write lots of notes."

Principal works of Sir Charles Villiers Stanford:

OPERA: *The Veiled prophet of Khorassan; Savonarola; The Canterbury pilgrims; Shamus O'Brien; Much ado about nothing; The Critic,* etc.

CHORAL: *The Three holy children; Eden;* Psalms; *Mass in G; Requiem; Stabat Mater; The Revenge; The Battle of the Baltic; The Last post; Fairy day; Elegiac ode; The Bard; East to West; Songs of the sea; Song of faith; Wellington ode; Welcome song; Songs of the fleet;* services; motets, etc.

ORCHESTRA: Seven symphonies; *Festival overture; In the style of a tragedy overture;* Four Irish rhapsodies; Eight Irish dances; *Serenade in G;* Two concertos for the piano and orchestra; *Concerto for violin and orchestra; Variations on an English theme* (for piano and orchestra); Incidental music to many plays including those of Aeschylus, Sophocles, Tennyson, etc.

CHAMBER MUSIC: *Nonet-serenade;* Two string quintets; *Piano quintet;* Six string quartets; Two piano quartets; Two piano trios; Two sonatas for violin and piano; Two sonatas for violoncello and piano; sonata for clarinet and piano, etc.

Songs, pieces for the piano, arrangements of Irish folk songs, etc.

About Sir Charles Villiers Stanford:

Fuller-Maitland, J. A. *The Music of Parry and Stanford;* Greene, Harry Plunket. *Charles Villiers Stanford;* Porte, John F. *Sir Charles Villiers Stanford;* Stanford, Sir Charles Villiers. *Pages from an Unwritten Diary;* Willeby, Charles. *Masters of English Music.*

Monthly Musical Record 48:98 May 1918; *Music and Letters* 5:193 July 1924; *Musical Opinion* 47:797 May 1924; *Musical Times* 68: 258 March 1927; *Proceedings of the Musical Association* 53:41 (1926-1927).

Important recordings of music by Sir Charles Villiers Stanford:

CHORAL: *Songs of the sea,* complete (GRAMOPHONE); *Songs of the fleet,* "Farewell" (GRAMOPHONE); "The Little Admiral" (GRAMOPHONE); *Morning Service in B-flat,* "Benedictus" (GRAMOPHONE); "Magnificat" and "Nunc dimittis" (GRAMOPHONE); "Te Deum" (COLUMBIA).

Alessandro Stradella　*1645-1682*

ALESSANDRO STRADELLA was born in or about 1645. The place of his birth is unknown, but it is believed to have been Naples. His father, Marcantonio Stradella, was governor of

Vignola who, in 1643—upon the siege of the town by the Papal troops—retreated to Montefestino.

The life of Stradella has been so colored by legend and romance that it is difficult to trace the boundary where truth ends and fiction begins. The most familiar version has been recorded by Bourdelot in the *Histoire de la musique et ses effets,* and there is reason to believe that at least part of this version is true.

Stradella, who had acquired a considerable reputation as a musician in his youth, was invited to Venice to compose operas for the Carnival season; some historians, like Burney, believe that he had come to Venice not to compose operas but to teach singing. In any case, while in Venice he was engaged by Senator Alvise Contarini to teach his beautiful mistress, Hortensia, the art of song. Stradella and his pupil fell in love with each other, finally deciding to escape from Venice together. When their flight was discovered by the Senator, he bitterly vowed that he would kill the musician. He engaged two assassins to follow the fleeing pair, who traced their movements as far as Rome. There, the assassins learned that Stradella's oratorio, *San Giovanni Battista* was being given at the church of St. John the Lateran, and they planned to accost the composer after the performance and murder him. While waiting for Stradella, they entered the Church, where they were so moved by the beauty of the music, and by the poignancy of Stradella's singing that—instead of murdering him—they warned him of the Senator's plans. The amorous pair, therefore, fled from Rome to Turin. In Turin, they received the protection of the Duchess of Savoy who, having heard their story, decided to help them. She placed Stradella's beloved in a convent, and by employing Stradella as her personal musician kept a vigilant eye over him. However, the lovers were only temporarily safe. One evening, taking less precaution than usual, Stradella was waylaid on the street and stabbed. The wound was not fatal, and after several weeks the composer recovered. The Duchess, finally, decided to have the couple marry in her palace and live with her. For one year, the pair knew happiness. Then, while in Genoa on the occasion of a performance of one of Stradella's operas, Stradella and his wife were accosted in the street late one night and murdered. The year of Stradella's death is believed to be 1682.

This life story of the composer has served as the libretto for an opera by Flotow, entitled *Stradella.*

Stradella's most famous work was his oratorio, *San Giovanni Battista,* whose principal importance rests in the fact that it represents an important link between the abortive oratorio form of Carissimi and the mature artistic creation of Handel. "The recitative is in general excellent," was Burney's critical opinion of the work, "and there is scarce a movement among the airs in which genius, skill and study do not appear." It is interesting to mention that this oratorio is one of the first works in which the proper accidentals—sharps and flats—were placed at the clef.

Discussing Stradella in relation to his eminent contemporaries, Alberto Gentili wrote: "Stradella by no means stands apart from his predecessors. But if in certain ariosos which spring up in the recitatives he reminds us closely of Cavalli—if the facile but well-turned stream of melody in certain pages takes us back to Cesti's nobility of form . . . . there is no denying, on the whole, Stradella's originality and creative force. He quite outdistances Cavalli by the greater amplitude of his forms and his breadth of outlook, which is capable of taking in a series of interdependent scenes. He excells Cesti by his variety of accent, by the nervous vigor of his utterance, by his melodic versatility, by his greater dramatic intensity."

Principal works by Alessandro Stradella:

OPERA: *La Forza dell amor paterno,* etc.

CHORAL: *San Giovanni Battista; Esther; San Pelagio; San Giovanni Crisostomo; Susanna,* etc.; Religious and secular cantatas; motets; madrigals; serenades, etc.

INSTRUMENTAL: String concertos.

About Alessandro Stradella:

Bourdelot. *Histoire de la Musique et ses Effets;* Burney, Charles A. *General History of Music;* Hess, Heinz. *Die Opern Alessandro Stradellas.*

Musical Times 68:507 June 1927; *Sammelbänder Internationalen Musik Gesellschaft* 8:566 (1906-1907).

Important recordings of music by Alessandro Stradella:

VOCAL: *Pietà, signore,* air (VICTOR-Gigli).

Johann Strauss, II *1825-1899*

FOR more than one hundred years, the Johann Strauss family were the waltz-kings of Vienna.

The first Johann Strauss, the father of the composer of *The Blue Danube waltz,* was born in Vienna in 1804. While still a boy, a goading wanderlust urged him to run away from his apprenticeship, bookbinding; for a while he was a homeless waif on the streets of Vienna. Good fortune brought him into contact with a sympathetic stranger, who decided to adopt him and give him musical training.

As a boy of fifteen, Johann joined the then celebrated band of Josef Lanner. Ambition, however, stirred restlessly in his bosom. It was not long before he broke all relationship with his employer in order to assemble his own orchestra. He made his debut as *Kapellmeister* in the Bock Café with instantaneous success. From the Bock, he went to the *Zwei tauben.* There he introduced the first of his captivating waltzes, the *Täuberl-wälzer,* and his fame in Vienna was firmly established.

When he reached the prime of life, an unhappy marriage drove him to desert his family for Emilie Trampusch, a beautiful and wealthy widow. The remainder of his years were, therefore, spent in wealth, luxury and love while, at the same time, he was achieving an enormous reputation as conductor of light music in France, England and Austria. While he was tasting success and adulation, his family suffered appalling penury. When, in 1849, he lay on his death-bed, his abandoned son —Johann Strauss, the second—was at his side. And the father died, knowing well that his son was greater than he, that the son would avenge himself for the desertion of the family by his father by surpassing his predecessor completely in his every effort as *Kapellmeister* and composer.

The fame of Johann Strauss, senior, as conductor was enormous. As a leader, he had a magnetism that was irresistible. "I shall never forget," wrote Richard Wagner, then in his nineteenth year, "the passion bordering on mad fury with which the wonderful Johann Strauss conducted. This Daemon of the ancient Viennese folk spirit trembled at the beginning of a new waltz like a python preparing to spring, and it was more the ecstasy produced by the music than the drinks among the enchanted audience that stimulated that magical first violin to almost dangerous flights."

While the elder Strauss was a prolific composer, producing an enormous quantity of music, some of which possesses charm and bewitching ingenuity, very little of it is of real importance. He is best known for his *Radetzky-march, Strains of the Lorelei and the Rhine,* and *Black, red and gold.* Had Johann Strauss, the older, been more self-critical, more discriminating in his selection of musical ideas, he might have ranked with the great waltz composers of all time. As it is, he is best remembered as a captivating *Kapellmeister*—and as the father of the greatest waltz composer of all time.

It was the younger Johann Strauss who immortalized the family name of Strauss, making it synonymous with great waltzes. The second Johann Strauss was born in Vienna on October 25, 1825, the first born of the marriage between the older Johann and Anna Streim. For some mysterious reason, father Johann was viciously opposed to his son becoming a musician. With violent threats and lashes of the whip he attempted to keep his son from any musical preoccupation. However, young Johann was too magnetically attracted to music to permit threats to discourage him. While his father was at the café, he attempted to draw pleasant sounds from his father's violin. Then, encouraged by his mother, he studied the violin and composition surreptitiously under Amon, a violinist in the father's orchestra. It was not until his father deserted his family that young Johann could turn his entire devotion and effort to music study.

JOHANN STRAUSS II

On October 15, 1844, Johann Strauss, the second, made his debut as *Kapell-meister*, at Dommayer's Casino, near Schönbrunn. He played the overture to Auber's *The Mute of Portici*, his father's waltz, *Strains of the Lorelei and the Rhine*, and a waltz of his own creation, *Die Gunstwerber*. *Die Gunstwerber* met such approval that young Strauss played several other morsels of his own creation—including the *Debutsquadrill* and the *Herzenlist* polka. Finally, his waltz *Sinngedichte* aroused such delirium among those in the audience that it was repeated eighteen times.

The older Johann Strauss was, at the time of this concert, sick at the home of his mistress. But, from the lips of friends, he heard the tidings that his son's triumph had been unprecedented in Vienna, and that young Johann was now an idol of the café-house.

From his debut on, young Johann Strauss' importance in Vienna swelled to prodigious proportions. He became the cynosure for all eyes, the envy of all young men, the idol of all young men. His music was on every one's lips and in each one's heart. "The Strauss madness," as it has been called by his biographers, was now at its height. Before long, Johann Strauss visited Russia, France and England where, too, his fame knew no boundaries.

On August 27, 1862 Johann Strauss married Henrietta Treffz, of notorious reputation. Strange to say, she made him a remarkable wife. Under her warm encouragement, Johann Strauss rose to new heights as a composer of waltzes; it was during this marriage that he composed some of his most imperishable masterpieces.

The world-famous *Blue Danube waltz* was composed sometime in 1867 while Strauss was living in the Praterstrasse. Its première took place on February 13, 1867, at a concert of the Wiener Männergesangverein at the Diana Saal. It was a sensation.

But Henrietta not only inspired her husband to compose his greatest waltzes. It was also her coaxing which made Strauss turn to more ambitious creative fields—the operetta. On February 10, 1871, the first performance of *Indigo and the forty thieves*, Strauss' first operetta, was performed at the Theatre-an-der-Wien. Critics were unanimous in agreeing that Johann Strauss had surpassed himself. Two years later, Johann Strauss composed his famous *Die Fledermaus*.

In June of 1872, Johann Strauss came to America, at the invitation of Boston to help commemorate the centenary of American independence. He made his American debut by conducting a monster concert. An orchestra of a thousand instruments and a chorus of a thousand voices, directed by no less than a hundred conductors, were all guided by a brightly illuminated baton in the hand of Johann Strauss. In America, as well, Johann Strauss met idolatry. During the next few weeks, he directed fourteen concerts—principally in Boston and New York, scoring unforgettable triumphs.

Henrietta Strauss died suddenly of a heart attack on April 8, 1878. Strauss' second wife, Angelika Diettrich, was an incorrigible coquette and strumpet. Their marriage, soon culminating in divorce, was sordid from the first. Johann Strauss married a third time—Adele Deutsch, who made his last days comfortable and happy. Adele survived her famous husband by more than three decades.

Late in 1894, Vienna became festive in honor of the fiftieth anniversary of Johann Strauss' first appearance as a *Kapellmeister*. For an entire week the festivities took place. On October 14, there was a festival concert in the Music Hall conducted by Johann Strauss himself; that evening there took place a Promenade concert. The following day, exactly fifty years after Johan Strauss made his memorable debut, the Haupt theatre presented a ballet accompanied by the music of Strauss' most famous melodies. Late that same night, a torchlight parade took place, with thousands of Viennese taking part. Telegrams and messages poured in from all over the world. America sent Strauss a silver loving cup with fifty silver leaves on it, the names of fifty of Strauss' most famous waltzes engraved, one on each leaf. Russia sent him a magnificent floral wreath. Word came from Berlin, Hamburg and Munich that similar festivities were observed in those cities. At the final concert of this celebration, Johann Strauss made his final speech to his public: "If it is true that I have talent, I owe it, above everything else, to my beloved city, Vienna."

On May 22, 1899, Johann Strauss conducted a performance of *Die Fledermaus*. After the performance, he caught cold and was confined to bed. Bronchitis set in. It was soon apparent that Strauss was a mortally sick man. Late one night, he sat up in bed, and gesturing extravagantly as though he were conducting an orchestra, he sang at the top of his voice:

So beautiful the sun shines yet,
Alas, this sun now soon must set!

On June 3, at four o'clock, his heart stopped beating.

The news of his death reached the *Volksgarten*. The conductor at once stopped the music he was performing in the middle of a bar, and broke the news to the audience. Then, after a few minutes of reverent silence, the orchestra played the *Blue Danube waltz*, pianissimo.

His funeral was as grandiose as though an Emperor had died. He was buried in the Vienna cemetery, near the other three glories of Vienna's musical life —Beethoven, Franz Schubert and Johannes Brahms.

To a certain extent, Johann Strauss' enormous appeal to his Viennese caféhouse public was the result of the fascination of his personality. He was strikingly attractive, with soft effeminate lines of the face, and rhythmic, graceful curves of the body. On the platform, conducting his orchestra, or off it, he made a profound impression. He was all grace and poise—the last word in elegance, sauveness and self-assurance. His charm was unquestioned.

But this only partially explains Strauss' great success. Equally important was the fact that he could produce sensuous qualities in the music he conducted, evoking new voices and new beauties from the texture of the harmonies. "You must go to the *Volksgarten* on Friday evening when Johann Strauss will conduct his waltzes," wrote no one less than Johannes Brahms. "There is a master, such a master of the orchestra that one never loses a single tone of whatever instrument." It should be remembered that altho Strauss conducted light music extensively, he was one of the first to feature extracts of Richard Wagner's music on his programs at a time when Wagner met antagonism and opposition in Vienna.

Altho Strauss' appeal as conductor cannot be doubted, it is as a composer of waltzes and operettas that his name lives. There were some critics, in his day and in our own, who cannot accept Strauss' music seriously. Eduard Hanslick objected to the "heavy Lisztian chords" and to the "Wagnerism" of the waltzes. Another critic of Strauss' day wrote: "Let it be stated that the waltzes, polkas and quadrilles of Herr Strauss lack not only freshness of invention but even the particular character of dance music; the continual syncopation of the themes, the noisy orchestration, the frequent employment of drums and whistles completely obscures the dance rhythm and makes his music truly horrible to the ear."

However, the greatest number of famous musicians have respected Strauss' music considerably. Hans von Bülow once wrote that a Johann Strauss waltz should be featured on symphony programs because of their intrinsic musical value. It is well-known that when Johannes Brahms autographed a picture for Adele Strauss, he scrawled in a corner a few bars of the *Blue Danube* and added: "Not by me—unfortunately." Jacques Offenbach, Verdi, Delibes, Gounod, Goldmark were only a few of the great composers who expressed great admiration for Strauss' charm and talent.

Strauss' outstanding importance as a conductor rests in the development he brought to the waltz-form. Wrote Paul Bechert: "His reform of the waltz as a species had reached a stage where it could not be improved upon. The originally simple form had been developed by him into a thing of subtle art; it was no longer pure ¾ rhythm, supported by simple broken chords in the bass and endowed with native melodic equipment. He had made it an instrument for the expression of varying moods of the widest scope. Just as Schubert had created the *Lied* out of the rudiments of simple folk songs, Strauss had made of the waltz an art form in the highest sense."

"To be sure, faults manifest themselves in Strauss' works," wrote this editor in an extensive article on Strauss in the *Musical Quarterly*. "Sometimes he resorts to melodic material of the most stilted kind; sometimes he uses *oom*-pah *oom*-pah kapellmeister accompaniments; harmonic crudities and clumsy modulations are not infrequent intruders in his scores; and his embellishment of melodies with octaves, trills and mordents may occasionally cloy. But even though one may recognize these defects and deplore them, one must concede that he frequently swept to greatness. . . . Strauss' ability to give elasticity and suppleness to three-quarter time was nothing short of miraculous. He could speak of pain and ecstasy, joy and suffering, all to the lilting rhythm of the waltz. And he was endowed with a melodic genius capable of bearing favorable comparison with his rhythmic gift."

Both brothers of Johann Strauss were waltz-composers in their own right.

Joseph Strauss (1827-1870) is the composer of such favorites as the *Aquarellen waltzes,* the *Delirienwälzer* and *Aus der ferne.* Eduard Strauss (1835-1916) is known principally for his *Doctrinenwälzer, Lilienkränze* and *Myrthen-Sträusschen* waltzes. There were times when the three brothers collaborated: The *Trifolienwälzer* and the *Schützenquadrill* were composed by Johann, Josef and Eduard; the *Pizzicato* polka, the *Vaterländischer* march and the *Monstrequadrill* were the works of Johann and Joseph. Without exception the works produced in collaboration were inferior to those created single-handed.

There is also a Johann Strauss III, nephew of the younger Johann Strauss, who in recent years has become well-known in Vienna as a conductor of light music. Neither Richard Strauss, the world-famous modern composer of tone-poems, nor Oscar Straus, the composer of such operettas as *The Chocolate soldier* is related to the waltz-family.

Principal works of Johann. Strauss, II:

OPERETTA: *Die Fledermaus; Carnival in Rome; Gypsy baron; A Night in Venice,* etc.

ORCHESTRA: About five hundred dance-works including such world-famous waltzes as the *Blue Danube; Tales from the Vienna woods; Morning journals; Wine, woman and song; Vienna blood; Artist's life,* etc.

Also polkas, quadrilles, etc.

About Johann Strauss, II:

Decsey, Ernst von. *Johann Strauss;* Ewen, David. *Wine, Women and Waltz.*

Important recordings of music by Johann Strauss, II:

OPERETTA: Fledermaus, abridged (BRUNSWICK-Berlin State Opera).

ORCHESTRA: *Music of Johann Strauss,* including the *Blue Danube, Acceleration* and *Tales from Vienna* waltzes, and overtures to the *Fledermaus* and *Gypsy baron* (VICTOR-Ormandy). *Waltzes of Johann Strauss,* including *Artist's life, Village swallows, A Thousand and one nights* waltzes (VICTOR-Krauss, Kleiber). Brunswick Strauss Collection, no. 2, including *Morning journals, Wine, woman and song* waltzes (BRUNSWICK).

Joseph Suk *1874-1935*
(See *Composers Of Today*)

Sir Arthur Sullivan *1842-1900*

"Sullivan was as much a satirist in musical notes as Gilbert in the verbal test. Their repartees in collaboration often reminded of the sarcasms of Voltaire."
—Saint-Saëns

SIR ARTHUR SEYMOUR SULLIVAN, one of the greatest composers of comic opera, was born in London on May 13, 1842. His father, a bandmaster, soon discovered that his son was unusually gifted: At the age of eight, Arthur could play tolerably well on almost every instrument in the band. When, therefore, Arthur finished four years of preliminary academic study at a private school in Bayswater, he received an appointment as a member of the Chapel Royal school. He possessed a striking voice, and was frequently called upon to sing solos. More important, however, is the fact that during his three years as a chorister he composed many anthems and songs, one of which was sufficiently talented to reach publication in 1855.

By 1856, Sullivan was promoted to the rank of "first boy" in the Chapel choir. He had shown such adaptability for music study that, when announcement was made that a Mendelssohn prize had been inaugurated, he was tempted to become a candidate. When the examinations were over it was discovered that, of the nineteen applicants, he was tied with one other young musician for first award—the other student being Joseph Barnby, later a well-known conductor. A second test was inaugurated to decide between these two applicants; from this, Arthur Sullivan emerged the victor. As a result, Arthur Sullivan became a pupil at the Royal Academy of Music where his teachers included Goss and Sterndale Bennett. He remained there until the Fall of 1858. During this period, he composed an overture which was performed at one of the concerts of the Academy.

On leaving the Royal Academy of Music, Arthur Sullivan went to Leipzig to enroll in the Conservatory. Under Hauptmann, Plaidy, Moscheles and Richter, he made rapid strides towards musical maturity. A string quartet and an orchestral overture, *The Light of the harem*—both of which were performed —attested to his growing strength as a composer.

Leipzig was an all-important influence in Sullivan's artistic development, as he himself recognized. "I often try to think what would have become of me had I never come to Germany," he wrote in a communication home. "In England there was very little more for me to learn. I had heard and knew well almost all the small stock of music which is ever performed in London (and it is very little compared to what one hears here!). I should have made very little improvement in pianoforte playing, whereas now, thanks to Messrs. Moscheles and Plaidy, I am a tolerably decent player." In Leipzig, too, Arthur Sullivan first tried his hand at conducting, with a certain measure of success.

Early in 1862 he was back in London. On April 15, his orchestral suite to Shakespeare's *The Tempest* was performed at the Crystal Palace with so much acclaim that Sullivan found himself a much-discussed composer. Charles Dickens was one of the celebrities at the concert. After the performance the distinguished novelist approached Sullivan and said: "I am not a music critic, but I do know that I have just listened to some very remarkable music." Some months later, Sullivan visited Paris in the company of Dickens. While there, he met Rossini for whom he played parts of his *Tempest,* to the enthusiasm and delight of the great composer.

The next few years saw Sullivan's prestige as a composer mounting rapidly. In 1863, after a visit to Ireland, he composed his *Symphony in E-flat* (more familiarly known as the *Irish symphony*) which, upon its first performance at the Crystal Palace in March of 1866, was a decided success. The same year, the death of his father inspired him to compose his orchestral overture, *In Memoriam,* featured at the Norwich Festival. Other important performances of his works included that of his *Concerto for violoncello and orchestra* at the Crystal Palace, on November 24, 1866, his orchestral overture *Marmion* by the Royal Philharmonic Society on June 3, 1867, an oratorio, *The Prodigal son,* at the Worcester Festival of 1870 and several shorter hymns and songs.

SIR ARTHUR SULLIVAN

the most famous of which are *Onward, Christian soldiers* and *The Lost chord.*

At this same time, Arthur Sullivan was successfully holding two positions as organist in London. Between 1874 and 1887 he expanded his activities by officiating regularly as conductor of the Leeds Festival and the Royal Philharmonic of London. From 1876 to 1881 he officiated as principal of the National Training School in London.

But it was not in serious music that Sullivan attained immortality, even though his religious music achieved tremendous popularity. For, as Isaac Goldberg wrote of Sullivan's religious music, "sweetness it has and light; never power, never depth, never loftiness." As a matter of fact, what Percy Fitzgerald wrote of Sullivan's oratorios might very well apply to the bulk of Sullivan's serious works, including his opera *Ivanhoe.* They are, wrote Fitzgerald, "excellent, scholarly works, but they seem to lack inspiration and are academical in style and treatment."

It was, rather, in efforts which Sullivan took less seriously, which, so to speak, he considered his musical slummings that Sullivan achieved greatness. In the lighter vein of song, Sullivan proved himself to be incomparable.

His first effort in this direction came in 1867, *Cox and Box,* based upon a famous farce of Madison Morton's.

However, it was not until Sullivan met his great collaborator, W. S. Gilbert, that he came into his own as a composer of comic opera. In 1871, Sullivan was introduced to Gilbert by a singer, Fred Clay; it was not long before an enterprising impresario, John Hollingshead of the Gaiety Theatre, commissioned the pair to compose a comic opera for his theatre. *Thespis* was the first of the Gilbert and Sullivan comic operas. While they were merely groping in this first collaborative effort, it was clearly disclosed that they were bringing comic opera into new territories. *Trial by jury* came in 1875, the first of their operas to be composed for Richard D'Oyly Carte, the impresario who was responsible for their greatest achievements; and *Trial by jury*—with its stinging satire on law—definitely proved that both composer and librettist had found themselves and each other. From this time on, their collaborative efforts were to be a "marriage of true minds," one of the most felicitous wedlocks of music and libretto that the history of operas has known.

In 1876, Richard D'Oyly Carte formed his own comic-opera company, and on November 17, 1877 launched his new venture with *The Sorcerer* of Gilbert and Sullivan. *The Sorcerer* was followed, six months later, by *Pinafore,* which played for two years to crowded and enthusiastic houses. That was the beginning of the Gilbert and Sullivan craze. In 1879, Gilbert and Sullivan came to America in order to protect their copyrights, which were being flagrantly stolen. While in this country, they introduced their *Pirates of Penzance* at the Fifth Avenue Theatre. *The Pirates* took New York by storm.

Meanwhile, D'Oyly Carte was erecting a new theatre, the Savoy, henceforth the home of the Gilbert and Sullivan operetta. To inaugurate the opening of the Savoy, *Patience*—that pungent attack on Oscar Wilde—was performed under the baton of Arthur Sullivan. Its success was tempestuous. A few months later, Arthur Sullivan was knighted by Queen Victoria.

After this, each new Gilbert and Sullivan comic opera was more successful than its predecessor. *Iolanthe* came in 1882, *Princess Ida* in 1884, *The Mikado* in 1885, *Ruddigore* in 1887, the *Yeomen of the guard* in 1888 and *The Gondoliers* in 1889.

In analyzing the scores which Sir Arthur Sullivan composed for these operas, Thomas Frederick Dunhill discovers the following outstanding characteristics of Sullivan's style in the lighter vein: (1) his avoidance of any manufactured music, (2) his complete unpretentiousness, (3) the unaffected simplicity and striking lucidity, (4) his pungent sense of humor and satire which "almost invariably are coexistent with a sense of beauty," and (5) his genius "for abounding provision of good melodies." Cecil Forsyth points out still another quality, which he considers most important of all, namely Sullivan's "recognition of the fact that it was not only necessary to set his text to music which was pleasing in itself, but to invent melodies in such close alliance with the words that the two things become indistinguishable. . . . In this respect, Sullivan did more for the English stage than any musician of his time."

In his scores, Sullivan is rarely the experimenter or innovator; he does not blaze new tonal trails. "He used no harmonies that composers before him had not used over and over again," wrote T. F. Dunhill. "His melodies were perfectly proportioned in an unorthodox way, and he seldom attempted to arrest our attention by oddities of shape or rhythm. His orchestration, skilful and pat as it invariably is, was never in the least degree experimental. And yet, within such circumscribed limits, his art is always recognizable for its personal quality. The Sullivan touch is unmistakable and can be felt instantly."

It was after the composition of *The Gondoliers* that the famous rupture between Gilbert and Sullivan took place, a rupture that had been pending for several years. They had not been harmonizing so smoothly in their personal relationship as they had in their artistic alliance. Each ridiculed the pretenses and poses of the other; each was slightly envious of the acclaim the other received; and each was not above criticizing the other. The final breach, it is said, was caused by the cost of a carpet

for the Savoy. The expenses of the Savoy Theatre were to be shared by Gilbert, Sullivan and D'Oyly Carte equally. Carte had purchased a new carpet for his theatre at a price exceeding $500, an expenditure which Gilbert thought unforgivable. A squabble between Gilbert and Carte ensued. At first, Sullivan was neutral in the dispute. Then, when Gilbert demanded to know his position, Sullivan said he was on the side of Carte. There followed hot and ugly words; Gilbert relieved himself of some ugly epithets. Shortly afterwards, Gilbert wrote his historic note to Sullivan: "The time for putting an end to our collaboration has at last arrived. In accordance, therefore, with the contents of my note to you of this morning, I am writing a letter to Carte (of which I enclose a copy) giving him notice that he is not to produce or perform any of my libretti after Christmas 1890. In point of fact, after the withdrawal of *The Gondoliers,* our united work will be heard in public no more."

In 1893, however, the rift was momentarily cemented. Once again, Gilbert and Sullivan collaborated on a comic opera. *Utopia limited* was a success, though both Gilbert and Sullivan realized that in this work neither one had succeeded in recapturing his former genius. One more collaborative effort saw the light of day, *The Grand duke* in 1896. With that opera, the most famous collaborators in musical history called it a day.

Sullivan's last works were an opera, *Ivanhoe,* which came in 1891, and three more operettas (to none of which Gilbert supplied a libretto). The last of these operettas, *The Emerald isle,* was never finished by Sullivan, but was brought to completion after his death by Sir Edward German.

Ivanhoe was Sullivan's most ambitious creation, the one upon which he expended most energy and devotion. "Sullivan wrote *Ivanhoe,* so to speak, with his lifeblood," we are informed by Herman Klein. "He slaved at it steadily from May until December, and put into it only of his best. For weeks before he finished it he was inaccessible; the Christmas of 1890 was no holiday for him." Despite all this devotion to his task, *Ivanhoe* was a dismal failure when it was given its first performance. And it failed dismally only because Sullivan as an artist had failed. "*Ivanhoe*," as Percy Fitzgerald pointed out, "was certainly a ponderous work, more like a vast symphony protracted thru several acts of an opera." Nor can it be said that Sullivan did not know that he had missed the mark. In Dr. Isaac Goldberg's *The Story of Gilbert and Sullivan* we are informed that Reginald De Koven, the American composer, attended the performance of *Ivanhoe* and told Sullivan that he liked the opera very much, indeed. "That's more than I do," was Sullivan's retort. "A cobbler should stick to his last."

The last years of Sullivan's life were a drab contrast to the former years of glory and splendor he had known. He drifted to Monte Carlo where he indulged in extravagant gambling and dissipation of energy. His health, moreover, had disintegrated: he was almost in perpetual pain, and his face had become haggard and deeply lined thru the overuse of morphine. It was a shabby close to a brilliant career; and no one realized this more forcefully than Sullivan himself.

His last days were spent in an agony which not even morphine could relieve. In the Fall of 1900 he caught a chill. Bronchitis set in, and his already weakened heart could not withstand the strain. Sir Arthur Sullivan died in London on November 22, 1900. It was a lonely death. None of his formerly close friends or associates was at his bedside. Gilbert, who was on the Continent, heard of his former collaborator's death thru the morning newspaper. D'Oyly Carte was sick in bed, too sick to be told of Sullivan's passing. It is a curious phenomenon, however, that Carte, from his bedside, saw thru the window a funeral cortège pass. It was Sullivan's funeral, but Carte had no way of knowing it. "After it had gone by, some one went to D'Oyly Carte's room and found him out of bed and prostrate by the window. Asked what he was doing there he replied, 'I have just seen the last of my old friend, Sullivan.'" Four and a half months later, D'Oyly Carte followed

his friend to the grave. W. S. Gilbert died on May 29, 1911.

B. W. Findon has described Sullivan as follows: "His face impressed at once, because it was the outward indication of the sweetness of his nature. The wide but somewhat low forehead and the pallor of his complexion were relieved by the eyes which were brimful of sensibility and radiant with quiet humor. . . . But soft and mild as were his eyes, there was a straight forward look in them which indicated the resolution of the man, and this trait was enhanced by the strength of the nose and chin. . . . Though below medium height, and with a figure inclined to corpulence, he carried with him a suggestion of dignity and power that were at once recognized. . . . His voice was musical and persuading, and he had a pleasing directness of speech which never failed to reach its mark. His personal charm was infinite."

Composition came easily to Sullivan. As Hesketh Pearson explained: "Many of his melodies came to him in the noise and bustle of a social crush, when he would pull out a notebook and commit them to paper. He scored with great rapidity, smoking cigarette after cigarette and chatting without effort to the visitor of the moment."

Extravagance was one of his most characteristic traits as a personality. Money came easily to him, and he spent it with reckless abandon, a fact which often irritated the more frugal Gilbert. As Gilbert once said: "My cook gets eighty pounds a year and gives me kipper. Sullivan's cook gets five hundred pounds a year for giving him the same thing in French." Amiability and generosity endeared him to all of his friends. He was, like all gamblers, hopelessly superstitious. He believed in hoodoos, lucky stars and lucky days. He was an inveterate smoker, drank copiously and lived richly and fully.

It should not be forgotten that, together with Sir George Grove, Sir Arthur Sullivan discovered the lost partbooks of Franz Schubert's *Rosamunde* as well as forty songs never before printed. Spurred on by a hint in the *Life of Franz Schubert* by Kreissle von Hellborn, Grove and Sullivan had come to Vienna in 1867 and there found the musical treasure, dusty and forgotten, in the attic of a Dr. Schneider.

Principal works by Sir Arthur Sullivan:

OPERAS: *Ivanhoe*; *The Beauty stone*; *The Rose of Persia*; *The Emerald Isle*; *Cox and Box*; *Trial by jury*; *The Sorcerer*; *H.M.S. Pinafore*; *The Pirates of Penzance*; *Patience*; *Iolanthe*; *Princess Ida*; *The Mikado*; *Ruddigore*; *The Yeomen of the guard*; *The Gondoliers*; *Utopia Limited*.

BALLET: *L'Ile enchantée*; *Victoria and Merrie England*.

ORCHESTRA: *Irish symphony*; *The Sapphire necklace overture*; *In Memoriam*; *Di Ballo overture*; *Marmion*; *Concertino for violoncello and orchestra*; *Marches*; incidental music to plays by Shakespeare, Tennyson, etc.

CHORAL: *The Prodigal son*; *The Light of the world*; *The Martyr of Antioch*; *Kenilworth*; *On shore and sea*; *The Golden legend*; *Festival Te Deum*; morning service; anthems, hymns; Fifteen part-songs.

Songs, pieces for the piano.

About Sir Arthur Sullivan:

Dunhill, Thomas Frederick. *Sullivan's Comic Operas: A Critical Appreciation*; Findon, B. W. *Sir Arthur Sullivan*; *His Life and Music*; Goldberg, Isaac. *The Story of Gilbert and Sullivan*; Pearson, Hesketh. *Gilbert and Sullivan*; Sullivan, Herbert (with Newman Flower). *Sir Arthur Sullivan*; *His Life, Letters and Diaries*; Wyndham, H. Saxe. *Arthur Sullivan*.

Important recordings of music by Sir Arthur Sullivan:

OPERA: Complete recordings of *The Gondoliers, Trial by jury, Pinafore, Pirates of Penzance, Iolanthe, Yeomen of the guard, Mikado* and *Patience* (HIS MASTERS VOICE-D'Oyly Carte).

ORCHESTRA: *In Memoriam* (GRAMOPHONE-Sargent); *Di Ballo overture* (GRAMOPHONE-Sargent).

VOCAL: *The Lost chord* (VICTOR-Crooks); *Onward, Christian soldiers* (VICTOR).

Franz von Suppé *1820-1895*

FRANZ VON SUPPÉ, one of the founders of German comic-opera, was born at Spalato on April 18, 1820, of Belgian descent. He was christened Francesco Ezerchiele Ermenegildo Cavaliere Suppé Demelli.

He was an unusually precocious child where music was concerned. At the age of eleven he began the study of the flute, making such progress that he was soon able to perform on the instrument with considerable talent. In his fifteenth year—innocent though he was of all technical knowledge—he composed a mass which was performed at the Franciscan church at Zara.

He was entered in the University of Padua where he continued his study of music. Upon the death of his father, he left for Vienna, where his mother had already settled. There, for a while, he taught Italian, and practised medicine. Then, convinced that his future belonged to music, he entered the Vienna Conservatory where he became a pupil of Seyfried and Sechter.

His first professional post as musician was as conductor of the Josephstadt Theatre in Vienna, a post that brought with it no pay. There followed conductorial engagements in Pressburg and Baden which were so successful that, in 1862, Suppé was appointed conductor of the important Theatre-an-der-Wien. In 1865, he became conductor of the Leopoldstadt Theatre in Vienna, a position he held until the end of his life.

By the time he received his appointment as conductor of the Leopoldstadt Theatre, he had already gained a formidable reputation as composer of comic-operas. In 1847, his *Das Mädchen vom Lande* was introduced in Vienna when it was a phenomenal success. Suppé's singable melodies enchanted the Viennese music-public. In 1858, another tremendous Suppé success thrilled Vienna, *Paragraph 3*. From that time on, Suppé composed more than one hundred fifty comic-operas, many of which attained tremendous vogue. The most famous of these included *Franz Schubert* (1864) which utilized several famous Schubert *Lieder*, *Die schöne Galathea* (1865), *Fatinitza* (1876) and *Boccaccio* (1879). Both *Fatinitza* and *Boccaccio* were adapted for the American stage by Harry B. Smith.

Franz von Suppé died in Vienna on May 21, 1895. Today, he is perhaps best known not for his comic-operas but for his two orchestral overtures, *Poet and peasant* and *Light cavalry* whose popularity seems deathless. *Poet and peasant* has been arranged for fifty-nine different combinations of instruments.

Discussing Suppé's qualities as a composer, Arthur Pougin wrote: "Suppé is

Johan Svendsen   *1840-1911*

FRANZ VON SUPPÉ

not only a musician full of the verve of youth and gaiety when he wrote for the theatre. Eclectic in temperament, supported by an excellent education, he joined Italian grace with German profundity, writing several important and serious works which reveal a happily inspired and richly endowed artist."

Principal works by Franz von Suppé:

OPERA: *Das Mädchen vom Lande*; *Paragraph 3*; *Franz Schubert*; *Die schöne Galathea*; *Fatinitza*; *Pique dame*; *Das Pensionat*; *Boccaccio*, etc.

CHORAL: *Mass*; *Requiem*.

ORCHESTRA: Symphonies; overtures (including *Poet and peasant, Light cavalry,* and *Morning, noon and night in Vienna*).

CHAMBER MUSIC: String quartets.

About Franz von Suppé:

Keller, Otto. *Franz von Suppé der Schopfer der Deutschen Operette*; Rieger, Erwin. *Offenbach und seine Wiener Schule.*

Important recordings of music by Franz von Suppé:

SELECTIONS FROM OPERA: *Boccaccio,* "Overture" (POLYDOR); "Hab' ich nur deine liebe" (VICTOR-Rethberg); "Florenz hat schöne frauen" (GRAMOPHONE). *Die schöne Galathea,* "Overture" (PARLAPHONE-Bodanzky); "Man trägt wieder treue augen" (GRAMOPHONE).

ORCHESTRA: *Poet and peasant* (COLUMBIA-Mengelberg); *Light cavalry overture* (VICTOR-Boult); *Morning, noon and night in Vienna* (VICTOR-Heger).

JOHAN SEVERIN SVENDSEN was born in Christiana on September 30, 1840. His father, a good musician, gave him his first lessons on the violin. When Johan was eleven years old, he turned to composition. The Svendsen family, however, was too indigent to permit Johan to follow a musical career. Circumstance compelled them to enlist Johan in the army in his fifteenth year. There, proving himself adept at playing the violin, flute and clarinet, he soon became bandmaster. During this period he supplemented his income by playing at town dances, frequently improvising Kreutzer studies into country dances.

In his twenty-first year, he left the army. For two years, he traveled in principal cities of Europe with a minstrel orchestra. His musical talent came to the notice of Charles XV who decided to give this young musician an annual stipend to enable him to perfect his violin technique. Thus, in 1863, Svendsen went to Leipzig where he studied under David, Hauptmann, Richter and Reinecke. Unfortunately, at this time, paralysis of the hand brought an abrupt end to his violin career. But it also opened the door for an even more important future, that of composer. Unable to play on his instrument, Svendsen turned to composition with great assiduity. During his Leipzig period he composed a *Symphony in D* and several large works for chamber groups, including an octet, a quintet and a quartet.

With the termination of his studies in 1867, Svendsen traveled extensively in Denmark, Iceland, Scotland and England, finally coming to Paris where he earned a living by playing in Musard's orchestra. He was back in Leipzig in 1870, then becoming acquainted with such eminent musicians as Liszt and Tausig who encouraged him in his work and gave him valuable counsel. One year later, Svendsen became the conductor of the Leipzig Euterpe concerts; in that year he also made his mark as a composer when the Leipzig Gewandhaus Orchestra performed his *Symphony in D,* a performance which attracted much notice.

JOHAN SVENDSEN

In 1872, Svendsen went to Bayreuth, becoming acquainted with Richard Wagner and intimately associated with the Bayreuth Festival. From there he traveled to his native country, assuming the direction of the Philharmonic concerts in Christiania for five years, between 1872 and 1877. During this time, Svendsen's talent was officially recognized in his own country. In 1874, he received an annuity from the government and a decoration from the king. This recognition of his talent, no doubt, was strongly instrumental in encouraging him to produce his most ambitious works. During the years that followed he composed the works that have made him famous, including four Norwegian rhapsodies, his *Romeo and Juliette overture* and the *Zorahayde legend* for orchestra.

In 1877, Svendsen returned to Germany for an extended visit. The year following, he went to Paris and London. Finally back in his own country, he once again became an important factor in its musical life, becoming court conductor in Christiania, in 1883. He assumed his last important position three years later, when he accepted an appointment as musical director of the Royal Theatre of Copenhagen.

Johan Svendsen died in Copenhagen on June 14, 1911. It was generally accepted that, although Svendsen was not a

Norwegian composer of the importance of Grieg, he had produced music of considerable attractiveness. His works have been praised for the workmanship and "sustained nobility of conception. His wide experience made his style more cosmopolitan than national."

Principal works by Johan Svendsen:

ORCHESTRA: *Symphony in D*; *Symphony in B-flat*; *Zorahayde legend*; *Romeo and Juliette overture*; Four Norwegian rhapsodies; *Funeral march* (for Charles XV); *Coronation march* (for Oscar II); *Concerto for violin and orchestra*; *Festival polonaise*; *Carnival in Paris*; *Romance* (for violin and orchestra).

CHAMBER MUSIC: *String octet*; *String quintet*; *String quartet*.

CHORAL: *Wedding cantata*; part-songs.

About Johan Svendsen:

Romain, Louis de. *Essais de Critique Musicale*.
Boston Symphony Orchestra Program Notes (1917-1918), p.1336; *Musical Courier* 62:40 June 21, 1911; *Musician* 9:185 May 1904.

Important recordings of music by Johan Svendsen:

ORCHESTRA: *Carnival in Paris* (GRAMOPHONE-Ronald); *Festival polonaise* (GRAMOPHONE); *Romance*, for violin and orchestra (COLUMBIA-Sammons).

Jan Sweelinck *1562-1621*

JAN PIETERZOON SWEELINCK, one of the important members of the Netherland school of contrapuntal music, was born in Amsterdam in 1562. His early lessons in music were procured from his father, an organist of the Old Church in Amsterdam, and from the local pastor. By his fifteenth year, Sweelinck had made sufficient progress to be able to go to Venice for a continuation of his studies; it is believed that, at this time, he studied under such famous masters as Zarlino, in theory, and Andrea Gabrieli, in organ playing.

In 1580, Sweelinck was back in Amsterdam, where he was appointed to the organ post vacated by his father at the Old Church, at a salary of one hundred gulden a year. In this position, Sweelinck acquired so great a prestige composer, teacher and organist that, in 1586, his salary was doubled; by 1590 his income had been increased to three hundred gulden together with the free use of a house. There is a story extant to the effect that several rich merchants in Amsterdam, deeply attached to Sweelinck, decided to create a special purse for him, with which they speculated for him. When the purse bulged to 40,000 gulden it was given as a gift to the musician.

Sweelinck was unquestionably the greatest of all Dutch organists. As the teacher of many famous organists—including the founders of the North German organ school of the seventeenth century, Praetorius and Samuel Scheidt—his influence was felt for more than a generation after his death. Johann Heintsch, a pupil of Sweelinck, spoke as follows about his master: "Sweelinck was considered a 'wonder of music.' When the fame of his greatness went abroad, the young talent of Germany flocked to him, and Hamburg called him the 'organist maker.' The two Hamburg masters, Praetorius and Scheidemann, honored him as a father. They learned from him not only music, but also principles of contact, and carried away from their association with him a lifelong ideal, which they kept ever before their eyes, and which they set before their famous pupils."

Considered historically, Sweelinck is one of the most important of the Netherland group. He brought the fugue form to its highest technical development; as a matter of fact, in the opinion of Karl Nef, only Johann Sebastian Bach excelled him in this form. Moreover, in some of Sweelinck's works, instrumental music makes its appearance for the first time. As a composer for the organ, he increased its resources immeasurably, and his works had a vital influence on all future organ composition.

Jan Sweelinck died in Amsterdam on October 16, 1621. He has been described by a contemporary as having a "handsome, manly face, from whose features speak a deep earnestness, but also goodness and kindness."

Between 1894 and 1901 Breitkopf and Härtel, published the complete works of Jan Sweelinck in twelve volumes, under the editorial guidance of Max Seiffert.

JAN SWEELINCK

Principal works by Jan Sweelinck:

CHORAL: Psalms; cantiones sacrae; chansons (for 5 voices); *Rimes françoises et italiennes,* etc.

INSTRUMENTAL: Pieces for the organ; pieces for the clavier, etc.

About Jan Sweelinck:

Seiffert, Max. *Sweelinck und seine Direkten Deutschen Schüler;* Sollitt, E. R. *From Dufay to Sweelinck;* Stainer, John R. *Dufay and his Contemporaries* (foreword).

Important recordings of music by Jan Sweelinck:

CHORAL: *Hodie Christus natus est* (POLYDOR); *Psalm 138* (COLUMBIA); *Tu as tout seul,* madrigal (COLUMBIA).

Thomas Tallis *1510-1585*

THOMAS TALLIS, the "father of English Cathedral Music," was born in England in or about 1510. Grove places Tallis' birth in 1505, but more recent researches find the year of 1510 more accurate. The early years of his life are veiled in obscurity, but it is believed that early in his life he came under the influence of the Netherland school of counterpoint.

Between 1532 and 1540, Tallis served as organist of Waltham Abbey. Upon the dissolution of the monastery he came to the post which he held with great prestige for the remainder of his life— under the reigns of Edward, Mary and

Elizabeth—namely, that of organist of Chapel Royal. There, he was in high favor with royalty, the recipient of many honors. In 1547, he received his livery for the coronation of Edward VI. In 1557, he was granted by Queen Mary the special reward of a lease of a manor on the Isle of Thanet. Queen Elizabeth continued the royal bounty in the first year of her reign with a grant of $2,000 a year.

In 1572, William Byrd joined Tallis at the Chapel Royal as pupil and fellow organist. From that time on the two great musicians became close friends. Three years later, they obtained from Queen Elizabeth an exclusive patent for printing and selling of music paper. The venture was a financial failure because neither one boasted great business acumen. But the venture resulted in at least one important event—the publication of *Cantiones sacrae,* containing sixteen motets by Tallis and eighteen by Byrd.

Shortly after this publication, Tallis resigned his post at the Chapel Royal and spent the last years of his life in retirement in Greenwich. During his last years, his fame as a musician had reached its height. He was generally regarded the foremost composer in England.

Thomas Tallis died in Greenwich on November 23, 1585, and was buried in the Greenwich Parish Church.

Much of Tallis' importance as a composer rested in his ability to make his musical style conform to the religious faith and forms of worship of his day. It will be recalled that Tallis lived thru the Reformation. The break with the Catholic Church compelled all English Church composers to write in a new style: from formerly ornate motets and masses, these English Church composers were compelled to produce anthems and offertories of a simple and unpretentious type suitable for the new services. It was Tallis' success in adapting himself to the new idiom that gave him his pre-eminent position in English music.

But Tallis was also an important creator, the composer of much music of compelling quality. "The majestic and

THOMAS TALLIS

architectural splendor of [his] works . . . may quite fitly claim for them a place beside all but the very highest flights of contemporary Italian art," wrote Ernest Walker. "In massive music . . . we see Tallis at his grandest; there are none of the angularities of phrasing that . . . mar the effect of occasional works by Tye. . . . But Tallis also could, when he so pleased, employ with equal success a tender and more expressively graceful style."

Tersely analyzing Tallis' style of composition, W. H. Hadow commented: "Tallis' music has little intimacy, little involution; it is strong, simple, dignified, caring more for solidity of structure than amenity of decoration."

The celebrated modern English composer, Ralph Vaughan-Williams has composed a *Fantasia on a theme of Thomas Tallis,* for double string orchestra, which has been prominently featured on symphony programs.

Principal works by Thomas Tallis:
CHORAL: Motets; anthems; prayers; psalms; litanies; services; masses; tunes, etc.

About Thomas Tallis:
Terry, Richard Runciman. *A Forgotten Psalter*; *Tudor Church Music,* vol. 6; Walker, Ernest. *A Short History of Music in England.*

Music and Letters 10:152 April 1929; *Musical Times* 66:800 September 1925.

Sergei Taneiev *1856-1915*

SERGEI IVANOVICH TANEIEV was born in Vladimir on November 25, 1856. His uncle, Alexander Sergeievitch Taneiev (1850-1918) was a brilliant musical amateur who composed many operas, symphonies and string-quartets of talent; he held high positions in the government, including that of chief chancellor.

Sergei Taneiev inherited his love for music from his father, a prosperous landowner, who was a devoted amateur. Displaying unusual talent, Sergei was given instruction at the piano at an early age by a lady, Miropolsky by name, who was so impressed with his talent that she took him to Nicholas Rubinstein, director of the Moscow Conservatory. Rubinstein recognized a spark of genius, and decided to take the boy under his care. He entrusted him to E. L. Langer for studies in harmony and piano, and personally supervised his general education.

By 1869 Rubinstein became convinced that he had made no mistake about the boy's talent. He urged Sergei Taneiev's father to permit the boy to give up all academic study and turn completely to music. For six years, Taneiev studied music intensively—pursuing a piano course under Nicholas Rubinstein, the study of theory under Hubert, and harmony and composition from Tschaikovsky. Finally, as a winner of a gold medal, he emerged, a fully equipped musician, ready to enter upon a professional career.

In 1875, Taneiev made his first public appearance as pianist, performing the Brahms *D-minor concerto* and receiving instantaneous recognition. A few months later, his friend Tschaikovsky entrusted to him the first public performance of his famous *Concerto in B-flat minor.*

There followed extensive tours, first with Leopold Auer, the violinist, and then with Nicholas Rubinstein, extending as far as Turkey and Greece. For a short period, Taneiev settled in Paris, where he became intimately acquainted with Gounod, Saint-Saëns, Vincent d'Indy and Fauré.

On returning to Russia, Taneiev undertook a concert tour of the Baltic provinces. He finally settled in Moscow where he was appointed professor of theory at the Moscow Conservatory. In 1881, on the death of Nicholas Rubinstein, he became director of the piano class, rising to the rank of director of the Conservatory four years later. For four years, he held this position with admirable distinction, after which he decided to retire in order to devote himself entirely to composition. He retained a few classes until 1906, when disagreements with Safonov—at that time director of the Conservatory—forced him to retire completely from pedagogy.

Performances of Taneiev's music were not frequent during his lifetime. In 1892, a cantata, *John of Damascus*—composed in memory of Nicholas Rubinstein—was performed in Moscow, Taneiev's first major work to receive performance. Three years later, his operatic trilogy, *Orestes*, strongly imitative of Wagner, was produced at the Maryinsky Theatre in Petrograd. *Orestes* consisted of three small operas, *Agamemnon, Choephorai* and *Eumenides.* On its first performance Chesikin found that its greatest fault was in its total absence of archaic coloring, feeling strongly that a judicious employment of ancient modes would have improved the work considerably. "If he does not achieve Wagnerian effects, he has written many beautiful pages." Rimsky-Korsakoff speaks in his autobiography of the many pages of "extraordinary beauty and expressiveness" in *Orestes.*

Sergei Taneiev died of a heart attack at Moscow on June 19, 1915. As a personality, he was best admired for his flaming idealism. He took teaching as a sacred duty; composition was to him a rite. He never gave a thought to marketing his music, being quite content to compose it, for composition's sake alone, and permitting it to lie dusty on the shelf. As a matter of fact, he was bewildered to learn that Belaiev was willing to publish his opera, *Orestes,* and some chamber music, and was even prepared to pay him for the privilege. Taneiev expressed similar surprise whenever anyone manifested interest in his music.

A man of retiring disposition, his greatest happiness came from cultural pursuits. He was a linguist, a lover of art-works and a profound student of literature. He had a passion for rare books. In two respects, at least, he stands apart from most Russian composers: He never touched alcohol, and he was a celibate.

As a composer, he worked carefully and slowly; *Orestes* took him ten years. He was not interested in experimental composition or in originality. As he once wrote to Tschaikovsky: "Least of all do I care to represent in my works samples of a style that was not invented before me, or to create new, unheard of music." He had an obsession for counterpoint, spending many hours in writing contrapuntal exercises on original themes in his copy books. As a matter of fact, his method of composition was to precede it with elaborate contrapuntal exercises. "Before starting the actual writing of some composition," we are informed by Rimsky-Korsakoff, "Taneiev used to prepare a vast number of sketches or studies; he wrote fugues, canons and different contrapuntal combinations upon a simple theme and motifs of his future composition. Only then, after sufficient practice in the principal parts, did he begin the general outline of his composition, knowing well

the material at his command and what he could build from this material."

The composer whom Taneiev adored most was Tschaikovsky.

Discussing the qualities of Taneiev's compositions, M. Montagu-Nathan pointed out their high contrapuntal skill, their perfection of form and mastery of construction both as to the whole and the details, and his recognizable themes which are symbols of expressiveness.

Taneiev is, perhaps, at his best in his chamber works where he succeeded in achieving his most personal style. "In respect to his style," wrote Leonid Sabaneyev, "Taneiev stands out as a master of the highest rank. It is hardly possible to mention another composer after Beethoven, save perhaps Brahms, who can stand comparison to him in respect to maturity of style in the sense of making the most of the instruments and creating a tonal web that commands interest. But at the same time there are apparent the characteristic faults of the melody, lack of inner emotional temperament, an occasional odd blindness to artistic differences of style, a blindness that permits Taneiev in one and the same composition to combine imitative traces of Mozart and Tschaikovsky."

Taneiev is also the author of two important volumes on counterpoint.

Principal works by Sergei Taneiev:

OPERA: *Orestes.*

CHORAL: *John of Damascus.*

ORCHESTRA: Four symphonies; *Overture on Russian themes*; *Suite* (for violin and orchestra); *Solemn overture.*

CHAMBER MUSIC: Two string quintets; Eight string quartets; *Piano quartet*; Three string trios; *Piano trio.*

Pieces for the piano; songs; choruses, etc.

About Sergei Taneiev:

Montagu-Nathan, Montagu. *Contemporary Russian Composers*; Rimsky-Korsakoff, Nicholas. *My Musical Life*; Sabaneyev, Leonid. *Modern Russian Composers.*
Musical Quarterly 13:540 October 1927.

Giuseppe Tartini *1692-1770*

GIUSEPPE TARTINI, successor of Corelli as composer for the violin, was born in Pirano on April 8, 1692. His parents were prosperous and able to

SERGEI TANEIEV

give him a good education. Planning a clerical career for him, they sent him to the Oratorio Saint Philip Neri for his early studies. From there, he went to the Padri delle Scuole, where he received his first lessons in music. Religion appealed so little to Tartini that he decided to turn to law. For this purpose he was sent to the University of Padua in 1770. Jurisprudence proved to be equally unappealing to the young student and he squandered his time in making love, fencing and playing the violin.

At this time he fell in love with a beautiful girl, believed to be a relative of the powerful Bishop of Padua, the Cardinal Giorgio Cornaro. They were married secretly—a fact which so infuriated the Bishop that to save his life, Tartini was forced to flee from Padua disguised as a pilgrim. For a period, he made his home in a monastery in Assisi. It was there that he studied the violin assiduously for the first time, acquiring a remarkable technique.

At the same time, he turned to composition, and early in 1713 he produced one of his best-known masterpieces, the *Devil's trill sonata* for the violin. Tartini has himself recorded the origin of this famous work. "One night in 1713 I dreamt that I had made a compact with the devil, who promised to be at my service on all occasions. Everything succeeded. . . . At last I thought I would offer my violin to the devil, in order to discover what kind of musician he was, when to my great astonishment I heard him play a solo so singularly beautiful and with such superior taste and precision that it surpassed all the music I had ever heard or conceived in the whole course of my life. I was so overcome with surprise and delight that I lost my power of breathing, and the violence of the sensation awoke me. Instantly, I seized my violin in the hopes of remembering some portion of what I had heard, but in vain! The work which this dream suggested, and which I wrote at that time, is doubtless the best of all my compositions. I call it the *Devil's trill sonata*."

In 1715, Tartini received the forgiveness of the Bishop of Padua. He returned to his native city where he ba-

came a violinist in the San Antonio Church. His fame as a violinist soon became so great that, in 1716, he was invited to Venice to enter into a contest with Veracini, the great Italian violinist. Tartini performed first, giving so remarkable a demonstration that Veracini decided discreetly to withdraw from the contest.

"Indeed, Tartini was a great violin-player," said Quantz, the great flautist in the court of Frederick the Great. "He produced a beautiful tone from his instrument, and he had an equal mastery over fingers and bow. He overcame the greatest difficulties without effort."

In 1721, Tartini was appointed musical leader at the San Antonio Church in Padua. Except for brief intermissions—during one of which he served as a musician to Count Kunsky in Prague—Padua remained his home for the remainder of his life. His salary in Padua was a modest one, only 400 ducats a year, but it satisfied him; he frequently refused a king's ransom to leave Italy and give performances in France and England. "I have no children, and a wife who thinks as I do," he once wrote in explanation to an Englishman, in refusing to accept an offer of 3 000 pounds to come to England. "We are satisfied with our circumstances, and if we have any wish, it is not the wish to possess more earthly goods."

GIUSEPPE TARTINI

In 1728, Tartini established his violin school in Padua which became world-famous, attracting violin students from all of Europe.

His fame, however, rests more securely upon his violin compositions than on his violin playing. In his works, he brought music for the violin to new stages of development. His works for his instrument are numerous, some of which—particularly the *Devil's trill sonata* and the *Sonata in G-major*—are favorite repertoire pieces of great violinists even in our own day. In these works, as we are informed by Arthur M. Abell, "he built upon the foundation laid by his great predecessor, Corelli, but . . . he greatly enlarged upon his models. He employed broader and more pregnant themes, while his passage work reveals organic development. Tartini understood the importance of light and shade; his passages stand out in bold contrast to the melodic passages, and they are not a mere collection of notes for the sake of variety; but they reveal a certain kinship to the whole structure."

Tartini, who was a great lover of poetry, received his inspiration for composition from verse. He always read a poem by one of his favorite writers when he wished to get into the mood for composition; and, before playing his work in public, he would always reread the poem.

By 1768, Tartini's health began to degenerate. An attack of convulsive paralysis was followed by a malignant growth of the foot which physicians found to be incurable. For many months, he suffered intensely.

Giuseppe Tartini died in Padua on February 26, 1770. He was buried in St. Catherine's Church.

As a personality, Tartini was a man of great piety, whose happiness, as he frequently told his friends, consisted in submission to the will of the Almighty. Simplicity of character, unpretentiousness and kindness endeared him to many friends. His generosity was famous. He distributed his property and belongings to friends and family during his lifetime so that there was very little left when he died. He possessed great culture, being a lover of every field of art and a professional student of the sciences; one of his favorite studies was in the field of acoustics.

Tartini likewise distinguished himself as a musical theorist, producing several important works in the field of harmony and violin playing.

Principal works by Giuseppe Tartini:
An entire library of music for the violin including eighteen concertos, fifty sonatas and many smaller pieces.
Music for violoncello; trios; quartets, etc.

About Giuseppe Tartini:
Musical Courier 57:8 July 29, 1908; *Musical Times* 73:988 November 1932; *Strad* 16:46 June 1905; *Strad* 40:283 October 1929.

Important recordings of music by Giuseppe Tartini:
VIOLIN AND PIANO: *Devil's trill sonata* (VICTOR-Menuhin); *Sonata in G-major* (COLUMBIA-Szigeti); *Sonata in G-minor*, "Grave" (COLUMBIA); *Fugue*, arranged by Kreisler (VICTOR-Kreisler).
ORCHESTRA: *Concerto in D-major*, for violoncello and orchestra (PARLAPHONE).

Georg Telemann *1681-1767*

"A Lully fame has won;
Corelli may be praised;
But Telemann alone,
Above all praise be raised."
—MATTHESON

GEORG PHILIPP TELEMANN was born in Magdeburg on March 14, 1681, the son and grandson of Lutheran pastors. At an early age, he showed a remarkably retentive memory. He could grasp several languages (including Latin and Greek), was able to memorize German poetry with facility and acquired musical instruction with ease. His only music instruction he received from an organist in his native town for a short period. For, though Telemann showed unusual aptitude for music (as a child he could perform on the zither, flute and violin; and at the age of twelve he composed an opera which reached performance) he was impatient of routinized study. He abandoned his teacher to devote himself more unrestrainedly to composition, and never again received systematic instruction from any master.

In his thirteenth year, Telemann went to school in Zellerfeld, in the Harz mountains, where he specialized in ge-

GEORG TELEMANN

ometry. There, at one time, a festival took place for which a special music-master was engaged to compose and direct the music. The master fell ill before he could fulfill his commission. Despite his youth, Telemann asked for an opportunity to substitute. He not only composed the musical score but directed it himself, a performance which made so deep an impression upon the mountaineers that they carried him away on their shoulders in triumph. The head-master of the school was particularly impressed by this achievement, and urged young Telemann to concentrate more upon music and less upon mathematics.

Four years later, Telemann was enrolled at the Gymnasium in Hildesheim, studying logic. But this was soon neglected for the sake of music. Not only the hours of recreation but the hours allotted to study of logic were spent in a feverish spurt of composition. Telemann's mother, however, would not permit her son to become a musician. Finally deciding to prepare him for law, she sent him to Leipzig in 1701. En route, Telemann stopped at Halle to pay his respects to George Frederic Handel.

In Leipzig, Telemann devoted himself to his law-study, keeping his musical passion a secret even from his closest friend. A roommate, however, accidentally discovered a psalm which Telemann had composed, and brought it to the attention of important musicians in Leipzig who succeeded in having it performed at St. Thomas Church. The burgomaster was so impressed with the music that he gave Telemann a gift, commissioning him at the same time to compose music for the St. Thomas Church every fortnight. This commission definitely influenced Telemann to discard the study of law and enter the profession of music.

There followed a bitter rivalry between Telemann and that eminent composer and chapel-master of St. Thomas, Kuhnau. Kuhnau was piqued that a young law student should be commissioned to compose music regularly for his Church. When, shortly afterwards, Telemann was engaged as chapel-master of the New Church (1704) with the provision that he direct the choir of the St. Thomas Church from time to time (so that, when Kuhnau passed away, Telemann might become successor automatically) Kuhnau's displeasure mounted to genuine resentment. From resentment he passed on to undisguised hostility when Telemann was chosen director of the opera house in Leipzig, thereby having the limelight of fame and attention focused upon him. From this time on, Kuhnau made every effort to have his young competitor displaced, but his efforts were futile. Telemann had become an idol of Leipzig music lovers, and his hold upon them was too secure.

In 1705, Telemann went to Sorau to become chapel-master to Graf Erdmann von Promnitz. Graf Erdmann von Promnitz was a great lover of French music, and it was in his honor that Telemann began to compose music in the French style. During two years of his stay in Sorau, Telemann composed more than two hundred French overtures.

From Sorau, Telemann went to Eisenach—a court which was more French in spirit than German—where he continued his composition of French music, particularly concertos and trios. In Eisenach, Telemann became acquainted with Johann Sebastian Bach and, in 1714, served as godfather to Philipp Emanuel Bach.

Telemann was, by temperament, too restless to remain in any one place indefinitely. By 1712, he was in Frankfurt as chapel-master of several churches. One year later, he founded the celebrated Collegium Musicum which, each week, gave concerts for the public; for these, Telemann composed an imposing amount of chamber and orchestral works.

Telemann's wanderings from one musical post to another came to an end in 1721 when he was engaged as chapel-master and cantor for the Johanneum in Hamburg. One year later, Leipzig made attractive offers to him to come to the St. Thomas Church to succeed the late Kuhnau. Hamburg—which esteemed Telemann highly—was so eager to retain its chapel-master permanently that it acceded to every demand of the composer. It was only after Telemann had refused the post at the St. Thomas Church in Leipzig that Johann Sebastian Bach was chosen.

His wanderings over, Telemann was absorbed in a whirlwind of music activity. He undertook the composition of music for five of the principal churches in Hamburg, and superintended musical education at the Gymnasium and the Johanneum. He directed the Opera in Hamburg which, thru his efforts and energies, was restored to its feet in 1722. He founded the Collegium Musicum which gave weekly concerts for the public. He started the first musical journal to be published in Germany. And, in addition to these many efforts, he composed music on commission for Eisenach, Bayreuth and Frankfurt.

In 1737, Telemann paid a visit to Paris, where he remained for eight months, attending many performances of his works. He died in Hamburg on June 25, 1767. His consolations, in old age, were music and flowers.

Telemann was succeeded in Hamburg by his own godson, Philipp Emanuel Bach.

In a monumental essay on Telemann, Romain Rolland emphatically pointed out the importance of this German composer in musical history. Telemann was

one of the first to initiate German comic opera, in which his gifts as a humorist were widely recognized. Likewise, he was among the first champions in Germany of the "French overture." [1] His Church music was of monumental stature, brought to an almost unprecedented technical mastery; some of its pages, in the opinion of Romain Rolland, "are worthy of Beethoven, while in the orchestral accompaniments there are some touches that remind one of Berlioz." Indeed, it is Rolland's opinion that "if Telemann had been more careful of his genius, if he had not written so much, accepted so many tasks, his name would perhaps have left a deeper mark on history than that of Gluck."

Great composers and critics have always esteemed Telemann's genius highly. Handel so valued Telemann's technical skill that he once said that Telemann could write a motet in eight parts as easily as anyone else could write a letter. Franz Schubert referred to Telemann as "the peerless master," and Schiebe considered him one of the greatest composers of the century.

Principal works by Georg Telemann:

CHORAL: Twelve cycles of cantatas; Forty-four passions; oratorios; 100 services; motets, etc.

INSTRUMENTAL: French overtures; French concertos; sonatas; trios; serenades; quartets. About Forty operas, 3000 pieces for the organ, pieces for harpsichord, etc.

About Georg Telemann:

Rolland, Romain. *A Musical Tour Thru the Land of the Past*; Valentin, Erich. *Georg Philipp Telemann: Ein Biographie.* *Die Musik* 23:317 March 1931.

Important recordings of music by Georg Telemann:

CHORAL: *St. John Passion*, "Lu, o ewiges Erbarmen," and "Wie trotzig erscheinet mit schwestern" (KANTOREI).

INSTRUMENTAL: *Suite in A-major* (VICTOR); *Quartet in B-minor* (TREASURY OF MUSIC); *Quartet in E-minor* (ANTHOLOGIE SONORE); *Fantasia,* for harpsichord (COLUMBIA).

Ambroise Thomas *1811-1896*

CHARLES LOUIS AMBROISE THOMAS, distinguished composer of French opera, was born in Metz on August 5, 1811. His parents, who were

---

[1] For comment on the "French overture" as distinguished from the "Italian" see sketch on Alessandro Scarlatti.

teachers of music, gave him his first lessons, and in 1828 Ambroise was able to enter the Paris Conservatory. He was a particularly good student; after one year in Zimmerman's piano class he won first prize. The following year, he studied harmony and accompaniment under Dourken, once again receiving first award. Completing his studies under Lesueur—whose favorite pupil he was—Thomas won the Prix de Rome with a cantata entitled *Hermann et Ketty*.

He went to Rome in 1832, where he spent three industrious years at the Villa Medici. The fruits of these years were several talented compositions, including *Caprices* for trio, a *Requiem* and *Souvenirs d'Italie*. The *Caprices* attracted the notice of Robert Schumann who commented that they were "neither heavy nor light, neither deep nor superficial, not classical nor romantic, but always euphonious and in certain parts full of beautiful melody."

Back in Paris, in 1836, Thomas turned his creative talent exclusively to the theatre. His first opera, *La Double échelle*, was given a performance at the Opéra Comique in 1837. While some critics found much to praise in this first fruit (Berlioz commented upon its "grace, fire, finesse of dramatic intentions, and tact in employment of instrumental masses") the work was not successfully received by the Paris music public. This was followed, a year later, by *Le Perruquier de la Régence,* which in turn was succeeded by a ballet, *La Gipsy*. Between 1840 and 1844, Thomas' productive pen created four more operas, all performed. But it was not until *Mina* (1843) that Thomas' work began to appeal to Parisians. *Mina* ran for fifty-six performances, bringing considerable publicity and attention to its composer's name.

During the political disturbances of 1848, Thomas enlisted in the Garde nationale. Fortunately, he was not compelled to remain for long in uniform. In 1849 he produced *Le Caïd*, a witty satire of Italian opera which is regarded by some critics as the forerunner of the Offenbach *opéra-bouffe*. Two more operas came in 1851, one of which is remembered today only because of its

AMBROISE THOMAS

overture, *Raymond*. *Raymond* was followed by five more operas, bringing the total of Thomas' work for the theatre to eighteen. A degree of recognition was now his. In 1851, he became a member of the Institut. In 1856, he was appointed professor at the Conservatory, and three years later he was made an officer of the Legion of Honor.

In 1860, Thomas decided to take a much-needed rest from composition. When he returned to creation, several years later, he seemed to have acquired an altogether new vitality and freshness. In 1866, the Opéra Comique presented *Mignon,* based upon Goethe's *Wilhelm Meister*. For the first time, Thomas touched permanent importance in his composition. This was his first thrust towards greatness, a thrust which insured him operatic fame.

The success of *Mignon* was not only sensational in its own day. Within twenty-eight years, Paris saw no less than one thousand performances of the opera. On that occasion, in 1894, Thomas was raised to the rank of Grand Cross of the Legion of Honor. On the night the Paris Opéra Comique was consumed by fire, in 1887, the opera performed was *Mignon*.

"If this opera is successful and popular," noted Henri de Curzon, "it is because it offers many things to many people: laughter and tears, sincere emotion·and frivolity, character and facility. . . . Its banal pages are relieved by an inspiration of exquisite grace. Conventional effects are balanced by the poignant truth of still another effect."

What the distinguished German critic, Eduard Hanslick, wrote concerning *Mignon* upon its first performance in Germany, still holds true. "This opera is in no place powerfully striking, and it is not the work of a richly organized, original genius. Rather does it appear to us as a work of a sensitive and refined artist, showing the practical ability of a master hand. Occasionally somewhat meagre and tawdry . . . the music to *Mignon* is nevertheless mostly dramatic, spirited and graceful, not of deep, but of true, and, in many instances, warm feeling."

Mignon was succeeded by another imposing achievement, *Hamlet,* performed with great success at the Paris Opéra in 1868. These two operas made Thomas the idol of the French music public. His name was spoken of with great admiration. He was a favorite at the Court of Napoleon III. It was, therefore, not surprising that when Auber died, the position of the director of the Paris Conservatory passed on to Thomas.

Although Thomas produced several more works for the theatre after *Hamlet,* he had lost the magic touch, and they were strongly imitative of his earlier and fresher style.

Ambroise Thomas died at his residence in the Paris Conservatory on February 12, 1896 after an illness of ten days.

Henri de Curzon described Thomas as a man of great timidity and reserve who was invariably absorbed in revery. "I need to dream," Thomas used to say, "just as other people need to sleep and walk." His sensitive face—with soft eyes which continually spoke of pain— bore an almost ineffaceable expression of sadness, a sadness which, as De Curzon commented, "was touched with poetry."

An eminent critic of Thomas' day, Adolphe Jullien, esteemed the composer's talent harshly. "The principal talent of Thomas consists in having been able to bend himself to the taste of the public by serving up in turn the style of music that suited it best. . . . In one word, he is a musician of science and worth, absolutely devoid of art initiative, and who turns to all the four quarters of the winds when these blow in the direction of success."

While it is true that Jullien's criticism was too severe, in that it failed to acknowledge Thomas' unquestionable talent for sentiment and tenderness, it must be confessed that Thomas too frequently catered to public taste. Dramatic taste he possessed to a great degree, skill in instrumentation, as well; and with them an ability, from time to time, to express a melody of great charm. But he was too easily satisfied with his efforts, too little inclined to edit and revise, too eager to catch the applause of his audiences with a catching phrase. As a result, he is more charming than original. However, the popular appeal of *Mignon* among opera audiences thruout the world cannot be questioned.

Principal works by Ambroise Thomas:

OPERA: *La Double échelle*; *Le Perruquier de la Régence*; *Le Panier fleuri*; *Carline*; *Mina*; *Le Caïd*; *Le Songe d'une nuit d'été*; *Raymond*; *Psyché*; *Le Carnaval de Venise*; *Mignon*; *Hamlet*; *Françoise de Rimini*, etc.

BALLET: *La Gipsy*; *Betty*; *La Tempête.*

CHORAL: *Hermann et Ketty*; *Requiem*; *Messe solennelle*; *Marche religieuse*; motets.

ORCHESTRA: *Fantasia* (for piano and orchestra).

CHAMBER MUSIC: *String quintet*; *String quartet*; *Piano trio.*

About Ambroise Thomas:

Boschot, Adolphe. *La Musique et la Vie*; Delaborde, Henri. *Notice sur la Vie et les Oeuvres de M. Ambroise Thomas*; Hervey, Arthur. *Masters of French Music.*

Ménestral 82:493 December 17, 1920.

Important recordings of music by Ambroise Thomas:

OPERA: *Mignon*, abridged (COLUMBIA-Théâtre de la Monnaie).

SELECTIONS FROM OPERA: *Hamlet*, "Vain regrets" and "Doute de la lumière" (COLUMBIA); "Invocation" (GRAMOPHONE); "Sa main, depuis hier" and "Adieu, dit-il, ayez foi!" (GRAMOPHONE); "Dans son regard plus sombre" (ODEON); "Comme une pâle fleur" (GRAMOPHONE). *Raymond*, "Overture" (VICTOR).

Ludwig Thuille *1861-1907*

L UDWIG WILHELM ANDREAS MARIA THUILLE was born in Bozen, in the Tyrols, on November 30, 1861. As a child he showed unmistakable musical talent, beginning composition at the age of eight. Both his parents died while he was still very young. After the death of his father, he was enrolled as a chorister in Kremsmünster. At the same time he was given instruction upon the violin and piano.

He was particularly fortunate at this time in attracting the attention of the well-to-do widow of a Tyrolese composer, Nagiller, who became his patron. Under her guidance, Thuille became a piano pupil of Josef Pembaur, Sr. In 1879, he was enrolled as a student of the Royal School of Music in Munich where he received thorough technical training under Josef Rheinberger. It was thru Frau Nagiller, too, that Thuille was introduced to another young composer, Richard Strauss. From that time on a close friendship developed between Thuille and Strauss. Strauss' first important tone-poem, *Don Juan,* is dedicated to Ludwig Thuille.

In 1866, Alexander Ritter, the poet, settled in Munich and—having become acquainted with both Thuille and Strauss some years before—now became closely attached to them, and aroused the enthusiasm of both composers for the gospel of Liszt and Wagner. Both Strauss and Thuille determined, in their composition, to continue along the path struck by Wagner and Liszt. In 1897, Thuille composed his first opera, *Theuerdank,* which was performed in that year in Munich under the baton of Richard Strauss. *Theuerdank,* which was strongly imitative of Wagner's style, received the Luitpold prize.

One year later, Thuille composed a second opera, *Lobetanz,* which brought him great prestige as a composer. *Lobetanz* was introduced by Felix Mottl in Munich on February 6, 1898, receiving so enthusiastic a response that it was soon afterwards performed in Berlin under Karl Muck. When *Lobetanz* was performed at the Metropolitan Opera House in New York in

LUDWIG THUILLE

1911, Herbert F. Peyser discussed it in the following manner: "Thuille shows unmistakably that he, too, has imbibed at the Wagnerian fount. The general color of his instrumentation and harmony of the first two acts bear witness to this. But even though he has chosen the loftiest possible model, it cannot be said that his score is a product of the highest inspiration. . . . Thuille reveals little original creativeness. There are passages of fluent grace and charm in the first two acts, but one misses the element of individuality and general distinction."

In 1900, Thuille produced his third opera, *Gugeline,* in which he began to draw sharply away from Wagnerian traditions and which, consequently, many critics esteem more satisfying artistically than his two previous operas.

However, Thuille's great reputation as a musician rests not with his creative work but with his influence as a teacher. In 1883, he was appointed professor at the Munich Royal School of Music. For more than twenty years he held his professorial post with eminence. His disciples were many, and were frequently referred to as the *Jung-Münchner Schule;* they included Walter Braunfels, Paul von Klenau and Josef Pembaur, Jr.

Ludwig Thuille died in Munich on February 5, 1907.

Principal works by Ludwig Thuille:

OPERA: *Theuerdank; Lobetanz; Gugeline.*

ORCHESTRA: *Romantic overture; Symphonischer festmarsch.*

CHORAL: *Traumsommernacht;* Men's choruses; Women's choruses, etc.

CHAMBER MUSIC: *Sextet* (for piano and wind); *Quintet;* Two sonatas for violin and piano; *Sonata for violoncello and piano.*

Pieces for the organ, for the piano; songs.

About Ludwig Thuille:

Daniels, Mabel W. *An American Girl in Munich;* Munster, Friedrich. *Ludwig Thuille: Ein erste Versuch;* Seidl, Arthur. *Neuzeitliche Tondichter und Zeitgenössiche Tonkünstler.*

Musical Quarterly 18:463 July 1932.

Sir Francesco Tosti *1846-1916*

SIR FRANCESCO PAOLO TOSTI was born in Ortona, Abruzzi, on April 9, 1846. At the age of eleven he was sent to Naples by his parents to study music at the Royal College of St. Pietro a Majella, where his instructors included Pinto for the violin and Conti and Mercadante in composition. Mercadante discovered young Tosti's talent, and soon made him a pupil teacher at the meagre salary of sixty francs a month.

In 1869, ill-health brought Tosti back to his native city where for many months he was confined to bed. During this period, he began the composition of several songs with great industry. On their completion, he submitted two of them for a prize offered by the Florentine Art Society, and two others to the publisher Ricordi. All four were refused.

Recovering from his illness, Tosti left Ortona and came to Ancona. Here, his poverty was great; he was forced to live on oranges and stale bread. Finally, his journey brought him to Rome where he met Sgambati, the great pianist and composer. Sgambati became so interested in the young musician that he offered to become his patron. Sgambati arranged for Tosti to give a vocal concert at which royalty was present. The Princess Margherite was so delighted with his songs and with his singing that she appointed him her teacher. With this appointment, the tide turned. Soon after this, he sold to Ricordi two songs which appealed strongly to the public; at the same time

SIR FRANCESCO TOSTI

he was appointed Keeper of the Musical Archives of Italy at the Court.

In 1875, Tosti went to England where he was fortunate in procuring the cooperation of several powerful friends who introduced him to the highest society. For many months, Tosti was a favorite in the fashionable drawing-room. Before long, he received an appointment as singing-master to the royal family of England. His fame as a composer was likewise mounting. Tosti had brought with him to England a song, *For ever and ever,* which was introduced by Violet Cameron at the Globe Theatre. The song became a sensation overnight; its composer found suddenly an enormous demand for his songs. He supplied this demand during the next few years with many of the songs that brought him world-fame—including *At vespers, Mother, That day, Good-bye* and *Forever!*

By 1885, he was the most famous song composer in England, and one of the best loved song writers in the world. He was an intimate friend of Italian and English dukes and duchesses, and a frequent visitor to Queen Victoria. His popularity was so great that his publishers, Ricordi, paid him $500 a week as a retaining fee for twelve songs a year.

Tosti, now established in England, decided to make it his permanent home.

For many years he was a member of the faculty of the Royal Academy of Music. In 1906, he was honored by England with the Commander of the Victorian Order, and two years later he was knighted by King Edward. The fact that Tosti became a British subject created considerable criticism and antagonism against him in Italy where it was felt that, for the sake of glory, he had renounced his own country.

In 1913, however, feeling that he had not much longer to live, Tosti, returned to his native country to spend his last years there. He died in Rome on December 2, 1916.

In his songs, Tosti revealed a natural flow of melody and a strong sentimentality which have given him a prominent position among composers of the Romantic song. The Italian critic, Robert Bracco, has pointed out that the chief characteristics of Tosti's songs are "a modest simplicity marked with an inborn dignity and an untrammeled elegance that are due more to instinct than to culture," and which have succeeded in retaining the "imprint of the purest and most traditional forms of Italian music."

Sir Francesco Paolo Tosti was a glamorous figure in high English society; his wit and pungent irony were well-known. He possessed modesty and kindness to a great degree which endeared him strongly to all those with whom he came into contact. His composition was seasonal, the bulk of his creative work being done at the seaside during warm weather. The winter was almost entirely devoted to social functions. However, he gathered his ideas at all times and in all places. It was a frequent sight to see him suddenly, irrespective of where or with whom he was, jot down hurriedly a few bars of music on a scrap of paper which he would stuff into his pocket.

Tosti is likewise known for his valuable edition of Italian folk songs of his native town, entitled *Canti popolari Abruzzesi*.

Principal works by Sir Francesco Tosti:

VOCAL: An entire library of famous songs including *Mattinata*, *Good-bye*, *Forever*, *Mother*, *At vespers*, *For ever and ever*, *Amore*, *April*, *Serenata*, *Vorrei morire*, *That day*, etc.

About Sir Francesco Tosti:

Collins, W. F. *Laurel Winners.*
Musical America 25:5 December 16, 1916; *Musical Opinion* 54:1030 September 1931; *Musical Times* 58:129 March 1917.

Important recordings of music by Sir Francesco Tosti:

SONGS: *Serenata* (VICTOR-Ponselle); *Good-bye* and *Forever* (VICTOR-Ponselle).

Peter Ilitch Tschaikovsky   1840-1893

"He has brought the East to the West on wings of art, uniting the sheer glory and magnificence of color of the one to the instinct for form and design of the other."—R. A. STREATFEILD

PETER ILITCH TSCHAIKOVSKY was born at Votinski, in the government of Viatka, on May 7, 1840. His mother had sprung from an old French Protestant family which, coming to Russia as refugees after the revocation of the Edict of Nantes, settled there permanently. In 1833, she married Ilya Petrovitch Tschaikovsky, a mining engineer in affluent circumstances. They had seven children, of which Peter Ilitch was the third.

As a child, Peter showed unusual interest in music. The family owned a mechanical instrument called an orchestrion which would tinkle Zerlina's air from Mozart's *Don Giovanni*. The beautiful air so thrilled the child that, after hearing it a first time, he persistently groped for musical expression of his own. He was given some lessons on the piano; his spare hours from this time on were devoted to indefatigable improvisations.

Despite his musical adaptibility, he was discouraged from devoting his time to his art—his parents having planned a legal career for him. In his tenth year, therefore, he went to a preparatory school in St. Petersburg for the study of jurisprudence. He completed his law studies nine years later. In the meanwhile, he did not forget his love for music. His mother's sister sang to him famous operatic arias, rekindling in him his early passion for the art. He also had access to a vocal score of Mozart's *Don Giovanni* which inflamed his im-

PETER ILITCH TSCHAIKOVSKY

agination; he frequently said in later life that Mozart was the greatest single influence in bringing him to music. However, it was not until the close of his legal study period that Tschaikovsky was permitted by his father to resume the study of the piano. His teacher, Rudolf Kündinger, found but little talent in Tschaikovsky. As a matter of fact, when Tschaikovsky's father asked of Kündinger, at one time, whether Peter should give up legal study for music, the teacher's answer was a firm and decisive negative.

When Peter Tschaikovsky left the school of jurisprudence, he was given a clerkship in the Ministry of Justice, a position he retained for three years. He was known to have been a sloppy worker, inattentive to his duties and uninterested in his task. At the same time, he was drifting more and more towards music. In 1861, he joined the class of Nicolas Zaremba (a pedantic theorist who was frequently the object of Balakirev's scorn), making such progress that the following year he was able to enter Anton Rubinstein's class in orchestration at the Conservatory. By this time, he had definitely decided to give up law for music. "Do not for a moment think that I expect ever to be a great artist," he wrote to his sister. "Whether I become a famous composer or a poor music-teacher is a matter of

indifference to me; at all events my conscience will be clear and I shall no longer have the right to complain about my lot."

As a graduating exercise for the Conservatory, Tschaikovsky composed a cantata based upon Schiller's *Ode to Joy.* Altho the work won a silver medal, none of his masters—including Anton Rubinstein, Rimsky-Korsakoff and Serov —esteemed it highly. There was, however, one prophetic opinion voiced by Hermann Laroche, Tschaikovsky's close friend, who later became a famous critic. Laroche wrote to Tschaikovsky: "In you, I see the greatest, or rather the only hope of our musical future. Your real works will perhaps only begin five years hence, but those mature works will surpass all that we have had since Glinka."

The cantata likewise made a favorable impression upon Nicholas Rubinstein, director of the newly opened Conservatory of Music in Moscow, who called to Tschaikovsky to become professor of harmony. The appointment came at a critical moment. Tschaikovsky's father had suffered severe financial reverses and was unable to support his son any longer. The salary at the Conservatory was a meagre one, but it protected Tschaikovsky from actual starvation. And it enabled him to devote a considerable amount of his time to composition, frequently even to make visits to France and Germany to acquaint himself with the music of these countries.

Overwork and worry, caused by the composition of his first symphony, brought Tschaikovsky to the brink of a nervous breakdown. He suffered from an agonizing hammering in the head which, he felt, heralded the approach of insanity. At other times, he was convinced that he was dying. Recovery came after several terrifying months, but the sickness left indelible fingerprints in the form of a permanent nervousness. When Tschaikovsky conducted, for example, he supported his chin with his left hand because he was afraid his head might fly off!

In February of 1867, two movements of the first symphony were performed in St. Petersburg (Anton Rubinstein stubbornly refused to have the whole work performed), where it was received with coldness. This reception embittered Tschaikovsky, but it did not discourage his productivity. A few piano pieces, an overture and his first opera, *Voyevod,* which followed, failed to increase his fame to any appreciable degree. Even his first great composition, the orchestral fantasy, *Romeo and Juliette*—which he composed in 1869 on the advice of Balakirev and which was first performed in Moscow in 1870 under Nicholas Rubinstein's direction—was a dismal failure. In 1872, therefore, Tschaikovsky was compelled, in order to support himself, to accept a position as music critic which he held—and detested—for four years.

What is believed to have been Tschaikovsky's only love-affair took place sometime in 1869. Désirée Artôt was a music-student, five years Tschaikovsky's senior. "I love her with all my heart and soul, and I feel I can't live without her," he wrote in one of his letters. Yet he vacillated a long time in proposing marriage. Desirée's betrothal to a Spaniard, finally, made marriage with Tschaikovsky out of the question, causing the composer no little anguish.

There took place in 1877 one of the major tragic incidents in Tschaikovsky's life. Tschaikovsky had been receiving letters of ardent affection from a pupil at the Moscow Conservatory, Antonina Milyoukova, who begged for an opportunity to meet him. Flattered by these letters, Tschaikovsky granted the girl an interview, during which she fell on her knees, expressing her great love for the composer and asking to become his humble servant. Embarrassed by this protestation of love and sympathizing with the girl, Tschaikovsky—who did not love her, and confessed as much—offered to marry her. In vain, Tschaikovsky's brother Anatol attempted to dissuade him from entering upon so ridiculous a bargain; but Tschaikovsky had given his word and refused to recant. The marriage was a sordid experience. After nine harrowing weeks, it brought Tschaikovsky to the verge of another nervous breakdown. At one desperate moment, he attempted to commit suicide by standing up to his neck in the ice-cold Neva River. His physicians ordered a change of scene. For an entire year, therefore, Tschaikovsky traveled in Switzerland and Italy, attempting to forget his bitter experience.

Escape from haunting memories, he found to a great degree in musical composition. During this period he produced an abundance of important works which revealed his increasing greatness as a creator—including his first piano concerto, the second and third symphonies, two string quartets, an opera, *Vakoula,* the *Variations on a rococo theme,* for violoncello and orchestra, and the orchestral fantasy, *Francesca da Rimini.*

While he was traveling in Switzerland and Italy, greatly troubled not only by his memories but also by financial problems, a stroke of good fortune came his way. He received word from Russia that an influential patron, Nadejda Filaretovna von Meck, had interested herself so deeply in his music that she offered the composer a yearly pension of three thousand dollars to free him from all pecuniary worry. That was the beginning of a thirteen year relationship between Tschaikovsky and his patron (whom he never spoke to personally), a relationship sealed by an exchange of letters in which Tschaikovsky bared his heart and soul to his "best friend," as he referred to her in his dedication of the *Fourth symphony.*

The pension made Tschaikovsky financially independent, able to travel extensively and to hurl all of his energy into composition. The first important products of his new freedom were his opera *Eugen Onegin,* the *Concerto for violin and orchestra* and the *Fourth symphony.* The first performance of the *Fourth symphony* took place in Moscow in 1878 under Nicholas Rubinstein. *Eugen Onegin* was introduced in Moscow in 1879. Both performances were moderately successful.

By this time, Tschaikovsky's fame as a composer was mounting. In 1884, he was honored by the Tsar with the decoration of the Order of St. Vladimir. Four years later, he received a government annual pension of fifteen hundred dollars for the remainder of his life.

Towards the close of 1887, Tschaikovsky began an extensive concert tour, during which he was accorded great honor in such important music centers as Leipzig, Berlin and Paris. In his letters, he wrote enthusiastically of the great praise showered upon him, of the enormous quantities of money which he was earning and spending. His trip stretched to Italy, where he began work upon his last opera, *Pique-Dame*. From Italy he went on to the Russian Caucasus, where he received word from his patron and friend, Nadejda Filaretovna von Meck that financial reverses compelled her to rescind her pension. Tschaikovsky wrote immediately speaking his deep sorrow in learning that his patron was suffering financially and expressing the wish that their friendship might continue unimpaired. Both this letter, and other letters to von Meck, remained unanswered. When Tschaikovsky returned to Moscow he learned that von Meck had not been in financial difficulty at all, but that she had used it as a pretext to sever a relationship that had begun to bore her. The realization that he had only been a fad for his patroness was a hard blow to Tschaikovsky.

In 1891, Tschaikovsky came to America on a concert tour, conducting orchestras in New York, Baltimore and Philadelphia. He was regally welcomed. It astonished him to learn how well the new world knew his music.

The principal work of Tschaikovsky's last years was, undoubtedly, the *Symphonie pathétique* (the title for which was provided by Tschaikovsky's brother, Modest). Composed in 1893, it was performed the same year in St. Petersburg, under the baton of the composer, with only moderate success. "There was applause and the composer was recalled," recorded Modest Tschaikovsky, "but with no more enthusiasm than on previous occasions." In this symphony, Tschaikovsky poured the tragedy of his own existence—his life sorrows, his bitterness and despair. Rarely has a musical work been more autobiographical in expressing the inmost feelings of a composer. Tschaikovsky himself was delighted with the work, his confidence in it remaining unimpaired by its uneventful reception.

On November 2, 1893 Tschaikovsky—at a luncheon with several friends—incautiously drank a glass of unboiled water, against the advice of his brother who dreaded cholera. That very night, Tschaikovsky was so violently attacked by illness that he said to his brother, Modest: "I think this is death, Goodbye." A physician was summoned; the illness was diagnosed as cholera.

After a day, delirium set in. He recognized no one, and in his unconscious state he frequently repeated the name of his former patron, Nadejda Filaretovna von Meck. A priest was called but, because of Tschaikovsky's unconscious state, it was not possible to administer the Communion. Finally, "Peter Ilitch suddenly opened his eyes," wrote Modest Tschaikovsky. "There was an indescribable expression of unclouded consciousness. Passing over the others standing in the room, he looked at the three nearest him, and then towards heaven. There was a certain light for a moment in his eyes, which was soon extinguished, at the same time with his breath. It was about three o'clock in the morning." The day was the sixth of November. After Tschaikovsky's death, a rumor arose to the effect that he had committed suicide, a rumor which has long ago been discounted.

Twelve days after Tschaikovsky's death, Nápravnik conducted, in memory of a great composer, the *Symphonie pathétique*. At that time, the performance of the symphony made a profound impression upon the audience.

Tschaikovsky has been described as a charming man of the world—a good linguist, and keenly intelligent. His lifelong morbidity has long been designated as the most prevailing attribute of his personality. To this might be added his excessive nervousness and irritability. Women played a small rôle in his life, and his greatest attachments were platonic. He drank enormously. Frequently, the activity of an entire day is tersely summed up in his diary by the one word: "Drunk." He had a tender, almost feminine, love for flowers. "When I am old and past composing," he once confided to von Meck, "I shall spend the whole of my time in growing them."

His life-long ambition was to become a prosperous landowner.

His great adoration in music was Mozart, but he likewise admired Beethoven, Wagner and Berlioz. He detested the music of Brahms. Among his own symphonies, curiously enough, he esteemed most highly (with the exception of the *Pathétique*) the first symphony.

James Gibbons Huneker has discerningly discussed Tschaikovsky's orchestral works. "His feelings for hues, as shown in his instrumentation, is wonderful. His orchestra fairly blazes at times. . . . He was not a great symphonist like Brahms; he had not the sense of formal beauty, preferring instead to work in free fashion within the easy and loosely flowing lines of the overture-fantasie. . . . He takes small, compact themes, nugget-like motives, which he subjects to the most daring and scrutinizing treatment. He polishes, expands, varies and develops his ideas in a marvelous manner, and if the form is often wavering the decoration is always gorgeous. . . . He is first and last a dramatic poet. He delineates the human soul in the convulsions of love, hate, joy and fear; he is an unique master of rhythms and of the torrential dynamics that express primal emotions in the full flood. . . . Give Tschaikovsky one or two large figures, give him a stirring situation, and then hark to the man as his dramatic impulse begins to play havoc."

It is the opinion of R. A. Streatfeild that the *Symphonie pathétique* is the composer's "most characteristic work, that into which he put most of himself. The fourth symphony may excel it in point of sheer picturesqueness, the fifth in poetic feeling, but in the sixth we feel that strongly personal note which rarely fails to appeal to sympathetic souls. Tschaikovsky affixed no program to it, but the story of a tortured soul, seeking an anodyne for its misery in the rapture of pleasure and in the ecstasy of battle, and finally sinking to hopeless pessimism and suicide, is scarcely to be misread. . . . When Tschaikovsky wrote the *Symphonie pathétique* he had attained such mastery of his material as gives him right to rank among great musicians. Whatever he chose to say he could express with absolute certainty of touch. In the *Symphonie pathétique* there are no effects that miss fire, no details that do not 'come off'. . . . It must stand as a very interesting and complete picture of a certain frame of mind, probably the completest expression in music of the *fin de siècle* pessimism that has ever been written."

Tschaikovsky has frequently been criticized for his oversentimentalism, his occasional ingenuousness and his frequent emotional extravagances. But, as Philip Hale has admirably explained, "the heart of Tschaikovsky was that of a little child; the brain was that of a man weary of the world and all its vanities. And so we have the singular phenomenon of naivete, accompanied by superrefined skill—and all this in the body and mind of a man fundamentally oriental in his tastes and especially in his love of surprising or monotonous rhythms and gorgeous colors. . . . When faith returns again to the world, his music may be studied with interest and curiosity as an important document in sociology. But in the present we are under his mighty spell."

Principal works by Peter Ilitch Tschaikovsky:

OPERA: *Voyevod*; *Undine*; *The Guardsman*; *Vakoula*; *Eugen Onegin*; *The Maid of Orleans*; *Mazeppa*; *The Enchantress*; *Pique-Dame*; *Iolanthe*.

BALLET: *The Swan lake*; *The Sleeping beauty*; *Nutcracker*.

ORCHESTRA: Six symphonies; *La Tempête*; *Francesca da Rimini*; *Manfred*; *Fatum*; *Roméo et Juliette*; *Hamlet overture*; *Triomphale ouverture*; *Mozartiana*; Suites from *Nutcracker* and *Sleeping beauty* ballets; *Suite caractéristique*; Two concertos for piano and orchestra; *Concerto for violin and orchestra*; *Variations on a rococo theme* (for violoncello and orchestra); *Serenade for strings*; *Marche solennelle*; *Capriccio Italien*; *Sérénade mélancholique,* for violin and orchestra, etc.

CHAMBER MUSIC: *String sextet*; Three string quartets; *Piano trio in A-minor*.

Choral pieces; pieces for the piano; Songs, etc.

About Peter Ilitch Tschaikovsky:

Blom, Eric. *Tschaikovsky's Orchestral Works*; Evans, Edward. *Tschaikovsky*; Huneker, James Gibbons. *Mezzotints in modern music*; Knorr, Ivan. *Tschaikovsky*; Mason, Daniel Gregory. *From Grieg to Brahms*;

Newmarch, Rosa. *Tschaikovsky, his Life and Works*; Stein, Richard H. *Tschaikovsky*; Tschaikovsky, Modest. *The Life of Peter Ilitch Tschaikovsky*; Weingartner, Felix. *Symphony Writers since Beethoven.*

Important recordings of music by Peter Ilitch Tschaikovsky:

SELECTIONS FROM OPERA: *Eugen Onegin*, "I love you Olga" (VICTOR); "Letter scene" (PARLAPHONE); "Written words" (POLYDOR); "Waltz" (VICTOR-Goossens); "Faint echo of youth" (COLUMBIA-Kullman); "Polonaise" (GRAMOPHONE-Goossens); "Prince Gremin's aria" (GRAMOPHONE). *Mazeppa*, "Cossack dance" (COLUMBIA-Harty). *Pique-Dame*, "Forgive me, bright celestial visions" (COLUMBIA); "It is night" (COLUMBIA); "When you choose me for your husband" (POLYDOR-Schlusnus); "My darling friend" (VICTOR); "It is near to midnight" (DECCA).

ORCHESTRA: *Symphony no. 3 in D-major* (VICTOR-Coates); *Symphony no. 4 in F-minor* (COLUMBIA-Mengelberg); *Symphony no. 5 in E-minor* (COLUMBIA-Mengelberg); *Symphonie pathétique* (VICTOR-Koussevitzky); *Francesca da Rimini* (VICTOR-Coates); *Roméo et Juliette* (VICTOR-Stokowski); *Nutcracker suite* (VICTOR-Stokowski); *Hamlet overture* (GRAMOPHONE-Coates); *The Swan lake suite* (VICTOR-Barbirolli); *Concerto no. 1 in B-flat minor*, for piano and orchestra (VICTOR-Rubinstein); *Concerto for violin and orchestra* (VICTOR-Elman); *Marche solennelle* (VICTOR-Stokowski); *Capriccio Italien* (VICTOR-Stokowski); *Sérénade mélancholique* (VICTOR-Elman).

CHAMBER MUSIC: *Quartet in F-major* (VICTOR-Budapest); *Quartet in D-major*, "Andante cantabile" (COLUMBIA-Lener); *Trio in A-minor* (COLUMBIA).

Christopher Tye 1498-1572

CHRISTOPHER TYE, the distinguished English Church composer of the Reformation, was born in or about 1498. Between 1510 and 1515 he was a member of the choir of King's College, Cambridge, rising to the rank of lay-clerk in 1527. After receiving his degree of Bachelor of Music, he was accorded, on September 10, 1541, an appointment as organist and master of the choristers at the Ely Cathedral. He held this position with distinction for twenty years. During these years, he composed his celebrated masses—including the *Euge bone*, the *Western wynd* and the *Mass*, for five voices—which brought him considerable prominence as a composer.

It is the opinion of many musicologists that these masses represent the richest creative output of Tye's musical career.

"His most important composition in Latin words . . . shows him to have been unquestionably the first English composer of his time," wrote H. B. Collins, "at least from the point of view of technique. The counterpoint is fluent and melodious to a remarkable degree."

In 1545, Tye received his doctorate from Oxford, shortly after which he became a Gentleman of the Chapel Royal. He was held in high esteem by royalty; for several years, he was the private music tutor of Prince Edward.

Like his distinguished contemporary, Tallis, Tye embraced the doctrines of the Reformation under Edward VI, completely changing his style of musical composition to conform to the new church services. It was not an easy task to renounce his artistic past and to adopt a completely new idiom, but like Tallis, Tye succeeded in doing this with unique felicitousness. For this reason, he was an all-important figure in the Church music of the Reformation. He now composed anthems, offertories and hymns with skill and taste. He succeeded in setting a standard for the composition of anthems which English composers after his time were to adopt, and which has tempted posterity to consider Tye "the father of the anthem."

Of his church music, in this new idiom, the most important was no doubt the *Actes of the Apostles*, composed by him in 1552, three tunes of which were later to furnish the material for three celebrated English hymns.

"Tye composed much for the reformed service," we learn from H. E. Wooldridge, "and seems, of all the composers of this period of enforced transition, the one most at ease in adapting himself to the new conditions. Many of his small offertory anthems are almost perfect examples of the Anglican ideal of good musicianship and directed by good sense. . . . He could supply the official demands for simplicity and directness of word-setting while yet preserving an independent musical interest of the finished part-writing and melodic propriety. To combine simplicity and distinction is at no time a common achievement; but in order to appreciate Tye's work in this kind at its full value, it must be remembered that he came at a period when the impulse of musical development has been towards magnificence and complexity, and that in his post-Reformation music he was handicapped by many of the difficulties of the pioneer."

With the accession of Queen Mary, Tye—because of his unorthodox views—retired from the Chapel Royal. In 1560, he was ordained deacon by Bishop Cox, and the following November he was made a priest. He died in or about 1572.

Principal works by Christopher Tye:

CHORAL: Masses; motets; Latin services; anthems; English services; In nomines, etc.

About Christopher Tye:

Walker, Ernest. *A Short History of Music in England*; Wooldridge, H. E. *Oxford History of Music*, vol. 2.
Musical Times 66:718 August 1925.

Important recordings of music by Christopher Tye:

CHORAL: *O, come, ye servants of the Lord* (GRAMOPHONE).

Orazio Vecchi *1551-1605*

ORAZIO VECCHI was born in 1551, probably at Modena. After completing music study in Bologna, he took holy orders and in 1586 became Canon of Correggio, rising to the rank of deacon in 1591. By this time, he had composed a considerable amount of sacred music which brought him such fame that, in 1591, ecclesiastical authorities appointed him (together with Giovanni Gabrieli and Luigi Balbi) to revise the "Roman Gradual," published the same year.

Excitable and quarrelsome by nature, Vecchi frequently came into disrepute with Church authorities. In 1593, he was involved in a street brawl during which he received a severe wound from a stiletto. Two years later, he was once again the principal in a brawl, in which his adversary received two serious wounds in the head. On another occasion, a scene took place at the Cathedral between Vecchi, who was intoning a chant, and his organist; at one point, each musician was under the impression that the other had a few moments of silence in his music and, since both men were stubborn, each attempted to drown out the other until the performance ended in laughter among the congregation and outraged horror among the clergy.

It was propably because of these offenses, and many others, that, in 1595, Vecchi was relieved of his ecclesiastical functions. His reputation as a musician, however, was so great that, in 1596, he was appointed chapel master in Modena. His importance as a composer continued to grow until his name was well known thruout Europe.

Vecchi died in Modena on February 19, 1605. It was said that his death was brought on directly by his aggrieved pain in learning that he had been deprived of his musical post in Modena by the bishop. He died leaving a considerable fortune, as well as a fine collection of books and pictures.

Vecchi's fame as a composer has persisted until our time, not because of his sacred music, despite its excellence, but because of *L'Amfiparnasso*, performed in Modena in 1594. *L'Amfiparnasso* has for a long time been the subject of much debate and speculation among musical historians. It was termed by its composer a *"commedia harmonica"* or comic opera—and for this reason the musical historian has for a long time designated it as one of the first examples in musical history of opera. But in form and artistic content it was far removed from the

ORAZIO VECCHI

operatic realm. It is a series of fourteen madrigals for five unaccompanied voices, linked together by a "libretto" which has almost no outline of a plot.

It was Romain Rolland who, in *Les Origines du théâtre lyrique moderne,* first pointed out that *L'Amfiparnasso* is not so much a primitive opera at it is a primitive program-symphony. Elaborating upon this very point, Edward J. Dent wrote: 'For Orazio Vecchi and his contemporaries, the most perfect instrument was the human voice, and the polyphonic madrigal, the style over which they had the greatest mastery. . . . Vecchi set the comedy of masks to music not because he wished to be dramatic, but because music without words was practically unthinkable. The comedy of masks was familar to his singers in such a way that his setting became virtually wordless. The characters represented would not be made real to their minds thru what they said on one particular occasion; they were not individuals, but eternal types, personifications of phases of character that every hearer could recognize more or less in some aspect of his own personality. Similarly in *Ein Heldenleben,* the 'hero' may be supposed by writers of analytical programs to be the ideal hero, or by facetious critics to be Richard Strauss himself; but it is more reasonable and more poetical to consider the work as the expression of what all of us have at some time thought and suffered. To admit this is simply to recognize that the *Amfiparnasso* and the *Heldenleben* are attempts of the remote past and the immediate present to express in music what the classical age expressed in Beethoven's symphonies."

Cecil Gray, in examining Vecchi's music has found in it "intrinsic beauty, wit and verse," which is "as fresh now as the day it was written."

Principal works by Orazio Vecchi:

CHORAL: Masses; motets; hymns; lamentations; madrigals; canzonets; *L'Amfiparnasso.*

About Orazio Vecchi:

Henderson, William James. *Some Forerunners of Italian Opera*; Rolland, Romain. *Les Origines du Théâtre Lyrique Moderne.*

Dominant 1:11 July 1928; *Monthly Musical Record* 36:50 March 1906.

Francesco Veracini *1685-1750*

"The Beethoven of the eighteenth century."—TORCHI

FRANCESCO MARIA VERACINI was born in Florence in 1685. He began the study of the violin at an early age, taught by his uncle Antonio Veracini, a well-known violinist and composer of the time.

In 1714, Veracini received his first important musical post, when he was summoned as violinist for the orchestra of St. Mark's Cathedral in Venice. There, he entered into a competitive concert with the eminent Tartini at the palace of Donna Pisano Mocenigo. Tartini played first, and when Veracini heard his impeccable performance he discreetly withdrew from the duel.

But Veracini's reputation as a violinist was formidable, and he was soon recognized as one of the eminent virtuosos of the day. He went to England, making a sensational debut at the King's Theatre. In 1716, he was back in Venice where the Crown Prince of Saxony heard him play and invited him to come to Dresden. The following year, therefore, Veracini was appointed solo violinist and composer to the Elector of Saxony at Dresden, a position he held for several years.

In 1722, Veracini was suddenly stricken with a fit of madness in which he jumped out of a window, breaking his leg and hip. Mattheson explained that the madness was caused by overstudy, intensive preoccupation with composition and slavish application to alchemy. However, a far different explanation is offered by other musical historians. Veracini, it is known, was a man of offensive arrogance and conceit. To humiliate him, a Dresden musician, Pisandel by name, challenged Veracini in court to play at sight a technically complex concerto which the former had composed. Veracini accepted the challenge, playing the work with great competence. Pisandel, however, minimized Veracini's achievement, calling upon one of the violinists in the court orchestra (whom he had secretly coached in this very concerto for several months) to perform the work. The obscure violinist gave, of course, a masterful exhibition.

FRANCESCO VERACINI

Veracini's humiliation was so great, it is said, that he was seized by fevers and temporary insanity.

In any case, by 1723, Veracini recovered fully from his accident and joined the chapel of Count Kunsky in Prague. In 1735, he was once again in London, the leader of the orchestra at the King's Theatre in Haymarket. The same year, his opera *Adriano* was first performed in London, and was sufficiently successful to enjoy seventeen performances.

Towards the end of his life, Veracini returned to Italy. En route, he was shipwrecked. His life was saved by a miracle, but he lost all of his belongings, and reached his native land a pauper. During his closing years, Veracini knew great poverty. He died in Pisa in 1750.

Veracini was a far greater composer than most of his contemporaries realized. His works, particularly those for the violin, were so far ahead of their time that most musicians of his day failed to appreciate or recognize their greatness. "His bold modulations, the wealth of his delicately worked out harmonies, his originality in expressing his conceptions," wrote Edmund van der Straeten, "differed too widely from anything that had been heard before, with the result that, for over a century, his compositions were entirely neglected. Only since the second half of last century, violinists

and the music public have become aware of their rare beauty. In form, they show a progress over their predecessors, but it is especially in thematic material and in its bold harmonic treatment and the characteristic chromatic passages that he appears quite modern. Some of his slow movements are truly enchanting, while his allegros often fascinate by their brightness and natural flowing form."

Principal works by Francesco Veracini:

OPERA: *Adriano*; *Roselinda*; *L'Errore di Salomone*.

CHORAL: *Nice e Tirsi*; *Parla al ritratto dell'amante*.

INSTRUMENTAL: Twenty-four sonatas for violin; quintet-concertos; symphonies for two violins, viola, violoncello and bass; sonatas for violin and flute, etc.

About Francesco Veracini:

Phipson, Thomas Lambe. *Biographical Sketches of Celebrated Violinists*; Reuchsel, Maurice. *L'École Classique du Violon*; Straeten, Edmund Sebastian Joseph van der. *The History of the Violin*.

Important recordings of music by Francesco Veracini:

INSTRUMENTAL: *Sonata in E-minor,* for violin and harpsichord (POLYDOR); *Largo,* for violin and piano (COLUMBIA-Szigeti).

Giuseppe Verdi *1813-1901*

GIUSEPPE VERDI, frequently called the "purest glory of Italian genius," was born in Roncole, a village in the duchy of Parma, on October 9, 1813. His father, an inn-keeper, was in reality a peasant, descended from a long line of peasants. Giuseppe Verdi, therefore, sprang from humble origins.

Shortly after his birth, Giuseppe Verdi hovered in the shadow of death when a troop of Cossacks descended upon Roncole, stormed the church in which were concealed the women and children, and spread death and havoc. Fortunately, little Giuseppe and his mother were hidden in the belfry where the Cossacks did not penetrate, thereby being safe from the slashing sabers.

An interest in music was aroused in Giuseppe at an early age. As a child, he manifested unusual curiosity for musical sounds when the organ of the church was playing or when a wandering violinist drew merry tunes from his strings. Giuseppe's father, finally—moved by the pleas of the boy—bought an old spinet. This was Giuseppe's closest friend during his boyhood days, and from it he acquired his first musical proficiency. "One day," related a friend of Verdi's father, "the boy was in the greatest delight at having found the major third and fifth of the key of C. The next day, however, he could not find the chord again. He fell into such a temper that he seized a hammer and proceeded to break the spinet into pieces."

In his tenth year, Giuseppe—who had been studying the organ from the village organist—was appointed to officiate over the musical services at the church. Simultaneously, he was sent by his father to the neighboring town of Busseto for regular instruction in letters. Thus, each week-end, young Verdi trudged the six miles from Busseto to Roncole to fulfill his duties as organist. Then, his duties over, he would walk the six miles back to Busseto. Once, while walking this distance in early dawn, he missed his road and fell into a canal. But for the fact that a peasant woman passed by fortuitously and heard his cries he would, no doubt, have drowned.

A friend of Giuseppe's father, Antonio Barezzi, a grocer in Busseto, offered the boy employment, at the same time making it possible for him to study music more intensively under Giovanni Provesi, organist of the Busseto Cathedral and director of the Busseto Philharmonic. Giuseppe's musical progress was so swift that, before long, Provesi permitted his student to substitute for him at the Cathedral organ and over the Philharmonic orchestra. At this same time, Verdi turned to composition, producing a formidable number of works for chorus, orchestra and piano. These pieces made so profound an impression upon the Busseto townsfolk that a fund was raised to enable Verdi to go to Milan to continue his music study in that important centre.

Verdi came to Milan in May of 1832 with the intention of entering the Conservatory. Strange to say, Verdi's application was rejected. The directors of the Conservatory felt that Verdi showed no particular aptitude for music. Undiscouraged, young Verdi sought private teachers, becoming a student of Vincenzo Lavigna, a composer of opera. "He is a fine young man," Lavigna said, "Giuseppe is discreet, studious and intelligent, and will prove a great honor to me and to our country."

The death of Giovanni Provesi in 1833 brought Verdi back to Busseto to assume the direction of the Philharmonic. Two years after his return, Verdi married Margherita Barezzi, the beautiful daughter of his one-time employer and friend.

His duties at the head of the Busseto Philharmonic came to a termination in 1839. Together with his wife and two children, Verdi returned to Milan with the hope of finding production for his first opera, which he had written in Busseto. Fortune was with him. On November 17, 1839, La Scala introduced Verdi's first opera, *Oberto*. Though *Oberto* ran for only several performances, it was successful, so successful that Ricordi, the publishers, paid Verdi two thousand lire for the publication rights, and the director of La Scala commissioned the composer to produce another opera for the following season.

For his second opera, Verdi selected a rousingly comic libretto. Never was a comic-opera written under greater stress of tragedy than *Un Giorno di Regno*. At first, Verdi fell ill. Then, his son, stricken by a mysterious ailment, died suddenly. Two days later, Verdi's daughter died just as mysteriously. And, after a few months, Verdi's young wife followed her children to the grave.

As might be expected, *Un Giorno*—written as it was under overwhelming emotional stress—was not a good opera, and upon its performance it was a complete failure. For a while, Verdi seriously thought of giving up composition completely and permanently. Only the encouragement of the director of La Scala, and the inspiration of a new imaginative and colorful libretto, succeeded in restoring to him his former zest for work. In 1842, Verdi composed his opera, *Nabucco*. Upon its first performance at La Scala on March 9,

GIUSEPPE VERDI

Rigoletto, based upon Victor Hugo's *Le Roi s'amuse.* *Rigoletto* was sensationally successful. It is said that Verdi knew well the contagious appeal of his score, for he refused to give the music of the aria *La Donna è mobile* to the singer until the eve of the performance, for fear that the appealing melody might become known before the performance of the opera. *La Donna è mobile,* as Verdi expected, took the audience by storm; it emphasized the striking victory of *Rigoletto.* Victor Hugo, himself, who had at first been violently prejudiced against opera, confessed that Verdi's music had won him over.

"We can still sense the extraordinary quality of this music in which orchestra and voice alike combine to heighten the poignancy of the situations," wrote Francis Toye. "The famous quartet in the last act remains to this day one of the acknowledged masterpieces of the world, so truly does every character express itself in the music. . . . There is something sombre and rugged in the simplicity of *Rigoletto* which entitles it to be called truly great, and it always remained one of Verdi's especial favorites."

Having found his stride, Verdi produced two other operas immediately following *Rigoletto* which are inevitably associated with his name. *Il Trovatore,* introduced in Rome in 1853, surpassed even the success of *Rigoletto* and established more firmly Verdi's reputation as the foremost operatic composer of his time. *La Traviata,* produced in Venice in 1853, was, curiously enough, a failure —principally the result of a 'poor performance. However, upon its revival a year later, *La Traviata* came to its own, joining *Rigoletto* and *Il Trovatore* in the high esteem of the opera-public.

His success enabled Verdi to achieve a life-long ambition. He bought himself spacious farmlands at Sant' Agata, near Busseto, where he spent a great portion of his time farming, supervising over the buying and feeding of his cattle, and watching over the produce of his crops. "I am and always will be a peasant," he once confessed. Certainly, he derived his greatest pleasure and relaxation from his farming activities.

it was a triumph. Verdi definitely became one of the most popular operatic composers of the day. Clothing, food, delicacies were named after him. He had definitely begun his march towards fame.

This success inspired in Verdi a breath-taking productivity. During the next few years, he composed no less than twelve operas, ranging from such effete productions as *I Masnadieri*— which had been commissioned by London for Jenny Lind—to such creations as *Ernani,* first produced in Venice in 1844, and *Luisa Miller,* composed in 1849 and based upon Schiller's *Kabale und Liebe.* These operas, even, at their best, give only furtive indications of the great Verdi that was soon to emerge. They consisted, for the most part, of a "string of passionate tunes bracketed in the conventional *cavatina-cabaletta* style," as James Gibbons Huneker pointed out, with "little attempt at following the book—such awful books!— and the orchestra, a huge, strumming machine, strumming without color, appositeness, rime or reason. And then the febrile, simian-like restlessness of the music! It was written for people of little musical intelligence, people who must hum a tune or ever after view it with contempt."

In 1851, Verdi composed the first of the operas that made him an immortal,

·In 1855, Verdi was invited by France to compose an opera to a libretto of Scribe for the Great Exposition. *I Vespri Siciliani* was not one of Verdi's preeminent successes, but it was well received by the French music-public. Upon his return to Sant' Agata, Verdi devoted himself to the composition of *Simon Boccanegra* which, though it is one of his most important works, was received coldly when first performed in Venice in 1857.

In 1859, Verdi married a second time, this time the beautiful singer Giuseppina Strepponi. During the next two years he was more active in politics than in music. Upon the inauguration of the first Italian parliament by Cavour, Verdi was elected deputy, remaining in this office for several years. He did not like politics and continually attempted to free himself from its yoke. This he did in 1865. Ten years later the King of Italy appointed Verdi a senator of the Kingdom, but though Verdi took the oath he never held the seat.

In 1861, Verdi received a commission from the Imperial Theatre of St. Petersburg for an opera. Upon the first performance of *La Forza del destino* in Russia it was received apathetically, partially because of its morbid theme, and partially because a strong Nationalist movement in St. Petersburg was opposed to Italian opera. The next important opera was *Don Carlos* composed in 1867 upon a commission from the Paris Opéra.

Early in 1869, Verdi was offered a munificent sum of money to compose an opera for Egypt. After refusing this offer upon two different occasions, Verdi was finally induced into accepting it by a glimpse at the libretto, whose theatrical qualities Verdi sensed instantly. Innumerable difficulties arose to delay the first performance of this new opera, principally the Franco-Prussian War which prevented for a while the shipping of the scenery from Paris, where it was being constructed, to Egypt. Finally, on Christmas Eve of 1871, Verdi's opera —it was *Aïda*—was magnificently performed in Cairo. Critics had been specially sent from France and Italy to cover the event, and they were unanimous in proclaiming this work as Verdi's masterpiece. When, however, *Aïda* was first performed in Italy, a few weeks after its world's première, it was received apathetically. The Italian music-public did not find the exotic theme of *Aïda* appealing. Moreover, it accused Verdi of becoming overcomplicated and abstruse, of bending the knee to the golden calf of Wagnerism—a strange criticism when one considers the Italianism of this opera!

Aïda brought Verdi's second period as an operatic composer to a close. It was a period in which he did not develop operatic forms or travel in new directions. He merely enriched those operatic forms and speech which he had inherited from Donizetti, Bellini and Rossini—but enriched them immeasurably. In this period, Verdi disclosed—as H. C. Colles pointed out—"an extraordinary power of depicting a graphic situation in a vocal melody." Many of the works of this period "have an irresistible grip upon the imagination by their sheer force of melody, and *Aïda* . . . is a unique example of a romantic story told entirely in a series of broad and intensely expressive tunes."

After *Aïda*, Verdi took a sixteen year holiday from the composition of operas. He did not neglect composition altogether, producing at least two important works. The first of these was the *String quartet*, composed in 1873. Of far greater artistic significance, however, was the *Requiem* created by Verdi as his gesture of honor and respect to the novelist Manzoni, who died in 1873. Verdi's *Requiem* was first performed under his own direction at the church of St. Mark in Milan, when it made so profound an impression that arrangements were made whereby it might be introduced to the leading music centres of Europe. There were some to criticize the *Requiem* for being more operatic than religious in style. But none could deny that it was music of poignant intensity, a profound expression of grief.

During the years that followed, Verdi devoted himself more industriously than before to the activities of his farm, music beginning to occupy less and less of an important rôle in his life. As a matter of fact, he had seriously considered never again to compose an opera.

In 1879, however, Verdi came into contact with Arrigo Boito, brilliant composer, critic and poet, whom he had first met many years before. Boito offered Verdi a libretto from Shakespeare's *Othello,* a libretto so uniquely adaptable to music that Verdi decided to return to creative work.

Otello was first produced at La Scala on February 5, 1887. With that work, a new and far different Verdi emerged. It was no longer the Verdi whose final and ultimate goal was the composition of endlessly flowing melodies. It was a Verdi, considerably matured by Wagnerian influence, who was much more interested in composing dramatic music that would express the action of the stage and heighten it, it was a Verdi who was keenly interested in musical characterization for the first time.

Despite the change in Verdi's style, *Otello* was a sensation. It was agreed that this was the greatest Verdi of all, a Verdi who had ripened into one of the foremost dramatic geniuses of all time. *Otello* brought Verdi back to the limelight; once again he found himself the most popular composer of his day.

At this time, Verdi was old, sick, smothered by feverish depressions. However, Boito's enthusiasm and zest were instrumental in turning him to the composition of one more opera. Once again, Boito fashioned an incomparable libretto —this time from Shakespeare's *The Merry Wives of Windsor.* And into this sparkling, merry libretto, Verdi was to pour the freshness and vitality of an inspiration that seemed unable to recognize old age. The composition of this last opera was a labor of love for Verdi. On February 9, 1893, La Scala in Milan gave the first performance of *Falstaff.* The general music-public was, perhaps, not so keenly impressed with this opera as it had been with *Otello.* But musicians and critics generally agreed that Verdi had produced his most spontaneous, youthful and immortal music. It is one of the amazing phenomenae in music that this score of such verdant freshness and youthful zest could have come from a composer eighty years old.

In discussing *Otello* and *Falstaff,* R. A. Streatfeild has written: "In *Otello* Verdi advanced to undreamed-of heights of freedom and beauty. *Aïda* was a mighty step towards the light, but with *Otello* he finally shook off the trammels of convention. His inexhaustible stream of melody remained as pure and full as ever, while the more declamatory parts of the opera, down to the slightest piece of recitative, are informed by a richness of suggestion, and an unerring instinct for truth, such as it would be vain to seek in his earlier work . . . . *Falstaff* is the very incarnation of youth and high spirits. . . . He has combined a schoolboy's sense of fun with the grace and science of a Mozart. The part-writing is often exceedingly elaborate, but the most complicated concerted pieces flow on as naturally as a ballad. The glorious final fugue is an epitome of the work. It is really a marvel of contrapuntal ingenuity, yet it is so full of bewitching melody and healthy animal spirits that an uncultivated hearer would probably think it nothing but an ordinary jovial finale. In the last act Verdi strikes a deeper note. He has caught the charm and mystery of the sleeping forest with exquisite art. There is an unearthly beauty about this scene, which is new to students of Verdi. In the fairy music, too, he reveals yet another side of his genius. Nothing so delicate nor so rich in imaginative beauty has been written since the days of Weber."

In 1897, Verdi's beloved wife died, leaving him a sad and lonely man. His grief sapped his strength, and from that time on he began to complain bitterly of his health. "Altho the doctors tell me I am not ill," he wrote to a friend in 1900, "I feel that everything tries me; I can no longer read or write; my sight is not good, my hearing is worse still; and above all, my limbs no longer obey me. I do not live; I vegetate."

He was on a visit to Milan when a paralytic stroke attacked him while he was dressing in his hotel room. Six days later—on January 27, 1901—he died. He was accorded the funeral of a national hero; almost a quarter of a million of his compatriots lined the streets to pay their last silent respects to the body as it was carried to the oratory of the Musicians' Home where it was buried.

In his will, Verdi had specified that he wished a simple burial without any music or pompous ceremony. Until the very end, therefore, Verdi remained a man of the utmost simplicity and unpretentiousness. Not even a lifetime of glory could rob him of his unaffected modesty. Charles Villiers Stanford, who attenued the first performance of *Otello*, has noted with surprise that even at that time Verdi could retain his simplicity of character, "so devoid was he of all self-assertion that he even expressed his regret that so vast a concourse of strangers should have taken the trouble to come from all parts of Europe for the première."

Verdi did not like the society of people; he was happiesι when he was alone. Comment has already been made that he found greatest satisfaction and delight in caring for his farm. He frequently said that, if he had been born stronger, he would have been a farmer rather than a composer. At any rate, throughout the latter ρart of his life he rose at an early hour and devoted the entire morning to visiting the horses and cattle, seeing that they were fed properly, to superintending the development of his elaborate crops. Except for his farm, his only diversion consisted in occasional games of cards or billiards.

He was excessively generous and exceedingly honest. He was also a good business man, shrewd in bargaining for terms and able to win his points at all times. Intensely patriotic, he was said to have accomplished as much as any other one man in bringing about the freedom and unity of Italy.

Principal works by Giuseppe Verdi:

ORCHESTRA: Two symphonies; marches.

CHAMBER MUSIC: *String quartet in E-minor.*

CHORAL: *Requiem*; *Ave Maria*; *Pater Noster*; *Four pezzi sacri*; *Stabat Mater*, etc.

OPERA: *Ernani*; *Macbeth*; *Luisa Miller*; *Rigoletto*; *Il Trovatore*; *La Traviata*; *I Vespri Siciliani*; *Simon Boccanegra*; *Un Ballo in maschera*; *La Forza del destino*; *Don Carlos*; *Aïda*; *Otello*; *Falstaff.*

Arias, duets; terzets; etc.

About Giuseppe Verdi:

Bellaigue, Camille. *Verdi*; Bonavia, F. *Verdi*; Gatti, Carlo. *Verdi*; Pougin, Arthur. *Verdi*; Toye, Francis. *Giuseppe Verdi; His Life and Works*; Werfel, Franz. *Verdi.*

Important recordings of music by Giuseppe Verdi:

OPERA: *Aida*, complete (VICTOR-La Scala); *Ernani*, abridged (COLUMBIA-La Scala); *Falstaff*, complete (COLUMBIA-La Scala); *Otello*, complete (VICTOR-La Scala); *Rigoletto*, complete (COLUMBIA-La Scala); *La Traviata*, complete (VICTOR-La Scala); *Il Trovatore*, complete (VICTOR-La Scala).

CHORAL: *Requiem*, complete (VICTOR).

Tomás Luis De Victoria   *1535-1611*

TOMÁS LUIS DE VICTORIA, whom J. B. Trend has designated as "the greatest figure in the music of Spanish history," is often considered second in importance only to Palestrina in the music of the sixteenth century.

For a long time it was believed that Victoria's birth occurred in 1540, but the researches of Felipe Pedrell placed the year as somewhere near 1535, in the diocese of Avila in Old Castile. Victoria's musical education is unknown; it is, however, reasonably certain that he procured it in Spain where he steeped himself deeply in the church music of Spanish composers.

In 1565, Victoria received a grant of money from Philip II, which enabled him to go to Rome. There he was appointed cantor of the Collegium Germanicum, which had been founded fifteen years previously by St. Ignatius Loyola.

His first published work consisted of a volume of motets, which he had composed as early as 1569 to 1570, and which appeared in 1572. "This work," commented W. H. Grattan-Flood, "displays the master almost in the plenitude of his powers." In 1575, Victoria was appointed chapel master of St. Apollinare. He held this position, however, for only four years. In 1579, he left Rome as a chaplain to the Empress Doña Maria, daughter of Charles V, who was on her way to enter a monastery in Spain.

Victoria then remained in Spain for the remainder of his life. In 1586, he was appointed music director of the Convent of the Descalzar Reales in Madrid, three years after the publication of his first book of masses. Victoria died in Madrid on August 7 or August 27, 1611.

The complete works of Victoria were published in eight volumes by Breitkopf and Härtel, under the editorship of Felipe Pedrell.

In discussing the characteristics of Victoria's music, J. B. Trend pointed out its intrinsically Spanish flavor. "Spanish musicians feel his music to be intensely Spanish; they find in him a peculiar attitude of mind which is immediately intangible and makes them feel that he is one of themselves. He is as unmistakably and inimitably Spanish —Castillian, even—as a portrait of El Greco or a dusty road in La Mancha. . . . The gruesome cries of the crowd in his passions are the musical expression of those characteristic groups of colored, wooden statuary, carried in procession thru the streets; the sensuous morbidity of motets like *Vere languores* or *Jesu dulcis memoria* is less congenial to him than the swirling rhythms and the flowing contrapuntal texture of those masses and motets which have their counterpart in the Assumptions and Resurrections of El Greco."

Principal works by Tomás Luis de Victoria:

CHORAL: Passions; masses; motets; cantiones; magnificats, etc.

About Tomás Luis de Victoria:

Collet, Henri. *Le Mysticisme Musical Espagnol du XVIe Siècle*; Pedrell, Felipe. *Tomás Luis de Victoria Abulense.*
Catholic Choirmaster 6:120 October 1920; *Musical Times* 66:311 April 1, 1925.

Important recordings of music by Tomás Luis de Victoria:

CHORAL: *Ave Maria* (BRUNSWICK); *Domine, non sum dignis* (GRAMOPHONE); *O magnum mysterium* (GRAMOPHONE); *O quam gloriosum* (GRAMOPHONE); *O vos omnes* (COLUMBIA); *Popule meus* (POLYDOR); *Quae est ista* (GRAMOPHONE); *Tantum ergo* (PARLAPHONE); *Tenebrae factae sunt* (VICTOR).

Henri Vieuxtemps *1820-1881*

HENRI VIEUXTEMPS was born in Verviers, Belgium, on February 20, 1820. He studied the violin at an early age with his father. At seven, he made a successful debut in his native town. In the same year, Charles de Bériot heard him perform, and was so im-

HENRI VIEUXTEMPS

pressed by the performance that he decided to take the prodigy under his wing. De Bériot secured for young Vieuxtemps a stipend from the King of Belgium, and personally gave him intensive training in violin technique and the violin literature of Corelli, Tartini, Viotti, etc.

In 1830, De Bériot took Vieuxtemps with him to Paris where, in many of De Bériot's concerts, Vieuxtemps was a fellow-performer. One year later, De Bériot started an extensive concert tour, leaving Vieuxtemps in Paris to his own resources. Vieuxtemps gave performances in Paris which were sensational. In 1833, he undertook an extensive concert tour thru Germany and Austria. "Vieuxtemps is the greatest genius of the young masters," wrote Robert Schumann when Vieuxtemps performed in Leipzig. "His playing has the brilliancy and perfume of the flower." In Vienna, Vieuxtemps had the distinction of being the first to perform the Beethoven *Concerto for violin and orchestra* in public. From Vienna, he went to London where he heard Paganini play; from that time on, he was strongly influenced both by Paganini's style of violin playing and by his style of composition.

In 1843, Vieuxtemps—now a world-famous violinist—visited America, in a tour which took him as far as Mexico. The tour was not successful, principally because another violinist, Ole Bull, was at that time the idol of the American music public. "I came too soon," was Vieuxtemps' own explanation. He played to half-empty houses, often going to absurd extremes to arouse the interest of Americans in his playing. At one time, he composed a series of pyrotechnical variations on *Yankee Doodle* which he featured extensively in his American concerts with the hope of attracting American curiosity towards his art. In New Orleans, it is said that he ordered the life-size photographs of him plastered upside-down so that the public might come to the concert hall in the belief that he would perform his music standing on his head!

Vieuxtemps, however, was not discouraged by the chilling failures of his first American tour. In 1857 and 1870 he made two more visits to America which were overwhelmingly successful.

Shortly after his first American tour, Vieuxtemps visited St. Petersburg where his concerts were so successful that he was appointed solo-violinist to the Czar. For six years, he remained in Russia.

In 1871, Vieuxtemps was appointed professor at the Brussels Conservatory for the chair formerly held by De Bériot. Two years later, paralysis of the arm compelled him to give up all concert work and pedagogy. Believing that the warm climate would relieve his paralysis, he went to Algiers. There, at Mustapha-les-Alger, he died on June 6, 1881.

Gay and light-hearted in spirit, Vieuxtemps was almost as appealing for the charm of his personality as for the genius of his violin playing. By temperament, he was restless and nervous; his greatest passion, in consequence, was for travel. He frequently expressed his contempt for a life of stability, affirming that his philosophy of living consisted of freedom of movement.

As a composer for the violin, Vieuxtemps was strongly influenced by Paganini. Like his celebrated predecessor, he filled his music with pyrotechnical effects diluted with warm sentiment. He is most famous for his six concertos for violin and orchestra. "We can search in vain," wrote the violinist, Arthur Hartmann, "for works which in dramatic intensity, in daring virtuosity and

effectiveness equal the first, third, fourth and fifth concertos. And when we recall that the first great concerto was written by Vieuxtemps when but eighteen years of age, the case may well stand as being without parallel. To my critical judgment, the fifth concerto represents a unique achievement in violinistic art, and is exemplary for its beautiful symmetry, skill and art of construction and for its wealth of noble and musically dramatic utterances."

Principal works by Henri Vieuxtemps:

ORCHESTRA: Six concertos for violin and orchestra; *Overture on the Belgian national anthem*; Two concertos for violoncello and orchestra.

VIOLIN AND PIANO: *Violin suite*; Fantasies; *Sonata for violin and piano.*

Transcriptions; Three cadenzas for the Beethoven *Violin concerto, etc.*

About Henri Vieuxtemps:

Bergmans, Paul. *Henri Vieuxtemps*; Lahee, Henry C. *Famous Violinists of Today and Yesterday*; Radoux, J. Théodore. *Vieuxtemps: Sa Vie, ses Oeuvres.* *Musical Courier* 57:5 September 16, 1908; *La Revue musicale* 40:50 November 1922.

Important recordings of music by Henri Vieuxtemps:

ORCHESTRA: *Concerto in D-minor*, for violin and orchestra (VICTOR-Heifetz); *Concerto in A-minor* (COLUMBIA-Dubois).

VIOLIN AND PIANO: *Ballade et Polonaise* (GRAMOPHONE); *Rêverie* (COLUMBIA); *Sérénité* (VICTOR).

Giovanni Viotti *1753-1824*

GIOVANNI BATTISTA VIOTTI, the son of a blacksmith, was born in Fontanetto, Piedmont, on May 23, 1753. On his eighth birthday, he was given the gift of a small violin on which he soon succeeded, without any instruction, in producing pleasant melodies. His father, an amateur horn player, began to teach him the elements of music; these lessons were supplemented by others given by Giovanni, a wandering lute player.

When Viotti was thirteen years old, he was recommended by a friend to the Marquesa of Voghera, in Turin, who was in search of a musical companion for her eighteen-year old son, the Prince of Cisterna. Because of Viotti's youth, the Marquesa refused to consider him. Another musician, Colognetti—who had heard Viotti play at sight—spoke so enthusiastically of him to the Prince, that the latter decided to give the young musician a trial. As a result, Viotti came to live in the palace of the Marquesa, and was placed under the instruction of the distinguished violinist, Pugnani. The Prince spent more than 20,000 francs in Viotti's violin education, but as he confessed: "I do not regret the money. We cannot pay too highly for the existence of such an artist."

In 1770, Viotti set out with his master, Pugnani, on an extensive concert tour which took them to Germany, Poland, Switzerland and, finally, France. In Paris, he gave a private concert in which he made an extraordinary impression. Finally, in 1782, he made his debut at the Concert Spirituel where his performance was described as phenomenal. His reputation now firmly established, he was offered fortunes to give further concerts, to accept important musical posts and to perform at the most exclusive Paris salons.

Then, at the height of his fame, Viotti suddenly decided to retire from active concertizing, despite the fabulous offers. What caused this sudden withdrawal from public performances, no one could explain. It is believed, however, that the indiscriminate applause of ignorant audiences so piqued him that he vowed never again to perform except for musicians. For the next few years, while living together with his bosom friend, Cherubini, Viotti gave charming Sunday musicales in which he performed his new works for his circle of musician-friends.

Invited to court to give a special performance for Queen Marie Antoinette, Viotti so delighted the Queen that she appointed him court-musician. At this time, Viotti—together with Léonard, hairdresser to the Queen—entered into business negotiations to re-establish opera in Paris with great artists. Unfortunately, the Revolution brought an end to this incipient endeavor. When, in 1792, the King and Queen were about to be executed, Viotti left for London. His fortune gone, he was now compelled to rescind his vow and once again make public appearances. He per-

formed at the Salomon concerts which at that time were honoring Joseph Haydn as guest. He also replaced Cramer as head of the Italian Opera in London.

In 1798, as a result of several innocent letters which Viotti sent to Paris and into which invidious messages were read, Viotti was accused of being in league with the revolutionary party. He was forced to leave London, and become an exile in Germany. For three years, he led a solitary existence in Schönfeldt, near Hamburg, where he spent his time in composition and teaching.

In 1801, he was permitted to return to England. He entered once again into business—this time by setting up a wine business to which he clung tenaciously until 1813 when it left him a financially ruined man.

Poverty compelled him to return to music. He now became active in the newly-founded Royal Philharmonic Society, playing in the orchestra under Salomon's leadership. He also visited Paris where he was warmly welcomed by his old friends. On one of his visits to the French capital, Viotti was appointed director of the Paris Opéra. But misfortune was dogging his footsteps. Shortly after his appointment, the Duc du Barry, nephew of the king, was assassinated at the Opéra, bringing on the immediate closing of the theatre. The Opéra was removed to a smaller

GIOVANNI VIOTTI

house where it encountered innumerable difficulties. Viotti was accused of mismanagement, and, in 1822, he was compelled to retire from his post with an annual pension of 600 francs.

He returned to London virtually penniless. The last years of his life were passed in obscurity, darkened by remorse and grief. He died on March 3, 1824. Something of the bitterness of his last years might be guessed by an item in his will which stated that he did not wish anything to be spent for his funeral because "a little earth will suffice for such a miserable creature as myself."

Viotti had a distinguished manner and considerable personal charm which made him the cynosure of female eyes. Strange to say, he never married; stranger still, women never played an important rôle in his life. His existence was not entirely dominated by music, literature and science sharing his interest. He was a passionate lover of nature. As a contemporary of Viotti, M. Eymar, pointed out: "A violet hidden under the leaves transported him with the liveliest of joy. . . . He would spend hours lying on the grass admiring a carnation, or breathing the fragrance of a rose."

As a composer, Viotti is most famous for his violin concertos, of which he composed twenty-nine. Of these, the one in A-minor (no. 22) is world-famous. In these concertos, he did not develop violin-technique, but succeeded in being among the first to give full treatment to the violin concerto. A contemporary critic of Viotti wrote as follows about Viotti's music in 1794: "His themes are splendid; they are developed with intelligence, tastefully contrasted with passages. . . . His harmonies are rich. . . . His rhythms are marked. . . . In a word, both Viotti's compositions, as well as his playing, are enchanting."

Pierre Baillot, the famous French violinist of the eighteenth century, said of Viotti's concertos: "These concertos exalt the soul. It is impossible not to discover in them a poetic feeling, not to see in them some of the heroes of Homer."

Principal works by Giovanni Viotti:

ORCHESTRA: Twenty-nine concertos for violin and orchestra.
CHAMBER MUSIC: Twenty-one string quartets; Twenty-one trios (for violins and viola); Fifty duos for unaccompanied two violins; Eighteen sonatas for violin and bass, etc.

About Giovanni Viotti:

Hart, George. *The Violin and Its Music*; Pincherle, Marc. *Feuillets d'histoire du Violon*; Pougin, Arthur. *Viotti et l'école Moderne*.
Ménestral 86:185 April 24, 1924; *Musical Courier* 57:9 August 5, 1908; *Quarterly Musical Magazine* 2:52 (1820); *Strad* 41:23 May 1930.

Important recordings of music by Giovanni Viotti:

VIOLIN AND PIANO: *Concerto in A-minor*, with piano accompaniment, "Adagio" (GRAMOPHONE).

Antonio Vivaldi *1678-1743*

THE biographical material that exists about Antonio Vivaldi is slight. Modern research has placed the locale of his birth as Venice, and 1678 as the year. In Venice, his father, Giovanni Battista, was a violinist in the ducal palace of San Marco. From him, and subsequently from Giovanni Legrenzi, young Vivaldi acquired his early musical education.

Despite the unusual talent for music that Vivaldi disclosed from the very first, he was directed by his father towards the Church. In his fifteenth year, he submitted to the tonsure. Three years later, he received his minor orders. The major orders came three years after that. On March 23, 1703 he was ordained priest.

During this period, he had not abandoned music. As a matter of fact he had not merely become a composer of some reputation but also a violin virtuoso of considerable greatness. Music soon dominated his entire life. In the *Dictionnaire historique des musiciens* of Choron and Fayolle, there is related an amusing anecdote which illustrates the growing importance that music was beginning to acquire in Vivaldi's life. "One day, when Vivaldi was at Mass, there occurred to him a theme for a fugue. He left the altar immediately, came to his sacristy to write out his theme. Then he returned to the altar to finish his Mass. Brought before an investigation, Vivaldi was excused because he was a musician, that is to say a little mad; and was, moreover, excused from saying Mass in the future."

While it is doubtful if this is more than a legend, it is illuminating in disclosing the great prominence music soon attained in Vivaldi's life, and why he turned away from the Church to devote himself exclusively to the art. He went to Germany where his performances on the violin aroused considerable admiration, and where he procured a position in the court of the Landgrave of Hesse-Darmstadt. In 1713, Vivaldi returned to Venice to become music master of a foundling hospital for girls—the Ospedale della Pietà—where he not only directed the orchestra and chorus, but also composed music for its concerts.

Antonio Vivaldi—who was known in his day as "the red priest"—was, as Marc Pincherle pointed out, a man of strange contradictions. Pincherle described Vivaldi as "feeble and sick, yet lively as gunfire," "quick to anger and just as quick to become calm," "passing from profanity to superstitious piety," "docile, when necessary, and at other times obstinate," "mystic, ready however to come back to earth when his interests demanded it."

In his composition, he worked easily and swiftly. As De Brosses, Vivaldi's friend, wrote: "The old man composes like wildfire. I have heard him boast of being able to compose a concerto, complete in all parts, in less time than it takes a copyist to write it out."

While Vivaldi composed with fecundity for theatre and church, his major importance in musical history rests with his instrumental music. Together with Corelli, he was one of the forefathers of the modern concerto; in his voluminous writings in this form—for violin, for the piano, and for orchestra—he brought it to altogether new stages of technical development in which the form was considerably solidified, and its artistic expressiveness greatly expanded.

Discussing the Vivaldi music in general, Julien Tiersot wrote: "His style is rich, natural and learned. . . .

ANTONIO VIVALDI

The expositions of his allegros possess a great freshness, and their developments evolve with a perfect logic and irreproachable feeling for outline. His slow movements form the central part of his concerto, offering varied and formerly unheard beauties."

"Vivaldi represented the tendency of Italian art towards harmonic form," wrote C. Hubert Parry, "such as were met with in Italian opera, in which, so far, simple clearness of design and superficial effectiveness were the principal virtues. He was essentially a violinist, and at times, especially in slow movements when the aptness of the violin for expressive melody invited him, he wrote really beautiful music."

It is well-known that Johann Sebastian Bach admired Vivaldi's concertos enormously, and that he arranged sixteen of his violin concertos for piano, four for organ and one for four pianos and string quartet.

After Vivaldi's death, almost all of his compositions suddenly disappeared and for two centuries lay completely forgotten in a private library. It is only in recent memory that Vivaldi's music has emerged from its obscurity and assumed the importance in musical history that it so well deserves.

Principal works by Antonio Vivaldi:

INSTRUMENTAL: Concerti grossi for chamber orchestra; concertos for violin and chamber orchestra; concertos for piano and chamber orchestra; concertos for organ; sonatas for violin and bass, etc.

Twenty-eight operas; cantatas; motets, etc.

About Antonio Vivaldi:

Choron et Fayolle. *Dictionnaire Historique des Musiciens*; Parry, C. Hubert. *Evolution of the Art of Music*; Schering, Arnold. *Geschichte der Instrumental-Konzert. Ménestral* 91:246 May 31, 1929; *La Revue de Musicologie* 14:11 August 1930.

Important recordings of music by Antonio Vivaldi:

INSTRUMENTAL: *Concerto grosso no. 2* (GRAMOPHONE); *Concerto grosso no. 5* (VICTOR-Pro Arte); *Concerto grosso no. 8* two movements (COLUMBIA); *Concerto grosso no. 9,* arranged for violoncello and piano (COLUMBIA); *Concerto grosso no. 10,* three movements (COLUMBIA); *Concerto grosso no. 11* (VICTOR-Stokowski); *Sonata in A-major,* for violin and piano (GRAMOPHONE-Busch, Serkin); *Sonata in E-minor,* for violoncello and string quartet (NATIONAL GRAMOPHONIC SOCIETY); *Trio sonata in G-minor* (PRO MUSICA).

Robert Volkmann *1815-1883*

FRIEDRICH ROBERT VOLK-MANN was born in Lommatzsch, in Saxony, on April 6, 1815. As a boy he was quiet and retiring by nature, revealing unusual intelligence and mental alertness. His father, a cantor and organist, trained him musically at an early age, teaching him the elements of piano playing and the organ. At the age of nine, Robert turned to composition; at twelve he was already sufficiently adept at the organ to substitute for his father at Church services.

He was, however, not intended for music but for pedagogy. For this purpose, he was sent to the Gymnasium at Freiberg, then to the Seminary in that city. At the latter institution, his musical gifts came to the notice of the musical director, A. F. Anacker, who gave him further instruction and urged him to follow the study of music more seriously. For this purpose, Volkmann came to Leipzig, in 1836, where he met, and was strongly influenced by, Robert Schumann. In Leipzig, his first published work, *Phantasiebilder* for piano, appeared.

After three years, he went to Prague, settling there as a teacher of music. A countess, who had heard of his talent, summoned him to her country seat in Szeméréd to teach her two daughters music. There, Volkmann had considerable leisure to devote himself to composition. But he lacked the artistic environment which only a large city can offer. Before long, he became subject to spells of melancholy. In the Spring of 1841, he decided to resign from his position and settle in Pesth. He took with him several compositions—including a *Sonata for violin and piano,* some songs, an overture for orchestra—which, when they came to the notice of prominent musicians, aroused considerable attention.

For many years, Volkmann led the uneventful life of a music teacher in Pesth, devoting himself at the same time to composition. His first significant work did not make an appearance until 1852, when Volkmann completed his *Piano trio in B-flat minor.* This composition, as Viktor von Herzfeld has pointed out, "was the first revelation of the master's genius. . . . The themes and motives are plastic, original, and for all their kinship with Beethoven, highly personal. . . . What is essential to perfection in music is there."

Several distinguished musicians—like Franz Liszt and Hans von Bülow—recognized the talent of this work and endeavored to bring attention to its composer. Despite their efforts, Volkmann was still working in comparative obscurity. Shortly afterwards, however, several of his string quartets were performed in Vienna and received high praise. Believing that Vienna would accord him that recognition which Hungary failed to do, Volkmann came to the Austrian capital in 1854, settling there for four years. A certain amount of attention was focused upon him in Vienna. But general recognition was still lacking, and Volkmann returned to Pesth in 1858, a disappointed and dejected artist.

For the remaining years of his life in the Hungarian capital, Volkmann continued his prolific composition. He never achieved great fame, but from time to time important performances of his works—such as the première of his *Symphony in D-minor* by the Leipzig

ROBERT VOLKMANN

Gewandhaus Orchestra—brought him the high praise of great musicians. He was honored by the Vienna Musik-freunde and the Berlin Academy. In 1875, Volkmann was appointed professor of composition at the Royal Academy of Music. Eight years later, on October 30, 1883, he died in Buda-pest, an unhappy and disappointed composer.

W. Beatty-Kingston, who met Volk-mann in Pesth in 1867, described the composer as follows: "A glance at the great Hungarian composer sufficed to convince any observant person that he had before him a man of sorrow, acquainted with grief. His bowed shoulders and sad, lustreless eyes told a tale of excessive application, toil at the desk and immoderate consumption of the 'midnight oil.' A heavy, drooping grizzled moustache enhanced the melan-choly expression of his countenance, furrowed by the pencil of care rather than time. . . . His chief characteristic appeared to be an invincible shyness almost amounting to painful timidity. To me, he conveyed the impression of a nature, originally gentle and diffident that had been subdued by ill-luck and unkind usage to a chronic condition of self-depreciation and hopelessness. . . . His black clothes . . . were threadbare and of strangely antiquated cut."

Discussing the quality of Robert Volk-mann's music, his nephew—Dr. Hans Volkmann—has written in his authorita-tive biography: "His works have only a very few qualities in common; the unfailing nobility of his artistic taste, a strange, almost ethereal sweetness of sound, the glamor of which is only too often discernable to the expert alone; and the severe logic in the development of ideas. . . . Strictly speaking, Volk-mann cannot be ranged in any group of composers. He was neither exclusively a disciple of Beethoven nor of Mozart, neither a classicist like Mendelssohn nor a romanticist like Schumann—and yet he was all this at times. He absorbed all these influences and assimilated them completely to his own nature. A self-dependent personality that cannot be compared to any other, speaks in his works."

Principal works by Robert Volkmann:

ORCHESTRA: Two symphonies; Three over-tures; Three serenades for string orchestra; *Concerto for violoncello and orchestra*; *Konzertstück* (for piano and orchestra).

CHORAL: *Sappho* (for soprano and orches-tra); Two masses; offertories; sacred choruses; part-songs, etc.

CHAMBER MUSIC: Six string quartets; Two piano trios; *Schlummerlied* (for harp, clarinet and horn).

Pieces for the violin, for violoncello, for piano, etc.

About Robert Volkmann:

Beatty-Kingston, W. *Music and Manners*; Preiss, Cornelius. *Robert Volkmann*; Volk-mann, Hans. *Robert Volkmann*.

Monthly Musical Record 13:273 December 1883; *Musical Quarterly* 1:336 July 1915.

Richard Wagner *1813-1883*

"In the whole range of [opera] . . . . will be found no greater name than that of Wagner. He has clothed it with a new life, he has taught it to deliver a new message, and the echoes of his voice will last, not only in his own work but in the days to come."—W. H. HADOW

THE foremost genius in the history of opera, Richard Wilhelm Wagner, was born in Leipzig on May 22, 1813.

His parentage has been subject to much speculation and controversy. Ernest Newman, who has done more research on Wagner than any other living musicologist, has written that "on his father's side, the parentage of Richard Wagner is still a matter of dubiety." It is generally believed that Richard Wagner was the son of Karl Friedrich Wagner, a police court clerk, and Johanna Bertz Wagner. However, there is evidence to point suspiciously to the fact that Richard Wagner might well have been the illegitimate son of Johanna Wagner and her dear friend Ludwig Geyer, an actor and playwright of Jewish origin—thereby. paradoxically, making one of the most vicious anti-Semites in music a Jew by birth. This evidence is further fortified by the fact that Wagner resembled Geyer in physical features, that certain of his personal characteristics were more Oriental than German. Ernest Newman has deduced from many documents that Wagner himself believed in the possibility of Geyer's having been his father."

Karl Friedrich Wagner died of typhoid shortly after Richard's birth. The following year, the widow was married to Ludwig Geyer, transferring her family from Leipzig to Dresden. Geyer was a tender and solicitous step-father, as Wagner himself has mentioned in his autobiography. "This excellent man . . . . undertook my education with the greatest of care and love." Unfortunately, Geyer died when Wagner was only seven years old.

The mother placed Richard in the Kreuzschule in Dresden where he acquired an education in the classical languages, history and mythology. Literature was his great interest at the time. He could write verse with a facile pen, at one time winning first prize in school for an original poem. He even went so far as to study English so that he might read Shakespeare in the original. At the age of eleven, he wrote a grandiose drama in verse, a compound of *Hamlet* and *King Lear* in which forty-two characters suffered death during the course of the tragedy.

Music was, at first, only of secondary importance. He had begun the study of the piano, for which he showed astonishing ineptitude. However, his enthusiasm for the art was not to be mistaken. As a child, he was introduced to portions of Weber's *Freischütz* which thrilled him.

One of his profoundest musical experiences occurred in his fourteenth year, when the Wagner family had removed to Leipzig. There, young Richard heard the performance of a Beethoven symphony for the first time (it was the *Seventh*), an event that had a far-reaching influence upon him. "I thereupon fell ill," he recorded in his autobiography, "and when I recovered I was a musician." He began the study of harmony and thorough-bass, becoming so preoccupied with music that he neglected academic study, sometimes failing to go to his classes for weeks at a stretch. He soon began to put to paper his first creative thoughts. First an embryo piano sonata and string quartet left his pen. Then he turned to more pretentious composition. One of these, an overture for orchestra, was performed in Leipzig under the direction of Heinrich Dorn. The manuscript of this overture was written in three different colored inks; the music was as bizarre as the appearance of the manuscript. The performance was something of a fiasco.

In 1830, Wagner entered the University of Leipzig where, as he himself confessed, he was more interested in drinking, gambling and dissipation than in study. Music, however, still absorbed him. He became a student of composition of Theodor Weinlig, cantor of the St. Thomas Schule, working under him so assiduously that in six months he acquired an imposing technical equipment. The fruits of this study were several overtures and a symphony, performed by the Gewandhaus Orchestra in Leipzig and in Prague. These works showed the strong influence that Beethoven exerted on the young composer at the time.

Shortly after the performance of Wagner's symphony in Leipzig, he was offered a position as chorus master of the Würzburger Theatre, which he accepted. This post probably turned his interest more forcefully to the theatre. He had before this attempted the composition of an opera, *Die Hochzeit*, which he discarded after several attempts. In Würzburg, however, he found the enthusiasm and strength to bring to completion his first opera, *Die Feen*, completed in 1834. *Die Feen* was succeeded by a second opera, *Das Liebesverbot,* based upon Shakespeare's *Measure for measure* which Wagner converted into a glorification of free love. To Wagner's intense disappointment, neither opera reached performance.

At this time, Wagner was in miserable financial straits. To alleviate this pressing condition, he accepted an artistically unsatisfying post as director of a small opera company in Magdeburg. One of the principal actresses of the company was Minna Planer, a charming, self-sufficient, attractive young girl, a few years Wagner's senior, already the mother of an illegitimate child. Minna Planer and Wagner became lovers. When the Magdeburg opera company collasped financially (leaving Wagner more sadly in debt than before) Minna Planer secured a post in Königsberg, whither Wagner, insane with jealousy, followed her. They were married on November 24, 1836.

In 1837, Wagner accepted a post as music-director in Riga. There he went from bad to worse where finance was concerned. He became so inextricably involved in debt that, to save himself, he was forced to flee. Wagner and his wife were smuggled across the Russian border, their passports having been confiscated by the debtors, and after a trying journey prolonged several weeks by violent storms, they reached London. After a short period, the Wagners crossed the Channel.

Wagner reached Paris with high hopes for the future. In his pocket was a letter of introduction to Meyerbeer, the Parisian favorite among the operatic composers of the time. In his valise was the score of a new opera, *Rienzi,* based upon a novel of Bulwer Lytton, the spectacular subject of which Wagner felt would appeal strongly to French taste.

But the three years Wagner spent in Paris were not crowned with the recognition and success for which he had hoped. They were, as a matter of fact, some of the most trying years in Wagner's life. Meyerbeer, upon his interview with Wagner, was polite, but not very helpful. *Rienzi* did not appeal to the directors of the Opéra, who refused it. Wagner was, therefore, reduced to a state of poverty even more appalling than he had known in Germany and Russia. To keep alive he was compelled to undertake the most sordid type of hackwork. Twice he was imprisoned for debt. The rest of the time he evaded starvation only narrowly.

It is the opinion of Ernest Newman that these trying years in Paris did much to warp Wagner's personality permanently. A noble character he had never been, it is true. Starvation and disappointment in Paris, however, combined to make him even more ruthlessly selfish than he had been before, more unscrupulous than ever before where money, women or friends were concerned. His ego became inflated—his armor of protection from a callous world. He began to harbor resentment against everybody, became antagonistic to society, adopted a pose of opposition against its codes of ethics and morals.

A new opera was now beginning to absorb his interests, an opera on the subject of the famous legend of the "flying Dutchman." Wagner sketched the libretto and sent it to Léon Pillet, manager of the Opéra, with the hope that he might receive the commission to prepare the opera. Pillet was interested in the libretto, but his only offer was to buy it for the use of some other composer for five hundred francs. Five hundred francs was a formidable sum to Wagner at that time. Moreover, its acceptance did not prevent him from composing an opera on the same book. He, therefore, eagerly accepted the sum. Guaranteed momentary recess from starvation, he now set to work upon his opera. "To compose music," wrote Wagner in his autobiography, "I needed a piano; for, after a nine months' interruption of all kinds of musical production, I had to work myself back to the musical atmosphere. I hired a piano, but when it came I walked round and round it in an agony of anxiety; I feared to find I was no longer a musician. I began with the *Sailor's chorus* and the *Spinning song*; everything went easily, fluently, and I actually shouted for joy as I felt through my whole being that I

RICHARD WAGNER

was still an artist. In seven weeks the opera was finished."

The tide was now to turn for Wagner. In 1842, *Rienzi* was accepted for performance by the Dresden Opera. The success of this performance was so great that Wagner received an appointment as conductor at the opera house. The following year, the Dresden Opera presented the *Flying Dutchman* to less appreciative audiences. In April of 1845, Wagner introduced *Tannhäuser* at the Dresden Opera, when it received an apathetic performance and a still more indifferent reception. *Lohengrin* was composed in 1848, but was not produced until 1850 when Franz Liszt presented it in Weimar.

In the operas from *Rienzi* to *Lohengrin,* Wagner's revolution of the long-accepted operatic form and conventions was slow and subtle. "As he himself put it," wrote Ernest Newman, "in *Rienzi* his sole aim had been to write an 'opera'; in the *Flying Dutchman* he made his first tentative step towards the musical drama. In the older opera the music was the first consideration, the libretto being constructed in such a way as to provide the composer with the conventional opportunities for aria, duet, trio, ensemble, and so on. In the musical drama as Wagner came to conceive it, the drama is the first consideration, and it is from the drama that the music must

take its expression, its color and its form. It is true, as Wagner himself admitted, that to all intents and purposes the old divisions of aria, duet, etc. still exist in the *Flying Dutchman,* but they are not there for their own sakes, merely as so many 'numbers'; they are not imposed arbitrarily upon the dramatic subject, but grow naturally out of it. In *Tannhäuser,* he got further away than in the *Flying Dutchman* from the opera of 'numbers'; and in *Lohengrin* further still. . . . We are so familiar with Tannhäuser today, and even inclined to regard it, in comparison with Wagner's later opera, as a little old-fashioned, that it is somewhat difficult to realize that in its own day it was an effort on the composer's part to do several things that had hardly been attempted in opera before. In the first place, the dramatic motive was every whit as important in his eyes as the music; in the second place, the old distinction between song and recitative had been completely swept away." It should also be mentioned that even in these early operas, Wagner's use of the *leit-motif*—a repetitious musical phrase to identify a character, situation or emotion—is already an important technical device.

The revolutionary uprising of 1848 awakened Wagner's political consciousness. He became so intimately associated with the revolutionary movement that, when the uprising was smothered, he was forced to flee to save his life. For a short while he found a haven at the home of Franz Liszt, thereby cementing a relationship in which Liszt was to devote the remainder of his life to spread propaganda for the Wagnerian music-drama. Then, learning that a price had been placed on his head, he escaped to Paris, finally settling in Zürich where he began a twelve year period as political exile.

During these years of exile, Wagner temporarily abandoned musical composition to devote himself to voluminous theoretical writings in which he propounded his revolutionary artistic doctrines. In the most important of these writings—principally *Die Kunst und die Revolution, Das Kunstwerk der Zukunft* and *Oper und Drama*—he formulated for the first time his principles of the opera, namely as a music-drama in which all the arts are synthesized. He affirmed that the nineteenth century could produce a theatre which would epitomize its own culture just as that of the ancient Athens had summed up Greek thought and art. In *Oper und Drama* he condemned opera because its sole aim and end was musical instead of dramatic expression, and he clearly and forcefully outlined the opera of the future as he saw it, where old conventions of aria and recitative were permanently discarded, where opera and libretto complemented each other, in which the other arts joined in a unified artistic expression.

To bring these aesthetic theories to practice, Wagner decided to return to operatic composition. In Dresden, he had interested himself so deeply in the sagas of Scandinavia, Iceland and Germany that he had already prepared, from this copious material, a lengthy poem entitled *Siegfried's Death*. It is this poem which he intended to convert into an operatic libretto, later renamed *The Dusk of the Gods*. However, as Wagner worked upon his poetical drama he realized that the subject was much too great for any one opera. In 1851, he prefixed *Siegfried's Death* with a second, explanatory work, entitled *Young Siegfried*. Still feeling that too much had been left unsaid, Wagner prefixed still another opera to this duet in 1852, the *Valkyrie*. Finally, still feeling that a "prelude" was needed to round out the whole, he prepared the book of the *Rhinegold*. In 1853, the libretto of this poetical series was published and distributed privately.

Between 1853 and 1857, Wagner worked intensively upon the composition of the musical scores to his poetical cycle, *The Ring of the Nibelungen*. He had completed all of the *Rhinegold*, *Valkyrie* and the first act of *Siegfried* when he decided, for the time being at any rate, to abandon the project. He had received an offer from the opera house in Rio de Janeiro to prepare a work especially for the company. Since Wagner felt strongly that his *Ring* was too gargantuan a venture for production in an ordinary opera-house and since he felt that, in any case, several more years were required to bring this mammoth work to completion, he decided to turn from the Nibelungen legend to another subject, that of Tristan and Isolde, based upon a Celtic legend.

It was peculiarly appropriate that, in composing this epic of love, Wagner should himself have been deeply in love. The object of his ardent affection at this time was Mathilde Wesendonck, the wife of a close friend and patron. However, as Ernest Newman takes pains to point out, *Tristan and Isolde* was by no means the effect of Wagner's love-affair. As a matter of fact, Ernest Newman goes so far as to suggest the paradox it might have been the cause, that Wagner fell in love with Mathilde Wesendonck only because at the time he was composing *Tristan*!

In August of 1859, Wagner brought *Tristan* to completion. *Tristan*, however, did not receive its first performance until June 10, 1865 when Hans von Bülow introduced it in Munich.

Meanwhile, in 1855, Wagner interrupted his many labors to visit England and conduct eight concerts of the Royal Philharmonic Orchestra. This visit was unsuccessful principally because England could not forget Wagner's devastating remarks about their beloved Mendelssohn in his vitriolic attack on the Jew in music. In September of 1856 Wagner came to Paris to conduct three concerts of his own music where, too, his performances were received coldly. In 1861, he was once again in Paris, this time to help in the preparation of a grandiose performance of *Tannhäuser*, sponsored by Prince Metternich. *Tannhäuser* was given more than one hundred and fifty rehearsals and was mounted in lavish style. It is said that more than $40,000 was expended in its production. On March 17, 1861, therefore, *Tannhäuser* was presented at the Opéra in the French language, equipped with new Venusberg music to please French love for the ballet. The reception it received —inspired by political reasons—was scandalous. The Parisian Jockey Club sent its members to hoot, howl, whistle. After three performances, the opera was removed from the repertoire—to Wagner's intense humiliation and bitterness.

In 1860, Wagner received official governmental pardon for his radical activity in Saxony twelve years before. After the *Tannhäuser* "debacle" Wagner returned to the land of his birth for the first time in twelve years. He undertook a long and extensive tour as conductor not only in his own works but also in the symphonies of Beethoven, achieving a magnificent reputation as a conductor and earning an all-important place in the history of conducting. It was at this time, too, that Wagner first received the friendship of the new king of Bavaria, the eighteen year old Ludwig II who, for many years, was Wagner's most influential patron.

Wagner's life was once again enmeshed in amatory difficulties. In 1862, after a trying period of misunderstanding, Richard Wagner and his wife, Minna, were permanently separated. Wagner was already strongly attracted to someone else. She was Cosima, daughter of Franz Liszt, and wife of Wagner's devoted friend and disciple, the conductor-pianist, Hans von Bülow. The love-affair between Wagner and Cosima developed during the next few years under the very eyes of the unsuspecting von Bülow. In 1865, Cosima bore Wagner a daughter, Isolde, whom von Bülow believed to be his own. When, in 1866 Minna Wagner died, and, one year later, Cosima bore him another daughter, Wagner was determined to have Cosima for his own. In the autumn of 1868, Richard and Cosima fled to Triebschen, near the Lake of Lucerne, to establish their home there. Franz Liszt was infuriated, for a long while refusing to forgive Wagner. Hans von Bülow was heart-broken. "If it had been anyone but Wagner," Hans von Bülow remarked, "I would have shot him." It is, however, a sublime example of the artistic integrity of both musicians that—though this betrayal embittered them against Wagner personally—they did not interrupt their indefatigable labors to bring the Wagnerian music-drama to recognition.

In the midst of this involved complication, Wagner completed and saw the first production of a new music-drama, *Die Meistersinger*. The theme of *Die Meistersinger*—glorifying the triumph of inspiration over formulistic and pedantic art—attracted Wagner as early as 1845. He completed the libretto in 1862, but the score did not receive its final strokes until 1867. On June 21, 1868, *Die Meistersinger* was given its first performance in Munich under the baton of Hans von Bülow. It is generally conceded that the character of the villain Beckmesser, was intended by Wagner as a satirical portrait of Eduard Hanslick, the eminent Viennese critic, bitter enemy of Wagner.

In June of 1869, a son was born to Cosima and Richard—called Siegfried—and on August 25, 1870 the lovers were married. As a birthday gift to his beloved Cosima, Wagner composed the deathless *Siegfried idyll*. On the dawn of Christmas morning of 1870, Wagner gathered a small orchestra at his home, the instruments tuned up in the kitchen, and then assembling at the foot of the staircase they awakened Cosima with the tones of one of the most tender serenades in music.

After *Die Meistersinger,* Wagner returned to the composition of his *Ring of the Nibelungen,* resuming the creation of *Siegfried* where he had suddenly left off twelve years before this. The composition fired Wagner with grandiose plans and dreams. In his mind he envisioned a special festival theatre where his gargantuan creation might be produced to best advantage. In these dreams he was encouraged and inspired by a young professor of philosophy at Basel, Friedrich Nietzsche. Soon a campaign was inaugurated in all parts of the music-world to raise money for this venture. Wagner societies were formed everywhere to create enthusiasm for this nympholeptic scheme. Three hundred thousand dollars was raised in this manner. On Wagner's birthday in 1872 the cornerstone for a festival theatre was laid in the small Bavarian town of Bayreuth. To commemorate this event, Wagner himself conducted a performance of Beethoven's *Ninth symphony*.

In supervising the construction of the festival theatre, Wagner applied many of his theories of the ideal opera-house. The orchestra was concealed from view, protected by a steel armor, thereby not only blending its tone more sonorously but also hiding the conductor from public attention. Moreover, the auditorium was so constructed that a full view of the stage was procured from every seat in the house.

Finally, in 1876 the *Ring of the Nibelungen* was performed in its entirety in Bayreuth. Hans Richter was the conductor; Wilhelmj, world-famous violinist, was concertmaster. It had been prepared with the most scrupulous fastidiousness. Expenses were not considered in procuring the scenery, costumes or arranging for stage-effects. As a result, a brilliant audience, gathered from all parts of the world, acclaimed the *Ring* and Wagner.

In 1877, Wagner revisited London to receive that ovation and triumph which had formerly been denied him. Returning to Germany, he established his home permanently in Bayreuth, at the villa Wahnfried, so called because there his fancies found rest. Another music-drama was absorbing his attention, built upon the theme of the redemption of the Holy Grail. On the twenty-eighth of June of 1882, *Parsifal* was introduced at Bayreuth. It was so successful that sixteen performances were necessary, bringing in a handsome profit.

Shortly after the performances of *Parsifal,* Wagner, who was suffering from heart disease, left for a vacation in Venice. He died there suddenly on February 13, 1883. It is known that death was brought on by a violent fit of temper. What inspired the rage has never been satisfactorily explained, altho it is believed that Wagner, in planning new performances of *Parsifal,* insisted upon including a charming singer of his acquaintance in the cast, to which the jealous Cosima objected violently.

Delegates from Wagnerian societies escorted the remains from Venice to Bayreuth where, after a magnificent and noble ceremony, the body was buried in the garden of Villa Wahnfried.

The police record of 1849, issued shortly after Wagner's escape from Saxony as a political enemy, gives us a minute description of the composer. "Wagner is thirty seven to thirty-eight years old, of middle height, has brown hair, wears glasses; open forehead; eye-brows brown; eyes grey-blue; nose and mouth well proportioned; chin round. Particulars: in moving and speaking he is hasty. Clothing: surtout of dark-green buckskin, trousers of black cloth, velvet waistcoat, silk neckerchief, the usual felt hat and boots." His lips were firm, the ends of which suggested hardness. A prominent chin and high cheekbones spoke of strength. His eyes were particularly brilliant, of a piercing intensity which electrified those whom they scrutinized. His face was deeply lined, fingerprints of his many trials and disappointments. Of medium stature in build, his large head seemed out of proportion with the rest of his body. His carriage had dignity.

Many of his personal traits have already been commented upon—his ruthless selfishness, his iron will, his complete disregard of any code of ethics or morals, his bitter antagonism towards society. Vain, irritable, nervous, always impatient, he was by no means a pleasant comrade. And yet, despite his hardness, his magnetic appeal was great. Too frequently he was capable of duplicity, betrayal, hypocrisy; he made enemies more freely than friends.

His frailty was, of course, Woman; his life was an endless succession of amatory relationships. He had an Oriental love for color and splendor. He wore expensive and brightly colored silk underclothing. His home was always cluttered with luxuriously brilliant tapestries, cushions, rugs and silks. He was uncontrollably extravagant, spending lavishly on impractical decorations, pendants, furnishings. He took particular pride in his dress. He had a wide assortment of satin trousers with jackets and slippers to match, and he possessed no less than twenty-four dressing gowns of different colors.

Richard Wagner's wife, Cosima, survived him by fifty years. Until the end of her life she was the guiding spirit of the Bayreuth festival, which each summer presented the Wagnerian music-drama. Siegfried Wagner, the son of Richard and Cosima, died in 1930 after achieving a world reputation as a Wagnerian conductor.

W. H. Hadow has discussed keenly the strength and weakness of Wagner's greatest music-dramas. Of the four works in the *Ring of the Nibelungen,* wrote Hadow, "*Rhinegold* is undoubtedly the weakest, *Siegfried* undoubtedly the finest. The latter, indeed, is the strongest in construction and the most vigorous in workmanship of all Wagner's creations, and its gold is studded with such gems as the *Schmiedelied,* the *Waldwebung* and the magnificent duet on which the *Siegfried idyll* was subsequently founded. *Valkyrie* is a very unequal work. It contains, perhaps, as many supremely fine numbers as *Siegfried* itself; but, except for the closing scene, the second act is rather tedious, and some of the other monologues stand in need of judicious curtailment. *The Dusk of the Gods* gives a little the impression that its first two acts were written for the sake of the third. But the whole scene of Siegfried's death, the superb funeral march, in which *motif* after *motif* tells the story of the murdered hero, the blazing pyre upon which Brünnhilde dies amid the wreck of Valhalla, and the overthrow of the very gods themselves, these form a climax of epic grandeur, presented with a vividness of reality which no epic can ever attain.

"If *Siegfried* is the strongest of the music-dramas *Tristan* is the most musical. . . . From the fascinating theme with which the overture opens . . . there is scarcely a page which does not contain some imperious appeal to the artistic sense. The whole composition is as full of melody as *Romeo and Juliette.* It is all set in one mood—the love of man for woman. There are two reasons why *Parsifal* has a claim to be considered Wagner's masterpiece. In the first place its emotional level is more sublime than that of its predecessors. The central conception of the *Ring* is strength, that of *Tristan* is passion, that of *Parsifal* is goodness. . . . In the second place, it is the most homogeneous of the music-dramas: that in which the different elements are most completely fused into unity. . . . In other words, it is the most complete embodiment of Wagner's dramatic theory, and so may be regarded as in a sense the climax of his work. . . . The music may be less rich than that of *Tristan,* but it is more dignified and restrained. The characters may be less distinct than those of *Siegfried,* but they are more significant and suggestive.

"*Meistersinger* has purposely been kept to the end, since, among Wagner's artistic products, it stands on a special footing of its own. It may be said to belong to both his creative periods, for the first sketches were written in 1845, about the time of *Lohengrin,* and the work was finished twenty-two years later. . . . Again, there are certain details of workmanship which are implied in its character of a comedy. . . . *Meistersinger* is full of more or less detachable melodies: Walther's three songs, Hans Sach's ballad, Beckmesser's absurd serenade, and the like. They do not in the least interfere with the continuity of the story, but a comic story allows more room for them than a tragic. The more conventional form of the music is in no sense a recantation: it is entirely consistent with Wagner's principles, and forms the natural outcome of his plot. But the drama is too well known and too popular to need any defence. From first to last it is a thoroughly genial work, with plenty of sound comedy, plenty of good-humored satire, plenty of tune, and an astonishing display of recondite rhythm and ingenious polyphony."

No doubt there are many weaknesses to the Wagnerian music-drama. Wagner was too frequently prolix, bombastic, pompous. His dramatic action suffers too frequently from over-elaborate and repetitious monologues to explain the background of the action. Finally, as H. C. Colles pointed out, the union of the arts could never be successfully realized by Wagner because he "was infinitely greater as a musician than as a poet or dramatist."

However, for all his faults, Wagner remained one of the supreme geniuses of the opera. Single-handed he evolved a new operatic form in which stilted conventions were permanently discarded and in which a new art form emerged. His luxuriously rich harmonic and contrapuntal writing influenced an entire generation of composers throughout the world. He brought a dramatic intensity to musical expression such as it had never before known. Most important of all, however, he created a world of enchantment which is entirely his own— the world of Siegfried and Brünnhilde, Tristan and Isolde, Hans Sachs and Eva, Parsifal and Kundry which has enthralled lovers of great art for a half a century and will continue to exert its contagious appeal for a long time to come.

Principal works by Richard Wagner:

OPERA: *Die Feen; Das Liebesverbot; Rienzi; The Flying Dutchman; Tannhäuser; Lohengrin; Tristan and Isolde; Die Meistersinger; The Ring of the Nibelungen (Rhinegold, Valkyrie, Siegfried, Dusk of the Gods); Parsifal.*
ORCHESTRA: *Symphony in C; A Faust overture; Trauermusik (for wind); Huldigungsmarsch; Siegfried idyll; Kaisermarsch; Grosser festmarsch.*
CHORAL: *Neujahrskantate; Volksymne; La Descente de la courtille; Weihegruss; An Webers grabe,* etc.
Pieces for the piano; songs.

About Richard Wagner:

Bekker, Paul. *Richard Wagner;* Chamberlain, Houston Stewart. *Richard Wagner;* Hadow, W. H. *Richard Wagner;* Henderson, W. J. *Richard Wagner;* Kapp, Julius. *The Women in Wagner's Life;* Krehbiel, H. E. *Studies in Wagnerian Drama;* Lavignac, Albert. *The Music Dramas of Richard Wagner;* Lavignac, Albert. *An Artistic Voyage to Bayreuth;* Mann, Thomas. *Past Masters;* Newman, Ernest. *The Life of Richard Wagner;* Newman, Ernest. *Wagner as Man and Artist;* Pourtalès, Guy de. *Richard Wagner;* Shaw, George Bernard. *The Perfect Wagnerite;* Wagner, Richard. *My Life.*

Important recordings of music by Richard Wagner:

OPERA: *Lohengrin,* abridged (BRUNSWICK); *Tannhäuser,* slightly abridged (COLUMBIA-Bayreuth Festival); *Tristan and Isolde,* abridged (COLUMBIA-Bayreuth Festival); *Rhinegold,* "Excerpts" (VICTOR-Stokowski); *Valkyrie,* abridged (VICTOR); *Valkyrie,* complete Act I (VICTOR-Bruno Walter); *Siegfried,* 3 albums (VICTOR); *The Dusk of the Gods,* abridged (VICTOR); *Parsifal,* act III (VICTOR); *Parsifal,* Miscellaneous excerpts (COLUMBIA).
SELECTIONS FROM OPERA: *Rienzi,* "Overture" (VICTOR-Stokowski); "Erstehe, hohe Roma, neu!" (BRUNSWICK); "Rienzi's gebet" (BRUNSWICK). *The Flying Dutchman,* "Overture "(GRAMOPHONE-Muck); "Wie oft in meeres tiefsten schlund" (VICTOR-Schorr); "Spinnchor" (VICTOR); "Senta's ballad" (VICTOR-Rethberg); "Wie aus der ferne" (GRAMOPHONE-Schorr). *Die Meistersinger,* "Prelude" (VICTOR-Muck); "Kirchenchor" (VICTOR); "Das schöne fest, Johannistag" (VICTOR-Kipnis); "Am stillen herd" (VICTOR-Lorenz); "Kein' regel wollte da passen" (VICTOR-Schorr); "Ich seh', 'swar nur" (VICTOR-Schorr, Ljundberg); "Schusterlied" (PARLAPHONE-Bohnen); "Prelude, Act III" (VICTOR-Stokowski); "Wahn, wahn" (VICTOR-Schorr); "Hat man mit dem schuhwerk" (VICTOR-Schorr, Rethberg); "Aha! Da streicht die Lene" (VICTOR-Schorr); "Quintet" (VICTOR); "Dance of the apprentices" (COLUMBIA-Bruno Walter); "Procession of the Mastersingers" (COLUMBIA); "Euch macht ihr's leicht" (VICTOR-Schorr); "Preislied" (GRAMOPHONE-Melchior); *Wagner album,* including preludes to Act I and Act III of *Lohengrin,* "Dawn and Rhine journey" from *Dusk of the gods* (VICTOR-Toscanini).
ORCHESTRA: *Siegfried idyll* (VICTOR-Toscanini); *Huldigungsmarsch* (VICTOR-S. Wagner); *Kaisermarsch* (GRAMOPHONE); *A Faust overture* (VICTOR-Coates).

Karl Maria von Weber *1786-1826*

"The most German of German composers."—RICHARD WAGNER

KARL MARIA FRIEDRICH ERNST, FREIHERR VON WEBER, was born at Eutin on December 18, 1786. His father, Franz Anton, was known to have been an adventurer. A violinist of considerable talent, and a composer of some commendable songs, Franz Anton first served as financial councilor and district judge to the Elector of Cologne. Upon the death of the Elector, Franz Anton was dismissed from his post. Having meanwhile lavishly squandered the wealth of his wife, he was compelled to become an impresario of an itinerant operatic company and, at other intervals, a violinist in small-town theatre orchestras. His wife died from a broken heart, brought on by this startling reverse of fortune. In 1785, Franz Anton, now in his fiftieth year, married a girl of sixteen. Their first child was Karl Maria.

Karl Maria had been born with a disease of the hip which made it impossible for him to move his legs until after his fourth year, and which fated him to limp for the remainder of his life. Despite the delicacy of his health, Karl Maria was forced to lead a nomadic life, following his father wherever a position as violinist or impresario was available. This, in its way, was a stroke of fortune for Karl Maria. As a child, he breathed the atmosphere of the theatre, became a part of it, acquiring by experience a knowledge of its mechanism which he was to use so advantageously in his operatic composition.

Franz Anton Weber, impressed by the tales of the wealth and honor which were being accorded to the prodigy, Wolfgang Amadeus Mozart, determined to develop his own son along similar lines. The piano and singing were taught him before he could even speak. At first, Karl Maria learned his lessons so slowly that his older brother Fritz prophesied that the child would become anything but a musician. However, Franz Anton's determination to make his son a prodigy was not relaxed. At the age of nine, Karl Maria was given lessons on the organ by Heuschkel in Hildburghausen, under whose influence Karl Maria produced his first known composition, *Von himmel hoch*, for organ. Shortly after this, a theatre manager in Carlsbad, impressed by the boy's talent, commissioned him to compose a comic-opera, *Das Waldmädchen*. This work was performed in Freiberg, Chemnitz and Vienna.

When Karl Maria was eleven, he became a pupil of Michael Haydn, the brother of the great composer. At this time, several other compositions were created by the young composer, including a second comic-opera, and a set of little fugues which the proud father published. The following autumn, Karl Maria was

KARL MARIA VON WEBER

studying the piano and composition in Munich. Weber's last teacher was Abbé Vogler in Vienna who subjected him to two intensive years of study.

Abbé Vogler's influence succeeded in procuring for young Weber an appointment as conductor in Breslau. He reached there in 1804, devoting himself to his new task with great devotion and integrity. He subjected his musicians to such rigid disciplining and severe training that he made many enemies. At one time, he accidentally drank some nitric acid, mistaking it for wine. When he recovered, after two months of illness, he learned that his many enemies had succeeded in having him removed from his post. During this Breslau period, Weber composed the sketches for an opera, *Rübezahl*, which it is believed he never finished, and an orchestral overture, *Turandot*.

For a short period, Weber found employment with Duke Eugen Friedrich of Württemberg, as conductor of his private orchestra. In this post, Weber composed two symphonies.

In 1807, Weber became private secretary of Duke Ludwig of Württemberg. His principal task seemed to have been to raise funds for his indigent master. It was a sordid post. Weber moved in dissolute company and, influenced by it, he surrendered himself to dissipation. This position came to a catastrophic close in 1810. At that time, Weber's father arrived in Württemberg, his reputation greatly damaged by the many debts in which he had become involved. Finding a sum of money in his son's bureau, which belonged to the Duke, he appropriated it. On February 9, 1810, while in the midst of rehearsing his opera *Silvana*, Weber was arrested for stealing. After a short period in prison, Weber was released on the condition he leave the kingdom permanently.

Weber settled for a brief period in Darmstadt where his former teacher, the Abbé Vogler, now had his home. Renewal of friendship with Vogler sobered Weber. During the following year he devoted himself industriously to composition, producing a piano concerto, six sonatas for violin and piano and a sparkling operetta *Abu Hassan*. At this time,

Weber became an intimate friend of Meyerbeer who was then a pupil of Vogler.

Early in 1811, Weber left Darmstadt. There followed a period of extensive travel and concert-work. In March of 1811, he came to Munich where his operetta, *Abu Hassan,* was presented. There followed concert engagements in Prague, Dresden and Leipzig. In Gotha, Weber was employed for a brief span by the eccentric Duke Emil Leopold. In Weimar, Weber met Goethe, who was but little impressed with the composer. After a short stay in Berlin, where his opera *Silvana* reached production, Weber revisited Gotha, Weimar, Leipzig, finally coming to Prague where he was given the post of director of the Opera House. For three years, Weber held this position, applying his enormous energy, devotion and artistic integrity to reorganizing every phase of operatic performances at that institution. The many exacting tasks of direction so sapped his vitality and so absorbed his time that he found little time for composition. During this period, he composed only several rousing patriotic songs, whose popularity spread like contagion, and a cantata.

In 1816, Weber was appointed chapel master of German Opera at Dresden. He assumed the post on January 13, 1817. On September 13 of the same year, his appointment at the Dresden Opera was confirmed for life. The following November, Karl Maria von Weber was married to Caroline Brandt.

Weber's new position inevitably turned his enthusiasm and interest towards German opera. He was now fired with the ambition of composing a German opera. One day, he accidently picked up a volume of ghost stories by Apel, one of which seemed to him particularly suited for operatic treatment. He referred it to Friedrich Kind, a poet, who promised to prepare a suitable libretto. The result was *Der Freischütz,* Weber's first masterpiece. *Der Freischütz* absorbed several years of hard work. Completed in 1820, it was given its first performance in Berlin on June 18, 1821. It was greeted with unprecedented enthusiasm. The audience, inflamed by German nationalism, rousingly accepted the opera as a masterpiece. Curiously

enough, the critics and some musicians were less enthusiastic, but they could not dampen the enthusiasm of the public. *Der Freischütz* was performed fifty times in less than eighteen months, drawing abundant receipts into the coffers of the opera-house.

On the day following the magnificent triumph of *Der Freischütz,* Weber composed his famous *Konzertstück,* for piano and orchestra, which he himself introduced one week later.

Der Freischütz made Weber famous throughout Europe. It was performed in Dresden in 1822 with a success that duplicated the triumph of Berlin. In Vienna, *Der Freischütz* was given fifty consecutive performances. Inevitably, offers poured in upon him. From the Elector of Hesse-Cassel he received an appointment as director of opera, an appointment which he declined, recommending Spohr for the position. From Vienna he received a commission to prepare a new opera, on a libretto by Helmina von Chezy. The new opera, *Euryanthe,* was given its first performance at the Kärthnerthor Theatre on October 25, 1823 and—despite its ridiculous libretto—was given a magnificent reception by a brilliant audience.

During his visit to Vienna to superintend the rehearsals of *Euryanthe,* Weber met Beethoven for the first time. "He received me with a love which was touching, embraced me certainly six or seven times in the most affectionate way," Weber wrote to his wife. "We spent the afternoon together in great joy and content. This rugged, repellent man actually paid me as much attention as if I were a lady he was courting, and served me at dinner with the most delicate care."

In 1824, Weber received a commission from Covent Garden, England, for an opera. He selected the theme of *Oberon,* and—harboring a strong presentiment that he was on the verge of death—he applied herculean energy upon what he felt would be his last work. Delays prevented the completion of the opera until January of 1826. Despite the fact that Weber's health had degenerated startlingly—he was suffering from diseased lungs—he insisted upon making the trip to England to supervise personally the rehearsals and performances. "I have heard his coffin-lid shut!" Frau Weber exclaimed when her husband took leave of her.

On April 12, 1826 *Oberon* was given its first performance under the baton of the composer to thunderous cheers of acclaim. But this grandoise success was bought at a terrible price. The strain and enervation of preparing the work for production undermined his heart completely. On June 6, 1826, Weber died in sleep. He was in the very prime of life, at the height of his creative powers.

He was buried in Moorfield Chapel. Eighteen years later, his remains were disinterred and transferred to the Catholic Cemetery in Dresden.

Karl Maria von Weber was described as a "small, narrow-chested man, with long arms, refined but large hands, thin, pale, irregular face, with brilliant blue eyes flashing through his spectacles; 'mighty forehead, fringed by a few straggling locks'; awkward and clumsy, but charming in spite of all, especially when he smiled. His dress was a blue frock-coat with metal buttons, tight trousers, Hessian boots with tassels, a cloak with several capes, and a broad round hat."

His was a genial and lovable nature which made many close bonds of friendship. His intimate friends laughingly called him *Kreutsalat* ("cabbage-salad"). He possessed a sparkling wit which expressed itself in well-turned *mots* and pungent satirical thrusts; his conversation and letters sparkled with a zestful humor. He even wrote clever satirical verse. By temperament he was restless; a nervous driving force compelled him to indulge in continual movement. He was a devout Roman Catholic. Over his bedside there hung a crucifix and several images of the Saints. During High Mass, he often went on his knees in front of his conductor's stand, keeping his hearers waiting while he prayed.

Richard Wagner has referred to Weber as the creator of the Romantic Opera. While certain elements of Romanticism appeared in operas before *Die Freischütz* electrified the music world, Weber definitely and unmistakably launched the Romantic Opera in the strictest sense of the term.

Discussing Weber's operas, R. A. Streatfeild has written as follows: "*Der Freischütz* is, upon the whole, the most thoroughly characteristic of Weber's works. The famous passage for the horns, with which the overture opens, strikes the note of mystery and romance which echoes through the work. The overture itself is a notable example of that new beauty which Weber infused into the time-honored form. . . . The inspiration of *Der Freischütz* is drawn so directly from the German *Volkslied* that at its production Weber was roundly accused of plagiarism by many critics. Time has shown the folly of such charges. *Der Freischütz* is German to the core, and every page of it bears the impress of German inspiration, but the glamour of Weber's genius transmuted the rough material he employed into a fabric of the richest art. Of the imaginative power of such scenes as the famous incantation it is unnecessary to speak. It introduced a new element into music, and one which was destined to have an almost immeasurable influence upon modern music. Weber's power of characterization was remarkable. . . . But in imaginative power and in the minute knowledge of orchestral detail, which enabled him to translate his conceptions into music, he has never been surpassed among writers for the stage. Modern opera, if we may speak in general terms, may be said to date from the production of *Der Freischütz*.

"After *Der Freischütz*, the libretti which he took in hand were of the most unworthy description, and even his genius had not been able to give them immortality. . . . To tell the truth, much of the libretto of *Euryanthe* borders upon the incomprehensible. . . . Puerile as this libretto is, it inspired Weber with some of the finest music he ever wrote. The spectacular portions of the opera are animated by the true spirit of chivalry, while all that is connected with the incomprehensible Emma and her secret is unspeakably eerie. . . The resemblance between the general scheme of the plot of *Euryanthe* and that of *Lohengrin* should not be passed over, nor the remarkable way in which Weber had anticipated some of Wagner's most brilliant triumphs.

"Weber's last opera, *Oberon*, is one of the few works written in recent times by a foreign composer of the first rank for the English stage. . . . The fairy music is exquisite throughout, but the human interest of the story is after all slight, and Weber, on whom the hand of death was heavy as he wrote the score, failed to infuse much individuality into his characters. . . .

"The changes which Weber . . . . effected, though less drastic were in their results fully as important as those of Gluck. In the orchestra as well as on the stage he introduced a new spirit, a new point of view. What modern music owes to him may be summed up in a word. Without Weber, Wagner would have been impossible."

Principal works by Karl Maria von Weber:

OPERA: *Silvana*; *Abu Hassan*; *Der Freischütz*; *Euryanthe*; *Oberon*; *Die drei pintos* (sketches only, completed into an opera by Mahler).

CHORAL: *Der erste Ton*; *In seiner ordnung schafft der Herr*; *Kampf und Sieg*; *Natur und Liebe*; *Jubel-cantata*; Two masses; Thirty part songs; Seven canons, etc.

ORCHESTRA: Two symphonies; *Jubel-ouvertüre*; various other overtures; Two concertos for piano and orchestra; *Konzertstück* (for piano and orchestra); Two concertos for clarinet and orchestra; *Concerto for bassoon and orchestra*; *Horn concertino*; *Invitation to the waltz* (originally for piano, orchestrated by Berlioz and Weingartner), etc.

CHAMBER MUSIC: *Quintet in B-flat* (for clarinet and strings); Six sonatas for violin and piano; *Duo concertant* (for clarinet and piano).

PIANO: Four sonatas; Eight sets of variations; Two rondo brillantes (the second being the *Invitation to the waltz*); Eighteen waltzes; Six fughetti, etc.

Over 80 songs.

About Karl Maria von Weber:

Benedict, Sir Jules. *Weber*; Coeuroy, André. *Weber*; Jähns, F. W. *Karl Maria von Weber in seinen Wirken*; Weber, Max Maria von. *Weber, ein Lebensbild*.

Important recordings of music by Karl Maria von Weber:

OPERA: *Der Freischütz*, abridged recording (POLYDOR-Berlin State Opera). *Euryanthe*, "Overture" (COLUMBIA-Mengelberg); "Jägerchor" (GRAMOPHONE). *Oberon*, "Overture" (COLUMBIA-Mengelberg); "Ocean, thou mighty monster" (COLUMBIA-Lehmann).

ORCHESTRA: *Invitation to the waltz*, orchestrated by Berlioz (VICTOR-Stokowski); *Konzertstück*, for piano and orchestra (COLUMBIA-Cassadesus); *Jubel-ouvertüre* (GRAMOPHONE-Bloch).

Thomas Weelkes 1575-1623

"Weelkes certainly surpassed all his contemporaries in wealth of imagination and originality."—E. H. FELLOWS

ONE of the greatest of English madrigalists, Thomas Weelkes, was born in or about 1575; the place of his birth has not been discovered.

The first authentic date in his life which has come down to us is 1597, when Weelkes published the first volume of his madrigals for three, four, five and six voices. One year later, he was appointed organist of Winchester College, a post he retained for four years.

In 1602, Weelkes received his bachelor's degree in music from Oxford. Leaving Winchester College, he became organist of the Chichester Cathedral. This office he held until the end of his life. He died while on a visit to London, at the home of a friend, on November 30, 1623. He was buried in St. Bride's Church.

Weelkes composed copiously in many forms of choral and instrumental music. "No one in any age or country has expressed so many different ideas and moods in pure choral music," wrote Gustav Holst, "and . . . he always expressed them beautifully and well. . . . Weelkes is the true English artist. He is an individualist as opposed to the Latin artist who tends to be a member of a school. . . . There is nothing to suggest that Weelkes hated conventionality. It simply did not exist for him. When his treatment of a subject happened to coincide with the convention of the day, it just coincided, and there is only the superb craftsmanship to show us which is his work. In everything he wrote this craftsmanship enabled him to express all he felt in his own inimitable manner, whether simply or with elaboration, whether in a style that was to vanish from the earth after his day, or in a style similar to that which most people regard as belonging to the twentieth century."

Ernest Walker has analyzed the distinguishing qualities of Weelkes' works. "His music is hardly ever perfectly free from a sort of quaint angularity and slight stiffness, which, in his best compositions, seems somehow to add a very pleasant tinge of piquancy, but which, in his less happy moments, produces a certain hard and unsympathetic impression. He has a fondness for a kind of agreeably antique restraint of style; and, though harmonically fully as advanced as any of his fellows, he occasionally diverges into a method which comes closer than is natural with most of them to the rigid ecclesiastical tonality, as in the expressively strong and massive six-part *Elegy in remembrance of the Ho, the Lord Borough,* or the fine five-part madrigal *Your beauty it allureth,* which is pure Mixolydian. But these features do not in the least detract from the charm of his music, which is among the most strongly individual of the period."

Edmund Horace Fellowes has pointed out that it is in his madrigals that Weelkes rises to highest importance. As a composer of the madrigal, Weelkes is of preeminent importance because "he struck out a new and brilliant line of his own," "introduced novel harmonic effects," "displayed a keen dramatic sense" and "provided some of the earliest examples of the constructive principles of musical form."

Principal works by Thomas Weelkes:

CHORAL: Anthems; services; ballets; Five sets of Madrigals; ayres, etc.

INSTRUMENTAL: Pieces for viols; pavans for viols; In nomines, etc.

About Thomas Weelkes:

Fellowes, Edmund Horace. *English Madrigal Composers*; Walker, Ernest. *A Short History of Music in England.*

Midland Musician 1:4 January 1926; *Proceedings of the Musical Association* 42:117 (1915-1916).

Important recordings of music by Thomas Weelkes:

CHORAL: *A Vesta was descending* (COLUMBIA); *Hark all ye lovely saints* (ROYCROFT); *O care thou wilt despatch me* (COLUMBIA); *On the plains* (COLUMBIA); *Sing we at pleasure* (GRAMOPHONE); *To shorten winter's sadness* (GRAMOPHONE).

INSTRUMENTAL: *Fantasy for a chest of viols* (COLUMBIA).

Henri Wieniawski *1835-1880*

HENRI WIENIAWSKI was born in Lublin, a small town in Poland, on July 10, 1835. His father was a physician; his mother, a woman of great intelligence. As a child, he revealed such musical gifts that it was decided to give him thorough training on the violin. Wieniawski made such progress that in his eighth year he was brought to Paris. After a year of preparatory study under Claval, Wieniawski was admitted into the Paris Conservatory as a pupil of the celebrated Massart. Once again his progress was swift; after two years, he won first prize in violin playing.

Shortly thereafter, he launched on an extensive concert tour thru the principal cities of Europe, as far as Russia, in which he dazzled audiences with his remarkable technique. On his return from the tour, he continued studies in harmony and composition under Colet in Paris. Then, at the amazing age of fifteen, he was pronounced ready to assume an artistic career. His teachers had confessed that there was nothing more they could teach him.

For the next few years, Wieniawski concertized extensively thruout Europe. His reputation grew and expanded until he was accepted as one of the great virtuosos of his time. Anton Rubinstein, the great pianist and composer, went so far as to write in his *Memoirs* that "Henri Wieniawski is, without doubt, the greatest violinist of our time."

Wieniawski's tours of triumph brought him once again to Russia where, in 1860, he was lionized by music lovers. The Czar was so delighted with his performances that he engaged Wieniawski as solo-violinist. For twelve years, Russia was Wieniawski's home; these were, without doubt, the happiest years of his life. Appreciation and fame were his; he lived in a musical environment surrounded by such friends as Rubinstein and Tschaikovsky. It was during this prolonged stay in Russia that he came into contact with Russian folk songs and dances, many of which he transcribed brilliantly for the violin.

In 1872, Wieniawski left Russia for America in the company of Anton Rubinstein. The two artists toured the country from one coast to the other. Once again Wieniawski knew triumph, and when Rubinstein returned to Russia the violinist remained behind in America to give additional concerts. He made more than two hundred appearances in America, earning a hundred thousand francs. Unfortunately, the bulk of this fortune was lost during the panic of 1873 when one of America's large banks failed.

The loss of a part of his wealth in America marked the beginning of a sharp decline in Wieniawski's fortune. Ill-health was now weakening his heart. Henceforth, he knew physical fatigue, nervous strain and pains which sapped his energy and vitality. Moreover, gambling had ineluctably drawn him into debt; at one time he was forced to pawn his beloved Amati violin which, fortunately was immediately redeemed by a good friend.

In 1874, Wieniawski was invited to assume the professorial post in violin teaching at the Brussels Conservatory, left vacant by Vieuxtemps. For three years he held this position. Then, the lure of travel called him once again to a concert tour. He was, however, little suited physically to undertake a strenuous journey. During this period, his health deteriorated to such an extent that there were concerts when he was compelled to sit while performing. In Berlin, at one engagement, an acute heart attack compelled him to stop in the midst of his performance; it is well-known how Joseph Joachim, who was seated in the audience, leaped upon the platform and, taking the violin and bow from the hand of the sick man, continued the program where Wieniawski had left off.

The end was not far off. Reaching Odessa, Wieniawski collapsed completely; he was now an irremediably broken shell. A sentimental urge to see Moscow once more—the city of his greatest success—drove him on. He reached Moscow, where the Baroness von Meck took him to her home. There he died on April 2, 1880, at the age of forty-five.

In his many works for the violin, Wieniawski has exhausted the technical possibilities of his instrument. They are brilliant technically, yet endowed with many melodic beauties. Wieniawski's violin works reveal, according to Arthur M. Abell, "true inspiration, a most sympathetic lyric and melodic invention, brilliant passage work and an admirable adaptation to the violin."

Joseph Wieniawski (1837-1912), brother of Henri was a well-known pianist who composed many works of great appeal, including a *Concerto for piano and orchestra,* a string quartet, a trio, several piano sonatas and smaller pieces for the piano.

Principal works by Henri Wieniawski:

An entire library of music for violin and orchestra and violin and piano including two concertos, two polonaises, two mazurkas, Fantasy on themes from *Faust, Scherzo-Tarantelle, Souvenir de Moscou,* caprices, themes and variations, etc.

About Henri Wieniawski:

Lahee, Henry C. *Famous Violinists of Today and Yesterday.*
Etude 33:667 September 1915; *Musical Courier* 57:5 September 23, 1908.
VIOLIN AND ORCHESTRA: *Concerto in D-minor* (VICTOR-Heifetz).
VIOLIN AND PIANO: *Souvenir de Moscou* (POLYDOR); *Scherzo-Tarantelle* (GRAMOPHONE-Heifetz); *Polonaise brilliante, no. 2* (PARLAPHONE); *Kuiawiak* (GRAMOPHONE); *Légende* (VICTOR-Elman); *Étude caprice* (VICTOR-Elman).

HENRI WIENIAWSKI

John Wilbye 1574-1638

THE life of John Wilbye, one of the great English madrigalists, is enshrouded in considerable obscurity which modern musical research has been unable to penetrate. It is believed that he was born in or about 1574 in Diss, and it is known that he was director of music at Hengrave, where he remained until 1626. In that year he migrated to the home of Lady Rivers who seems to have become his patroness; in her home, he lived during the last twelve years of his life. Dr. Edmund H. Fellowes conjectures that since Wilbye never married and since the majority of his madrigals spoke of unrequited love, that Wilbye was silently enamored of Lady Rivers. John Wilbye died in September of 1638 in Colchester. Of his two books of madrigals, the first was published in 1598, and the second in 1609.

Wilbye's madrigals—of which *Sweet honey-sucking bees* and *Flora gave me fairest flowers* are famous to this day—are among the finest specimens in that form of vocal art. "It was in the directness and purity of the style," wrote an anonymous critic in the *Musical Times,* "the strong sense of beauty in sound, the admirably vocal nature of the part-writing that impressed themselves irresistibly on the mind of the musician. . . . In the serious madrigal, Wilbye surpassed all his contemporaries. It afforded him scope not only for the ingenious devices by which he gave dramatic color to his words, as well as for more freedom and sometimes complexity of rhythm, but also for the varied emotional sentiment which he treated with such depth, although with such true artistic reserve that his work has never been tainted with anything approaching sentimentalism."

Comparing Wilbye with that other great madrigalist of the period, Weelkes, Edmund Horace Fellowes wrote: "Wilbye undoubtedly wrote in a more polished style with a greater delicacy of expression; he also showed a rather more subtle sense of beauty than Weelkes."

"Wilbye," in the opinion of Karl Nef, "is one of the greatest figures in English

music, both from the point of view of technique and from that of expression."

Principal works of John Wilbye:
CHORAL: Two sets of madrigals; *Lady Oriana* madrigal.

About John Wilbye:
Fellowes, Edmund Horace. *English Madrigal Composers*; Walker, Ernest. *A Short History of Music in England.*
Musical Times 56:223 April 1925; *Proceedings of the Musical Association* 41:63 (1914-1915).

Important recordings of music by John Wilbye:
CHORAL: *Adieu, sweet Amaryllis* (COLUMBIA); *Lady, when I behold* (COLUMBIA).

Adrian Willaert 1488-1562

ADRIAN WILLAERT, one of the glories of the Netherland School of contrapuntal music, was born in Roulers, West Flanders, between 1488 and 1490. His parents designated him for law, and he was sent to Paris about 1514 to begin the study of jurisprudence. In Paris he came into contact with Jean Mouton, gifted Netherland musician, pupil of Josquin des Prés, who was in Paris as chapel master to Louis XII. Mouton began to teach Willaert music. Willaert showed such enthusiasm for the art that he immediately decided to discard all thought of law.

From Paris, Willaert went to Rome where, in 1518, he accidentally heard a performance of one of his hymns in a Church. Upon inquiry, he learned that it had been assumed in Rome that the hymn had been composed by Josquin des Prés. Upon proving conclusively to the singers that it was he, and not Josquin, who created the work, the singers refused to perform it any longer.

He remained in Rome for a short period, then passed on to Venice. From Venice, he went to the court of Ludwig, King of Bohemia and Hungary, where he held the office of chapel-master. His position terminated when Ludwig was killed in battle in 1526. One year later, however, Willaert received an appointment as chapel-master of San Marco in Venice. There his influence upon an entire generation of musicians was profound. It was thru his influence that

ADRIAN WILLAERT

there grew, under his wing, the well-known school of Venetian composers. His pupils included the distinguished theorist, Zarlino and the celebrated contrapuntist, Gabrieli.

Both as composer and as chapel-master, Willaert enjoyed great prestige. He was honored by his fellow Venetians —who referred to his music as "drinkable gold"—in poems and celebrations. It was, therefore, to be expected that when Willaert, towards the close of his life, expressed the wish to return to his native country and live the end of his days in quiet retirement, the Venetians should prevail upon him to remain among them. Willaert, therefore, never returned to the Netherlands. He died in Venice on December 7, 1562.

Willaert created the style of contrapuntal composition which utilized two or more choirs, achieving remarkable effects for divided and answering choruses. "As the Venetian painters suffused their work with a transfiguring light," wrote the historian Ambros, "so the Venetian composers achieved marvels of lovely sound with the colorful interplay of antiphonal choirs, and later with the mingling of glowing instrumental tones."

Willaert is likewise esteemed in musical history as among the first of the great composers to create madrigals. His madrigals, in the opinion of H. E.

Wooldridge are "studiously simple both in form and style of melody, and the music following the metrical structure closely, yet enriching it . . . with graceful points of imitation and simpler forms of ornamental cadence."

Principal works by Adrian Willaert:
CHORAL: Motets; masses; madrigals, etc.

About Adrian Willaert:
Ambros, August Wilhelm. *Geschichte der Musik*; Sollitt, E. R. *From Dufay to Sweelinck*; Wooldridge, H. E. *Oxford History of Music*, vol. 2.

Hugo Wolf *1860-1903*

HUGO WOLF, one of the greatest composers of the German *Lied*, was born in a small town of Styria, Windischgraz, on March 13, 1860. His father, a currier by profession, was a proficient amateur musician who, curiously enough, was violently opposed from the very first to young Hugo's desire to study music. The reason may have been a disastrous fire which, in 1867, reduced the family possessions to ashes; father Wolf, consequently, may have been determined that his son pursue a profession which might make him self-supporting much sooner than the making of music could.

As a result, Hugo Wolf, at the age of ten, became a pupil at Graz Gymnasium, where he was a deplorable student in every course except that of music. In 1873, Hugo's father, in despair, transferred him to the Mittelschule in Marburg, with the hope that a change of scene might benefit the boy. Two years later, Hugo was expelled because, as the officials of the school complained, he was too preoccupied with music to devote his attention elsewhere. There was little left for Herr Wolf to do but to yield to his son's indefatigable wish to become a musician. Receiving a promise from his sister that she would support Hugo during his musical schooling, Herr Wolf sent his son to the Vienna Conservatory in 1875.

Unfortunately, it cannot be said that Hugo Wolf was more of a shining example of scholarship at the Conservatory than he had been in previous schools. The routine of the music schools smothered his spirit; his temperament rebelled against the sterile exercises to which he was subjected day by day. Once again he was a lackadaisical and dull student, and two years after his entrance he was dismissed from the Conservatory.

He turned, now, for his musical knowledge to text books and musical scores. Too poor to possess a piano, he would borrow the masterpieces of piano literature, particularly the Beethoven sonatas—and, sitting for hours on a park bench, he would study them visually. His harmony and counterpoint he derived from a painstaking dissection of great symphonies, oratorios, chamber works and piano compositions. During this period, too, he read voraciously, particularly poetry of which he was a passionate lover. He knew lyrics of Goethe, Grillparzer and Mörike by heart. In addition, he studied English and French in order to gain greater intimacy with the poetry in those languages.

Shortly after his entrance into the Conservatory—in 1875—Hugo Wolf met the one contemporary composer whom he worshipped, Richard Wagner. Wagner had come to Vienna to conduct *Tannhäuser* and *Lohengrin,* and Wolf, eagerly seeking an opportunity of exchanging a few words with the master, waited patient hours outside of the Imperial Hotel, where Wagner was staying, in order to open the door for him. Finally, thru the efforts of the hotel manager, Wolf was given the looked-for opportunity of meeting the great composer. Wolf brought with him a few of his manuscripts, begging for criticism. "My dear child," Wagner told him, "I cannot give you an opinion of your compositions; I have far too little time. . . . When I was your age and composing music, no one could tell me whether I should ever do anything great. . . . When you are older, and when you have composed bigger works, and if by chance I return to Vienna, you will show me what you have done. But that is no use now; I cannot give you an opinion of them yet."

Thus ended the only interview Hugo Wolf ever had with Wagner. However, until the end of his life Wolf was Wag-ner's devoted disciple. Wolf not only made frequent pilgrimages to Bayreuth but also committed to memory every important page of music Wagner composed.

A close friend of Hugo Wolf, Dr. Heinrich Wener, has given us a vivid insight into the adoration of Wagner by Wolf, by describing for us Wolf's behaviour on February 14, 1883, the day after Wagner's death. "Without a word, without any notice of me, he went to the piano and played the Funeral March from the *Götterdammerung.* Then he shut down the piano, and went—silently as he came. In the evening he reappeared in a subdued and deeply sorrowful mood: 'I have wept like a child,' he told me."

The years between 1877 and 1881, which Hugo Wolf spent in study, were marked by great poverty. He taught music to private pupils, but earned only enough to buy himself one meal a day. In 1881, his distressing condition was momentarily relieved when he received a position as second chapel-master in Salzburg, where his work consisted in rehearsing choruses in the operettas of Millöcker and Johann Strauss. This work did not appeal to him, and before long he preferred to return to the poverty and cold of Vienna.

In 1884, he was appointed music critic of the *Salonblatt,* a fashion-journal. For three years he distinguished himself with his critical writings which were fearless and pungent, often witty, often scathingly devastating, often uniquely penetrating. He vigorously fought the battle for the music of Wagner, Bruckner and Berlioz who, he knew, were not sufficiently appreciated. And he was brave enough to swim against the tide: he viciously attacked the music of Brahms, whose symphonies and songs he felt were greatly overestimated. For this latter offense, he suffered considerable abuse. His *Quartet in D-minor,* for example, was refused a performance only because disciples of Brahms exerted their influence against him. And his *Penthesilea* was accepted by Hans Richter for rehearsal with the Vienna Philharmonic so that—permitting the players to perform it once with mistakes —Richter could comment acidly:

"Gentlemen, I would not have played this piece until the end; I was merely interested in knowing what sort of a composer this is who dares write against the master, Brahms."

During this difficult period, Hugo Wolf began to compose his *Lieder*. In 1887, thru the efforts of a friend, Friedrich Eckstein, two volumes of Wolf's songs were published by the small Viennese film of Wetzler. This publication—the first sign of appreciation his music received—encouraged Wolf, filling him with renewed strength. After giving up his position with the *Salonblatt*, he secluded himself in Perchtoldsdorf, near Vienna, in 1888, and devoted himself assiduously to the composition of *Lieder*. It was during this year that he produced, with an amazing fecundity, that series of masterpieces which have placed his name among the greatest composers of the *Lied*—the *Mörike Liederbuch*, the *Goethe Liederbuch*, the *Spanisches Liederbuch*, the *Keller Lieder* and *Alte weisen*.

Then, for some mysterious reason, his inspiration ran dry. Again and again he turned to his composition only to find that his inventiveness was gone, his imagination parched. "I have given up all idea of composing," he wrote to a friend in May of 1891. "Heavens knows how things will finish. Pray for my poor soul!"

This obituary to his inspiration was, however, premature. By the end of the year, freshness and vitality returned. He was composing the first of his *Italien lieder,* in which his former genius expressed itself once again in forms of cameo perfection. Another period of sterility followed to be continued by another period of rich creation. In 1895, he composed his opera *Der Corregidor* (first performed in Mannheim in 1896 when it was a dismal failure). In 1896, came the second volume of his *Italien lieder*. His energy was now uncontrollable, and in 1897 he was working with furious application on a new opera, *Manuel Venegas,* and more songs.

Suddenly, without warning, a catastrophe struck him. On September 20, 1897, Hugo Wolf ment mad.

He was sent by kind and solicitous friends to a private hospital where he

HUGO WOLF

was tenderly looked after. There, rest and quiet worked a miraculous cure. By February 1898, he was sufficiently well to undertake a holiday voyage to Italy. He returned to Vienna rejuvenated in body and mind, a little more sedate and despondent, it was true, and unable to return to his composition, but otherwise his former, healthier self.

But a new attack of madness soon seized him. One morning he attempted to drown himself in the Traunsee. He was taken to the Lower Austrian Mental Hospital. Paralysis set in, crippling his speech and body. For more than two weeks he was a lamentable spectacle of a human being. Frequently, he had strange illusions that he was someone else and would mutter to himself: "If only I were Hugo Wolf!" He seemed to be oblivious of everyone and everything—except his pain.

Death finally came in the form of peripneumonia on February 22, 1903.

His funeral was an impressive ceremony. Those, who would not honor him when he was alive, were ready to do him homage now that he was dead. The foremost musicians of Vienna attended, including delegations from the Royal Opera and the Conservatory. A chorale of Bruckner's accompanied his body to its grave. Immediately after his death, the city of Vienna decreed that an honorary tomb be erected in his honor.

As a personality, Hugo Wolf was known for his tactlessness, his ingenuous ignorance of how best to further his own ends, his almost savage honesty which knew neither expediency nor opportunism. He was particularly sensitive to noises. He was capable of subtle and pointed humor. His friends informed us that he was always in a hurry.

He was of a very excitable nature; his enthusiasms often bordered upon frenzy. Hermann Bahr, the distinguished Viennese critic, has written of Wolf's neurotic preoccupation with Kleist's poetry, for example. "He raved about it; his hands shook if he read only a couple of verses from it; his eyes glittered; he appeared as one transfigured, as though he saw a higher and brighter sphere whose gates had opened suddenly." Once—when Bahr and Wolf were living together—Bahr returned home late at night. Suddenly "the door opened and from the other room appeared. . . Hugo Wolf in a very long shirt, with candle and book in his hand, a most pale and fantastic apparition. . . . He laughed a shrill laugh and jeered. . . . Then he came to the middle of the room, waved his candle and. . . began to read to us, chiefly from *Penthesilea*."

He recognized his own importance and was sublimely indifferent to what anyone else thought of him. "What I write now I write for the future," he once said. "They are masterpieces. There has been nothing like it since Schubert and Schumann."

What might have been sheer arrogance has, instead, become astute prophecy. Today, we know that Hugo Wolf's *Lieder* are in a class by themselves and that there have been only few song composers worthy of joining his company. At his best, he stood at the side of Schubert and Schumann; and he was at his best in a preponderance of his *Lieder*.

Perhaps the most authoritative criticism of Hugo Wolf's songs has come to us from Ernest Newman. "It is because I believe Wolf to have said a larger number of beautiful things in the lyric, and a greater variety of beautiful things, than any other composer before or since, that I rank him above all other song-writers. . . . Within the small sphere of the song, Wolf exhibits an architectonic faculty that, I daresay, has not its superior in the whole history of music. No music could be surer in its sense of balance, in the knowledge of when to cease and when to continue; no music conveys more surely the impression that it simply *had* to begin just here and end just there. . . . Equally admirable, equally eloquent of the big mind that visualizes the whole work of art at a glance, sees the whole in all the detail, and each detail in reference to the whole, is the certainty with which each new touch is introduced here and there in a melody or accompaniment, that seems to flash a momentary . . . light on this word or that, without disturbing the unity and inevitableness of the thematic development. This betokens not only quick psychological perception but a consummate sense of form and a consummate mastery of technique."

Principal works by Hugo Wolf:

OPERA: *Der Corregidor.*

ORCHESTRA: *Penthesilea*; *Italian serenade* (arranged for chamber-orchestra).

CHAMBER MUSIC: *String quartet*; *Italian serenade.*

CHORAL: *Six sacred songs* (for unaccompanied voices); *Christnacht*; *Elfenlied*; *Der Feuerreiter*; *Dem Vaterland.*
An entire library of immortal songs.

About Hugo Wolf:

Bahr, Hermann. *Gesammelte Aufsätze uber Hugo Wolf*; Decsey, Ernest. *Hugo Wolf*; Grunsky, Karl. *Hugo Wolf*; Newman, Ernest. *Hugo Wolf.*

Important recordings of music by Hugo Wolf:

VOCAL: Four volumes of songs, including some of the *Spanisches Liederbuch, Italien Lieder,* the Mörike, Goethe and Michelangelo *Lieder* (HUGO WOLF SOCIETY).

CHAMBER MUSIC: *Italian serenade* (VICTOR-Budapest).

APPENDICES

APPENDIX I

Composers Grouped By Nationality

Austria
Bruckner, Anton, *b.* Ansfelden.
Czerny, Karl, *b.* Vienna.
Dittersdorf, Karl von, *b.* Vienna.
Ernst, Heinrich, *b.* Brünn.
Haydn, Joseph, *b.* Rohrau.
Mahler, Gustav, *b.* Kalischt, Bohemia.
Mozart, Wolfgang Amadeus, *b.* Salzburg.
Strauss, Johann, II, *b.* Vienna.
Suppé, Franz von, *b.* Spalato.
Thuille, Ludwig, *b.* Bozen (see Germany).
Wolf, Hugo, *b.* Windischgratz.

Belgium
Bériot, Charles de, *b.* Louvain.
Franck, César, *b.* Liège (see France).
Gossec, François, *b.* Vergnies (see France).
Grétry, André Ernest, *b.* Liège (see France).
Monte, Philippe de, *b.* Malines.
Vieuxtemps, Henri, *b.* Verviers.

Bohemia
Biber, Heinrich von, *b.* Wurtemburg (see Germany).
Dussek, Johann, *b.* Časlav.
Dvořák, Antonín, *b.* Nelahozevec.
Fibich, Zdeněk, *b.* Vseboric.
Hammerschmidt, Andreas, *b.* Brüx, (see Germany).
Kuhnau, Johann, *b.* Geising (see Germany).
Mahler, Gustav, *b.* Kalischt (see Austria).
Nápravnik, Eduard, *b.* Beischt (see Russia).
Smetana, Bedřich, *b.* Leitomischl.

Denmark
Gade, Niels, *b.* Copenhagen.
Kuhlau, Friedrich, *b.* Ülzen, Hanover, Germany.
Reinecke, Karl, *b.* Altona (see Germany).

France
Adam, Adolphe, *b.* Paris.
Auber, Daniel François, *b.* Caen, Normandy.
Berlioz, Hector, *b.* La-Côte-Sainte-André.
Bizet, Georges, *b.* Paris.
Boieldieu, François, *b.* Rouen.
Chabrier, Emmanuel, *b.* Ambert, Auvergne.
Chausson, Ernest, *b.* Paris.
Cherubini, Luigi, *b.* Florence, Italy.
Chopin, Frédéric, *b.* Zelazowa Wola, Poland.
Couperin-le-Grand, François, *b.* Paris.
David, Félicien, *b.* Cadenet.
Delibes, Léo, *b.* St.-Germain-du-Val.
Duparc, Henri, *b.* Paris.
Franck, César, *b.* Liège, Belgium.
Gossec, François, *b.* Vergnies, Belgium.

Gounod, Charles, *b.* Paris.
Grétry, André Ernest, *b.* Liège, Belgium.
Halévy, Jacques, *b.* Paris.
Heller, Stephen, *b.* Pesth, Hungary.
Hérold, Ferdinand, *b.* Paris.
Lalo, Édouard, *b.* Lille.
Leclair, Jean Marie (l'aîné), *b.* Lyon.
Lecocq, Charles, *b.* Paris.
Lekeu, Guillaume, *b.* Hensy.
Lesueur, Jean François, *b.* Plessier.
Lully, Jean Baptiste, *b.* Florence, Italy.
Massenet, Jules, *b.* Montaud.
Méhul, Étienne Henri, *b.* Givet.
Messager, André, *b.* Montluçon.
Meyerbeer, Giacomo, *b.* Berlin, Germany.
Monsigny, Pierre Alexander de, *b.* Framquembergues, near St. Omer.
Offenbach, Jacques, *b.* Cologne, Germany.
Rameau, Jean Philippe, *b.* Dijon.
Reyer, Ernest, *b.* Marseilles.
Rode, Joseph, *b.* Bordeaux.
Saint-Saëns, Camille, *b.* Paris.
Thomas, Ambroise, *b.* Metz.

Germany
Albert, Eugène d, *b.* Glasgow, Scotland.
Bach, Johann Christian, *b.* Leipzig.
Bach, Johann Sebastian, *b.* Eisenach.
Bach, Philipp Emanuel, *b.* Weimar.
Bach, Wilhelm Friedemann, *b.* Weimar.
Beethoven, Ludwig van, *b.* Bonn.
Biber, Heinrich von, *b.* Wurtemberg, Bohemia.
Brahms, Johannes, *b.* Hamburg.
Bruch, Max, *b.* Cologne.
Buxtehude, Dietrich, *b.* Helsingborg, Sweden.
Cornelius, Peter, *b.* Mayence.
Cramer, Jean Baptist, *b.* Mannheim (see Great Britain).
Flotow, Friedrich von, *b.* Mecklenburger.
Franz, Robert, *b.* Halle.
Froberger, Johann, *b.* Halle.
Gluck, Christoph Williband, *b.* Neumarkt.
Graun, Karl Heinrich, *b.* Wharenbrück, Saxony.
Graupner, Christoph, *b.* Kirchberg, Saxony.
Hammerschmidt, Andreas, *b.* Brüx, Bohemia.
Handel, George Frederick, *b.* Halle.
Hasse, Johann Adolph, *b.* Bergedorf, near Hamburg.
Hassler, Hans Leo, *b.* Nuremberg.
Hiller, Johann Adam, *b.* Wendisch-Ossig.
Hoffman, E. T. A., *b.* Königsberg.
Hummel, Johann, *b.* Pressburg. Hungary.
Humperdinck, Engelbert, *b.* Siegburg.
Jensen, Adolph, *b.* Königsberg.
Keiser, Reinhard, *b.* Teuchern, near Weissenfels, Leipzig.

Kuhlau, Friedrich, *b.* Ülzen, Hanover.
Kuhnau, Johann, *b.* Geising, Bohemia.
Loewe, Karl, *b.* Löbejün.
Lortzing, Albert, *b.* Berlin.
Mendelssohn, Felix, *b.* Hamburg.
Meyerbeer, Giacomo, *b.* Berlin (see France).
Moszkowski, Moritz, *b.* Breslau.
Nicolai, Otto, *b.* Königsberg.
Offenbach, Jacques, *b.* Cologne (see France).
Raff, Joachim, *b.* Lachen, Switzerland.
Reger, Max, *b.* Brand.
Reinecke, Karl, *b.* Altona, Denmark.
Rheinberger, Josef, *b.* Vaduz.
Rigel, Henri Joseph, *b.* Wertheim (see France).
Schütz, Heinrich, *b.* Köstritz, Saxony.
Schumann, Robert, *b.* Zwickau, Saxony.
Spohr, Louis, *b.* Brunswick.
Stamitz, Johann Wenzel, *b.* Deutschbrod.
Telemann, Georg, *b.* Magdeburg.
Thuille, Ludwig, *b.* Bozen, Austria.
Volkmann, Robert, *b.* Lommatzsch, Saxony (see Hungary).
Wagner, Richard, *b.* Leipzig.
Weber, Karl Maria von, *b.* Eutin.

Great Britain
Arne, Thomas, *b.* London.
Attwood, Thomas, *b.* London.
Balfe, Michael, *b.* Dublin, Ireland.
Bennett, Sterndale, *b.* Sheffield, Ireland.
Blow, John, *b.* North Collingham.
Boyce, William, *b.* London.
Bull, John, *b.* England.
Byrd, William, *b.* Lincolnshire.
Clementi, Muzio, *b.* Rome, Italy.
Coleridge-Taylor, Samuel, *b.* London.
Cramer, John Baptist, *b.* Mannheim, Germany.
Dowland, John, *b.* near Dublin, Ireland.
Dunstable, John, *b.* Dunstable, Bedfordshire.
Farnaby, Giles, *b.* England.
Field, John, *b.* Dublin, Ireland.
Gibbons, Orlando, *b.* Cambridge.
Locke, Matthew, *b.* Exeter.
Mackenzie, Sir Alexander, *b.* Edinburgh, Scotland.
Morley, Thomas, *b.* England.
Parry, Sir Charles Hubert, *b.* Bournemouth.
Purcell, Henry, *b.* Westminster.
Stainer, Sir John, *b.* London.
Stanford, Sir Charles Villiers, *b.* Dublin, Ireland.
Sullivan, Sir Arthur, *b.* London.
Tallis, Thomas, *b.* England.
Tosti, Sir Francesco, *b.* Ortona, Abruzzi, Italy.
Tye, Christopher, *b.* England.
Weelkes, Thomas, *b.* England.
Wilbye, Thomas, *b.* England.

Hungary
Goldmark, Karl, *b.* Keszthely.
Heller, Stephen, *b.* Pesth (see France).
Hummel, Johann, *b.* Pressburg (see Germany).
Joachim, Joseph, *b.* Kittsee.
Liszt, Franz, *b.* Raiding.
Volkmann, Robert, *b.* Lommatzsch, Saxony.

Ireland
Balfe, Michael, *b.* Dublin (see Great Britain).
Dowland, John, *b.* near Dublin (see Great Britain).
Field, John, *b.* Dublin (see Great Britain).
Herbert, Victor, *b.* Dublin (see United States).
Stanford, Sir Charles Villiers, *b.* Dublin (see Great Britain).

Italy
Allegri, Gregorio, *b.* Rome.
Bellini, Vincenzo, *b.* Catania, Sicily.
Boccherini, Luigi, *b.* Lucca.
Boito, Arrigo, *b.* Padua.
Bossi, Marco Enrico, *b.* Salò.
Busoni, Ferruccio, *b.* Empoli, Tuscany.
Caccini, Giulio, *b.* Rome.
Carissimi, Giacomo, *b.* Marino.
Cavalli, Francesco, *b.* Crema.
Cesti, Marcantonio, *b.* Arezzo.
Cherubini, Luigi, *b.* Florence (see France).
Cimarosa, Domenico, *b.* Aversa, Naples.
Clementi, Muzio, *b.* Rome (see Great Britain).
Corelli, Arcangelo, *b.* Fusignano, Bologna.
Donizetti, Gaetano, *b.* Bergamo.
Frescobaldi, Girolamo, *b.* Ferrara.
Gabrieli, Giovanni, *b.* Venice.
Galuppi, Baldassaro, *b.* Burano.
Geminiani, Francesco, *b.* Lucca.
Gesualdo, Carlo, *b.* Naples.
Jommelli, Niccolo, *b.* Aversa.
Leoncavallo, Ruggiero, *b.* Naples.
Locatelli, Pietro, *b.* Bergamo.
Lully, Jean Baptiste, *b.* Florence (see France).
Marcello, Benedetto, *b.* Venice.
Martini, "Padre," *b.* Bologna.
Martucci, Giuseppe, *b.* Capua.
Monteverdi, Claudio, *b.* Cremona.
Nardini, Pietro, *b.* Fibiana.
Paganini, Niccolo, *b.* Genoa.
Paisiello, Giovanni, *b.* Taranto.
Palestrina, Giovanni Pierluigi da, *b.* Palestrina.
Pergolesi, Giovanni, *b.* Jesi.
Piccinni, Nicola, *b.* Bari.
Ponchielli, Amilcare, *b.* Cremona.
Puccini, Giacomo, *b.* Lucca.
Pugnani, Gaetano, *b.* Turin.
Rossini, Giacchino, *b.* Pesaro.
Scarlatti, Alessandro, *b.* Palermo.
Scarlatti, Domenico, *b.* Naples.
Sgambati, Giovanni, *b.* Rome.
Spontini, Gasparo, *b.* Majolati.
Stradella, Alessandro, *b.* Naples (?).
Tartini, Giuseppe, *b.* Pirano.
Tosti, Sir Francesco, *b.* Ortona, Abruzzi (see Great Britain).
Vecchi, Orazio, *b.* Modena (?)
Veracini, Francesco, *b.* Florence.
Verdi, Giuseppe, *b.* Roncole, Parma.
Viotti, Giovanni Battista, *b.* Fontanello.
Vivaldi, Antonio, *b.* Venice.
Willaert, Adrian, *b.* Roulers, the Netherlands.

Netherlands
Dufay, Guillermus, *b*. Hainault.
Josquin des Prés, *b*. Hainault.
Lasso, Orlando de, *b*. Mons, Hainault.
Sweelinck, Jan, *b*. Amsterdam.
Willaert, Adrian, *b*. Roulers (see Italy).

Norway
Grieg, Edvard, *b*. Bergen.
Svendsen, Johan, *b*. Christiana.

Poland
Chopin, Frédéric, *b*. Zelazowa Wola (see France).
Moniuszko, Stanislaus, *b*. Ubiel.
Wieniawski, Henri, *b*. Lublin.

Russia
Arensky, Anton Stepanovitch, *b*. Nijny-Novgorod.
Balakirev, Mily, *b*. Nijny-Novgorod.
Borodin, Alexander, *b*. St. Petersburg.
Cui, César, *b*. Vilna.
Dargomijsky, Alexander, *b*. Toula.
Glinka, Michael, *b*. Novospasskoï, Smolensk.
Kalinnikov, Vassily, *b*. Voima.
Liadov, Anatol, *b*. St. Petersburg.
Liapunov, Serge, *b*. Yaroslav.
Moussorgsky, Modest, *b*. Karevo.
Nápravnik, Eduard, *b*. Beischt, Bohemia.
Rimsky-Korsakoff, Nicholas, *b*. Tikhin.
Rubinstein, Anton, *b*. Volhynia.
Serov, Alexander, *b*. St. Petersburg.
Taneiev, Sergei, *b*. Vladimir.
Tschaikovsky, Peter Ilitch, *b*. Votinski, Viatka.

Scotland
Albert, Eugène d', *b*. Glasgow (see Germany).
Mackenzie, Sir Alexander, *b*. Edinburgh (see Great Britain).

Spain
Albéniz, Isaac, *b*. Camprodón, Gerona.
Bréton, Tomás, *b*. Salamanca.
Granados, Enrique, *b*. Lérida.
Morales, Cristobal, *b*. Seville.
Pedrel, Felipe, *b*. Tortosa.
Sarasate, Pablo, *b*. Pamplona.
Victoria, Tomás Luis de, *b*. Avila.

Sweden
Buxtehude, Dietrich, *b*. Helsingborg (see Germany).

Switzerland
Raff, Joachim, *b*. Lachen (see Germany).

United States
Billings, William, *b*. Boston.
Chadwick, George, *b*. Lowell, Mass.
De Koven, Reginald, *b*. Middletown, Conn.
Foster, Stephen, *b*. Pittsburgh.
Gilbert, Henry F. *b*. Somerville.
Griffes, Charles Tomlinson, *b*. Elmira, N.Y.
Herbert, Victor, *b*. Dublin, Ireland.
Hopkinson, Francis, *b*. Philadelphia.
Macdowell, Edward, *b*. New York City.
Nevin, Ethelbert, *b*. Sewickley, Pa.
Paine, John Knowles, *b*. Portland, Maine.
Parker, Horatio W., *b*. Auburndale, Mass.

APPENDIX II

A Synthetic Outline of Musical History

I. THE AGE OF COUNTERPOINT: 15th and 16th Centuries

A. **Church Music**
1. AN ENGLISH FORERUNNER: Dunstable (1370-1453)
2. THE NETHERLAND SCHOOL: Dufay (1400-1474); Josquin dès Pres (1445-1521)
3. THE FLEMISH SCHOOL: Orlando de Lasso (1532-1594); Philippe de Monte (1521-1603)
4. THE VENETIAN SCHOOL: Willaert (1488-1562); Gabrieli (1557-1612)
5. THE ROMAN SCHOOL: Morales (1500-1553) from Spain; Victoria (1535-1611), from Spain; Palestrina (1525-1594); Allegri (1582-1652)
6. THE GERMAN SCHOOL: H. L. Hassler (1564-1612)
7. THE REFORMATION OF ENGLAND: Tallis (1510-1585); Tye (1498-1572)

B. **Secular Music**
1. THE GROWTH OF THE MADRIGAL
   a. ORIGINS IN ITALY: Willaert (1480-1562); Vecchi (1551-1605); Gesualdo (1560-1614); Monteverdi (1567-1643)
   b. THE ENGLISH MADRIGAL: Byrd (1543-1623); Morley (1557-1603); Bull (1562-1628); Gibbons (1583-1625); Weelkes (1575-1623); Wilbye (1574-1638)

II. HOMOPHONIC MUSIC OF THE SIXTEENTH CENTURY

A. **Instrumental Music in Infancy**
1. EARLY ORGAN MUSIC: Gabrieli (1557-1612); Sweelinck (1562-1621); Frescobaldi (1583-1643)
2. EARLY VIRGINAL MUSIC: Byrd (1543-1623); Bull (1562-1628)
3. EARLY CONCERTED MUSIC: Dowland (1563-1626); Byrd (1543-1623); Bull (1562-1628); Farnaby (1560-1600); Weelkes (1575-1623)

B. **Origin of the Opera**
1. BEGINNINGS IN FLORENCE: Caccini (1550-1618)
2. THE EARLY VENETIANS: Cavalli (1602-1676); Cesti (1620-1669)
3. THE FIRST GREAT OPERA COMPOSER: Monteverdi (1567-1643)

C. **The Oratorio** (modeled after operatic forms): Carissimi (1604-1674); Stradella (1645-1682)

III. THE SEVENTEENTH CENTURY

A. **Opera Reaches Development**
1. THE FRENCH OPERA: Lully (1632-1687)
2. EARLY ENGLISH OPERA: Locke (1630-1677); Purcell (1658-1695)
3. EARLY GERMAN OPERA: Schütz (1585-1672); Keiser (1674-1739)
4. NEAPOLITAN SCHOOL OF OPERA: A. Scarlatti (1659-1725)

B. **The Development of Instrumental Music**
1. ORGAN FORMS REACH INTEGRATION: Froberger (died 1667); Buxtehude (1637-1707)
2. FIRST HARPSICHORD (OR PIANO) SONATAS: Kuhnau (1660-1722); Froberger (1616-1667); Purcell (1658-1695)
3. CONCERTED MUSIC: Heinrich von Biber (1644-1704)
4. FIRST VIOLIN SONATAS: Corelli (1653-1713)
5. FIRST CONCERTOS, OR CONCERTI GROSSI: Corelli (1653-1713)

C. **Contrapuntal Music:** Hammerschmidt (1602-1675); Schütz (1585-1672)

IV. THE EIGHTEENTH CENTURY

A. **Further Development for the Opera**
1. THE RISE OF THE COMIC OPERA: Pergolesi (1710-1736) ; Galuppi (1706-1785) ; Monsigny (1729-1817) ; Cimarosa (1749-1801) ; Paisiello (1741-1816) ; Grétry (1741-1813) ; Gossec (1734-1829) ; Méhul (1763-1817)
2. SERIOUS OPERA IN FRANCE: Rameau (1683-1764)
3. SERIOUS OPERA IN GERMANY: Graun (1701-1759) ; Graupner (1683-1760) ; Telemann (1681-1767) ; J. A. Hasse (1699-1783)
4. THE RISE OF THE "GERMAN" OPERA: J. A. Hiller (1728-1804) ; Mozart (1756-1791)
5. OPERA VERSUS MUSIC-DRAMA: Gluck (1714-1787) versus Piccinni (1728-1800) ; Cherubini (1760-1842) ; Spotini (1774-1851)

B. **The Growth of the Instrumental Concerto** (also early violin music): Vivaldi (1678-1743); Tartini (1692-1770); Locatelli (1693-1764); Leclair (1697-1764), etc.

C. **Development of Piano Music:** Daquin (1694-1772); Couperin (1668-1733); Domenico Scarlatti (1685-1757)

D. **The Age of Counterpoint Is Brought to Magnificent Culmination:** J. S. Bach (1685-1750) ; Handel (1685-1759)

E. **The Early Symphony**
1. THE MANNHEIM SCHOOL: Stamitz (1717-1757)
2. THE BACH FAMILY: J. C. Bach (1735-1782) ; W. F. Bach (1710-1784) ; Philipp Emanuel Bach (1714-1788)
3. EARLY DEVELOPMENT: Graupner (1683-1760) ; von Dittersdorf (1739-1799)
4. Josef Haydn (1732-1809) and W. A. Mozart (1756-1791)

F. **The Early String Quaret:** Boccherini (1743-1805); von Dittersdorf (1739-1799); Haydn (1732-1809) : Mozart (1756-1791)

G. **Classicism in England:** Arne (1710-1778); Attwood (1765-1838); Boyce (1710-1779)

H. **Classicism in America:** Billings (1746-1800); Hopkinson (1737-1791).

V. THE NINETEENTH CENTURY

A. **The Full Enrichment of Symphony, String Quartet and Sonata:** Ludwig van Beethoven (1770-1827)

B. **Opera Reaches Further Development**
1. ITALIAN OPERA: Rossini (1792-1868) ; Bellini (1802-1835) ; Donizetti (1797-1848) ; Verdi (1813-1901) ; Boito (1842-1918) ; Puccini (1858-1924) ; Leoncavallo (1858-1919) ; etc.
2. FRENCH OPERA: Meyerbeer (1791-1864) ; Halévy (1799-1862) ; Gounod (1818-1893) ; Thomas (1811-1896) ; Bizet (1838-1875) ; Massenet (1842-1912), etc.
3. GERMAN OPERA: Weber (1786-1826) ; Spohr (1784-1859) ; Wagner (1813-1883) ; Humperdinck (1854-1921), etc.

C. **Further Growth of the Comic-Opera**
1. FRANCE: Boieldieu (1775-1834) ; Auber (1782-1871) ; Adam (1803-1856) ; Hérold (1791-1833) ; Lecocq (1832-1918) ; Offenbach (1819-1880)
2. GERMANY: Nicolai (1810-1849) ; Cornelius (1824-1874) ; von Suppé (1820-1895) ; Lortzing (1801-1851) ; Johann Strauss, II (1825-1899), etc.
3. ENGLAND: Balfe (1808-1870) ; Sullivan (1842-1900)
4. AMERICA: Herbert (1859-1924) ; de Koven (1859-1920)

D. **Early Romanticism:** E. T. A. Hoffmann (1776-1822); Lesueur (1760-1837); John Field (1782-1837) ; Loewe (1796-1869)

E. **Romanticism in Full Flower:**
1. GERMANY: Schubert (1797-1828) ; Schumann (1810-1856) ; Mendelssohn (1809-1847) ; Robert Franz (1815-1892)
2. FRANCE: Chopin (1810-1849) ; Berlioz (1803-1869) ; David (1810-1876) ; Reyer (1823-1909)
3. AMERICA: Stephen Foster (1826-1864)
4. ENGLAND: Tosti (1846-1916)

F. Late Romanticism:
1. GERMANY: Brahms (1833-1897) ; Bruch (1838-1920) ; Bruckner (1824-1896) ; Mahler (1860-1911) ; D'Albert (1864-1932) ; Wolf (1860-1903) ; Reger (1873-1916), etc.
2. FRANCE: Franck (1822-1890) ; Chabrier (1841-1894) ; Chausson (1855-1899) ; Duparc (1848-1933) ; Lalo (1823-1892) ; Saint Saëns (1835-1921) ; Lekeu (1870-1894), etc.
3. ITALY: Busoni (1866-1924) ; Martucci (1856-1909) ; Sgambati (1843-1914)
4. ENGLAND: Coleridge-Taylor (1875-1912) ; Mackenzie (1847-1933) ; Parry (1848-1918) ; Stanford (1852-1924) ; Stainer (1840-1901)
5. AMERICA: Chadwick (1854-1931) ; Griffes (1884-1920) ; Macdowell (1861-1908) ; Nevin (1862-1901) ; Paine (1839-1906)

G. Program Music: Berlioz (1803-1869); Liszt (1811-1886)

H. The Development of Violin Music: Viotti (1753-1824); Paganini (1782-1840); Rode (1774-1830) ; Ernst (1814-1865) ; de Bériot (1802-1870) ; Sarasate (1844-1908) ; Vieuxtemps (1820-1881) ; Wieniawski (1835-1880), etc.

I. The Development of Piano Music: Hummel (1778-1837); Cramer (1771-1858); Czerny (1791-1857) ; Field (1782-1837) ; Chopin (1810-1849) ; Liszt (1811-1886) ; Rubinstein (1830-1894)

J. The Development of the Lied: Schubert (1797-1828); Schumann (1810-1856); Franz (1815-1892) ; Jensen (1837-1879) ; Wolf (1860-1903) ; Cornelius (1824-1874) ; Reger (1873-1916)

K. Nationalism in Music:
1. RUSSIA: Glinka (1804-1857) ; Dargomijsky (1813-1869) ; Balakirev (1837-1910) ; Cui (1835-1918) ; Borodin (1883-1887) ; Moussorgsky (1839-1881) ; Rimsky-Korsakoff (1844-1908) ; Arensky (1861-1906) ; Rubinstein (1830-1894) ; Tschaikovsky (1840-1893), etc.
2. SCANDINAVIA: Gade (1817-1890) ; Grieg (1843-1907) ; Svendsen (1840-1911)
3. BOHEMIA: Dvořak (1841-1904) ; Smetana (1824-1884) ; Fibich (1850-1900)
4. SPAIN: Pedrell (1841-1922) ; Albéniz (1860-1909) ; Bretón (1850-1923) ; Granados (1867-1916)
5. POLAND: Moniuszko (1819-1872)
6. AMERICA: Gilbert (1868-1928) ; Griffes (1884-1920)

APPENDIX III

A Selected Bibliography

I. GENERAL HISTORIES OF MUSIC

Adler, Guido. Handbuch der musikgeschichte. Berlin. Heinrich Kellar Verlag. 1930.

Ambros, August Wilhelm. Geschichte der musik. Leipzig. F. E. C. Leuckart. 1909.

Bachrach, A. L. (editor). The musical companion. London. Victor Gollancz. 1934.

Bekker, Paul. The story of music. New York. W. W. Norton. 1927.

Bellaigue, Camille. Les époques de la musique. Paris. C. Delagrave. 1909.

Bonnet, Jacques. Histoire de la musique et de ses effets. Paris. J. Cochart. 1715.

Burney, Charles. A general history of music. New York. Harcourt, Brace & Co. 1935.

Busby, Thomas. A general history of music. London. G. & B. Whittaker. 1819.

Colles, Henry C. The growth of music. Oxford. The Clarendon Press. 1912.

Combarieu, J. Histoire de la musique. Paris. A. Colin. 1919.

Crowest, Frederick J. The story of the art of music. New York. D. Appleton. 1902.

Dumesnil, René. Histoire de la musique. Paris. Éditions d'histoire et d'art. 1934.

Einstein, Alfred. Geschichte der musik. Leipzig and Berlin. B. G. Teubner. 1920.

Ewen, David (editor). From Bach to Stravinsky. New York. W. W. Norton. 1933.

Fétis, François Joseph. Histoire générale de la musique. Paris. Firmian Didot Frères. 1869-1870.

Finney, Theodore M. A history of music. New York. Harcourt Brace & Co. 1935.

Goddard, Joseph. The rise of music. London. W. Reeves. 1908.

Gray, Cecil. A history of music. London. K. Paul, Trench, Trubner & Co. 1928.

Hadow, Sir William Henry. Music. London. Williams and Norgate. 1925.

Hall, Leland and Saerchinger, César. The art of music. vol 1-3, New York. The National Society of Music. 1915.

Hawkins, Sir John. A general history of the science and practice of music. London. T. Payne and Son. 1776.

Henderson, William James. How music developed. New York. F. A. Stokes & Co. 1898.

Hogarth, George. Musical history, biography and criticism. London. J. W. Parker. 1838.

Hull, Arthur Eaglefield. Music: classical, romantic and modern. London. J. M. Dent & Sons. New York. E. P. Dutton & Co. 1927.

Landormy, Paul. A history of music. New York. Chas. Scribner's Sons. 1934.

Lavoix, Henri Marie François. Histoire de la musique. Paris. A. Quantin. (no date).

Naumann, Emil. History of music. London. Cassell. 1901.

Nef, Karl. An outline of the history of music. New York. Columbia University Press. 1935.

Oxford History of Music. London. Oxford University Press.
vol. 1 and 2. Wooldridge, H. F. The polyphonic period. 1901-1905.
vol. 3. Parry, Sir Charles Hubert. The music of the seventeenth century. 1902.
vol. 4. Fuller-Maitland, J. A. The age of Bach and Handel. 1902.
vol. 5. Hadow, Sir William Henry. The Viennese period. 1905.
vol. 6. Dannreuther, Edward George. The romantic period. 1905.
vol. 7. Colles, Henry C. Symphony and drama: 1850-1900. 1934.

Parry, Sir Charles Hubert. The evolution of the art of music. New York. D. Appleton. 1930.

Prunières, Henri. Nouvelle histoire de la musique. Paris. Rieder. 1934.

Riemann, Hugo. Geschichte der musik zeit Beethoven. Berlin and Stuttgart. Verlag von W. Spemann. 1901.

Riemann, Hugo. Handbuch der musikgeschichte. Leipzig. Breitkopf und Härtel. 1904-1913.

Rockstro, William Smyth. A general history of music. New York. Chas. Scribner and Weltord. 1886.

Schering, Arnold. Geschichte der musik in beispielen. Leipzig. Breitkopf und Härtel. 1931.

Scott, Cyril. Music; its secret influence throughout the ages. Philadelphia. David McKay Co. London. Rider & Co. 1933.

Soubies, Albert. Histoire de la musique. Paris. E. Flammarion. 1899.

Stahford, Sir Charles Villiers and Forsyth, Cecil. A history of music. New York. Macmillan Co. 1924.

II. HISTORIES OF SPECIAL TRENDS, PERIODS, SCHOOLS OF MUSIC, ETC.

Abraham, Gerald. Studies in Russian music. New York. Chas. Scribner's Sons. 1936.

Anderton, H. Orsmond. Early English music. London. The Musical Opinion. 1920.

Apthorp, William Foster. The opera past and present. New York. Chas. Scribner's Sons. 1901.

Bach, Albert B. The art ballad: Loewe and Schubert. Edinburgh. W. Blackwood. 1890.

Barrett, William Alexander. English church composers. New York. Scribner. 1911; London. Sampson, Low, Marston & Co. Ltd. 1925.

Becker, Oscar. Die englischen madrigalisten. Leipzig. Druck von L. Seidel. 1901.

Bekker, Paul. The changing opera. New York. W. W. Norton. 1935.

Blaze, François Henri Joseph (Castil-Blaze). Le l'opéra en France. Paris. Janet et Cotelle. 1820.

Blaze de Bury, Ange Henri. Les débuts de la musique à Venise. Brussels. T. Lombaerts. 1914.

Blaze de Bury, Ange Henri. La musique dans le nord. Paris. Revue des deux mondes. (no date).

Blaze de Bury, Ange Henri. Les origines de la musique en Angleterre. Brussels. Librarie des deux mondes. 1912.

Borren, Charles van den. Sources of keyboard music. London. Novello & Co. 1914.

Bruneau, Alfred. Les musiciens de Russie et musiciens de France. Paris. Bibliothèque Charpentier. 1903.

Bruneau, Alfred. Musiques d'hier et de demain. Paris. E. Fasquelle. 1900.

Bruneau, Alfred. La musique française. Paris. E. Fasquelle. 1901.

Buehl, James W. The great operas. Philadelphia. Société Universelle Lyrique. 1899.

Calvocoressi, M. D. and Abraham, Gerald. Masters of Russian music. New York. Alfred A. Knopf. 1936.

Charbonnel, Raoul. La danse. Paris. Garnier frères. 1900.

Chouquet, Gustave. Histoire de la musique dramatique en France. Paris. Firmian Didot. 1873.

Coeuroy, André. La musique française moderne. Paris. Kra. 1928.

Collet, Henri. L'essor de la musique espagnol au XXᵉ siècle. Paris. Editions M. Eschig. 1929.

Collet, Henri. Le mysticisme musical espagnol du XVIᵉ siècle. Paris. F. Alcan. 1913.

Cucuel, Georges. La pouplinière et la musique du chambre au XVIIIᵉ siècle. Paris. Fischbacher. 1913.

Cui, César. La musique en Russie. Paris. Fischbacher. 1880.

Curzon, Henri. Musiciens du temps passé. Paris. Fischbacher. 1893.

Dumesnil, René. Musiciens romantiques. Paris. Editions du Trianon. 1928.

Elsòn, L. C. The history of American music; rev. to 1925 by Arthur Elson. New York. Macmillan Co. 1925.

Fellowes, Edmund Horace. The English madrigal. London. Oxford University Press. 1925.

Fellowes, Edmund Horace. English madrigal composers. Oxford. Clarendon Press. 1921.

Finck, Henry T. Songs and song writers. New York. Charles Scribner's Sons. 1900.

Fouqué, Octave. Les révolutionnaires de la musique. Paris. Calmann Lévy. 1882.

Gilman, Lawrence. Phases of modern music. New York. Harper & Bros. 1904.

Glyn, Margaret H. About Elizabethan virginal music and its composers. London. W. Reeves. 1924.

Goddard, Joseph. The rise and development of opera. London. W. Reeves. 1912.

Graves, Charles Larcom. Post Victorian music. London. Macmillan. 1911.

Gray, Cecil, Survey of contemporary music. London. Oxford University Press. 1924.

Hadow, Sir William Henry. Church music. London. Longmans Green. 1926.

Hadow, Sir William Henry. English music. London. Longmans Green. 1931.

Hadow, Sir William Henry. Studies in modern music. London. Seeley & Co. 1893.

Hantich, Henri. La musique tchèque. Paris. Librarie Nilsson. 1908.

Hart, George. The violin and its music. London. Dulan and Co. 1885.

Henderson, William James. Masters of French music. New York. Mentor Association. 1919.

Henderson, William James. Some forerunners of Italian opera. New York. Henry Holt. 1911.

Hervey, Arthur. Masters of French music. New York. Chas. Scribner's Sons. 1894.

Heseltine, Philip. The English ayre. London. Oxford University Press. 1926.

Hiller, Ferdinand. Aus dem tonleben unserer zeit. Leipzig. H. Mendelssohn. 1868.

Hipsher, Edward Ellsworth. The American opera and its composers. Philadelphia. Theodore Presser Co. 1927.

Hogarth, George. Memoirs of the music drama. London. R. Bentley. 1838.

Hogarth, George. Memoirs of the opera in Italy, France, Germany and England. London. R. Bentley. 1851.

Howard, John Tasker. Our American music. New York. Thos. Y. Crowell. 1931.

Hughes, Rupert. American composers. Boston. Page and Co. 1914.

Jean-Aubry, Georges. French music of to-day. London. K. Paul, French, Trubner and Co. 1919.

Jullien, Adolphe. Le Cour et l'opéra sous Louis XVI. Paris. Didier et Cie. 1878.

Jullien, Adolphe. Musiciens d'aujourd'hui. Paris. Librarie de l'art. 1892-94.

Jullien, Adolphe. Musiciens d'hier and d'aujourd'hui. Paris. Eischbacher. 1910.

Jullien, Adolphe. La musique et les philosophes du XVIIIᵉ siècle. Paris. J. Baur. 1873.

Jullien, Adolphe. Paris dilettante au commencement du siècle. Paris. Firmian Didot. 1884.

Jullien, Adolphe. La ville et le cour au XVIIIᵉ siècle. Paris. E. Rouveyre. 1881.

Kilburn, Nicholas. The story of chamber music. London. W. Reeves. 1932.

Korngold, Julius. Deutsches opernschaffen der gegenwart. Leipzig. Leonhardt Verlag. 1921.

Krehbiel, Henry Edward. Chapters of opera. New York. Henry Holt. 1908.

Krehbiel, Henry Edward. Makers of modern opera. New York. Mentor Association. 1914.

Krehbiel, Henry Edward. More chapters of opera. New York. Henry Holt. 1919.

Kretzschmar, Hermann. Geschichte der oper. Leipzig. Breitkopf und Härtel. 1919.

Landowska, Wanda. The music of the past. New York. Alfred A. Knopf. 1924.

Laserre, Pierre. The spirit of French music. London. K. Paul, Trench, Trubner & Co. 1921.

Laurencie, Lionel de la. Les créateurs de l'opéra français. Paris. F. Alcan. 1930.

Laurencie, Lionel de la. L'école française du violon. Paris. Librarie Delagrave. 1922.

Lavignac, Albert. Music and musicians. New York. Henry Holt. 1903.

Lavoix, Henri. Histoire de la musique française. Paris. Libraries-Imprimeries Réunies. 1891.

Leichentritt, Hugo. Geschichte der motette. Leipzig. Breitkopf und Härtel. 1908.

Locke, Arthur Ware. Music and the romantic movement in France. London. K. Paul, Trench, Trubner & Co. 1920.

Mackinlay, Sterling. The origin and development of light opera. London. Hutchinson & Co. 1927.

Menil, Félicien de. L'école contrapuntique flamande du XVᵉ et au XVIᵉ Siècle. Paris. E. Demets. 1905.

Mitjana y Gordon, Rafael. Estudios sobre algunos músicos españoles del siglo XVI. Madrid. Libreria de los succesores de Hernando. 1918.

Montagu-Nathan, Montagu. A history of Russian music. New York. Chas. Scribner's Sons. 1914.

Montagu-Nathan, Montagu. An introduction to Russian music. Boston. I.⁰ Phillips. 1916.

Morris, Reginald Owen. Contrapuntal technique in the sixteenth century. Oxford. Clarendon Press. 1922.

Naylor, Edward W. Shakespeare and music. New York. E. P. Dutton & Co.; London. J. M. Dent & Sons. 1931.

Newmarch, Rosa. The Russian opera. New York. E. P. Dutton & Co. 1914.

Niecks, Frederick. Program music in the last four centuries. London. Novello and Co. 1907.

Pannain, Guido. Modern composers. London. J. M. Dent and Sons. 1932; New York. E. P. Dutton & Co. 1933.

Pincherle, Marc. Feuillets d'histoire du violon. Paris. G. Legouix. 1927.

Pincherle, Marc. Les violinistes; compositeurs et virtuoses. Paris. H. Laurens. 1922.

Pougin, Arthur. Musiciens de XIXᵉ siècle. Paris. Fischbacher. 1911.

Pougin, Arthur. A short history of Russian music. London. C. Windus. 1915.

Prunières, Henri. Cavalli et l'opéra vénetian au XVIIᵉ siècle. Paris. Rieder. 1931.

Prunières, Henri. L'opéra italien de France avant Lulli. Paris. E. Champion. 1913.

Reuchsel, Maurice. L'école classique du violon. Paris. Fischbacher. 1906.

Riesemann, Oskar von. Monographien zur Russichen musik. München. Drei Masken Verlag. 1923.

Rolland, Romain. A musical tour through the land of the past. London. K. Paul, Trench, Trubner and Co. 1922.

Rolland, Romain. Les origines du théâtre lyrique moderne. Paris. E. de Boccard. 1931.

Salazar, Adolfo. La música contemporanea en España. Madrid. Ediciones La Nave. 1930.

Saminsky, Lazare. Music of our day. New York. Thos. Y. Crowell. 1932.

Schering, Arnold. Geschichte der instrumental-konzert. Leipzig. Breitkopf und Härtel. 1927.

Schering, Arnold. Geschichte der oratoriums. Leipzig. Breitkopf und Härtel. 1911.

Seidl, Arthur. Neuzeitliche tondichter und zeitgenössiche tonkünstler. Regensburg. G. Bosse. 1926.

Seiffert, Max. Geschichte der klaviermusik. Leipzig. C. F. Weitzmann. 1899.

Seiffert, Max. Sweelinck und seine direkten deutschen schüler. Leipzig. Breitkopf und Härtel. 1891.

Seré, Octave (Jean Poueigh). Musiciens français d'aujourd'hui. Paris. Mercure de France. 1911.

Smith, Leo. Music of the seventeenth and eighteenth centuries. London. J. M. Dent. 1931.

Sollitt, E. R. From Dufay to Sweelinck. New York. Ives Washburn. 1933.

Straeten, Edmund Sebastian Joseph van der. The history of the violin. London. Cassel & Co. 1931.

Streatfeild, R. A. The opera. London. George Routledge & Sons. (no date).

Tiersot, Julien. Un demi siècle de musique française. Paris. Librarie F. Alcan. 1924.

Trend, John Brande. Manuel de Falla and Spanish music. New York. Alfred A. Knopf. 1929.

Trend, John Brande. The music of Spanish history. London. Oxford University Press. 1926.

Trend, John Brande. A picture of modern Spain: men and music. Boston. Houghton; London. Constable. 1921.

Truinet, Charles Louis and Roquet, A. E. Les origines de l'opéra français. Paris. E. Plon, Nourrit et Cie. 1886.

Vechten, Carl van. The music of Spain. New York. Alfred A. Knopf. 1918.

Villalba, Muñoz Luis. Últimos músicos espagñoles del siglo XIX. Madrid. I. Alier. 1914.

Walker, Ernest. A short history of music in England. London. Oxford University Press. 1924.

Weingartner, Felix. The symphony since Beethoven. Boston. Oliver Ditson Co. 1904.

Willeby, Charles. Masters of English music. London. James R. Osgood, McIlvain Co. 1896.

III. COLLECTIVE BIOGRAPHIES

Bachman, Alberto. Les grands violinistes du passé. Paris. Fischbacher. 1913.

Bacharach, A. L. (editor). Lives of the great composers. London. V. Gollancz. 1935.

Baptie, David. Sketches of English glee composers. London. W. Reeves. 1896.

Bellaigue, Camille. Musical studies and silhouettes. New York. Dodd, Mead & Co. 1901.

Blaze de Bury, Ange Henri. Musiciens contemporains. Paris. M. Lévy frères. 1856.

Blaze de Bury, Ange Henri. Musiciens du passé, du présent et de l'avenir. Paris. Calmann Lévy. 1881.

Blom, Eric. Stepchildren in music. London. G. T. Foulis. 1925.

Boschot, Adolphe. Chez les musiciens. Paris. Plon, Nourrit. 1922.

Bridge, Frederick. Twelve good musicians. New York. E. P. Dutton & Co. 1920.

Chantavoine, Jean. De Couperin à Debussy. Paris. F. Alcan. 1921.

Crowest, Frederick. The great tone poets. London. Macmillan & Co. 1893.

Dole, Nathan Haskell. Famous composers. New York. Thos. Y. Crowell. 1936.

Elson, L. C. Great composers and their work. Boston. L. C. Page & Co. 1898.

Elson, Louis (editor). Modern music and musicians. New York. The University Society. 1912.

Engel, Carl, Alle breve: from Bach to Debussy. New York. G. Schirmer. 1921.

Ferris, George T. Great German composers. New York. D. Appleton & Co. 1882.

Ferris, George T. Great Italian composers. New York. D. Appleton & Co. 1903.

Ferris, George T. Great violinists and pianists. New York. D. Appleton & Co. 1895.

Flood, William Henry Grattan. Late Tudor composers. London. Oxford University Press. 1931.

Fuller-Maitland, J. A. English music of the XIX century. London. G. Richards. 1902.

Fuller-Maitland, J. A. Masters of German music. New York. Chas. Scribner's Sons. 1894.

Grew, Sidney. Makers of music. London. G. T. Foulis & Co. 1935.

Hadden, James Cuthbert. Composers in love and marriage. London. John Long. 1913.

Hargreave, Mary. Earlier French musicians. London. K. Paul, Trench, Trubner & Co. 1917.

Imbert, Hughes. Profils d'artistes contemporains. Paris. Fischbacher. 1897.

Keddie, Henrietta. Musical composers and their works. Boston. Roberts Bros. 1878.

Klauser, Karl; Paine, John Knowles; Thomas, Theodore (editors). Famous composers and their works. Boston. J. B. Millet & Co. 1901.

Lahee, Henry C. Famous violinists of today and yesterday. Boston. L. C. Page & Co. 1899; rev. ed. 1925.

Mason, Daniel Gregory. Beethoven and his forerunners. New York. The Macmillan Co. 1930.

Mason, Daniel Gregory. Contemporary composers. New York. The Macmillan Co. 1918.

Mason, Daniel Gregory. From Grieg to Brahms. New York. The Macmillan Co. 1927.

Mason, Daniel Gregory. The Romantic composers. New York. The Macmillan Co. 1906.

Metcalf, Frank, J. American writers and compilers of sacred music. New York. The Abingdon Press. 1925.

Oldmeadow, Ernest. Great musicians. Philadelphia. George W. Jacobs & Co. 1908.

Parker, John R. A musical biography. Boston. Stone and Fovell. 1824.

Parry, Sir Charles Hubert. Studies of great composers. London. G. Routledge. 1904.

Phipson, Thomas Lambe. Biographical sketches and anecdotes of celebrated violinists. London. Richard Bentley & Sons. 1877.

Rolland, Romain. Musicians of today. New York. Henry Holt. 1914.

Rolland, Romain. Some musicians of former days. New York. Henry Holt. 1915.

Sharp, R. Farquharson. Makers of music. London. W. Reeves. 1901.

Streatfeild, R. A. Masters of Italian music. New York. Chas. Scribner's Sons. 1895.

IV. INDIVIDUAL BIOGRAPHIES

(See bibliographical section at the conclusion of each individual sketch).

V. CRITICAL WRITINGS

Apthorp, William Foster. Musicians and music lovers. New York. Chas. Scribner's Sons. 1894.

Bellaigue, Camille. Études musicales. Paris. C. Delagrave. 1903.

Bellaigue, Camille. Impressions musicales et littéraires. Paris. C. Delagrave. 1900.

Berlioz, Hector. Gesammelte schriften. Leipzig. G. Heinze. 1864.

Boschot, Adolphe. La musique et la vie. Paris. Librairie Plon. 1931.

Boschot, Adolphe. Le mystère musical. Paris. Librairie Plon. 1929.

Burk, John (editor). Philip Hale's Boston symphony program notes. New York. Doubleday, Doran & Co. 1935.

Foss, Hubert J. (editor). The heritage of music. London. Oxford University Press. 1927-1935.

Gilman, Lawrence. Nature in music. New York. John Lane. 1914.

Gilman, Lawrence. Program notes for the New York Philharmonic Symphony Society, and for the Philadelphia Symphony Orchestra.

Grétry, André Ernest Modeste. Mémoires, ou essais sur la musique. Paris. L'Imprimerie de la République. 1797.

Hadow, William Henry. Collected essays. London. Oxford University Press. 1928.

Henderson, William James. Preludes and studies. New York. Longmans, Green and Co. 1892.

Hiller, Ferdinand. Musikalisches und personliches. Leipzig. Breitkopf und Härtel. 1876.

Huneker, James Gibbons. Melomaniacs. New York. Chas. Scribner's Sons. 1905.

Huneker, James Gibbons. Mezzotints in modern music. New York. Chas. Scribner's Sons. 1899.

Huneker, James Gibbons. Unicorns. New York. Chas. Scribner's Sons. 1917.

Jean-Aubry, Georges. La musique et les nations. Paris. Éditions de la Sirène. 1922.

Krehbiel, Henry Edward. Music and manners. New York. Chas. Scribner's Sons. 1899.

Liszt, Franz. Pages romantiques. Paris. F. Alcan. 1912.

Marliave, Joseph. Études musicales. Paris. F. Alcan. 1917.

Meugy, A. La poésie de la musique. Paris. Hacette et cie. 1875.

Newman, Ernest. Musical studies. London. John Lane. 1905.

Romain, Louis de. Essais de critique musicale. Paris. A. Lemerre. 1890.

Rousseau, Jean Jacques. Écrits sur musique. Paris. P. Pourrat frères. 1838.

Schumann, Robert. Music and musicians. New York. E. Schuberth & Co. 1877.

Servières, Georges. Épisodes d'histoire musicale. Paris. Fischbacher. 1914.

Servières, Georges. La musique française moderne. Paris. G. Havard. 1897.

Sonneck, Oscar Georg. Miscellaneous studies in the history of music. New York. The Macmillan Co. 1921.

Standford, Sir Charles Villiers. Interludes. London. J. Murray. 1922.

Stanford, Sir Charles Villiers. Studies and memoirs. London. Constable & Co. 1908.

Upton, George P. Musical pastels. Chicago. A. C. McClurg. 1902.

Vechten, Carl van. In the garret. New York. A. A. Knopf. 1920.

Wagner, Richard. Prose works. London. K. Paul, Trench & Co. 1892-1899.

Weissman, Adolf. Music come to earth. London. J. M. Dent & Sons. 1930.

Weissman, Adolf. The problems of modern music. London. J. M. Dent & Sons. 1925.

Wortham, H. E. A musical odyssey. London. Methuen & Co. 1924.

VI. MEMOIRS, AUTOBIOGRAPHIES, ETC.

Adam, Adolphe Charles. Souvenirs d'un musicien. Paris. M. Lévy frères. 1857.

Beatty-Kingston, William. Music and manners. London. Chapman & Hall. 1887.

Berlioz, Hector. Autobiography. London. Macmillan & Co. 1884.

Chorley, Henry. Autobiography. London. R. Bentley & Son. 1873.

Daniels, Mabel. An American girl in Munich. Boston. Little Brown & Co. 1905.

Fay, Amy. Music-study in Germany. Chicago. Jansen, McClurg & Co. 1882. New York. The Macmillan Co. 1882.

Goldmark, Karl. Notes from the life of a Viennese composer. New York. A. & C. Boni. 1927.

Gounod, Charles. Memoirs of an artist. Chicago and New York. Rand McNally & Co. 1895.

Halévy, Jacques. Souvenirs et portraits. Paris. M. Lévy frères. 1861.

Kelley, Michael. Musical reminiscences. London. H. Colburn. 1826.

Mendelssohn, Felix. Letters from Italy and Switzerland. London. Longmans, Green & Roberts. 1862.

Ponte, Lorenzo da. Memoirs. Philadelphia. J. B. Lippincott. 1929.

Rimsky-Korsakoff, Nicholas. My musical life. New York. A. A. Knopf. 1923.

Rubinstein, Anton. Autobiography. Boston. Little Brown & Co. 1890.

Spohr, Louis. Autobiography. London. Reeves and Turner. 1878.

Stanford, Sir Charles Villiers. Pages from an unwritten diary. New York. Longmans, Green & Co. 1914.

Wagner, Richard. My life. London. Constable & Co. 1911.

Walker, Bettina. My musical experiences. New York. Chas. Scribner's Sons. 1893.

VII. BOOKS OF REFERENCE

Abert, Hermann. Illustrietes musiklexikon. Stuttgart. J. Engelhorns. 1927.

Bachmann, Alberto. An encyclopedia of the violin. New York. D. Appleton & Co. 1925.

Blaze, François Henri Joseph (Castil-Blaze). Dictionnaire de musique moderne. Brussels. J. J. Cantaerts. 1828.

Choron, Alexandre Étienne and Fayolle, F. Dictionnaire historique des musiciens. Paris. Chimot. 1817.

Cobbett, Walter Willson. Cyclopedic survey of chamber music. London. Oxford University Press. 1930.

Darrell, Robert D. The Gramaphone Shop encyclopedia of recorded music. New York. The Gramaphone Shop, Inc. 1936.

Eitner, Robert. Biographisch-bibliographisches quellen-lexikon. Leipzig. Breitkopf und Härtel. 1900-1904.

Fétis, François Joseph. Biographie universelle des musiciens. Paris. F. Didot frères. 1864.

Gerber, Ernst Ludwig. Historisch-biographisch lexikon der tonkünstler. Leipzig. J. G. I. Breitkopf. 1790-1792.

Grove, Sir George. Dictionary of music and musicians. New York. The Macmillan Co. 1927.

Hull, Arthur Eaglefield. A dictionary of modern music and musicians. London. J. M. Dent & Sons. 1924; New York. Dutton. 1924.

Pratt, Waldo Selden. The new encyclopedia of music and musicians. New York. The Macmillan Co. 1934.

Pulver, Jeffrey. A biographical dictionary of old English music. London. K. Paul, Trench, Trubner & Co. 1927.

Riemann, Hugo. Musik-lexikon. Berlin. M. Hesse. 1929.

Rousseau, Jean Jacques. A dictionary of music. London. J. French. 177-?.

INDEX